COMMENTARIES

ON THE

CONFLICT OF LAWS,

FOREIGN AND DOMESTIC,

IN REGARD TO

CONTRACTS, RIGHTS, AND REMEDIES,

AND ESPECIALLY IN REGARD TO

MARRIAGES, DIVORCES, WILLS, SUCCESSIONS, AND JUDGMENTS.

BY JOSEPH STORY, LL. D.,

DANE PROFESSOR OF LAW IN HARVARD UNIVERSITY.

"Il régnera donc toujours entre les nations une contrariété perpétuelle de loix; peutêtre régnera-t-elle perpétuellement entre nous sur bien des objets. Delà la nécessité de s'instruire des règles, et des principes, qui peuvent nous conduire dans la décision des questions, que cette variété peut faire naître."

Boullenois, Traité de la Personalité, &c. des Loix, Préface.

THE LAWBOOK EXCHANGE, LTD.
Clark, New Jersey

ISBN 9781584777731 (hardcover)
ISBN 9781616190989 (paperback)

Lawbook Exchange edition 2010

The quality of this reprint is equivalent to the quality of the original work.

The Lawbook Exchange, Ltd.
33 Terminal Avenue
Clark, New Jersey 07066-1321

Please see our website for a selection of our other publications and fine facsimile reprints of classic works of legal history:
www.lawbookexchange.com

Library of Congress Cataloging-in-Publication Data

Story, Joseph, 1779-1845.
Commentaries on the conflict of laws, foreign and domestic, in regard to contracts, rights, and remedies, and especially in regard to marriages, divorces, wills, successions, and judgments / Joseph Story.
p. cm.
Originally published: Boston : Hilliard, Gray, and Company, 1834.
Includes bibliographical references and index.
ISBN-13: 978-1-58477-773-1 (cloth : alk. paper)
ISBN-10: 1-58477-773-7 (cloth : alk. paper)
1. Conflict of laws--United States. 2. Conflict of laws. I. Title.
KF411.S76 2007
340.90973--dc22 2006035985

Printed in the United States of America on acid-free paper

COMMENTARIES

ON THE

CONFLICT OF LAWS,

FOREIGN AND DOMESTIC,

IN REGARD TO

CONTRACTS, RIGHTS, AND REMEDIES,

AND ESPECIALLY IN REGARD TO

MARRIAGES, DIVORCES, WILLS, SUCCESSIONS, AND JUDGMENTS.

By JOSEPH STORY, LL. D.,

DANE PROFESSOR OF LAW IN HARVARD UNIVERSITY.

"Il régnera donc toujours entre les nations une contrariété perpétuelle de loix; peutêtre régnera-t-elle perpétuellement entre nous sur bien des objets. Delà la nécessité de s'instruire des règles, et des principes, qui peuvent nous conduire dans la décision des questions, que cette variété peut faire naître."

Boullenois, Traité de la Personalité, &c. des Loix, Préface.

BOSTON:
HILLIARD, GRAY, AND COMPANY.
1834.

CAMBRIDGE:
CHARLES FOLSOM,
PRINTER TO THE UNIVERSITY.

TO THE

HONORABLE JAMES KENT, LL. D.

SIR,

IT affords me very sincere satisfaction to have the opportunity of dedicating this work to you. It belongs to a branch of international jurisprudence, which has been long familiar to your studies, and in which you have the honor of having been the guide and instructer of the American youth. I can trace back to your early labours in expounding the civil and the foreign law the motive and encouragement of my own far more limited researches. I wish the present work to be considered as a tribute of respect to a distinguished Master from his grateful pupil.

It is now about thirty-six years since you began your judicial career on the Bench of the Supreme Court of the State of New York. In the intervening period between that time and the present, you have successively occupied the offices of Chief Justice and of Chancellor of the same State. I speak but the common voice of the Profession and the public, when I say, that in each of these stations you have brought to its duties a maturity of judgment, a depth of learning, a fidelity of purpose, and an enthusiasm for justice, which have laid the solid foundations of an imperishable fame. In the full vigor of your intellectual powers, you left the Bench only to engage in a new task, which of itself seemed to demand by its extent and magnitude a whole life of strenuous diligence. That task has been accomplished. The "Commentaries on American Law" have already acquired the reputation of a juridical Classic, and have placed their author in the first rank of the benefactors of the Profession. You have done for America, what Mr. Justice Blackstone in his invaluable Commentaries has done for England. You have embodied the principles of our law in pages as attractive by the persuasive elegance of their style, as they are instructive by the fulness and accuracy of their learning.

You have earned the fairest title to the repose, which you now seek, and which at last seems within your reach. It is, in the noblest sense, *otium cum dignitate*. May you live many years to enjoy it! The consciousness of a life, like yours, in which have been blended at every step public spirit and private virtue, the affections, which cheer, and the taste, which adorns the domestic circle, cannot but make the recollections of the past sweet, and the hopes of the future animating.

I am, with the highest respect,

Your obliged friend,

JOSEPH STORY.

Cambridge, Massachusetts,
January 1, 1834.

PREFACE.

I now submit to the indulgent consideration of the profession and the public another portion of the labours appertaining to the Dane Professorship of Law in Harvard University. The subject is one of great importance and interest; and from the increasing intercourse between foreign States, as well as between the different States of the American Union, it is daily brought home more and more to the ordinary business and pursuits of human life. The difficulty of treating such a subject in a manner suited to its importance and interest can scarcely be exaggerated. The materials are loose and scattered, and are to be gathered from many sources, not only uninviting, but absolutely repulsive, to the mere Student of the Common Law. There exists no treatise upon it in the English language; and not the slightest effort has been made, except by Mr. Chancellor Kent, to arrange in any general order even the more familiar maxims of the Common Law in regard to it. Until a comparatively recent period, neither the English Lawyers, nor the English Judges seem to have had their attention drawn towards it, as a great branch of international jurisprudence, which they were required to administer. And, as far as their researches appear as yet to have gone, they are less profound and satisfactory, than their admirable expositions of municipal law.

The subject has been discussed with much more fulness, learning, and ability by the foreign Jurists of continental Europe. But even among them there exists no systematical Treatise embracing all the general topics. For the most part, they have discussed it only with reference to some few branches of jurisprudence, peculiar to the civil law, or to the customary law (almost infinitely varied) of the neighbouring States of Europe, or of the different Provinces of the same Empire. And it must be confessed, that their writings are often of so controversial a character, and abound with so many nice distinctions (not very intelligible to Jurists of the school of the Common Law) and with so many theories of doubtful utility, that it is not always easy to extract from them such principles, as may afford safe guides to the judgment. Rodemburg, Boullenois, Bouhier, and Froland have written upon it with the most clearness, comprehensiveness, and acuteness. But they rather stimulate than satisfy inquiry; and they are far more elaborate in detecting the errors of others, than in widening and deepening the foundations of the practical doctrines of international jurisprudence. I am not aware, that the works of these eminent Jurists have been cited at the English Bar; and I should draw the conclusion, that they are in a great measure, if not altogether, unknown to the studies of Westminster Hall. How it should happen, that, in this age, English Lawyers should be so utterly indifferent to all foreign jurisprudence, it is not easy to conceive. Many occasions are constantly occurring, in which they would derive essential assistance from it, to illustrate the questions, which are brought into contestation in all their Courts.

In consulting the foreign Jurists, I have felt great embarrassment, as well from my own imperfect knowledge of the jurisprudence, which they profess to discuss, as from the remote analogies, which it sometimes bears to the rights, titles, and remedies recognised in the Common Law. To give their opinions at large upon many topics would fill volumes; to omit all statements whatever of their opinions would be to withhold from the reader many most important lights, to guide his own studies, and instruct his own judgment. I have adopted an intermediate course; and have laid before the reader such portions of the opinions and reasonings of foreign Jurists, as seemed to me most useful to enable him to understand their doctrines and principles, and to assist him with the means of making more ample researches, if his leisure or his curiosity should invite him to the pursuit. Humble as this task may appear to many minds, it has been attended with a labour truly discouraging and exhausting. I dare not even now indulge the belief, that my success has been at all proportionate to my wishes or my efforts. I feel, however, cheered by the reflection (is it a vain illusion?), that other minds, of more ability, leisure, and learning, may be excited to explore the paths, which I have ventured only to point out. I beg, in conclusion, to address to the candour of the Profession my own apology in the language of Strykius; — "Crescit disputatio nostra sub manibus; unum enim si absolveris jus, plura se offerunt consideranda. At nos temporis, quod nimis breve nobis fit, rationem habentes, accuratius illa inquirere haud possumus. Hinc sufficerit, in presens sparsisse quædem saltem adhuc jura, quidque de iis statuamus, vel obiter dixisse." *

JOSEPH STORY.

Cambridge, Massachusetts,
January, 1, 1834.

---

* Strykii Disputatio 1. ch. 2. § 92. Tom. II. p. 24.

CONTENTS.

LIST OF AUTHORS CITED.

THE following list of some of the more important Authors, whose works have been cited, may assist the student in his researches.

D'AGUESSEAU, HENRY FRANCIS, Chancellor of France, born at Limoges, 1668, and died 1751. His works are collected and published in 13 vols. 4to.

ALEXANDER AB ALEXANDRO, a Neapolitan lawyer, born 1461, and died at Rome about the age of 62.

D'ARGENTRÉ, BERTRAND, President of the *Présidial* of Rennes, born in 1519, and died in 1590. His works are entitled *Commentarii in Patrias Britonum Leges, seu Consuetudines generales Ducatûs Britaniæ.*

BALDUS, UBALDUS, born about 1324, died 1400. His works are comprised in 4 vols. fol.

BARTOLO, or BARTHOLUS, born at Sasso Ferrato, in the March of Ancona, 1313, and died in his 46th year. He was called "the star and luminary of lawyers, the master of truth, the lantern of equity, the guide of the blind," &c. His works were printed at Venice, 1499, in 4 vols. fol., according to Camus; in 1599 in 10 or 11 vols. fol., according to Watt.

BOUHIER, J., President of the Parliament of Dijon, born at that place, 1673, and died 1746. His works, relating to the present subject, are published in two vols. fol., and entitled, *Les Coutumes du Duché de Bourgogne, avec les Observations du Président Bouhier.*

BOULLENOIS, LOUIS, advocate in the Parliament of Paris, born at Paris, 1680, and died 1762. There are two works by him, on the present subject; *Traité de la Personalité et de la Réalité des Lois, Coutumes, Statuts, par forme d'Observations*, in 2 vols. 4to., and *Dissertations sur des Questions, qui naissent de la Contrariété des Loix et des Coutumes.* 4to. This last was published first, and is the original outline of the larger work, which afterwards appeared.

BRETONNIER, BARTHOLEMEW JOSEPH, advocate of the Parliament of Paris, born at Montrotier, near Lyons, 1656, and died 1727. He is the author of a work in 2 vols. 12mo., entitled *Recueil des principales Questions de Droit qui se jugent diversement dans les différens Tribunaux du Royaume, avec des Réflexions pour concilier la Diversité de la Jurisprudence.* He also edited the works of HENRYS.

BURGUNDUS, BURGUNDIUS, or BOURGOIGNE, NICOLAUS, jurisconsult, born at Enghien in Hainault, 1586. He is the author of a work, entitled, *Tractatus Controversiarum ad Consuetudinem Flandriæ.*

BYNKERSHOEK, CORNELIUS VAN, born at Middlebourg, 1673, and died 1743. His works are well known.

CASAREGIS, JOSEPH LAURENTIUS DE, born at Genoa, 1670, and died 1737. His works are entitled, *Discursus legales de Commercio*, and are published in 2, 3, and 4 vols. fol.

CHRISTINÆUS, PAULUS, born at Malines, 1533, and died 1638. His works are, *Practicarum Quæstionum Rerumque in Supremis Belgarum Curiis actarum et Observationum Decisiones;* and *Commentarii in Leges Municipales Mechlinienses.*

COCHIN, HENRY, advocate in Parliament, born at Paris, 1687, and died 1747. His works are collected in 6 vols. 4to.

COQUILLE, GUI, advocate of the Parliament of Paris, born at Decise in Nivernois, 1523, and died 1603. There is a work by him, *Des Coutumes des Nivernois.*

CUJAS, JAMES, born at Thoulouse, 1520, and died 1590. His voluminous works need not be particularly mentioned.

DENISART, J. B., jurisconsult, born 1712, and died 1765. He published *Collection de Décisions nouvelles relatives à la Jurisprudence.*

DOMAT, JOHN, born at Clermont in Auvergne, 1625, and died 1696. His *Civil Law in its Natural Order* is well known through the translation of Dr. Strahan.

DUMOULIN, (in Latin, MOLINÆUS,) CHARLES, born 1500 and died 1560. What he has written upon the present subject is to be found in his Commentary on the first book of the Code, verb. *Conclusiones de Statutis*, in his 53d *Consilium*, and in his notes on *Alexander*, *Decius*, and *Chasseneuz.*

DURANTON, A., Professor of Law at Paris. His works are, *Cours de Droit Français, suivant le Code civil*, in 16 vols. 8vo.

EMÉRIGON, BALTAZARD MARIE, advocate of the Parliament of Aix, born about 1725 and died 1784. His *Traité des Assurances*, 2 vols. 4to. is referred to in the present Commentaries.

ERSKINE, JOHN, Professor of Law at Edinburgh. His principal work is entitled *Institutes of the Laws of Scotland.*

EVERHARD, NICHOLAS, born in the island of Walcheren, 1462, and died 1532. His works are *Topica Juris, sive Loci Argumentorum Legales;* and *Consilia, sive Responsa Juris.*

FROLAND, LOUIS, advocate of the Parliament of Rouen, died 1746. His works, relating to the present subject, in two 4to. vols., are entitled, *Mémoire concernant la Nature et la Qualité des Statuts.*

GAILL, ANDREW, born at Cologne, 1525, and died 1587. He was called the Papinian of Germany.

GROTIUS, HUGO, born at Delft, 1583, and died 1645. His works are well known.

HEINECCIUS, JOHANNES GOTLEIB, Professor of Philosophy and Law at Halle, born at Eisenburg, 1681, and died 1741. His works need not be particularly mentioned.

HENRYS, CLAUDE, jurisconsult, born at Montbrison, 1615, and died 1662. His works are collected in four vols. fol.

HERTIUS, JOHANNES NICOLAUS, born near Giessen, 1651, and died 1710. His treatise, *De Collisione Legum* is to be found in his select works in two vols. 4to.

HUBERUS, ULRICUS, a lawyer, historian, and philologer, born at Dockum, in the Dutch territories, 1635, and died 1694. His treatise *De Conflictu Legum* is to be found in his *Prælectiones Juris Civilis*, 3 vols. 4to.

KAIMS, LORD, (HENRY HOME,) born at Kaims, in Berwickshire, 1696, and died 1782. The reader is referred to his *Principles of Equity.*

LE BRUN, DENIS, advocate, died 1708, before the publication of his principal work, *Traité de Communautés.*

LEEUWEN, SIMON VAN, born at Leyden, 1625, and died 1682. His work referred to, in the present Commentaries, is translated into English, with the title of *Commentaries on the Roman-Dutch Law.*

LIVERMORE, SAMUEL, of New Orleans, died, 1833. He is the author of *Dissertations on the Contrariety of Laws.*

MASCARDUS, JOSEPHUS, an ecclesiastic and Italian jurisconsult, born at Sarzana towards the end of the 16th century, and died about 1630. He is the author of an extensive work, entitled, *De Probationibus Conclusiones.*

MERLIN, M. (de DOUAI.) His voluminous works are entitled, *Répertoire Universel et Raisonné de Jurisprudence;* and *Questions de Droit.*

MORNAC, ANTOINE, born near Tours, first appeared before the Parliament of Paris in 1580; and died 1620. His works are comprised in 4 vols. fol.

PARDESSUS, J. M. *Cours de Droit Commercial.* 5 vols. 8vo. Paris. 1831.

POTHIER, ROBERT JOSEPH, born at Orleans, 1699, and died 1772. His works need not be particularly mentioned.

PECK, PETER, born at Zirckzee, in Zealand, 1529, and died 1589. His works are collected in one vol. fol.

PUFFENDORF, SAMUEL, born in Upper Saxony, 1632; and died 1694. His works are well known.

RODEMBURG, was a judge of the Supreme Court of Utrecht and flourished about the middle of the 17th century. His treatise, *De Jure quod oritur ex Statutorum vel Consuetudinum Diversitate,* is to be found at the end of Boullenois's *Traité de la Personalité et de la Réalité des Loix.*

STOCKMANS, PETER, born at Antwerp, 1608, and died 1671. His works are comprised in one vol. 4to.

STRYKIUS, SAMUEL, born 1640, and died 1710. His son, JOHN SAMUEL, was born 1668, and died 1715. Their works, with those of RHETIUS, are collected in 14 vols. fol.

VOET, PAUL, (the father,) born at Heusden, in Brabant, 1619, and died 1677. His work on the present subject is entitled, *De Statutis et eorum Concursu.*

VOET, JOHN, son of Paul, born at Utrecht, 1647, and died 1714. His Commentary on the Pandects contains a short chapter, *de Statutis.*

INDEX TO CASES CITED.

C.

D.

O.

P.

Q.

R.

ERRATA.

Page	22,	*line*	21,	*for*	national	*read*	natural
"	134,	"	20,	"	is	"	are
"	208,	"	12,	"	were	"	where
"	241,	"	31,	"	Ridgman	"	Bridgman
"	300,	"	30,	"	Tyrush	"	Tyrwhit
"	339,	"	34,	"	found	"	founded
"	343,	"	19,	"	equanimity	"	unanimity
"	385,	"	18,	"	*qui*	"	*que*

COMMENTARIES

ON THE

CONFLICT

BETWEEN FOREIGN AND DOMESTIC LAWS.

CHAPTER I.

INTRODUCTORY REMARKS.

§ 1. The Earth has long since been divided into distinct Nations, inhabiting different regions, speaking different languages, engaged in different pursuits, and attached to different forms of government. It is natural that, under such circumstances, there should be many variances in their institutions, customs, laws, and polity; and that these variances should result sometimes from accident, and sometimes from design, sometimes from superior skill, and knowledge of local interests, and sometimes from a choice founded in ignorance, and supported by the prejudices of imperfect civilization. Climate, and geographical position, and the physical adaptations springing from them, must at all times have had a powerful influence in the organization of each society, and have given a peculiar complexion and character to many of its arrangements. The bold, intrepid, and hardy natives of the North of Europe, whether civilized or barbarous, would scarcely desire, or tolerate, the indolent inactivity and luxurious indulgences of the Asiatics. Nations inhabiting the borders of the ocean, and accustomed to maritime intercourse with other nations, would naturally require institutions and laws, adapted to their pursuits and enterprises, which would be wholly unfit for those, who should be placed in the interior of a continent, and should maintain very different relations with their neighbours, both in peace and war. Accordingly we find, that, from the earliest records of authentic history, there has been (as far at least as we can trace any,) little uniformity in the laws, usages, policy, and institutions, either of contiguous or of distant nations. The Egyptians, the Medes, the Persians, the Greeks, and the Romans, differed not more in their characters and employments from each other, than in their institutions and laws. They had little desire to learn, or to borrow, from each other; and indifference, if not contempt, was the habitual state of almost every ancient nation in regard to the internal polity of all others.

§ 2. Yet even under such circumstances, from their intercourse with each other, questions must sometimes have arisen, as to the operation of the laws of one nation upon the rights and remedies of parties in the domestic tribunals, especially when they were in any measure dependent upon, or connected with foreign transactions. How these questions were disposed of, we do not know; but it is most probable, that they were left to be decided by the analogies of the municipal code, or were abandoned to their fate, as belonging to that large class of imperfect rights, which rests wholly on personal confidence, and is left without any appeal to remedial justice. It is certain, that the nations of antiquity did not recognise the existence of any general or universal rights and obligations, such as among the moderns constitute, what is now emphatically called, the Law of Nations. Even among the Romans, whose jurisprudence has come down to us in a far more perfect and comprehensive shape, than that of any other nation, there cannot be traced out any distinct system of principles applicable to international cases of mixed rights. This has been in some measure accounted for by Huberus[1] upon the supposition, that at the time, to which the Roman jurisprudence relates, the Roman dominion extended over so great a portion of the habitable world, that frequent cases of contrariety or conflict of laws could scarcely occur.[2] But this is a very inadequate account of the matter; since the antecedent jurisprudence of Rome must have embraced many such cases at earlier periods; and if there had been any rules, even traditionally known to govern them, they could scarcely have failed of being incorporated into the civil codes of Justinian. In many of the nations, over which the Romans extended their dominion, the inhabitants were left in possession of their local institutions, usages, and laws, to a large extent; and commercial, as well as political, intercourse must have brought many diversities of laws and usages in judgment before the tribunals of justice.[3] We have the most abundant evidence on this head, in relation to the Jews, after they had submitted to the Roman yoke, who were still permitted to follow their own laws in

---

1 2 Hub. lib. 1, tit. 3, p. 538.

2 The language of Huberus is, "In jure Romano non est mirum nihil hac de re extare, cum populi Romani per omnes orbis partes diffusum, et æquabili jure gubernatum imperium conflictui diversarum legum non æque potuerit esse subjectum." — Hub. lib. 2, tit. 3, sect. 1.

3 See, 1 Hertii Opera, § 4, de Collis. leg. p. 119, § 2.

the times of our Saviour, and down to the destruction of Jerusalem.[1]

§ 3. The truth is, that the Law of Nations, strictly so called, was in a great measure unknown to antiquity, and is the slow growth of modern times, under the combined influence of Christianity and Commerce.[2] It is well known, that when the Roman Empire was destroyed, the Christian world was divided into many independent sovereignties, acknowledging no common head, and connected by no uniform civil polity. The invasions of the Barbarians of the North, the establishment of the feudal system in the middle ages, and the military spirit and enterprise cherished by the Crusades, struck down all regular commerce, and surrendered all private rights and contracts to mere despotic power. It was not until the revival of Commerce on the shores of the Mediterranean, and the revival of Letters and the study of the Civil Law by the discovery of the Pandects, had given an increased enterprise to maritime navigation, and a consequent importance to maritime contracts, that any thing like a system of international justice began to be developed. It first assumed the modest form of commercial usages ; it was next promulgated under the more imposing authority of royal ordinances ; and it finally became by silent adoption a generally connected system, founded in the natural convenience, and asserted by the general comity of the commercial nations of Europe. The system, thus

1 There are traces to be found in the Digest of the existence and operation of the Lex Loci. See, Dig. lib. 50, tit. 1, l. 21, § 7 ; Id. lib. 50, tit. 6, l. 5, § 1 ; Id. tit. 4, l. 18, § 27 ; Id. tit. 3, l. 1 ; Livermore's Dissert. p. 1, note a.

2 See, 1 Ward's Law of Nations, ch. 6, p. 171 to p. 200 ; Id. ch. 3, p. 120 to 130.

introduced for the purposes of commerce, has gradually extended itself to other objects, as the intercourse of nations has become more free and frequent. New rules, resting on the basis of general convenience, and an enlarged sense of national duty, have been, from time to time, promulgated by jurists, and supported by courts of justice, by a course of juridical reasoning, which has commanded almost universal confidence, respect, and obedience, without the aid, either of municipal statutes, or royal ordinances, or international treaties.

§ 4. Indeed, in the present times, without some general rules of right and obligation, recognised by civilized nations to govern their intercourse with each other, the most serious mischiefs and most injurious conflicts would arise. Commerce is now so absolutely universal among all countries; the inhabitants of all have such a free intercourse with each other; contracts, marriages, nuptial settlements, wills, and successions, are so common among persons, whose domicils are in different countries, having different and even opposite laws on the same subjects; that without some common principles adopted by all nations in this regard there would be an utter confusion of all rights and remedies; and intolerable grievances would grow up to weaken all the domestic relations, as well as to destroy the sanctity of contracts and the security of property.[1]

---

[1] Boullenois in his preface (1 vol. p. 18,) says, "Il regnera donc toujours entre les nations une contrariété perpetuelle de loix ; peut-être regnera-t-elle perpetuellement entre nous sur bien des objects. Delà la nécessité de s'instruire des règles et des principes, qui peuvent nous conduire dans la décision des questions, que cette variété peut faire naître."

§ 5. A few simple cases will sufficiently illustrate the importance of some international principles in matters of mere private right and duty. Suppose a contract, valid by the laws of the country, where it is made, is sought to be enforced in another country, where such a contract is positively prohibited by its laws; or, *vice versâ*, suppose a contract, invalid by the laws of the country, where it is made, but valid by that of the country, where it is sought to be enforced; it is plain, that unless some uniform rules are adopted to govern such cases, (which are not uncommon,) the grossest inequalities will arise in the administration of justice between the subjects of the different countries in regard to such contracts. Again; by the laws of some countries marriage cannot be contracted until the parties arrive at twenty-one years of age; in other countries not until they arrive at the age of twenty-five years. Suppose a marriage to be contracted between two persons in the same country, both of whom are over twenty one years but less than twenty-five, and one of them is a subject of the latter country. Is such a marriage valid, or not? If valid in the country, where it is celebrated, is it valid also in the other country? Or the question may be propounded in a still more general form, Is a marriage, valid between the parties in the place, where it is solemnized, equally valid in all other countries? Or is it obligatory only as a local regulation, and to be treated every where else as a mere nullity?

§ 6. Questions of this sort must be of frequent occurrence, not only in different countries wholly independent of each other; but also in provinces of the same empire, governed by different laws, as was the case in France before the Revolution; and also in countries acknowledging a common sovereign, but yet organized as distinct communities, as is still the case in regard to the communities composing the British Empire, the Germanic Confederacy, the States of Holland, and the Domains of Austria and Russia.[1] Innumerable suits must be litigated in the judicial forums of these countries and provinces, in which the decision must depend upon the point, whether the nature of a contract should be determined by the law of the place, where it is litigated; or by the law of the domicil of one or both of the parties; or by the law of the place, where the contract was made; whether the capacity to make a testament should be regulated by the law of the testator's domicil, or that of the location of his property; whether the form of his testament should be prescribed by the law of his domicil, or of that of the location of his property, or of that of the place, where the testament is made; and in like manner, whether the law of the domicil, or what other law should govern in cases of succession of intestate estates.[2]

§ 7. It is plain, that the laws of one country can have no intrinsic force, *proprio vigore*, except within the territorial limits and jurisdiction of that country. They can bind only its own subjects, and others, who are within its jurisdictional limits; and the latter only while they remain there. No other nation, or its subjects, are bound to yield the slightest obedience to those laws. Whatever extra-territorial force they are to have, is the result, not of any original power to extend them abroad, but of that respect, which from motives of public policy other nations are disposed to

---

1 See, 1 Froland, Mémoires sur les Statuts, P. 1. ch. 1. § 5 to § 10.

2 Livermore, Dissert. 3, 4; Merlin, Répert. Statut.

yield to them, giving them effect, as the phrase is, *sub mutuæ vicissitudinis obtentu*, with a wise and liberal regard to common convenience and mutual necessities. Boullenois has laid down the same exposition as a part of his fundamental maxims. "Of strict right," says he, "all the laws made by a sovereign have no force or authority except within the limits of his domains. But the necessity of the public and general welfare has introduced some exceptions in regard to civil commerce." *De droit étroit, toutes les lois, que fait un souverain, n'ont force et autorité que dans l'étendue de sa domination; mais la nécessité du bien public et général des nations a admis quelques exceptions dans ce, qui regarde le commerce civil.*[1]

§ 8. This is the natural principle flowing from the equality and independence of nations. It is an essential attribute of every sovereignty, that it has no admitted superior, and that it gives the supreme law within its own domains on all subjects appertaining to its sovereignty. What it yields, it is its own choice to yield; and it cannot be commanded by another to yield it as matter of right. And accordingly it is laid down by all publicists and jurists, as an incontestable rule of public law, that one may with impunity disregard the law pronounced by a magistrate beyond his territory. *Extra territorium jus dicenti impune non paretur*, is the doctrine of the Digest;[2] and it is equally as true in relation to nations, as the Roman law held it to be in relation to magistrates. Vattel has deduced a similar conclusion from the general independence and equality of nations, very properly holding, that relative

---

1 1 Boullenois, Prin. Gén. 6. p. 4.

2 Dig. lib. 2. tit. 1. l. 20.

strength or weakness cannot produce any difference in regard to public rights and duties, and that whatever is lawful for one nation is equally lawful for another; and whatever is unjustifiable in one is equally so in another.[1] And he affirms in the most positive manner (what indeed cannot well be denied) that sovereignty, united with domain, establishes the exclusive jurisdiction of a nation within its territories, as to controversies, crimes, and rights arising therein.[2]

§ 9. The jurisprudence, then, arising from the conflict of the laws of different nations, in their actual application to modern commerce and intercourse, is a most interesting and important branch of public law, To no part of the world is it of more interest and importance than to the United States, since the union of a national government with that of twenty-four distinct, and in some respects independent states, necessarily creates very complicated relations and rights between the citizens of those states, which call for the constant administration of extra-municipal principles. This branch of public law may be fitly denominated private international law, since it is chiefly seen and felt in its application to the common business of private persons, and rarely rises to the dignity of national negotiations, or national controversies.[3]

§ 10. The subject has never been systematically treated by writers on the common law of England; and, indeed, seems to be of very modern growth in that

---

[1] Vattel, Prelim. § 15 to § 20; Id. B. 2, ch. 3, § 35, 36; The St. Louis, 2 Dodson R. 210.

[2] Vattel, B. 2, ch. 7, § 84, 85.

[3] The civilians are accustomed to call the questions arising from the conflict of foreign and domestic laws mixed questions, *questions mixtes*. 1 Froland, Mémoires des Statuts, ch. 1, § 9, p. 13; Id. ch. 7, § 1, p. 155.

kingdom; and can hardly, as yet, be deemed to be there cultivated, as a science, built up and defined with entire accuracy and precision of principles. More has been done to give it form and symmetry within the last fifty years, than in all preceding time. But much yet remains to be done to make it, what it ought to be, in a country of such vast extent in its commerce, and such universal reach in its intercourse and polity.[1]

§ 11. The civilians of continental Europe have examined the whole subject in all its bearings with a much more comprehensive philosophy, if not with a more enlightened spirit. Their works, however, abound with theoretical distinctions, which serve little other purpose than to provoke idle discussions, and with metaphysical subtilties, which perplex, if they do not confound, the inquirer. As precedent has no absolute authority in their juridical discussions, it is unavoidable, that many differences of opinion should exist among them, even in relation to leading principles. But the strong sense and critical learning of the best minds among them have generally maintained those doctrines, which at the present day are deemed most persuasive and satisfactory, as well for the solid grounds, on which they rest, as for the universal approbation, with which they are entertained by courts of justice.[2]

---

1 Mr. Chancellor Kent has remarked, that these topics of international law were almost unknown in the English courts prior to the time of Lord Hardwicke and Lord Mansfield; and that the English lawyers seem generally to have been strangers to the discussions on foreign law by the celebrated jurists of continental Europe. 2 Kent's Comm. Lect. 39 p. 455, 2d edition.

2 The late Mr. Livermore, in his learned Dissertations on the Contrariety of Laws, printed at New Orleans in 1828, has enumerated the principal continental writers, who have discussed this subject at large. I gladly refer the reader to these Dissertations, as very able and clear. There is also a catalogue of the principal writers in Boullenois,

§ 12. In their discussions upon this subject the civilians have divided statutes into three classes, personal, real, and mixed. By statutes, they mean, not the positive legislation, which in England and America is known by the same name, viz. the acts of parliament and of other legislative bodies, as contradistinguished from the common law; but the whole municipal law of the particular state, from whatever source arising.[1] Sometimes the word is used by them in contradistinction to the imperial Roman law, which they are accustomed to style by way of eminence the COMMON LAW, since it constitutes the general basis of the jurisprudence of all continental Europe, modified and restrained by local customs and usages, and positive legislation.[2] Voet says, *Sequitur jus particulare, sive non commune, quod uno vocabulo usitatissimo* statutum *dicitur, quasi statum publicum tuens. Appellatur etiam* jus municipale. *Etiam in jure nostro dicta* lex, *seu* lex municipii, *quemadmodum in genere signat jus commune.* And he defines it thus, *Est jus particulare ab alio legislatore quam Imperatore constitutum. Dico,* jus particulare, *in quantum opponitur juri communi, non prout est gentium et naturale, sed prout est jus civile Romano-*

Traité des Statuts, Préface, Vol. 1. p. 29, note (1.); in Dupin's edition of Camus, Profession d'Avocat, Vol. 2, tit. 7, § 5, art. 1561 to 1566; in Froland, Mémoires concernans les Qualités des Statuts, Vol. 1, P. 1, ch. 2, p. 15; and in Bouhier, Coutum. de Bourg. Vol. 1. ch. 23, p. 450. In the preparation of these Commentaries I have availed myself chiefly of the writings of Rodemburg, the Voets (father and son), Froland, Boullenois, Bouhier, and Huberus, as embracing the most satisfactory illustrations of the leading doctrines. My object has not been to engage in any critical examination of the comparative merits or mistakes of the different commentators; but rather to gather from each of them what seemed most entitled to respect and confidence.

[1] Bouhier Coutum. de Bourg. Vol. 1, p. 174 to 179, § 9 to 32; 1 Hertii Opera. De Collisione Legum § 4, art. 5 p. 121.

[2] Bouhier Coutum. de Bourg. Vol. 1, p. 175, 178, § 16, 28, 29.

rum, populo Romano commune, et omnibus, qui illo populo parebant. Additur, ab alio legislatore, *cum qui statuta condit, recte et suo modo legislator appelletur, ut ipsa statuta leges dicuntur municipiorum. Et quidem*, ab alio, *quia regulariter statuta non condit Imperator; excipe, nisi municipibus jura det, statuta præscribat, secundum quæ ipsi sua regant municipia. Denique adjicitur*, quam imperatore, *quod licet Imperator solummodo dicatur legislator, id tamen non alio sensu obtineat, quam quod suis legibus non hunc aut illum populum, verum omnes constringat, quos suæ clementiæ regit imperium.*[1] Merlin says, "that this term, *statute*, is generally applied to all sorts of laws and regulations. Every provision of law is a statute, which permits, ordains, or prohibits any thing." *Ce terme*, (statut,) *s'applique en général à toutes sortes de lois et de réglémens. Chaque disposition d'une loi est un statut, qui permet, ordonne, ou défend quelque chose.*[2]

§ 13. The civilians have variously defined the different classes of statutes or laws. The definitions of Merlin are sufficiently clear and explicit for all the purposes of the present work, and will therefore be here cited. The distinctions between the different classes are very important to be observed in consulting the foreign Jurists, since they have been adopted from a very early period, and pervade all their discussions. Personal statutes are held by them to be of general obligation and force every where; and real statutes to have no extra-territorial force or obligation.[3]

---

1 Voet. De Statut. § 4, ch. 1, p. 112; Id. § 1, ch. 4, p. 35; Liverm. Dissert. II, p. 21, note (b).

2 Merlin, Répertoire, art. *Statut*. Saul *v.* His Creditors, 17 Martin. R. 569, 589.

3 Rodemburg, De Statut. Divers. c. 3. p. 7. 1 Froland, Mémoires des Statuts, ch. 7, § 1, 2.

"Personal statutes," says Merlin, "are those, which have principally for their object the person, and treat only of property (*biens*)[1] incidentally (*accessoirement*); such are those, which regard birth, legitimacy, freedom, the right of instituting suits, majority as to age, incapacity to contract, to make a will, to plead in proper person, &c.[2] Real statutes are those, which have principally for their object property (*biens*), and which do not speak of persons, except in relation to property; such are those, which concern the disposition, which one may make of his property, either alive, or by testament.[3] Mixed statutes, are those, which concern at once persons and property. But Merlin adds, "that in this sense almost all statutes are mixed, there being scarcely any law relative to persons, which does not at the same time relate to things."[4] He therefore deems the last classification unnecessary, and holds, that every statute ought to receive its denomination according to its principal object. As that is real, or personal, so ought the quality of the statute to be determined.[5] But this distribution into three classes is usually adopted, precisely as it is stated by Rodemburg; — *Aut enim statutum simpliciter disponit de personis; aut solummodo de rebus; aut conjunctim de utrisque.*[6]

---

1 The term "biens," in the sense of the civilians and continental jurists comprehends not merely goods and chattels, as in the common law, but real estate. But the distinction between movable and immovable property is nevertheless recognised by them, and gives rise in the civil, as well as in the common law, to many important distinctions as to rights and remedies.

2 See Pothier, Coutum. d'Orléans, ch. 1, § 1, art. 6.

3 See Pothier, Coutum. d'Orléans, ch. 1, § 2, art. 21.

4 Merlin, Répertoire, Statut; Id. Autorization Maritale, § 10.

5 Ibid.

6 Rodemburg, De Statut. Diversitate, c. 2, p. 4; Le Brun, Traité de la Communauté, Liv. 2, ch. 3, § 20 to 48; Bouhier, Coutum. de Bourg. ch.

§ 14. In the application of this classification to particular cases, there has been no inconsiderable diversity of opinion among the civilians. What particular statutes are to be deemed personal, and what real; when they may be said principally to regard persons, and when principally to regard things; these have been vexed questions, upon which much subtilty of discussion, and much heat of controversy, have been displayed. The subject is in itself full of intrinsic difficulties; but it has been rendered more perplexed by metaphysical niceties, and over-curious learning.[1] Hertius admits,

---

21 to ch. 37; Voet de Statut. § 4, ch. 2, p. 116 to 124; Livermore's Dissert. § 65 to 162; 1 Froland, Mém. Qual. des Statuts, P. 1, ch. 3, p. 25; Id. ch. 4, p. 49, ch. 5, p. 81, ch. 6, p. 114; Boullenois, Traité des Statuts, vol. 1, préface, p. 22; Pothier, Coutum. d'Orléans, ch. 1, § 1, art. 6, 7, 8. — Boullenois distributes all statutes into three classes: "Ou le statut dispose simplement des personnes; ou il dispose simplement des choses; ou il dispose tout à la fois des personnes et des choses." 1 Boullenois, Traité des Statuts réels et personnels. Princ. Gén. pp. 4, 6; and tit. 1, ch. 2, obs. 2, p 25. Mr. Henry, in his Dissertation on Personal, Real, and Mixed Statutes, has adopted the like distribution, without any acknowledgment of the source, (Boullenois,) from which he has drawn all his materials. See Henry on Personal and Real Statutes, ch. 1, § 2 to ch. 3 § 1, p. 2 to p. 33. See also Livermore's Dissert. 2, § 65 to 162, p. 62 to 106; Id. § 168, p. 109. The Supreme Court of Louisiana have said, that foreign jurists, by a personal statute, mean that, which follows, and governs the party subject to it, wherever he goes; and a real statute is that, which controls things, and does not extend beyond the limits of the country, from which it derives its authority. Saul v. His Creditors, (17 Martin's R. 569, 590.) Is not this a description of the effect of of such statutes, rather than a definition of their nature? See Id. 593.

[1] See 1 Boullenois, tit. 1, ch. 1, observ. 2, p. 16, &c; Id. ch. 2, obs. 5, p. 114, to p. 122; 1 Froland, Mém. ch. 2, p. 15; 2 Kent's Comm. Lect. 39, p. 453 to 457, (2d edit.); Saul v. His Creditors, 17 Martin's R. 569 to 596; Henry on Foreign Law, ch. 3. p. 23, &c. — The Supreme Court of Louisiana have made some very just remarks on this subject. "We are led," say the Court, "into an examination of the doctrine of real and personal statutes, as it is called by the continental writers of Europe; a subject the most intricate and perplexed of any, that has occupied the attention of lawyers and courts; one on

that these subtilties have so perplexed the subject, that it is difficult to venture even upon an explanation. His language is, *De collisu legum anceps, difficilis, et late diffusa est disputatio, quam nescio, an quisquis explicare totam aggressus fuerit.*[1] And in another place, he adds, *Junioribus plerisque placuit distinctio inter statuta, realia, personalia, et mixta. Verum in iis definiendis mirum est, quam sudant doctores.*[2] Bartholus, or Bartolus, has furnished a memorable example of these niceties. If, says he, a statute declares that, "the estate of the intestate shall descend to the eldest son," (*bona decedentis deveniant in primogeni-*

---

which scarcely any writers are found entirely to agree, and on which it is rare to find one consistent with himself throughout. We know of no matter in jurisprudence so unsettled, or none, that should more teach men distrust of their own opinions, and charity for those of others." Saul v. His Creditors. (17 Martin's R. 569, 588.) Chancellor D'Aguesseau has attempted a definition, or test, of real and personal laws. He says, "The true principle in this matter is, to examine, if the statute has *property* directly for its object, or its destination to certain persons, or its preservation in families, so that it is not the interest of the person, whose rights or acts are examined, but the interest of others, to whom it is intended to assure the property, or the real rights, which were the cause of the law. Or if, on the contrary, all the attention of the law is directed towards the person, to provide in general for his qualifications, or his general absolute capacity, as when it relates to the qualities of major or minor, of father or son, legitimate or illegitimate, ability or inability to contract, by reason of personal causes. In the first hypothesis, the statute is real; in the second, it is personal." Cited Id. p. 594. How unsatisfactory is this description, when applied in practice.

1 1 Hertii Opera, De Collis. Legum, § 1, p. 91; Id. § 4, p. 121, 122, § 5.

2 1 Hertii Opera, § 4, n. 3, p. 120. See also 1 Froland, Mém. Qualité des Statut, ch. 3, to ch. 7; Bouhier, Coutum. de Bourg. ch. 23, § 58, 59. — Mr. Livermore has given a concise view of the various opinions of foreign jurists on this subject, which will well reward a diligent perusal. Livermore's Dissert. 2, § 65 to 162. His own opinions, which exhibit great acuteness, will also be found in the same work from § 163 to § 214. The subject is very amply discussed in Froland, Boullenois, Bouhier, Le Brun, and Rodemburg.

tum,) it is a real statute; if it says, "the eldest son shall succeed to the estate," *(primogenitus succedat,)* it is a personal statute.[1] This distinction has been justly exploded by other civilians, as the mere order and construction of the words of the statute, and not its objects, would otherwise decide its character.[2]

§ 15. Le Brun says, that in order to ascertain, whether a statute is personal or not, it is necessary to examine, whether it universally governs the state of the person, independent of property. If it does not universally govern the state of the person, but only particular acts of the person, it is not personal. Thus, a statute, which prohibits married persons from making donations to each other, is purely real, because it regulates a particular act only. And a statute, to be personal, must regulate the state of the person without speaking of property, *(biens.)* Thus, a statute, which excludes females from inheriting fiefs, in favor of males; or, which excludes a beneficiary heir from the succession, in favor of the simple heir; or which excludes a daughter, who is endowed, from the succession, is real; for all these statutes speak of property. For the same reason, he holds the *Senatûs-consultum Velleianum,* by which a married woman was prohibited from binding herself for the debt of another person,[3] (and which was borrowed from the Roman Law into the customary jurisprudence of some of the French provinces,) to be a real statute, because it regulates a particular

---

1 1 Boullenois, tit. 1, ch. 1, obs. 2, p. 17; Livermore's Dissert. 2, § 67, 68.

2 Ibid. p. 19; Livermore's Dissert. 2, § 67 to § 77; 1 Froland, Mém. Statut. P. 1, ch. 3, § 3, 4; 17 Martin's R. 569, 591; Bouhier, Coutum. de Bourg. ch. 53, § 58 to 99.

3 Dig. lib. 16, tit. 1, l. 1; Id. l. 16, § 1.

act of the person only. And he adds, that the definition of a real statute results from that of a personal statute. In one word, a statute is real, which regulates a particular act of the person, or which speaks of property.[1] Other jurists of distinguished reputation (among whom is Boullenois,) have denied this to be a sound distinction; and have especially held the *Senatûs-consultum Velleianum* to be a personal statute.[2]

§ 16. It is not my design to engage in the controversy, as to what constitutes the true distinction between personal and real statutes, or to examine the merits of the various systems propounded by foreign jurists. It would carry me too far from the immediate purpose of these commentaries, even if I felt myself possessed (which I certainly do not) of that critical skill and learning, which such an examination would require, in order to treat the subject with suitable dignity. My object is rather to present the leading principles upon some of the more important topics, and to use the works of the civilians, to illustrate, confirm, and expand the doctrines of the common law, so far at least, as the latter have assumed a settled form. If, in referring to the authority of the civilians, I should speak of the personality of laws, *(personalité des statuts,)* and the reality of laws, *(réalité des statuts,)* let it not be attributed to a spirit of innovation upon the received usages of language; but rather to a desire to familiarize expressions, which in this peculiar sense have already found their way into our juridical discussions, and are becoming daily more and more im-

---

1 Le Brun, Traité de la Communauté, Liv. 2, ch. 3, § 5, n. 20 to n. 48.

2 1 Boullenois, p. 40, 43, 49, 78, 79, 82, 101, 103, 105, 106, 118; Henry on Foreign Law, 31, 50.

portant to be understood by American lawyers, since they are incorporated into the very substance of the jurisprudence of some of the States in the Union.[1] By the personality of laws foreign jurists generally mean all laws, which concern the condition, state, and capacity of persons; by the reality of laws, all laws, which concern property or things; *quæ ad rem spectant.*[2] Whenever they wish to express, that the operation of a law is universal, they compendiously announce, that it is a personal statute; and whenever, on the other hand, they wish to express, that its operation is confined to the country of its origin, they simply declare it to be real.

---

1 See note to 2 Kent's Comm. Lect. 39, p. 456, 2d edition.

2 Mr. Livermore, in his Dissertations, used the words, *personality* and *reality*; Mr. Henry, in his work, the words *personalty* and *realty*; I have preferred the former, as least likely to lead to mistakes, as "personalty" is in our law confined to personal estate, and "realty" to real estate.

CHAPTER II.

GENERAL MAXIMS OF INTERNATIONAL JURISPRUDENCE.

§ 17. Before entering upon any examination of the various heads, which a treatise upon the Conflict of Laws will naturally embrace, it seems necessary to advert to a few general maxims or axioms, which constitute the basis, upon which all reasonings on the subject must necessarily rest; and without the express or tacit admission of which, it will be found impossible to arrive at any principles to govern the conduct of nations, or to regulate the due administration of justice.

§ 18. I. The first and most general maxim or proposition is that, which has been already adverted to, that every nation possesses an exclusive sovereignty and jurisdiction within its own territory. The direct consequence of this rule is, that the laws of every state affect, and bind directly all property, whether real or personal, within its territory; and all persons, who are resident within it, whether natural born subjects, or aliens; and also all contracts made, and acts done within it.[1] A state may, therefore, regulate the manner and circumstances, under which property, whether real, or personal, or in action, within it, shall be held, transmitted, bequeathed, or transferred, or enforced; the condition, capacity, and state, of all persons within it; the validity of contracts, and other acts, done within it;

---

1 Henry on Foreign Law, P. 1, ch. 1, § 1, p. 1; Huberus, Lib. 1 tit. 3, § 2; Hall v. Campbell, Cowper R. 208; Ruding v. Smith, 2 Hagg. Consist. R. 383.

the resulting rights and duties growing out of these contracts and acts; and the remedies, and modes of administering justice in all cases calling for the interposition of its tribunals to protect, vindicate, and secure the wholesome agency of its own laws within its own domains.

§ 19. Accordingly, Boullenois has laid down the following among his general principles, *(principes généraux.)* He says, (1.) He, or those, who have the sovereign authority, have the sole right to make laws; and these laws ought to be executed in all places within the sovereignty, where they are known, in the prescribed manner. (2.) The sovereign has power and authority over his subjects, and the goods, which they possess within his dominions. (3.) The sovereign has also authority to regulate the forms and solemnities of contracts, which his subjects make within the territories under his dominions; and to prescribe the rules for the administration of justice. (4.) The sovereign has also a right to make laws, to govern foreigners in many cases; for example, in relation to property, which they possess within the reach of his sovereignty; in relation to the formalities of contracts, which they make within his territories; and in relation to judiciary proceedings, if they institute suits before his tribunals. (5.) The sovereign may in like manner make laws for foreigners, who even pass through his territories; but these are commonly merely laws of police, made for the preservation of order within his dominions, whether they are perpetual or temporary.[1] The same doctrine is either tacitly, or expressly, conceded by every other jurist, who has discussed the subject at large, whether he has written upon municipal law, or upon public law.[2]

---

[1] 1 Boullenois, Des Statuts, p. 2, 3, 4. [2] Vattel, B. 2, ch. 7, § 84, 85.

§ 20. II. Another maxim, or proposition, is, that no state or nation can, by its laws, directly affect, or bind property out of its own territory, or persons not resident therein, whether they are natural born subjects, or others. This is a natural consequence of the first proposition; for it would be wholly incompatible with the equality and exclusiveness of the sovereignty of any nation, that other nations should be at liberty to regulate either persons or things within its territories. It would be equivalent to a declaration, that the sovereignty over a territory was never exclusive in any nation, but only concurrent with that of all nations; that each could legislate for all, and none for itself; and that all might establish rules, which none were bound to obey. The absurd results of such a state of things need not be dwelt upon. Accordingly Rodemburg has significantly said, that no sovereign has a right to give the law beyond his own dominions; and if he attempts it, he may be lawfully refused obedience; for wherever the foundation of laws fails, there their force and jurisdiction fail also. *Constat igitur extra territorium legem dicere licere nemini, idque si fecerit quis, impune ei non pareri, quippe ubi cesset statutorum fundamentum, robur, et jurisdictio.*[1] P. Voet speaks to the same effect: *Nullum statutum sive in rem, sive in personam, si de ratione juris civilis sermo instituatur, sese extendit ultra statuentis territorium.*[2] Boullenois, (as we have seen,) announces the same rule: *De droit étroit, toutes les loix, que fait un souverain, n'ont force et autorité que dans l'étendue de sa domination*; and, indeed, it is the common language of jurists.[4] Mr. Chief Justice

---

[1] Rodemb. de Stat. ch. 3, § 1, p. 7. [2] Voet de Stat. § 7, ch. 2, § 7, p. 124.

[3] 1 Boullenois, Des Statut. Princip. Gén. 6, p. 4. — Id. ch. 3, Observ. 10, p. 152. [4] Id.

Parker has recognised the doctrine in the fullest manner. "That the laws," says he, "of any state cannot by any inherent authority be entitled to respect extra-territorially, or beyond the jurisdiction of the state, which enacts them, is the necessary result of the independence of distinct sovereignties."[1]

§ 21. Upon this rule there is often engrafted an exception of some importance to be rightly understood. It is, that although the laws of a nation have no direct, binding force, or effect, except upon persons within its territories; yet every nation has a right to bind its own subjects by its own laws in every other place.[2] In one sense, this exception may be admitted to be correct, and well founded in the practice of nations; in another sense it is incorrect, or, at least, it requires qualification. Every nation has hitherto assumed it as clear, that it possesses the right to regulate and govern its own native born subjects everywhere; and consequently, that its laws extend to, and bind, such subjects at all times, and in all places. This is commonly adduced as a consequence of what is called national allegiance, that is, of allegiance to the government of the territory of a man's birth. Thus, Mr. Justice Blackstone says, "Natural allegiance is such as is due from all men, born within the king's dominions, immediately upon their birth." "Natural allegiance is, therefore, a debt of gratitude, which cannot be forfeited, cancelled, or altered, by any change of time, place, or circumstance. An Englishman, who removes to France, or to China, owes the same allegiance to the king of England there, as at home, and twenty years hence, as well as now."[3] And he pro-

1 Blanchard v. Russell, 13 Mass. R. 4.

2 Henry on Real and Personal Statut. P. 1, ch. 1, p. 1.

3 1 Black. Comm. 369, 370; Foster, C. L. 184.

ceeds to distinguish it from local allegiance, which is such as is due from an alien, or stranger born, for so long a time as he continues within the dominions of a foreign prince. The former is universal and perpetual; the latter ceases the instant the stranger transfers himself to another country;[1] and it is, therefore, local and temporary. Vattel, on the other hand, seems to admit the right of allegiance not to be perpetual even in natives; and that they have a right to expatriate themselves, and, under some circumstances, to dissolve their connexion with the parent country.[2]

§ 22. Without entering upon this subject, (which properly belongs to a general treatise upon public law,) it may be truly said, that no nation is bound to respect the laws of another nation, made in regard to subjects, who are non-residents. The obligatory force of such laws cannot extend beyond its own territories. And if such laws are incompatible with the laws of the country, where they reside, or interfere with the duties, which they owe to the country, where they reside, they will be disregarded by the latter. Whatever may be the obligatory force of such laws upon such persons, if they should return to their native country, they can have none in other nations, where they reside. They may give rise to personal relations between the sovereign and subjects, to be enforced in his own domains; but they do not rightfully extend to other nations. *Clauduntur territorio.* Nor, indeed, is there, strictly speaking, any difference in this respect, whether such laws concern the persons, or the property of native subjects. A state has just as much intrinsic right, and no more, to give to its own laws an extra-

1 Black. Comm. 369, 370; Foster C. L. 184.

2 Vattel, B. 1, ch. 19, § 220 to 228.

territorial force, as to the property of its subjects situated abroad, as it has in relation to the persons of its subjects domiciled abroad. That is, as sovereign laws, they have no obligation or power over either. When, therefore, we speak of the right of a state to bind its own native subjects everywhere; we speak only of its own claim and exercise of sovereignty over them, and not of its right to compel or require obedience to such laws on the part of other nations. On the contrary every nation has an exclusive right to regulate persons and things within its own territory according to its own sovereign will and polity.

§ 23. III. From these two maxims or propositions, there flows a third, and that is, that whatever force and obligation the laws of one country have in another, depends solely upon the laws, and municipal regulations of the latter, that is to say, upon its own proper jurisprudence and polity, and upon its own express or tacit consent.[1] A state may prohibit the operation of all foreign laws, and the rights growing out of them, within its own territories. It may prohibit some foreign laws, and admit the operation of others. It may recognise, and modify, and qualify some foreign laws; it may enlarge, or give universal effect to others. It may interdict the administration of some foreign laws; it may favour the introduction of others. When its code speaks positively on the subject, it must be obeyed by all persons, who are within the reach of its sovereignty. When its customary, unwritten, or common law speaks directly on the subject, it is equally to be obeyed; for it has an equal obligation with its positive code. When both are silent, then, and then only, can the question properly arise, what law is to

[1] Huberus, Lib. 1, tit. 3, § 2.

govern in the absence of any clear declaration of the sovereign will. Is the rule to be promulgated by a legislative act of the sovereign power? Or is it to be promulgated by courts of law, according to the analogies, which are furnished in the municipal jurisprudence? This question does not admit of any universal answer; or rather, it will be answered differently in different communities, according to the organization of the departments of each particular government.

§ 24. Upon the continent of Europe some of the principal states have silently suffered their courts to draw this portion of their jurisprudence from the analogies furnished by the civil law, or by their own customary or positive code. France, for instance, composed, as it formerly was, of a great number of provinces, governed by different laws and customs, was early obliged to sanction such exertions of authority by its courts, in order to provide for the constantly occurring claims of its subjects, living and owning property in different provinces, in a conflict of the different provincial laws. In England and America the courts of justice have hitherto exercised the same authority in the most ample manner; and the legislatures have in no instance (it is believed) in either country interfered to provide any positive regulations. The common law of both countries has been expanded to meet the exigencies of the times, as they have arisen; and so far as the practice of nations, or the *jus gentium privatum*, has been supposed to furnish any general principle, it has been followed out with a wise and manly liberality.

§ 25. The real difficulty is to ascertain, what principles in point of public convenience ought to regulate the conduct of nations on this subject in regard to each other; and in what manner they can be best applied to the infinite variety of cases, arising from the complicated concerns of human society in modern times. No nation can be justly required to yield up its own fundamental policy and institutions in favour of those of another nation. Much less can any nation be required to sacrifice its own interests in favour of another; or to enforce doctrines, which, in a moral, or political view, are incompatible with its own safety or happiness, or conscientious regard to justice and duty. In the endless diversities of human jurisprudence many laws must exist in one country, which are the result of local or accidental circumstances, and are wholly unfit to be engrafted upon the institutions and habits of another. Many laws, adapted to heathen nations, would be totally repugnant to the feelings, as well as to the justice, of those, which embrace Christianity. A heathen nation might justify polygamy, or incest, contracts of moral turpitude, or exercises of despotic cruelty over persons, which would be repugnant to the first principles of Christian duty. The laws of one nation may be founded upon a narrow selfishness, exclusively adapted to promote the personal or proprietary interests of its own subjects, to the injury or even ruin of those of the subjects of all other countries. A nation may refuse all reciprocity of commerce, rights, and remedies to others. It may assume a superiority of powers and prerogatives for the very purpose of crushing those of its neighbours, who are less fortunate or less powerful. In these, and in many other cases, which may easily be put, without any extravagance of supposition, there would be extreme difficulty in saying, that other nations were bound to enforce laws, institutions, or customs, so subversive of their own morals, justice, interest, or polity. Who, for instance, (not to multiply cases), who would contend, that any nation in Christendom ought to carry into effect to its utmost range the paternal power of the ancient Romans in their early jurisprudence, extending to the life and death of their children?[1] Or that terrible power (if it ever really existed) under the law of the Twelve Tables, which enabled creditors to cut their debtor's body into pieces, and divide it among them?[2]

§ 26. The jurists of continental Europe have with uncommon skill and acuteness endeavoured to collect principles, which ought to regulate this subject among all nations. But it is very questionable, whether their success has been at all proportionate to their labour; and whether their principles, if universally adopted, would be found either convenient or desirable under all circumstances. Their systems, indeed, have had mainly in view the juridical polity fit for the different provinces and states of a common empire, though they are by no means limited to them. It is easy to see, that in a nation, like France, before the revolution, governed by different laws in its various provinces, some uniform rules might be adopted, which would not be equally fit for the adoption of independent nations possessing no such common interests, or such common basis of jurisprudence. The leading positions maintained by many of the French jurists are, that the laws of a country, which concern persons, who reside within, and are subject to its territorial jurisdiction, ought to be deemed

---

1 Laws of the Twelve Tables, Table 4, ch. 1, 1 Pothier, Pandects, and Id. § 1, 2, (8vo edit. Paris, 1818, p. 386, 387); 1 Black. Comm. 452; Fergusson. on Marr. and Divorce, 411; Grotius, B. 2, ch. 5, § 7.

2 Table 3, ch. 4; 1 Pothier, Pandects, and Id. Comm. § 2, (8vo edit. Paris, 1818, p. 372, 380, 381); 2 Black. Comm. 472, 473.

of universal obligation in all other countries; that the laws, which concern the property of such persons, ought to be deemed purely local, and the laws of a mixed character, concerning such persons and property, ought to be deemed local, or universal, according to their predominant character. Thus, Boullenois lays down these rules in pointed terms. *Les loix pures personelles, soit personnelles universelles, soit personelles particulières, se portent partout; c'est à dire, que l'homme est partout de l'état, soit universel, soit particulier, dont sa personne est affectée, par la loi de son domicil. Les loix réelles n'ont point d'extension directe, ni indirecte hors la jurisdiction et la domination du legislateur. Le sujet et le materiel dominant direct et immediat du statut en determine la nature et qualité; c'est à dire, que le sujet et le materiel le font être réel, ou personnel.*[1]

§ 27. Independent of the almost insurmountable difficulties, in which the continental jurists admit themselves to be involved, in the attempt to settle the true character of these mixed cases of international jurisprudence, and about which they have been engaged in endless controversies with each other, there are certain exceptions to these rules, generally admitted, which shake the very foundation, on which they rest, and admonish us, that it is far easier to give simplicity to systems, than to reconcile them with the true duties and interests of all nations in all cases. Take, for example, two neighbouring states, one of which admits, and the other of which prohibits, the existence of slavery, and the rights of property growing out of it; what help would it be to either, in

[1] 1 Boullenois, Traité des Statuts, Prin. Gén. 18, 23, 27, p. 6, 7.

ascertaining its own duties and interests in regard to the other, to say, that their laws, so far as they regard the persons of the slaves, were of universal obligation; and, so far as they regard the property in slaves, they were real, and of no obligation beyond the territory of the lawgiver?[1]

§ 28. There is indeed great truth in the remarks, which have been judicially promulgated on this subject by a learned court. "When so many men of great talents and learning are thus found to fail in fixing certain principles, we are forced to conclude, that they have failed, not from want of ability, but because the matter was not susceptible of being settled on certain principles. They have attempted to go too far, to define and fix that, which cannot, in the nature of things, be defined and fixed. They seem to have forgotten, that they wrote on a question, which touched the comity of nations, and that that comity is, and ever must be, uncertain. That it must necessarily depend on a variety of circumstances, which cannot be reduced to any certain rule. That no nation will suffer the laws of another to interfere with her own to the injury of her citizens. That, whether they do or not, must depend on the condition of the country, in which the foreign law is sought to be enforced; the particular nature of her legislation, her policy, and the character of her institutions. That in the conflict of laws, it must often be a matter of doubt, which should prevail; and that whenever a doubt does exist, the court, which decides, will prefer the law of its own country to that of the stranger."[2]

---

1 See Somerset's case, and Hargrave's note to Co. Lit. 79, *b*, note 44.

2 Saul *v.* His Creditors, 17 Martin. R. 569, 595, 596.

§ 29. Huberus has laid down three axioms, which he deems sufficient to solve all the intricacies of the subject. The first is, that the laws of every empire have force only within the limits of its own government, and bind all, who are subjected to it, but not beyond those limits. The second is, that all persons, who are found within the limits of a government, whether their residence is permanent or tempórary, are to be deemed subjects thereof. The third is, that the rulers of every empire from comity admit, that the laws of every people in force within its own limits, ought to have the same force every where, so far as they do not prejudice the power or rights of other governments, or of their citizens.[1] "From this," he adds, "it appears, that this matter is to be determined, not simply by the civil laws, but by the convenience and tacit consent of different people; for since the laws of one people cannot have any direct force among another people, so nothing could be more inconvenient in the commerce and general intercourse of nations, than that what is valid by the laws of one place should become without effect by the diversity of laws of another; and that this is the true reason of the last axiom, of which no one hitherto seems to have entertained any doubt."[2]

§ 30. Hertius seems to have been dissatisfied with these rules; and especially with the last; and he doubts

---

1 Huberus, Lib. 1, tit. 3, de Conflictu Legum, § 2, p. 538.

2 Ibid. — These axioms of Huberus are so often cited, that it may be well to give them in his own words. "(1) Leges cujusque imperii vim habent intra terminos ejusdem reipublicæ, omnesque ei subjectos obligant, nec ultra. (2) Pro subjectis imperio habendi sunt omnes, qui intra terminos ejusdem reperiuntur, sive in perpetuum, sive ad tempus ibi commorentur. (3) Rectores imperiorum id comiter agunt, ut jura cujusque populi intra terminos ejus exercita teneant ubique suam vim, quatenus nihil potestati aut juri alterius imperantis ejusque civium præjudicetur." 2 Huberus, Lib. 1 tit. 3; De Conflictu Legum. § 2.

exceedingly, whether this comity of nations, founded upon the notion of mutual convenience and utility, can furnish any sufficiently solid basis of a system. *Ob reciprocam enim utilitatem, in disciplinam juris gentium abiisse, ut civitas alterius civitatis leges apud se valere patiatur, adeoque exemplum hoc, ut evidentissimi argumenti ad probandum, quod jus gentium revera a jure naturæ distinctum sit, vult observari. Verum enim nos valde dubitamus, num res hæc ex jure gentium, sine mutuâ earum indulgentiâ, possit definiri, presertim cum in unâ eâdemque civitate collisio sæpissime fiat. Nôrunt etiam periti ex solis exemplis jus gentium adstruere, quam sit fallax; tum si solâ populorum convenientiâ id niti dicamus, quæ juris erit efficacia?* He adds, that he is disposed to search deeper into the matter; *nobis paullo altius libet repetere;*[1] and he proceeds to enunciate his own views under the known distinctions of personal and real statutes, and then lays down the following rules. 1. "When a law is directed, or has regard, to the person, we are to look to (be governed by) the laws of the country, to which he is personally subject." *Quando lex in personam dirigitur, respiciendum est ad leges illius civitatis, quæ personam habet subjectam.* 2. "If a law bears directly upon things, it is local, in whatever place and by whomsoever the act is done." *Si lex directo rei imponitur, ea locum habet, ubicunque etiam locorum et a quocunque actus celebratur.* 3. "If a law gives the form (prescribes the form) to the act, then the place of the act, and not of the domicil of the party, or of the situation of the thing, is to be regarded." *Si lex actui formam dat, inspiciendus est locus actûs, non domicilii, non rei sitæ.*[2]

---

[1] 1 Hertii Opera, De Collis. Leg. § 4, art. 3 and 4, p. 120.
[2] Id. § 4, art. 8, 9, 10, p. 123 to 126.

Now, after the admission of Hertius himself, that the usage of nations must furnish a very fallacious guide on such a subject, it is not a little difficult to perceive, what superior authority or value his own rules have over those of Huberus. The latter has at least this satisfactory foundation for his most important rule, that he is mainly guided in it by the practice of nations; and he thus aimed, as Grotius had done before him, to avail himself of the practice of nations, as a solid proof of the acknowledged law of nations.[1]

§ 31. Some attempts have been made, but without success, to undervalue the authority of Huberus. It is certainly true, that he is not often spoken of, except by jurists belonging to the Dutch School. Boullenois, however, has quoted his third and last axiom with manifest approbation.[2] But it will require very little aid of authority to countenance his merits, if his maxims are well founded; and if they are not, no approbation, founded on foreign recognitions, can disguise their defects. It is not, however, a slight recommendation of his works, that hitherto he has possessed an undisputed preference on this subject over other continental jurists, as well in England as in America. Indeed, his two first maxims will in the present day scarcely be disputed by any one; and the last seems irresistibly to flow from the right and duty of every nation to protect its own subjects against injuries resulting from the unjust and prejudicial influence of foreign laws; and to refuse its aid to carry into effect any foreign laws, which are repugnant to its own interests and polity.

---

1 The Scottish courts seem constantly to have held the doctrine of Huberus in his third axiom to be entirely correct. See Fergusson, on Marr. and Div. 395, 396, 410.

2 1 Boullenois, Traité des Statuts, ch. 3, Obser. 10, p. 155.

§ 32. It is difficult to conceive, upon what ground a claim can be rested, to give to any municipal laws an extra-territorial effect, when those laws are prejudicial to the rights of other nations, or their subjects. It would at once annihilate the sovereignty and equality of the nations, which should be called upon to recognise and enforce them; or compel them to desert their own proper interest and duty in favour of strangers, who were regardless of both. A claim, so naked of principle and authority to support it, is wholly inadmissible.

§ 33. It has been thought by some jurists, that the term, "comity," is not sufficiently expressive of the obligation of nations to give effect to foreign laws, when they are not prejudicial to their own rights and interests. And it has been suggested, that the doctrine rests on a deeper foundation; that it is not so much a matter of comity, or courtesy, as of paramount moral duty.[1] Now, assuming, that such a moral duty does exist, it is clearly one of imperfect obligation, like that of beneficence, humanity, and charity. Every nation must be the final judge for itself, not only of the nature and extent of the duty, but of the occasions, on which its exercise may be justly demanded. And, certainly, there can be no pretence to say, that any foreign nation has a right to require the full recognition and execution of its own laws in other territories, when those laws are deemed oppressive or injurious to the rights or interests of the inhabitants of the latter, or where their moral character is questionable, or their provisions impolitic.[2] Even in other cases, it is difficult to perceive a clear foundation in morals, or in natural

1 Livermore's Dissert. p. 26 to 30.

2 See Saul *v.* His Creditors, 17 Martin R. 569, 596 to 599.

law, for declaring, that any nation has a right (all others being equal in sovereignty) to insist, that its own positive laws shall be of superior obligation in a foreign realm to the domestic laws of the latter, of an equally positive character. What intrinsic right has one nation to declare, that no contract shall be binding, which is made by any of its subjects in a foreign country, unless they are twenty-five years of age, more than another nation, where the contract is made, to declare, that such contract shall be binding, if made by any persons of twenty-one years of age? One should suppose, that if there be any thing clearly within the scope of national sovereignty, it is the right to fix, what shall be the rule to govern contracts made within its own territories.

§ 34. That a nation ought not to make its own jurisprudence an instrument of injustice to other nations, or their subjects, may be admitted. But in a vast variety of cases, which may be put, the rejection of the laws of a foreign nation may work less injustice, than the enforcement of them will remedy. And, here again, every nation must judge for itself, what is its true duty in the administration of justice. It is not to be taken for granted, that the rule of the foreign nation is right, and that its own is wrong.

§ 35. The true foundation, on which the administration of international law must rest, is, that the rules, which are to govern, are those, which arise from mutual interest and utility, from a sense of the inconveniences, which would result from a contrary doctrine, and from a sort of moral necessity to do justice, in order that justice may be done to us in return.[1] This

---

1 Livermore Dissert. p. 28; Blanchard *v.* Russell, 13 Mass. R. 4.

is the ground upon which Rodemburg puts it. *Quid, igitur,* (says he) *rei in causâ est, quod personalia statuta territorium egrediantur? Unicum hoc ipsa rei natura ac necessitas invexit, ut cum de statu et conditione hominum quæritur, uni solummodo judici, et quidem domicilii, universum in illâ jus sit attributum; cum enim ab uno certoque loco statum hominis legem accipere necesse est, quod absurdum, earumque rerum naturaliter inter se pugna foret, ut in quot loca quis iter faciens, aut navigans, delatus fuerit, totidem ille statum mutaret aut conditionem; ut uno eodemque tempore hic sui juris, illic alieni futurus sit; uxor simul in potestate viri, et extra eandem sit; alio loco habeatur quis prodigus, alio frugi.*[1] President Bouhier expounds the ground with still more distinctness. *Mais avant toutes choses, il faut se souvenir, qu'encore que le règle étroite soit pour la restriction des coutumes dans leurs limites, l'extension en a néanmoins été admise en faveur de l'utilité publique, et souvent même par une espèce de nécessité, &c. Ainsi, quand les peuples voisins ont souffert cette extension,* ce n'est point, *qu'ils se soient vus soumis à un statut étranger; c'est seulement, parce qu'ils y ont trouvé leur interêt particulier. On peut donc dire, que cette extension est sur une espèce de droit des gens,* et de bienséance, *en virtu duquel les différens peuples sont tacitement demeurés d'accord, de souffrir cette extension de coutume à coutume, toutes les fois que l'equité et l'utilité commune le demanderoient; à moins que celle, où l'extension seroit demandée, ne contînt en ce cas une disposition prohibitive.*[2]

§ 36. But of the nature, and extent, and utility of this recognition of foreign laws, respecting the state and

---

1 Rodemburg, De Stat. Diversit. tit. 1, c. 3, § 4, p. 8.

2 Bouhier, Cout. de Bourg. ch. 23, § 62, 63, p. 457.

condition of persons, every nation must judge for itself, and certainly is not bound to recognise them, when they would be prejudicial to its own interests. The very terms, in which the doctrine is commonly enunciated, carry along with them this necessary qualification and limitation of it. Mutual utility presupposes, that the interest of all nations is consulted, and not that of one only. Now, this demonstrates, that the doctrine owes its origin and authority to the voluntary adoption and consent of nations. It is, therefore, in the strictest sense a matter of the comity of nations, and not of absolute paramount obligation, superseding all discretion on the subject.[1]

§ 37. Vattel has with great propriety said, "that it belongs exclusively to each nation to form its own judgment of what its conscience prescribes to it; of what it can, or cannot do; of what is proper, or improper for it to do. And of course it rests solely with it to examine and determine, whether it can perform any office for another nation, without neglecting the duty, which it owes to itself."[2] Lord Stowell has pointed out the same principle in his usual felicitous manner. Speaking with reference to the validity of a Scotch marriage, in controversy before him, he remarked; "Being entertained in an English court it (the cause) must be adjudicated according to the principles of English law, applicable to such a case. But the only principle, applicable to such a case, by the law of England is, that the validity of the marriage rights must be tried by reference to the law of the country, where, if they exist at all, they had their origin. Having furnished this principle, the law of England withdraws

1 2 Kent's Comm. Lect. 39, p. 457, 458, (2d edition.)

2 Vattel, Prelim. Disc. p. 61, 62, § 14, 16.

altogether, and leaves the legal question to the exclusive judgment of the law of Scotland."[1]

§ 38. There is, then, not only no impropriety in the use of the phrase "comity of nations," but it is the most appropriate phrase to express the true foundation and extent of the obligation of the laws of one nation within the territories of another.[2] It is derived altogether from the voluntary consent of the latter; and is inadmissible, when it is contrary to its known policy, or prejudicial to its interests. In the silence of any positive rule, affirming, or denying, or restraining the operation of foreign laws, courts of justice presume the tacit adoption of them by their own government, unless they are repugnant to its policy, or prejudicial to its interests. It is not the comity of the courts, but the comity of the nation, which is administered, and ascertained in the same way, and guided by the same reasoning, by which all other principles of the municipal law are ascertained and guided. The doctrine of Huberus would seem, therefore, to stand upon just principles; and though, from its generality, it leaves behind many grave questions as to its application, it has much to commend it, in point of truth, as well as of simplicity. It has accordingly been sanctioned both in England and America by a judicial approbation, as direct and universal, as can fairly be desired for the purpose of giving sanction to it, as authority, or as reasoning.[3]

---

1 Dalrymple *v.* Dalrymple, 2 Hagg. Consist. R. 59. See Scrimshire *v.* Scrimshire, Id. 407, 416.

2 See Robinson *v.* Bland, 2 Burr. R. 1077, 1079; Blanchard *v.* Russell, 13 Mass. R. 4.

3 Out of the great variety of authorities, in which the rules of Huberus are directly or indirectly approved, the reader is referred to the

following. — Co. Lit. 79, b, Hargrave's note 44; Robinson *v.* Bland, 2 Burr. R. 1077, 1078; Holman *v.* Johnson, Cowper, 341; 2 Kent's Comm. Lect. 39, p. 453 to 463, (2d edition); Pearsall *v.* Dwight, 2 Mass. R. 84, 90; Desesbats *v.* Berquier, 1 Binn. R. 336; Holmes *v.* Remsen, 4 John. Ch. R. 469; Cowen's note, 4 Cowen's Rep. 510; Saul *v.* His Creditors, 17 Martin. R. 569, 596, 597, 598; Greenwood *v.* Curtis, 6 Mass. R. 358.

CHAPTER III.

NATIONAL DOMICIL.

§ 39. HAVING disposed of these preliminary considerations, it is proposed, in the further progress of these Commentaries, to examine the operation and effect of foreign laws; first, in relation to persons, their capacity, state, and condition; secondly, in relation to contracts; thirdly, in relation to property, personal, mixed, and real; fourthly, in relation to wills, successions, and distributions; fifthly, in relation to persons acting *in autre droit*, such as guardians, executors, and administrators; sixthly, in relation to remedies and judicial sentences; seventhly, in relation to penal laws and offences; and eighthly, in relation to evidence and proofs.

§ 40. As, however, in all the discussions upon this subject, perpetual reference will be made to the domicil of the party, it may be proper to ascertain, what is the true meaning of the term "domicil"; or rather, what constitutes the national domicil of a party, according to the understanding of publicists and jurists.

§ 41. By the term "domicil," in its ordinary acceptation, is meant the place, where a person lives, or has his home. In this sense the place, where a person has his actual residence, inhabitancy, or commorancy, is sometimes called his domicil. In a strict and legal sense, that is properly the domicil of a person, where he has his true, fixed, permanent home, and principal establishment, and to which, whenever he is absent, he has the intention of returning, (*animus revertendi.*)[1]

---

[1] Dr. Lieber's Encyc. Americ. art. *Domicil.*

§ 42. In the Roman law it is said, "there is no doubt, that every person has his domicil in that place, which he makes his family residence and principal place of his business; from which he does not depart, unless some business requires; when he leaves it, he deems himself a wanderer; and when he returns to it, he deems himself no longer abroad." *In eodem loco singulos habere domicilium non ambigitur, ubi quis larem rerumque ac fortunarum summam constituit; unde cursus non sit discessurus, si nihil avocet; unde cum profectus est, peregrinari videtur; quod si rediit, peregrinari jam destitit.*[1] "And again the place, which is the principal seat of the fortunes or property, which any person possesses, is deemed his domicil." *Domicilium facit potissimum sedes fortunarum suarum, quas quis in aliquo loco habet.* And in another place it is said, "If any one always carries on his business, not in a colony, but in a municipality, or city, where he buys, sells, and contracts; where he makes use of, and attends the forum, the public baths, and public shows; where he celebrates the holidays, and enjoys all municipal privileges, and none in the colony; he is deemed there to have his domicil, rather than in the place (colony), in which he sojourns for purposes of agriculture." *Si quis negotia sua non in coloniâ, sed in municipio semper agit, in illo vendit, emit, contrahit, eo in foro, balneo, spectaculis utitur, ibi festos dies celebrat; omnibus denique municipii commodis, nullis coloniarum, fruitur; ibi magis habere domicilium, quam ubi colendi causâ diversatur.*[2] And again, "He is deemed an inhabi-

---

[1] Cod. Lib. 10, tit. 39, l. 7; Pothier, Pand. Lib. 50, tit. 1, § 2, n. 15, p. 308.

[2] Dig. Lib. 50, tit. 1, l. 27; Pothier, Pand. Lib. 50, tit. 1, § 2, art. 2, n. 18; 2 Domat, Public Law, B. 1, tit. 16, § 3, art. 4.

tant, who has his domicil, in any place, and whom the Greeks call *πάροικον*, that is to say, a neighbour, or person inhabiting near to a village. For those are not alone to be deemed inhabitants, who dwell in a town; but those also, who cultivate grounds near its limits, so that they conduct themselves, as if their place of abode were there." *Incola est qui aliquâ regione domicilium suum contulit, quem Græci πάροικον (id est,* juxta habitantem) *appellant. Nec tantum hi, qui in oppido morantur, incolæ sunt; sed etiam, qui alicujus oppidi finibus agrum habent, ut in eum se, quasi in aliquam sedem, recipiant.*[1] Some, at least, of these are more properly descriptions, than definitions of domicil.

§ 43. The French jurists have defined it to be the place, where a person has his principal establishment. Thus Denizart says, "The domicil of a person is the place, where a person enjoys his rights, and establishes his abode, and makes the seat of his property." *Le domicile est le lieu, où une personne jouissant de ses droits, établit sa demeure et la siége-de sa fortune.*[2] The Encyclopedists say, "that it is, properly speaking, the place, where one has fixed the centre of his business." *C'est, à proprement parler, l'endroit où l'on a placé le centre de ses affaires.*[3] Pothier says, "It is the place, where a person has established the principal seat of his residence and of his business." *C'est le lieu où une personne à etabli la siége principale de sa demeure et de ses affaires.*[4] And the modern French Code declares, that the domicil of every Frenchman,

---

1 Dig. Lib. 50, tit. 16, l. 239, § 2; Id. l. 203; Pothier, Pand. Lib. 50, tit. 1, § 2, art. 1, n. 16.

2 Denizart, art. *Domicil.*

3 Encyclop. Moderne, art. *Domicil.*

4 Pothier, Cout. d'Orléans, ch. 1, § 1, art. 8.

as to the exercise of civil rights, is the place, where he has his principal establishment, (*est le lieu, où il à son principal établissement.*)[1] Vattel has defined domicil to be a fixed residence in any place with an intention of always staying there.[2] But this is not an accurate statement. It would be more correct to say, that that place is properly the domicil of a person, in which his habitation is fixed, without any present intention of removing therefrom.[3]

§ 44. Two things, then, must concur to constitute domicil; first, residence; and secondly, intention of making it the home of the party. There must be the fact, and the intent; for, as Pothier has truly observed, a person cannot establish a domicil in a place, except it be *animo et facto.*[4] And in many cases actual residence is not indispensable to retain a domicil, after it is once acquired; but it is retained, *animo solo*, by the mere intention not to change it, or adopt another. If, therefore, a person leave his home for temporary purposes, but with an intention to return to it, this change of place is not in law a change of domicil. Thus, if a person go on a voyage to sea, or to a foreign country, for health, or pleasure, or business of a temporary nature, with an intention to return, such transitory residence does not constitute a new domicil, or amount to an abandonment of the old one; for it is not the mere act of inhabitancy in a place, which makes it the domicil, but the fact coupled with the intention of remaining there, *animo manendi.*[5]

---

1 Cod. Civ. art. 102. See also Merlin, Répert. art. *Domicil.*

2 Vattel, B. 1, ch. 19, § 22.

3 Dr. Lieber's Encyc. Amer. *Domicil;* 10 Mass. R. 488.

4 Pothier, Cout. d'Orléans, ch. 1, § 1, art. 9. See Scrimshire *v.* Scrimshire, 2 Hagg. Ecc. R. 405, 406.

5 Pothier, Cout. d'Orléans, ch. 1, § 1, art. 9; Encyclop. Amer. art. *Domicil;* Cochin, Œuvres, Tom. 5, p. 4, 5, 6.

§ 45. It is sometimes a matter of great difficulty to decide, in what place a person has his domicil. The residence is often of a very equivocal nature; and the intention still more obscure.[1] Both are sometimes to be gathered from slight circumstances of mere presumption, and conflicting acts. An intention of permanent residence may often be engrafted upon an inhabitancy for a special or fugitive purpose.[2] And, on the other hand, an intention to change the domicil may be fully announced, and yet no correspondent change of inhabitancy be actually made.[3] *Domicilium re et facto transfertur, non nudâ contestatione.*[4] The Roman lawyers were themselves greatly puzzled by cases upon this subject of an equivocal nature; and Ulpian, and Labeo, and others, held different opinions respecting them.[5] Thus, to the question, where a person had his domicil, who did his business equally in two places, Labeo answered, that he had no domicil in either place. But other jurists, and among them was Ulpian, were of opinion, that a man might in such a case have two domicils, one in each place. Celsus seems to have thought, that, in such a case, which place was the domicil of the party depended upon his own choice and intention. And Julian doubted, whether, if he had no fixed choice, and intention, he could have two domicils.[6]

---

[1] Pothier, Cout. d'Orléans, ch. 1, art. 20; Merlin, Répertoire, *Domicil*, § 2, 6; Bouhier, Cout. de Bourg. ch. 22, § 196 to 206.

[2] The Harmony, 2 Robinson R. 322, 324; Pothier, Cout. d'Orléans, ch. 1, art. 15.

[3] See Harvard College *v.* Gore, 5 Pick. R. 370.

[4] Dig. Lib. 50, tit. 1, l. 20.

[5] Dig. Lib. 50, tit. 1, l. 5, b. 27; Pothier, Pand. Lib. 50, tit. 1, § 2, art. 1, n. 16; Id. art. 2.

[6] Dig. Lib. 50, tit. 1, l. 5, 27; Pothier, Pand. Lib. 50, tit. 1, § 2, art. 2, n. 2; Somerville *v.* Somerville, 5 Vesey, 750, 786, 790; 2 Domat, Public Law, B. 1, tit. 16, § 3, p. 462; Id. art. 6.

§ 46. Without speculating upon all the various cases, which may be started upon this subject, it may be useful to collect together some of the more important rules, which have been generally adopted, as guides in cases of most familiar occurrence. First, the place of birth of a person is considered as his domicil, if it is at the time of his birth the domicil of his parents. *Patris originem unusquisque sequitur.*[1] This is usually denominated the domicil of nativity, *domicilium originis.* But, if the parents are then on a visit, or on a journey (*in itinere*), the home of the parents (at least if it is in the same country) will be deemed the domicil of nativity.[2] If he is an illegitimate child, he follows the domicil of his mother. *Ejus, qui justum patrem non habet, prima origò a matre.*[3] Secondly, the domicil of birth of minors continues, until they have obtained a new domicil. Thirdly, minors are generally deemed incapable, *proprio marte,* of changing their domicil during their minority; and therefore retain the domicil of their parents; and if the parents change their domicil, that of the infant children follows it; and if the father dies, his last domicil is that of the infant children.[4] *Placet etiam filium-familias domicilium habere posse, non utique ibi, ubi pater habuit, sed ubicunque ipse constituit.*[5] Fourthly,

---

[1] Cod. Lib. 10, tit. 31, l. 36; 2 Domat, Public Law, B. 1, tit. 16, § 3, art. 10; 1 Boullenois, Observ. 4. p. 53. See Scrimshire *v.* Scrimshire, 2 Hagg. Eccl. R. 405, 406; Cochin, Œuvres, Tom. 5, p. 5, 6; Id. 698.

[2] Dr. Lieber's Encyc. Amer. art. *Domicil;* Pothier, Cout. d'Orléans, ch. 1, art. 10, 12; Somerville *v.* Somerville, 5 Vesey, 750, 787; 1 Boullenois, Observ. 4, p. 53.

[3] Dig. Lib. 50, tit. 1, l. 9.

[4] Id.; Pothier, Cout. d'Orléans, ch. 1, art. 12, 16; 2 Domat, Public Law, B. 16, tit. 16, § 3, art. 10; Guier *v.* O'Daniel, 1 Binn. R. 349, 351.

[5] Dig. Lib. 50, tit. 1, l. 3, 4.—Whether a guardian, or father can change the domicil of a minor, or idiot, or insane person, under his

a married woman follows the domicil of her husband. This results from the general principle, that a person, who is under the power and authority of another, possesses no right to choose a domicil.[1] *Mulierem, quamdiu nupta est, incolam ejusdem civitatis videri, cujus maritus ejus est.*[2] Fifthly, a widow retains the domicil of her deceased husband, until she obtains another. *Vidua mulier amissi mariti domicilium retinet.*[3] Sixthly, *primâ facie*, the place, where a person lives, is taken to be his domicil, until other facts establish the contrary.[4] Seventhly, every person of full age, having a right to change his domicil, it follows, that if he removes to another place, with an intention to make it his permanent residence (*animo manendi*), it becomes instantaneously his place of domicil.[5] Eighthly, if a person has actually removed to another place, with an intention of remaining there for an indefinite time, and as a place of present domicil, it becomes his place of domicil, notwithstanding he may entertain a

---

charge, has been matter of doubt, upon which different opinions have been expressed by jurists. In the affirmative there may be found among others, Bynkershoeck, Boullenois, Bretannier. In the negative Pothier, and Mornac.—See Pothier, Coutumes d'Orléans, ch. 1, art. 17. Bynker. Quæst. Privat. Juris, Lib. 1, ch. 16; Merlin, Répertoire, *Domicil*, § 5, art. 2, 3; Boullenois, Quest. de la Contrariété des Lois, Quest. 2 p. 40, edit. 1732. See also Guier *v.* O'Daniel, 1 Binn. R. 349, note. Somerville *v.* Somerville, 5 Ves. 750, 787; Potinger *v.* Wightman, 3 Merivale R. 67; Cutts *v.* Haskins, 9 Mass. R. 543; Holyoke *v.* Haskins, 5 Pick. R. 20.

1 Dr. Lieber's Encyc. Amer. *Domicil*; Pothier, Cout. d'Orléans, ch. 1, art. 10; 2 Domat, Public Law, B. 1, tit. 16, § 3, art. 11, 13; Merlin, Répertoire, *Domicil*, § 5.

2 Dig. Lib. 50, tit. 1, l. 38, § 3; Id. Lib. 5, tit. 1, l. 65; 2 Domat, Public Law, B. 1, tit. 16, § 3, art. 12.

3 Dig. Lib. 50, tit. 1, l. 22, § 1.

4 Bruce *v.* Bruce, 2 Bos. and Pull. 228, note; Id. 230; Bempde *v.* Johnstone, 3 Ves. 198, 201; Stanley *v.* Bernes, 3 Hagg. Eccles. R. 374, 437.

5 Pothier, Cout. d'Orléans, ch. 1, art. 13.

floating intention to return at some future period.[1] Ninthly, the place, where a married man's family resides, is generally to be deemed his domicil.[2] But it may be controlled by circumstances; for if it is a place of temporary establishment for his family, or for transient objects, it will be otherwise.[3] Tenthly, if a married man has his family fixed in one place, and he does his business in another, the former is considered the place of his domicil.

§ 47. Eleventhly, if a married man has two places of residence at different times of the year, that will be esteemed his domicil, which he himself selects, or describes, or deems, to be his home, or which appears to be the centre of his affairs, or where he votes, or exercises the rights and duties of a citizen.[4] Twelfthly, if a man is unmarried, that is generally deemed the place of his domicil, where he transacts his business, exercises his profession, or assumes municipal duties or privileges.[5] But this rule is of course subject to some qualifications in its application.[6] Thirteenthly, residence in a place, to produce a change of domicil, must be voluntary. If, therefore, it be by constraint or involuntarily, as by banishment, arrest, or imprisonment, the antecedent domicil of the party remains.[7] Fourteenthly, mere intention to acquire a

---

1 Bruce *v.* Bruce, 2 Bos. and Pull. 228, note; Id. 230; Stanley *v.* Bernes, 3 Hagg. Eccles. R. 374.

2 Pothier, Cout. d'Orléans, ch. 1, art. 20; Bempde *v.* Johnstone, 3 Ves. 198, 201.

3 Pothier, Cout. d'Orléans, ch. 1, art. 15.

4 Pothier, Cout. d'Orléans, ch. 1, art. 20; Somerville *v.* Somerville, 5 Ves. 750, 788, 789, 790; Harvard College *v.* Gore, 5 Pick. R. 370; Cochin, Œuvres, Tom. 3, p. 702.

5 Somerville *v.* Somerville, 5 Ves. 750, 788, 789.

6 Id.

7 2 Domat, Public Law, B. 1, tit. 16, § 3, art. 14; Merlin, Répertoire, *Domicil*, § 4, art. 3; Bempde *v.* Johnstone, 3 Ves. 198, 202.

new domicil without the fact of removal avails nothing; neither does the fact of removal without the intention. Fifteenthly, presumptions from circumstances will not prevail against positive facts, which fix, or determine the domicil.[1] Sixteenthly, a domicil once acquired remains, until a new one is acquired.[2] It is sometimes laid down, that a person may be without any domicil; as if he quits a place with an intent to fix in another place, it is said, that while he is *in transitu*, he has no domicil. Julian, in the Roman law, has so affirmed. *Si quis domicilio relicto naviget, vel iter faciat, quærens quo se conferat, atque ubi constituat; hunc puto sine domicilio esse.*[3] But the more correct principle would seem to be, that the original domicil is not gone, until a new one has been actually acquired, *facto et animo.*[4] Seventeenthly, if a man has acquired a new domicil, different from that of his birth, and he removes from it with an intention to resume his native domicil, the latter is re-acquired, even while he is on his way, *in itinere*, for it reverts from the moment the other is given up.[5]

§ 48. The foregoing rules principally relate to changes of domicil from one place to another within the same country, although many of them are applicable to residence in different countries. In respect to the

---

[1] Dr. Lieber, Encyc. Amer. *Domicil.*

[2] Somerville v. Somerville, 5 Ves. 750, 787; Merlin, Répertoire, *Domicil*, § 2; Harvard College v. Gore, 5 Mass. R. 370; Cochin, Œuvres, Tom. 5, p. 5, 6.

[3] Dig. Lib. 50, tit. 1, l. 27, § 2; 2 Domat, Public Law, B. 1, tit. 16, § 3, art. 9.

[4] See Jennison v. Hapgood, 10 Pick. R. 77; Bruce v. Bruce, 2 Bos. and Pull. 228; Cochin, Œuvres, Tom. 5, p. 5, 6.

[5] The Indian Chief, 3 Rob. 12; La Virginie, 5 Rob. 98. — On the subject of Domicil the learned reader is referred to Fergusson on Marriage and Divorce, Appendix, p. 277 to 362; and Henry on Foreign Law, Appendix A. p. 181, &c.; Cochin, Œuvres, Tom. 5, p. 4, 5, 6; Ex parte Wrigby, 8 Wend. R. 134.

latter, there are certain principles, which have been generally recognised by tribunals, administering public law, as of unquestionable authority. First — Persons, who are born in a country, are generally deemed citizens and subjects of that country. A reasonable qualification of this rule would seem to be, that it should not apply to the children of parents, who were *in itinere* in the country, or abiding there for temporary purposes, as for health, or occasional business. It would be difficult, however, to assert, that in the present state of public law such a qualification is universally established. Secondly — Foreigners, who reside in a country for permanent or indefinite purposes, *animo manendi*, are treated universally as inhabitants of that country.[1] Thirdly — A national character, acquired in a foreign country by residence, changes, when the party has left the country *animo non revertendi*; and if he be *in itinere* to his native country with that intent, his native domicil revives. The moment a foreign domicil is abandoned, the native domicil is re-acquired. But a mere return to the native country, without an intent to abandon the foreign domicil, does not work any change of domicil.[2] Fourthly — Ambassadors and other foreign ministers retain their domicil in the country, which they represent, and to which they belong. But a different rule generally applies to Consuls, and other commercial agents, who are presumed to remain in a country for purposes of trade, and therefore acquire a domicil, where they

---

1 Vattel, Lib. 1, ch. 19, § 213.

2 The Venus, 8 Cranch, 278, 281; The Frances, 8 Cranch, 335; The Indian Chief, 3 Rob. 12; Bempde *v.* Johnstone, 3 Ves. 198, 202; The Friendschaft, 3 Wheaton R. 14; Ommany *v.* Bingham, cited 5 Ves. jr. 756, 757, 765.

reside.[1] Fifthly — Children born upon the sea are deemed to belong, and have their domicil in the country, to which their parents belong.[2]

§ 49. From these considerations and rules the general conclusion may be deduced, that domicil is of three sorts; domicil by birth, domicil by choice, and domicil by operation of law. The first is the common case of the place of birth, *domicilium originis*; the second is that, which is voluntarily acquired by a party, *proprio marte*. The last is consequential, as that of the wife arising from marriage.[3]

---

1 Vattel, B. 1, ch. 19, § 217; The Indian Chief, 3 Rob. 13, 27; The Josephine, 4 Rob. 26.

2 Vattel, B. 1, ch. 19, § 216; Dr. Lieber's Encyc. Amer. art. *Domicil.*

3 Pothier, Cout. d'Orléans, ch. 1, art. 12. — Whoever wishes to make more extensive researches upon this subject may consult Denizart's Dictionary, art. *Domicil.* Encyclopédie Moderne, tom. 10, art. *Domicil.* Merlin, Répertoire, *Domicil;* 2 Domat (by Strahan), p. 484, Lib. 1, tit. 16, § 3, of Public Law; Dig. Lib. 50, tit. 1, per tot.; Cod. Lib. 10, tit. 30, l. 2 to l. 7; Voet. ad Pandect. Lib. 5, tit. 1, § 90 to 92; Bynkershoeck, Quæst. Priv. Juris. Lib. 1, ch. 11, and the authorities cited in Dr. Lieber's Encyclopedia Americana, *Domicil;* Henry on Foreign Law, Appendix A, on *Domicil*, p. 181, &c. to p. 209.

CHAPTER IV.

CAPACITY OF PERSONS.

§ 50. We now come to the consideration of the operation and effect of foreign laws in relation to persons, their capacity, state, and condition.

§ 51. All laws, which have for their principal object the regulation of the capacity, state, and condition of persons, have been treated by foreign jurists generally as personal laws.[1] They are by them divided into two sorts; those, which are universal, and those, which are special. The former regulate universally the capacity, state, and condition of persons, such as their minority, majority, emancipation, and power of administration of their own affairs. The latter create an ability or a disability to do certain acts, leaving the party in all other respects with his general capacity or incapacity.[2] But, whether laws purely personal belong to

---

1 See, Saul v. His Creditors, 17 Martin. R. 569, 596. — Boullenois enumerates, as personal, all laws, which regard majority or minority, emancipation, interdiction for lunacy or prodigality, subjection of married women to the marital power, subjection of minors to the power of their parents and guardians, legitimacy and illegitimacy, excommunication, civil death, infamy, nobility, foreigners and strangers, and naturalization.* See, also, Merlin, Répert. Statut. Pothier enumerates among personal laws, those respecting the paternal power, the guardianship of minors, and their emancipation, the age required to make a will, and the marital authority. Pothier, Cout. d'Orléans, Introd. ch. 1, art. 6. See, also, Rodemburg, De Div. Stat. tit. 2, ch. 5, § 14. Le Brun enumerates among personal statutes those respecting majority, legitimacy, guardianship, and the paternal power. Le Brun, Traité de la Communauté, Liv. 2, ch. 3, § 5, n. 25. See, also, Bouhier, Cout. de Bourg. ch. 23, § 64.; 1 Boullenois, ch. 2, Observ. 5, p. 74 to 122.

2 See Henry on Foreign Law, 2, 3; 1 Froland, Mém. ch. 5, p. 81.

* 1 Boullenois, Observ. 4, p. 46, 51; Id. 78; Id. 800.

the one class or the other, they are for the most part held by foreign jurists to be of absolute obligation every where, when they have once attached upon the person by the law of his domicil. Boullenois has stated the doctrine among his general principles. Personal laws (says he) affect the person with a quality, which is inherent in him, and his person is the same every where. Laws purely personal, whether universal or particular, extend themselves every where; that is to say, a man is every where deemed in the same state, whether universal or particular, by which he is affected by the law of his domicil. *Ces loix personelles affectent la personne d'une qualité, qui lui est inhérente, et la personne est telle partout.* And again, — *Les loix pures personelles, soit personnelles universelles, soit personnelles particulières, se portent par tout; c'est à dire, que l'homme est partout de l'état, soit universel soit particulier, dont sa personne est effectée par la loi de son domicil.*[1] *Habilis vel inhabilis in loco domicilii, est habilis vel inhabilis in omni loco.*[2] Rodemburg says, Whenever inquiry is made as to the state and condition of a person, there is but one judge, that of his domicil, to whom the right appertains to settle the matter. *Cum de statu et conditione hominum quæritur, uno solummodo judici, et quidem domicilii, universum in illâ jus sit attributum.*[3] Hence (says Hertius) the state and quality of a person are governed by the law of the place, to which he is by his domicil subjected. Whenever a law is directed to the person, we are to refer to the law of the place, to

---

[1] Boullenois, Prin. Gén. 10, 18, p. 4, 6; Observ. 4, 10, 12, 14, 46.

[2] Boullenois, Quest. Mixt. Disc. Prél. p. 20, pr. 11.

[3] Rodemburg, De Div. Stat. ch. 3, § 4 to 10; 1 Boullenois, 145; Id. Observ. 14, p. 196.

which he is personally subject. *Hinc status et qualitas personæ regitur a legibus loci, cui ipsa sese per domicilium subjecit. Quando lex in personam dirigitur, respiciendum est ad leges illius civitatis, quæ personam habet subjectam.*[1] Froland, Bouhier, Voet, Pothier, and others, lay down a similar rule.[2] Merlin has expressed it in equally comprehensive terms.[3]

§ 52. The result of this doctrine is admitted to be, that a person, who has attained the age of majority by the law of his native domicil, is to be deemed every where to be of age; and on the other hand, a person, who is in his minority by the law of his native domicil, is to be deemed every where in the same condition.[4] Thus, for example, if by the law of the place of original domicil a person cannot make a will of his property, before he is twenty-one years of age, he cannot, if under that age, make a valid will, even of such property as is situate in a place, where the law allows persons of the age of fourteen years to make a will of the like property.[5] So, if by the law of the original domicil

---

1 Hertius, De Coll. Leg. § 4, p. 122, § 5; Id. p. 123, § 8; Id. p. 128, § 12.

2 1 Froland, Mém. ch. 7, § 2, p. 156; Id. Vol. 2, ch. 33, § 8, 9, 10, p. 1574; Bouhier, Cout. de Bourg. ch. 23, § 92; Id. p. 461, ch. 24, § 11, p. 463; Id. ch. 22, § 5 to 11, p. 418; Voet. De Stat. ch. 2, § 4, p. 123; Henry on Foreign Law, ch. 4, p. 34; Pothier, Cout. d'Orléans, ch. 1, art. 7; 1 Hert. Opera, De Coll. § 4, p. 121, § 5, p. 123, § 8.

3 Merlin, Répert. Statut.; Id. Majorité, § 5; Id. Autorisation Maritale, § 10.—The like rule is maintained by Burgundus, Stockmans, and D'Argentré as to personal property and covenants. See Livermore, Diss. p. 34, 35, 50. See, Merlin, Répert. Majorité, § 5; Id. Autorisation Maritale, § 10.

4 1 Boullenois, p. 103, &c.

5 Pothier, Cout. d'Orléans, ch. 1, art. 7; 1 Boullenois, Prin. Gén. 19, p. 7; Id. Observ. 16, p. 205; 1 Froland, Mém. ch. 7, p. 156; Bouhier, Cout. de Bourg. ch. 22, § 5 to 11; ch. 24, § 7 to 13; Merlin, Répert. Majorité, § 5; Id. Autorisation Maritale, § 10.

a married woman cannot dispose of her property, except with the consent of her husband, she is equally prohibited from disposing of her property situate in another place, where no such consent is requisite.[1] And many jurists apply this doctrine indiscriminately to moveable, and to immoveable property. Thus, Boullenois says, "if a man has immoveable property situate in a place, where the age of majority is fixed at twenty-five, and by the law of his own domicil he is of age at twenty, he may at twenty sell, or alienate such immoveable property. On the other hand, if by the law of the place, where the immoveable property is situate, he is of age at twenty, but by the law of his domicil not until twenty-five, he cannot sell, or alienate such property, until the age of twenty-five."[2] But other jurists distinguish between moveable and immoveable property, applying the law of *situs* to the latter, and the law of the domicil to the former.[3] This will hereafter come more fully under consideration.

§ 53. But, although the doctrine is thus generally stated, foreign jurists are compelled to make many exceptions in its application, which go far to limit, if not to impair, its force and efficiency.[4] Indeed, the language held by some of them on this subject has not always such a precision, as to its designed extent and operation, as to free the mind from all doubt in regard to its true meaning. Merlin says,[5] "The law of the domicil

---

1 Ibid. Henry on Foreign Law, § 1, p. 31.

2 Boullenois, Dissert. Mixtes, Quest. 1, p. 19. See, also, Merlin, Répert. Majorité, § 4, 5.

3 Voet, Burgundus, Stockmans, and Peckius, cited in Merlin, Répert. Majorité, § 5, p. 189, (edit. 1827.)

4 See, Livermore, Diss. p. 62 to 106.

5 Merlin, Répert. Statut.; See, also, Id. Majorité, § 5; Id. Autorisation Maritale, § 10.

governs the state of the person, and his personal capacity and incapacity. It also governs personal actions, moveables, and moveable effects, in whatever place they may in fact be situated. The power of the law of the domicil extends every where, to every thing within its province; so that he, who is of majority by the law of his domicil, is of that age every where. The law of the place, where the property *(biens)* is situate, regulates the quality and disposition of it. When the law of the domicil, and that of the situation *(situs)*, are in conflict with each other, if the question is respecting the state and condition of the person, the law of the domicil ought to prevail; if it is respecting the disposition of property *(biens)*, the law of the place, where they are situate, is to be followed." Now, this language of Merlin is sufficiently broad to cover moveable as well as immoveable property; and yet it is very clear, that the disposition of moveable property, and the capacity to dispose of it, are by foreign jurists generally, and by Merlin himself, held to be governed by the law of the domicil, according to the maxim, that moveables follow the person, *mobilia sequuntur personam.*[1] What, perhaps, Merlin intends here to assert, may be, that, where a person is incapable by the law of his domicil, he cannot dispose of his property any where, the incapacity extending even to places, where he is not domiciled, and where, by the local law, he would otherwise have capacity. But that, where he is capable by the law of his domicil, and the question does not respect the capacity to dispose of property,

1 Pothier, Cout. d'Orléans, ch. 1. art. 7; 1 Boullenois, Prin. Gén. 16, p. 7; Id. Observ. 19, p. 338, &c.; Rodemburg. ch. 3, § 4, 9, 10, p. 7 to 9; Id. ch. 2, p. 6; Voet. de Stat. § 4, ch. 2, p. 125, § 8; Pothier, De Choses, P. 2, § 3; Livermore's Dissert. 82.

but the extent, to which it may be exercised by persons, who are capable, there the law of the place, where it is situate, will govern. Yet he would seem also to intimate, that there is some distinction between personal property and real property, (moveables and immoveables) as to the effect of the operation of the *lex domicilii*.

§ 54. In another place Merlin lays down the rule, that a law respecting majority, full and entire, is personal, and extends to property *(biens)* situate out of the territory. Thus, if by custom a person is of age at twenty, and he has the faculty of disposing of his immoveable property, it extends to that in a foreign country, where a different rule exists. He admits, however, that the Voets, Burgundus, Stockmans, and Peckius, while they admit such a law to be personal, insist, that it does not extend to the disposal of immoveables.[1] Merlin in another place says, "If the law of the domicil declares a person incapable to sell, alien, contract, or to bind himself in any manner to another, it is impossible, that his immoveables, in whatever country they may be situated, can be aliened, bound, or hypothecated by him. Who has ever doubted, that the interdiction pronounced against a prodigal, or a madman, by the judge of his domicil, was an obstacle to the alienation of his property *(biens)*, which is situate within the reach of another jurisdiction? Who has ever doubted, that the tutor (guardian), named by the judge of the domicil, has the right to administer the property *(biens)*, which is within the territory of another judge?[2]" This is very bold and uncomprom-

[1] See, Merlin, Répert. Majorité, § 5; Id. Autorisation Maritale, § 10.

[2] Merlin, Répert. Autorisation Maritale, § 10, art. 2.

ising language; but it will be very difficult to sustain it without many qualifications. In the progress of our inquiries, it will be found, that many exceptions are admitted to exist, as to the operation of personal laws, and that the practice of nations by no means justifies the doctrine in the extent, to which it is ordinarily laid down by foreign jurists.

§ 55. Hitherto we have been considering cases, where there has been no change of domicil; as to which, as we have seen, the doctrine of foreign jurists is, that the law of the original domicil is to prevail, where there is a conflict of personal laws. But suppose, that a person has had different domicils, a domicil by birth, and a subsequent domicil by choice, when he is *suo jure*, which is to prevail? Hertius does not hesitate to say, that the law of the new domicil is to prevail. *Status et qualitas regitur a legibus loci*, (says he,) *cui ipse sese domicilium subjecit; atque inde etiam fit, ut quis major hic, alibi, mutato scilicet domicilio, incipit fieri minor.*[1] The like opinion is held by Paul Voet.[2] Froland thinks this question cannot be answered universally; but he puts a distinction. "If," says he, "the question is purely as to the state of the person, abstracted from all consideration of property, or subject-matter *(matière réelle)*, in this case the law, which first commenced to fix his condition, (that is, the law of the domicil of his birth,) will preserve its force and authority, and follow him, wherever he may go. Thus, if by the law of the domicil of origin a person attains his majority at twenty years,

1 1 Hertii Opera, § 4, p. 123, § 8.

2 Rodemburg, De Div. Stat. p. 2, ch. 1, p. 57, § 5, 6; Merlin, Répert. Majorité, § 4; Merlin, Retroactif. § 3, art. 9, n. 3; Voet. de Stat. § 4, ch. 2, p. 123.

and he goes to reside in another place, where the age of majority is twenty-five years, he is held to be of the age of majority every where; and, notwithstanding he is under twenty-five years, he may in his new domicil sell, alien, hypothecate, and contract, as he pleases."[1] "But," he adds, "when the question is as to the ability or disability of a person, who has changed his domicil, to do a certain thing, there the law of his original domicil falls, and gives place to the law of his new domicil. Thus, if a married woman, by the law of the country of her birth, is not allowed to pass property by will without the consent of her husband, and she acquires a domicil in another country, where such power is allowed, she may, notwithstanding, dispose of her property in the latter country by will.[2] This is a very nice, if it be not in many cases an evanescent, distinction; and Froland admits, that a different doctrine is held by many jurists. But he is not singular in his opinion.[3] Bouhier insists, that in case of a transfer of the domicil, the law of the original domicil ought in all cases to regulate the personal capacity; and he enlarges on the subject with much ability.[4]

§ 56. On the other hand, Burgundus does not hesitate to hold, that the law of the new or actual domicil ought to prevail; *si mutaverit domicilium, novi domicilii conditionem induere.*[5] Rodemburg is of the same opinion, upon the ground, that the state and condition

---

1 Froland, Mém. ch. 7, § 13, 14, p. 171; See, 2 Boullenois, Observ. 32, p. 7 to 11; Bouhier, Cout. de Bourg. ch. 22, § 4 to 10.

2 1 Froland, Mém. ch. 7, § 15, p. 172.

3 See, Rodemburg, De Div. Stat. tit. 2, ch. 1, 2, 3, 4, tit. 3, ch. 1, 2, 3, 4, tit. 4, ch. 1, 2, 3, 4; 2 Boullenois, ch. 1, Obs. 32, p. 1 to 53; Merlin, Répert. Effet. Retroactif. § 111, p. 2, art. 5, n. 3.

4 Bouhier, Cout. de Bourg. ch. 22, § 4 to 10.

5 Cited in Merlin, Répert. Effet Retroactif, § 5.

of the person is wholly governed by the law of the domicil; and when that is changed, the state and condition change with it; *personæ enim status et conditio cum tota regatur a legibus loci, cui illa sese per domicilium subdiderit, utique mutato domicilio, mutari et necesse est personæ conditionem.*[1] And he applies the rule indiscriminately to the case of minors and married women.[2]

§ 57. Boullenois (whose opinions will be stated more fully hereafter) admits the general principle to be, as Rodemburg states it, and asserts, that the whole world acknowledges, that the state of the person depends on his actual domicil. But then he makes a distinction between the state and condition of persons, which give rights, founded in public reasons, admitted by all nations, and which have a cause absolutely unconnected with domicil, so that the moment a man is affected with this state and condition, the domicil has no influence upon them, but public reasons superior to those of domicil, to which all nations pay respect; and other subordinate states and conditions, which are founded in truth in public rights, but only for one nation, or some provinces of a nation. Among the former he enumerates interdiction, or prohibition, to do acts, by reason of insanity, prodigality, emancipation by royal authority, legitimacy of birth, nobility, infancy, &c.; and these, he contends, are never altered by any change of domicil; but are for ever fixed. Among the latter he enumerates, community of property between husband and wife; the state of the husband, as to the marital power; the state of the father as to the pater-

---

1 Rodemburg, De Div. Stat. tit. 2, P. 2, ch. 1, n. 3; 2 Boullenois, p. 2, 5, 7.

2 Id. n. 5, n. 6.

nal power, &c.; and these, he contends, are sometimes affected by a change of domicil, and sometimes not. He holds, that the capacity of married women is governed by the law of the new domicil; but that of minors by the law of their domicil of birth.[1] He also holds, that the paternal power is regulated by the domicil of birth. But, here, again, he distinguishes between moveable and immoveable property; holding, that the law of the domicil of birth governs as to the former, and the law of the situation *(situs)* as to the latter.[2]

§ 58. Merlin, after citing the opinions of other jurists, formerly came to the conclusion, that the law of the place of birth, and not that of the new domicil, ought to govern equally in all these cases, of minority, of paternal power, and of marital power after marriage; and he expressed surprise, and not without reason, that Boullenois should have attempted to distinguish between them.[3] It is not for us to interfere in such grave controversies; *non nostrum inter vos tantas componere lites.* Yet Merlin himself, after having stated this doctrine to be best founded in principle, though involving some inconveniences, still insisted, that upon such a removal the capacity of a person to dispose of his moveable property by a testament is to be governed by the law of the new domicil, because the state of a person, has no influence, as to the distribution of his moveable property after his death; and the capacity to make a will, resulting from age, has nothing in common with what is properly called the state of the per-

---

1 2 Boullenois, 9, 10, 11, 12, 13, 19, 20, 31 to 53; Id. Dissert. Mixtes, Quest. 2, p. 40 to 62; Id. Quest. 20, p. 406 to 447.

2 Boullenois, 32, 33 to 53; Id. Dissert. Mixtes, Quest. 20, p. 406 to 447.

3 Merlin, Répert. Autorisation Maritale, § 10, art. 4.

son; which is so true that his state is governed by the domicil, and the situation decides solely concerning the age, at which a person may dispose of moveable property upon his death.[1]

§ 59. It seems, however, that Merlin has since, upon farther reflection, come to a different conclusion; and he may be now numbered among those, who support the doctrine, that the law of the new domicil ought to govern in such cases. Be this as it may, Pothier[2] holds the doctrine in the most unqualified terms, that the law of the new or actual domicil ought in all cases to govern, and that the change of domicil discharges the party from the law of his former domicil, and subjects him to that of his new domicil. Whatever doubts may be suggested of the correctness of his opinion in a juridical sense, it must be admitted to possess the strong recommendation of general convenience and certainty of application.

§ 60. Huberus, instead of relying upon the mere quality of laws, as personal, or real, lays down the following doctrine. Personal qualities *(qualitates personales)*, impressed by the laws of any place upon a person, accompany him, wherever he goes, with this effect, that in every place he enjoys, and is subject to the same law, which other persons there enjoy, or are subject to. Therefore, he adds, those, who with us are under tutelage or guardianship, as minors, prodigals, and married women, are every where deemed to be persons subject to such guardianship; and possess, and enjoy the rights, which the law of the place attributes to persons under guardianship. Hence, he,

---

1 Merlin, Répert. Majorité, § 4; Id. Effet Retroactif, § 3, 2, art. 5, n. 3; Id. Autorisation Maritale, § 10, art. 4, edit. 1827, at Brussels.

2 Pothier, Cout. d'Orléans, ch. 1, art. 1, § 12.

who in Friezeland has obtained the immunity of his age *(veniam ætatis)*, contracting in Holland, is not deemed restored to full capacity *(non restituitur in integrum)*. He, who is declared a prodigal here, cannot enter into a valid contract in another place. Again, in some provinces, those, who are twenty-one years of age, are deemed of majority, and may alienate their immoveable property, and exercise less important rights in those places, where no one is deemed of majority, until he has attained twenty-five years; because all other governments give effect by comity to the laws and adjudications of other cities in regard to their subjects, so, always, that there be no prejudice to their own subjects, or their own law.[1]

§ 61. He goes on to remark. "There are persons, who thus interpret the effect of laws respecting the quality of persons, that he, who in a certain place is a major, or minor, in puberty, or beyond it, a son subject to paternal power, or a father of a family under or out of guardianship, every where enjoys, and is subject to the same law, which he enjoys, and to which he is subject, in that place, where he first becomes, or is reputed such. So that whatever he could, or could not do in his own country, the same is allowed, and prohibited to him to do. This seems to me unreasonable, and would occasion too great a confusion of laws, and a burthen upon neighbouring nations, arising from the laws of others. Thus, if an unemancipated son *(filius-familiâs)*, who cannot in Friezeland make a will, goes into Holland, and there makes a will; and it is asked, whether it has any validity? I suppose it has, &c.; because the laws bind all those, who are in any ter-

---

1 Huberus, lib. 1, tit. 3, § 12.

ritory; neither is it proper *(civile)*, that Hollanders, in respect to business done among themselves, should, neglecting their own laws, be governed by foreign laws. But it is true, that this will would not have effect in Friezeland, &c.; because otherwise nothing would be more easy than for our citizens to elude our laws, as they are evaded every day. But such a will would be of validity elsewhere, even where an unemancipated son could not make a will; for there the reason of evading the laws of a country by its own citizens ceases; for in such a case the fact would not be committed."[1]

§ 62. This doctrine of Huberus cannot in its full extent be maintained; and especially in relation to immoveable property it is universally repudiated by the common law, and in many cases by foreign jurists.[2] Lord Stowell has expressly said, that he does not mean to say, that Huberus is correct in laying down, as universally true, that being of age in one country a man is of age in any other country, be their law of majority what it may.[3]

§ 63. Without venturing further into the particular opinions maintained by foreign jurists on this subject, (a task, which would be almost endless,) it may perhaps be useful to place before the reader some of those doctrines, which appear best established, or at least, which have the sanction of such authority, as gives them a superior weight and recommendation, in the continental jurisprudence.

---

1 Huberus, Lib. 1, tit. 3, § 13.

2 See the Authors cited by Merlin, Répert. Majorité, § 5.

3 Ruding *v.* Smith, 2 Hagg. Ecc. Rep. 391, 392.

§ 64. In the first place, the acts of a person, done in the place of his domicil, are to be judged of by the laws of that place, and will not be permitted to have any other legal effect elsewhere, than they have in that place.[1] There are exceptions to this rule; but they result from some direct or implied provisions of law in the customary or positive code of the country, in which the act comes in judgment, applying to the very case; for it is competent for a country, if it pleases, to prescribe its own rule for all cases, arising out of transactions in foreign countries, whenever any rights under them are brought into controversy in its own tribunals. If, therefore, a person has a capacity to do any act, or has an incapacity to do an act, by the law of the place of his domicil, the act, when done there, will be governed by the same law, wherever its validity may come into contestation. Thus, an act done by a minor, without the consent of his guardian, if valid by the law of the place of his domicil, where it is done, will be recognised as valid in every other place; if invalid there, it will be held invalid in every other place. So, if a married woman, disabled by the law of the place of her domicil from entering into a contract, or transferring property, without the consent of her husband, makes a contract, or transfers property there, it will be held invalid, and a nullity every where.[2] This seems to be a principle generally recognised in the absence of all positive or implied municipal regulations to the contrary; according to the maxim, *quando*

---

1 "Statutum personale (says Voet) ubique locorum personam comitatur, in ordine ad bona intra territorium statuentis sita, ubi persona affecta domicilium habet." Voet. De Statut. § 4, ch. 2, § 6. p. 123.

2 1 Boullenois, Prin. Gén. 6; 1 Froland, Mém. ch. 7, p. 156.

lex in personam dirigitur, respiciendum est ad leges illius civitatis, quæ personam habet subjectam.[1]

§ 65. In the next place, another rule, directly connected with the former, is, that personal capacity, or incapacity, attached to a party by the law of his domicil, is deemed to exist every where, *(qualitas personam sicut umbra sequitur,)* so long as his domicil remains unchanged, even in relation to transactions in a foreign country, where they might otherwise be obligatory.[2] Thus, a minor, a married woman, a prodigal, or spendthrift, a person *non compos mentis*, or other person, who is deemed incapable of transacting business *(sui juris)*, in the place of his or her domicil, will be deemed incapable every where, not only as to

---

1 1 Hertii Opera, § 4, art. 8. p. 123. — The learned reader is referred for proofs to Huberus, De Conflict. Leg. Lib. 1, tit. 3, § 12, 13. 15; 1 Boullenois, Prin. Gén. 10, 12, 16, 17; Id. tit. 1, ch. 3, Observ. 8, p. 145, &c.; 2 Boullenois, tit. 2, ch. 1, p. 1 to 53; Rodemburg, De Divers. Statut. ch. 3. p. 7; Id. tit. 2, ch. 1, p. 10; Voet. De Statut. § 4. ch. 2; Id. ch. 3; 1 Hertii Opera, De Collis. Leg. § 4, 8, p. 123; Froland, Mém. P. 1, ch. 5, 7; Id. P. 2, ch. 33; Bouhier, Cout. de Bourg. ch. 22, 23, 24.

2 "Conditio personæ a causa domicilii tota regitur. Proinde, ut sciamus, quâ ætate minor contrahere possit, respicere oportet ad legem domicilii." Burgundus, Trac. 2, n. 6; 1 Boullenois, Observ. 4, p. 53. "C' est ainsi, (says Boullenois,) que la majorité et la minorité du domicil ont lieu partout, même pour les biens situés ailleurs;" 1 Boullenois, Prin. Gén. ch. 6; Id. Observ. 10, 12, and 46. "Celui qui est majeur (says Froland) suivant la coutume, où il a pris naissance, et sous laquelle il réside, est majeur partout, et peut comme tel, aliener, hypotequer, vendre ses biens, sans considérer, si suivant la loi de leur situation il seroit mineur." 1 Froland, Mém. ch, 7, p. 156. Rodemburg holds the same doctrine. Rodemburg, De Divers. Stat. tit. 2, ch. 1. So D'Argentré: "Quotiescunque de habilitate aut de inhabilitate personarum quæratur, toties domicilii leges et statuta spectanda." 1 Livermore's Diss. 34. So, J. Voet: "Potius domicilii leges observandas existimem; quoties in quæstione, an quis minor vel majorennis sit, obtinuit, id dijudicandum esse ex lege domicilii; sic ut in loco domicilii minorennis, ubique terrarum pro tali habendus sit." Voet. ad Pand. lib. 4, tit. 1, § 29.

transactions in the place of his or her domicil, but as to transactions in every other place.[1]

§ 66. Thus, if an American citizen, domiciled in an American State, as for instance in Massachusetts, where he would be of age at twenty-one years, should order a purchase of goods to be made for him in France, where he would not be of age until twenty-five, the contract would nevertheless be obligatory upon him. On the other hand a person, domiciled in France, of twenty-one years of age, who should order a like purchase of goods in Massachusetts, would not be bound by his contract; for he would be deemed incapable of making such a contract.[2] The same rule will govern in relation to the disposition of personal or moveable property by a person, who is a minor or major in the place of his domicil; for it will be valid, or not, according to the law of the place of his domicil, wherever the property may be situate.[3] There are exceptions also to the rule; but they stand upon peculiar grounds.

§ 67. The ground, upon which this rule has been generally adopted, is doubtless that suggested by Rodemburg, the extreme inconvenience, which would otherwise result to all nations from a perpetual fluctuation of capacity, state, and condition, upon every accidental change of place or moveable property.[4]

§ 68. The modern law of France, as it is laid down by Pardessus, is to the same effect. "No act, what-

---

1 1 Boullenois, Principes Généraux, 10, 19, et Observ. 4, 12, 16, p. 5; 1 Froland, Mém. ch. 7, p. 155, 156; Rodemburg, De Divers. Stat. tit. 2, ch. 1.

2 Huberus, De Conflictu Legum, Lib. 1, tit. 3, § 12.

3 1 Froland, Mém. ch. 7, p. 157, 158; 1 Boullenois, Princ. Gén. 6, 19; Id. Observ. 4, 12; Rodemburg, De Divers. Stat. tit. 2, ch. 1.

4 Rodemburg, De Divers. Stat. tit. 1, ch. 3, n. 4; See also 1 Boullenois, Obs. 4, p. 48. 49.

soever may be its nature," says he, "can be stipulated, but by persons capable of binding themselves; and the general consent of civilized nations has left the law, which regulates the capacity of an individual, to the country, to which he belongs. A person, declared incapable by the law of the country, of which he is a subject, cannot be relieved of that incapacity, except by the law of that country, as well in regard to the acts, which it permits him to do, as to the conditions, which it prescribes in doing them. Thus, French minors, incapable of binding themselves by engagements of commerce, unless they are emancipated or authorized, cannot bind themselves in commercial transactions in a foreign country, even when the law of that country does not require the like conditions, &c. For the same reason, the French tribunals will not consider valid the commercial engagements, entered into in France by minors, or persons of either sex, who, by the law of their own country, are rendered incapable, even though the law, to which they are subject, prescribes other conditions, than those required by the law of France. For it is the interest of a government to respect, in favor of the subject of another government, when he is cited before its tribunals, the laws, upon the faith of which the foreigner has contracted, and not to tolerate him in withdrawing himself, by a mere change of jurisdiction, from the laws, which regulate his capacity, and to which he is bound by his allegiance, wherever he may inhabit. Without this the government would expose its own subjects to be treated with a like injustice by what is denominated the right of retaliation or reprisals."[1] Yet he is compelled to admit, that there may

[1] 5 Pardessus, P. 6, tit. 7, ch. 2, § 1, art. 1482; Henry on Foreign Law, Appendix, p. 221, 222. See Cochin, Œuvres, Tom. 1, p. 154.

be exceptions to the doctrine. The *Code Civil* (art. 3) lays down the rule in the broadest terms: *Les loix concernant l'état et la capacité des personnes régissent les François même résidant en pais étranger.*

§ 69. In the third place, another rule is, that upon a change of domicil, the capacity or incapacity of the person is regulated by the law of the new domicil. Pothier lays down this rule, as we have seen, in emphatic terms. "The change of domicil," says he, "delivers persons from the empire of the laws of the place of the domicil they have quitted, and subjects them to those of the new domicil they have acquired." *Le changement de domicile délivre les personnes de l'empire des lois du lieu du domicile qu'elles quittent, et les assujettit à celles du lieu de nouveau domicile, qu'elles acquièrent.*[1] Burgundus adopts the same rule: *Consequenter dicamus, si mutaverit domicilium persona, novi domicilii conditionem induere.*[2] So Rodemburg, *Personæ enim status et conditio cum tota regatur a legibus loci, cui illa sese per domicilium subdiderit, utique mutato domicilio, mutari et necesse est personæ conditionem.*[3] Froland, indeed, (as we have already seen,) maintains a different doctrine, in which to some extent he is followed by Bouhier and others.[4] The doctrine, however, which is most generally approved, is that, which has been maintained by Pothier, though it is contradicted by the modern code of France.[5]

---

1 Pothier, Coutum. d'Orléans, ch. 1, art. 1, § 13.

2 1 Boullenois, Obs. 4, p. 53.

3 Rodemburg, De Divers. Stat. tit. 2, P. 2, ch. 1, p. 56; 2 Boullenois, ch. 1, and Obs. 32.

4 1 Froland, Mém. ch. 7, § 13, 14, 15, p. 171, 172; Id. ch. 33, § 4, 5, 6, 7, p. 1575 to 1582; Bouhier, Coutum. de Bourg. ch. 22, § 17 to 20, 31, p. 419 to 421. See also Henry on Foreign Law, Appendix A, p. 196. See, 2 Boullenois, p. 1 to 53; Merlin, Répertoire, Majorité, § 5; Autorisation Maritale, § 10; Effet Retroactif, § 3, 2, art. 5.

5 Code Civil, art. 3. See also Cochin, Œuvres, Tom. 1, p. 154.

§ 70. Having stated these rules, it may be proper to notice a distinction, which in many cases may have a material operation. So far as respects the capacity or incapacity of the person, the law of the new domicil would probably prevail in the tribunals of the country of that domicil, as to all rights, contracts, and acts, done or litigated there. The same law would probably have a like recognition in every other country, except that of the original or native domicil. The principal difficulty, which would arise, would be, how far any rights, contracts, and acts, would be recognised by the latter, where they were dependent upon the law of the new domicil, which should be in conflict with its own law on the same subject. It is precisely under circumstances of this sort, that the third axiom of Huberus may be presumed to have a material influence, viz. that a nation is not under any obligation to recognise rights, contracts, or acts, which are to its own prejudice, or in opposition to its own settled policy.

§ 71. Boullenois was sensible of this distinction, as we have already seen, and says, "that on this point it is necessary to distinguish from others the states and conditions of persons, as to rights founded upon public reasons, admitted among all nations, and which have a foundation, or cause, foreign from the domicil; so that the domicil, from the moment a man is affected with these states or conditions, not influencing it in any manner, the new domicil ought not to influence it, but public reasons, superior to those of the domicil, to which all nations pay respect. Such are incapacity from insanity or prodigality, emancipation from the paternal power by royal authority, legitimacy, nobility, infamy, &c. These states do not change with a change of domicil; and of these it is properly said, that, having at first fixed the condition of the person, the change of domicil does not put an end to them."[1] And he adds: "But there are states and conditions more subordinate, and which are in fact public rights *(des droits publics)*, but for one nation only, or for several provinces of the same nation. Such are the state of community (of property), or non-community among married persons *(conjoints)*; the state of the husband as to his marital power; the state of the father, as to the rights of property from the paternal power; and other subordinate states, which are almost infinitely various." In regard to these latter states, he admits the embarrassment of laying down any general rules, as to the effect of a change of domicil. And he concludes his remarks by affirming, first, that the law of the domicil ought to be followed, as to the state and condition of the person; secondly, that it ought not to be derogated from, except so far as the spirit of justice, and the necessity of not injuring the rights of parties, require a departure; thirdly, that the general rule ought not to be impaired, when the law will otherwise furnish means to remedy any injury, which the change of domicil may occasion.[2] He goes on to declare, what he supposes to be perfectly consistent with this doctrine, that when a person has, in the domicil of his birth *(domicilium originis)*, arrived of age, and he afterwards removes to another place, where, after the same age, he would still be a minor, the law of the domicil of his birth ought to prevail. For instance, if a person, who by the law of the domicil of his birth is of age at twenty, removes to another place after that age, where the minority extends to twenty-five years, he does not lose his majority, and become a minor in his new domi-

---

[1] 2 Boullenois, Obs. 32. p. 10, 11, 19.
[2] Id. Obs. 32, p. 11, 12, 13, 19.

cil.[1] And, on the other hand, if the same person is a minor by the law of the place of his birth, and not so by that of his new domicil, his state of minority continues notwithstanding his removal. Yet Boullenois does not hesitate to declare the general principle to be incontestable, that the law of the actual domicil decides the state and condition of the person; so that a person by changing his domicil changes at the same time his condition.[2] Perhaps a better illustration of the intrinsic difficulties of laying down general rules for all cases could not well be imagined; for Boullenois himself, as we have seen, holds laws respecting the majority and minority of age, to be laws affecting the state and condition of persons, and, as such, governed by the law of the domicil.[3]

§ 72. The reason, given by civilians, for a preference of the law of the domicil of birth over the law of the actual domicil, in fixing the age of majority, is, that each state is presumed to be the best capable of judging from the physical circumstances of climate or otherwise, when the faculties of its citizens are morally or civilly perfect for the purposes of society. And with respect to cases of lunacy, idiocy, and prodigality, it is supported by them upon the argument from inconvenience, and the great confusion and mischief, which would arise from the same person being considered as capable to contract in one place, and incapable in another; and so he were to change his civil character with every change of domicil.[4] There may be great reason for giving such a universal operation to certain classes of personal incapacities; but it would be difficult to

---

1 2 Boullenois, Obs. 32, p. 12, 19. 2 2 Boullenois, Obs. 32, p. 13.

3 1 Boullenois, Princ. Gén. 8, 10, 11, 17, 18; Id. Obs. 4, p. 51, 52.

4 Henry on Foreign Law, p. 5, 6; Rodemburg, tit. 1, ch. 3, n. 4, p. 8.

allow the same reason to prevail in regard to all. And, even in relation to those of the most general application, it is by no means so clear, that the argument from inconvenience is not equally strong on the other side.

§ 73. The truth seems to be, that there are, properly speaking, no universal rules, by which nations are morally or politically bound on this subject. Each adopts for itself such modifications of the doctrine, as it deems most convenient, and most in harmony with its own institutions, interests, and policy. It may suffer the same rule, as to the capacity, state, and condition of foreigners, to prevail within its own territory, as does prevail in the place of their domicil; and may at the same time refuse to allow any other rule, than its own, to prevail, in respect to the capacity, state, and condition of its own subjects, wherever they may reside. It may adopt a more limited doctrine, and recognise the law of the domicil, both as to foreigners and its own subjects, in respect to transactions and property in that domicil, and at the same time exclude any operation, except of its own law, as to transactions and property within its own territory. It may adopt the most general doctrine, and allow the rule of the domicil, as to capacity, state, and condition, to prevail under every variety of change of domicil. But whatever it allows, or withholds, will always be measured by its own opinion of convenience and benefit, or of prejudice and injury. Probably the law of the actual domicil *(domicilium habitationis)* will be found in most cases to furnish the most convenient and least prejudicial rule, at least in regard to transactions and property out of the country of birth *(domicilium originis.)* As to transactions and property within the country of birth, the policy of most nations will naturally incline them to hold their own laws conclusive over their own subjects, wherever they may be domiciled, so far as regards minority and majority, and other capacity, or incapacity, to do acts.

§ 74. Illustrations may be easily found to confirm these remarks in the actual jurisprudence of many countries. Thus, Pardessus, while he contends, that the law of France, as to personal incapacity generally, ought to prevail as to French subjects every where, at the same time admits, that it ought not to govern in relation to certain disabilities. Thus, the law of France, which forbids nobles, or persons of official dignity, to sign bills of exchange or other engagements, which authorize an arrest of the body, he thinks, ought not to extend to such acts of the same persons in other countries. For, though it may be urged, that it is a personal law, which follows the person every where, as in the case of a minor, or a married woman under the marital power, and every person is bound to know the state and condition of the person, with whom he contracts; yet, he contends, that the rule ought not to be applied, except to the universal state of the person, as a minor or major, or of a woman subject to, or free from, the marital power; and that all nations are agreed in fixing the capacity to contract to a certain age, and in placing women in dependence upon their husbands.[1] Every one will at once perceive, how exceedingly loose the distinction is, by which this exception is attempted to be maintained.

§ 75. Now, it so happens, that, what Pardessus (and many other jurists are certainly of his opinion) supposes to be very clear doctrine, has been held directly

[1] 5 Pardessus, P. 6, tit. 7, ch. 2, § 1, art. 1483; Henry on Foreign Law, Appendix, 222.

otherwise by the supreme court of Louisiana. That court, in a very learned opinion, have said, "The writers on this subject, with scarcely an exception, agree, that the laws or statutes, which regulate minority and majority, and those, which fix the state or condition of man, are personal statutes, and follow, and govern him, in every country. Now, supposing the case of our law, fixing the age of majority at twenty-five, and the country, in which a man was born and lived previous to his coming here, placing it at twenty-one, no objection could perhaps be made to the rule just stated. And it may be, and, we believe, would be true, that a contract, made here at any time between the two periods already mentioned, would bind him. But, reverse the facts of the case; and suppose, as is the truth, that our law placed the age of majority at twenty-one; that twenty-five was the period, at which a man ceased to be a minor in the country, where he resided; and that, at the age of twenty-four, he came into this state, and entered into contracts; would it be permitted, that he should in our courts, and to the demand of one of our citizens plead, as a protection against his engagements, the laws of a foreign country, of which the people of Louisiana had no knowledge? And would we tell them, that ignorance of foreign laws, in relation to a contract, made here, was to prevent him from enforcing it, though the agreement was binding by those of their own state? Most assuredly we would not."[1]

[1] Saul *v.* His Creditors, 17, Martin, R. 596 to 598.—A like doctrine was held by the same Court in another case. The Court on that occasion said, "A foreigner coming into Louisiana, who was twenty-three years old, could not escape from a contract with one of our citizens, by averring, that, according to the laws of the country he left, he was not a major until he reached the age of twenty-five." Baldwin *v.* Gray, 16 Martin, R. 192 193. See also, Fergusson on Divorce, Appendix, p. 276

§ 76. The case first put seems founded upon a principle entirely repugnant to that, upon which the second rests. In the former, the law of the domicil of origin is allowed to prevail; in the latter, that of the domicil of the contract. Such a course of decision certainly may be adopted by a government, if it shall so choose; but then it would seem to stand upon mere arbitrary legislation and positive law, and not upon principle. The difficulty is in seeing, how a court, without such positive legislation, could arrive at both conclusions. General reasoning would lead us to the opinion, that both cases ought to be decided the same way; that is, either by the law of the domicil of origin, or by that of the domicil of the contract. Many foreign jurists maintain the former opinion;[1] many the latter. It is not very easy to decide, which rule would, on the whole, be most convenient for any nation to adopt. It may be said, that he, who contracts with another, ought not to be ignorant of his condition, *qui cum alio contrahit, vel est, vel esse debet, non ignarus conditionis ejus.*[2] But this rule, however reasonable to be applied to the condition of a man by the law of the country, where he is domiciled, is not so clear in point of convenience or equity, when applied to the condition of a person by the law of a foreign country. How are the inhabitants of any country to ascertain the condition of such person by the law of a foreign country, or the law of his domicil of origin? Even courts of justice do not assume to know, what the laws of a foreign country are;

---

to 363; Hertius, De Collisione, Tom. 1, § 4, p. 120, 121. Grotius seems to have been of opinion, that the *lex loci contractus* ought to govern in cases of minority. Grotius, B. 2, ch. 11, § 5.

1 See Livermore's Dissert. p. 33.

2 Dig. Lib. 50, tit. 17, l. 17. See Livermore's Diss. p. 38.

but require them to be proved. How then shall private persons be presumed to have better means of knowledge? On the other hand, it may be said with great force, that contracts ought to be governed by the law of the country, where they are made, as to the competence of the parties to make them, and as to their validity. Such a rule has certainty and simplicity in its application. It would not, therefore, be matter of surprise, if the country of the party's birth should hold such a contract valid or void according to its own law, and that, nevertheless, the country, where it was made, should hold it valid or void according to its own law. It has been well observed by an eminent judge, that "with respect to any ignorance arising from foreign birth and education, it is an indispensable rule of law, as exercised in all civilized countries, that a man, who contracts in a country, engages for a competent knowledge of the law of contracts of that country. If he rashly presumes to contract without such knowledge, he must take the inconveniences resulting from such ignorance upon himself; and not attempt to throw them upon the other party, who has engaged under a proper knowledge and sense of the obligation, which the law would impose upon him by virtue of that engagement."[1]

§ 77. In another case the supreme court of Louisiana have adopted the doctrine of the law of the domicil of origin under peculiar circumstances. The plaintiff was born in Louisiana in 1802, and the laws of the state at that time fixed the age of majority at twenty-five. In the year 1808 the period of majority was altered to twenty-one. The plaintiff in 1827, and for several years

1 Lord Stowell, in Dalrymple v. Dalrymple, 2 Hagg. Consist. R. 61.

before, was a Spanish subject, and a resident in Spain, where minority ceases at twenty-five. A suit being brought by her to recover her share in the succession to her grandmother in Louisiana, before she was twenty-five, the question arose, whether she was competent to maintain the suit; and that turned upon another, whether she was to be deemed a minor, or not. The court upon that occasion decided, that she was to be deemed a major; and said; "The general rule is, that the laws of the domicil of origin govern the state and condition of the minor, into whatever country he removes. The laws of Louisiana, therefore, must determine at what period the plaintiff became of age; and by them she was a major at twenty-five. Admitting that her removal into another country, before the alteration of our law, would exempt her from its operation, and that her state and condition were fixed by the rules prevailing in the place, where she was born, at the time she left it, a point by no means free from difficulty, no proof has been given that the plaintiff was taken out of Louisiana before the change made in 1808."[1] The question did not here arise, as to the effect of any contract, made in Louisiana (as in the preceding case), but the simple question of the state of minority or majority. But it is difficult to perceive, why the same rule should not apply to a like case of contract; and if it would apply, it is not easy to reconcile this with the preceding doctrine, unless upon the ground, that the courts of the native domicil ought to follow their own law, as to minority and majority.

§ 78. There is an earlier case in the same court, in which it would seem to have been held, as a part

---

[1] Barrera v. Alpuente, 18 Martin R. 69.

of the law of nations, that "personal incapacities, communicated by the laws of any particular place, accompany the person, wherever he goes. Thus, he, who is excused from the consequences of contracts for want of age in his country, cannot make binding contracts in another."[1] This doctrine is certainly at variance with that maintained by the same court at later periods.[2] It is somewhat curious, that it was avowed in the case of what is called a runaway marriage, celebrated in Mississippi, with a female minor of Louisiana, of thirteen years of age, without the consent of her parents; and which, by the law of Louisiana, would seem to have been void without such consent, if celebrated in Louisiana. It was not, however, the main point in the case; and the decision itself was placed, (as we shall hereafter see,) upon a broader foundation.

§ 79. In respect to contracts of marriage, the English decisions have established the rule, that a foreign marriage, valid according to the law of the place where celebrated, is good every where else.[3] But they have not, *e converso*, established, that marriages of British subjects, not good according to the law of the place where celebrated, are universally, and under all possible circumstances, to be regarded as invalid in England.[4] And accordingly Lord Stowell has decided, that a marriage, had under peculiar circumstances at the Cape of Good Hope, during British occupation, was valid, though not in conformity to the Dutch law. In that case the

1 Le Breton *v.* Nouchet, 3 Martin R. 60, 70.

2 Saul *v.* His Creditors, 17 Martin R. 597, 598; Baldwin *v.* Gray, 16 Martin R. 192, 193.

3 Ryan *v.* Ryan, 2 Phill. Ecc. R. 332; Herbert *v.* Herbert, 3 Phill. Ecc. R. 58; S. C., 2 Hagg. Ecc. R. 263, 271; Lacon *v.* Higgins, 3 Starkie R. 178; S. C., 1 Dowl. and R. N. P. R. 38. See Ryan and Mood. R. 80.

4 Ruding *v.* Smith, 2 Hagg. Consist. R. 390, 391.

husband (an Englishman) was a person entitled by the laws of his own country to marry without the consent of parents or guardians, being of the age of twenty-one; but by the Dutch law he could not marry without such consent until thirty years of age. The lady (an Englishwoman) was under the age of nineteen, her father was dead, her mother had married a second husband, and she had no guardian. Upon that occasion Lord Stowell said, "Suppose the Dutch law had thought fit to fix the age of majority at a still more advanced period than thirty, at which it then stood, at forty, it might surely be a question in an English court, whether a Dutch marriage of two British subjects, not absolutely domiciled in Holland, should be invalidated in England on that account; or, in other words, whether a protection intended for the rights of Dutch parents, given to them by Dutch law, should operate to the annulling a marriage of British subjects, upon the ground of protecting rights, which do not belong in any such extent to parents living in England, and of which the law of England could take no notice, but for the severe purpose of this disqualification. The Dutch jurists (as represented in this libel), would have no doubt whatever, that this law would clearly govern a British court. But a British court might think that a question, not unworthy of further consideration, before it adopted such a rule for the subjects of this country." "In deciding for Great Britain upon the marriage of British subjects, they (the Dutch jurists) are certainly the best and only authority upon the question, whether the marriage is conformable to the general Dutch law of Holland; and they can decide that question definitely for themselves and for other countries. But questions of a wider extent may lie beyond this;

whether the marriage be not good in England, although not conformable to the general Dutch law; and whether there are not principles leading to such a conclusion? Of this question, and of those principles, they are not the authorized judges; for this question, and those principles, belong either to the law of England, of which they are not the authorized expositors at all, or to the *jus gentium*, upon which the courts of this country may be supposed as competent as themselves; and certainly, in the case of British subjects, much more appropriate judges."[1]

§ 80. In another case, where two British subjects, being minors, and in France solely for purposes of education, intermarried, it was held by the court, that the marriage, being void by the law of France, was a mere nullity. The court (Sir Edward Simpson) said, "The only question before me is, whether this be a good or bad marriage by the law of England, &c. The question being in substance, whether by the law of this country marriage contracts are not to be deemed good or bad according to the laws of the country, in which they are formed; and whether they are not to be construed by that law. If such be the law of this country, the rights of English subjects cannot be said to be determined by the laws of France, but by

[1] Ruding *v.* Smith, 2 Hagg. Consist. R. 389, 390. — That there are other excepted cases from the operation of foreign law, seems to have been directly held by Sir George Hay, in Harford *v.* Higgins, 2 Hagg. Consist. R. 423. He there said, "I do not mean, that every domicil is to give jurisdiction to a foreign country, so that the laws of that country are necessarily to obtain and attach upon a marriage solemnized there. For, what would become of our factories abroad, at Leghorn, or elsewhere, where the marriage is only by the law of England, and might be void by the law of that country? Nothing will be admitted in this court to affect such marriages, so celebrated, even where the parties are so domiciled." Id. 432.

those of their own country, which sanction and adopt this rule of decision. By the general law all parties contracting gain a forum in the place, where the contract is entered into. All our books lay this down for law," &c. "There can be no doubt, then, that both the parties in this case obtained a forum, by virtue of the contract in France. By entering into the marriage there, they subjected themselves to have the validity of it determined by the laws of that country."[1] And he afterwards proceeded to add, "This doctrine of trying contracts, especially those of marriage, according to the laws of the country, where they were made, is conformable to what is laid down in our books, and what is practised in all civilized countries, and what is agreeable to the law of nations, which is the law of every particular country, and taken notice of as such."[2] And the learned judge proceeded to cite the opinions of civilians to the precise effect; and he afterwards concluded with these remarks; "All nations allow marriage contracts. They are *juris gentium;* and the subjects of all nations are concerned in them; and from the infinite mischief and confusion, that must necessarily arise to the subjects of all nations with respect to legitimacy, successions, and other rights, if the respective laws of different countries were only to be observed, as to marriages contracted by the subjects of those countries abroad, all nations have consented, or must be presumed to consent, for the common benefit and advantage, that such marriages should be good or not, according to the laws of the country, where they are made. It is of equal consequence to

---

1 Scrimshire *v.* Scrimshire, 2 Hagg. Consist. R. p. 407, 408.

2 Ibid, p. 412.

all, that one rule in all these cases should be observed by all countries; that is, the law of the countries, where the contract is made. By observing this law no inconvenience can arise; but infinite mischief will ensue, if it is not."[1] "So that in cases of this kind *the matter of domicil makes no sort of difference in determining them*, because the inconvenience to society, and the public in general is the same, whether the parties contracting are domiciled or not. *Neither does it make any difference, whether the cause be that of contract or marriage;* for if both countries do not observe the same law, the inconveniences to society must be the same in both cases."[2]

§ 81. Here, then, we have a doctrine laid down of the *jus gentium*, or at least of the *jus gentium*, as understood and recognised in England, in regard to contracts generally, and especially in regard to contracts of marriage, very different from the rule, as laid down by foreign jurists, that the law of the domicil of origin, or of the actual domicil, is of universal obligation as to the capacity, state, and condition of persons. The same doctrine has been formally promulgated upon other occasions.[3] In the great case of Dalrymple *v.* Dalrymple,[4] which turned upon the validity of a Scotch marriage, where one of the parties was an English minor, Lord Stowell said, "Being entertained in an English court, it (the cause) must be adjudicated according to the principles of English law applicable to such a case. But the only principle applicable to such

---

1 Scrimshire *v.* Scrimshire, 2 Hagg. Consist. R. p. 417.

2 Id. 419. See Lord Meadowbank's Opinion, Fergusson on Marr. and Divorce, Appendix, p. 361, 362.

3 Doe *v.* Vardill, 5 B. and Cresw. 438, 452, 453.

4 2 Hagg. Consist. R. 54.

a case by the law of England is, that the validity of the marriage rights must be tried by reference to the law of the country, where, if they exist at all, they had their origin."[1]

§ 82. In regard to other contracts made by minors a similar rule has prevailed. In a case where money had been advanced for a minor during his stay in Scotland (who seems to have had his general domicil in England), it was held by Lord Eldon, that the question, whether in an English court a recovery could be had for the money so advanced, depended upon the law of Scotland; for the general rule was, that the law of the place, where the contract is made, must govern the contract.[2]

§ 83. Foreign jurists have entertained a very different opinion on this very point of the capacity of a person to contract in another country, when he is disabled, as a minor, by the law of his own country and domicil. Thus it has been said by them, that where the law of Modena enabled a minor of fourteen years of age to contract, that would not enable a minor of Bologna of the same age to make a valid contract at Modena.[3] And Rodemburg asserts the same doctrine in the most emphatic terms; in which he is followed by Boullenois.[4]

---

1 Id. 58, 59. See also Conway v. Beasley, 3 Hagg. Ecc. R. 639; Middleton v. Janverin, 2 Hagg. Consist. R. 437, 446.

2 Male v. Roberts, 3 Esp. N. P. R. 163. See also Thompson v. Ketcham, 8 John. R. 189; Grotius, Lib. 2, ch. 11, § 5. See also Dalrymple v. Dalrymple, 2 Hagg. Consist. R. 60, 61.

3 D'Argentré cited in Livermore's Dissert. p. 34, § 21 to 32; Id. p. 42, § 33 to 56; 1 Froland, Mém. 112, 156, 159.

4 Rodemburg, De Div. Stat. tit. 2, § 1; 1 Boullenois, Obs. 16, p. 205; Bouhier, ch. 23, n. 92; 1 Froland, Mém. p. 112, 159; 2 Froland, Mém. p. 1576 to 1582.

§ 84. Bouhier, although he holds to the doctrine of the capacity and incapacity by the law of the domicil extending every where else,[1] is manifestly startled, when it is applied to the case of marriages. He admits, that in such cases it is commonly held, that the law of the place, where the marriage is celebrated, ought to prevail. But he propounds a doubt, whether it ought in regard to subjects, who contract marriage in a foreign country, in order to evade the domestic law. But at the same time he seems to admit, that a marriage so celebrated ought to be held valid, if there is no such intention to evade the domestic law, although the husband may be a minor.[2] D'Argentré thus propounds the general doctrine. "When the question is, as to the right or capacity of any person to do civil acts generally, it is to be referred to the judge, who exercises judicial functions in the place of his domicil; that is to say, to whom his person is subject, and who has authority so to pronounce respecting him, that whatever he shall promulgate, adjudge, or ordain respecting the rights of persons ought to obtain, and be of force, in every place, to which he may transfer himself, on account of this authority over the person." *Cum de personæ jure aut habilitate quæritur ad actus civiles, in universum ea judicis ejus potestas est, qui domicilio judicat, id est, cui persona subjicitur, qui de eo sic statuere potest, ut quod edixerit, judicârit, ordinârit de personarum jure, ubicunque obtineat, quocumque persona contulerit propter afficentiam personæ.*[3] Froland asserts the same doctrine, and expressly ex-

[1] Bouhier, Cout. de Bourg, ch. 24, § 11, p. 463.
[2] Id. ch. 28, § 59 to 67, p. 556 to 557; Id. ch. 24, § 11, p. 463.
[3] 1 Froland, Mém. 112.

tends it to cases of contract.[1] Mr. Henry in his judicial capacity has given it a like extent in the English colony of Demarara; for he declares, that in the cases of prodigals, minors, idiots, and lunatics, the law of the domicil accompanies the party every where.[2] Cochin lays down the doctrine with great boldness, that a marriage contracted in a foreign country by French subjects, although contracted in the form prescribed by the foreign law, is void, if it violates the laws of France. The subjects of the King of France (says he) are always his subjects. And the parties contracting at D. (in Brabant), have only that capacity to contract, which is given by the laws of their country. It is a personal statute, which follows them every where.[3]

§ 85. Huberus, although he seems in some places to affirm an equally extensive doctrine, in others manifestly deems it too broad.[4] In regard to the contract of matrimony he holds, that it is to be governed by the law of the place, where the marriage is celebrated, with the exception, however, of cases of incest. "If," says he, "it is lawful in the place, where it is contracted and celebrated, it will be held valid and have effect every where, with this exception, that it does not prejudice others. To which it may be added, that it is not of an evil example, as if it should be a case of incest within the second degree according to the law of nations." *Si licitum est eo loco, ubi contractum et celebratum est, ubique validum erit, effectumque habebit, sub eâ exceptione prejudicii aliis non creandi. Cui licet*

1 1 Froland, Mém. 112, 156 to 160. See also 1 Hertii Opera, § 4, n. 8, p. 123; Id. n. 5, p. 122.

2 Henry on Foreign Law, p. 38, 39; Odwin *v.* Forbes; Id. p. 95, 96, 97.

3 Cochin, Œuvres, Tom. 1, p. 153, 154.

4 Huberus, De Conflictu Legum, Lib. 1, tit. 3, § 12, 13.

addere, si exempli nimis sit abominandi, ut si incestum juris gentium in secundo gradu contingeret. And he puts another exception, where persons belonging to one country go into another to be married, merely to evade the law of their own country, in which case he holds the marriage void, though good by the law of the place, where it is celebrated.[1]

§ 86. This latter doctrine has upon the most solemn consideration been overturned in England, as we shall hereafter see;[2] and such a marriage has been held valid. But we are not, therefore, to conclude, that every marriage by and between British subjects in foreign countries, will be held valid, because it is celebrated according to the laws of such countries. On the contrary, where the laws of England create a personal incapacity to contract marriage, that incapacity will, in some cases, be held to have a universal operation, so as to make a subsequent marriage in a foreign country a mere nullity, when litigated in a British court.[3]

§ 87. Indeed, the general principle adopted in England in regard to cases of this sort appears to be, that the *lex loci contractus* shall be permitted to prevail, unless when it would work injustice, or be *contra bonos mores*, or be repugnant to the settled principles and policy of its own laws. An illustration of this principle, may be found in the known difference between the Scottish and the English law, on the subject of the legitimation of antenuptial offspring. By the law of Scotland illegitimate children become by the subsequent marriage of the parents legitimate, and may inherit as heirs.

---

1 Huber. Lib. 1, tit. 3, § 8.

2 See 2 Kent. Comm. Lect. 26, p. 91, 92, (2d edit.)

3 Conway *v.* Beasley, 3 Hagg. Ecc. R. 639, 647, 652; Lolley's Case, 1 Russell and Ryan, Cr. Cas. 236.

But the law of England is otherwise; and, therefore, a person, born *ante justas nuptias* of parents domiciled in Scotland, and subsequently marrying there, cannot inherit landed property in England. So it was expressly decided in Doe dem. Birthwhistle *v.* Vardell (5 B. and Cresw. 438.)[1] The court there admitted, that the *lex loci* governs in questions of marriage; but not as to the consequences of marriage. And one of the learned judges on that occasion said; "The very rule, that a personal *status* accompanies a man every where, is admitted to have this qualification, that it does not militate against the law of the country, where the consequences of that *status* are sought to be enforced."[2] Yet the law of foreign countries as to legitimacy is so far respected in England, that a person, illegitimate by the law of his domicil of birth, will be held illegitimate in England.[3]

§ 88. Another illustration, touching the capacity of persons to contract marriage, may be stated from English jurisprudence. By the law of England marriage is an indissoluble contract, except by the transcendent power of Parliament. Hence it has been held, that a marriage, once celebrated between British subjects in an English domicil, cannot be dissolved by a divorce obtained under the laws of a foreign country, to which the parties may temporarily remove. Thus, an English marriage cannot be dissolved, under such circumstances, by a Scotch divorce, regularly obtained according to the law of Scotland, by persons going thither for that

---

1 See 2 Inst. 97; Glanville, B. 7, ch. 15. See also Voet. de Statut. § 4, c. 3, n. 15, p. 138; 1 Hertii Opera, De Collis. Leg. § 4, p. 129, § 15.

2 Per Littledale, J. 5 B. and Cres. 455.

3 See Shedden *v.* Patrick, and the Strathmore Peerage, cited in 5 Barn. and Cres. 444; 3 Hagg. Ecc. R. 652.

purpose, who have their domicil in England. And a second marriage in Scotland after such divorce will be held unlawful, and will subject the parties to the charge of bigamy. And it yet remains an undecided question in the English law (as we shall hereafter see), whether a *bonâ fide* change of domicil, and a divorce subsequently obtained, would change the legal predicament of the parties in an English tribunal.[1]

§ 89. In the American courts the doctrine, as to capacity or incapacity to marry, has been held to depend generally on the law of the place, where the marriage is celebrated, and not on the place of domicil of the parties. An exception would doubtless be applied to cases of incest and polygamy. But in affirmance of the general principle it has been held, that if a person, divorced from his first wife, is rendered by the law of the place of the divorce incapable of contracting a second marriage, still, if he contracts marriage in another state, where the disability does not exist, the marriage will be held valid. And a marriage, celebrated in a foreign state, to evade the law of the place of domicil, is on the same account held valid.[2] Mr. Chancellor Kent has indeed laid down the doctrine in regard to contracts generally in terms, which may admit of a different interpretation. He says, "The personal incompetency of individuals to contract, as in the case of infancy, and the general capacity of parties to contract, depend upon the law of the domicil."[3] But he is to

---

1 See Rex *v.* Lolley, 1 Russ. and Ryan, C. 236; Tovey *v.* Lindsay, 1 Dow R. 124; Beazley *v.* Beazley, 3 Hagg. Ecc. R. 639. See also Fergusson on Marr. and Div. Appendix, 269.

2 2 Kent. Comm. 91 to 93, (2d edit.); Id. 458, 459; Putnam *v.* Putnam, 8 Pick. 433; West Cambridge *v.* Lexington, 1 Pick. R. 504; De Couche *v.* Savatier, 3 John. Ch. R. 190.

3 2 Kent Comm. Lect. 39, p. 458, (2d edition.)

be understood as referring to the law of the domicil, when it is the place, where the contract is made; for he has in the same paragraph stated, that the *lex loci contractus* governs in relation to the validity of contracts, and has applied it especially to nuptial contracts.[1]

§ 90. The difficulty of applying any other rule to the class of nuptial contracts will become still more clear by attending to the great extent of the parental power recognised by the continental nations of Europe, and derived by them from the civil law. Parental restraints upon the marriages of minors exist to a very great extent in Germany, Holland, France, and other civil law countries; to so great an extent indeed, that the marriages of minors, without the consent of parents, or at least of the father, are absolutely void; and the disability of minority is in these countries carried to a

---

1 2 Kent Comm. Lect. 39, p. 458, (2d edition), and De Couche *v.* Savatier, 3 John. Ch. R. 190. — The English authorities, cited by Chancellor Kent, justify this conclusion. One is, Male *v.* Roberts, in 3 Esp. R. 163, which was a case of a contract by a minor in Scotland, during his temporary residence there, and it was held to be governed by the law of Scotland. Another is, Ex parte Otto Lewis, 1 Ves. R. 298, where a lunatic heir of a mortgagee, who had been declared a *non compos* in Hamburg, and no commission of lunacy had been taken out in England, was ordered to convey the estate in payment of the mortgage in Hamburg, under Statute 4 Geo. ch. 10. Here, Lord Hardwicke manifestly acted upon the ground, that the mortgage money was personal property, and, the lunatic being domiciled in Hamburg, the court would take notice of his disability to convey there, by the law of that place. The remaining authority is Pardessus. His doctrine is certainly more broad. But it could not have been intended by Chancellor Kent to overrule the English doctrine, and his own prior statement, upon the authority of a foreign jurist. Pardessus is an authority in favour of the limited doctrine, that a person incapacitated by the law of his domicil cannot contract with validity there; but he carries his doctrine much farther. The cases of Saul *v.* His Creditors, 17 Martin R. 596, 598, and Baldwin *v.* Gray, 16 Martin R. 192, 193, already cited, establish a like limited doctrine, and decide, that a contract by a minor is to be governed by the *lex loci contractus.*

much greater age, than it is by the common law.[1] In some of these countries majority is not attained until thirty; and even at this day in France the age of majority of males is twenty-five and of females is twenty-one. Yet France has ventured upon the bold doctrine, that the marriages of Frenchmen in foreign countries shall not be deemed valid, if the parties are not by its own law competent to contract from their being under the parental power.[2] There can be little doubt, that foreign countries, where such marriages are celebrated, will follow their own law, and disregard that of France.

§ 91. If we pass from cases of minority to other disabilities, enforced by the law of the native or after acquired domicil, there will be still more reason to doubt, whether any rule of such law respecting personal capacity and incapacity ought to be declared to be of universal obligation and efficacy. Let us take the case of a person declared infamous by the law of the place of his domicil. It is said, that under such circumstances he is to be deemed every where infamous. *Hinc* (says Hertius) *in uno loco infamis, ubique infamis habetur.* Surely, it will not be contended, that, if a Protestant be declared a heretic in a Catholic country, and rendered infamous, and inhabilitated thereby, he is to be deemed under like infamy and disability in protestant countries. That would certainly be pressing the doctrine to a wanton extravagance.[3]

---

[1] 2 Kent Comm. Lect. 26, p. 86, (2d edition); 1 Black. Comm. 437; 2 Hagg. Consist. R. 372, 389; Id. 395; 1 Brown, Civ. Law, 59.

[2] 2 Kent Comm. Lect. 26, p. 93, note, (2d edit.); Code Civil, art. 170; Id. art. 148; 1 Toullier, Droit Civil, art. 576, 577.

[3] See 1 Hertii Opera, § 4, n. 8, p. 124; Liver. Diss. p. 30, 31.

Yet certainly the foreign jurists do press it to that extent.[1]

§ 92. In like manner, let us consider the civil disabilities imposed by the English laws in cases of outlawry, excommunication, civil death, and popish recusancy.[2] It would be difficult to maintain, that these accompanied the person to America, where no like disabilities exist, and where they are foreign to the whole genius of our laws. Yet foreign jurists strenuously maintain the doctrine.[3] We have no positive laws declaring, that such foreign disabilities shall not be recognised; but an American court would deem them purely local, and incapable of being enforced here. Even the conviction of a crime in a foreign country, which makes the party infamous there, and incapable of being a witness, has been held not to produce a like effect here.[4] The capacity or incapacity of any persons to do acts in their own country would undoubtedly under such circumstances be judged by their own laws; but not to do extra territorial acts.

§ 93. The foreign jurists, also, generally maintain, that the question of legitimacy or illegitimacy is to be decided exclusively by the law of the domicil of origin. They assert the general maxim to be of universal obligation, *Pater est, quem justæ nuptiæ demonstrant*, which is true only in a limited sense. They therefore hold, that if, by the law of a country (as of Scotland), a man, born

---

1 See Henry on Foreign Law, p. 30; 1 Boullenois, Observ. 4, p. 52 to 67.

2 See 3 Black. Comm. 101, 102, 283; 1 Black. Comm. 132; 4 Black. Comm. 54, 319, 320.

3 1 Boullenois, Observ. p. 59 to p. 67; 2 Boullenois, p. 9, 10, 19. But see, contra, Voet. De Statut. § 4, ch. 3, n. 17, 18.

4 Commonwealth v. Green, 17 Mass. R. 515, 540, 541.

a bastard, becomes legitimate by a subsequent marriage of his parents, he ought to be deemed legitimate every where. And so, on the contrary, if a man so born would by the law of his own country be deemed illegitimate (as in England), he ought to be deemed illegitimate every where, even in another country, where he would by its law be deemed legitimate.[1] We have already seen, that this doctrine has been expressly overruled in England.[2]

§ 94. Another case may be put of persons, whose marriages are void or voidable by reason of their profession. Thus, by the law of England, until after the reformation, monks and nuns were deemed incapable of contracting marriage (as they still are in many parts of the continent), and their contracts for this purpose were held nullities. The marriages of priests also were in law voidable, as contrary to their office, at any time during their lives.[3] And to this very day in Catholic countries, marriages are prohibited to the priesthood, and to persons in monastic orders. Yet it would be extremely difficult to maintain, that the marriage of a nun, or monk, or priest, celebrated in America, where no such prohibition exists, ought, *causâ professionis*, to be held a mere nullity on account of such foreign prohibitions, especially where the other party is entitled to the protection of our laws.

§ 95. By the laws of some countries the subjects thereof are prohibited from intermarrying with foreign-

---

1 1 Boullenois, Obser. 4, p. 62 to 64. But see Voet. De Statut. § 4, ch. 3, n. 15, p. 138; 1 Hertii Opera, § 4, p. 129, § 14, 15.

2 Doe *v.* Vardell, 5 B. and Cres. 438, 452, 453; 1 Hertii Op., De Collis. Leg. § 4, p. 129, § 15.

3 2 Inst. 686, 687; Com. Dig. Baron and Feme, B. 2; 1 Woodes. Lect. 16, p. 422.

ers, or with persons of another sect; and some civilians have held, that such laws are of universal obligation, and accompany the person every where.[1] But it can hardly be supposed, that any other nation would suffer such a marriage celebrated in its own dominions, with one of its own subjects, according to its own laws, to be deemed a nullity in its own courts. Such a narrow prohibition would be justly deemed odious, and be rejected.

§ 96. Another case may be put of even a more striking character. Suppose a person to be a slave in his own country, having no personal capacity to contract there, is he upon his removal to a foreign country, where slavery is not tolerated, to be still deemed a slave? If so, then a Greek or Asiatic, held in slavery in Turkey, would, upon his arrival in England, or in Massachusetts, be deemed a slave and be there subject to be treated as mere property, and under the uncontrollable despotic power of his master. The same rule would exist as to Africans and others, held in slavery in foreign countries. We know, how this point has been settled in England. It has been decided, that the law of England abhors, and will not endure the existence of slavery within the nation; and consequently, as soon as a slave lands in England, he becomes *ipso facto* a freeman, and discharged from the state of servitude.[2] Independent of the provisions of the constitution of the United States, for the protection of the rights of masters in regard to domestic fugitive slaves,

---

1 Voet. De Stat. § 5, ch. 2, n. 1, p. 155, 156; Vattel, B. 2, ch. 8, § 115.

2 Somersett's Case, Lofft's R. 1; S. C. 11; State Trials, (Hargrave edit.) 340; 20 Howell, State Trials, 79; Co. Lit. 79; Harg. note, 44; 1 Black. Comm. 424, 425, Christian's note; Forbes *v.* Cochrane, 2 B. and Cres. 448; The Amedie, 1 Acton R. 240; S. C. 1 Dodson R. 84; Id. 91, 95; The St. Louis, 2 Dodson R. 210.

there is no doubt, that the same principle pervades the common law of the non slave holding states in America; that is, foreign slaves would no longer be deemed such after their removal thither.[1] It is quite a different question, how far rights acquired, and wrongs done to slave property, or contracts made respecting such property, in countries, where slavery is permitted, may be allowed to be redressed, or recognised in the judicial tribunals of governments, which prohibit slavery.[2]

§ 97. Struck with the inconveniences of the doctrine of the ubiquity of the law of the domicil, as to the capacity, state, and condition of persons, a learned judge in the Scottish courts[3] has not hesitated to hold an opposite doctrine to belong to Scotland. "Would a marriage here," says he, "be declared void, because the parties were domiciled in England, and were minors, when they married here, and of course incapable by the law of that country of contracting marriage? This category of law does not affect the contracting individuals only, but the public, and that in various ways. And the consequences would prove not a little inconvenient, embarrassing, and probably even inextricable, if the personal incapacities of individuals, as of majors and minors, the competency to contract marriages, and infringe matrimonial engagements, the rights of domestic authority and service, and the like, were to be qualified and regulated by foreign laws and customs, with which the mass of the

1 See Saul *v.* His Creditors, 17 Martin R. 598; In re Francisco, 9 Amer. Jurist, 490; Butler *v.* Hopper, 1 Wash. C. C. R. 499; Ex parte Simmons, 4 Wash. C. C. R. 390.

2 Madrazo *v.* Willes, 3 B. and Ald. 353; Forbes *v.* Cochrane, 2 B. and Cres. 448; The St. Louis, 2 Dodson R. 210; The Antelope, 10 Wheaton R. 66; Wharton's Digest, Servants and Slaves, A. D.

3 Lord Meadowbank.

population must be utterly unacquainted. Accordingly, the laws of this description seem no where to yield to those of foreign countries; and accordingly, it is believed, no nation has hitherto thought of conferring powers and forms on its courts of justice, adequate for enabling them to execute over foreigners regular authority for enforcing the observance by them of the laws of their own country, when expatriated. In fact, the very same principles, which prescribe to nations the administration of their own criminal law, appear to require a like exclusive administration of law relative to the domestic relations. Hence, both in England and Scotland, the most regular constitution abroad of domestic slavery was held to afford no claim to domestic service in this country, though restrictions for only such service, and under such domestic authority, as our laws recognised. The whole order of society would be disjointed, were the positive institutions of foreign nations concerning the domestic relations, and the capacities of persons regarding them, admitted to operate universally, and form privileged castes, living each under separate laws, like the barbarous nations during many centuries after their settlement in the Roman Empire." [1]

§ 98. These diversities in the practical jurisprudence of different countries, as to the effect of personal ability and disability, capacity or incapacity, abundantly establish, in the first place, that there is no general rule on the subject, which is admitted by all nations; and, in the next place, that the very exceptions introduced, or conceded, by those, who most strenuously contend for the universal operation of the law of the domicil in

---

[1] Lord Meadowbank; Fergusson on Marr. and Divorce, App. 361, 362.

cases of this nature, as satisfactorily establish, that no general rules, have been or can be established, which may not work serious inconvenience to the interests or institutions of some countries. The proper conclusion, then, to be drawn from this review of the subject is, that the rule of Huberus is correct, that no nation is under any obligation to give effect to the laws of another nation, which are prejudicial to itself or its citizens; that in all cases it must judge for itself, what foreign laws are so prejudicial or not; and that, in cases not so prejudicial, a spirit of comity and a sense of mutual utility ought to induce every nation to allow full force and effect to the laws of every other nation. This is the doctrine asserted by Chancellor Kent, and it certainly has a most solid foundation in the actual practice of nations. "There is no doubt," says he, "of the truth of the general proposition, that the laws of a country have no binding force beyond its own territorial limits; and their authority is admitted in other states, not *ex proprio vigore*, but *ex comitate*, *&c.* Every independent community will judge for itself, how far the *comitas inter communitates* is to be permitted to interfere with its domestic interests and policy, &c. It is a maxim, that *locus regit actum*, unless the intention of the parties to the contrary be clearly shown. It is, however, a necessary exception to the universality of the rule, that no people are bound to enforce, or hold valid in their courts of justice any contract, which is injurious to their public rights, or offends their morals, or contravenes their policy, or violates a public law."[1]

---

[1] 2 Kent Comm. Lect. 39, p. 457, 458, (2d edit.) See also Greenwood *v.* Curtis, 6 Mass. R. 378, 379.—This subject is a good deal

§ 99. In discussing this subject our attention has been more particularly drawn to the common cases of incapacity, resulting from minority, and marriage. But the principles, which apply to them, are not materially different from those, which apply to cases of idiocy, insanity, and prodigality. The extent of the rights and authorities of guardians, curators, parents, and masters, over persons subjected to their control, or committed to their charge, may, in a general sense, be said to depend, so far as they are to be recognised, or enforced by and in foreign nations, upon the same common international jurisprudence.

§ 100. In concluding this discussion, as to the operation of foreign laws on questions relating to the capacity, state, and condition of persons, it may be useful to bring together those rules, which seem best established in the jurisprudence of England and America, leaving others of a more doubtful character and extent to be decided, as they may arise in the proper forum.

§ 101. First. The capacity, state, and condition of persons according to the law of their domicil will generally be regarded, as to acts done, rights acquired, and contracts made in the place of their domicil. If these acts, rights, and contracts have validity there, they will be held equally valid every where. If invalid there, they will be held invalid every where.[1]

§ 102. Secondly. But as to acts done, and rights

---

discussed in Fergusson on Marriage and Divorce; and the opinions in the case of Gordon *v.* Pye, in 1815, and of Edmonstone and others, in 1816, before the Scottish courts, are particularly worthy of examination, from their comprehensive learning and ability; Fergusson, Appendix, p. 276 to 363. See also, Id. p. 384 to 422.

[1] See Male *v.* Roberts, 3 Esp. R. 63; Thompson *v.* Ketcham, 8 John. 189.

acquired, and contracts made in other countries, the law of the country, where they are done, acquired, or made, will generally govern in respect to the capacity, state, and condition of persons.

§ 103. Thirdly. Hence we may deduce, as a corollary, that in regard to questions of minority or majority, competency or incompetency to marry, incapacities incident to coverture, guardianship, emancipation, and other personal qualities and disabilities, the law of the domicil of birth, or of other fixed domicil, is not generally to govern, but the *lex loci contractûs aut actûs*, the law of the place, where the contract is made, or the act done. Therefore a person, who is a minor, until he is of the age of twenty-five years by the law of his domicil, and incapable, as such, of making a valid contract there, may nevertheless in another country, where he would be of age at twenty-one years, generally make a valid contract at that age, even a contract of marriage.

§ 104. Fourthly. Personal disqualifications not arising from the law of nature, but from the principles of the customary or positive law of a foreign country, and especially such as are of a penal nature, are not generally regarded in other countries, where the like disqualifications do not exist. Hence, the disqualifications resulting from heresy, excommunication, Popish recusancy, infamy, and other penal disabilities, are not enforced in any other country, except that, in which they originate. They are strictly territorial. So the state of slavery will not be recognised in any country, whose institutions and policy prohibit slavery.[1]

§ 105. Fifthly. In questions of legitimacy, the *lex*

[1] Co. Lit. 79, b.; Harg. note, 44.

loci of the marriage will generally govern, as to the issue subsequently born. If the marriage is valid by the *lex loci*, it will generally be held valid every where for the purpose of heirship. If invalid there, it will generally (not universally) be held invalid every where.

§ 106. Sixthly. No nation being under any obligation to yield up its own laws, in regard to its own subjects, to the laws of other nations, it will not suffer its own subjects to evade the operation of its own fundamental policy or laws, or to commit frauds in violation of them, by acts or contracts made in a foreign country; and it will judge for itself, how far it will adopt, or reject such acts or contracts. Hence, the acts of prodigals, minors, idiots, lunatics, and married women, escaping into foreign countries, are not to be deemed as, of course, absolutely obligatory, even if sanctioned by the foreign law, unless the laws of their own country adopt such foreign law, as a rule in such cases.[1]

---

1 An apt illustration of this rule may be found in the present law of France. By that law, a marriage contracted in a foreign country between Frenchmen, or a Frenchman and a stranger, is valid, if celebrated according to the forms used in that country, provided it is preceded by a proper publication of banns, and the Frenchman does not contravene the other provisions of the French law. Upon this law Toullier remarks, that the conditions, required to be complied with, are those of the code respecting the contract of marriage; for as the laws respecting the person follow a Frenchman every where, it results, that even in a foreign country he is held to conform to the French laws relative to the age of the contracting parties, their family, and the impediments to marriage. 1 Toullier, Droit Civil François, art. 576, p. 484. So that French minors, who are incapable of contracting a marriage in France, are disabled every where, even though the marriage would be good by the law of the place, where the marriage is celebrated. The English and American law hold such a marriage good. Code Civil, art. 144, 148, 170; Merlin, Répert. tit. Loi. § 6, n. 1. See also 2 Kent Comm. Lect. 26, p. 93, note, (2d edition.) The doctrine of France, in this

So a person born before wedlock, who in the country of his birth is deemed illegitimate, may not, by a subsequent marriage of his parents in another country, where such marriage would make him legitimate, cease to be illegitimate in the country of his birth. Hence also, if a marriage is by the laws of a country indissoluble, when once contracted between its own subjects, they may not, by a mere removal into another country, at least without a change of domicil, be deemed capable of contracting a new marriage after a divorce, lawful by the law of the place, to which they have removed.[1] But this will be more fully considered in the succeeding chapters.

---

respect, is but an illustration of the general rule, prescribed by the Civil Code (art. 3.), that the laws respecting the state and condition of Frenchmen govern them even when resident in a foreign country.

1 See Rex *v.* Lolley, 1 Russ. and Ryan's Case, 236; Tovey *v.* Lindsay, 1 Dow R. 124; Beazley *v.* Beazley, 3 Hagg. Eccl. R. 639; McCarthy *v.* De Loix, 1831, 2 Russell and Mylne R.

CHAPTER V.

MARRIAGE.

§ 107. Having treated of the capacity and incapacity of persons, as affected by foreign law, we shall next proceed to consider more fully the nature and effect of the relation of marriage contracted by and between persons, who are admitted to possess competent capacity. We shall then discuss the manner, in which that relation may be dissolved, and the effect of such dissolution.

§ 108. Marriage is treated by all civilized nations as a peculiar and favored contract. It is in its origin a contract of natural law. It may exist between two individuals of different sexes, although no third person existed in the world, as happened in the case of the common ancestors of mankind. It is the parent, and not the child of society; *principium urbis et quasi seminarium reipublicæ*. In civil society it becomes a civil contract, regulated and prescribed by law, and endowed with civil consequences. In most civilized countries, acting under a sense of the force of sacred obligations, it has had the sanctions of religion superadded. It then becomes a religious, as well as a natural and civil contract; for it is a great mistake to suppose, that because it is the one, therefore it may not likewise be the other.[1] The common law of England (and the like law exists in America) considers marriage in no other light than as a civil contract. The holiness

---

[1] Dalrymple *v.* Dalrymple, 2 Hagg. Consist. R. 63; Linclo *v.* Belisario, 1 Hagg. Consist. R. 231.

of the matrimonial state is left entirely to ecclesiastical and religious scrutiny.[1] In the Catholic and in some of the Protestant countries of Europe, it is treated as a sacrament.[2]

§ 109. There are some remarks on this subject made by a distinguished Scottish judge, so striking, that they deserve to be quoted at large. "Marriage being entirely a personal *consensual* contract, it may be thought, that the *lex loci* must be resorted to in expounding every question, that arises relative to it. But it will be observed, that marriage is a contract *sui generis*, and differing, in some respects, from all other contracts, so that the rules of law, which are applicable in expounding and enforcing other contracts, may not apply to this. The contract of marriage is the most important of all human transactions. It is the very basis of the whole fabric of civilized society. The *status* of marriage is *juris gentium*, and the foundation of it, like that of all other contracts, rests on the consent of parties. But it differs from other contracts in this, that the rights, obligations, or duties, arising from it, are not left entirely to be regulated by the agreements of parties, but are, to a certain extent, matters of municipal regulation, over which the parties have no control, by any declaration of their will. It confers the *status* of legitimacy on children born in wedlock, with all the consequential rights, duties, and privileges, thence arising; it gives rise to the relations of consanguinity and affinity; in short, it pervades the whole system of civil society. Unlike other contracts, it cannot, in general, amongst civilized

[1] 1 Black. Comm. 433.

[2] 2 Hagg. Consist. R. 63 to 65.

nations, be dissolved by mutual consent; and it subsists in full force, even although one of the parties should be for ever rendered incapable, as in the case of incurable insanity, or the like, from performing his part of the mutual contract.

§ 110. "No wonder that the rights, duties, and obligations, arising from so important a contract, should not be left to the discretion or caprice of the contracting parties, but should be regulated, in many important particulars, by the laws of every civilized country. And such laws must be considered as forming a most essential part of the public law of the country. As to the constitution of the marriage, as it is merely a personal, consensual contract, it must be valid every where, if celebrated according to the *lex loci;* but, with regard to the rights, duties, and obligations, thence arising, the law of the domicil must be looked to. It must be admitted, that, in every country, the laws relative to divorce are considered as of the utmost importance, as public laws affecting the dearest interests of society.

§ 111. "It is said, that, in every contract the parties bind themselves, not only to what is expressly stipulated, but also to what is *implied* in the nature of the contract; and that these stipulations, whether express or implied, are not affected by any subsequent change of domicil. This may be true in the general case, but, as already noticed, marriage is a contract *sui generis,* and the rights, duties, and obligations, which arise out of it, are matters of so much importance to the well-being of the State, that they are regulated, not by the private contract, but by the public laws of the State, which are imperative on all, who are domiciled within its teritory. If a man in this country were to confine his wife in an iron cage, or to beat her with a rod of the thickness of the Judge's finger, would it be a justification in any court, to allege, that these were powers, which the law of England conferred on a husband, and that he was entitled to the exercise of them, because his marriage had been celebrated in that country?

§ 112. "In short, although a marriage, which is contracted according to the *lex loci*, will be valid all the world over, and although many of the obligations incident to it are left to be regulated solely by the agreement of the parties; yet many of the rights, duties, and obligations, arising from it, are so important to the best interests of morality and good government, that the parties have no control over them; but they are regulated and enforced by the public law, which is imperative on all, who are domiciled within its jurisdiction, and which cannot be controlled or affected by the circumstance, that the marriage was celebrated in a country, where the law is different. In expounding or enforcing a contract entered into in a foreign country, and executed according to the laws of that country, regard will be paid to the *lex loci*, as the contract is evidence, that the parties had in view the law of the country, and meant to be bound by it. But a party, who is domiciled here, cannot be permitted to import into this country a law peculiar to his own case, and which is in opposition to those great and important public laws, which our Legislature has held to be essentially connected with the best interests of society."[1]

§ 113. The general principle certainly is, (as we have already seen,) that between persons, *sui juris*, marriage is to be decided by the law of the place, where it is

[1] Lord Robertson, in Fergusson on Marr. and Div. 397, 398, 399.

celebrated. If valid there, it is valid every where. It has a legal ubiquity of obligation. If invalid there, it is equally invalid every where.[1] The most prominent, if not the only known exceptions to the rule, are those respecting polygamy and incest; those positively prohibited by the public law of a country, from motives of policy; and those celebrated in foreign countries by subjects entitling themselves under special circumstances to the benefit of the laws of their own country. Cases, illustrative of each of these exceptions, have been already alluded to.

§ 114. Christianity is understood to prohibit polygamy and incest; and therefore no Christian country would recognise polygamy, or incestuous marriages.[2] But when we speak of incestuous marriages, care must be taken to confine the doctrine to such cases, as by the general consent of Christendom are deemed incestuous. It is difficult to ascertain exactly the point, at which the law of nature, or Christianity, ceases to prohibit marriages between kindred; and nations are by no means agreed on this subject.[3] In most of the countries of Europe, in which the canon law has had authority or influence, marriages are prohibited between near relations by blood or marriage; and the canon and the common law seem to have made no distinction on this point between con-

---

1 Ryan *v.* Ryan, 2 Phill. Eccl. R. 332; Herbert *v.* Herbert, 3 Phill. Eccl. R. 58; Dalrymple *v.* Dalrymple, 2 Hagg. Consist. R. 54; Ruding *v.* Smith, 2 Hagg. Consist. R. 390, 391; Scrimshire *v.* Scrimshire, 2 Hagg. Consist. R. 395; Ilderton *v.* Ilderton, 2 H. Bl. 145; Middleton *v.* Janverin, 2 Hagg. R. 437; Lacon *v.* Higgins, 3 Stark. R. 178; 2 Kent Comm. Lect. 26, p. 91, (2d edit.); 2 Kaims on Eq. B. 3, ch. 8, § 1.

2 See Paley on Moral Phil. B. 3, ch. 6; 2 Kent Comm. Lect. 26, p. 81, (2d edit.); 1 Black. Comm. 436. See Grotius, B. 2, ch. 5, § 9; Greenwood *v.* Curtis, 6 Mass. R. 378.

3 Grotius, B. 2, ch. 5, § 12, 13, 14. See 1 Brown Civ. Law, 61 to 65.

sanguinity, or relation by blood and affinity, or relation by marriage, though there certainly is a very material difference in the cases.[1] Marriages between relations by blood, in the lineal ascending or descending line, are universally held by the common, the canon, and the civil law, to be unnatural and unlawful.[2] And a marriage between an uncle and niece by blood has been held in England to be incestuous, upon the ground, that it is against the law of God and sound morals, that it would tend to endless confusion, and that the sanctity of private life would be polluted, and the proper freedom of intercourse in families would be destroyed, if such practices were not discountenanced in the strongest manner.[3]

§ 115. In England it has been declared by statute, that all persons may lawfully marry, but such as are prohibited by God's law, that is, such as are within the Levitical degrees.[4] And it has been there held, that a marriage between a father-in-law and the daughter of his first wife is incestuous and unlawful.[5] In the collateral line, marriages between brother and sister by blood are deemed incestuous and void, and indeed seem repugnant to the first principles of social order and morality.[6] Beyond this, it seems difficult to ex-

---

1 2 Kent Comm. Lect. 26, p. 81, 82, (2d edit.); 1 Bl. Comm. 434.

2 Wightman *v.* Wightman, 4 John. Ch. R. 343; 2 Kent Comm. Lect. 26, p. 81, (2d edit.); Harrison *v.* Burwell, Vaughan R. 206; S. C. 2 Vent. R. 9; Grotius, B. 2, ch. 5, § 12, 13, 14; Grotius, B. 2, § 12, n. 2; 2 Heinecc. Elem. Juris Natur. B. 2, ch. 2, § 40, by Turnbull.

3 Burgess *v.* Burgess, 1 Hagg. Consist. R. 384, 386; 1 Black. Comm. 435; Butler *v.* Gastrill, Gilbert R. 156, 158; 2 Kent Comm. Lect. 26. p. 84, (2d edit.)

4 Com. Dig. Baron and Feme, B. 2, B. 4.

5 1 Hagg. Consist. R. 393, note.

6 Wightman *v.* Wightman, 4 John. Ch. R. 343; 2 Kent Comm. Lect. 26, p. 83, (2d edit.)

tend the prohibition upon principle. Incestuous marriages by the English law are not absolutely void; but are voidable only during the lives of the parties; and, if not so avoided, are deemed after their death to all intents and purposes valid.[1] But upon the point, whether a marriage between a man and the sister of his deceased first wife is lawful, there has been a diversity of opinion and practice. In England it would be held invalid.[2] In many of the American states, it is held clearly valid, not merely in a civil sense, but in a moral and Christian sense; in others, the English rule prevails.[3]

§ 116. It would be a strong point to put, that a marriage, perfectly valid between such parties in all New England, should be held invalid in Virginia, or England, even though the parties originally belonged to

---

1 1 Black. Comm. 434, 435.

2 Burn Eccl. Law, Marriage, I; 1 Black. Comm. 434, 435, Christian's note (2), citing Gibson's Cod. 412; Harris v. Hicks, Salk. 548; Hall v. Good, Vaughan R. 302, 312; Burn Eccl. Law, Marriage, I.; Com. Dig. Baron and Feme, B. 2, B. 4; 2 Inst. 683; Bac. Abridg. Marriage A.

3 Lord Chief Justice Vaughan, in delivering the opinion of the court in Harrison v. Burwell (Vaughan R. 206; S. C. 2 Vent. R. 9), says, that a man is prohibited by the statute, 32 Henry 8, [ch. 38,] to marry his wife's sister. But within the meaning of Leviticus, (ch. 18, v. 14,) and the constant practice of the Commonwealth of the Jews, a man was prohibited to marry his wife's sister only during her life; after he might. So the text is. Vaughan R. 241; S. C. 2 Vent. 17. There seems a discrepancy between what is here said, and his judgment in the subsequent case of Hall v. Good, Vaughan R. 302, 312, 320. The opinion of Lord Chief Justice Vaughan, in both cases, and the case of Butler v. Gastrill, Gilbert Eq. R. 156, are full of learning and instruction on the subject of the canonical and ecclesiastical prohibitions of marriage. Dr. John H. Livingston, of New Jersey, has written an elaborate dissertation upon the subject of the marriage of a man with his sister in law (wife's sister), which was printed at New Brunswick, N. J., in 1816. It holds the doctrine, that such marriages are scripturally incestuous. The opposite doctrine has been maintained by many able writers. See also 2 Kent Comm. Lect. 26, p. 85, (2d edition,) note.

the latter country or state. But as to persons not so belonging, it would be of most dangerous consequence to suppose, that either of them would assume the liberty to hold such marriages a nullity, merely because their own jurisprudence would not, in a local transaction, uphold it. This distinction between marriages incestuous by the law of nature, and such as are incestuous by the positive code of a state, has been fully recognised by one of our most learned American courts. "If," say the court, "a foreign state allows of marriages incestuous by the law of nature, as between parent and child, such marriage would not be allowed to have any validity here. But marriages not naturally unlawful, but prohibited by the law of one state and not of another, if celebrated where they are not prohibited, would be holden valid in a state where they are not allowed. As in this state a marriage between a man and his deceased wife's sister is lawful; but it is not so in some states; such a marriage celebrated here would be held valid in any other state, and the parties entitled to the benefits of the matrimonial contract."[1] Indeed, in the diversity of religious opinions in Christian countries, a large space must be allowed for interpretation as to religious duties, rights, and solemnities.[2] In the Catholic countries of continental Europe, there are many prohibitions of marriage, which are connected with religious establishments and canons; and in most countries there are positive or

---

1 Greenwood *v.* Curtis, 6 Mass. R. 378, 379; Medway *v.* Needham, 16 Mass. R. 157, 161. But see Huberus, Lib. 1, tit. 3, § 9; Wightman *v.* Wightman, 4 John. Ch. R. 343.

2 See on this point, 2 Kent Comm. Lect. 26, p. 85, (2d edition); Harrison *v.* Burwell, Vaugh. R. 206; S. C. 2 Vent. R. 9; Co. Litt. 149; Grotius, B. 2, ch. 5, § 12, 13, 14; Rutherf. Inst. B. 1, ch. 15, § 10; Wightman *v.* Wightman, 4 John. Ch. R. 343.

customary prohibitions, which involve peculiarities of religious opinion or conscientious doubt. It would be most inconvenient to hold all marriages celebrated elsewhere void, which were not in scrupulous accordance with local institutions.[1]

§ 117. In respect to the second exception, the prohibitions depending upon positive law, they of course can apply strictly only to the subjects of a country. An illustration of this nature may be found in the Civil Code of France, which annuls (art. 174) marriages by Frenchmen, in foreign countries, who are under incapacity by the laws of France.[2] A law of a similar nature may be found in the Act of 12 Geo. 3, ch. 11, respecting the royal family, by which they are prohibited from contracting marriage, unless under special circumstances, pointed out in the act;[3] and the provisions of this act have been actually applied to a foreign marriage, contracted by one of the royal princes. The doctrine of the English courts, already alluded to, in regard to the indissolubility of English marriages celebrated in England, notwithstanding a subsequent divorce in a foreign country, affords a still more striking illustration, as, in its practical effects, it may render the issue of a second marriage illegitimate; so that a son, the issue of the second marriage in Scotland, may be legitimate there and illegitimate in England, — may be a

---

1 Huberus says, that if a Brabanter, who should marry within the prohibited degrees, under a dispensation from the Pope, should remove here (into Holland), the marriage would be considered valid. Yet if a Frizian should marry the daughter of his mother in Brabant, and celebrate the nuptials there, returning here, he would not be acknowledged as a married man, because, in this way, our laws might be evaded. Huberus, Lib. 1, tit. 3, § 9.

2 2 Kent Comm. Lect. 26, p. 93, (2d edit.); Code Civil, art. 170; Merlin, Répert. Loi, § 6, n. 1.

3 1 Black. Comm. 226.

lawful Scotch Peer, and yet lose the English estates, which support his peerage.[1]

§ 118. In respect to the third exception, it has been deemed to arise in cases of moral necessity, and has been applied to persons, residing in factories, in conquered places, and in desert or barbarous countries, or in countries of an opposite religion, who are permitted to contract marriage there according to the laws of their own country. In short, wherever there is a local necessity from the absence of laws, or the presence of prohibitions or obstructions, not binding upon other countries, or from peculiarities of religious opinion and conscientious scruples, or from circumstances of exemption from local jurisdiction, marriages will be allowed to be valid according to the law of the native domicil.[2]

§ 119. The doctrine, upon which this exception from necessity is founded, will be best explained by a quotation from an opinion of Lord Stowell, in a case, already referred to, in which the question of the validity of a marriage, celebrated at the Cape of Good Hope between English subjects, by a chaplain of the British forces, then occupying that settlement under a capitulation, recently made, came before him for decision. After citing the rule, that the law and legislative government of every dominion equally affect all persons and all property within the limits thereof, and remarking, that to such a proposition, expressed in very general terms, only general truth can be ascribed, (for it is undoubtedly subject to exceptions,) he proceeded to say, that even the native and resident inhabitants

---

1 See Beazley *v.* Beazley, 3 Hagg. Ecc. Rep. 639; Rex *v.* Lolley, 1 Russell and Ryan c. 236; Tovey *v.* Lindsay, 1 Dow, 124; McCarthy *v.* De Croix, cited 3 Hagg. 642, note.

2 See Ruding *v.* Smith, 2 Hagg. Consist. R. 371, 384, 385, 386; Lautour *v.* Teesdale, 8 Taunt. R. 830; S. C. 2 Marshall R. 243; The King *v.* Inhab. of Brampton, 10 East. R. 282.

are not all brought strictly within the pale of the general law. And in illustration of this remark, he referred to the fact, that even in England, there is a numerous and respectable body (referring to the Jews), distinguished by great singularity of usages, who, though native subjects, under the protection of the general law, are, in many respects, governed by institutions of their own; and particularly in their marriages; for, it being the practice of mankind to consecrate their marriages by religious ceremonies, the differences of religion in all countries, that admit residents, professing religions essentially different, unavoidably introduce exceptions in that matter to the universality of the rule, which makes mere domicil the constituent of an unlimited subjection to the ordinary law of the country. He then added, "What is the law of marriage in all foreign establishments settled in countries professing a religion essentially different? In the English factories at Lisbon, Leghorn, Oporto, Cadiz, and in the factories in the East, Smyrna, Aleppo, and others? In all of which (some of these establishments existing by authority, under treaties, and others under indulgence and toleration,) marriages are regulated by the law of the original country, to which they are still considered to belong. An English resident at St. Petersburg does not look to the ritual of the Greek Church, but to the rubric of the Church of England, when he contracts a marriage with an Englishwoman. Nobody can suppose, that whilst the Mogul empire existed, an Englishman was bound to consult the Koran for the celebration of his marriage. Even where no foreign connexion can be ascribed, a respect is shown to the opinions and practice of a distinct people. The validity of a Greek marriage in the extensive dominions of Turkey is left to depend, I presume, upon their own canons, without any reference to Mahometan ceremonies. There is a *jus gentium* upon this matter, a comity, which treats with tenderness, or, at least, with toleration, the opinion and usages of a distinct people, in this transaction of marriage. It may be difficult to say *a priori*, how far the general law should circumscribe its own authority in this matter. But practice has established the principle in several instances; and where the practice is admitted, it is entitled to acceptance and respect. It has sanctioned the marriages of foreign subjects in the houses of the ambassadors of the foreign country, to which they belong.[1] I am not aware of any judicial regulation upon this point. But the reputation, which the validity of such marriages has acquired, makes such a recognition by no means improbable, if such a question was brought to judgment." "It is true, indeed, that English decisions have established this rule, that a foreign marriage, valid according the law of the place where celebrated, is good every where else. But they have not *e converso* established, that marriages of British subjects, not good according to the law of the place where celebrated, are universally, and under all possible circumstances, to be regarded as invalid in England. It is, therefore, certainly to be advised, that the safest course is, always to be married according to the law of the country; for then no question can be stirred. But if this cannot be done on account of legal or religious difficulties, the law of this country does not say, that its subjects shall not marry abroad." And he accordingly held the marriage valid, on the distinct British character of the parties, on their independence of the Dutch law in their own British transactions, on the insuperable obstacles of obtaining

---

1 See Pertreis *v.* Tondear, 1 Hagg. Consist. R. 136.

any marriage conformable to the Dutch law, on the countenance given by British authority and British administration to this transaction, and upon the whole country being under British dominion.[1]

§ 120. In regard to marriages by British subjects in their foreign settlements, the general rule is, that marriages, good by the laws of England, will be valid there; for they carry those laws with them into such settlements, and are not to be governed by the laws or customs of the natives. Thus, it has been held, that a marriage between British subjects at Madras is good, if conformable to the British laws, and not to the laws of the natives of India.[2]

§ 121. The ground, however, upon which the general rule of the validity of marriages, according to the *lex loci contractûs*, is maintained, is easily vindicated. It cannot be better expressed, than in language already quoted. All civilized nations allow marriage contracts. They are *juris gentium;* and the subjects of all nations are equally concerned in them. Infinite mischief and confusion must necessarily arise to the subjects of all nations with respect to legitimacy, successions, and other rights, if the respective laws of different countries were only to be observed, as to marriages contracted by the subjects of those countries abroad; and therefore all nations have consented, or are presumed to consent, for the common benefit and advantage, that such marriages shall be good or not, according to the laws of the country where they are celebrated. By observing this rule, few, if any, inconveniences can arise. By disregarding it, infinite mischiefs must ensue.[3] Suppose, for instance, a marriage celebrated in

1 Ruding *v.* Smith, 2 Hagg. Consist. R. 371.

2 Lautour *v.* Teesdale, 8 Taunt. R. 830; S. C. 2 Marsh. R. 243.

3 2 Hagg. Consist. R. 417, and ante, § 80.

France, according to the law of that country, should be held void in England, what would be the consequences. Each party might marry anew in the other country. In one country the issue would be deemed legitimate; in the other illegitimate. The French wife would in France be held the only wife, and entitled as such to all the rights of property appertaining to that relation. In England, the English wife would hold the same exclusive rights and character. What, then, would be the confusion in regard to the personal property of the parties, in its own nature transitory, passing alternately from one country to the other! Suppose there should be issue of both marriages, and then all the parties should become domiciled in England or France, what confusion of rights, what embarrassments of personal and conjugal relations, must necessarily be created! [1]

§ 122. Foreign jurists have as strenuously supported the general rule, as the tribunals sitting to administer the common law; and undoubtedly from a common sense of the pernicious consequences, which would flow from a different doctrine. Thus, Sanchez holds, that a marriage is void, where it wants the solemnities prescribed by the local law; "what," says he, "the law of the place requires, where the contract is made, and what are the solemnities, which are to be followed in contracts, are to be decided solely by the laws of the place, in which the contract is celebrated;" *quæ petunt leges loci, ubi contractus initur, et quoad solennitatem adhibendam in contractibus, solæ leges loci, in quo contractus celebratur, inspiciuntur.*[2] John Voet affirms the

---

[1] Scrimshire *v.* Scrimshire, 2 Hagg. Consist. R. 417, 418.

[2] 2 Hagg. Consist. R. 413.

same doctrine, holding, that a marriage of an inhabitant of Holland in Flanders, or Brabant, according to the laws of the latter, would be valid in Holland; "because," says he, "it is sufficient in contracts to follow the solemnities of the place, in which the contract is celebrated, although the solemnities are not observed, which are prescribed in the place of the domicil of the parties, or of the situation of the property, in executing the act;" *eo quod sufficit in contrahendo adhiberi solennia loci illius, in quo contractus celebratur, etsi non inveniantur observata solennia, quæ in loco domicilii contrahentium, aut rei sitæ, actui gerendo prescripta sunt.*[1] Paul Voet holds the same opinion.[2] Huberus says, that a marriage valid by the law of the place, where it is celebrated, is binding every where, under the exception, which he generally applies, that it is not prejudicial to others, or that it is not incestuous.[3] Bouhier adopts the general rule, hesitating as to the nature and extent of the exceptions.[4] Hertius lays down the following axiom. "If the law prescribes a form for the act, the place of the act, and not the domicil of the parties, or of the situation of the property, is to be considered." *Si lex actui formam dat, inspiciendus est locus actûs, non domicilii, non rei sitæ.* And he puts the following as an example; "A marriage contracted according to the solemnities of any place, where the married couple are commorant, cannot be rescinded upon the pretext, that, in the domicil or country of the husband, other solemnities are required."

1 2 Hagg. Consist. R. 415, cites J. Voet, in Dig. Lib. 23, tit. 2, n. 4, p. 20.

2 Voet. De Statut. § 9, ch. 2, n. 9, p. 267.

3 Huberus, Lib. 1, tit. 3, n. 8.

4 Bouhier, Cout. de Bourg. ch. 27, § 59 to 66.

Matrimonium juxta solennitates loci alicujus, ubi sponsus et sponsa commorabantur, contractum non potest prætextu illo rescindi, quod in domicilio aut patriâ mariti aliæ solennitates observentur.[1] He puts exceptions afterwards to this general axiom; one of which is, that a contract between foreigners belonging to the same country, is to be governed by the law of their own country, and not by that of the *lex loci contractûs.* In this exception, he has to encounter many distinguished adversaries.[2] The French jurists seem generally to support the doctrine, that marriage is to be held valid or not, according to the law of the place of celebration, except in cases positively prohibited by their own law to their own subjects. And Merlin says, that it is a contract so completely of natural and moral law, that when celebrated by savages, in places where there are no established laws, it will be recognised as good in other countries.[3]

§ 123. A question has been much discussed, how far a marriage regularly celebrated in a foreign country, between persons belonging to another country, who have gone thither from their own country for that purpose, is to be deemed valid, if it is not celebrated according to the law of their own country. Huberus puts the case, and does not hesitate to pronounce such a marriage invalid, because it is an evasion, or fraud upon the law of the country, to which the parties belong.[4] Bouhier has adopted the same opin-

---

1 1 Hertii Opera, De Collis. Leg. § 4, p. 126, § 10.

2 Id. p. 128, § 10. Non Valet (6.)

3 Merlin, Répertoire, Mariage, § 1, p. 343. See also 2 Boullenois, 458; 1 Froland, Mém. p. 177, ch. 1; Pardessus, Vol. 5, P. 6. tit. 7, ch. 2, art. 1481 to 1495.

4 Huberus, Lib. 1, tit. 3, § 9.

ion;[1] and it is also maintained by Paul Voet.[2] In opposition to this doctrine, it has, however, been settled, after some struggle, both in England and America, that such a marriage is good. The question in England was first decided by the High Court of Delegates, in 1768;[3] and having been subsequently recognised, notwithstanding the doubts of Lord Mansfield, may now be there deemed beyond controversy.[4] In Massachusetts, the doctrine is as firmly established. It is admitted, that the doctrine is repugnant to the general principles of law relating to contracts; for a fraudulent evasion of the laws of the country, where the parties have their domicil, would not be protected. But the exception in favour of marriages is maintained upon principles of public policy, with a view to prevent the disastrous consequences to the issue of such a marriage, which would result from the loose state, in which persons so situated would live.[5] The doctrine has been carried even farther, so as to admit the legitimacy of the issue of a person, who had been divorced *a vinculo* for adultery, and was declared by the local law incompetent to marry again, but who had gone into a neighbouring state, and there contracted marriage, and had issue.[6] And the like

---

1 Bouhier, Cout. de Bourg. ch. 28, § 60, 61, 62, p. 557.

2 Voet. De Statut. § 9, ch. 2, p. 268.

3 Compton *v.* Bearcroft, Bull. N. P. 114; 2 Hagg. Consist. R. 443, 444.

4 See Harford *v.* Morris, 2 Hagg. Consist. R. 423; Robinson *v.* Bland, 2 Burr. R. 1077 to 1080; Fergusson on Marr. and Div. 63, 64, 65.

5 Medway *v.* Needham, 16 Mass. R. 157, 161; Putnam *v.* Putnam, 8 Pick. R. 433.

6 West Cambridge *v.* Lexington, 1 Pick. R. 506; 2 Kent Comm. Lect. 26, p. 92, 93, (2d edition.) See Fergusson, on Marr. and Div., note R. p. 469.

rule has been applied in favour of the widow by such second marriage, so as to entitle her to dower in the real estate of her deceased husband, situate in Massachusetts.[1]

§ 124. The English doctrine in relation to Scotch marriages, by parties domiciled in England, and going to Scotland to marry, though a plain violation of the English marriage act, has been upheld unquestionably upon a like policy. It is the least of two evils, in a political, a civil, and a moral sense. We have already seen, that the positive code of France has promulgated an opposite doctrine, with unrelenting severity. The wisdom of such a course remains to be established; and it will be no matter of surprise, if hereafter we shall find a Frenchman, with two lawful wives, one according to the law of the place of the marriage, and the other according to that of his domicil of origin.[2] The English doctrine has, indeed, stopped short of the moral mischief; for it has maintained, as we have seen, that a second marriage, after a divorce, in Scotland, of a marriage originally celebrated in England between English subjects, is void, though such divorce and second marriage would be unquestionably good by the law of Scotland. So that here there may be two lawful wives of the party, living at the same time, in different countries, and two families of children, one of which is deemed legitimate by the law of the one country, and illegitimate by the law of the other.[3] It is easy to see, what various difficulties may grow out of such a state

---

1 Putnam *v.* Putnam, 8 Pick. R. 433.

2 1 Toullier, Droit Civil, art. 576; Code Civil, art. 144, 148, 170; Merlin, Répertoire, tit. Loi. § 6, n. 1, and ante note § 84, 117.

3 Beazley *v.* Beazley, 3 Hagg. Eccl. R. 639; Rex *v.* Lolley, 1 Russell and Ryan, c. 236.

of things. A son, by the second marriage, may be entitled to the whole real and personal estate of the father in Scotland, and incapable of touching either in England. The Massachusetts doctrine escapes from these incongruities.

CHAPTER VI.

MARRIAGES — INCIDENTS TO.

§ 125. HAVING considered, how far the validity of marriages is to be decided by the law of the place, where they are celebrated, we are next led to consider the operation of foreign law upon the incidents of marriage. These may respect the personal capacity and powers of the husband and wife, or the rights of each in regard to the property, personal or real, acquired, or held by them during the coverture.

§ 126. The jurisprudence of different nations contains almost infinitely diversified regulations upon this subject; and the task of enumerating all of them would be as hopeless, as it would be useless. Before the revolution in France, there were a multitude of such diversities in the local and customary law of her own provinces; and in Germany, and the states of Holland and Italy, and the vast domains of Austria and Russia, the like diversities existed, and probably still continue to exist. Froland has enumerated a few of each, by way of illustrating the endless embarrassments, arising from the conflict of laws;[1] and his ample work is mainly devoted to a consideration of the mixed questions, arising from the conjugal relation, as affected by different laws. In some of the French provinces a married woman had a power to contract; in others not.[2] In Holland, the husband has a power to dispose of all the property of his wife; and she is

[1] 1 Froland, Mémoires, ch. 1, § 7, 8.

[2] Id.; Henry on Foreign Law, 31. See also 1 Boullenois, 421, ch. 1; Id. p. 467, 468; Merlin, Répertoire, Autorisation Maritale, § 10.

wholly deprived of any power over it. In Utrecht her consent is necessary, where there are no children; and in some other places, where there are. In Utrecht the husband and wife are disabled from making donations to each other; in Holland they may make them.[1] In some states there is a community of property between husband and wife; in others none; and in others again, mixed rights and qualified claims.[2]

§ 127. Boullenois has put several cases, showing the practical difficulties of this conflict of laws. Suppose a husband domiciled in a place, where he cannot bind his wife, if he contracts alone, and without her, although she is under marital power and authority; and the husband goes to, and contracts in a place, where, by reason of this authority, he can bind his wife, by binding himself; will the latter contract bind her? He answers in the negative, because the obligation of the wife does not spring from the nature of the contract, nor from the place of the contract, but from the marital authority, which has no such effect in the place of his domicil.[3] In Brittany, when a husband and wife are each bound *in solido* for the same contract or debt, payment must be first sought out of the effects of the husband. But in Paris, upon a like contract, the effects of the husband and wife are indiscriminately bound. Suppose, then, that married persons, domiciled in Brittany, should go to Paris and contract, or that married persons domiciled in Paris should go to Brittany and contract, in what manner is the creditor to seek payment? Boullenois seems to hold, that in such a case, the laws are to

---

1 1 Froland, Mém., ch. 1, § 7, 8.

2 Id. ch. 2 to 15; Henry on Foreign Law, ch. 1, § 3, p. 10, 36, note; Id. 95; Boullenois, Obs. 15, p, 198; Id. Princ. Gén. 8, p. 8.

3 2 Boullenois, Obs. 46, p. 467.

be followed, which regulate the estate and condition of the wife, that is to say, the laws of her domicil.[1]

§ 128. It is hardly possible to enumerate the different rules, adopted in the customary or positive law of different provinces, upon the subject of the rights of husband and wife. In some places the laws, which place the wife under the authority of her husband, extend to all her acts, as well *inter vivos*, as testamentary. In others, the former only are prohibited. In some, the consent of the husband is necessary, to give effect to the contracts of the wife. In others, the contract is valid, but suspended in its execution during the life of the husband. In some, the wife has no power over the administration of her own property. In others the prohibition is confined to property merely *dotal*, and she has the free disposal of her other property, which is called *paraphernal*.[2]

§ 129. But not to perplex ourselves with cases of a provincial and unusual nature, let us attend to the differences on this subject in the existing jurisprudence of two of the most polished and commercial states of Europe, in order to realize the variety of questions, which may spring up, and embarrass the administration of justice.

§ 130. The present Code of France does not undertake to regulate the conjugal association as to property, except in the absence of a special contract, which the husband and wife may, under certain limitations, make, as they shall judge proper. When no special stipulations exist, the case is governed by what

1 2 Boullenois, Obs. 46, p. 468, 469.

2 2 Boullenois, p. 11; 1 Domat, B. 1, tit. 9, p. 166, 167; Id. § 4, p. 179, 180, &c. See also 1 Froland, Mém. per tot.; Merlin, Répertoire, Autorisation Maritale, § 10.

is denominated the rule of community, *le régime de la communauté*. This community, or nuptial partnership, generally extends to all the moveable property of the husband and wife, and the fruits, income, and revenues thereof, whether in possession, or in action, at the time of the marriage, or subsequently acquired; to all immoveable property acquired during the marriage; but not to such immoveable property, as either possessed at the time of the marriage, or which came to them afterwards by title of succession, or by gift.[1] The property thus acquired by this nuptial partnership, is liable to the debts of the parties existing at the time of the marriage, to the debts contracted by the husband during the community, or by the wife, with the consent of the husband; and to the maintenance of the family, and other charges of the marriage. As in common cases of partnership, recompense may be had for charges, which ought to be borne exclusively by either party. The husband alone is entitled to administer the property of the community; and he may sell, alien, and mortgage it, without the concurrence of the wife. He cannot dispose, *inter vivos*, by gratuitous title, of the immoveables of the community, or of the moveables, except under particular circumstances; and testamentary dispositions made by him cannot exceed his share in the community.[2] The community is dissolved by natural death, by civil death, by divorce, by separation of body, or by separation of property. Upon separation of body, or property, the wife resumes her free administration of her moveable property, and may alien it. But she cannot alien her immoveable

1 Code Civil of France, art. 1387 to 1408; Id. art. 1497 to 1541.
2 Id. art. 1409 to 1440.

property without the consent of her husband, or without being authorized by law upon his refusal. Dissolution by divorce gives no right of survivorship to the wife; but it may occur on the civil or natural death of the husband. Upon the death of either party, the community being dissolved, the property belongs equally to the surviving party, and the heirs of the deceased, after the due adjustment of all debts, and charges, and claims on the fund, in equal moieties.[1]

§ 131. Such is a very brief outline of some of the more important particulars of the French Code, in regard to the property of married persons, in cases of community. They may vary these rights by special contract, or they may marry under what is called the *dotal* rule, *le régime dotal;* but it would carry us too far to enter upon the consideration of these peculiarities, as our object is only to point out the more broad distinctions between the English and French law.

§ 132. In regard to personal rights, independent of the ordinary rights and duties of conjugal fidelity, succour, maintenance, and assistance, the husband becomes the head of the family; and the wife can do no act in law without the authority of her husband. She cannot, therefore, without his consent give, alien, mortgage, or acquire property. No general authority, even though stipulated by a marriage contract, is valid, but as to the administration of the property of the wife. But the wife may make a will without the authority of her husband. If the wife is a public trader, she may, without the authority of her husband, bind herself in what concerns her business; and in such case

---

[1] Code Civil of France, art. 1441 to 1496.

she also binds her husband, if there is a community between them.[1]

§ 133. If we compare this nuptial jurisprudence, brief and imperfect as the outline necessarily is, with that of England, it presents, upon the most superficial examination, very striking differences. In the first place, as to personal rights and disabilities, the law of England, with few exceptions, which it is unnecessary to mention, places the wife completely under the guardianship and coverture of the husband. The husband and wife are, in contemplation of law, one person. He possesses the sole power and authority over the person and acts of the wife; so that, as Mr. Justice Blackstone has well observed, the very being, or legal existence of the wife, is suspended during the marriage, or at least, is incorporated and consolidated into that of the husband.[2] For this reason, a man cannot grant any thing to his wife, or enter into a covenant with her during his life, though he may devise to her by will. She is incapable of entering into any contract, executing any deed, or doing any other valid act, in her own name. All suits, even for personal injuries to her, must be brought in the name of her husband and herself, and with his concurrence. Upon the marriage, the husband becomes liable to all her debts; but neither the wife, nor her property, is liable for any of his debts. In the civil law, and, as we have seen, in the French law, the husband and wife are, for many purposes, considered as distinct persons, and may have separate estates, contracts, rights, and injuries.[3]

---

1 Code Civil of France, art. 212 to 226, art. 1426; 2 Toullier, Droit Civ. art. 618 to 655.

2 1 Black. Comm. 441.

3 Id., 1 Brown, Civ. Law, 82; 2 Kent. Comm. Lect. 28, p. 129, &c. (2d edition.)

§ 134. In respect to property, the husband, by the marriage, independent of any marriage settlement, becomes *ipso facto* entitled to all her personal property of every description, in possession, and in action, and may dispose of it at his pleasure. He has also a freehold in her real estate during their joint lives; and if he has issue by her, and survives her, during his own life also; and an exclusive right to the whole profits of it during the same period. There is not any community between them in regard to property, as in the French law. Upon his death she is simply entitled to dower of one third of his real estate during her life; and she may, at his pleasure, by a testamentary disposition, be deprived of all right and interest in his personal estate, although it came to him from her by the marriage. During the coverture she is also incapable of changing, transferring, or in any manner disposing of her real estate, except with his concurrence; and she is incapable of making an effectual testament.[1]

§ 135. Now, these differences, (which are by no means all, which exist) exemplified in the French and English laws, are, for the most part, the very same, as exist in America between the States settled under the common law, and those settled under the civil law; between those deriving their origin from Spain or France, and those deriving their origin from England.[2] We may see at once, then, upon a change of domicil, or even of temporary residence, from a state or country governed by the one law, to one governed by the

---

1 2 Kent Comm. Lect. 28, p. 129, &c., (2d edit.); 2 Black. Comm. 433.

2 Id., p. 183 and note, (2d edition.) See 1 Domat, B 1, tit. 9; Id. tit. 10. See Christy's Louisiana Digest, art. *Husband* and *Wife*, and Louisiana Code, art. ad idem.

other, what various questions of an interesting and practical nature may, nay must, grow up from this conflict of local jurisprudence.

§ 181. It is extremely difficult upon the subject of the personal disabilities of the wife to lay down any satisfactory rule as to the extent, to which they are recognised by foreign nations. In general, she is deemed to have the same domicil as her husband; and can during the coverture acquire none other, *suo jure.*[1] Her acts, done in the place of her domicil, will have validity or not, as they are, or are not valid there. But as to her acts done elsewhere, there is much room for diversity of opinion and practice among nations. We have seen, that many of the civilians and jurists of continental Europe hold, that the capacity and incapacity of married women, as in other cases of the personality of laws, accompany them every where, and govern their acts.[2] And Mr. Chancellor Kent has said, that as personal qualities and civil relations of a universal nature, such as infancy and coverture, are fixed by the law of the domicil, it becomes the interest of all nations mutually to respect, and sustain that law.[3] This is true in a general sense. But every nation will judge for itself, what its own interest requires, and, in framing its own jurisprudence, will often hold acts valid within its territories, which the laws of a foreign domicil might prohibit, or disable the parties from doing.

§ 137. In considering this point, it is material, at least so far as foreign jurists are concerned, to distinguish cases, where there has been a change of domicil

---

1 Ante, § 46.

2 See Henry on Foreign Law, p. 50; Fergusson, on Mar. and Div. 334 to 336; Merlin, Répertoire, Autorisation Maritale, § 10.

3 2 Kent Comm. Lect. 39, p. 419, (2d edit.)

of the parties, from those, where there has not. Where the domicil of marriage remains unchanged, the acts of the wife, and her power over her property in a foreign country, are held by many jurists, (among whom are Merlin and Pothier,) to be exclusively governed by the law of her domicil; in other words, her acts are valid, or not, as the law of her domicil gives her capacity or incapacity to do them. And the rule is applied to immoveable, as well as to moveable property. Thus, if by the law of her domicil she cannot alien property, or contract, except by the consent of her husband, she cannot alien her property, or contract, without such consent, in a foreign country, where no such restriction exists.[1] But suppose, that the parties afterwards remove to a new domicil, where the consent of the husband is not necessary, is the law of the new domicil, as to the capacity of the wife, to prevail, or that of the matrimonial domicil? This a question upon which foreign jurists have been greatly divided in opinion.[2]

§ 138. For example, the law of England disables a married woman from making a will in favour of her husband, or others; the law of France allows it. Suppose a husband and wife, married in and subjects of England, should temporarily or permanently become domiciled in France; would a will of the wife in France, in regard to property in England, in favour of her husband or others, be held valid in England?[3] Froland, would answer this question upon principle in the affirmative; for he holds, that the capacity and inca-

[1] Merlin, Répertoire, Autorisation Maritale, § 10, art. 2; Pothier, Cout. d'Orléans, ch. 1, art. 7.

[2] See Merlin, Répertoire, Effet Rétroactif, § 2, 3, art. 5; Autorisation Maritale, § 10.

[3] See Merlin, Répertoire, Testament, § 1, 5, art. 1, 2, p. 309 to 319.

pacity of married women to do things changes with their domicil; and that acts, valid by the law of their original domicil, if done in a new domicil, by whose laws they are void, are to be deemed nullities. Thus, he says, a married woman, who is incapable by the law of her domicil of entering into a suretyship for another, or contracting with her husband, as in Normandy, if she goes to reside at Paris, where no such law exists, is deprived of that exception; and, on the other hand, a woman married at Paris, and afterwards going to reside in Normandy, or in any other country, where the Roman law prevails (*Droit écrit*), loses her capacity to enter into any such contract, which she previously possessed.[1]

§ 139. Other jurists would give a different response; for we have already seen, that in regard to personal laws, there is much conflict of opinion, how far they are affected by changes of domicil.[2] Merlin, in an especial manner, at one time bent the whole strength of his

---

[1] 1 Froland, Mém. 172; 1 Boullenois, p. 61; 2 Boullenois, p. 7, 13. — Froland has some subtile distinctions on this subject, which, to say the least of them, are not in a practical sense very clear. Lest I should misstate the purport of his remarks, I will quote them in the original, having already referred to them in another place. "Quand il s'agit de l'état universel de la personne, abstraction faite de toute matière réelle, *abstractè ab omni materiâ reali*, en ce cas le statut, qui a commencé à fixir sa condition, conserve sa force et son authorité, et la suit par tout en quelque endroit, qu'elle aille — Mais quand il est question de l'habilité ou inhabilité de la personne, qui a changé de domicile *à faire une certaine chose*, alors le statut, qui avoit réglé son pouvoir, tombe entièrement à son égard, et cède tout son empire à celui dans le territoire duquel elle va demeurer." 1 Froland, Mém. 171, 172. See 2 Boullenois, p. 7 to 10.

[2] See 1 Boullenois, p. 187, 188 to 196; Id. 200; 2 Boullenois, p. 2, 14, 15, 17, 19 to 204; Rodemburg, De Div. Stat. tit. 2, ch. 1, § 3; Id. P. 2, ch. 1, § 1, and Observ. 32, p. 22 to 28; Henry on Foreign Law, p. 50, 51; Merlin, Répertoire, Autorisation Maritale, § 10; Id. Effet Rétroactif, § 3, 2, art. 3.

acknowledged ability, to establish the doctrine, (which is supported by Bouhier,[1]) that the law of the matrimonial domicil, and not of the new domicil, as to the capacity and incapacity of the wife, ought to prevail. He reasoned it out principally in his examination of the subject of the marital power, or the incapacity of the wife, according to certain local laws, to do any valid act, make any conveyance, or engage in any contract, without the consent and authorization of her husband. And he then held, that this incapacity is not changed by a change of domicil to a place, in whose laws it has no existence. After maintaining this opinion (as he says) for forty years, he has recently changed it, and adhered to the doctrine, that the law of the new domicil ought to govern.[2] In discussing the nature and extent of the paternal authority, conferred by the domicil of birth, in regard to foreign property, he seems to have been aware of the difficulties of his early doctrine; and he has said, with great truth, that to put an end to all the difficulties of such cases, it is necessary to make a uniform law, not for France only, but for the world; for the settlement of a foreigner in France, or of a Frenchman in a foreign country, would at once raise them anew, notwithstanding all the regulations of the present Civil Code of France.[3] His reasoning upon the testamentary power, and the manner, in which it is affected by the *situs* of the property, also affords strong proof of the intrinsic infirmity of all general speculations.[4]

---

[1] Bouhier, Cout. de Bourg. ch. 22, § 22 to 32, 45.

[2] Merlin, Répertoire; Effet Rétroactif., § 3, 2, art. 5, p. 15; Id. Autorisation Maritale, § 10, art. 4, p. 243, 214; Id. Majorité, § 5.

[3] Merlin, Répertoire, Puissance Paternelle, § 7, art. 1, 2, 3.

[4] Id. Testament, § 1, § v, art. 1, 2, p. 309 to 319.

§ 140. Hertius puts the following case. By the law of Utrecht married persons are incapable of making a will of property in favour of each other; not so in Holland. Is such a will of property in Utrecht, made by married persons in Holland, valid? Or, *e contra*, is such a will, made by married persons in Utrecht, of property in Holland, valid? He answers the former question in the negative, and the latter in the affirmative.[1] Yet other jurists maintain the contrary.[2]

§ 141. Rodemburg distinguishes the cases into two sorts; (1) those, in which there is no change of domicil of the married parties; (2) and those, in which there is a change of domicil. In the former case he holds, that the capacity and incapacity by the law of the domicil extend every where. In the latter case, that the capacity and incapacity of the new domicil attach. So that according to him the disabilities of a wife by the law of her domicil attach to all her acts wherever done, at home, or abroad, as long as the domicil exists. But upon a *bonâ fide* change of domicil by her husband, she loses all disabilities not existing by the law of the new domicil, and acquires all the capacities allowed by the latter.[3] In this doctrine he is supported by Boullenois.[4] Hence if a husband, who by the law of his domicil has his wife subject to his authority, changes his domicil to a place, where no such law exists; or *e contra*, if he changes his domicil from a place, where the wife is exempt from the marital power, to one, where it exists;

---

1 Hertii Op. De Collis. Leg. § 4, p. 142, § 43.

2 See 1 Boullenois, 194 to 204; Id. 205 to 222; Rodemburg, De Div. Leg. tit. 2, ch. 1, § 1, 3.

3 Rodemburg, De Div. Stat. tit. 2, ch. 1, § 1, p. 10, 11; Id. P. 2, ch. 1, § 1, p. 55, 56, ch. 4, § 1.

4 1 Boullenois, p. 61; Id. 205, &c.; 2 Boullenois, p. 1, &c. p. 7, &c.; Id. p. 93 to 112.

in each case the wife has the capacity or incapacity of the new domicil. Rodemburg puts another case. By the law of Holland married persons may make a will in favour of each other; by the law of Utrecht, not. Suppose a man and wife, who are married in Holland, move to Utrecht, is the will between them, previously made, good? And he decides in the negative.[1]

§ 142. But Boullenois himself puts a case, which he seems to decide upon a ground, which breaks in upon the general doctrine. Suppose a woman domiciled, and married in a country, using the Roman Law (*Droit écrit*), to a man belonging to the same country. She has the right and capacity by that law to enjoy her *paraphernal* property there, and alienate it independently of her husband,[2] and without his being entitled to intermeddle in the administration of it in any manner. If her husband goes to reside at Paris (where no such right exists), does she fall under the marital authority, so as to lose from that period the administration and alienation of her *paraphernal* property? Boullenois admits, that she falls under the marital authority; but at the same time contends, that she has, notwithstanding, the right of administering and alienating her *paraphernal* property; because it was given her by the contract of marriage, supported by the law of her matrimonial domicil; and that her husband cannot by a change of domicil extinguish her right founded upon such authentic titles. And though she cannot act without the consent of her husband in such administration and alienation, he is bound to give such consent.[3]

---

1 Rodemburg, De Div. Stat. P. 2, tit. 2, ch. 4, § 1; 2 Boullenois, 81; Id. 93 to 112.

2 1 Domat, B. 1, tit. 9, p. 167; Id. § 4, p. 179, 180.

3 2 Boullenois, p. 20, 21; Id. 22 to 28.

But Boullenois is compelled to admit other exceptions to the doctrine, where other considerations are mixed up in the case. Thus, he says, that if a woman is married at Paris, and has a community of property with her husband there, and she has goods at Aix or Toulouse, where she is not under the marital authority; and her husband goes to reside at either of these places, she cannot sell her property there without the consent of her husband. But, if there were no such community, then she might sell.[1]

§ 143. Passing from the consideration of personal capacities, disabilities, and powers, let us next examine into the effects of marriage upon the property of the husband and wife, and their rights over it. The marriage may have taken place with an express contract, or arrangement, as to the property of the parties; or it may have taken place without any such contract, or arrangement. The principal difficulty is not so much to ascertain, what rule ought to govern in cases of express contract, (at least, where there is no change of domicil,) as what rule ought to govern in cases, where there is no contract, or no contract, which provides for the emergency. Where there is an express contract, that, if it speaks fully to the point, will generally be admitted to govern all the property of the parties, not only in the matrimonial domicil, but in every other place, under the same limitations and restrictions as apply to other cases of contract.[2] But where there is

---

1 2 Boullenois, 22, 23, 24. See 2 Froland, Mém. 1007 to 1064; Bouhier, Cout. de Bourg. ch. 22, § 5 to 10; Id. § 28 to 32; J. Voet, ad Pand. Lib. 5, tit. 1, § 101.

2 See Le Brun, Traité de la Communauté, Liv. 1, ch. 2, § 2; Murphy v. Murphy, 5 Martin R. 83; Lashley v. Hogg, Robertson's Appeal Cases. 4; Feaubert v. Turst. Preced. in Chan. 207, 208.

no express contract at all, or none speaking to the point, the question, what rule ought to govern, is surrounded with more difficulty. Is the law of the matrimonial domicil to govern? Or the law of the local situation of the property? Or the law of the actual domicil of the parties? Does the same rule apply to moveable, as to immoveable property, when in different countries?[1] Boullenois has remarked, that, even on the subject of marriage contracts, the law of the place of a contract will not always decide all the questions arising from it. Many of the questions must be decided by the law of the domicil of the parties, and sometimes even of one of them.[2]

§ 144. Two classes of cases naturally present themselves in considering this subject. First, where during the marriage there is no change of domicil; secondly, where there is such a change.

§ 145. And first, in cases, where there is no change of domicil, and no express contract. Huberus[3] lays down the doctrine, in broad terms, that not only the contract of marriage itself, properly celebrated in a place according to its laws, is valid in all other places; but that the rights and effects of the marriage contract, according to the laws of the place, are to be held equally in force every where. Thus, he says, in Holland married persons have a community of all their property, unless it is otherwise agreed in their nuptial

---

1 In some foreign codes, there are express provisions, that marriage contracts shall not fix the rights of the couple according to the law of foreign countries. In France, there is an effective prohibition of contracts regulating marriage rights by the old customs of the provinces, which it had abolished. Code Civil, art. 1390. See also Bourcier *v.* Lanusse, 3 Martin R. 581.

2 Boullenois, Prin. Gén. 48, p. 11. See also 1 Dig. Lib. 5, tit. 1, l. 65.

3 Huberus, Lib. 1, tit. 3, § 9.

contract; and, that this will have effect in respect to property situate in Friezeland, although in that province, there is only a community of the losses and gains, and not of the property itself. The example, he thus puts, obviously shows, that his doctrine is applied to cases, where there is no express contract. Mr. Chancellor Kent has applied the doctrine of Huberus in a case of express contract; and has laid down the rule, that the rights, dependent upon nuptial contracts, are to be determined by the *lex loci*.[1] This may be generally correct, in regard to cases of express or implied nuptial contracts; and it is probable, that none other were at the time in the mind of the learned judge. But we shall presently see, that as a mere question, in regard to the universal operation of the *lex loci*, there is much controversy upon the subject among foreign jurists.

§ 146. There are many distinguished jurists, who, in common with Huberus, maintain the opinion, that the incidents and effects of the marriage upon the property of the parties, wherever it is situate, is to be governed by the law of the matrimonial domicil, in the absence of all positive arrangements between the parties.[2] Thus, if English subjects are married in England, without any nuptial contract, the husband, being entitled by the law of England to all the personal property of his wife, will be entitled to it, wherever it may be, in England, or in any foreign country. And his rights, it would seem, in her immoveable property,

---

1 See De Couche *v.* Savatier, 3 John. Ch. R. 211; 2 Kent Comm. Lect. 39, p. 458, 459, (2d edit.) See also Feaubert *v.* Turst, cited in Robertson's Appeal Cases 1, and Lashley *v.* Hogg, 1804, cited Id. 4.

2 Merlin, Répertoire, Communauté de Biens, § 1, art. 3; 1 Boullenois, 660 to 673; Id. 732 to 818; Rodemburg, De Div. Stat. tit. 2, ch. 5, § 12, 13, 14, 15.

wherever situate, would, in the opinion of many of them, be exclusively regulated by the law of England.[1] So, on the other hand, French subjects, married in France, without any contract, would hold their property in community generally; and this rule would apply as well to that situate in foreign countries, as to that in France.

§ 147. The grounds, upon which this opinion is maintained, are various. Some jurists hold, that the law of the matrimonial domicil attaches all the rights and incidents of marriage to it, *proprio vigore*, and independent of any supposed consent of the parties.[2] Others hold, that there is in such cases an implied consent of the parties to adopt the law of the matrimonial domicil by way of tacit contract; and then the same rule applies, as is applied to express contracts. Dumoulin was the author, or most powerful advocate, of this latter doctrine. *Inest*, (says he) *tacitum pactum, quod maritus lucrabitur dotem conventam in casu, et pro proportione statuti illius domicilii, quod prævidetur et intelligitur; et istud tacitum pactum, nisi conventum fuerit, intrat in actionem ex stipulatu rei uxoriæ, et illam informat.* And he adds, that it applies to all property, wherever situate, and whether moveable or immoveable;

---

[1] Hertii Opera, De Collis. Leg. § 47, p. 143. — Many jurists make no distinction in the application of the doctrine of the tacit contract of marriage between moveable and immoveable property, and consider both to be governed by the law of the domicil of marriage. Others again distinguish between them. Foreign jurists commonly in the term, "biens," include all sorts of property, moveable and immoveable, in their discussions on this subject.*

[2] See 1 Boullenois, 741, 750, 757, 758; Huberus, Lib. 1, tit. 3, § 9.

* See Merlin, Répertoire, Autorisation Maritale, § 10, art. 2; Id. Majorité, § 5; Id. Communauté de Biens, § 1, art. 3; Voet. De Statut. § 4, ch. 2, n. 16; Rodemburg, De Div. Stat. P. 1, tit. 2, ch. 5, § 13, 14, 15; Id. P. 2, tit. 2, ch. 4, § 1; 1 Boullenois, 673, 683, 767; 2 Boullenois, 81, 88, 93, 94, 266, 277; 1 Hertii Opera, De Collis. Leg. § 46, 47, p. 143, 144; Livermore, Dissert. 73, 74; Huberus, Lib. 1, tit. 3, § 9; Bouhier, ch. 22, § 79, p. 429.

Sed locum habebit ubique etiam extra fines et territorium dicti statuti, etiam interim correpti, et hoc indistincte, sive bona dotalia sint mobilia, sive immobilia, ubicunque sita, sive nomina. Ratio punctualis specifica procedat in vim taciti pacti ad formam statuti; veluti, quod tacitum pactum pro expresso habetur.[1]

§ 148. The opinion of Dumoulin is adopted by Bouhier, Hertius, Pothier, Merlin, and other distinguished jurists.[2] It is opposed, however, by others of no small celebrity; and the doctrine of tacit contracts (as we shall see) is treated by some of them as a mere indefensible and visionary theory. D'Argentré is at the head of those, who maintain, that the law of the *situs* of the property constitutes the rule to decide the rights of the marriage couple at all times.[3]

§ 149. It may be useful to bring together in this place, in a more exact form, the opinions of some jurists of the highest reputation on this subject, for the purpose of exhibiting some of the differences, as well as the coincidences, of the doctrines maintained by them.

§ 150. Cochin holds the doctrine, that if the contract of marriage contains no stipulation for community of property, the law of the place, where the parties are domiciled, and to which they submit by the contract of marriage, must govern, not only as to property (*biens*) situate in that place, but as to property situate in all

---

1 1 Froland, Mém. 62, 218; Livermore, Dissert. 74.

2 Bouhier, Cout. de Bourg. ch. 23, § 69 to 75; Id. ch. 26, per tot.; 1 Froland, Mém. 61 to 63; Id. 178 to 211; Id. 214 to 222; Id. 274; Merlin, Répertoire, Communauté de Biens, § 1, art. 3; Pothier, Traité de la Communauté, art. 1, n. 10; 1 Hertii Opera, De Collis. Leg. § 47, p. 143.

3 1 Froland, Mém. 192 to 200; Id. 220, 222; 1 Boullenois, 673 to 690; Id. 732 to 736; Id. 740 to 750; Id. 757, 792; 2 Boullenois, 110; Merlin, Répertoire, Communauté de Biens, § 1, art. p. 110, 111.

other places. The rights of married persons, he adds, over the property, which they then have, as well as over that, which they afterwards acquire, ought to be regulated by a uniform rule. If they have established one by the contract of marriage, that ought to decide as to all; if they have made no stipulation, then the law of the place of their common domicil establishes a rule for them, since they are presumed to submit themselves to it, when they have not stipulated any thing to the contrary.[1]

§ 151. Le Brun is quite as explicit. After stating, that the community of property may be formed by an express contract, or by a tacit contract, he gives, as a reason for the latter, that, if the couple have not made any stipulation, and are domiciled in a place, where the law of community exists, when they are married, the conclusion is, that they have referred themselves to that law. And this presumption has its foundation in law, which often decides, that, as to things omitted in the contract, the parties have referred themselves to the usage or law.[2] And he adds, that as in cases of express contracts for community of property, the contract reaches all property of the parties, even in other countries, so in cases of tacit contracts, as those resulting by operation of law, the same rule applies. If the law of the place of domicil and marriage of the parties creates such a community, it applies to all property, wherever situate. It has, in short, all the character and effect of a personal law or statute, though it regulates property.[3]

§ 152. Hertius has put a number of cases to illus-

1 Cochin, Œuvres, Tom. 3, p. 703.

2 Le Brun, Traité de la Communauté, Lib. 1, ch. 2, § 2, 3, 4.

3 Id. Liv. 1, ch. 2, § 6, 36 to 42.

trate the general principle. At Liege, by law, the husband by marriage acquires the ownership of all the property of his wife of every nature. At Utrecht, it is otherwise. Is an inhabitant of Utrecht entitled, *jure connubii*, to take all the property of his deceased wife, situate in Liege? He answers in the negative, because the law of the place of marriage (Utrecht), does not confer it.[1] Again. A person, in whose domicil there is no community of property between married persons, possesses property in another territory, where such community of all property exists, and he contracts marriage in another country, where a qualified community only exists, (*ubi societas bonorum tantum, sive simpliciter ita dicta, obtinet.*) What law is to prevail? Some jurists hold, that the law of the domicil shall prevail. Others are of a different opinion. Hertius himself holds, that, as the case supposes the place of the marriage to be that of both parties, the law of the husband's domicil ought to prevail, as an implied contract between the parties.[2] Again. In the domicil of the husband, a community of property exists between married persons; will that community apply to immoveable property bought by either party in a territory, where such a law does not exist? Many jurists decide in the negative. Hertius holds the affirmative, upon the ground of an implied contract, resulting from the marriage.[3] The decision in the case

1 Hertii Op., De Collis. Leg., § 44, p. 142, 143.

2 Id. p. 143, § 46. — Froland puts the case of a man domiciled at Paris, who goes and marries a woman in a country governed by the Roman law, in Rheims, Auvergne, or Normandy, or *è contra*; and asks in such a case, what law is to prevail as to future acquisitions (conquests); the law of the domicil of the husband, or that of the wife, or that of the place of marriage, or of the location of the property? And he decides in favour of the latter. 1 Froland, Mém. 321. See also Voet. De Stat. § 4, ch. 3, p. 134, 135, § 9.

3 Id. p. 144, § 47.

of De Couche *v.* Savatier (3 John. Ch. R. 190, 211), treating it as a case of express or implied contract, would lead to the same conclusion.

§ 153. Froland has stated the question in a more general shape; whether, if a community of property exists by the law of the place of domicil and marriage of the parties, it extends to all property situate elsewhere, where no such law prevails? He gives the reasoning of different jurists, maintaining opposite opinions on the point, and concludes by stating, that the opinion of Dumoulin in the affirmative has finally prevailed, in cases where there is an express contract for such community; and Dumoulin equally contends for it in cases of tacit contract, resulting from the *lex loci.*[1] From this latter point, however, Froland dissents in a qualified manner. He deems the law of community, independent of an express contract, to be a real law; and therefore confined to the territory. As to acquests, or acquisitions, whether of moveable or immoveable property, made in foreign countries, where the law of

[1] 1 Froland, Mém. p. 178 to 200; Id. p. 211 to 271; Id p. 272 to 340. See also 1 Boullenois, 660 to 683; Id. 732 to 818. Dumoulin's words are, "Nullum dubium est, quin societas semel contracta complectatur bona ubique sita, sine ullâ differentiâ territorii, quemadmodum quilibet contractus, sive tacitus, sive expressus, ligat personam et res disponentis ubique. Non obstat, quod hujusmodi societas non est expressa, sed tacita; nec oritur ex contractu expresso partium, sed ex tacito vel præsumpto contractu a consuetudine locali introducto." 1 Froland, Mém. 274. See also Livermore's Dissert. p. 69, 71, 72, 73, 74; Saul *v.* His Creditors, 17 Martin R. 569, 599. The same doctrine is maintained by Bouhier. "Tout statut," says he, "qui est fondé sur une convention tacite et presumée des contractans est personel." Bouhier, Cout. de Bourg. ch. 23, § 69 to 74. And he expressly applies it to the case of tacit contracts of marriage, following out the reasoning of Dumoulin. Id. ch. 26, § 1 to 20. On the other hand, D'Argentré and Vander Meulen hold, that all laws respecting community are real, and not personal; and therefore, that they are governed by the law *rei sitæ.* 1 Boullenois, 758, 759, 760 to 765.

community extends, he agrees, that, in cases of express contract, the law of the matrimonial domicil ought to prevail. But as to foreign countries, where the law of community does not exist, he thinks the right does not extend either *in vim consuetudinis*, or *in vim contractûs*, for it is in vain to presume a tacit contract; and that, therefore, it is governed by the law *rei sitæ*. It would seem, however, from subsequent passages, that he applied his doctrine to the case of immoveables only; admitting that moveables should be governed by the law of the domicil of the parties.[1]

§ 154. Rodemburg seems to apply the same principle to cases, where there is a nuptial contract, as where there is none, holding, that, in the latter case, the law of the matrimonial domicil is adopted by a tacit contract. At the same time he asserts, that the law of community is not personal, but real; and hence, if it does not, or may not, directly act upon property *aliunde*, where no community exists; yet it will give a right of action, founded in tacit contract, which is to be enforced every where. And, therefore, the law of the matrimonial domicil in such a case, acts indirectly to give it universality. And he applies it equally to present and future acquisitions.[2]

§ 155. Boullenois holds an opinion somewhat different. He considers the law of community between married persons, as one regulating the state and condition of the person, and therefore not real, but personal. Hence he holds, that the law of community, if existing in the matrimonial domicil, extends to property

---

[1] 1 Froland, Mém. 316, 317, 321, 322, 323, 338, 341; 1 Boullenois, 758, 759.

[2] Rodemburg, De Div. Stat. tit. 2, ch. 5, § 12, 13, 14, 15; 1 Boullenois, p. 673 to 683; Id. 732 to 735; Id. 754 to 757.

wherever situate, and *vice versâ*; not upon the ground of tacit contract, but *proprio vigore*, as a law, both as to present property, and future acquisitions; unless by the law of the *situs* such future acquisitions are prohibited; and in that case the law of the *situs* as to them is to prevail.[1]

§ 156. Pothier has adopted the doctrine of tacit contract of Dumoulin; and therefore, in case there is no express contract, if the law of the matrimonial domicil creates a community, he holds, that it applies to all property, present and future, wherever situate, and even in provinces, which do not admit of a community.[2] Grotius is also stated to have held the same opinion in a case, where he was consulted.[3]

§ 157. It has been remarked by the Supreme Court of Louisiana, that the greater number of the jurists of France and Holland are of opinion, that in settling the rights of the husband and wife, on the dissolution of the marriage, to the property acquired, the law of the place, where it was contracted, and not of that, where it was dissolved, must be the guide. And that this opinion is by most of them founded on the idea first promulgated by Dumoulin, that, where the parties marry without an express contract, they must be presumed to contract in relation to the law of the country, where the marriage took place, and that this tacit contract follows them, wherever they go.[4] But that Court are of opinion, that the ground is unsatisfactory, especially when it is applied to cases of property acquired after a

---

[1] 1 Boullenois, 736, 741, 750, 751 to 754; Id. 754 to 757, 759, 760, 766, 769, 770; 2 Boullenois, 277.

[2] Pothier, Traité de la Communauté, Art. Prélim. n. 10, 11, 12, 13, 14.

[3] See Henry on Foreign Law, ch. 5, p. 36, 37, note.

[4] Saul *v.* His Creditors, 17 Martin R. 599.

subsequent change of domicil. Their view of the subject is, that if the doctrine of tacit contract be admissible, the contract is to be construed in the same way, as if the laws of the country of the marriage were inserted in it; and that, so far as they are to be deemed real, and not personal laws, they are necessarily territorial, and can be construed to apply to acquests or acquisitions only within that country. The extent of the tacit agreement depends on the extent of the law. If it had no force beyond the jurisdiction of the power, by which it is enacted; if it is real, and not personal; the tacit consent of the parties cannot turn it into a personal statute. They have not said so; and they are presumed to have contracted in relation to the law, such as it was, to have known its limitations, as well as its nature, and to have had the one as much in view as the other. In one word, the parties have agreed, that the law shall bind them, as far as that law extends, but no farther.[3]

§ 158. The result of this reasoning (and it certainly has great force) would seem to be, that in the case of a marriage without any express contract the *lex loci contractûs* (assuming that it furnishes the just basis of a tacit contract) will govern, as to all moveable and immoveable property within the country; and as to property in other countries, it will govern moveables, but not immoveables; the former having no *situs*, and the latter being governed by the *lex rei sitæ*.

§ 159. Perhaps the most simple and satisfactory exposition of the subject is, or at least, that, which best harmonizes with the analogies of the common law, is, that in a case of marriage, where there is no special

---

1 Saul *v.* His Creditors, 17 Martin R. 569, 603 to 605.

contract, and there has been no change of domicil, the law of the place of celebration should govern the rights of the parties in respect to all personal estate (moveables), wherever acquired, and wherever it may be situate; but real estate (immoveables) should be left to be adjudged by the *lex rei sitæ*, as not within the reach of any extra-territorial law.[1] Where there is a special contract, that furnishes a rule for the case, and as matter of contract, will be carried into effect every where, under the limitations and exceptions belonging to all other contracts.[2]

§ 160. In the next place, what is the principle to be adopted in cases, where there has been a change of

---

1 See Henry on Foreign Law, ch. 7, p. 48, 49.

2 P. Voet lays down the following doctrine. "Si statuto hujus loci inter conjuges *bona sint communia*, vel *pactis antenuptialibus* ita conventum sit, ut omnia, ubique locorum sita, communia forent, etiam ad illa, quæ in Frisià jacent, ubi non nisi quæsitorum est communio, dabitur actio ut communicentur." Voet, De Stat. § 4, ch. 2, p. 127, § 16; Id. ch. 3, p. 134, § 9. Yet he deems laws establishing a community of property to be real, and not personal laws. Id. § 4, ch. 3, p. 134, 135, § 9. See 1 Froland, Mém. 199, 200. This apparent discrepancy may be reconciled, by considering, that though the law of community be real; yet it may found a right of action for property situate elsewhere.* A distinction of this sort seems not unknown in the Scottish law. 1 Rose Cas. in Bank, 481. Lord Meadowbank, in a Scottish case of great importance, laid down the following doctrine as unquestionable. "In the ordinary case of transference by contract of marriage, when a lady of fortune, having a great deal of money in Scotland, or stock in the bank, or public companies there, marries in London, the whole property is *ipso jure* her husband's. It is assigned to him. The legal assignment of a marriage operates, *without regard to territory*, all the world over." Royal Bank of Scotland *v.* Smith, &c., 1 Rose Cas. Bank, Appx. 481. Lord Eldon has affirmed this doctrine to be correct, in relation to personal property; but not in relation to real property. And in cases ef bankruptcy, to which he applied it, he added, that there was no legal obligation on a bankrupt to convey his real estate, situate in a foreign country, to the assignees. Selkrig *v.* Davies, 2 Rose Bank Cas. 99, S. C. 2 Dow R. 230, 250.

* See also Rodemburg, De Divers. Stat. tit. 2, ch. 5, § 12 to 15.

domicil? And this admits of a double aspect; first, in relation to property acquired before the removal; and secondly, in relation to property acquired afterwards in the new domicil. In each instance, however, we are to be understood to speak of the operation of law, where there is no express nuptial contract.

§ 161. Upon this subject there is no small diversity of opinion among foreign jurists, as well in regard to the right to property acquired after the change of domicil, as in regard to the right to property antecedently acquired. Bouhier lays down the rule in general terms, that in relation to the beneficial and pecuniary rights (*les droits utiles et pécuniaires*) of the wife, which result from the matrimonial contract, either express or tacit, the husband has no power by a change of domicil to alter or change them, according to the rule, *Nemo potest mutare consilium suum in alterius injuriam;* and he insists, that this is the general opinion of jurists. Thus, if by the law of the matrimonial domicil there exists a community of property between the husband and wife, and they remove to another place, where no such community exists, the rights of neither party are changed, and the community applies in the same manner, as in the original domicil. And, on the other hand, if no such community exists in the matrimonial domicil, a transfer of domicil to a place, where it does exist, will not create it; for a change of domicil would not add any thing to the marriage rights in a case of express contract, and therefore ought not to do so in a tacit contract.[1] And this is also Dumoulin's opinion.[2] Bouhier makes no distinction whatsoever between moveable and immoveable

---

[1] Bouhier, Cout. de Bourg. ch. 22, § 63 to 72. [2] Id.

property.[1] Nor does he seem to recognise any between property antecedently acquired, and that acquired after the change of domicil.[2]

§ 162. Le Brun supports a like opinion. He insists, that, if there is no special contract of marriage, the law of the place, where the marriage is celebrated, and in which the parties are domiciled, governs as a tacit contract; and that no subsequent change of domicil can change the legal rights of the parties, even as to after acquired property. And he puts the case of a marriage in Paris, and a subsequent change of domicil of the parties to the province of Bar, where the survivor is by custom entitled to the whole property in moveables by survivorship; and holds, that if either die, the moveables, whether acquired before or after the removal, are governed by the law of community, and do not all remain to the survivor. *La raison est, qui ce seroit changer l'establissement de communauté fait par le contrat, ou par la coutume, selon lequel on a dû partager les meubles aussibien que les acquêts.*[3]

§ 163. Rodemburg puts the case of marriage, where the law of community of property between husband and wife prevails, and a subsequent removal to another place, where it has no existence; and asks, if the community still subsists in the new domicil? He observes, that most of the Dutch jurists are of opinion, that it does; and in this opinion, he concurs to this extent, that the community will continue, until the parties have, by some overt act, discarded it; and then it will cease.[4] And he applies the same principle to cases of dowry

---

1 Bouhier, Cout. de Bourg. ch. 22, § 79, 80. 2 Id. ch. 22, per tot.

3 Le Brun, Traité de la Communauté, Liv. 1, ch. 2, § 55, 56.

4 Rodemburg, De Div. Stat. P. 2, tit. 2, ch. 4, § 3, 4; 2 Boullenois, 85 to 87; Id. 173.

by the customary law, holding, that the matrimonial domicil ought to prevail.[1]

§ 164. Hertius puts the following question. A marriage is contracted in a place, where the civil law governs, (i. e. there is no community); and afterwards the couple remove to a place, where the law of community exists; and to the inquiry, whether in such a case there is a community in the acquisitions of the parties after the removal, he answers in the negative, adopting the doctrine of Rodemburg.[2] And in the more general form of presenting the question, whether in the case of married persons, removing from their matrimonial domicil, where a community of property exists, to a place, where it does not, they are to be governed by the law of the matrimonial domicil, he evidently adopts the affirmative, citing Rodemburg.[3] And he applies his doctrine to immoveable property, as well as to moveable, making an exception, however, of the case, where there is a prohibitory law of the country of the *situs*.[4]

§ 165. Paul Voet appears to maintain the doctrine generally, that a change of domicil does not change the effect of the marriage contract express or tacit. *Quia non eo ipso, qui domicilium transferat, censetur voluntatem circa facta nuptialia mutasse.*[5] Merlin maintains the like opinion, saying, that if a couple are married at Paris, meaning then to live there, and afterwards they remove to Lyons, in such case the community, formed at Paris, will continue as to property acquired at Lyons.[6]

---

1 Rodemburg, De Div. Stat. P. 2, tit. 2, ch. 4, § 5; 2 Boullenois, 87.

2 1 Hertii Opera, De Collis. Leg. § 49, p. 145.

3 Id. § 48, p. 145.

4 Id. § 47, p. 144, 145.

5 Voet. De Stat. § 9, ch. 2, n. 7, p. 266; Id. § 4, ch. 2, n. 16, p. 127.

6 Merlin, Répertoire, Communauté de Biens, § 1, p. 111.

§ 166. Boullenois holds the opinion, as we have seen, that the law regulating the community affects the state or condition of the parties, and is, therefore, personal; and accompanies them every where, and affects property, wherever situate[1]. He accordingly insists, that, if by the law of the matrimonial domicil a community of property exists, that community extends to all future acquisitions, whether moveable or immoveable, even in places, to which the parties have afterwards removed, and where no such community exists.[2] Pothier has adopted the opinion of Boullenois, that the law of community is to be deemed personal and not real; and he also adopts the doctrine of Dumoulin, as to tacit contracts. So, that he has no hesitation in declaring, as we have seen, that the law of the matrimonial domicil governs the property every where.[3] But he has omitted to put the case of a change of domicil, and the effects, which it would produce. In another place he has laid down as a general principle, that a change of domicil delivers all persons from the empire of the laws of their former domicil, and subjects them to the new.[4] What, then, ought to be the effect of a removal upon property acquired in the new domicil?

§ 167. Froland has given his opinion, after a good deal of hesitation on the subject, to this effect. In cases, where there is an express contract of community of property between the husband and wife, he holds, that a change of domicil does not alter the rights of the

---

1 1 Boullenois, 736, 741, 750 to 754; Id. 759 to 770; 2 Boullenois, 277; 17 Martin 607.

2 2 Boullenois, 277, 278, 283, 284, 285.

3 Pothier, Traité de la Communauté, Art. Prélim. n. 10, 11, 12, 13.

4 Pothier, Cout. d'Orléans, ch. 1, § 1, n. 13.

parties; and, that the community applies to property situate, where the community is unknown, as well as where it exists.[1] But where there is no express contract, he deems the law of community as purely real, and, therefore, as not extending beyond the matrimonial domicil. He treats the notion of Dumoulin, of a tacit contract in such a case, as a mere imaginary thing; words, and nothing else; a mere subtilty, phantom, and chimera. *Ce ne sont là que des paroles, et rien de là: mirificum illud Molinæi acumen; des subtilités d'esprit; des idées; des chimères; enfin dès moyens, que la seule imagination échauffée produit.*[2] The conclusion, to which he arrives, is, that, if two persons marry without any contract in a place, where the law of community exists, and remove to another place, where it does not exist, the change of domicil has no effect whatsoever; but the rights of each are the same, as if they had remained in their matrimonial domicil; and that the acquisitions of immoveable property, situate in the new domicil, do not fall into community, but are governed by the law *rei sitæ*. As to moveables, he holds, that the law of the actual domicil ought to govern.[3]

§ 168. There are many other jurists, who maintain, that the law of community among married persons is *real*, and not personal, and among these the most distinguished are D'Argentré, Paul Voet, and Vander

---

1 1 Froland, Mém. P. 2, ch. 1, § 10, 11, p. 200 to 210; Id. 341; Id. 190.

2 Id. P. 2, ch. 3, § 9, 10, 11, p. 315 to 338; Id. 341.

3 Id. p. 315 to 323; Id. 341. — I confess myself under some difficulty in reconciling what is here said, with what Froland seems to decide in the next chapter (4th), § 3, p. 345, &c., where he appears to hold, that a woman marrying in a place, where the law of community does not exist, does not, by removing with her husband to a place, where it does exist, acquire any right of community to his acquisitions or moveables in the latter.

Meulen.[1] According to them, the law *rei sitæ* will govern in all cases, where there is no express contract.

§ 169. Huberus does not hesitate to assert the doctrine, that, in case of a change of domicil, future acquisitions of married persons are governed by the law of their actual domicil, and not of their antecedent matrimonial domicil. Thus, after asserting, that in Holland there is a community of property, and in Friezeland not; he says, if the married couple remove from one province (Holland) to the other (Friezeland), whatever property is afterwards acquired, ceases to be common, and remains in distinct ownership (*distinctis proprietatibus*); and the property before held in community remains clothed with the same legal character, that it previously possessed. And he applies his doctrine to immoveable, as well as to moveable property, relying upon the doctrine of tacit consent, or tacit contract;[2] and holding with Dumoulin, *quia pactio bene extenditur ubique, sed non statutum merum, hoc est, solâ et merâ vi statuti.*[3]

§ 170. It would be endless to recount the diversities of opinion among foreign jurists on this subject, following out the almost infinitely varied cases, which the customs and laws of different provinces and countries have brought before them. According to the opinion of the Supreme Court of Louisiana, already cited, the greater number of foreign jurists are of opinion, that, in settling the rights of husband and wife, on the dissolution of mar-

---

1 1 Boullenois, 758, 759, 760, 761, 765; Voet. De Stat. § 4. ch. 3, p. 134, 135, § 9. See also J. Voet. ad Pand. Lib. 5, tit. 1, n. 101; Merlin, Communauté de Biens, § 1, art. 3, p. 104, 110; Bouhier, Cout. de Bourg. ch. 23, § 34. See Saul *v.* His Creditors, 17 Martin R. 598, 599; Id. 588.

2 Huberus, Lib. 1, tit. 3, § 9.

3 Livermore, Diss. 74; 1 Froland, Mém. 63.

riage, to the property acquired by them, the law of the domicil of the marriage, and not of the place, where it is dissolved, is to be the guide.[1] It is probably so; but there is more difficulty in affirming it, where there has been a change of domicil, than where there has been none. It may be inferred, that the Scottish law has adopted the rule, that in cases of community, where there is no written contract, the law of the domicil of the parties at the death of either of them regulates the disposal of the property.[2]

§ 171. No question appears to have arisen in the English courts upon the point, which we have been discussing; that is, what rule is to govern in cases of matrimonial property, where there is no express contract, and there has been a change of domicil. But there is a case,[3] in which Lord Eldon is reported to have said, that the case of Feaubert *v.* Turst, (Prec. Ch. 207) was founded in (the nuptial) contract; and that, if there had been no contract, the law of England (notwithstanding their domicil at the time of their marriage was in France) would have regulated the rights of husband and wife, who were domiciled in England at the dissolution (by death) of the marriage. So that, according to this doctrine, the law of the actual domicil will govern as to all property, without any distinction, whether it is property acquired antecedently, or subsequently, to the removal.

§ 172. In America there has been a general silence in the States governed by the common law. But in Louisiana, where the jurisprudence is framed upon the general basis of the Spanish and French law, the

1 Saul *v.* His Creditors, 17 Martin R. 599.

2 Fergusson on Marr. and Div. 346, 347; Id. 361.

3 Lashley *v.* Hogg, cited in Robertson's Appeal Cases, 4.

point has several times come under judicial decision. The law of community exists in that state;[1] and from the frequency of removals from and to it, it is scarcely possible, that some of the doctrines, which have so much perplexed foreign jurists, should not be brought under review.

§ 173. We have already had occasion to take notice of some of the views entertained by the Supreme Court of Louisiana upon this subject. They have very properly remarked, that questions upon the conflict of the laws of different states are the most embarrassing and difficult of decision of any, that can occupy the attention of courts of justice. And it may be added, almost in their own language, that the vast mass of learning, which the research of counsel can furnish, leaves the subject as much enveloped in obscurity and doubt, as it would be, if one were called upon to decide, without the knowledge of what others had thought and written upon it.[2]

§ 174. It is manifest, that the great body of foreign jurists, who maintain the ubiquity of the law of the matrimonial domicil, notwithstanding any change of domicil, found themselves upon the doctrine of a tacit contract, which, being once entered into, is of legal obligation every where. The remarks of the Supreme Court of Louisiana on this point have been already cited; and certainly they have a great tendency to shake its foundation.[3] If the law of community be a real, and not a personal law, it would seem to follow, that it ought to regulate things within the limits of the

---

1 Civil Code of Louisiana (1809), 336, art. 63; New Code, art. 2370.

2 Saul v. His Creditors, 17 Martin R. 571, 572.

3 Id. 599 to 608.

country, where it is in force, and not elsewhere.[1] The most strenuous advocate for the doctrine of tacit contract must admit, that, if by the statute of another country community is prohibited, as to property there, the law of the matrimonial domicil ought not to prevail in such country, in contradiction to its own. And the learned Court, above referred to, have said, that they can perceive no solid distinction between the case of a real statute, and a prohibitory statute, as to property in the country.[1]

§ 175. But if the law of community be personal, still there is strong ground to contend, that the personal laws of one country cannot control the personal laws of another, *ipso facto*, where they provide for property within the jurisdiction of the latter. No one can doubt, that a country has a right to say, that contracts for community, made in another country, shall have no operation in its own territory. The question, then, is reduced to the mere consideration, whether the law of the country does directly or indirectly provide for, or repudiate, the community as to property within it.[2]

§ 176. Upon this reasoning, after full consideration, the Supreme Court of Louisiana were of opinion, that the law of community should, upon just principles of interpretation, be deemed a real law, as it relates to things, more than to persons, and has, in the language of D'Aguesseau, the destination of property to certain persons, and its preservation, in view.[3] They therefore held, that, where a married couple had re-

---

1 Saul *v.* His Creditors, 17 Martin, 601, 602.

2 Id. 573, 574 to 588; 1 Hertii Opera, De Collis. Leg. § 47, p. 143, 144.

3 Saul *v.* His Creditors, 17 Martin R. 593, 594, 595, 606, 607; D'Aguesseau, Œuvres, Tom. 4, Pl. 54, p. 660.

moved from Virginia (their matrimonial domicil), where no community exists, into Louisiana, where a community does exist, the acquests and gains, acquired after their removal, were to be governed by the law of community in Louisiana.[1]

§ 177. This doctrine appears to be in full accordance with the laws of Spain. Those laws apply the same rule to cases of express contract, and to cases of tacit contract, or customary law. Where there is an express contract, that governs as to all acquisitions and gains before the removal. Where there is no express contract, the customary law of the matrimonial domicil governs in like manner. But in both cases all acquisitions and gains, made after the removal, are governed by the law of the actual domicil.[2] The present revised Code of Louisiana adopts a like rule; and declares, that a marriage, contracted out of the state between persons, who afterwards come to live within the state, is subject to the community of acquests, with respect to such property as is acquired after their removal.[3]

§ 178. This Code of course furnishes the rule for all future cases; but the discussions in Louisiana have arisen upon antecedent cases, and have involved a general examination of the doctrine upon principle and authority. The doctrine, which, with reference to public law, has been thus established in that state, resolves itself into two fundamental propositions. First; where there is

[1] The law of community existed in Louisiana under the Spanish law, and now exists under the Civil Code of that state; Bruneau v. Bruneau's Heirs, 9 Martin R. 217; Code Civil of Louisiana (1809), 336, art. 63; Revised Code, art. 2370; 17 Martin R. 573; 2 Kent Comm. Lect. 28, p. 183, note to 2d edition.

[2] Saul v. His Creditors, 17 Martin, 576 to 581, 607, 608.

[3] Code Civil of Louisiana, art. 2370.

an express contract, that there shall be a community of acquests and gains between the parties, even though they should reside in countries, where different laws prevail, that agreement will be held obligatory throughout, as matter of contract, in cases of removal; with this restriction, however, applicable to all contracts, that it is not to cause any prejudice to the citizens of the country, to which they remove, and that its execution is not incompatible with the laws of that country.[1] Secondly; where there is no such express contract, the law of the matrimonial domicil is to prevail as to the antecedent property; but the property acquired after the removal is to be governed by the law of the actual domicil.[2] This latter proposition has been laid down, in terms unusually strong, by its Supreme Court. "Though it was *once* a question (say the Court), it seems *now* to be a *settled* principle, that when a married couple emigrate from the country, where the marriage was contracted, into another, the laws of which are different, the property, which they acquire in the place, to which they have removed, is governed by the laws of that place."[3] Upon these propositions, the Court have accordingly decided, that, where a couple, who were married in North Carolina, where no community exists, had removed to Louisiana, where it does exist, the property acquired after the removal was to be held in community.[4] And in another case, where the marriage was in Cuba, and there was a special contract, that there should be a community according to the custom of Paris, wherever the parties

---

1 Murphy *v.* Murphy, 5 Martin 83; 17 Martin R. 605, 606.

2 Gale *v.* Davis, 4 Martin R. 645; 17 Martin 605, 606; Le Breton *v.* Nouchet, 3 Martin R. 60, 73.

3 Gale *v.* Davis, 4 Martin R. 649.

4 Id. 4 Martin R. 645.

might reside; and the parties removed to South Carolina, where none exists, the contract was held to govern the property acquired in the latter state.[1] The same doctrine has been maintained in New York, in case of a marriage between French subjects, under a similar stipulation of community, and mutual donation in case of survivorship.[2]

§ 179. An instance, illustrative of the exception in cases of express contract, may be drawn from other decisions in Louisiana. Upon a marriage celebrated in that state, the parties stipulated, that the rights of the parties should be governed by the custom of Paris. The question was, whether the parties, residing in the country, were competent to enter into a nuptial contract, stipulating, that the effects of it on their property should be governed by a foreign law. The Court held, that they had no such competency, and that the contract was void.[3]

§ 180. A still more striking case occurred in the same state, upon some of the doctrines of which, as stated by the Court, there may, perhaps, be some reason to pause; but the reasons are nevertheless stated with great force. A man in Louisiana run away with a young lady of thirteen years of age, without the consent of her parents or guardian, and married her in Mississippi, and then returned with her to Louisiana. After her death her mother demanded her property, as it would descend by the Louisiana law. The Court sustained the demand. From the elaborate opinion de-

---

1 Murphy v. Murphy, 5 Martin, 83; 17 Martin R. 605; Bourcier v. Lanusse, 3 Martin R. 581, 583.

2 De Couche v. Savatier, 3 John. Ch. R. 190, 211.

3 Bourcier v. Lanusse, 3 Martin R. 581. See Code Civil of France, art. 1390.

livered by the Court the following extract is made, as highly interesting. "With respect, (say the Court,) to the law of nations, the principle, recognised by most writers, may be reduced to this; that although no power is bound to give effect, within its own territory, to the laws of a foreign country; yet by the courtesy of nations, and from a consideration of the inconveniences, which would be the result of a contrary conduct, foreign laws are permitted to regulate contracts, made in foreign countries. But, in order that they may have such effect, it must, first, be ascertained, that the parties really intended to be governed by those laws, and had not some other country in contemplation at the time of the contract. This being previously recognised, the government, within the bounds of which such foreign laws claim admission, has next to consider, whether the enforcing of these laws will cause no prejudice to its rights, or to the rights of its citizens.

§ 181. "Let us take the first exception, and apply it to this case. Did the parties really intend to be governed by the laws of the Mississippi Territory, and had they not in contemplation, at the time of contracting marriage, their return to this country? If we were to judge from their acts alone, there could be no hesitation in saying, that they went to Natchez for the purpose only of contracting marriage, and intended to come back, as soon as it could conveniently be done. Their remaining at Natchez only a few weeks, and that in a tavern, their return to New-Orleans not long after, and the continuation of their residence there until the death of the wife, would amount to an irresistible proof, that they had this country in contemplation at the time of contracting their marriage. But it is alleged, that, however evident their intention may appear from these facts, the appellant had really taken the resolution to settle at Natchez. Evidence has been furnished of his declarations to that purpose, both before his departure, and after his arrival in the Mississippi Territory. One of his brothers has sworn, that, previous to his leaving New-Orleans, he told him and his other brothers, that he intended to stay at Natchez. Other persons have deposed, that letters, expressive of the determination of the appellant to remain there, were by them received from him, shortly after their dates. Without questioning the propriety of the admission of such testimony, the Court is satisfied, that it is insufficient to counterbalance the weight of the facts, which disclose the real intention of the parties.

§ 182. "But, should their intention still remain a subject of doubt, we have next to consider, whether by permitting the laws of the Mississippi Territory to regulate this case, this government would not injure its own rights, or the rights of its citizens. For, a foreign law having no other force, than that which it derives from the consent of the government, within the bounds of which it claims to be admitted, that government must be supposed to retain the faculty of refusing such admission, whenever the foreign law interferes with its own regulations. A party to this marriage was one of those individuals, over whom our laws watch with particular care, and whom they have subjected to certain incapacities for their own safety. She was a minor. Has she, by fleeing to another country, removed those incapacities? Her mother is a citizen of this state; she herself was a girl of thirteen years, who had no other domicil than that of her mother. Did she not remain, notwithstanding her flight to Natchez, under the authority of this government? Did not the protection of this government follow her, wherever she went? If so, this government cannot, without surrendering its rights, recognise the empire of laws, the effect of which would be, to render that protection inefficacious. But the laws of the Mississippi Territory, as stated by the parties, do not only interfere with our rights, but are at war with our regulations. By our laws a minor, who marries, cannot give away any part of his property without the authorization of those, whose consent is necessary for the validity of the marriage. By the laws of the Mississippi Territory all the personal estate of the wife (that would embrace, in this case, every thing, which she had) is the property of the husband. Again; according to our laws, we cannot give away more, than a certain portion of our property, when we have forced heirs. But what our laws thus forbid, is permitted in the Mississippi Territory. And shall our citizens be deprived of their legitimate rights by the laws of another government, upon our own soil? Shall the mother of Alexandrine Dussuau lose the inheritance of her deceased child, secured to her by our laws, because her daughter married at Natchez? Shall our own laws be reduced to silence within our own precincts, by the superior force of other laws? If such doctrine were maintainable, it would be unnecessary for us to legislate. In vain should we endeavour to secure the persons and the property of our citizens. Nothing would be more easy, than to render our precautions useless, and our laws a dead letter. But the municipal law of the Mississippi Territory, which is relied upon by the appellant, is not the law, which would govern this case, *even there*. The law of nations is law at Natchez, as well as at New-Orleans. According to the principles of that law, 'personal incapacities, communicated by the laws of any particular place, accompany the person, wherever he goes. Thus, he, who is excused the consequences of contracts for want of age in his country, cannot make binding contracts in another.' Therefore, even if this case were pending before a tribunal of the Mississippi Territory, it is to be supposed, that they would recognise the incapacity, under which Alexandrine Dussuau was labouring, when she contracted marriage, and decide, that such marriage could not have the effect of giving to her husband, what she was forbidden to give. If that be sound doctrine in any case, how much more so must it be in one of this nature; where the minor, almost a child, has, in all probability, been seduced into an escape from her mother's dwelling, and removed in haste out of her reach? We cannot, here, hesitate to believe, that the Courts of our neighbouring Territory, far from lending their assistance to this infraction of our laws, would have enforced them with becoming severity. For, if, when an appeal is made to those general principles of natural justice, by which nations have tacitly agreed to govern themselves in their intercourse with each other, while nations entirely foreign to one another feel bound to observe them, how much more sacred must they be between governments, who, though independent of each other in matters of internal regulation, are associated for the purposes of common defence, and common advantage, and are members of the same great body politic?" [1]

§ 183. The doctrines thus generally maintained in Louisiana will, most probably, form the basis of the American jurisprudence on this subject. They have

[1] Le Breton v. Nouchet, 3 Martin R. 60, 66, 71.

much to commend them in their intrinsic convenience and certainty, as well as in their equity; and they seem best to harmonize with the known principles of the common law in other cases. In concluding this topic, the following propositions may be laid down, as those, which, though not universally established, or recognised in America, have much of domestic authority for their support, and none in opposition to them.

§ 184. (1.) Where there is a marriage between parties in a foreign country, and an express contract respecting their rights and property present and future, that, as a matter of contract, will be held equally valid every where, unless, under the circumstances, it stands prohibited by the laws of the country, where it is sought to be enforced. It will act directly on moveable property every where. But as to immoveable property in a foreign territory, it will, at most, confer only a right of action, to be enforced according to the jurisprudence *rei sitæ*.[1]

§ 185. (2.) Where such an express contract applies in terms or intent only to present property, and there is a change of domicil, the law of the actual domicil will govern the rights of the parties as to all future acquisitions.

§ 186. (3.) Where there is no express contract, the law of the matrimonial domicil will govern as to all the rights of the parties to their present property in that place, and as to all personal property every where, upon the principle, that moveables have no *situs*, or rather that they accompany the person every where.[2] As to immoveable property the law *rei sitæ* will prevail.[3]

---

1 See Henry on Foreign Law, 48, 49; Id. 95.

2 See Stein's case, 1 Rose Cases, Appendix, 481; Selkrig *v.* Davies, 2 Rose Cas. 99; S. C. 2 Dow, 230, 250.

3 See Henry on Foreign Law, 48, 49.

§ 187. (4.) Where there is no change of domicil, the same rule will apply to future, as to present acquisitions. (5.) But where there is a change of domicil, the law of the actual domicil, and not of the matrimonial domicil, will govern as to all future acquisitions of moveable property; and, as to all immoveable property, the law *rei sitæ.*

§ 188. (6.) And here also, as in cases of express contract, the exception is to be understood, that the law of the place, where the rights are sought to be enforced, do not prohibit such arrangements. For if they do, as every nation has a right to prescribe rules for the government of all persons and property within its own territorial limits, in a case of conflict its own law is to prevail.[1]

§ 189. (7.) Although, in a general sense, the law of the matrimonial domicil is to govern in relation to the incidents and effects of marriage; yet this doctrine must be received with many qualifications and exceptions. No other nation will recognise such incidents or effects, when they are incompatible with its own policy, or injurious to its own interests. A marriage in France or Prussia may be dissolved for incompatibility of temper; but no divorce would be granted from such a marriage, for such a cause, in England, Scotland, or America.[2] "If," said a learned Scottish judge, in a passage already cited, "a man in this country were to confine his wife in an iron cage, or beat her with a rod of the thickness of the judge's finger, would it be any justification in any court to allege, that these were powers, which the law of England conferred on a husband, and

---

1 See Fergusson on Marr. and Div. 358 to 363; Id. 383, 392 to 422.

2 Id. 398.

that he was entitled to exercise them, because his marriage had been celebrated in that country?"[1] And he added, with great emphasis, that marriage is a contract *sui generis*; and the rights, duties, and obligations, which arise out of it, are matters of so much importance to the well-being of the state, that they are regulated not by the private contract, but by the public laws of the state, which are imperative upon all, who are domiciled within its territory.[2]

§ 190. (8.) The doctrine of tacit contract to regulate the rights and duties of matrimony, in cases, where there is no express contract, according to the law of the place, where the marriage has been celebrated, is questionable in itself; and, even if admitted, must be liable to many qualifications and restrictions. We have seen, that it has been much doubted in Louisiana;[3] and the Scottish Courts have utterly refused (as we shall fully see hereafter) to allow the doctrine of such a tacit contract to regulate the right of divorce.[4]

§ 191. But a question may sometimes occur, what is to be deemed in the sense of the rule the true matrimonial domicil? Is it the place, where the actual marriage is celebrated? Or where the contract of marriage is entered into? Or where the parties are domiciled, if the marriage is celebrated elsewhere? Or if the husband or wife have different domicils, whose is to be regarded? These, and many other perplexing inquiries may be raised; and foreign jurists have not passed them over without examination.

---

1 See Fergusson on Marr. and Div. 399, per Lord Robertson; Id. 361.

2 Id. 369; Id. 361.

3 Saul *v.* His Creditors, 17 Martin 598 to 607.

4 Fergusson on Marr. and Div, 358 to 363; Id. 382, 393 to 422.

§ 192. Where the place of domicil of both the parties is the same with that of the contract and the celebration of the marriage, no difficulty can arise. The place of celebration is clearly then the matrimonial domicil. But, let us suppose, that neither of the parties has a domicil in the place, where the marriage is celebrated; but it is a marriage *in transitu*, or during a temporary residence, or on a journey made for that sole purpose, *animo revertendi;* what is then to be deemed the matrimonial domicil?

§ 193. The principle maintained by foreign jurists, in such cases, is, that, with reference to personal rights and rights of property, the actual or intended domicil is to be deemed the matrimonial domicil; or, to express the doctrine in a still more general form, they hold, that the law of the place, where at the time of marriage the parties intend to fix their domicil, is to govern all the rights resulting from the marriage. Hence, they would answer the question proposed, by stating, that in such a case the law of the actual domicil of the parties is to govern, and not the place of the marriage *in transitu*.[1]

§ 194. But, suppose a man, domiciled in Massachusetts, should marry a lady, domiciled in Louisiana, what is then to be deemed the matrimonial domicil? Foreign jurists would answer, that it is the domicil of the husband, if the intention of the parties is to fix their residence there; and of the wife, if the intention is to fix their residence there; and if the residence is intended to be in some other place, as in New York, then the matrimonial domicil would be in New York.

---

1 2 Boullenois, 260; Pothier, Traité de la Communauté, Art. Prélim. no. 14, 15, 16; Voet. De Statut. § 9, ch. 2, § 5, 6.

Rodemburg lays down the doctrine in explicit terms; and gives as a reason, that the marriage is presumed to be contracted according to the laws of the place, where they intend to fix their domicil.[1] Boullenois states the same doctrine, and says, that ordinarily, where the domicils of the husband and wife are not the same, the law of the husband's domicil is to prevail, unless he means to establish himself in that of his wife.[2] This appears also to be the opinion of Dumoulin, Mascardus, Bartholus, Bouhier, Pothier, Merlin, and other distinguished jurists.[3]

§ 195. Cujas affirms the same doctrine. *Ex eo contractu mulier migravit in alium locum, id est, talis est contractus, ut ex eo mulier statim migret in alium locum. Ergo non is locus spectatur, sed ille, in quem sit migratio. Hac ratione, mulier non agit, ubi matrimonium contraxit; sed ubi ex matrimonio migravit, divertit, aut agit.*[4] And in so doing, he does no more than affirm the very doctrine of the Pandects. *Exigere dotem mulier debet illic, ubi maritus domicilium habuit, non ubi instrumentum dotale conscriptum est; nec enim id genus contractus est, ut eum locum spectari oporteat, in quo instrumentum dotis factum est, quam*

---

1 Rodemburg, tit. 2, ch. 5, § 15; 1 Boullenois, 11, 682, 683, 802; Voet. De Statut. § 9, ch. 2, § 5; Le Brun, Traité de la Communauté, Liv. 1, ch. 2, § 42, 43, 46, 47, 48.

2 1 Boullenois, 802; 2 Boullenois, 259, 260, 265; Voet. De Statut. § 9, ch. 2, § 5, 6.

3 2 Boullenois, 260 to 265; Pothier, Traité de la Communauté, Art. Prélim. n. 14, 15, 16; Bouhier, Cout. de Bourg, ch. 22, § 18 to 28; Merlin, Répertoire, Autorisation Maritale, § 10, art. 5, p. 244; Id. Communauté de Biens, § 1, p. 111.

4 Cujas ad Legem, Exigere dotem, 164, Cujacii Opera, Tom. 7, p. 164. See also 14 Martin R. 577; Le Brun, Traité de la Communauté, Liv. 1, ch. 2, § 41.

eum, in cujus domicilium et ipsa mulier per conditionem matrimonii erat reditura.[1]

§ 196. Huberus holds very decisive language on the same subject. "But (says he) the place, where a contract is made, is not so exactly to be looked at, but, that, if the parties have in contracting had reference to another place, that is to be rather regarded, *contraxisse unusquisque in eo loco intelligitur, in quo, ut solveret, se obligavit.*[2] Therefore, the place of the marriage contract is not so much to be deemed the place, where the nuptial contract is made, as that, in which the parties, contracting matrimony, intend to live. Thus, it daily happens, that men in Friezeland, natives or sojourners, marry wives in Holland, which they immediately bring into Friezeland. If this be their intention at the time of the contract, there is no community of property, although the marriage contract is silent, according to the law of Holland; but the law of Friezeland in this case is in the place of a contract." [3]

§ 197. Le Brun has discussed the question at considerable length, and arrives at the same conclusion. And he puts the case of a person domiciled in Normandy, where the law of community does not exist, who marries in Paris, without any contract, where the law of community does exist; and holds, that, if he has not changed his domicil, but returns immediately to Normandy, the law of Normandy will govern, and no community of property will exist between himself and his wife.[4]

---

1 Dig. Lib. 5, tit. 1, § 65.

2 Id. 44, tit. 7, l. 21.

3 Huberus, Lib. 1, tit. 3, § 10; S. P. Fergusson on Marr. and Div. 174; Voet. De Statut. § 9, ch. 2, § 5, 6.

4 Le Brun, Traité de la Communauté, Liv. 1, ch. 2, § 46, 47, 48, 49, 50, 51, 55.

§ 198. This doctrine has been repeatedly acted on by the Supreme Court of Louisiana. In one case of a runaway marriage in another state by parties domiciled in Louisiana, who immediately afterwards returned, the Court held, as we have seen, that the law of Louisiana governed the marriage rights and property.[1] In another case, where the parties were married in one state, intending immediately to remove into another, which intention was consummated, the Court held, that the marriage rights and property were governed by the law of the place of intended residence. On this last occasion, the Court said; "We think, that it may be safely laid down as a principle, that the matrimonial rights of a wife, who marries with the intention of an instant removal for residence into another state, are to be regulated by the laws of her intended domicil, when no marriage contract is made, or one without any provision in this respect." [2] In the same case, the Court also recognised the general rule, that, where the husband and wife have different domicils, the law of that of the husband is to prevail; because the wife is presumed to follow her husband's domicil.[3]

§ 199. Under these circumstances, where there is such a general consent of foreign jurists to the doctrine thus recognised in America, it is not, perhaps, too much to affirm, that a contrary doctrine will scarcely hereafter be established; for in England, as well as in America, in the interpretation of other contracts, the law of the place, where they are to be performed, has been held to govern.[4] Treated, therefore, as a mat-

---

1 Le Breton *v.* Nouchet, 3 Martin R. 60.

2 Ford's Curators *v.* Ford, 14 Martin R. 574, 578. 3 Id. 577.

4 Robinson *v.* Bland, 2 Burr. R. 1077; Lanusse *v.* Barker, 3 Wheaton

ter of tacit matrimonial contract (if it can be so treated), there is the rule of analogy to govern it. And treated as a matter to be governed by the municipal law, to which the parties were, or meant to be, subjected by their future domicil, the doctrine seems equally capable of a solid vindication.[1]

R. 101: 4 Cowen R. 513, note; 2 Kent Comm. Lect. 39, p. 459, (2d edition): Fergusson on Marr. and Div. 341, 342, 395, 396, 416.

[1] See Fergusson on Marr. and Div. 339 to 346.

CHAPTER VII.

FOREIGN DIVORCES.

§ 200. HAVING thus considered the operation of marriage upon the personal capacity, and the property of the parties, in the place of its celebration, and in foreign countries, we next come to the consideration of the important subject of divorce. Marriage is not treated as a mere contract between the parties, subject, as to its continuance, dissolution, and effects, to their mere pleasure and intentions. But it is treated as a civil institution, the most interesting and important in its nature of any in society. Upon it the sound morals, the domestic affections, and the delicate relations and duties of parents and children, essentially depend. On this account, it has, in many nations, the sanction and solemnity of religious obligation superadded to it. And it may be truly said, that Christianity, by giving to it a more affecting and sublime morality, has conferred upon mankind new blessings; and has elevated woman to the rank and dignity of an equal, instead of being a humble companion, or a devoted slave.

§ 201. It is not my design to enter into any discussion, as to the general right of the legislative power to authorize directly or indirectly a dissolution of the matrimonial state, and to release the parties from all future obligation. It is deemed by all modern nations to be within the competency of legislation to provide for such a dissolution and release, in some form and for some causes. And there is no doubt, that a divorce, regularly obtained according to the jurisprudence of the country, where the marriage was celebrated, and where the parties are domiciled, will be held a complete dissolution of the matrimonial contract in every other country.[1] I say, where the marriage is celebrated, and where the parties are domiciled; for both ingredients are, or may be material, and the presence of one and the absence of the other may change the legal predicament of the case.

§ 202. The real difficulty is to lay down appropriate principles to govern cases, where the marriage is celebrated in one place, and the parties are domiciled in another; where there is a change of domicil by one party, without a similar change by the other; where by the law of the place of celebration the marriage is indissoluble, or dissoluble only under peculiar circumstances, and by the law of another, it is dissoluble for various causes, and even at the pleasure of the parties. By the law of England marriage is indissoluble except by a special act of parliament.[2] By the law of Scotland a divorce may be had through the instrumentality of a judicial process, and a decree for adultery.[3] By the civil law an almost unbounded license was allowed to divorces; and wives were often dismissed by their husbands, not only for want of chastity, and for intolerable temper, but for causes of the most frivolous nature.[4] In France a divorce may be judicially obtained for the cause of adultery, excess, cruelty, or

---

1 2 Kent Comm. Lect. 27, p. 107, 108, (2d edition.)

2 1 Black. Comm. 440, 441.

3 Fergusson on Marr. and Div. 1, 18; Erskine's Instit. B. 1, tit. 6, § 38, 43.

4 2 Kent Comm. Lect. 27, p. 102, 103, (2d edition); 1 Brown Civ. Law, 89, 90, 91, 92; 1 Black. Comm. 441; Novellæ, 117, ch. 8; Cod. Lib. 5, tit. 17, l. 8; Merlin, Répertoire Divorce, § 2, p. 149, 150; Pothier, Traité de Mariage, art. 463; Van Leeuwen, Comm. B. 1, ch. 15, § 1, 2, 3.

grievous injuries of either party; and in certain cases by mutual and persevering consent.[1] In America an equal diversity of principle and practice exists. In some states, as in Massachusetts and New York, divorces are grantable by judicial tribunals for the cause of adultery.[2] In other states divorces are grantable judicially for causes of far inferior grossness and enormity, approaching sometimes almost to frivolousness. In other states divorces can be pronounced by the legislature only, and for such causes, as in its wisdom it may choose from time to time to allow.[3]

§ 203. Some of the most embarrassing questions belonging to international jurisprudence arise under the head of marriage and divorce. Suppose, for instance, a marriage celebrated in England, where marriage is indissoluble, and a divorce obtained in Scotland *a vinculo matrimonii*, as may be for adultery under its laws, will that divorce be operative in England, so as to authorize a new marriage there by either party? Suppose a marriage in Massachusetts, where a divorce may be had for adultery, will a divorce obtained in another state, for a cause unknown to the laws of Massachusetts, be held valid there? If, in each of these cases the divorce would be held invalid in the countries, where the marriage is celebrated, but valid, where the divorce is obtained, what rule is to govern in other countries as to such divorce? Is it to be

---

1 Code Civil, art. 229 to 233; Id. 275, &c. — See in Fergusson on Marriage and Divorce, Appendix, 448, the Prussian Code on the subject of Divorce; among others, incompatibility of temper, endangering life or health, is a good cause of divorce, art. 703.

2 This also is the law in Holland, in Prussia, and the Protestant states of Germany, in Sweden, Denmark, and Russia. Fergusson on Marr. and Div. 202.

3 See 2 Kent Comm. Lect. 27, 106 to 110; Id. 117, 118, (2d edition.)

deemed valid, or invalid there? Will a new marriage contracted there by either party be good, or not good? These and many other perplexing questions may be put; and it is difficult at the present moment to give any answer to them, which would receive the unqualified assent of all nations.

§ 204. Other most perplexing inquiries may grow out of the consideration of the national character of the parties; whether they are both citizens, or subjects, or both foreigners, or one a citizen, and the other a foreigner; whether the marriage is celebrated at home or abroad; whether the jurisdiction of any court to pronounce a decree of divorce is to be founded upon the national character of the parties, upon the celebration of the marriage within the territorial jurisdiction, upon the domicil of the parties within it, or upon the actual presence or temporary residence of one or both of them at the time, when the process is instituted. And if, upon any of these grounds, the jurisdiction is sustained, another not less important inquiry is, whether the law of divorce of the place of the marriage, or that of the place, where the suit is instituted, is to be administered.

§ 205. By the law of Scotland, to found a jurisdiction for divorce, it would seem, that nothing more is necessary than the presence of one of the parties within the kingdom, and proof of the fact of adultery, at home or abroad. A learned Scottish jurist, in remarking upon the embarrassments arising out of this state of the law of Scotland, has made the following powerful observations.

§ 206. "These conclusions evidently demonstrate, that, unless the remedy in this judicature shall be limited, either to that, which the *lex loci contractûs* affords, or to that, which the *lex domicilii*, taken in the same fair sense, as in questions of succession, might give, the public decrees of the only court of Scotland, which is competent to pronounce one in such consistorial causes, become proclamations to invite all the married, who incline to be free, not in the rest of the British empire alone, but in all countries, where marriage is indissoluble by judicial sentence, to seek that object in this tribunal. Adultery and presence within our territory are the only requisites to found the jurisdiction by citation. What numbers of foreign parties may accept such an offer, and may even commit the crime here, for the very purpose of affording ground for the action, it is impossible to conjecture. But it is manifest, that, in exact proportion to their number, injury to the morals of this country must follow; and, by setting at nought the laws of other nations, reproach must be brought upon our own. For all foreign parties, while matters stand upon this footing, have it in their power, with the help of evidence, as easily provided, as it may be disgusting and impure, to oblige the Scotch Consistorial Court to entertain the whole mass of their foreign causes, although there is no fair interest to insist, that the municipal law of Scotland shall decide these by its own peculiar rules. To what extent, therefore, the good order of society may eventually be disturbed by this compulsory abuse and pollution of its jurisdiction, in consequence of the doubts and contests, that must ensue as to rights of legitimacy and succession, no calculation can be made." [1]

§ 207. Upon the point, what is the rule of divorce, a learned Scottish judge has made the following re-

---

1 Fergusson on Marr. and Div. Introd., p. 18, 19.

marks, in a case depending before him in judgment.[1] "With us, the laws relative to divorce are founded on Divine authority. How can a person withdraw himself from obedience to such laws? Are these laws relaxed as to a person domiciled in Scotland, because his marriage is contracted in a country, where the law of divorce is different? If two natives of Scotland were married in France or Prussia according to the laws of those countries, the marriage would no doubt be valid here. But would they be entitled to come into the Commissary Court, and insist for a dissolution *a vinculo matrimonii*, merely because their tempers were not suitable, which, in France, was a ground of divorce, or for any of the numberless reasons for dissolving a marriage, which are allowed by the laws of Prussia? But, if we would not listen to the *lex loci*, when it facilitates divorce to a degree, which our law considers as inconsistent with the best interests of society, and as not warranted by the Divine law, on what principle are we to give effect to the *lex loci*, which prohibits divorce, even *adulterii causá*, though permitted in this country under the sanction of the Divine law?"

§ 208. These passages are sufficiently significant, as to the intrinsic difficulties of the subject, looking only to the law of divorce of a single country. But, when we look at the almost endless diversities of foreign continental jurisprudence on the same subject, and the little regard, which is habitually paid in that jurisprudence to the decrees of foreign courts, especially in matters, which concern persons belonging to any other continental sovereignty; it ought not to surprise us, if one nation should hold its own law of divorce of universal obligation and authority, and another should yield it up in favour of the law of the domicil of the parties.

[1] Lord Robertson; Fergusson, Appendix, 398. See also Id. 415.

§ 209. Upon the continent of Europe there has long existed a known distinction between the Catholics and Protestants on the subject of divorce. The former, according to the doctrine of the Romish Church, consider marriage as a sacrament, and in its effects to be governed by the Divine law; and according to their interpretation of that law it is indissoluble.[1] The Protestants, on the contrary, have not always considered it as a sacrament; but many, if not most of them, have considered it mainly as a civil institution, subject to the legislative authority, as matter of public police and regulation.[2]

§ 210. In Catholic France, we are informed, that until some time after the revolution, (until 1792,) marriage was always treated as indissoluble.[3] "Our Church," says Merlin, "never approved of divorce, properly so called. It has always regarded it as contrary to the precept, *Quod Deus conjunxit, homo non separet;* What God hath joined together, let not man put asunder.[4] It is, therefore, a perpetual maxim among us, that marriage cannot be dissolved by means of a divorce."[5] Pothier says, marriage is not dissolved, but by the natural death of one of the parties; while they live, it is indissoluble.[6] He adds, that, though divorce

---

1 See Fergusson on Marr. and Div. Appendix, note M. p. 443; Heinecc. Elem. Juris Germ. tit. 14, § 328 to 332; Dalrymple *v.* Dalrymple, 2 Hagg. Consist. R. 63, 64, 67.

2 1 Black. Comm. 433; 2 Hagg. Consist. R. 63, 67.

3 We have already seen, that by the Code Civil of France, art. 229 to 233, divorce is allowed in a variety of cases. Upon the restoration of the Royal Family, in 1816, it seems, that the law of divorce was abolished. Merlin, Répertoire, Divorce, § 4, p. 161. Whether, since the revolution of 1830 it has been reinstated, I am not at this moment able to say. See Duranton, Cours de Droit Français, Vol. 14, p. 535, note.

4 Matthew, ch. 19, v. 6. 5 Merlin, Répertoire, Divorce, § 3, p. 151.

6 Pothier, Traité du Mariage, art. 462.

was permitted by the Christian Emperors, the Church regarded it as prohibited by the Gospel; and that it is not permitted by the French law for any cause whatsoever.[1]

§ 211. Protestants have dealt differently by it.[2] In Scotland, which proposes on this subject to be governed exclusively by the Scriptures, divorce is allowed for the Scriptural causes, for adultery, and for wilful desertion.[3] In many other Protestant countries, it is not treated as indissoluble, except for Scriptural causes; but it may be dissolved for other causes. In England, it is never dissolved except by an act of Parliament, and for adultery. In the Protestant continental nations of Europe many other causes of divorce are known; and in America, as we have seen, it is generally treated as a matter of civil regulation.[4]

§ 212. The conflict of laws on the subject of divorce does not seem to have undergone much discussion among the continental jurists; at least, I have not been able to trace any systematic examination of the subject in those works, which are within my reach, and in which almost all other topics of the conflict of laws are so amply treated. The silence of the French jurists may be accounted for, in a great measure, from the uniformity of operation of the Catholic religion and its canons over all the provinces of that kingdom; from the strong probability, that few cases of foreign divorces between French subjects were ever judicially examined; and from the natural conclusion, that, as in their

---

1 Pothier, Traité du Mariage, 464. 2 Id. art. 465

3 Erskine's Instit. B. 1, tit. 6, § 43, 44; Fergusson on Marr. and Div. Apppendix, note H. p. 423.

4 See 1 Black. Comm. 441; Code Civil of France, art. 229 to 233; Fergusson on Marr. and Div. Appendix, note N. p. 448; 2 Kent Comm. Lect. 27, p. 95 to 106; Van Leeuwen's Comm. B. 1, ch. 15, § 1 to 6.

view Christianity made the marriage union indissoluble, no earthly tribunal, either foreign or domestic, could rightfully pronounce a sentence of divorce. The silence of other Catholic countries may be accounted for in the same way. But it is not so easy to assign a satisfactory reason for the omission of the Protestant countries of the continent, to discuss the subject at large. It is highly probable, that, in those countries, the parties have been referred to their matrimonial forum, either to furnish the true rule to expound the contract, or to administer the law of divorce, or for both purposes. This course has not been without example, even in our own country, upon cases bearing a close affinity.[1]

§ 213. Merlin has treated the question purely as one arising under the French law, either with reference to the allowance of divorces under the legislation of 1792, or with reference to the prohibition of divorces after the restoration of the Bourbons in 1816. He asks the question, whether, in virtue of the new law (of 1792), which introduced divorce, a marriage celebrated under the old law, which prohibited divorce, could be dissolved; and, *vice versâ*, whether a marriage celebrated after the new law, which permitted divorce, could be dissolved after the promulgation of the law (of 1816), which prohibited divorce. He says, that if divorce was, as the state of the parties (*l'état des époux*), the immediate effect and simple consequence of the marriage, the question might be easily answered. Upon this hypothesis, as the state of the parties, the right of divorce would depend altogether upon the law at the time, when the marriage was celebrated; because then,

---

[1] 2 Kent Comm. Lect. 27, p. 108, (2d edition.)

in the first-case put, the contract must be deemed one for an indissoluble union; and in the second case, a contract dissoluble for the proper causes of divorce. But, he goes on to state, that divorce does not depend upon the intention of the parties, nor is it a consequence, or interpretation of it. The legislature, in allowing or prohibiting divorce, has regard only to considerations of public order, and not to the mere contract of the parties. They are not permitted by private agreement to change the laws, or to make a marriage dissoluble or indissoluble in contravention of the policy of the state. He, therefore, comes to the conclusion, that in a French court a divorce in such case would be granted, or denied, according to the law of France at the time of the suit.[1]

§ 214. The question, how a marriage in a foreign country between French subjects, or foreigners, would be affected by a naturalization or domicil in France, is not here touched. In another work, however, treating of moot questions, he has recently discussed the point. He asks, whether French subjects, married in France since the repealing act of 1816, who have abandoned their country, and become naturalized in a country, where divorce is allowed, could institute a suit there, and dissolve their marriage by a decree of divorce pronounced there by mutual consent. He supports the affirmative upon the general reasoning, by which he has sustained the doctrine in the preceding paragraph.[2] It would seem, however, from his own statement, that this is quite an open question in France.

---

1 Merlin, Répertoire, Effet Rétroactif, § 3, 2, art. 6, p. 19.
2 Merlin, Questions de Droit, Divorce, § 11, p. 350.

§ 215. It is to the decisions of the English and Scottish courts, that we must look for the most thorough and exact discussions of this subject. From the different nature of their respective laws on the subject of divorce, from their national union, and from their constant and easy intercourse, the courts of both countries have been frequently called upon to pronounce very elaborate judgments on the jurisdiction and law of divorce in contestations before them.

§ 216. Several questions on this subject have been recently discussed in the courts of Scotland. One is, whether a permanent domicil of the parties is indispensable to found a jurisdiction in cases of divorce in the Scottish tribunals; or whether a citation given formally to the party defendent, or left at his dwelling-place in Scotland, after he has been forty days there, is sufficient to subject him to the jurisdiction of those courts in a suit for divorce. In the case, in which this question was principally discussed, the marriage was celebrated in England; the husband many years afterwards abandoned his wife, and went to Scotland to reside; and the wife commenced a suit for divorce against her husband in the Scottish Consistorial Court. The Court were of opinion, that as the parties were English, and never cohabited as husband and wife in Scotland, and there was no proof, that the husband had taken up a fixed and permanent residence in Scotland, the suit ought to be dismissed upon the ground of a want of jurisdiction. Upon appeal, the decree was reversed by the superior tribunal, and a decree of divorce was ultimately pronounced.

§ 217. The leading grounds of the reversal were, "that the relation of husband and wife is a relation acknowleged *jure gentium*; that the duties, obligations, and rights to redress wrongs incident to that relation, as recognised by the law of Scotland, attach on all married persons living within the territory, and subject to that law, wheresoever their marriage may have been celebrated; that jurisdiction, or the right and duty of the courts of Scotland to administer justice in such matters, over persons not natural born subjects, arises from the person sued being resident within the territory at the time of their citation and appearance, or being duly domiciled, and being properly cited accordingly, at the instance of a person having a sufficient interest and title, and proceeding in due form of law."[1] The result of this decision is, that permanent domicil, or the *animus remanendi*, is not necessary to found the jurisdiction. In several other succeeding cases, the Court have followed up the doctrine, affirming that a temporary residence is sufficient to found the jurisdiction, notwithstanding the permanent jurisdiction of the parties is in another country.[2]

§ 218. This doctrine has been maintained with great ability and learning, and no one can read the reasoning without admitting its force. It has not, however, been deemed satisfactory in England. In a very important case before the twelve judges, where English subjects were married in England, and afterwards the husband went to Scotland, and procured a divorce *a vinculo* there, and then returned to England, and married another wife, it was decided, that the second marriage was void; and the husband was guilty of bigamy.

---

[1] Utterton *v.* Tewsh, Fergusson on Marr. and Div. 1, 55, 56.

[2] Duntze *v.* Levett, Fergusson on Marr. and Div. 63 to 167: Edmonstone *v.* Lockhart, Id. 168 to 208, Butler *v.* Forbes, Id. 209 to 225; Kibblewhite *v.* Rowland, Id. 226 to 248; Gordon *v.* Pye, Id. 276 to 362; Id. 383 to 423.

It has been commonly supposed, that this decision proceeded upon the broad and general ground, that an English marriage is incapable of being dissolved under any circumstances by a foreign divorce; and so it was understood by Lord Eldon on a later occasion.[1] But it has been stated by a learned judge, in a very recent case, that it turned upon the distinction, in point of jurisdiction, between a temporary and fugitive residence for the purpose of a divorce, and a *bonâ fide* change of domicil by the husband and wife, *animo remanendi.* And upon the ground of that distinction, in a case, where there was no change of domicil, and the parties were not at any time *bonâ fide* domiciled in Scotland, he declared a Scottish divorce from an English marriage utterly void.

§ 219. The language of his opinion is so important, that it deserves to be quoted at large. "A case," says he, "in which all the parties are domiciled in England, and resort is had to Scotland (with which neither of them have any connexion) for no other purpose, than to obtain a divorce *a vinculo,* may properly be decided on principles, which would not altogether apply to a case differently circumstanced; as where, prior to the cause arising, on account of which a divorce was sought, the parties had been *bonâ fide* domiciled in Scotland. Unless I am satisfied, that every view of this question had been taken, the Court cannot, from the case referred to (Lolley's case), assume it to have been established as a universal rule, that a marriage had in England, and originally valid by the law of England, cannot, under any possible circumstances, be dissolved by the decree

---

1 Tovey *v.* Lindsay, 1 Dow R. 117. See also McCarthy *v.* De Caix, 1831, cited 3 Hagg. Eccles. R. 642, note.

of a foreign court. Before I could give my assent to such a doctrine (not meaning to deny, that it may be true), I must have a decision, after argument, upon such a case, as I will now suppose, viz. a marriage in England, the parties resorting to a foreign country, becoming actually *bonâ fide* domiciled in that country, and then separated by a sentence of divorce pronounced by the competent tribunal of that country. I am not aware, that that point has ever been distinctly raised; and, I think, I may say with certainty, that it has never received any express decision. I believe the course of decision in Scotland up to the present hour has been to consider, that the Scotch courts have a right to entertain jurisdiction with respect to marriages had in England, after the parties had been residents for a certain period in Scotland, though that period had been infinitely too short to constitute, what we should call a legal domicil; and that those courts have proceeded in such cases to divorce *a vinculo*. It is obvious, that many most important differences may arise in cases of this description. Two Scotch persons, married in England, may afterwards go to reside in Scotland. Again; one of the contracting parties may be English, and the other Scotch. If the law of Scotland continue such, as their courts have hitherto held it to be, and if the decision in Lolley's case be of universal application, the issue of the second marriage may be legitimate in Scotland, and illegitimate in England. The son may take the real estate in Scotland, and not the real estate in England. He might possibly be a Scotch peer, and lose his English title, and with it the English estates, the only support of his Scotch peerage."[1]

---

[1] Conway v. Beazley, 3 Hagg. Eccles. R. 639, 645, 646, 647, 653.

§ 220. Independent of this point of jurisdiction, which is left at the present moment in a state of distressing uncertainty, as well as to the effect of a permanent, as to that of a temporary domicil, to found a sentence of divorce, the Scottish courts have been called on to decide other questions of a broader character, and involving more extensive consequences. In the first place, the general question already hinted at, whether an English marriage between English subjects, being indissoluble by the law of England, can under any possible circumstances be dissolved by a decree of divorce in Scotland. In the next place, whether a marriage in Scotland by English subjects, domiciled at the time in England, is dissoluble under any circumstances by a decree of divorce in Scotland. In the next place, whether, in case of a marriage in England, it will make any difference, that the parties are both Scotch persons, domiciled in Scotland, or afterwards become *bonâ fide* and permanently domiciled there.

§ 221. Upon these questions, the highest tribunals in Scotland have come to the following conclusions. First, that a marriage between English subjects in England, and indissoluble there, may be lawfully dissolved by the proper Scottish court for a cause of divorce, good by the law of Scotland, when the parties are within the process and jurisdiction of the court; or, in other words, that it is not a valid defence against an action of divorce in Scotland for adultery committed there, that the marriage had been celebrated in England. Secondly, that a Scotch marriage by persons, domiciled at the time in England, is dissoluble in like manner by the proper Scottish court; or, in other words, that it is not a valid defence, that the parties had been domiciled in England, when the marriage had been celebrated in Scotland. Thirdly, that in case of a marriage in England, it will make no difference, that the parties are Scottish persons, domiciled in Scotland, or are afterwards *bonâ fide* and permanently domiciled there; or, in other words, that it is not a valid defence, that the parties are Scottish persons, happening to be in England, when their marriage was celebrated, but who, thereafter, have returned to Scotland, and cohabited, and continued domiciled there. The result of these opinions (the unanimous opinions of the judges of the Court of Sessions) is, that the mere fact of the marriage having been celebrated in England, whether between English or Scottish parties, is not *per se* a defence against an action of divorce for adultery committed there.[1]

§ 222. The reasoning, by which these opinions are maintained, as it may be gathered from comparing the arguments of the different judges, is to the following effect. The relation of husband and wife, wherever originally constituted, and the parties therein connected, are entitled to the same protection and redress from the courts of justice in Scotland, as to wrongs committed in Scotland, that belong of right to that relation by the law of Scotland.[2] By marrying in England parties do not become bound to reside for ever in England, or to treat one another in every other country, where they may reside, according to the law of England. Their obligation is to fulfil the duties of husband and wife to each other in every country, to which they may be called in the course of Providence; and they neither promise, nor have power to engage, that they will carry

---

1 Cases of Edmonstone, Levett, and Forbes, Fergusson on Marr. and Div. 383, 392, 393; Id. 114, 115.

2 Fergusson on Marr. and Div. 358.

the law of England along with them to regulate, what the duties and powers shall be, which they shall fulfil and exercise, or the redress, which the violation of those duties, or abuse of those powers, may entitle them to. All these functions belong to the law of the country, where they may eventually reside, and to which they unquestionably contract the duties of obedience and subjection, whenever they enter its territories. Even, if it had been the will of the parties by any stipulation, however express, to make the *lex loci* the law of their marriage, it would derive no force from that circumstance. An action of divorce could not be dismissed, because the parties, when intermarrying, had in the most formal manner renounced the benefit of divorce, and had become bound, that their marriage should be indissoluble. It would be no objection to a divorce at the instance of a Roman Catholic, that his marriage was to him a sacrament, and therefore by its own nature indissoluble. These are all *facta privatorum*, and cannot impede or embarrass the steady, uniform course of the *jus publicum*, which with regard to the rights and obligations of individuals, affected by the three great domestic relations, enacts them from motives of political expediency and public morality; and in no wise confers them as private benefits, resulting from agreements concerning *meum et tuum*, which are capable of being modified and renounced at pleasure.[1]

§ 223. If this supposed obligation of indissolubility, resulting from contract, can derive no force from the will of the parties, it cannot derive any from the dictates of the municipal law, where the relation of mar-

---

[1] Fergusson on Marr. and Div. 359, 360; Id. 398, 399, 402.

riage originated, so as to give it efficacy *ultra territorium*, where *jus dicenti impune non paretur*. In the fulfilment of ordinary contracts, as to *meum et tuum*, the *lex loci contractûs* forms an implied condition of the contract, and is accordingly adopted, as furnishing the means of construing it aright. But this is merely a proceeding in execution of the will of the parties, and not in the least a recognition of the authority of a foreign law. The case is, therefore, quite different, where the will of the parties only constitutes, and does not modify the relation or its rights; and where of course the municipal law, deriving nothing from stipulation or agreement, is merely the positive institution of the sovereign, and cannot direct the decisions of foreign courts, or circumstances occurring within their own jurisdiction. Matrimonial rights and obligations, so far as they are *juris gentium*, admit of no modification by the will of parties; and foreign courts are, therefore, in no wise called upon to inquire after that will, or after any municipal law, to which it may correspond.[1]

§ 224. Foreigners equally with natives, while residents, are subject to the law here, and of course are under the protection of the law. The relations, in which they stand towards one another, and which have been duly constituted before they came here, if relations recognised by all civilized nations, must be observed; and the obligations created by them must be fulfilled agreeably to the dictates of the law of Scotland. If the law refused to apply its rules to the relation of husband and wife, parent and child, master and servant, among foreigners in this country, Scotland could

[1] Fergusson on Marr. and Div. 360, 361, 402, 410, 412, 414.

not be deemed a civilized country, as thereby it would permit a numerous description of persons to traverse it, and violate with utter impunity all the obligations, on which the principal comforts of human life depend. If it assumed jurisdiction, but applied not its own rules, but the rules of the law of a foreign country, the supremacy of the law of Scotland within its own territories would be compromised; its arrangements for domestic comfort would be violated, confounded, and perplexed; and powers of foreign courts, unknown to its law and constitution, would be usurped and exercised.[1] In every country the laws relative to divorce are considered of the utmost importance, as positive laws affecting the domestic interests of society; and in some places are treated as of divine authority.[2] A party domiciled here cannot be permitted to import into this country a law peculiar to his own case, and which is in opposition to those great and important public laws, which are held to be connected with the best interests of society.[3]

§ 225. That there is great force in this reasoning, cannot well be denied. As yet, however, it has obtained no positive sanction in England; and, as far as judicial opinions have gone, they may be said to be against the doctrine, that an English marriage is dissoluble by a Scottish divorce.[4] The reasoning, by which this latter view is sustained, seems to be, that the law of the place, where the marriage is celebrated, furnishes a just rule for the interpretation of its obligations and rights, as it does in the case of other contracts, which

---

1 Fergusson on Marr. and Div. 57, 58, 414, 418.

2 Id. 398, 402, 403.

3 Id. 399, 400, 412, 418.

4 Lolley's Case, 1 Russell and Ryan Cas. 236; Tovey *v.* Lindsay, 1 Dow R. 124; McCartey *v.* De Caix, 3 Hagg. Eccles. R. 642, note; 2 Kent Comm. Lect. 27, p. 116, 117, (2d edition.)

are held obligatory according to the *lex loci contractûs*.[1] It is not just, that one party should be able at his option to dissolve a contract by a law different from that, under which it was formed, and by which the other party understood it to be governed. If any other rule, than the *lex loci contractûs*, is adopted, the law of marriage, on which the happiness of society so mainly depends, must be completely loose and unsettled;[2] and the marriage state, whose indissolubility is so much favored by Christianity, and by the best interests of society, will become subject to the mere will, and almost to the caprice, of the parties as to its duration. The courts of the nations, whose laws are most lax upon this subject, will be constantly resorted to for the purpose of procuring divorces; and, thus, not only frauds will be encouraged, but the common cause of morality and religion be seriously injured, and conjugal virtue and parental affection become corrupted and debased.[3] Thus, a dissatisfied party might resort to one foreign country, where incompatibility of temper is a ground of divorce; or to another, which admits of divorce upon even more frivolous pretences, or upon mere consent.

§ 226. In this manner a nation may find its own inhabitants throwing off all obedience to its own laws and institutions, and subverting, by the interposition of a foreign tribunal, its own fundamental policy. Nay, a stronger case may be put of a marriage deemed, as a sacrament, indissoluble by the public religion of the nation, which is yet dissolved at the will of a foreign

---

1 Fergusson on Marr. and Div. 283, 284, 285, 311, 312, 313, 318, 325, 335, 339.

2 Id. 283, 298, 312.

3 Id. 103, 104, 283, 284, 318, 319, 353, 355, 356.

nation, in violation of the highest of all human duties, a perfect obedience to the Divine law. There is no solid ground, upon which any government can be held to yield up its own fundamental laws and policy, as to its own subjects, in favour of the laws or acts of other countries. Parties contracting in a country, where marriage is indissoluble, voluntarily submit to the jurisdiction and laws of that country, if they are foreigners domiciled there. If they are natural subjects, they are bound by the laws of the country in virtue of the general duty of allegiance. Why should England permit her subjects, by a foreign domicil, to escape from the indissolubility of a marriage contracted in England, and thus permit them to defeat a fundamental policy of the realm?[1] Such is the reasoning on each side.

§ 227. If in any nation the doctrine shall ever be established, in regard to marriages, that the law of the place of its celebration shall prevail, not only as to its original validity, but also as to its mode of dissolution, some interesting questions will still remain for decision. In the first place, will any foreign court have a right to entertain jurisdiction to decree a divorce for causes justified by the law of the matrimonial domicil? Will the like right exist, where no divoree is grantable by the *lex loci* for a similar cause in case of a domestic marriage? For instance, could a consistory court of England entertain a suit for a divorce *a vinculo* for the cause of adultery in case of a Scottish marriage? Or in such cases is the remedy to be exclusively pursued in the domestic forum of the marriage? Whoever

---

[1] Mr. Chancellor Kent has given an excellent summary of the reasoning on each side in his Commentaries; 2 Kent Comm. Lect. 27, p. 110 to 117. My own duty required me to follow out his doctrine by some additional sketches.

shall diligently consider these questions, will not find them without serious embarrassment. They are incidentally treated in the Scottish decisions already alluded to; and the reasoning on each side is worthy of an exact perusal.[1] The attempt to engraft foreign remedial justice upon domestic institutions has always been found extremely difficult; and, as we shall hereafter see, has led to the conclusion, that the safest and best rule is, to give remedies only to the extent, and in the manner, which the *lex loci* justifies and approves.[2]

§ 228. In America, questions respecting the nature and effect of foreign divorces upon domestic marriages, and *vice versâ*, have, as might be expected, been under discussion in our courts. In Massachusetts, in some early cases, the Supreme Court refused to interfere, and grant a divorce, where the parties lived in another state at the time the adultery was charged to have been committed, and the libellant had since that time removed into the state. These decisions seem mainly to have proceeded upon the construction of the local statutes, which conferred jurisdiction upon the Court in matters of divorce; but it was admitted, that the state, to which the parties belonged, had jurisdiction, and could exercise it, if it appeared expedient.[3] In a later case, where a marriage, celebrated in Massachusetts, had been dissolved in Vermont, upon a suit by the husband for a divorce, for the cause of extreme cruelty of his wife (a cause inadmissible by the laws of Massachusetts to dissolve a marriage), it appearing, that

---

1 See Fergusson on Marr. and Div. Appendix, 383 to 422.

2 See in 6 Law (Eng.) Magazine, 32, a review of the English law as to Divorces.

3 Hopkins *v.* Hopkins, 3 Mass. R. 158; Carter *v.* Carter, 6 Mass. R. 268.

the parties had not at the time any permanent domicil in Vermont, but that the husband had gone there for the purpose of obtaining a divorce, the divorce was held a mere nullity, upon the ground, that there was no real change of domicil. "If," said the Court, "we were to give effect to this decree, we should permit another state to govern our citizens in direct contravention of our own statutes; and this can be required by no rule of comity."[1]

§ 229. In another case, the general question came before the Court, whether a marriage, celebrated in Massachusetts, could be dissolved by a decree of divorce of the proper State Court of Vermont, both parties being at the time *bonâ fide* domiciled in that State, and the cause of divorce being such, as would not authorize a divorce *a vinculo* in Massachusetts. The Court decided in the affirmative, upon the ground, that the law of the actual domicil must regulate the right. The reasoning of the Court was to the following effect. "Regulations on the subject of marriage and divorce are rather parts of the criminal, than of the civil code; and apply not so much to the contract between the individuals, as to the personal relations resulting from it, and to the relative duties of the parties, to their standing and conduct in the society, of which they are members; and these are regulated with a principal view to the public order and economy, the promotion of good morals, and the happiness of the community. A divorce, for example, in a case of public scandal and reproach, is not a vindication of the contract of marriage, or a remedy to enforce it; but a

---

1 Inhabitants of Hanover *v.* Turner, 14 Mass. R. 227, 231. See also Barber *v.* Root, 10 Mass. R. 265, 266.

species of punishment, which the public have placed in the hands of the injured party to inflict, under the sanction, and with the aid of the competent tribunal; operating as a redress of the injury, when, the contract having been violated, the relation of the parties, and their continuance in the marriage state, have become intolerable or vexatious to them, and of evil example to others. The *lex loci*, therefore, by which the conduct of married persons is to be regulated, and their relative duties are to be determined, and by which the relation itself is to be in certain cases annulled, must be always referred, not to the place where the contract was entered into, but where it subsists for the time, where the parties have had their domicil, and have been protected in the rights resulting from the marriage contract, and especially where the parties are, or have been amenable for any violation of the duties incumbent upon them in that relation."[1]

§ 230. In New York, so far as decisions have gone, they coincide with those of Massachusetts. Thus, in a case, where the marriage was in that state, and afterwards the wife went to Vermont, and instituted a suit for divorce there, for a cause not recognised by the laws of New York, against her husband, who remained domiciled in New York, the Supreme Court of the latter state refused to carry the decree into effect in regard to alimony, notwithstanding the husband had appeared in the cause,[2] upon the ground, that, there being no *bonâ fide* change of the domicil of the parties, it was an attempt fraudulently to evade the force

---

1 Barber v. Root, 10 Mass. R. 265.

2 This does not appear in the statement of facts; but it is averred by counsel, to appear upon exemplification of the record of the decree of Vermont; 1 John. R. 431.

and operation of the laws of New York.[1] The Court, however, abstained from declaring, what was the legal effect of the divorce so obtained. In another case, where the marriage was in Connecticut, and the husband afterwards went to Vermont, and instituted a suit there for divorce against his wife, who never resided there, and never appeared in the suit, it was held, that the decree of divorce obtained in Vermont was invalid, being *in fraudem legis* of the state, where the parties were married, and had their domicil. It was further held, that the Courts of Vermont could not possess a proper jurisdiction over the case, both parties not being within the state, and the wife not having had personal notice of the suit.[2] What would be the effect of a marriage in Connecticut, a subsequent *bonâ fide* change of domicil to New York, and then a divorce in Connecticut, both parties appearing in the suit, remains as yet undecided.[3]

---

1 Jackson *v.* Jackson, 1 John. R. 424.

2 Borden *v.* Fitch, 15 John. R. 121. See 2 Kent Comm. Lect. 27, p. 108, (2d edition.)

3 Pawling *v.* Bird's Ex'ors, 13 John. R. 192, 208, 209.

CHAPTER VIII.

FOREIGN CONTRACTS.

§ 231. WE next come to the consideration of the highly important branch of international jurisprudence, arising from the conflict of laws in matters of contract generally. This subject has been very much discussed, not only by foreign jurists, and foreign courts, but in our own domestic tribunals. The general principles, which regulate it, have, therefore, acquired a high degree of certainty; although there remain, upon so complex a topic, many intricate and difficult questions yet unsettled.

§ 232. It is easy to see, that, in the common intercourse of different countries, many circumstances may be required to be taken into consideration, before it can be clearly ascertained, what is the true rule, by which the validity, obligation, and interpretation of contracts are to be governed. To make a contract valid, it is a universal principle, admitted by the whole world, that it should be made by parties capable to contract; that it should be voluntary; upon a sufficient consideration; lawful in its nature; and in its terms reasonably certain. But upon some of these points there is a diversity in the positive and customary laws of different nations. Persons, capable in one country, are incapable by the laws of another; considerations, good in one, are insufficient or invalid in another; the public policy of one permits or favours certain agreements, which are prohibited in another; the forms, prescribed by the laws of one, to ensure validity and obligation, are unknown in another; and the rights, acknowledged by one, are not commensurate with those belonging to another. A person sometimes contracts in one country, and is domiciled in another, and is to pay in a third; and sometimes the property, which is the subject of the contract, is situate in a fourth; and each of these countries may have different, and even opposite laws. What then is to be done in this conflict of laws? What law is to regulate the contract, either to determine the rights, the actions, and the defences growing out of it; or the consequences flowing from it; or to interpret its terms, and ascertain its stipulations? Boullenois has very justly said, that these are questions of great importance, and embrace a wide extent of objects.[1]

§ 233. There are two texts of the civil law, which treat of this subject, which have been supposed by civilians to involve an apparent antinomy. One seems to require, that the place, where the contract is entered into, should alone govern the contract. *Si fundus væn ierit, ex consuetudine ejus regionis, in quâ negotium gestum est, pro evictione caveri oportet*;[2] if land shall be sold, it is to be warranted against eviction according to the law of the country, in which the business is transacted. The other, on the contrary, seems to require, that the place, where the contract is to be executed should govern it. *Contraxisse unusquisque in eo loco intelligitur, in quo, ut solveret, se obligavit*; every one is understood to have contracted in the place, in which he has bound himself to perform the contract.[3]

§ 234. Dumoulin has endeavoured to reconcile these

1 2 Boullenois, 445.

2 Dig. Lib. 21, tit. 2, l. 6.

3 Dig. Lib. 44, tit. 7, l. 21. — To the same effect is the text; "Contractum autem non utique eo loco intelligitur, quo negotium gestum est, sed quo solvenda est pecunia." Dig. Lib. 42, tit. 5, l. 3.

texts, by supposing, that, in the first case, the land lies in the place, where the contract is made, and the parties are domiciled; and that, in the other case, the party has bound himself to execute the contract throughout in another place, than that, in which he contracts. But the generality of French authors have reconciled these laws in a different manner; by considering, that the place of a contract admits of a double meaning, viz. the place, where the contract is entered into, *ubi verba proferuntur*, and that, where the contract is to be executed, *ubi solutio destinatur*. They think, therefore, that the law, *Si fundus*, is to be understood of the place, where the contract is entered into, *ubi verba prolata sunt;* and, that it applies to cases, where it is necessary to decide upon the form, either of the proof, or substance, or mode of the contract, or of its extrinsic ceremonies or solemnities; and, that the law, *Contraxisse*, applies to the case, where the question is respecting the rights, which spring from the contract, of which the execution and performance are referred to another place.

§ 235. Boullenois holds both interpretations unsatisfactory, and insufficient for many occasions; for they suppose, that two places only are to be examined in resolving all questions, the place of the making, and the place of the performance of the contract; and in effect, they put aside the law of the place of the *situs* of the thing *(rei sitæ)*, and that of the domicil of the parties, which are often imperative, and on many occasions deserve a preference.[1] And he informs us, that the foreign jurists have warned us against the errors, which constitute the quicksands of the law on this

---

[1] 2 Boullenois, 445, 446, 447.

subject. One of these errors is, the confounding of those things, which belong to the solemnities of the acts, and the effects, which result from the nature of the acts, on the one side, with the charges or liens, which spring up after the acts, purely by accident, on the other side; another is, the refusal, in any case, to pay deference to the law of the *situs* of the thing.[1]

§ 236. Mævius has asserted the following system. The law of the place of the contract is to govern, first, as to the solemnities of the act or contract; and secondly, as to the effects caused thereby; but as to the charges (*onus*) and extrinsic accidents, that it is not to govern. In this system he is not generally followed; and Boullenois has observed, that it is very difficult to say, what ought to be deemed to belong to the solemnities of contracts; what are the effects caused by them; and what are the changes and extrinsic accidents resulting from them.[2]

§ 237. Burgundus has offered the following system. In relation to express contracts two things are to be considered, the form, and the matter of the contract, (*Omnis obligandi ratio habeat necesse est rem et verba, hoc est, formam et materiem.*) But he adds, it is not indiscriminately permitted to contract in all times and places, that is to say, to apply in all times and places the form and matter to contracts (*sed nec omni loco et tempore contrahere licet*); but one must take care with whom he contracts; and, also, that the contract is conformable to law. These things being premised, Burgundus lays down the following rules; first, in every thing, which regards the form of contracts, and the perfecting of them, the law of the place, where the

---

1 2 Boullenois, 447, 449.

2 Id. 448, 449.

contract, is entered into is to be followed. *Et quidem in scripturâ instrumenti, solemnitatibus et ceremoniis, et generaliter in omnibus, quæ ad formam ejusque perfectionem pertinent, spectanda est consuetudo regionis, ubi fit negotiatio.* These, he denominates, the substantials of the contract (*substantialia contractûs*); and among them he includes the necessity of giving caution or security upon a sale, according to any customary law. So the laws, which determine the place and time, where and when contracts ought to be made, belong to the form; *Conditio loci et temporis perfectionem formæ quoque respiciunt, et ideo regione contractûs pariter diriguntur.* In like manner, special stipulations for a limited responsibility, as of particular heirs only, belong to the form. And he concludes by observing, that all questions touching the obligation of the contract, *vinculum obligationis*, or its interpretation, as whom it binds, and to what extent; what is included, what is excluded from it; also, all actions, and all ambiguities, arising out of the contract; these are all questions respecting the formalities of the contract. Hence, he passes to the consideration of the matter of the contract, by which he means the things, of which it disposes; and he affirms, in respect to the matter, that the law of the situation ought to govern. He applies the same rule to *quasi* contracts, as to express contracts; *Idem in quasi contractibus quod, in contractibus obtinet.*[1]

§ 238. Hertius has laid down three general rules

---

[1] 2 Boullenois, 450 to 454. — Not having access to Burgundus's original work, I have drawn this sketch entirely from that given by Boullenois. Burgundus, in exemplifying what he means by the matter of the contract, where the law of the *situs* governs, confines himself to real estate, or immoveable property.

upon the subject of the operation of foreign law; the first is, that when the law respects persons, the law of the country, to which the party is a subject, is to be followed; secondly, when the law repects things, the law of the *situs;* and thirdly, when the law imposes any form upon the business (*actus*), the law of the place, where it is transacted, and not of the domicil, or of the *situs*, is to govern. This last, in an especial manner, he applies to contracts even when they regard property situated in a foreign country.[1]

§ 239. Huberus lays down the following doctrine. All business and transactions in court, and out of court, (or, as we should say, in *pais*, or judicial) whether testamentary, or *inter vivos*, regularly executed according to the law of the place, are valid every where, even in countries, where a different law prevails, and where, if transacted, they would have been invalid. On the other hand, business and transactions, contrary to the law of the place, where they are executed, as they are in their origin invalid, never acquire any validity. And this rule applies not only to persons, who are domiciled in the place of the contract, but to those, who are commorant there. There is this exception, however, to be understood, that if the rulers of another people would be affected with any notable inconvenience thereby, they are not bound to give any effect to such business and transactions.[2] And he applies this doctrine equally to contracts, and to other acts.[3] He adds, that the place, where a contract is entered into, is not to be regarded, if the parties had another country in view in making the contract; *Verum ta-*

---

1 1 Hertii Opera, De Collis. Leg. § 4, p. 126, § 10.

2 Huberus, Lib. 1, tit. 1, § 3.

3 Id. § 5, 7.

men non ita precise respiciendus est locus, in quo contractus est initus, ut, si partes alium locum respexerint, ille non potius sit considerandus. But here the same restriction is to apply, that no injury arise thereby to the citizens of the foreign country in regard to their own rights.[1] And he deduces the following general conclusion, that if the law of another country is in conflict with the law of our country, in which a contract is also entered into, conflicting with another contract, which is entered into elsewhere, in such a case our law is to prevail, and not the foreign law; *Si jus loci in alio imperio pugnet cum jure nostræ civitatis in quá contractus etiam initus est, confligens cum eo contractu, qui alibi celebratus est, magis est, ut jus nostrum, quam jus alienum, servemus.*[2]

§ 240. Boullenois has discussed this subject in a most elaborate manner; and has laid down a number of rules, which are entitled to great consideration.[3] First. The law of the place, where a contract is entered into, is to govern as to every thing, which concerns the proof and authenticity of the contract, and the faith, which is due to it, that is to say, in all things, which regard its solemnities or formalities. Secondly. The law of the place of the contract is generally to govern in every thing, which forms the obligation of the contract (*le lien du contrat*), or what is called *vinculum obligationis.* Thirdly. The law of the place of the contract is to govern as to the intrinsic and substantive form of the contract. Fourthly. When

---

1 Huberus, Lib. 1, tit. 1, § 11. 2 Id. tit. 3, § 11.

3 Mr. Henry has laid down the first eight rules of Boullenois, as clear law, without the slightest acknowlegment of the source, whence they are taken. In fact, his Treatise is in substance taken from Boullenois, whose name, however, occurs only once or twice in it.

the law has attached certain formalities to things themselves, which are the subject of the contract, the law of their situation is to govern. This rule is applicable to contracts respecting real estate. Fifthly. When the law of the place of the contract admits of dispositions or acts, which do not spring properly from the nature of the contract, but have their foundation in the state and condition of the person, there the law, which regulates the person, and upon which his state depends, is to govern. Sixthly. In questions, whether rights, which arise from the nature and time of the contract, are lawful or not, the law of the place of the contract is to govern. Seventhly. In questions concerning moveable property, of which the delivery is to be instantly made, the law of the place of the contract is to govern. Eighthly. If the rights, which accrue to the profit of one of the contracting parties, in fact accrue under a contract, valid in itself, and not subject to recission, but from a new cause purely accidental, and *ex post facto*; in this case, the law of the place, where these rights accrue, is to govern, unless the parties have otherwise stipulated. Ninthly. These rules are to govern equally, whether the contestation be in a foreign tribunal, or in the domestic tribunal, proper for the controversy. Tenthly. In questions upon the true interpretation of clauses in a contract, the accompanying circumstances ought ordinarily to decide them.[1]

§ 241. Without entering farther into the examination of the opinions and doctrines of foreign jurists, we shall now proceed to the consideration of those doctrines, which appear to be recognised and settled

---

[1] 2 Boullenois, 458, 467, 472, 475, 477, 489.

in the jurisprudence of the common law. The law, which is to govern in relation to the capacity of the parties to enter into a contract, has been already fully considered. It has been shown, that, though the foreign jurists generally hold, that the law of the domicil ought to govern in regard to the capacity of persons to contract;[1] yet the common law holds a different doctrine, viz. that the *lex loci contractûs* is to govern.[2]

§ 242. (1.) Generally speaking, the validity of a contract is to be decided by the law of the place, where it is made. If valid there, it is by the general law of nations, *jure gentium*, held valid every where, by tacit or implied consent.[3] The rule is founded, not merely in the convenience, but in the necessities of nations; for otherwise, it would be impracticable for them

[1] In addition to the foreign authorities already cited, we may add that of Cochin and D'Aguesseau. The former says, that the subjects of the King of France are always subjects, and they cannot break the bonds, which attach them to his authority; and parties, contracting in a foreign country, cannot possess any capacity to contract, but according to the law of their own country. It is a personal law, which follows them every where. Cochin, Œuvres, Tom. 1, p. 153, 154; Id. 545: Id. Tom. 4, p. 555. "When," says D'Aguesseau, "the question is, as to an act purely personal, we consider only the law of the domicil. That alone commands all persons, who are subject to it. Other laws cannot make those capable or incapable, who do not live within their reach. And this is what Bartolus intended to remark, when he said, Statutum non potest habilitare personam sibi non subjectam." D'Aguesseau, Œuvres, Tom. 4, p. 639.

[2] See ante, ch. 4, § 51 to 54, § 100 to 106. See also Male *v.* Roberts, 3 Esp. R. 163; Thompson *v.* Ketcham, 8 John. R. 189; Livermore's Diss. p. 34, § 21, p. 35, § 22, 23, 24, p. 38, § 26, 27, p. 40, § 31, p. 42, § 33, p. 43, § 35.

[3] Pearsall *v.* Dwight, 2 Mass. R. 88, 89. See Casaregis Disc. 179; Willing *v.* Conseequa, 1 Peters R. 317; 2 Kent Comm. Lect. 39, p. 457, 458, (2d editition.) De Sobry *v.* De Laistre, 2 Harr. and John. R. 193, 221, 228; Smith *v.* Mead, 3 Connect. R. 253; Medbury *v.* Hopkins, 3 Connect. R. 472; Houghton *v.* Page, 2 N. Hamp. R. 42; Dyer *v.* Hunt, 5 New Hamp. R. 401; Erskine's Instit. B. 3, tit. 2, § 39, 40, 41, p. 514 to 516.

to carry on an extensive intercourse and commerce with each other. The whole system of agencies, purchases and sales, credits, and negotiable instruments, rests on this foundation; and the nation, which should refuse to acknowledge the common principles, would soon find its whole commercial intercourse reduced to a state, like that, in which it now exists with savage tribes, with the barbarous nations of Sumatra, and with other portions of Asia, washed by the Pacific. *Jus autem gentium* (says the Institute of Justinian) *omni humano generi commune est; nam usu exigente, et humanis necessitatibus. Et ex hoc jure gentium, omnes pene contractus introducti sunt, ut emptio, venditio, locatio, conductio, societas, depositum, mutuum, et alii innumerabiles.*[1] And no more forcible application can be propounded of this imperial doctrine, than to the subject of international private contracts.[2] In this, as a general principle, there seems a universal consent of courts and jurists, foreign and domestic.[3]

---

1 1 Inst. Lib. 1, tit. 2, § 2.

2 2 Kent Comm. Lect. 39, p. 454, 455, and note, (2d edition); 10 Toullier, art. 80, note; Pardessus, Droit Comm. Vol. 5, art. 1482; Charters *v.* Cairnes, 16 Martin R. 1.

3 The cases, which support this doctrine, are so numerous, that it would be a tedious task to enumerate them. They may, generally, be found collected in the Digests of the English and American Reports, under the head of Foreign Law, or Lex Loci. The principal part of them are collected in 4 Cowen Rep. 510, note; and in 2 Kent Comm. Lect. p. 39, 457, et seq. in the notes. See also Fonblanque, on Eq. B. 5, ch. 1, § 6, note t. p. 443; Brackett *v.* Norton, 4 Connect. R. 517; Medbury *v.* Hopkins, 3 Connect. R. 472; Smith *v.* Mead, 3 Connect. R. 253; De Sobry *v.* De Laistre, 2 Harr. and John. R. 193, 221, 228; Trasher *v.* Everhart, 3 Gill. and John. R. 234. The foreign jurists are equally full, as any one will find upon examining the most celebrated of every nation. They all follow the doctrine of Dumoulin. "In concernentibus contractibus et emergentibus tempore contractûs, inspici debet locus, in quo contrahitur." See Bouhier, ch. 21, § 190; 2 Boullenois, 458.

§ 243. (2.) The same rule applies, *vice versâ*, to the invalidity of contracts; if void, or illegal by the law of the place of the contract, they are generally held void and illegal every where.[1]

§ 244. (3.) But there is an exception to the rule as to the universal validity of contracts, which is, that no nation is bound to recognise or enforce any contracts, which are injurious to their own interests, or to those of their own subjects.[2] This exception results from the consideration, that the authority of the acts and contracts done in other states, as well as the laws, by which they are regulated, are not, *proprio vigore*, of any efficacy beyond the territories of that state; and whatever is attributed to them elsewhere, is from comity, and not of strict right. And every independent community will, and ought to judge for itself, how far that comity ought to extend. The reasonable limitation is, that it shall not suffer prejudice by its comity.[3] Mr. Justice Best has with great force said, that in cases turning upon the comity of nations (*comitas inter communitates*), it is a maxim, that the comity cannot pre-

---

1 Huberus, Lib. 1, tit. 3, § 3, 5; Van Reimsdyk *v.* Kane, 1 Gallis. R. 375; Pearsall *v.* Dwight, 2 Mass. R. 88, 89; Touro *v.* Cassin, 1 Nott and McCord R. 173; De Sobry *v.* De Laistre, 2 Harr. and John. R. 193, 221, 225; Houghton *v.* Page, 2 N. Hamp. R. 42; Dyer *v.* Hunt, 5 N. Hamp. R. 401; Van Schaick *v.* Edwards, 2 John. Cas. 355; Robinson *v.* Bland, 2 Burr. R. 1077; Burrows *v.* Jemino, 2 Str. 732; Alves, *v.* Hodgson, 7 T. R. 237; 2 Kent Comm. Lect. 39, p. 457, 458, (2d edition.)

2 Greenwood *v.* Curtis, 6 Mass. R. 378, 379; Blanchard *v.* Russell, 13 Mass. R. 1, 6; Whiston *v.* Stodder, 8 Martin R. 95; De Sobry *v.* De Laistre, 2 Harr. and John. R. 193, 228; Trasher *v.* Everhart, 3 Gill. and John. R. 234.

3 Trasher *v.* Everhart, 3 Gill. and John. R. 234; Greenwood *v.* Curtis, 6 Mass. R. 378; 2 Kent Comm. Lect. 39, p. 457, (2d edition); Huberus, Lib. 1, tit. 3, § 2, 3; Pearsall *v.* Dwight, 2 Mass. R. 88, 89; Eunomus, Dial. 3, § 67.

vail in cases, where it violates the law of our own country, the law of nature, or the law of God.[1] Contracts, therefore, which are in evasion or fraud of the laws of a country, or the rights or duties of its subjects, contracts against good morals, or religion, or public rights, and contracts opposed to the national policy or institutions, are deemed nullities in every country, affected by such considerations; although they may be valid by the laws of the place, where they are made.

§ 245. Indeed, a broader principle might be adopted; and it is to be regretted, that it has not been universally adopted by all nations in respect to foreign contracts, as it has been in respect to domestic contracts, that no man ought to be heard in a court of justice to enforce a contract founded in, or arising out of, moral or political turpitude.[2] The civil law contains an affirmation of this wholesome doctrine. *Pacta, quæ contra leges constitutionesque, vel contra bonos mores fiunt, nullam vim habere indubitati juris est.*[3] *Pacta, quæ turpem causam continent, non sunt observanda.*[4] Unfortunately, from a very questionable subserviency to mere commercial gains, it has become an established formulary of the jurisprudence of the common law, that no nation will regard or enforce the revenue laws of any other country; and that the contracts of its own subjects, to evade or defraud the just rights of other

---

1 Forbes *v.* Cochrane, 2 B. and Cres. R. 448, 471.

2 Armstrong *v.* Toler, 11 Wheaton R. 258, 260; Chitty on Bills, (8th edit.), 1833, p. 143, note; Boucher *v.* Lawson, Cas., Temp. Hard. 84, 89, 194; Planche *v.* Fletcher, Doug. R. 250.

3 Cod. Lib. 6, tit. 3, l. 6.

4 Dig. Lib. 2, tit. 14, l. 27, § 4. See also 1 Chitty on Comm. and Manuf. ch. 4, p. 82, 83.

nations, will be enforced in its own tribunals.[1] Sound morals would seem to point to a very different conclusion.

§ 246. A few cases may serve to illustrate the exceptions under each of the foregoing heads.[2] First, contracts, which are in evasion or fraud of the laws of the country.[3] Thus, if a contract is made in France, to smuggle goods into America in violation of our laws, the contract will be treated by our courts as utterly void, as an intended fraud upon our laws.[4] And in such a case it is wholly immaterial, whether the parties are citizens or foreigners. So if a collusive capture and condemnation are procured in our courts in fraud of our laws by foreigners, who are even enemies at the time, their contract for the distribution of the prize proceeds will be held utterly void by our courts; though the acts are a mere stratagem of war. And it will make no difference, that the laws have since been repealed, or that the war has since ceased; for the contract being clearly in fraud of the laws existing at the time, the execution of it ought not to be enforced by the courts of the country, whose laws it was designed to evade.[5]

§ 247. The same principle applies, not only to contracts growing immediately out of, and connected with, an illegal transaction, but to new contracts, if they are in part connected with the illegal transaction, and grow

---

1 See Boucher *v.* Lawson, Cas. Temp. Hard. 85, 89, 194.

2 Many of the cases upon this subject, will be found referred to in the argument of Armstrong *v.* Toler, 11 Wheaton R. 265, 266.

3 See 1 Bell. Comm. 232 to 240; Kaims on Eq. B. 3, ch. 8, § 1.

4 See Holman *v.* Johnson, Cowper R. 341; Armstrong *v.* Toler, 11 Wheaton R. 258; Cambioso *v.* Maffit, 2 Wash. Cir. R. 98.

5 Hannay *v.* Eve, 3 Cranch R. 242; See Jaques *v.* Withy, 1 H. Black. R. 65; The Springfield Bank *v.* Merrick, 14 Mass. R. 322.

immediately out of it. Thus, for example, a man, who, under a contract made in a foreign country, imports goods for another, by means of a violation of the laws of his country, is disqualified from founding any action upon such illegal transaction for the value, or freight of the goods, or other advances made on them. He is justly punished for the immorality of the act; and a powerful discouragement from the perpetration of the act is thus provided. And if the importation is the result of a scheme to consign the goods to a friend of the owner with the security of the former, that he may protect, or defend them for the owner, in case they should be brought into jeopardy, a promise afterwards made by the owner, to the friend, to indemnify him for his advances and charges on account of any proceedings against the property, although it purport to be a new contract, will be held utterly void, as constituting a part of the *res gesta*, or original transaction. It will clearly be a promise growing immediately out of, and connected with, the illegal transaction.[1]

§ 248. But the principle stops here, and is not extended to new transactions after the illegal act. If the new promise is wholly unconnected with the illegal act, and is founded on a new consideration, and is not a part of the original scheme, it is not tainted by the illegal act, although it was known to the party, to whom the promise was made. Thus, if, after the illegal act is accomplished, a new contract (not being unlawful in itself) is made by the importer for a sale of the goods to a retail merchant, and the merchant afterwards

---

1 Armstrong *v.* Toler, 11 Wheaton, 261, 262. See Canaan *v.* Brice, 3 Barn. and Ald. 179.

sells the same to a tailor, or customer, all these new contracts will be valid, although the illegality of the original act is known to each of them at the time, when he entered into the new contract.

§ 249. And it will make no difference, that such new and independent contract is made with a person, who was the contriver and conductor of the original illegal act; for a new contract, founded on a new consideration, although in relation to property, respecting which there have been unlawful transactions between the parties, is not in itself unlawful. Thus, if A should, in a foreign country, during war, contrive a plan for importing goods from the country of the enemy on his own account by means of smuggling, or of a collusive capture, and goods should be sent in the same vessel by B; and A should, upon the request of B, become surety for the payment of the duties, or should undertake to become answerable for the expenses on account of a prosecution for the illegal importation, or should advance money to B, to pay these expenses; these acts, if they constituted no part of the original scheme, and if A was not to be concerned, nor in any manner instrumental in promoting the illegal importation of B, but he was merely engaged in a similar illegal transaction, devising the plan for himself, would be deemed a new contract upon a valid and legal consideration, unconnected with the original act, although remotely caused by it. And such new contract would not be so contaminated by the turpitude of the offensive act, as to turn A out of court, when seeking to enforce it in the courts of this country, although the illegal introduction of the goods into the country was the consequence of the scheme projected by A, in relation to his own goods.

§ 250. The same principle may be illustrated by another example. If A should become answerable for expenses on account of a prosecution for the illegal importation, or should advance money to B, to enable him to pay those expenses; these acts would constitute a new contract, on which an action might be maintained in our courts, if it constituted no part of the original scheme for the illegal importation, but it was subsequent to, and independent of it.[1]

§ 251. This general distinction has been asserted in many cases, which have undergone a legal adjudication. Thus, in a case were goods were sold in France by a Frenchman to an Englishman, for the known purpose of being smuggled into England, it was held, that the Frenchman could maintain a suit in England for the price of the goods, upon the ground, that the sale was complete in France, and the party had no connexion with the smuggling transaction. The contract (said the Court) is complete, and nothing is left to be done. The seller, indeed, knows, what the buyer is going to do with the goods; but he has no concern in the transaction itself.[2] But if it enters at all, as an ingredient, into the contract between the parties, that the goods shall be smuggled, or that the seller shall do some act to assist or to facilitate the smuggling, such as packing them in a particular way, there the seller is deemed active, and the contract will not be enforced. And the same doctrine has accordingly been held in other cases.[3]

---

1 Armstrong *v.* Toler, 11 Wheaton R. 258, 260, 268 to 271. But see Canaan *v.* Brice, 3 Barn. and Ald. 179.

2 Holman *v.* Johnson, Cowper R. 341.

3 Waynell *v.* Reed, 5 T. R. 599; Lightfoot *v.* Tenant, 1 Bos. and Pull. 551; Biggs *v.* Lawrence, 3 T. R. 459; Clugas *v.* Peneluna, 4 T. R. 466; Holman *v.* Johnson, Cowper, 341.

§ 252. Huberus puts a case illustrative of the same doctrine. In particular places certain merchandise is prohibited. If sold there, the contract is void. But, if the same merchandise is sold in another place, where there is no such prohibition, and a suit is brought in the place, where the prohibition exists, the buyer will be held liable (*condemnabitur*), because the contract was, in its origin, valid. But, if the merchandise is sold to be delivered in another place, where it is prohibited, the buyer will not be liable; because such a contract is repugnant to the law and interest of the country, which made the prohibition.[1]

§ 253. The result of these decisions certainly is, that mere knowledge of the illegal purpose, for which goods are purchased, will not affect the validity of the contract of sale of goods, intended to be smuggled into a foreign country, even in the courts of that country. But that there must be some participation or interest in the act itself. It is difficult, however, to reconcile them with the strong reasoning of Lord Chief Justice Eyre in an important case on the same subject; reasoning, which has much to commend it in point of sound sense, and sound morals. "Upon the principles of the common law," said he, "the consideration of every valid contract must be meritorious. The sale and delivery of goods, nay, the agreement to sell and deliver goods, is, *primâ facie*, a meritorious consideration to support a contract for the price. But the man, who sold arsenic to one, who, he knew, intended to poison his wife with it, would not be allowed to maintain an action upon his contract. The consideration of

---

1 Hub. Lib. 1, tit. 3, § 5; S. P., Greenwood *v.* Curtis, 6 Mass. R. 378; Ex'ors of Cambioso *v.* Assignees of Moffat, 2 Wash. Cir. R. 98.

the contract, in itself good, is there tainted with turpitude, which destroys the whole merit of it. I put this strong case, because the principle of it will be felt and acknowledged without further discussion. Other cases, where the means of transgressing a law are furnished, with the knowledge, that they are intended to be used for that purpose, will differ in shade more or less from this strong case; but the body of the colour is the same in all. No man ought to furnish another with the means of transgressing the law, knowing, that he intended to make that use of them."[1] The wholesome morality and enlarged policy of this passage make it almost irresistible to the judgment.

§ 254. The doctrine of Lord Chief Justice Eyre has been expressly adopted in other cases. In Langton *v.* Hughes,[2] the Court of King's Bench held, that a person, who sold drugs to a brewer, knowing, that they were intended to be used in the brewing of beer contrary to an act of Parliament, was held, not to be entitled to recover the money due upon the sale. Lord Ellenborough on that occasion said, "that a person, who sells drugs, with a knowledge, that they are meant to be so mixed, may be said to cause or procure, *quantum in illo*, the drugs to be mixed. So if a person sell goods with a knowledge, and in furtherance of the buyer's intention to convey them upon a smuggling adventure, he is not permitted by the policy of the law to recover such a sale." And the other members of the Court concurred in that opinion. Mr. Justice Bayley added, "If a principal sell articles in order to enable the vendee to use them for illegal purposes, he cannot recover the

---

1 Lightfoot *v.* Tenant, 1 Bos. and Pull. 351, 356.

2 1 Maule and Selw. 593.

price. The smuggling cases, which were decided on that ground, are very familiar." Although the case of Hodgson *v.* Temple[1] is the other way, the doctrine Langton *v.* Hughes has been most firmly upheld in the latest case upon the subject.[2]

§ 255. There seems a strong inclination at present in the courts of law to hold, that, if a contract is made in foreign parts by a citizen of a country to sell goods, which he knows at the time are to be smuggled in violation of the laws of his own country, he shall not be permitted to enforce it in the courts of his own country, although the contract of sale is complete, and might be enforced in a like case of a foreigner.[3]

§ 256. Pardessus has asked, whether, if Frenchmen have entered into a contract abroad, forbidden by the laws of the place, they can insist upon its execution in France; as, for example, a contract for contraband or smuggling. And he has answered, that he rather thinks they may, since this offence is only a violation of the law of the foreign state; and governments in this respect exercise a sort of mutual hostility; and, without openly favouring enterprises of a contraband nature, they do not proscribe them.[4] But this doctrine of Pardessus is certainly a departure from the general principle, that the validity of contracts depends upon the *lex loci contractûs;* for in the case supposed, the contract is clearly void by the laws of the country, where it is made.

---

1 5 Taunt. R. 183.

2 Canaan *v.* Bryce, 3 Barn. and Ald. 179, 181.

3 Biggs *v.* Lawrence, 3 T. R. 454; Clugas *v.* Penaluna, 4 T. R. 466; Weymell *v.* Reed, 5 T. R. 599; Eunomus Dial. 3, § 67; Ex'ors of Cambioso *v.* Assignees of Moffat, 2 Wash. Cir. R. 98.

4 5 Pardessus, art. 1492.

§ 257. It might be different, if the contract were made in some other country, or in the country, to which the parties belong; for it has been long laid down as a settled principle, that no nation is bound to protect, or regard the revenue laws of another country; and, therefore, a contract made in one country by residents to evade the revenue laws of another country, is not deemed illegal in the country of its origin.[1] Against this principle Pothier has argued strongly, as being inconsistent with good faith, and the moral duties of nations. Valin, however, supports it; and Émérigon defends it upon the unsatisfactory ground, that smuggling is a vice common to all nations.[2] An enlightened policy, founded upon national justice, as well as national interest, would seem to favour the opinion of Pothier in all cases, where positive legislation has not adopted the principle as a retaliation upon the narrow and exclusive revenue system of another nation.[3] The contrary doctrine is, however, firmly established

---

1 See Boucher v. Lawson, Cas. Temp. Hard. 84, 89, 194; Holman v. Johnson, Cowper R. 341; Biggs v. Lawrence, 3 T. R. 454; Clugas v. Penaluna, 4 T. R. 466; Ludlow v. Van Rensaellaer, 1 John. R. 94; Lightfoot v. Tenant, 1 Bos. and Pull. 551, 557; Planché v. Fletcher, Doug. R. 251; Lever v. Fletcher, 1 Marsh. Insur. 58 to 61.

2 Pothier, Assur. n. 58; 2 Valin Comm. art. 49, p. 127; 1 Émérig., ch. 8, § 5, p. 212, 215, (215 to 218, edité par Boulay-Paty,) and see note of Estrangin to Pothier ad loc.; 1 Marshall Ins. ch. 3, § 1, p. 59, 60.

3 It is gratifying to find that Mr. Marshall and Mr. Chitty have both taken side with Pothier on this point. The following passage from a work of the latter expounds the reasoning with considerable force. "There is something in these decisions, to which a liberal mind cannot readily assent; and the impropriety of them seems to have been hinted at by Lord Kenyon in the before-mentioned case of Weymell v. Reed. It is impossible not to feel a greater inclination towards the opinion of Pothier, who observes, 'that a man cannot carry on a contraband trade in a foreign country, without engaging the subjects of that country to commit an offence against the laws, which it is their duty to obey; and it is a crime of moral turpitude to engage a man to commit a crime; that a man,

in the actual practice of modern nations without any such discrimination.

§ 258. (2.) The second class of excepted contracts comprehends those against good morals, or religion, or public rights.[1] Such are contracts made in a foreign country for future illicit cohabitation and prostitution;[2] contracts for the printing or circulation of irreligious and obscene publications; contracts to pro-

---

carrying on commerce in any country, is bound to conform to the laws of that country; and therefore to carry on an illicit commerce there, and to engage the subjects of that country to assist him in so doing, is against good faith; and consequently a contract made to favour or protect this commerce is peculiarly unlawful, and can raise no obligation.'

"If our law be justifiable in protecting these transgressions, it can be only on the plea of necessity. But where is the necessity? Shall we be told, that it is impossible to ascertain in the English courts the complex provisions of another country's revenue law? Surely this argument can avail but little, when it is recollected, that in all cases where the argument is not convenient, the law of another country, however complex, is the rule, by which contracts negotiated in that country are tried and construed. It may be true, that the rule of our law was adopted by way of retaliation for the illiberal conduct of other states, and is continued from a cautious policy. But a cautious policy in a great state is but too often a narrow policy; and, after all, the best policy for a state, as well as for an individual, will perhaps be found to consist in honesty and honourable conduct. Indeed the system is so directly opposite to the clear principles of right feeling between man and man, that nothing could have withheld the states of Europe from concurring for its total abrogation, except the smallness of the gain or loss that attends upon it." 1 Chitty on Commerce and Manuf., p. 83, 84; 1 Marshall Insur. 59 to 61.

[1] 2 Bell Comm. 232.

[2] See 1 Selwyn's Nisi Prius, Assumpsit p. 59, 60; Walker *v.* Perkins, 3 Burr. 1568; Greenwood *v.* Curtis, 6 Mass. R. 379; Birmington *v.* Wallis, 4 Barn. and Ald. 650; Lloyd *v.* Johnson, 1 Bos. and Pull. 340; Jones *v.* Randall, Cowp. R. 37; Appleton *v.* Campbell, 2 Carr. and P. 347; De Sobry *v.* De Laistre, 2 Harr. and John. R. 193, 228. — Lord Mansfield, in the case of Robinson *v.* Bland, 2 Burr. 1084, puts the very case. In many countries (says he), a contract may be maintained by a courtesan for the price of her prostitution; and one may suppose an action to be brought here; but that could never be allowed in this country. Therefore, the *lex loci* cannot in all cases govern and direct.

mote or reward the commission of crimes; contracts to corrupt, or evade the due administration of justice; contracts to cheat the public agents, or to defeat the public rights; and, in short, all contracts, which in their own nature are founded in moral turpitude, and are inconsistent with the good order and interests of society.[1] All such contracts, even though they might be valid in the country, where they are made, would be held void elsewhere.

§ 259. (3.) The next class of excepted contracts comprehends those, which are opposed to the national policy and institutions. For example, contracts made in a foreign country to procure loans in our country, in order to assist subjects of a foreign state in the prosecution of war against a nation, with which we are at peace; for such conduct is inconsistent with a just and impartial neutrality;[2] contracts entered into with a foreign government (as for a loan of money), such government being a new government unacknowledged by the government, to which the party, entering into the contract, belongs;[3] for a like rule of public policy applies to such cases; contracts entered into in violation of a monopoly granted by any country to any subjects thereof;[4] contracts to carry on trade with the enemy, or to cover enemy property, or contraband of war;[5] contracts

---

1 See Com. Dig. Assumpsit, F. 7; Smith *v.* Stotesbury, 1 W. Bl. 204; S. C., 2 Burr. 924; Foxes *v.* Johnes, 4 Esp. R. 97; Willis *v.* Baldwin, Doug. R. 450; Walcot *v.* Walker, 7 Vesey R. 1; Southey *v.* Sherwood, 2 Merivale, 435, 441; Lawrence *v.* Smith, Jacob R. 471, 474, note; Jones *v.* Randall, Cowp. R. 37; Fergusson on Marr. and Div. 396, 397.

2 De Weitz *v.* Hendricks, 9 Moore R. 586; S. C., 2 Bing. R. 314.

3 Thompson *v.* Powles, 2 Simon R. 194. See also Jones *v.* Garcia del Rio, 1 Turner and Russ. R. 299.

4 Pattison *v.* Mills, 1 Dow and Clarke R. 342.

5 1 Marshall Insur., B. 1, ch. 3, § 3, p. 78, § 4, p. 85; Griswold *v.* Waddington, 16 John. R. 438; 2 Wheaton R. Appendix, 35; Richard-

to carry into effect the African slave trade, or the rights of slavery, in countries, which refuse to acknowledge its lawfulness, at least if entered into by subjects of such countries.[1] In all such cases the contracts would be held utterly void here, whatever might be their validity in the country, where they are made, as inconsistent with our duties, our policy, or our institutions.[2]

§ 260. (4.) Another rule naturally flowing from, or rather illustrative of, that already stated respecting the validity of contracts, is, that all the formalities, proofs, or authentications of them, which are required by the *lex loci*, are indispensable to their validity every where else. And this is in precise conformity to the rule laid down on the subject by Boullenois.[3] Hertius is equally direct. *Si lex actui formam dat, inspiciendus est locus actûs, non domicilii, non rei sitæ; id est, si de solenni-*

---

son *v.* Maine Ins. Co., 6 Mass. R. 102, 110, 112, 113; Musson *v.* Fales, 16 Mass. R. 332; Coolidge *v.* Inglee, 13 Mass. R. 26.

1 See Somerset's Case, Lofft's R. 1; 20 Howell's State Trials, 79; Fergusson on Marr. and Div. 396, 397; Madrazo *v.* Willes, 3 Barn. and Ald. 353; Forbes *v.* Cochrane, 2 Barn. and Cresw., 448; and especially the opinion of Best J.—I am not unaware of the bearing of the case of Greenwood *v.* Curtis, 6 Mass. R. 358, on this point; and without undertaking to examine its authority, it may be sufficient to say, that it is not without difficulty in its principles and application, as will abundantly appear from the elaborate argument of Mr. Justice Sedgwick in the same case (Id. 362, n.), and the later reasoning of Mr. Justice Best in 2 Barn. and Cresw. 448. I have given, in the text, what seems to me to be the just doctrine resulting from the modern cases, without meaning to assert, that the authorities cited are fully in point.

2 2 Bell. Comm. 234.

3 Erskine's Inst. B. 3, tit. 2, § 39, 40, 41, p. 514, 515; Boullenois, Quest. Mixt. p. 5; Bouhier, Cout. de Bourg. ch. 21, § 205; 2 Boullenois, 468; 1 Hertii Op. De Collis. Leg. § 4, n. 59. See also Voet. ad Pand. Lib. 5, tit. 1, § 51; 1 Boullenois, 523; Henry on Foreign Law, 37, 38; Id. 224; 5 Pardessus, art. 1485; Depau *v.* Humphreys, 20 Martin R. 1, 22.

bus quæratur, si de loco, de tempore, de modo actûs, ejus loci habenda est ratio, ubi actus sive negotium celebratur.[1] Thus, if by the laws of a foreign country a contract is void, unless it is written on stamp paper, it ought to be held void every where; for unless it be good there, it can have no obligation in any other country.[2] It might be different, if the contract had

---

[1] Hertii Opera, De Collis. Leg. § 10, p. 126; Id. p. 148, § 59. See also Cochin, Œuvres, Tom. 1, p. 72; Id. Tom. 3, p. 26; Id. Tom. 5, p. 697; D'Aguesseau, Œuvres, Tom. 4, p. 637, 722.

[2] Alves *v.* Hodgson, 7 T. R. 237; Clegg *v.* Levy, 3 Campb. R. 166. But see Chitty on Bills, (8th edit.) p. 143, note; and Wynne *v.* Jackson, 2 Russell R. 351. — The case of Wynne *v.* Jackson, 2 Russell R. 351, is certainly at variance with this doctrine. It was a bill brought to stay proceedings at law on a suit, brought in England by the holder, against the acceptor of bills of exchange, made and accepted in France, and which, in an action brought in the French courts, had been held invalid for want of a proper French stamp. The Vice-Chancellor held, "that the circumstance of the bills being drawn in France, in such a form, that the holder could not recover on them in France, was no objection to his recovering on them in an English court." This doctrine is wholly irreconcileable with that in Alves *v.* Hodgson, 7 T. R. 241, and Clegg *v.* Levy, 3 Camp. R. 166; and if by the laws of France such contracts were void, if not on stamped paper, it is equally unsupportable upon acknowledged principles. In the case of James *v.* Catherwood, 3 Dowl. and Ry. 190, where assumpsit was brought for money lent in France, and unstamped paper receipts were produced in proof of the loan, evidence was offered to show, that by the laws of France such receipts required a stamp to render them valid; but it was rejected by the court, and the receipts were admitted in evidence upon the ground, that the courts of England could not take notice of the revenue laws of a foreign country. But this is a very insufficient ground, if the loan required such receipt and stamp to make it valid as a contract. And, if the loan was good *per se;* but the stamp was requisite to make the receipt good as evidence, then another question might arise, whether other proof, than that required by the law of France, was admissible of a written contract. This case also is inconsistent with the case in 3 Camp. R. 166. Can a contract be good in any country, which is void by the law of the place, where it is made, because it wants the solemnities required by that law? Would a parol contract made in England, respecting an interest in lands, against the statute of Frauds, be held valid elsewhere? Would any court dispense with the written evidence required upon

been made payable in another country; or if the objection were, not to the validity of the contract, but merely to the admissibility of other proof of the contract in the foreign court.[1]

§ 261. The ground of this doctrine, as commonly stated, is, that every person, contracting in a place, is understood to submit himself to the law of the place, and silently to assent to its action upon his contract. *Quia censetur quis, semet contrahendo, legibus istius loci, ubi contrahit, etiam ratione solemnium subjicere voluisse. Ut quemadmodum loci consuetudo subintrat*

such a contract? On a motion for a new trial, the Court refused it, Lord Chief Justice Abbott saying, "The point is too plain for argument. It has been settled, or, at least, considered as settled, ever since the time of Lord Hardwicke, that in a British court we cannot take notice of the revenue laws of a foreign state. It would be productive of prodigious inconvenience, if, in every case, in which an instrument was executed in a foreign country, we were to receive in evidence, what the law of that country was, in order to ascertain, whether the instrument was, or was not, valid." With great submission to his Lordship, this reasoning is wholly inadmissible. The law is as clearly settled, as any thing can be, that a contract void by the law of the place, where it is made, is void every where. Yet, in every such case, whatever may be the inconvenience, courts of law are bound to ascertain, what the foreign law is. And it would be a perfect novelty in jurisprudence to hold, that an instrument, which, for want of due solemnities in the place, where it was executed, was void, should yet be valid in other countries. We can arrive at such a conclusion only by overturning well established principles. The case alluded to, before Lord Hardwicke, was probably Boucher *v.* Lawson, (Cases T. Hard. 85,) Id. 194, which was the case of a contract between Englishmen, to be executed in England, to carry on a smuggling trade against the laws of Portugal. Lord Hardwicke said, that such a trade was not only a lawful trade in England, but very much encouraged. The case is wholly distinguishable from the present case; and from that of any contract made in a country and to be executed there, which is invalid by its laws. A contract made in Portugal by persons domiciled there, to carry on smuggling against its laws, would, or ought to be held void every where.*

[1] Ludlow *v.* Van Rensselaer, 1 John. R. 93; James *v.* Catterwood, 3 Dow and Ryl. 190.

* See 3 Chitty on Comm. and Manuf. ch. 2, p. 166.

contractum, ejusque est declarativa, ita etiam loci statutum.[1] It would be more correct to say, that the law of the place of the contract acts upon it, independently of any volition of the parties, in virtue of the general sovereignty possessed by every nation to regulate all persons, property, and transactions within its own territory. And, in admitting the law of a foreign country to govern in regard to contracts made there, every nation merely recognises, from a principle of comity, the same right to exist in other nations, which it demands and exercises for itself.[2] Some foreign jurists make an exception from the general rule in cases of contracts, made in a foreign country by any persons, for the purpose of evading the revenue system, or local solemnities, prescribed by the laws of their own country, respecting such contracts.[3]

§ 262. Other illustrations of this rule might be easily multiplied. Thus, by the English and American law,

---

1 Voet. De Stat. § 9, ch. 2, p. 267, n. 9; Cochin, Œuvres, Tom. 5, p. 697; Fergusson on Marr. and Div. 397; 2 Boullenois, 475, 476; Id. 500, 501, 502; Casaregis Disc. 179, § 56. — Boullenois, and some other jurists contest the universality of this presumed assent to the law of the place of the contract; and assert, that the principle generally and broadly taken, *généralement et cruement* (*nuditer et indistincte*,) is not correct. But where no other place of performance is pointed out, it seems difficult to see, what other law is to govern. See 2 Boullenois, 457, 458, 459; Id. 501, 502 to 518; Bouhier, ch. 21, § 191, 192; Voet. De Stat. § 9, ch. 2, § 10, p. 269. Hertius even goes so far as to say, that the law of the place of a contract does not govern, where the party is a stranger, ignorant of its laws; "non valet, si exterus ignoravit statutum." 1 Hertii Opera, De Collis. Leg. § 4, p. 126, 127, § 10. See also 2 Boullenois, 502. Can a stranger, living in a country, plead ignorance of the laws of that country in his defence? Is he not bound by them, whether he knows them, or not? Huberus, on the contrary, holds, that the law of the place of the contract governs, not only in respect to those, who are domiciled, but those, who are commorant there. Huberus, Lib. 1, tit. 3, § 3.

2 Blanchard *v.* Russell, 13 Mass. R. 1, 4.

3 Voet. Id. p. 268, Excep. 3, 4.

contracts falling within the purview of what is called the Statute of Frauds, are required to be in writing; such are contracts respecting the sale of lands, contracts for the debts of third persons, and contracts for the sale of goods beyond a certain value. If such contracts, made by parol (*per verba*), are sought to be enforced elsewhere, they will be held void, exactly as they are held in the place, where they are made. And so the like rule applies, *vice versâ*, where parol contracts are good by the law of the place; but would be void, if originally made in another place, where they are sought to be enforced, for want of certain solemnities, or for want of being in writing.[1]

§ 263. (5.) Another rule, illustrative of the same general principle, is, that the law of the place of the contract is to govern, as to the nature, obligation, and interpretation of it; *Locus contractûs regit actum.*[2]

---

1 2 Boullenois, 459, 460; 1 Boullenois, 492 to 498; Id. 499; Id. 506; Id. 523; Erskine's Inst. B. 3, tit. 2, § 39, 40; Vidal *v.* Thompson, 11 Martin R. 23; Casaregis Disc. 179, n. 59, 60; 1 Hertii Opera, De Collis. Leg. p. 148, § 59; Boullenois, Quest. de la Contrar. des Loix. p. 5; Livermore Diss. p. 46, § 41; Alves *v.* Hodgson, 7 T. R. 241; Clegg *v.* Levy, 3 Camp. 166. But see Wynne *v.* Jackson, 2 Russell R. 251; and James *v.* Catterwood, 3 Dowl. and Ryl. 190; Ante, § 260, and note, p. 216. Hertius seems to think, that, if foreigners in another country make a contract according to the law of their own country (both belonging to the same country), in such a case, the contract will avail in their own country, even if not made according to the *lex loci contractûs* 1 Hertii Opera, De Collis. Legum. § 10, p. 126, 128. So is Voet. de Statut. § 9, ch. 2, Excep. 4, p. 268. But Boullenois has observed, that he does not find any authors, who are of opinion, that such a contract made elsewhere, according to the law of their own country, ought to have place even beyond the country. 2 Boullenois, 459.

2 1 Émér. Assur. ch. 4, § 8, p. 122, 125, 128. See Casaregis, Disc. 179, § 60; Erskine's Inst. B. 3, tit. 2, § 39, 40, p. 514, 515; Delvalle *v.* Plomer, 3 Camp. R. 444; Harrison *v.* Sterry, 5 Cranch, 289; Le Roy *v.* Crowninshield, 2 Mason R. 15; Van Reimsdyke *v.* Kane, 1 Gallis. R. 371; 2 Kent Comm. Lect. 37, p. 394, Lect. 39, p. 458 to 460, (2d edit.) — "Quod si de ipso contractu quæratur (says P. Voet), seu de naturâ

First, as to the nature of the contract; by which is meant those qualities, which properly belong to it, and by law or custom always accompany it, or inhere in it.[1] Such qualities foreign jurists are accustomed to call *naturalia contractûs; ea enim, quæ autoritate legis vel consuetudinis contractum comitantur, eidem adherent. Lex enim altera est quasi natura, et in naturam transit.*[2] Thus, whether a contract be a personal obligation or not; conditional or absolute; principal or accessary; of principal or of surety; of limited or universal operation; these are points properly belonging to its nature, and dependent upon the law and custom of the place of the contract, whenever there are no express terms in the contract itself. By the law of some countries, there are certain joint contracts, which bind each party for the whole, *in solido;* and there are other joint contracts, where the parties are, under circumstances, bound only for individual portions. In each case the law regulates the nature of the con-

---

ipsius, seu de iis, quæ ex naturâ contractûs veniunt, puta fidejussione, etc. etiam spectandum est loci statutum, ubi contractus celebratur; quod ei contrahentes semet accommodare præsumantur." P. Voet. De Stat. § 9, ch. 2, § 10, p. 269. J. Voet. is still more full on the same point. Voet. ad Pand. Lib. 14, tit. 1, § 29.

1 Pothier, as well as other jurists, distinguish between the essence, the nature, and the accidents of contracts; the former includes whatever is indispensable to the constitution of it; the next, whatever is included in it, without being expressly mentioned by operation of law, but is capable of a severance without destroying it: and the last, those things, which belong to it only by express agreement. Without meaning to contest the propriety of this division, I am content to include the two former in the single word, nature, as quite conformable to our English idiom. Cujas also adopts the same course. See Pothier, Oblig. n. 5. See also 2 Boullenois, 460, 461, 462; Bayou *v.* Vayasseur, 10 Martin R. 61; Merlin, Répertoire, Convention, § 2, n. 6, p. 357.

2 2 Boullenois, 460; Voet. De Statut. § 9, ch. 10, § 10, p. 287.

tract, in the absence of express stipulations.[1] These may be said to constitute the nature of the contract.[2]

§ 264. An illustration may be taken from a case often put by the civilians. By the law of some countries a warranty is implied in all cases of sale; by that of others, it is not. Suppose a contract of sale is made in the former, by parties domiciled in the latter. If the contract is to be executed in the country, where it is made, a warranty will be implied, as an incident arising from the nature of the contract; if it is to be executed in the place of the domicil of the parties, for reasons, which we shall presently see, no warranty will be implied.[3] By the civil law, there is an implied warranty, as to the quality and soundness of goods sold; by the common law, there is not.[4] A sale of goods in England, would be governed by the common law; a sale in a foreign country, under the civil law, would be governed by that law, as to implied warranty.

§ 265. Another illustration may be borrowed from an actual decision under the common law. By the

---

1 Pothier on Oblig. n. 261 to 268; Van Leeuwen Comm. B. 4, ch. 4, § 1; Fergusson *v.* Flower, 16 Martin R. 312; 2 Boullenois, 463; Code Civil of France, art. 1197, 1202, 1220, 1222; Id. Code of Comm. art. 22, 140.—One may see, how strangely learned men will reason on subjects of this nature, by consulting Boullenois. He puts the case of a contract made in a country, where all parties would be bound *in solido*, and by the law of their own domicil, they would be entitled to the benefit of a division, and *vice versâ*; and asks, What law is to govern? In each case he decides, that the law should govern, which is most favourable to the debtor. "Ainsi, les obligés solidaires ont contracté sous une loi, qui leur est favorable; j'embrasse cette loi; elle leur est contraire, j'embrasse la loi de leur domicile." 2 Boullenois, 463, 464. See also Bouhier, ch. 21, § 198, 199.

2 See Henry on Foreign Law, 39.

3 Pothier, Oblig. n. 7; 2 Boullenois, 475, 476; Id. 460 to 463; Code Civil of France, art. 1135; Voet. De Statut. § 9, ch. 2, § 10, p. 269.

4 Pothier, Pand. Lib. 19, tit. 1, art. 5, § 48 to 51; 2 Black. Comm. 451; 2 Kent Comm. Lect. 39, p. 478 to 481, (2d edition.)

law of England an acceptance of a bill of exchange binds the acceptor to payment at all events. By the law of Leghorn, if a bill be accepted, and the drawer fails, and the acceptor has not sufficient effects of the drawer in his hands at the time of acceptance, the acceptance becomes void. An acceptance in Leghorn is governed by this law; and under such circumstances it has been held void.[1]

§ 266. Secondly, the obligation of the contract, which, though often confounded with, is distinguishable from, its nature.[2] The obligation of a contract is the duty to perform it, whatever may be its nature. It may be moral, or legal, or both. But when we speak of obligation generally, we mean legal obligation, that is, the right to performance, which the law confers on one party, and the corresponding duty of performance, to which it binds the other.[3] This is what the French jurists call *le lien du contrat* (the legal tie of the contract), *onus conventionis*, and the civilians generally, *vinculum juris*, or *vinculum obligationis*.[4] The Institutes of Justinian have thus defined it. *Obligatio est juris vinculum, quo necessitate adstringimur alicujus rei solvendæ secundum nostræ civitatis jura.*[5] A contract may in its nature be purely voluntary, and possess no legal obligation. It may be a mere naked pact. It may possess a legal obligation; but the laws may limit the extent and force of that obligation *in personam*, or *in rem*. It may bind the party personally,

---

1 Burrows *v.* Jemimo, 2 Str. R. 733; 2 Eq. Abr. 526.

2 See 2 Boullenois, 454, 460, 462, 463, 464.

3 See 3 Story Comm. on Constitution, § 1372 to 1379; Ogden *v.* Saunders, 12 Wheaton, 213; Pothier on Oblig. art. 1, n. 1, 173, 174, 175.

4 2 Boullenois, 458, 459, 460.

5 Pothier. Pandect. Lib. 44, tit. 7, P. 1, art. 1, § 1; Inst. Lib. 3, tit. 14; Pothier, Oblig. n. 173, 174.

but not his estate; or it may bind his estate, and not his person. The obligation may be limited in operation or duration; or it may be revocable or dissoluble in certain future events, or under peculiar circumstances.[1]

§ 267. It would be easy to multiply illustrations under this head. Suppose a contract by the law of one country to involve no personal obligation (as was thought to be the law in the case of Melan *v.* Fitzjames),[2] but merely to confer a right to proceed *in rem;* such a contract would be held every where to involve no personal obligation. Suppose, by law, a mortgage for money borrowed, should, in the absence of any express contract to repay, be limited to a mere repayment out of the land, a foreign court would refuse to entertain a suit giving it a personal obligation. Suppose a contract for the payment of the debt of a third person, in a country, where the law subjected such a contract to the tacit condition, that payment must first be sought against the debtor and his estate; that would limit the obligation to a mere accessorial and secondary character; and it would not be enforced in any foreign country, except after a compliance with the requisitions of the local law. Sureties, indorsers, and guarantees, are, therefore, liable every where, only according to the law of the place of the contract. Their obligation, if treated by such local law, as an accessorial, could not any where else be deemed a principal, obligation.[3] So, if by the law of the place of a contract, its obligation is positively and *ex directo* extinguished after a certain period, it cannot be revived by a suit in a foreign

---

[1] See 2 Boullenois, 452, 454; Code Civil of France, art. 1168 to 1196.

[2] 1 Bos. and Pull. 138.

[3] See Pothier on Oblig. n. 407.

country.[1] To use the expressive language of a learned judge, it must be shown, what the laws of the foreign country are, and that they create an obligation, which our laws will enforce.[2]

§ 268. Let us take another case, which has actually passed into judgment. By the common law, heirs are not bound by the simple contract of their ancestor, but only by instruments under seal, declaring them expressly bound. By the law of Louisiana, the heirs are bound upon such simple contracts. If a simple contract is made in a state governed by the common law, it cannot be enforced in Louisiana against the heirs of the debtor, although they are domiciled in Louisiana. The remedy must be sought through the instrumentality of an administration of the assets there.[3]

§ 269. Cases sometimes occur, in which the tribunals of a foreign country are called upon to decide upon the law of another country, where the contract is made; and they misinterpret that law. In such a case, if they discharge the parties from the obligation of the contract, in consequence of such misinterpretation of the law, that discharge will not be held obligatory upon the courts of the country, where the contract was made. A recent case has occurred on this subject. A bill of exchange, drawn in France, and indorsed there, and accepted and payable in England at a banker's, was passed by an indorsee in discharge of an antecedent debt; and upon presentment for payment, it was dishonoured, and the banker's clerk by mistake cancelled the acceptance, and then wrote on it,

1 See Le Roy *v.* Crowninshield, 2 Mason R. 151; Pothier, Oblig. n. 636 to 639; Voet. ad Pand. Lib. tit. 1, § 29, ad finem.

2 Lord Chief J. Eyre, 1 Bos. and Pull. 141.

3 Brown *v.* Richardson, 13 Martin R. 202.

"cancelled by mistake." Afterwards the indorser, who had so passed the bill in discharge of his debt, cited all the parties, and, among others, the creditor and holder of the bill before the tribunals of France, who decreed, that the cancellation operated as a suspension of legal remedies against the acceptor, and consequently discharged the other parties, the indorsers, as well as the drawer. A suit was then brought by the creditor against the debtor-indorser in England; and it was held, that the courts of France had mistaken the law of England, as to the effect of the cancellation; and that the plaintiff was entitled to recover against the defendant the full amount of the debt, notwithstanding the decree in the French courts.[1]

§ 270. Thirdly. The interpretation of contracts. There are certain general rules of interpretation recognised by all nations, which form the basis of all reasoning on the subject of contracts. The object is to ascertain the real intention of the parties in their stipulations; and when these are silent, or ambiguous, to ascertain, what is the true sense of the words used, and what ought to be implied in order to give them full effect. The primary rule in all expositions of this sort is that, so well expressed in the Digest. *In conventionibus contrahentium voluntas potius quam verba spectari placuit.*[2] But in many cases the words used have different meanings in different places by law or by custom; and where the words are themselves ob-

[1] Novelli *v.* Rossi, 2 Barn. and Adolp. 757.

[2] Dig. Lib. 50, tit. 16, l. 219. — Many rules of interpretation are found in Pothier on Obligations, n. 91 to 102; in Fonblanque on Equity, B. 1, ch. 6, § 11 to 20, and notes; 1 Domat, Civil Law, B. 1, tit. 1, § 2; 1 Powell on Contracts, 370 et seq.; Merlin, Répertoire, Convention, § 7, p. 366.

scure or ambiguous, custom and usage in a particular place may give them an exact and appropriate meaning. Hence, the rule has found admission into almost all, if not all, systems of jurisprudence, that, if the common intention of the parties does not appear from the words of the contract, and if it can be interpreted by any custom or usage of the place, where it is made, that course is to be adopted. Such is the rule of the Digest. *Si non appareat, quod actum sit, erit consequens, ut id sequamur, quod in regione, in quâ actum est, frequentatur.*[1] Usage is, indeed, of so much authority in the interpretation of contracts, that a contract is understood to contain the customary clauses, although they are not expressed, according to the known rule, *In contractibus tacite veniunt ea, quæ sunt moris et consuetudinis.*[2] Thus, if a tenant is by custom to have the outgoing crop, he will be entitled to it, though not expressed in the lease.[3] And if a lease is entirely silent as to the time of the tenant's quitting, the custom of the country will fix it.[4] By the law of England, a month means ordinarily in common contracts, as in leases, a lunar month; but in mercantile contracts it means a calendar month. A contract, therefore, made in England for a lease of land for twelve months, would mean a lease for forty-eight weeks only.[5] A promissory note, to pay money in twelve months, would mean in

---

1 Dig. Lib. 50, tit. 17, l. 34; 1 Domat, Civil Law, B. 1, tit. 1, § 2, n. 9; 2 Boullenois, 490.

2 Pothier, Oblig. n. 95; Merlin, Répertoire, Convention, § 7; 2 Kent Comm. Lect. 39, p. 555, (2d edition.)

3 Wigglesworth *v.* Dallison, Doug. R. 201, 207.

4 Webb *v.* Plumer, 2 B. and Ald. 746.

5 2 Black. Comm. 141; Catesby's Case, 6 Coke R. 62; Lacon *v.* Hooper, 6 T. R. 224.

one year, or twelve calendar months.[1] If a contract of either sort were required to be enforced in a foreign country, its true interpretation must be everywhere the same, that is, according to the usage in the country, where the contract was made.

§ 271. The same word, too, has often different significations in different countries. Thus, the term *usance*, which is common enough in negotiable instruments, in some countries means a month, in others, two or more months, and in others, half a month. A note payable at one usance must be construed every where according to the meaning in the country, where the contract is made.[2] There are many other cases illustrative of the same principle. A note made in England for 100 pounds, would mean 100 pounds sterling; a like note made in America, would mean 100 pounds in American currency, which is one fourth less in value. It would be monstrous to contend, that on the English note, sued in America, the less sum only ought to be recovered; and on the American note, sued in England, one third more ought to be recovered.[3]

§ 272. The general rule then is, that, in the interpretation of contracts, the law and custom of the place of the contract is to govern.[4] And it is founded in wisdom, sound policy, and general convenience. Especially, in

---

[1] Chitty on Bills, (8th edit., 1833), p. 406; Lang *v.* Gale, 1 M. and Selw. 111; Cockell *v.* Gray, 3 B. and Bing. 187; Leffingwell *v.* White, 1 John. Cas. 99.

[2] Chitty on Bills, (8th edit. 1833), p. 404, 405. See also 2 Boullenois, 447.

[3] See also Powell on Contracts, 376; 2 Boullenois 498, 503; Henry on Foreign Law, Appendix, 233; Pardessus, Droit Comm. art. 1492.

[4] See Dessau *v.* Humphreys, 20 Martin R. 1, 8, 9, 13, 22, 23, 24; Morris *v.* Eves, 11 Martin R. 730; Courtois *v.* Carpenter, 1 Wash. Cir. R. 376.

interpreting ambiguous contracts, ought the domicil of the parties, the place of execution, the various provisions and expressions of the instrument, and other circumstances, implying a local reference, to be taken into consideration.[1] *Quidvis in dubio pro modo regionis agere et contrahere presumitur.*[2]

§ 273. Boullenois, while he admits the general propriety of the rule, contests its universality. He seems to think (and some other jurists adopt the same opinion), that, where a contract is made between foreigners of the same country, who are not domiciled, but merely transient persons, it might be governed by the law of their own country; and that it applies *a fortiori*, where they are ignorant of the laws of the place, where the contract is made.[3] Without undertaking to say, that the exception may not be well founded in particular cases, as to persons *in transitu*, it may unhesitatingly be said, that nothing but the clearest intention on the part of foreigners, to act upon their own domestic law, ought to change the application of the general rule.[4] And, indeed, even then, if the performance of the contract is to be in the same country, where it is made, it seems difficult, upon principle, to sustain the exception. Huberus has applied the same rule to those, who are domiciled, and to those, who are merely commorant in the place of the contract.[5]

§ 274. Grotius has also affirmed it in a general form. "If," says he, "a foreigner makes a bargain with a native, he shall be obliged by the laws of his state; be-

1 See Landsdowne *v.* Landsdowne, 2 Bligh. Parl. R. 60, 87.

2 Le Brun, Traité de la Communauté, Liv. 1, ch. 2, § 46.

3 2 Boullenois, 457, 458; Id. 495, 496, 497, 501, 502, 503; and note, ante § 263.

4 See Pardessus, Droit Comm. n. 191, 1492; 1 Émérigon, ch. 4, § 8.

5 Huberus, Lib. 1, tit. 3, § 2, 3; ante § 261, note. See Livermore's Diss. p. 46, § 42.

cause he, who enters into a contract in any place, is a subject for the time being, and must be obedient to the laws of that place." [1] Emérigon follows Grotius, and adopts his very language. "A stranger," says he, "who contracts in the territories of a state, is held as a temporary subject of the state, subject to the laws thereof. *L'étranger, qui contracte dans les terres d'un état, est tenu, comme sujet à terres de cet état, de se soumettre aux lois du pays.*[2] Lord Stowell, in a passage in one of his most celebrated judgments, has refused to acknowledge ignorance of the law of a foreign country to be any foundation to release a party from the obligation of a contract made there.[3]

§ 275. Cases, illustrative of the importance of this general rule, may be easily found in the jurisprudence of modern nations. "In some countries," says Boullenois, "the laws give a certain sense and a certain effect to clauses in an instrument, while the laws of another country give a sense and effect more extensive, or more restrained. For example, at Toulouse, the clause, *si sine liberis*, added to a substitution, means a gradual substitution; and in other places, it means only a condition, if other circumstances do not concur." [4] The full effect of this example may be felt only by a civilian. But an analogous one may be put from the common law. A contract in England for, or a conveyance of, an estate to A, and the heirs of his body begotten, would, before the statute *de donis*, have

---

1 Grotius, B. 2, ch. 11, § 5.

2 Émérigon, Diss. ch. 4, § 8, p. 124, 125. See also Casaregis, Disc. 179, n. 60, 61, 62.

3 Dalrymple *v.* Dalrymple, 2 Hagg. Consist. R. 60, 61.

4 2 Boullenois, 447, 518, 519.

been interpreted to mean a contract for, or conveyance of, a conditional fee simple, and, since that statute, of a fee tail.[1] The rights growing out of these different interpretations are, as every common lawyer knows, exceedingly different; and to construe them otherwise, than according to the common law, would defeat the intent of the parties, and uproot the solid doctrines of law. The sense of the terms, and the legal effect of the instrument ought, and it is to be presumed, would be everywhere ascertained by the same mode of interpretation, wherever the point should come directly or indirectly in judgment.

§ 276. The language of marriage contracts and settlements must, in like manner, be interpreted according to the law of the place, where they are contracted. A moment's consideration would teach us the inextricable confusion, which would ensue from disregarding the habitual construction put by courts of law upon instruments of this sort, executed in England, or France, and brought into controversy in other countries. The whole system of interpretation of the clauses of marriage contracts and settlements in England is in a high degree artificial; but it is built upon uniform principles, which could not now be swept away without innumerable difficulties. What could a foreign court do in interpreting the terms, *heirs of the body, children, issue*, connected with other words of limitation, or description, in a marriage settlement or a will made in England? The intricate branch of English jurisprudence, upon which the true exposition of such clauses depends, tasks the exhausting diligence and learning of the highest professional minds; and requires almost the study of a life to master it.[1] Probably the system of interpretation in France does not involve fewer difficulties, dependent upon the nice shades of meaning of words in different connexions, and the necessary complexity of matrimonial rights, and nuptial contracts, and prospective successions.[2] The general rule is in no cases more firmly adhered to, than in cases of nuptial contracts and settlements, which are construed and enforced according to the *lex loci contractûs*.[3]

§ 277. The same rule is also universally acknowledged in relation to commercial contracts.[4] Where the terms of an instrument, executed by foreigners in a foreign country, are free from obscurity, it will be construed according to the obvious import of those terms, unless there is some proof, that, according to the law of the foreign country, the true interpretation of them would be different.[5] But where a particular interpretation is established, that must be followed. Indeed, the courts of every country must be presumed to be the best expositors of their own laws, and of the terms of contracts made with reference to them. And no court on earth, professing to be governed by principle, would assume the power to declare, that a foreign court misunderstood the laws of their own country, or the operation of them on contracts made there.[6]

---

1 See Fearne on Contingent Remainders, passim.

2 See 2 Boullenois 489 to 494, 503, 504, 505, 513; Martyn *v.* Fabrigas, Cowper R. 174.

3 Feaubert *v.* Turst, Prec. ch. 207; De Couche *v.* Savatier, 3 John. Ch. R. 190.

4 Pardessus, Droit Comm. n. 191, 1492; 2 Kent Comm. Lect. 39, p. 457, 458, (2d edition.)

5 King of Spain *v.* Machado, 4 Russell R. 225.

6 Elmendorf *v.* Tayler, 10 Wheaton R. 159; Saul *v.* His Creditors, 17 Martin R. 587.

§ 278. The remarks upon this rule cannot be better enforced, than by a quotation from an opinion of the late learned Chief Justice Parker. "That the laws of any state cannot, by any inherent authority, be entitled to respect extraterritorially, or beyond the jurisdiction of the state, which enacts them, is the necessary result of the independence of distinct sovereignties. But the courtesy, comity, or mutual convenience of nations, amongst which commerce has introduced so great an intercourse, has sanctioned the admission and operation of foreign laws relative to contracts. So, that it is now a principle generally received, that contracts are to be construed and interpreted according to the laws of the state, in which they are made, unless from their tenor it is perceived, that they were entered into with a view to the laws of some other state. And nothing can be more just than this principle. For when a merchant of France, Holland, or England, enters into a contract in his own country, he must be presumed to be conusant of the laws of the place, where he is, and to expect, that his contract is to be judged of and carried into effect according to those laws; and the merchant, with whom he deals, if a foreigner, must be supposed to submit himself to the same laws, unless he has taken care to stipulate for a performance in some other country, or has in some other way excepted his particular contract from the laws of the country, where he is."

§ 279. It has been sometimes suggested, and especially by foreign jurists, that contracts, made between foreigners in a foreign country, ought to be construed according to the law of their own country, whenever they both belong to the same country; and, where they belong to different countries, some controversy has arisen as to the point, whether the law of the domicil of the debtor or creditor ought to prevail. Where a contract is made in a country between a citizen and a foreigner, it seems admitted, that the law of the place, where the contract is made, ought to prevail, unless the contract is to be performed elsewhere.[1] In the common law all these niceties are discarded. Every contract, whether made between foreigners, or between foreigners and citizens, is deemed to be governed by the law of the place, where it is made, and is to be executed.[2]

§ 280. The rules already considered suppose, that the performance of the contract is to be in the place, where it is made, either expressly or by tacit implication. But where the contract is either expressly or tacitly to be performed in any other place, there the general rule is, in conformity to the presumed intention of the parties, that the contract, as to its validity, nature, obligation, and interpretation, is to be governed by the law of the place of performance.[3] This would seem to be a result of natural justice; and the Roman law has (as we have seen) adopted it as a maxim; *Contraxisse unusquisque in eo loco intelligitur, in quo ut solveret, se obligavit.*[4] And again, in the law *Aut ubi quis contraxerit. Contractum autem non utique eo loco intelligitur, quo negotium gestum sit; sed quo solvenda est pecunia.*[4]

---

1 See Livermore's Dissert. § 42, p. 46; 1 Hertii Opera, De Collis. Leg. § 10, p. 126, 128; Voet. De Statut. § 9, ch. 2, Excep. 4, p. 268. But see contra; 2 Boullenois, 459; Ante § 273, 274.

2 Smith *v.* Meade, 3 Connect. R. 253; De Sobry *v.* De Laistre, 2 Harr. and John. R. 193, 228.

3 2 Kent Comm. Lect. 37, p. 393, 394, and Lect. 39, p. 459, (2d edit.); Casaregis. Disc. 179; 1 Émérigon, c. 4, § 8; Voet. De Stat. § 9, ch. 2, § 15; Boullenois, Quest. Contr. des Lois, p. 330, &c.

4 Dig. Lib. 44, tit. 7, l. 21; Id. Lib. 42, tit. 5.

§ 281. Voet has laid down the same rule. *Hinc ratione effectûs et complementi ipsius contractûs spectatur ille locus, in quem destinata est solutio; id quod ad modum, mensuram, usuras, et negligentiam, et moram post contractum initum accedentem, referendum est.*[1] So that, according to him, if a contract is for money or goods, the value is to be ascertained at the place of performance, and not at the place, where the contract is made.[2] And the same rule applies to the weight or measure of things, if there be a diversity in the different places.[3] Huberus adopts the same exposition. *Verum tamen non ita præcise respiciendus est locus, in quo contractus est initus, ut, si partes alium in contrahendo locum respexerint, ille non potius considerandus.*[4] And, indeed, it has the general consent of foreign jurists.[5] The same rule has been adopted both in England and America. In one of the earliest cases, Lord Mansfield stated the doctrine with his usual clearness. "The law of the place can never be the rule, where the transaction is entered into with an express view to the law of another country, as the rule, by which it is to be governed."[6] And it has uniformly been recognised as correct.[7]

§ 282. But although the general rule is so well es-

---

1 Voet. De Stat. § 9, ch. 2, p. 270, § 11, 14, 15, 16.

2 Voet. Id. p. 271, § 15.

3 Id. p. 271, § 16.

4 Huberus, Lib. 1, tit. 3, § 10.

5 2 Boullenois, 488; 1 Hertii Op. De Collis. Leg. § 4, n. 53, p. 147; Voet. ad Pand. Lib. 4, tit. 1, § 29.

6 Robinson *v.* Bland, 2 Burr. R. 1077, 1078.

7 Ludlow *v.* Van Rensselaer, 1 John. R. 94; Thompson *v.* Ketcham, 8 John. R. 189; Fanning *v.* Conseequa, 17 John. R. 511; Powers *v.* Lynch, 3 Mass. R. 77; 4 Cowen Rep. 510, note; Van Reimsdyk *v.* Kane, 1 Gall. R. 371; Cox and Dick. *v.* U. S. 6 Peters, 172, 203; 2 Fonbl. Eq. B. 5, ch. 1, § 6 and note; Prentiss *v.* Savage, 13 Mass. R. 20, 23, 24.

tablished, the application of it in many cases is not unattended with difficulties; for it is often a matter of serious question, in cases of a mixed nature, which rule ought to prevail, the law of the place, where the contract is made, or that of the place, where it is to be performed.[1] In general, it may be said, that, if no place of performance is stated, or the contract may indifferently be performed any where, it ought to be referred to the *lex loci contractûs*. But there are many cases, where this rule will not be a sufficient guide; and as the subject is important in its practical bearing, it may be well to illustrate it by some cases.

§ 283. One of the most simple cases is, where two merchants, doing business with each other, reside in different countries, and have mutual accounts of debt and credit with each other for advances and sales. What rule is to be followed as to the balance of accounts from time to time between them? Is it the law of the one country, or of the other, if there is a conflict of laws? If the transactions are all on one side, as in case of sales and advances by a commission merchant in his own country for his principal abroad; there, the contracts may well be referred to the country of the commission merchant, and the balance be deemed due

---

1 See 2 Kaims, Eq. B. 3, ch. 8, § 4; Voet. De Statut. § 9, ch. 2, § 10. — Hertius puts some questions under this head. A condition is added to a contract in Belgium, which is performed by the debtor in Germany; if the laws of the countries are different, which are to prevail? Hertius says, those of Belgium, because the condition performed relates back to the time of making the contract. Again, a contract made in one place is confirmed in another; what laws are to govern? He answers, if the confirmation is to give greater *credit* to the contract, as putting it in writing for the sake of proof, the law of the place of the contract is to prevail. If to give *validity* to the contract, the law of the place of the confirmation.*

* 1 Hertii Opera, De Collis. Leg. p. 147, § 54, 55.

according to its laws.[1] For, although it may be truly said, that the debt is due from the principal, and he is generally expected to pay it, where he dwells; yet it is equally true, that the debt is due, where the advances are made, and payment may be insisted on there.

§ 284. But suppose the advances have been made in the country of the principal, and the goods sold in the other country; is the same rule to prevail? Or, are the advances to be governed by the law of the place, where advanced, and the sales of the goods, by that of the place, where received by the commission merchant? Suppose both the merchants, in different countries, sell goods and make advances mutually for each other; and upon the accounts a balance is due from one to the other; by the law of what place is such balance to be ascertained and paid? In these and many other like mixed cases, the amount of the balance, and the true principle of the adjustment of the mutual accounts, may materially depend upon the operation of the *lex loci*, when that of one conflicts with the other. The habits of business and trade between the parties may sometimes decide the points; but if none are established, the cases must be reasoned out upon principle. And, upon principle, it may perhaps be found most easy to decide, that each transaction is to be governed by the law of the place, where it originated; advances by the law of the place, where advanced; and sales of goods by the law of the place, where received.[2] The importance of the true rule is peculiarly felt in all cases of interest to be paid on balances.

---

1 Coolidge *v.* Poor, 15 Mass. R. 427; Conseequa *v.* Fanning, 3 John. Ch. R. 587, 610. See also Bradford *v.* Harvard, 13 Mass. R. 18; Milne *v.* Moreton, 6 Binn. R. 353, 359, 365.

2 See Conseequa *v.* Fanning, 3 John. Ch. R. 587, 610; 17 John. R. 511; Casaregis Disc. 179.

§ 285. Another case may serve to illustrate this doctrine. A merchant in America orders goods to be purchased for him in England. In which country is the contract to be deemed complete, and by the laws of which is it to be governed? Casaregis has affirmed, that in such a case the law of England ought to govern, for there the final assent is given by the person, who receives and executes the order of his correspondent. *Pro hujus materiæ declaratione præmittenda est regula ab omnibus recepta, quod contractus vel negotium inter absentes gestum dicatur eo loco, quo ultimus in contrahendo assentitur, sive acceptat, quia tunc tantum uniuntur ambo consensus.*[1] This doctrine, so reasonable in itself, has been expressly affirmed by the Supreme Court of Louisiana.[2] It has also received sanction in a recent case in the House of Lords, where the Lord Chancellor said, "If I, residing in England, send down my agent to Scotland, and he makes contracts for me there, it is the same, as if I myself went there, and made them.[3]

§ 286. And if a like contract of purchase is made by an agent without orders, and the correspondent ratifies it, Casaregis says, "that the contract is not to be deemed a contract in the country of the ratification, but of the purchase; because the ratification has reference back to the time and place of the purchase." *Ratio est, quia ille ratificationis consensus, licet emittatur in loco ratificantis, et ibi videatur se unire cum altero precedenti gerentis consensu, qui venit a loco gerentis ad locum ratificantis, retro trahitur ad tempus et ad locum,*

---

[1] Casaregis Disc. 179, § 1, 2. See 1 Hertii Opera, De Collis. Leg. p. 147, § 56.

[2] Whiston *v.* Stodder, 8 Martin R. 93.

[3] Pattison *v.* Mills, 1 Dow and Clarke R. 342.

in quo fuit per gestorem initus contractus emptionis.[1] So, a like rule applies, if a merchant in one country agrees to accept a bill drawn on him by a person in another country. It is deemed a contract in the place, where the acceptance is to be made.[2] Voet adopts the same conclusion. *Quid si de literis cambii incedat questio, Quis locus spectandus? Is spectandus est locus ad quem destinatæ, et ibidem acceptatæ.*[3]

§ 287. Another class of cases may be stated. A merchant in one country sends a letter to a merchant in another, requesting him to purchase goods, and to draw on him for the amount of the purchase money by bills. In which country is the contract, if the purchase is made, to be deemed made? Is it in the country, where the letter is written, and on which the drafts are authorized to be drawn? Or where the goods are purchased? The decision has been, that when such advances are made, the undertaking is to replace the money at the same place; and, therefore, the party advancing will be entitled to interest on the advances according to the law of the place of the advances.[4] So, if advances are made for a foreign merchant at his request, or security given for a debt in like manner, the party paying or advancing is entitled to repayment in the place of the advances or security given, unless some other place is stipulated.[5] So, where a loan is made in one state, and security is to be given therefor in another state by way of mortgage; it may be asked, what law is to govern in relation to the contract and

1 Casaregis Disc. 179, § 20, 64, 76 to 80, 83.
2 Boyce v. Edwards, 4 Peters R. 111.
3 P. Voet. De Statut. § 9, ch. 2, § 14.
4 Lanusse v. Barker, 3 Wheaton R. 101, 146.
5 Bayle v. Zacharie, 6 Peters, 635, 643, 644.

its incidents? The decision has been, that the law of the place, where the loan is made is to govern; for the mere taking of foreign security does not (it is said) necessarily alter the locality of the contract. Taking such security does not necessarily draw after it the consequence, that the contract is to be fulfilled, where the security is taken. The legal fulfilment of a contract of loan on the part of the bondsman is repayment of the money; and the security given is but the means of securing, what he has contracted for, which, in the eye of the law, is to pay, where he borrows, unless another place of payment be expressly designated by the contract.[1] But if the mortgage is actually to be executed in a foreign country, and the money is to be paid there, the loan will be deemed to be there completely made, although the money may have been actually advanced elsewhere.[2]

§ 288. A case somewhat different in its circumstances, but illustrative of the principle, occurred formerly in England. By a settlement made upon the marriage of A in England, a term of five hundred years was created upon estates in Ireland, in trust to raise £12,000 for the portions of daughters. The parties to the settlement resided in England; and a question

---

1 De Wolf v. Johnson, 10 Wheaton R. 367, 383. See also Ranelagh v. Champant, 2 Vern. R. 395, and Raithby's note; Conner v. Bellamont, 2 Atk. 382, Post § 293.

2 De Wolf v. Johnson, 10 Wheaton R. 367; Hosford v. Nichols, 1 Paige R. 221. — Whether a contract, made in one state, for the sale of lands situate in another state, on credit, reserving interest at the legal rate of interest of the state, where the lands lie, but more than that of the state, where the contract is made, would he usurious, has been much discussed in the state of New York. In Van Schaick v. Edwards, 2 John. Cas. 355, the judges were divided in opinion upon the question. See also Hosford v. Nichols, 1 Paige R. 220, and Deevar v. Span, 3 T. R. 425.

afterwards arose, whether the £12,000 charged on the term should be paid in England, without any abatement or deduction for the exchange from Ireland to England. It was decided, that the portion ought to be paid, where the contract was made, and the parties resided, and not in Ireland, where the lands lay, which were charged with the payment; for it was a sum in gross, and not a rent issuing out of the land.[1]

§ 289. Let us take another case. A merchant resident in Ireland sends to England certain bills of exchange, with blanks for the dates, sums, times of payment, and names of the drawees. These bills are signed by the merchant in Ireland, indorsed with his name, and dated from a place in Ireland, and are transmitted to a correspondent in England, with authority to him to fill up the remaining parts of the instrument. The correspondent in England accordingly fills them up. Are the bills, when thus filled up, and issued, to be deemed English or Irish contracts? It has been held, that they are to be deemed Irish contracts, and of course to be governed, as to stamps and other legal requisitions, by the law of Ireland; and that, as soon as they were filled up, the whole transaction related back to the time of the original signature of the drawer.[2] And one of the court said, that if the drawer had died, while the bills were on their passage, and they were afterwards filled up and negotiated to an innocent indorser, the personal representatives of the drawer would be bound.

---

1 Phipps v. Earl of Anglesea, 5 Vin. Abridg. 209, pl. 8; 2 Eq. Abridg. 220, pl. 1; Id. 754, pl. 3; 1 P. Will. 696; 2 Bligh. Parl. R. 88, 89. See also Lansdowne v. Lansdowne, 2 Bligh Parl. R. 60; Stapleton v. Conway, 3 Atk. 327; S. C. 1 Ves. 427.

2 Snaith v. Mingay, 1 M. and Selw. 87.

§ 290. Bonds for the faithful discharge of the duties of office are often given with sureties, by officers, to the government of the United States; and it sometimes happens, that the bonds are executed by the principals in one state, and by the sureties in a different state. What law is in such cases to regulate the contract? The rights and duties of sureties are known to be different in different states. In Louisiana one system prevails, deriving itself mainly from the civil law; in other states a different system prevails, founded on the common law. It has been decided, that the bonds in such cases must be treated, as delivered, and to be performed, at the seat of the government of the Union, upon the ground, that the principal is bound to account there; and, therefore, by necessary implication, all the parties look to that, as the place of performance, by the law of which they are to be governed.[1]

§ 291. The question also often arises in cases respecting the payment of interest. The general rule is, that interest is to be paid on contracts according to the law of the place, where they are to be performed, in all cases where interest is expressly or impliedly to be paid.[2]

---

[1] Cox and Dick *v.* U. States, 6 Peters R. 172, 202; Duncan *v.* U. States, 7 Peters R. 435.

[2] Conner *v.* Bellamont, 2 Vern. R. 382; Cass *v.* Kennion, 11 Vesey R. 314; Robinson *v.* Bland, 2 Burr. R. 1077; Ekins *v.* East India Company, 1 P. W. 395; Ranelagh *v.* Champant, 2 Vern. R. 395, and note, ibid, by Raithby; 1 Chitty on Comm. and Manuf. ch. 12, p. 650, 651; 3 Chitty, Id. ch. 1, p. 109; Eq. Abridg. Interest, E.; Henry on Foreign Law, 43, note; Id. 53; 2 Kaims, Equity, B. 3, ch. 8, § 1; 2 Fonbl. Eq. B. 5, ch. 1, § 6, and note; Ridgman's Equity Digest, Interest, vii; Fanning *v.* Conseequa, 17 John. R. 511; S. C. 3 John. Ch. R. 610; Hosford *v.* Nichols, 1 Paige R. 220; Houghton *v.* Page, 2 N. Hamp. R. 42; Peacock *v.* Banks, 1 Minor. R. 387. — A case illustrative of this principle, recently occurred before the House of Lords. A widow in Scotland entered into an obligation to pay the whole of her deceased husbands debts. It was held, by the Court of Session in Scotland, that

Thus, a note made in Canada, where interest is six per cent. payable with interest, in England, where it is five per cent. bears English interest only.[1] Loans made in a place bear the interest of that place, unless payable elsewhere.[2] And, on this account, a contract for a loan

the English creditors, on contracts made in England, were entitled to recover interest in all cases, where the law of England gave interest, and not, where it did not. Therefore, on bonds, and bills of exchange, interest was allowed, and on simple contracts, not. And this decision was affirmed by the House of Lords. Montgomery *v.* Budge, 2 Dow and Clarke's Rep. 297.

The case of Arnott *v.* Redfern (2 Carr. and Payne, 88) may at first view seem inconsistent with the general doctrine. There, the original contract was made in London between an Englishman and a Scotchman. The latter agreed to go to Scotland as agent four times a year, to sell goods, and collect debts for the other party, remit the money, and guaranty one fourth part of the sales; and he was to receive one per cent. upon the amount of sales, &c. The agent sued for a balance of his account in Scotland, and the Scotch Court allowed him interest on it. The judgment was afterwards sued in England; and the question was, whether interest ought to be allowed. Lord Chief Justice Best said, "Is this an English transaction? For, if it is, it will be regulated by the rules of English law. But, if it is a Scotch transaction, then the case will be different." He afterwards added, "This is the case of a Scotchman, who comes into England, and makes a contract. As the contract was made in England, although it was to be executed in Scotland, I think it ought to be regulated according to the rules of the English law. This is my present opinion. These questions of international law do not often occur." And he refused interest, because it was not allowed by the law of England. The court afterwards ordered interest to be given, upon the ground, that the balance of such an account would carry interest in England. But Lord Chief Justice Best rightly expounded the contract, as an English contract, though there is a slight inaccuracy in his language. So far as the principal was concerned, the contract to pay the commission was to be performed in England. The services of the agent were to be performed in Scotland. But the whole contract was not to be executed exclusively there by both parties. A contract, made to pay money in England, for services performed abroad, is an English contract, and will carry English interest.

1 Scofield *v.* Day, 20 John. R. 102.

2 De Wolf *v.* Johnson, 10 Wheaton R. 367, 383; Conseequa *v.* Willing, Peter's Cir. R. 225; 2 Boullenois, 477, 478.

in a foreign country may stipulate for interest higher than that allowed at home.[1] If the contract for interest be illegal there, it will be illegal everywhere.[2] But if it be legal, where it is made, it will be of universal obligation, even in places, where a lower interest is prescribed by law.

§ 292. The question, therefore, whether a contract is usurious or not, depends not upon the rate of the interest allowed, but upon the validity of that interest in the country, where the contract is made, and is to be executed. A contract made in England for advances to be made at Gibraltar, at a rate of interest beyond that of England, would, nevertheless, be valid in England; and so a contract to allow interest upon credits in Gibraltar at such higher rate, in favour of an English creditor.[3]

§ 293. And in cases of this sort, it will make no difference (as we have seen), that the due performance of the contract is secured by a mortgage or other security upon property situate in another country,

---

[1] 2 Kent Comm. Lect. 39, p. 461, (2d edition); Hosford *v.* Nichols, 1 Paige R. 220; Houghton *v.* Page, 2 N. Hamp. R. 42; Thompson *v.* Powles, 2 Simons R. 194.

[2] 2 Kaims Equity, B. 3, ch. 8, § 1; Hosford *v.* Nichols, 1 Paige R. 220; 2 Boullenois, 477. — In the case of Thompson *v.* Powles (2 Simons R. 194), the Vice-Chancellor said, "In order to have the contract (for stock) usurious, it must appear, that the contract was made here, and that the consideration for it was to be paid here." See also Yrisarri *v.* Clement, 2 Carr. and Payne R. 223.

In Hosford *v.* Nichols (1 Paige R. 220), where a contract was made for the sale of lands in New York, by citizens then resident there, and the vender afterwards removed to Pennsylvania, where the contract was consummated, and a mortgage given to secure the unpaid purchase money with New York interest (which was higher than that of Pennsylvania), the Court thought the mortgage not usurious, it being only a consummation of the original bargain made in New York.

[3] Harvey *v.* Archbold, 1 Ryan and Mood. R. 184.

where the interest is lower. For it is collateral to such contract, and the interest reserved being according to the law of the place, where the contract is made, and to be executed, there does not seem to be any valid objection to giving collateral security elsewhere, to enforce and secure the due performance of a legal contract.[1] But, suppose a debt is contracted in one country, and afterwards, in consideration of farther delay, the debtor in another country enters into a new contract for the payment of interest upon the debt at a higher rate, than that allowed by the country, where the original debt was contracted, but not higher than that allowed by the law of the country, where it is so stipulated; it may be asked, whether such stipulation is valid? It has been decided, that it is.[2] On the other hand, suppose the interest so stipulated is according to the rate of interest allowed in the country, where the debt was contracted, but higher than that in the country, where the new contract is made; is the stipulation invalid? It has been decided, that it is.[3] In each of these cases the *lex loci contractûs* governs as to the proper rate of interest.

§ 294. In cases of express contracts for interest foreign jurists generally hold the same doctrine. Dumoulin, and after him Boullenois says, *In concernentibus contractum et emergentibus tempore contractûs, spectatur locus, in quo contrahitur.*[4] And hence the

---

1 Conner *v.* Bellamont, 2 Atk. 382; Stapleton *v.* Conway, 3 Atk. 727; 1 Vesey 427; De Wolf *v.* Johnson, 11 Wheaton R. 367, 383.

2 Conner *v.* Bellamont, 2 Atk. 382. See also Hosford *v.* Nichols, 1 Paige R. 220.

3 Dewar *v.* Span, 3 T. R. 435. See also Stapleton *v.* Conway, 3 Atk. 382; S. C. 1 Vesey, 427.

4 2 Boullenois, 472; Henry on Foreign Law, p. 53; Boullenois Quest. de la Contr. des Lois, p. 330 to 338.

latter deduces the validity of all contracts expressly made according to the *lex loci*. But, where there is no express contract, and interest is to be implied, foreign jurists are not so well agreed.[1] Some contend, that, if the contract is between foreigners, the law of interest of the domicil of the creditor ought to prevail; and others, that that of the debtor ought to prevail.[2]

§ 295. Boullenois is of opinion, that, where there is no express contract, the interest, for which a delinquent debtor is tacitly liable, on account of his neglect to pay the debt, is the interest allowed by the law of the place, where the debt is payable; because it is there, that the interest has its origin. And, in this, he follows the doctrine of Everard, who says, *Quia ubi certus locus solutionis faciendæ destinatus est, tunc non factâ solutione in termino et loco præfixo, mora dicitur contrahi in loco destinatæ solutionis, non in loco celebrati contractûs.* Strykius holds the same opinion. *Si lis oritur ex post facto, propter negligentiam et moram, consideratur locus, ubi mora contracta est.*[3] Boullenois puts a distinction, which also deserves notice, between cases, where the debt (for money loaned) is payable at a fixed day, and where no day is fixed for payment, but it is at the pleasure of the creditor, and no place of payment is mentioned. In the former case, he holds, that the debtor is bound, in order to avoid default, to seek the creditor and pay him; and therefore the neglect to make payment arises in the domicil of the creditor, and interest ought to be allowed according to the law of that place. In the latter case the creditor

---

1 2 Boullenois, 472, 477 to 479, 496.

2 Id.; Bouhier, Cout. de Bourg. ch. 21, § 194 to 199; Livermore's Dissert. p. 46, 47, § 42.

3 2 Boullenois, 477; Henry on Foreign Law, p. 53.

is to demand payment of the debtor; and, the neglect of payment is in the domicil of the debtor, and, therefore, interest ought to be allowed according to the law of his domicil. And, if, between the time of contracting the debt, and the demand of the creditor, the debtor has changed his domicil, Boullenois is of opinion, that, if the demand is in the new domicil, interest for neglect of payment should be according to the law of the latter; especially if the change of domicil is known to the creditor. And he applies the same rule to a case, where, by the law of the old domicil, a simple demand only is required, and, by the law of the new domicil, a demand by judicial process is necessary.[1] The distinction does not appear to have any foundation in our jurisprudence; for, whether the debt be payable at a fixed day, or upon demand of the creditor, if no place of payment is prescribed, the contract takes effect, as a contract of the place, where it is made; and, being payable generally, it is payable every where, and after a demand and refusal of payment, interest will be allowed according to the law of the place of the contract.

§ 296. It may, therefore, be laid down as a general rule, that, by the common law, the *lex loci contractûs* will, in all cases, give the rule of interest, following out the doctrine of the civil law; *Quum judicio bonæ fidei disceptatur, arbitrio judicis usurarum modus, ex more regionis, ubi contractum, constituitur; ita tamen ut legi non offendat.*[2] And if the place of performance is

---

1 2 Boullenois, 477, 478, 479.

2 Dig. Lib. 22, tit. 1, l. 1; Id. l. 37; 1 Eq. Abr. Interest, E.; Champant *v.* Ranelagh, Prec. ch. 128; De Sobry *v.* De Laistre, 2 Harr. and John. R. 193, 228.

different from that of the contract, the interest will be according to that of the former.[1]

§ 297. But, clear as the general rule, as to interest, is, there are cases, in which its application will be found not without embarrassments. Thus, where a consignor in China consigned goods for sale in New York, and delivered them to the agent of the consignee in China, and the proceeds were to be remitted to the consignor in China, and there was a failure to remit, the question arose, whether interest was to be computed according to the rate in China, or in New York. Mr. Chancellor Kent held, that it should be according to the rate in China. But the Appellate Court reversed his decree, and decided in favour of the sale in New York. Each Court admitted the general rule, that the interest should be according to the law of the place of performance, where no express interest is stipulated. But the Court of Chancery thought, that the delivery of the goods being in China, and the remittance being to be made there, the contract was not complete, until the remittance arrived, and was paid there. The Appellate Court thought, that the delivery of the goods in China, to be sold at New York, was not distinguishable in principle from a delivery at New York; and, that the remittance would be complete, in the sense of the contract, the moment the money was put on board the proper conveyance in New York for China; and it was then at the risk of the consignor. The duty

---

1 2 Kent Comm. Lect. 39, p. 460, (2d edit.); Robinson *v.* Bland, 2 Burr. R. 1077; Ekins *v.* East India Company, 1 P. W. 396; Boyce *v.* Edwards, 4. Peters R. 111; 2 Fonbl. Eq. B. 5, ch. 1, § 6; Fanning *v.* Conseequa, 17 John. R. 511; De Sobry *v.* De Laistre, 2 Harr. and John. R. 193, 228; Smith *v.* Mead, 3 Connect. R. 253; Winthrop *v.* Carlton, 12 Mass. R. 4; Foden *v.* Sharp, 4 John. R. 183; Henry on Foreign Law, p. 53.

of remittance was to be performed in New York, and the failure was there; and consequently New York interest only was due.[1]

§ 298. Another case has arisen of a very different character. A note was given in New Orleans, payable in New York, for a large sum, bearing an interest of ten per cent. being the legal interest of Louisiana, the New York legal interest being seven per cent. only. The question was, whether the note was tainted with usury, and therefore void, as it would be, if made in New York. The Supreme Court of Louisiana decided, that it was not usurious; and, that the interest might be stipulated for according to the law of Louisiana, or that of New York. The Court seem to have founded their judgment upon the ground, that in the sense of the general rule, there are, or may be, two places of contract; that, in which it is made; and that, in which it is to be performed; *Locus, ubi contractus celebratus est; locus destinatæ solutionis*; and therefore, that if the law of both places is not violated, the contract for interest will be valid.[2]

§ 299. There is no doubt, that the phrase *lex loci contractûs* may have a double meaning or aspect; and, that it may indifferently indicate the place, where the contract is actually made, or that, where it is virtually made according to the intent of the parties, that is, the place of performance. Everard, as well as other distinguished jurists, refer to this distinction.[3] Voet places it in a strong light. *Ne tamen hic oriatur confu-*

---

1 Conseequa *v.* Fanning, 3 John. Ch. R. 587, 610; S. C. 17 John. R. 511, 520, 521.

2 Depau *v.* Humphreys, 20 Martin R. 1. But see Van Schaike *v.* Edwards, 2 John. Cas. 355.

3 20 Martin R. 22, 23, 24.

sio, locum contractûs duplicem facio; alium, ubi fit, de quo jam dictum; alium, in quem destinata solutio. Illud locum verum, hunc fictum appellat Salicet. *Uterque tamen recte locus dicitur contractûs, etiam secundum leges civiles, licet postremus aliquid fictionis contineat.*[1] But for what purpose do foreign jurists refer to the distinction? Is it, that the validity of the same contract is to be at the same time ascertained in part by the law of one country, and in part by that of another? Let us attend to their own words.[2] *In scripturâ instrumenti, in ceremoniis et solemnitatibus, et generaliter in omnibus, quæ ad formam et perfectionem contractûs pertinent, spectanda est consuetudo regionis, ubi fit negotium. Debet enim servari statutum loci contractûs, quoad hæc, quæ oriuntur secundum statutum ipsius contractûs.*[3] Christinæus says, *Generaliter, in omnibus, quæ ad formam contractûs ejusque perfectionem pertinent, spectanda est consuetudo regionis, ubi fit negotiatio; quia consuetudo influit in contractus, et videtur ad eos respicere, et voluntatem suam eis commodare.*[4] Everard says. *Quoad perfectionem contractûs, seu solemnitatem adesse, seu substantiam ejus requisitam,* semper *inspicitur statutum seu consuetudo loci celebrati contractûs.*[5]

§ 300. Now, it is most manifest, that these writers in these passages speak exclusively, as to the formalities and solemnities and modes of execution of contracts, and hold, that to be good anywhere, the local

---

1 Voet. De Statut. § 9, ch. 2, § 11, p. 270. See also 2 Boullenois, 488; Boullenois, Quest. sur Contr. des Lois, p. 330 to 338.

2 Not having access to the works of Christinæus, Everard, Alexander, or Bartolus, I am compelled to quote them, as I find them, from 20 Martin R. 22, without any aid from the context.

3 20 Martin R. 22, 23. 4 Id. 23. 5 Id. 23.

law must be followed. As they state no exception, they would seem to apply the same rule to contracts to be performed in foreign countries, as in the place of the contract. They do not touch the question, now under consideration, as to the payment of interest. But Everard afterwards adds. *Sed ubi agitur de consuetudine solvendi, vel de iis, quæ veniunt implendi, diu ex post contractum, et in alieno loco impletione destinato, tunc inspicitur locus destinatæ solutionis.*[1] Whenever the question is, as to the usage of payment, or of those things, which are to be performed a long time after the contract, and in another place, where the performance is intended, there the law of the place of payment is to govern.[2] Now, this passage would seem as strictly to apply to the case of a payment of interest, as to the case of a payment of principal. If the parties have not stipulated a particular interest, the usage of the place of payment will certainly govern. If they have stipulated an interest, inconsistent with that of the *lex solutionis*, the question will still remain, whether it can be lawfully done.

§ 301. Bartolus says, *Aut quæris de his, quæ oriuntur secundum formam ipsius contractûs, aut de his, quæ oriuntur ex post facto, propter aut negligentiam vel moram. Primo casu intelligitur locus contractûs; et intelligo locus contractûs ubi celebratur, non ubi collata solutio.*[3] Now, whether Bartolus meant here wholly to repudiate, or not, the distinction above stated, as to the *lex loci contractûs*, and *lex loci solutionis*, is unimportant. He plainly goes no farther than to decide, that contracts, wherever payable, are not valid, except

1 20 Martin R. 25.
2 Id. See also Vidal *v.* Thompson, 11 Martin R. 23.
3 Id. 24.

the forms of the *lex loci celebrati contractûs* are followed.

§ 302. In one passage Burgundus says, that interest is to be allowed according to the place of the contract; and that, if the question comes under consideration in a foreign court, the interest stipulated, though higher than what is lawful by the *lex fori*, ought to be allowed. But where no interest is stipulated, there, the interest is to be *ex morâ*, according to the law of the place of payment.[1] In another place he says, *Idem de solutionibus dicendum, scilicet, ut in omnibus, quæ ex eâ sunt, aut inde oriuntur, aut circa illam consistunt, aut aliquo modo affinia sunt, consuetudinis loci spectemus, ubi eamdem implere convenit.*[2] So, that if this language is to be interpreted in its broad sense, the interest must be according to the law of the place of performance. Burgundus's opinion may be thought of less value, however, because he applies the like rule to prescriptions. *Affinia solutionis sunt præscriptio, oblatio rei debitæ.*[3]

§ 303. Boullenois, has no where, to my knowledge, directly treated the question, whether the interest may be stipulated according to the place of the contract, when payment is to be made in another place, where it would be illegal. The citations, supposed to countenance a different doctrine, put the case only of a rate of interest or annuity, good by the law of the place of the contract (and for aught that appears, payable there), and holds, that it will be good, although different from the law of the domicil of the creditor, or debtor, or even of the property pledged for security.[4]

---

1 20 Martin R. 22, 23, 25. See also Vidal *v.* Thompson, 11 Martin R. 23.

2 2 Boullenois, 488, 498.

3 Id.

4 Id. 472, 473.

§ 304. It may then be affirmed with some confidence, that the foreign jurists, who have been relied on, do not establish the asserted doctrine. On the other hand, there are other foreign jurists, whose doctrines lead to an opposite conclusion. Thus, Voet says, if in one place a stipulation for higher interest is allowed, than is allowed in another, the place, where the contract is made, is to decide, whether it is good, or whether it exceeds that, which is allowable. But we must remember, that, in point of law, that is not properly the place of the contract, where the business is transacted, but where the money is to be paid. But good faith must be observed; and the place of the contract, where higher interest is allowed, must not be sought for the purpose of evading the law. And, he adds, that an hypothecation of property, as security, in another place, where interest is lower, will not vary the rules, for the security will be treated as merely accessorial.[1]

§ 305. It has been said, that, if the principle be, that a contract, valid in the place, where the contract is celebrated, is void, if it is contrary to the law of the place of payment, it must establish the converse proposition, that a contract void by the law of the place, where it is made, is valid, if good by the law of the place of payment.[2] This would seem to be reasonable; and the doctrine is supported by modern cases, notwithstanding the old cases have been supposed to lead to a contrary conclusion. In Connor *v.* Bellamont (2 Atk. 381), a bond was executed in Ireland for a debt contracted in England; and because it constituted a security on lands in Ireland, Lord Chancellor Hard-

---

1 Voet. ad Pand. Lib. 22. tit. 1. § 6; Id. Lib. 4. tit. 1. § 29.

2 20 Martin R. 30.

wicke held, that it was valid, though it bore the Irish interest of seven per cent. But he thought it would have been otherwise, if it had been a simple contract debt; or if the bond had been executed in England.[1] Mr. Chancellor Kent has correctly laid down the modern doctrine, and is fully borne out by the authorities. "The law of the place, (says he,) where the contract is made, is to determine the rate of interest, when the contract specifically gives interest; and this will be the case, though the loan be secured by a mortgage on lands in another state, unless there be circumstances to show, that the parties had in view the law of the latter place in respect to interest. When that is the case, the rate of interest of the place of payment is to govern."[2]

§ 306. But it has been asked, if this be the established doctrine, of what use is it for any legislature to pass a law for the protection of the weak and necessitous?[3] And the case of minors has been mentioned, as exhibiting the inconvenience of the principle. But we have already seen, that minors in one country may lawfully contract in another, in which they are deemed of age.[4] The true answer to all such suggestions is, that no country can give to its own laws an extra-territorial authority, so as to bind other nations. If it undertakes to legislate in regard to acts or contracts performed elsewhere, it can claim for its own laws no other validity, than the comity of other nations may choose to allow

1 Stapleton v. Conway, 3 Atk. 727; S. C. 1 Ves. 427. See Dewar v. Span, 3 T. R. 425.

2 2 Kent Comm. Lect. 39, p. 460, 461, (2d edit.); 10 Wheaton R. 367; 20 John. R. 102; 2 Simon. R. 194; Robinson v. Bland, 2 Burr, 1077.

3 20 Martin R. 30.

4 12 Martin R. 597; Ante § 82.

towards them. It may, if it choose, deem all such acts and contracts valid or invalid, according to its own laws; but it cannot impose a like obligation on other nations.

§ 307. Analogous to the rules respecting interest, would seem to be the rule of damages in cases, where the contract is not strictly pecuniary, or where the right arises *ex delicto*. Thus, if a ship be illegally converted in the East Indies, the interest there will be allowed by way of damages.[1] So, the damages on a bill of exchange will be according to the *lex loci contractûs* of the particular party.[2] So, if a note, made in a foreign country, is for the payment of a certain sum in sugar, and by custom, such notes are payable in sugar at a valuation, the law of the place is to govern in the damages.[3]

§ 308. Where a contract is made in one country, and is payable in the currency of that country, and a suit is afterwards brought in another country, to recover on the contract, a question often arises, as to the manner, in which the amount of the debt is to be ascertained, whether at the existing or established par value of the currencies of the two countries, or according to the rate of exchange between them. For instance, a debt of £100 is contracted in England, and payable there; and afterwards a suit is brought in America for the recovery of the amount. The present par fixed by law between the two countries is, to estimate the pound sterling at four dollars and eighty cents; but the rate

---

1 Ekins *v.* East India Company, 1 P. Will. 395, 396; Conseequa *v.* Willing, Peters Cir. R. 225; Id. 303.

2 Slacum *v.* Pomeroy, 6 Cranch. 221; Hazlehurst *v.* Kean, 4 Yates R. 19; Pothier Oblig. n. 171.

3 Courtois *v.* Carpentier, 1 Was. Cir. R. 376.

of exchange, on bills drawn in America on England, is generally at from 8 to 10 per cent. advance. In a recent case, it was held by the King's Bench, in an action for a debt payable in Jamaica, and sued in England, that the amount should be ascertained by adding the rate of exchange to the par value; and so, *vice versâ*, deducting it, when the exchange is below the par. But this seems to have been against Lord Tenterden's judgment.[1] And it is difficult to reconcile it with the doctrine of some other cases.[2] In a late American case, where the payment was to be in Turkish piastres (but it does not appear from the Report, where the contract was made, or was payable), it was held to be the settled rule "where money is the object of the suit, to fix the value according to the rate of exchange at the time of the trial."[3] It is impossible to say, that a rule laid down in such general terms ought to be deemed of universal application; and cases may easily be imagined, which might justly form exceptions.

§ 309. The proper rule would seem to be, in all cases, to allow that sum in the currency of the country, where the suit is brought, which should approximate most nearly to the amount, to which the party is entitled in the country, where the debt is payable, calculated by the real, and not by the nominal par of exchange.[4]

---

1 Scott *v.* Bevan, 2 Barn. & Adolp. 78. See Delegal *v.* Naylor, 7 Bing. R. 460; Ekins *v.* East India Company, 1 P. Will. 396.

2 See Cockerell *v.* Barber, 16 Ves. 461.

3 Lee *v.* Wilcocks, 5 Serg. & R. 48.

4 In Cash *v.* Kenneon, (11 Vesey R. 314), Lord Eldon held, that if a man, in a foreign country, agrees to pay £100 in London, upon a given day, he ought to have that sum there on that day. And if he fails in that contract, wherever the creditor sues him, the law of that country ought to give him just as much, as he would have had, if the contract had been performed. — J. Voet says, "Si major, alibi minor, eorundem

In some countries there is an established par of exchange by law, as in the United States, where the pound sterling of England, is now valued at four dollars and eighty cents. In other countries, the original par has, by the depreciation of the currency, become merely nominal; and there, we should resort to the real par. And, where there is no established par from a depreciation of the currency, there, the rate of exchange may justly furnish a standard, as the nearest approximation of the relative value of the currencies. And where the debt is payable in a particular known coin, as Sicca rupees, or Turkish piastres, there the mint value of the coin, and not the mere bullion value, in the country, where the coin is issued, would seem to furnish the proper standard, since it is referred to by the parties in their contract.

§ 310. And in all these cases we are to take into consideration the place, where the money is payable; for wherever the creditor may sue for it, he is entitled to have an amount equal to what he must pay, in order to remit it to that country.[1] Thus, if a note were made in England, for £100 sterling, payable in Boston (Mass.), if a suit were brought in Massachusetts, the party would be entitled to recover four hundred and eighty dollars, that being the established par of exchange by our laws. But, if our currency had become depreciated by a debasement of our coinage, then the depreciation ought to be allowed for, so

---

nummorum valor sit, in solutione faciendâ; non tam spectanda potestas pecuniæ, quæ est in loco, in quo contractus celebratus est, quam potius quæ obtinet in regione illâ, in quâ contractus implementum faciendum est." *

[1] See 1 Chitty on Comm. and Manufact. ch. 12, p. 650, 651.

* Voet. ad Pand. Lib. 12. tit. 1. § 25. Henry on Foreign Law 43, note.

as to bring the sum to the real, instead of nominal par.[1] But, if a like note were given in England for £100, payable in England, or payable generally (which in legal effect would be the same thing); there, in a suit in Massachusetts, the party would be entitled to recover, in addition to the four hundred and eighty dollars, the rate of exchange between Massachusetts and England, which is ordinarily from eight to ten per cent. above par. And if the exchange were below par, a proportionate deduction should be made; so that the party would have his money replaced in England at exactly the same amount, which he would be entitled to receive in a suit there.

§ 311. This distinction may, perhaps, reconcile most of the cases, between which, there is, at first view, an apparent contrariety. It was evidently acted on in Dungannon *v.* Hackett,[2] where money, payable in Ireland, was sued for in England; and the Court allowed Irish interest, but directed an allowance to the debtor for the payment of it in England, and not in Ireland. It is presumable, that the money was of less value in Ireland, than in England. A like rule was adopted in Ekins *v.* The East India Company,[3] where money payable in India was recovered in England; and the charge of remitting it from India was directed to be deducted.

---

1 Voet has expressed an opinion upon this subject in general terms. "Quid si in specie de nummorum aut redituum solutione difficultas incedat, si forte valor sit immutatus, an spectabitur loci valor, ubi contractus erat celebratus, an loci, in quem destinata erat solutio? Respondeo, ex generali regulâ, spectandum esse loci statutum, in quem destinata erat solutio." Voet. De Stat. § 9, ch. 2, § 15, p. 271. And he applies the same rule, where contracts are for specific articles, the measures whereof are different in different countries. Id. § 16, p. 271.

2 1 Eq. Cas. Abr. 288, 289.

3 1 Peere Will. 396; S. C. 2 Bro. Par. Cas. 72.

§ 312. In Cockerill *v.* Barber,[1] by a will made in India, a legacy was given of 30,000 Sicca rupees, and the testator afterwards died in England, leaving personal property, both in England and India; upon a suit in chancery for the legacy, the master, to whom it was referred, estimated the Sicca rupees at 2*s.* 6*d.* per Sicca rupee, being the East India Company's rate of exchange between *India* and Great Britain (i. e. on bills drawn in India on Great Britain), at the time the legacy became due. At the same time, the par or sterling value of the Sicca rupees in India and England was 2*s.* 1*d.* per Sicca rupee; and the East India Company's rate of exchange between *Great Britain* and India (i. e. on bills drawn in England on India) was 2*s.* 3*d.* Upon exceptions taken, it was contended, that either the par of exchange, or the rate of exchange between Great Britain and India ought to have been adopted. Lord Eldon said, that in cases of foreign legacies, the Court have directed them "to be computed according to the (real) value of the currency of the country, to which the testator belonged, or where the property was; and no more was done in such cases, than ascertaining the value of so many pounds in the current coin of the country, and paying that amount out of the funds in court. I do not believe the Court have ever said, they would not look at the value of the current coin of the country, but would take it as bullion. At the time of Wood's half-pence in Ireland, whatever was their actual worth, yet payment in England must have been according to their nominal current value, not the actual value. So, whatever was the current value of the rupee at the time, when this legacy ought to be paid, is the ratio, according to

[1] 16 Ves. 461, 465.

which payment must be made here in pounds sterling. If twelve of Wood's half-pence were worth six pence in this Court, six pence must have been the sum paid. *And in a payment in this court, the cost of remittance has nothing to do with it.* So, if the value of 30,000 rupees, at the time the payment ought to have been made in India was £10,000, that is the sum to be paid here, *without any consideration as to the expence of remittance.*" And he accordingly directed the master to review his report, and the legacies to be paid, *according to the current value of the Sicca rupee in Calcutta.*

§ 313. In considering this decision, it is material to observe, that the will was made in India, and, of course, the legacy payable there; and the testator died in England, leaving personal assets in both countries. Under these circumstances, the legatee was not compellable to resort to England for payment of the legacy; but he elected of his own mere choice to receive it there. He might have resorted to India, if he had pleased;[1] and if so, he would have been entitled to the exact amount of 30,000 Sicca rupees, according to their current value there. He ought not, then, by resorting to a court in England to oblige the estate to bear the charge of remittance of the amount to England, which it was charged with by the master's report. Nor ought the estate, upon his mere election to receive the amount in England, to pay for the remittance of the same from England to India. The decree of the Court was, therefore, manifestly right,

---

[1] See Bourke *v.* Ricketts, 10 Ves. 332, and Raithby's Notes to Ranelagh *v.* Champant, 2 Vern. 395; Saunders *v.* Drake, 2 Atk. 466; Stapleton *v.* Conway, 1 Ves. 427.

and consistent with the principles above stated. But the language of the Court does not seem to put the case upon this clear ground; but to put it upon the ground, that the value, at the par of exchange (not indeed nominal, but real), without any reference to the place of payment, or remittance, was, in all cases, the true rule. It admits, however, of some doubt, whether the Court intended to make so general an application of its language, and did not intend to restrain it to the circumstances of the particular case. Suppose the executor in India had remitted all the funds to England, and had become domiciled there, and the legatee had always lived in India; would not the latter, having no other means of getting payment but by a suit in England, have been entitled to the charge of remittance to India? Without expressing any opinion upon the subject, it may, perhaps, be thought worthy of further consideration. And Scott *v.* Bevan,[1] already cited, is certainly at variance with the decision, as a doctrine of universal application.[2]

---

1 2 Barn. & Adolph. 78. See also Delegal *v.* Naylor, 7 Bing. R. 460.

2 In the case of mixed money, in Sir John Davies's Reports, [28], 48, there is a curious discussion, as to the nature and changes of English currency. A bond was given in England for the payment of "£100 sterling, current and lawful money of England," to be paid in Dublin, Ireland; and between the time of giving the bond, and its becoming due, Queen Elizabeth, by proclamation, recalled the existing currency in Ireland, and issued a *new debased coinage* (called mixed money), declaring it to be the lawful currency of Ireland. A tender was made in this debased coin, or mixed coin, in Dublin, in payment of the bond. The question, before the Privy Council of Ireland, was, whether the tender was good, or ought to have been in currency, or value, equal to the current lawful money, then current in England. The Court held the tender good; first, because the mixed money was current lawful of England, Ireland being within the sovereignty of the British crown; and secondly, because the payment being to be in Dublin, it could be made in no other currency, than the existing currency

§ 314. Negotiable Instruments often present questions of a like mixed nature. Thus, suppose a negotiable bill of exchange is drawn in Massachusetts on England, and is indorsed in New York, and again by the first indorsee in Pennsylvania, and by the second in Maryland, and the bill is dishonored; what damages will the holder be entitled to? The law as to damages in these states is different (in Massachusetts 10 per cent., in New York and Pennsylvania 20 per cent., and in Maryland 15 per cent.[1]); what rule then is to govern? The answer is, that, in each case, the *lex loci contractûs.* The drawer is liable, according to the law of the place, where the bill was drawn; and the successive indorsers, according to the law of the place of their indorsement, every indorsement being treated as a new and substantive contract.[2] The consequence is, that the indorser may render himself liable, upon a dishonor of the bill, for a much higher rate of damages, than he can recover from the drawer. But this results from

---

of Ireland, which was the mixed money. The Court do not seem to have considered, that the true value of the *English* current money might, if that was required by the bond, have been paid in Irish currency, though debased, by adding so much more, as would bring it to the par. And it is extremely difficult to conceive, how a payment of current lawful money of *England,* could be interpreted to mean current, or lawful money of *Ireland,* when the currency of each kingdom was different, and the royal proclamation made a distinction between them, the mixed money being declared the lawful currency of Ireland only. Perhaps the desire to yield to the royal prerogative of the Queen a submissive obedience, as to all payments in Ireland, may account for a decision so little consonant with the principles of law in modern times.*

1 3 Kent Comm. Lect. 44, p. 116 to 120, (2d edition.)

2 Powers *v.* Lynch, 3 Mass. R. 77; Prentiss *v.* Savage, 13 Mass. R. 20, 23, 24; Slacum *v.* Pomeroy, 6 Cranch, 221; Depau *v.* Humphreys, 20 Martin R. 1, 14, 15; Hicks *v.* Brown, 12 John. R. 142; Bayley on Bills, chap. A. p. 28, Phillips & Sewall's Edition.

* See Kearney *v.* King, 2 Barn. & Ald. 301; Sprowle *v.* Legg, 1 Barn. & Cres. 16.

his own voluntary contract; and not from any collision arising from the nature of the original contract.[1]

§ 315. It has sometimes been suggested, that this doctrine is a departure from the rule, that the law of the place of payment is to govern.[2] But correctly considered, it is entirely in conformity to the rule. The drawer and indorsers do not contract to pay the money in the foreign place, on which the bill is drawn; but only to guarantee its acceptance, and payment there by the drawee; and in default of such payment, they agree to reimburse the holder, in principal and damages, at the place, where they respectively entered into the contract.[3]

§ 316. Nor is it any departure from the rule to hold, that the time of payment of such a bill is to be according to the law of the place, where it is payable;

---

1 Pardessus has discussed this matter at large. He adopts the general doctrine here stated, that the law of the place of each indorsement is to govern, as each indorsement constitutes a new contract between the immediate parties. And he applies the same rule to damages; and says, that, if the law of the place, where a bill of exchange is drawn, admits of the accumulation of costs and charges on account of re-exchanges (as is the law of some countries), in such a case each successive indorser may become liable to the payment of such successive accumulations, if allowed by the law of the place, where they made their indorsement. He seems, indeed, to press his doctrine farther, and to hold, that, if the law of the place of such indorsement does not allow such accumulation of re-exchanges, but the law of the place, where the bill is drawn, does, the indorsers will be liable to pay, as the drawer would. But his reasoning does not seem satisfactory; and it is certainly inconsistent with the acknowledged doctrines of the common law. Pardessus, Droit Commerc. art. 1500. See, also, Henry on Foreign Laws, 53 Appx. 239 to 242; 3 Kent Comm. Lect. 44, p. 115, (2d edition.)

2 2 Kent Comm. Lect. 39, p. 459, 460; Chitty on Bills, p. 191 to 194, (8th edit. London.)

3 Potter *v.* Brown, 5 East R. 123, 130; Hicks *v.* Brown, 12 John. R. 142; Powers *v.* Lynch, 3 Mass. R. 77; Prentiss *v.* Savage, 13 Mass. R. 20, 24; Pardessus, Droit Comm. art. 1497.

as, that the days of grace are to be allowed, as, by law or custom, they exist there;[1] for such is the appropriate construction of the contract, according to the rule.[2]

§ 317. But suppose a negotiable note is made in one country and payable there, and it is afterwards indorsed in another country, and by the law of the former equitable defences are let in, in favour of the maker, and by the latter excluded; what rule is to govern, in regard to the holder? The answer is, the law of the place, where the note was made; for there the maker undertook to pay; and the subsequent negotiation did not change his obligation or right.[3] Acceptances of bills are governed by the same principles. They are deemed contracts in the place, where they are made, and are to be performed.[4] But, suppose a negotiable acceptance, or a negotiable note, made payable generally, without any specification of place; what law is to govern, in case of a negotiation of it by one holder to another in a foreign country, in regard to the acceptor or maker? Is it a contract, by them to pay in any place, where it is negotiated, so as to be deemed a contract of that place, and governed by its laws? The Supreme Court of Massachusetts have held, that it creates a debt payable any where, by the very nature of the contract; and it is a promise to whosoever shall be the holder of the bill or note.[5] Assuming this to be true; still it does not follow, that

---

1 See 2 Kent Comm. 459, 460; Chitty on Bills, p. 191, 8th edit. London; Pothier Contrat de Change, n. 15, 155; 5 Pardessus, § 1495.

2 Vedal v. Thompson, 11 Martin, 23, 24.

3 Ory v. Winter, 16 Martin, R. 277.

4 Lewis v. Owen, 4 B. & Ald. 654.

5 Braynard v. Maynard, 8 Pick. R. 194.

the law of the place of the negotiation is to govern; for the transfer is not, as to the acceptor or maker, a new contract; but it is under, and a part of, the original contract, and springs up from the law of the place, where that contract was made. A contract to pay generally is governed by the law of the place, where it is made; for the debt is payable there, as well as in any other place. To bring a contract within the general rule of the *lex loci*, it is not necessary, that it should be payable exclusively in the place of its origin. If payable every where, then it is governed by the law of the place, where it is made; for the plain reason, that it cannot be said to have the law of any other place in contemplation to govern its validity, obligation, or interpretation. All debts between the original parties are payable every where, unless some special provision to the contrary is made; and, therefore, the rule is, that debts have no *situs*; but accompany the creditor everywhere.[1] The holder, then, takes the contract of the acceptor or maker, as it was originally made, and as in the place, where it was made. It is there, that the promise is made to him to pay everywhere.

§ 318. A case a little more difficult in its texture, is, when a contract is made in one country, for payment of money in another country, and, by the laws of the latter, a stamp is required, and not by those of the former; whether it is governed by the *lex solutionis*, or not. And it has been held, that it is not; upon the ground, that an instrument, as to its form and

---

1 Blanchard *v.* Russell, 13 Mass. R. 1, 6; Slacum *v.* Pomeroy, 6 Cranch, 221.

solemnities, is to be governed by the *lex loci contractûs*; and that a stamp is not required by the principle.[1]

§ 319. But a case, still more difficult to reconcile with established principles, in its actual adjudication, has occurred in Massachusetts. A bill of exchange was drawn at Manchester, in England, upon a firm established at Boston, in Massachusetts, payable in London, and was accepted at Manchester by one of the firm, then there. The bill was, therefore, drawn in England, accepted in England, and payable in England. But, upon its dishonour, it was held, that it was to be deemed a bill accepted in Boston, because the domicil of the firm was there, and that damages were recoverable of 10 per cent., as they would be upon a like bill, accepted in Boston.[2] There was nothing upon the face of the bill, that alluded to an acceptance in Boston, and nothing in the circumstances, that pointed in that direction. It was certainly competent for the firm to contract in England, and accept in England; and, beyond all question, if the bill had been drawn solely on the person, who accepted it, the acceptance must have been deemed to be made in England, notwithstanding his domicil was in Boston. Is there any difference between an acceptance by a firm, and by a single person? Is not the general principle of law, that which is affirmed by Casaregis, that a contract or acceptance is to be deemed made, where the contract or acceptance is perfected, *eo loci, quo ultimus in contrahendo assentitur?*[3] It has certainly been put

---

1 Vidal *v.* Thompson, 11 Martin R. 23, 24, 25. But see ante, § 260, and note; Wynne *v.* Jackson, 2 Russell R. 351; Clegg *v.* Levy, 3 Camp. R. 166; James *v.* Catherwood, 3 Dowl. & Ryl. R. 190.

2 Grimshaw *v.* Bender, 6 Mass. R. 157.

3 Casaregis Disc. 179, n. 1.

upon that ground in many modern authorities.[1] And, therefore, if the acceptor be an accommodation acceptor, payments by him of the bills, drawn by the drawer in a foreign country, will be deemed payments under a contract, made with the drawer in the place of acceptance and payment.[2]

§ 320. The doctrine maintained in this case, (6 Mass. R. 157,) is directly in conflict with that maintained under similar circumstances by the Supreme Court of New York. The latter held, that the bill having been drawn in England, and made payable there, and accepted there, it was to be treated as an English contract, and the English interest of 5 per cent. only was allowable for the delay of payment.[3] This decision, being in entire harmony with the general principles on this subject, will probably obtain general credit in the commercial world.[4]

§ 321. In stating the foregoing rules, we have been necessarily led to the consideration of many of what are properly deemed the effects of contracts, which, like the validity of contracts, are dependent upon, and are to be governed by, the *lex loci contractûs*. These effects are, the right conferred on the party, for whose benefit the contract is made; the correspondent duty of the other party to fulfil it; the right of action, which arises from the non-fulfilment; and the consequential right to interest or damages, for the injury

---

1 Boyce *v.* Edwards, 4 Peters R. 111; P. Voet. De Statut. § 9, ch. 2, § 14. See also McCandish *v.* Cruger, 2 Bay R. 377; Bain *v.* Ackworth, 1 S. Car. R. 107; Lewis *v.* Owen, 4 B. & Ald. 654.

2 Lewis *v.* Owen, 4 B. & Ald. 654.

3 Foden *v.* Thorp, 4 John. R. 183.

4 See Bayley on Bills, (4th edition,) ch. A. p. 28 to 32.

done by such non-fulfilment to the injured party.[1] The manner, in which remedies are to be administered, will fall under another and distinct head.

§ 322. But there are some other effects, which may be deemed accompaniments, effects, or incidents of contracts, which may deserve a passing notice. They are properly collateral to them, and arise by operation of law, or by the act of the parties. Among these may be placed the liability of partners and part owners for partnership debts. If, by the law of the place, where the contract is made, they would be liable *in solido*, although, by the law of the domicil of the partnership, they might be liable only for a proportionate share, the law of the former will follow the debt everywhere; or in other words, the effect of the *lex loci* of the contract upon the liability of the partners and part owners will be of universal obligation.[2] By the law of some countries the acceptor of a bill of exchange is discharged from his acceptance, if, when he accepted, the drawer was bankrupt; and this effect of the acceptance regularly accompanies it everywhere, as an incident.[3] Such, also, is the incidental right of warranty, conferred by the civil law in cases of sales of merchandise, not merely as to title, but as to quality.[4] Such, also, is the lien of a vendor, upon a real estate sold for the payment of the purchase money, according to the law of England; the lien given for

---

[1] See Pothier. Oblig. n. 141 to 172; Voet. De Statut. § 9, ch. 2, § 12; Boullenois Ques. de la Contr. des Lois. p. 330 to 338.

[2] Ferguson *v.* Flower, 16 Martin, 312. See also Carroll *v.* Waters, 9 Martin R. 500; Pardessus, Droit Comm. art. 1495.

[3] Pardessus, Droit Comm. art. 1495.

[4] Ante, § 264; Henry on Foreign Law, 51, 52; 2 Boullenois, 475, 476; Voet. De Statut. § 9, ch. 2, § 10.

the purchase money, upon goods or merchandise sold, by the civil law, and the law of some modern countries;[1] the lien of a bottomry bond on the thing pledged; the lien of mariners on the ship for their wages; the priority of payment *in rem*, which the law sometimes attaches to peculiar debts, or particular persons. In these, and like cases, where the lien, or privilege, is created by the *lex loci contractûs*, it will generally, though not universally, be respected and enforced in all places, where the property is found, or the right can be beneficially enforced by the *lex fori*. And on the other hand, where the lien or privilege does not exist in the place of the contract, it will not be allowed in another country, although the local law, where the suit is brought, would otherwise sustain it. Thus, if goods are purchased in England by a citizen of Louisiana, in case of his insolvency, no lien or privilege will exist for the unpaid price, though the law of Louisiana allows it in common cases.[2] Nor would there seem to be any just ground of doubt, that a bottomry bond would be held valid *in rem* in all commercial countries, if the lien is good, by the law of the place of the contract.

§ 323. But the recognition of the existence and validity of such liens by foreign countries is not to be confounded with the giving them a superiority, or priority, over all other liens and rights justly acquired in such foreign countries under their own laws, merely because the former liens in the countries, where they first attached, had by law or custom such superiority, or priority. Such a case would present a very differ-

---

[1] 1 Domat, Civ. Law, B. 4, § 2, n. 3.

[2] Whiston *v.* Stodder, 8 Martin R. 95, 134, 135.

ent question, arising from a conflict of rights, equally well founded in the respective countries. "The law of the place, where a contract is made," said Mr. Chief Justice Marshall, in delivering the opinion of the Supreme Court, in an important case, "is, generally speaking, the law of the contract; i. e. it is the law, by which the contract is expounded. But the right of priority forms no part of the contract. It is extrinsic, and rather a personal privilege, dependent on the law of the place, where the property lies, and where the court sits, which is to decide the cause."[1] And the doctrine was, on that occasion, expressly applied to a contract, made in a foreign country with a person resident abroad.

§ 324. It is here, also, that Huberus has laid down his qualifying doctrine. If, says he, the law of another country is in conflict with that of our own state, in which also a contract is made, conflicting with a contract celebrated elsewhere, we should, in such a case, rather observe our own law, than the foreign law.[2] And he puts several cases to illustrate it. By the Roman law, and the law of Friezeland, an express hypothecation of a moveable, oldest in date, is entitled to a preference or priority, even against a third possessor. But it is not so among the Batavians. And, therefore, if, upon such an hypothecation, the party brings a suit in Holland against such third possessor, his suit will be rejected; because the right of such third possessor cannot be taken away by the law of a foreign country.[3]

§ 325. He also puts another case. In Holland, if a

---

1 Harrison v. Sterry, 5 Cranch, 289, 298; See 12 Wheaton R. 361, 362.

2 Huberus Lib. 1, tit. 3, § 11. 3 Ibid.

marriage contract is privately made, stipulating, that the wife shall not be liable for debts contracted solely by the husband, it is valid, notwithstanding it is to the prejudice of subsequent creditors. But in Friezeland such a contract is not valid, unless published; nor would the ignorance of the parties be an excuse, according to the Roman law and equity. And if the husband should contract debts in Friezeland; on a suit there, the wife would be held liable for a moiety to the Friezian creditors, and could not defend herself under her private dotal contract. But the Batavian creditors, suing in Friezeland, would not be entitled to a similar remedy; for, in such a case, the law of the place of their contract alone, and not the law of both countries, would come under consideration.[1] The Author was probably here treating of a case, where the debts were contracted in Friezeland, after the husband and wife had removed their domicil there; or, at least, if there was no change of domicil, where the property of the parties, to be affected by the marriage contract, was situate in Friezeland. Under any other aspect, it would be difficult to maintain the doctrine.

§ 326. Lord Ellenborough has laid down a similar doctrine. "We always import," says he, "together with their persons, the existing relations of foreigners, as between themselves, according to the laws of their own countries; except, indeed, where those laws clash with the rights of our own subjects here, and one or

1 Huberus, Lib. 1, tit. 3, § 11. — The sense of this passage in Huberus, is mistranslated in the note to 3 Dallas R. 375. The translator has translated the words, *in contractibus heic celebratis*, "where the marriage was contracted here," and *jus loci contractûs*, "the law of the place, where the marriage was contracted;" whereas the author in this clause is manifestly referring to the contracts (debts) of the respective creditors.

other of the laws must necessarily give way; in which case our own is entitled to the preference. This having been long settled in principle, and laid up among our acknowledged rules of jurisprudence, it is needless to discuss it farther."[1] The Supreme Court of Louisiana have adopted a more modified doctrine; "that, in a conflict of laws, it must often be a matter of doubt, which should prevail; and, that whenever that doubt does exist, the court, which decides, will prefer the law of its own country to that of the stranger.[2] And, if the positive laws of a state prohibit particular contracts from having effect according to the rules of the country, where they are made, the former must prevail."[3]

§ 327. Mr. Chancellor Kent undoubtedly intended to lay down the same rule in his Commentaries, as is stated by Huberus, and Lord Ellenborough, when he said, "that when the *lex domicilii* (*contractûs?*) and the *lex fori* (as to conflicting rights acquired in each?) come in direct collision, the comity of nations must yield to the positive law of the land. *In tali conflictu magis est, ut jus nostrum, quam jus aliorum, servemus.*"[4] He could not mean to say, that rights, acquired under the law of the place of domicil, were not to be enforced in another forum, because the laws of the latter did not recognise such rights or obligations in cases arising within its own territories.

§ 328. This subject will be resumed hereafter under other heads. But the remarks of a learned Scottish Judge,[5] may here be properly introduced. "The ap-

1 Potter *v.* Brown, 5 East, 124, 130.

2 Saul *v.* His Creditors, 17 Martin R. 596. 3 Id. p. 586, 587.

4 2 Kent. Comm. Lect. 39, p. 461, (2d edit.)

5 Lord Robertson, Fergusson on Marr. and Div. 397.

plication of the *lex loci* to contracts, though general, is not universal. It does not take place, where the parties, at the time of entering into the contract, had the law of another kingdom in view; or where the *lex loci* is in itself unjust, or *contra bonos mores;* or contrary to the public law of the state, as regarding the interests of religion, or morality, or the general well-being of society."

§ 329. It may also be stated, though the proposition has been already incidentally considered, that, when a debt is contracted in a foreign country, it is not to be deemed exclusively payable there, unless there is in the contract itself some stipulation to that effect. On the contrary, a debt contracted in a particular country, and not limited to a particular place of payment, is, by operation of law, payable everywhere, and may be enforced, wherever the debtor or his property can be found.[1]

§ 330. Having considered the principles applicable to the nature, validity, interpretation, and effect of contracts, we are next led to the consideration of the manner, in which they may be discharged, and what matters upon the merits will constitute a good defence to them. I say upon the merits; for the objections arising from the *lex fori,* such as the limitations of remedies, and the modes of suit, will constitute a separate head of inquiry.

§ 331. And, here, the general rule is, that a defence or discharge, good by the law of the place, where the contract is made, or is to be performed, is to be held of equal validity in every other place, where the question may be litigated.[2] Voet has laid down this doc-

---

1 See Blake *v.* Williams, 6 Pick. R. 286, 315.

2 2 Bell's Comm. B. 8, ch. 3, § 1, p. 692.

trine in the broadest terms. *Si adversus contractum aliudve negotium gestum factumve restitutio desideratur, dum quis aut metu, aut dolo, aut errore lapsus, damnum sensit contrahendo, transigendo, solvendo, fidejubendo, hereditatem adeundo, aliove simili modo; recte interpretes statuisse arbitror, leges regionis, in quâ contractum gestumve est id, contra quod restitutio petitur, locum sibi debere vindicare in terminandâ ipsâ restitutionis controversiâ; sive res illæ, de quibus contractum est, et in quibus læsio contigit, eodem in loco, sive alibi sitæ sint, &c. Si tamen contractûs implementum non in ipso contractûs loco fieri debeat, sed ad locum alium sit destinatum, non loci contractûs, sed implementi, leges spectandas esse ratio suadet; ut ita secundum cujus loci jura implementum accipere debuit contractus, juxta ejus etiam leges resolvatur.*[1] Casaregis in substance lays down the same doctrine;[2] and Huberus throughout implies it.[3]

§ 332. In England and America the same rule has been adopted, and acted on with a most liberal justice.[4] Thus, infancy, if a good defence by the *lex loci contractûs*, will be a valid defence everywhere.[5] A tender and refusal, good by the same law, either as a full discharge, or as a present fulfilment of the contract, will be respected everywhere.[6] Payment in paper money bills, or in other things, if good by the same laws, will be

1 J. Voet. ad Pand. Lib. 4, tit. 1, § 29.

2 See Casaregis, Disc. 179, § 60, 61.

3 Huberus, Lib. 1, tit. 3, § 3, 7; Voet. De Statut. § 9, ch. 2, § 20.

4 2 Kent Comm. Lect. 39, p. 459, (2d edit.); Potter *v.* Brown, 5 East 124; Dwarris on Stat. P. 2, p. 650, 651; 2 Bell Comm. 692.

5 Thompson *v.* Ketcham, 8 John. R. 189; Male *v.* Roberts, 3 Esp. R. 163.

6 Warder *v.* Arell, 2 Wash. Virg. R. 282, 293, &c.

deemed a sufficient payment everywhere.[1] And, on the other hand, where a payment by negotiable bills or notes is, by the *lex loci*, held to be conditional payment only, it will be so held, even in states, where such payments under the domestic law would be held absolute.[2] So, if by the law of the place of a contract (even though negotiable) equitable defences are allowed in favour of the maker, any subsequent indorsement will not change his rights in regard to the holder. The latter must take it *cum onere*.[3]

333. The case of an acceptance of a bill of exchange in a foreign country affords another illustration. Although by our law it is absolute, and binding in every event; yet, if by that of the foreign country it is merely a qualified contract, it is governed by that law in all its consequences.[4] Acceptances are deemed contracts in the country, where they are made; and the payments are regulated by the law thereof.[5]

§ 334. But, although the general rule is, as above stated, that a discharge by the law of a place, where a contract is made, is a discharge everywhere; yet there are exceptions to the rule, which every country will enforce or not, according to its own discretion and sense of justice. Thus, where a contract was made in England between two Danish subjects, one of whom was domiciled in England; and afterwards, during a war between England and Denmark, the Danish government con-

---

7 Warder *v.* Arell, 2 Wash. Virg. R. 282, 293; 1 Brown Ch. R. 376; Seabright *v.* Calbraith, 4 Dall. 325; Bartsth *v.* Atwater, 1 Connect. R. 409.

2 Bartsth *v.* Atwater, 1 Connect. R. 409.

3 Ory *v.* Winter, 16 Martin R. 277. See also Evans *v.* Gray, 12 Martin R. 475; Chartus *v.* Cairnes, 16 Martin R. 1.

4 Burrows *v.* Jemimo, 2 Str. R. 733; S. C., 2 Eq. Abrid. 525. See Van Cleff *v.* Terasson, 3 Pick. R. 12.

5 Lewis *v.* Owen, 4 B. & Ald. 654; 5 Pardessus, § 1495.

fiscated the debt, and required it to be paid by the debtor, who was then in Denmark, and he paid it accordingly; the English court on a suit, brought in England after the peace, by the creditor against the debtor, held, that the payment to the Danish government was no discharge, although it would have been so by the laws of Denmark, upon the ground, that such a confiscation was not justified by the law of nations.[1]

§ 335. The most important, or, at least, most frequent cases of discharge of contracts, occurring in practice, are those of discharges arising from matters *ex post facto;* such as a discharge from the contract upon the subsequent insolvency or bankruptcy of the contracting party. And, here, the general rule is, that a discharge from the contract according to the law of the place, where it is made, or where it is to be performed, is good everywhere, and extinguishes the contract.[2] This doctrine was fully recognised in the English law by Lord Mansfield (and it doubtless had a much earlier existence) in a formulary of language, which has often since been quoted, as a general axiom of jurisprudence. "It is a general principle," said he, "that, where there is a discharge by the law of one country, it will be a discharge in another."[3] The expression is too broad, and

1 Wolf *v.* Oxholm, 6 M. & Selw. R. 92. — It is wholly unnecessary here to consider, whether the confiscation of debts by an enemy is conformable, or not, to the law of nations. That is a point belonging to the public law of nations, and underwent very grave discussions in the American courts, during the late war with Great Britain. See the Emulous, 1 Gallison R. 563; S. C. on Appeal, Brown *v.* United States, 8 Cranch R. 110.

2 2 Kent Comm. Lect. 37, p. 392, 393, (2d edit.); 2 Bell Comm. 691 to 695; 1 Chitty on Comm. and Manuf. ch. 12, p. 654.

3 Ballantine *v.* Golding, 1 Coop. Bank. Laws, (5th edit.), p. 347, (4th edit.), p. 515; 13 Mass. R. 7; 2 Bell Comm. 692.

should have the qualification annexed, which the case before him required, and which has been uniformly understood, viz. that it is a discharge in the country, where the contract was made, or was to be performed. And so it was interpreted by Lord Ellenborough in a much later case. "The rule, (said he) was well laid down by Lord Mansfield, in Ballantine *v.* Golding, that, what is a discharge of a debt *in the country, where it was contracted,* is a discharge of it everywhere." [1] And this doctrine is firmly established, and generally recognised, in America.[2] By some judges the doctrine has been put upon the implied consent of the parties in making the contract, that they would be governed, as to all its effects, by the *lex loci.*[3] By others, it is put upon the more firm and solid basis of the sovereign operation of the local law upon all contracts made within its sovereignty; and the indispensable comity, which all other nations are accustomed to exercise towards such laws, whenever they are brought into question, either as to contracts, rights, or property.[4]

§ 336. The doctrine has been stated in a more

---

1 Potter *v.* Brown, 5 East, 124, 130. See Hunter *v.* Potts, 4 T. R. 182; Quin *v.* O'Keefe, 2 H. Bl. 553.

2 See on this point, Smith *v.* Smith, 2 John. R. 235; Hicks *v.* Brown, 12 John. R. 142; Van Reimsdyk *v.* Kane, 1 Gallis. R. 371; Blanchard *v.* Russell, 13 Mass. R. 1; Baker *v.* Wheaton, 5 Mass. R. 511; Watson *v.* Bourne, 10 Mass. R. 337; 4 Cowen's Rep., note, p. 515; Green *v.* Sarmiento, Peter's Cir. R. 74; McMenomy *v.* Murray, 3 John. Ch. R. 435, 440, 441; Walsh *v.* Nourse, 5 Binn. R. 381; Sturgis *v.* Crowninshield, 4 Wheaton R. 122; Ogden *v.* Saunders, 12 Wheaton R. 213, 358; 2 Kent Comm. Lect. 37, p. 392, 393; Id. Lect. 39, p. 459, (2d edit.); Atwater *v.* Townsend, 4 Connect. R. 47; Hempstead *v.* Reed, 6 Connect. R. 480; Houghton *v.* Page, 2 New Hamp. R. 42; Dyer *v.* Hunt. 5 New Hamp. R. 401.

3 See Ante § 261; Blanchard *v.* Russell, 13 Mass. R. 1, 4, 5; Prentiss *v.* Savage, 13 Mass. R. 20, 23.

4 Potter *v.* Brown, 5 East. R. 124; Ante § 261.

general form by a late learned Judge, who said, "that it may be assumed, as a rule affecting all personal contracts, that they are subject to all the *consequences* attached to contracts of a similar nature by the laws of the country, where they are made, if the contracting party is a subject of, or resident in, that country, where it is entered into, and no provision is introduced to refer to the laws of another country."[1] This is not, perhaps, in strictness of language, quite correct. There are many *consequences* flowing from contracts in the place, where they are made, which do not accompany them everywhere, and are not of universal obligation. Remedies are a consequence of contracts, when broken; but, as we shall hereafter see, they are governed by different rules from rights. And the rights, given by the law of the place of the contract, are not always deemed of universal obligation or validity. Marriage, for instance, is admitted to be a valid contract everywhere, when it is so by the law of the place, where it is celebrated. But, as we have seen, all the consequences, attached to marriage in one country, do not follow it into other countries.[2] In Scotland a subsequent marriage legitimates children antecedently born; but this consequence will not make such children legitimate in England, as to real estate.[3] So, the indissolubility of marriage by the law of one country will not attach to it everywhere.

§ 337. And even in regard to common contracts of a different nature, the general rule, as to the conse-

---

1 Blanchard *v.* Russell, 13 Mass. R. 1, 5.

2 See Ante § 145 to 190: Fergusson on Marr. and Div. 359, 360, 361, 397, 398, 399, 402, 414; Conway *v.* Beazley, 3 Hagg. Ecc. R. 639.

3 Doe *v.* Birtwhistle *v.* Vardill, 5 B. & Cresw. 438; 1 Hertii Opera, De Collis. Leg. § 4, p. 129, § 15.

quences of them, must receive many qualifications and limitations, resulting from the public policy, or the domestic laws of other states, where they are sought to be enforced, and the right and duty of self-protection against unjust foreign legislation. If, for example, a country, where a contract was made, should, under a pretence of a general bankrupt act, authorize a discharge from all contracts made with foreigners, and should, at the same time, exclude the latter from all participation with domestic creditors in the assets; it cannot be presumed, that such an act would be held a valid discharge in the countries, to which such foreigners belonged.[1] And, certainly, the priorities and privileges, annexed by the laws of particular states to certain classes of debts contracted therein, are not generally admitted to have the same pre-eminence over debts contracted in the country, which is called upon to enforce them.[2] Nor are the courts of any state under any obligation to give effect to a discharge of a foreign debtor, where, under its own laws, the creditor has previously acquired a right to proceed against his property within its own territory.[3]

§ 338. When we speak of a discharge of a debt in the country, where it is contracted, being a discharge everywhere, care must be taken to distinguish between cases, where, by the *lex loci*, there is a virtual or direct extinguishment of the debt itself; and where there is only a partial extinguishment of the remedy. By the bankrupt laws of England, and by the corresponding insolvent laws of some of the United States,

---

1 Blanchard *v.* Russell, 13 Mass. R. 1, 6.

2 See Ante § 322, 323; Hub. De Conflictu Leg. Lib. 1, tit. 3, § 11.

3 Tappan *v.* Poor, 15 Mass. R. 419; Le Chevalier *v.* Lynch, Doug. R. 170. But see Hunter *v.* Potts, 4 T. R. 182; S. P. 2 H. Bl. 402.

an absolute discharge from all rights and remedies of the creditors is provided for, as part of the system; and, therefore, the whole obligation of the contract is deemed, *ipso facto*, extinguished. But there are insolvent laws, and other special systems, both in Europe and America, which fall short of this extent and operation. In some cases, the person only is liberated from future imprisonment and responsibility; in others, particular portions of property are exempted; and in others again, a mixed system, embracing some postponed or modified liabilities both of the person and property, prevails.[1]

§ 339. Now, in all these cases, where there is not a positive, or virtual extinguishment of all rights and remedies of the creditors, the contract is not deemed extinguished; and, therefore, it may be enforced (as we shall hereafter more fully see) in other countries. By the Roman law a *Cessio Bonorum* of the debtor was not a discharge of the debt, unless the property ceded was to the full sufficient for that purpose. It otherwise operated only as a discharge, *pro tanto*, and exonerated the debtor from imprisonment. *Qui bonis cesserint*, (says the Code,) *nisi solidum creditor reciperit, non sunt liberati. In eo enim tantummodo hoc beneficium eis prodest, ne judicati detrahantur in carcerem.*[2] In Holland, Huberus informs us, that a *Cessio Bonorum* does not even exempt from imprisonment, unless the creditors assent. *Secundum jus nostrum Cessio Bonorum, invitis creditoribus, debitorem a carcere publico non*

---

[1] See 1 Domat, Civ. Law, B. 4, tit. 5, § 1; Morris v. Eves, 11 Martin R. 750. See Mather v. Bush, 16 John. R. 424, note; 2 Bell Comm. ch. 5, p. 563 to 567; Phillips v. Allan, 8 B. and Cres. 477.

[2] Cod. Lib. 7, tit. 71, l. 1; 1 Domat, Civ. Law, B. 4, tit. 5, § 1, n. 1, 2. See 16 John. R. 424; note (b.)

liberat;[1] and Heineccius proclaims the same, as the law of some parts of Germany.[2] The Scottish law conforms to the Roman Code in its leading outlines;[3] and the modern Code of France adopts the same system.[4] An Insolvent Act, or Bankrupt Act, or *Cessio Bonorum*, which only absolves the person of the debtor from imprisonment, but not his future property; or, which only suspends remedies against either the one, or the other, for a limited period, is not to be deemed a discharge from the contract; and its operation is (as we shall presently see) purely intra-territorial.[5]

---

1 Huberus, Lib. 42, tit. 3, § 1, 3, note; 1 Atk. R. 255; 3 John. Ch. R. 442; Voet. ad Pand. Lib. 42, tit. 3, § 8; Le Roy *v.* Crowninshield, 2 Mason R. 160. — Lord Mansfield is reported to have said, in Ballantine *v.* Golding, 1 Cooke Bank. Laws, p. 347, (5th edit.), p. 515, (4th edit.), "that he remembered a case in Chancery, of a *Cessio Bonorum* in Holland, which is held a discharge in that country, and it had the same effect here." The case alluded to is most probably Ex Parte Burton (1 Atk. 255.) The law of Holland is the reverse of what his Lordship is here supposed to affirm, as the case in 1 Atk. 225, and the citations from Huberus and Voet establish. Whether the error is in the Reporter, or in Lord Mansfield himself, may well be questioned. Mr. Henry has given a sketch of the present law of France, as to the *Cessio Bonorum* in cases of foreign contracts, which certainly has some peculiarities, not conforming to the general principles of international law adopted in other nations. Henry on Foreign law, Appendix, 250. See Pardessus, art. 1324 to 1328. The *Cessio Bonorum* of Scotland is (it seems) a mere discharge of the person. See 2 Bell Comm. ch. 5, p. 563, &c.; Phillips *v.* Allan, 8 B. & Cresw. 479.

2 Heinecc. Elem. Jur. Civ. ad Pand. p. 6, Lib. 42, tit. 3, § 252, 254; 3 John. Ch. R. 441, 442.

3 Erskine's Inst. B. 4, tit. 3, § 26, 27.

4 Code Civil of France, art. 1265 and 1270; Merlin, Répertoire, Cession de Biens.

5 Tappan *v.* Poor, 15 Mass. R. 419; Morris *v.* Eves, 11 Martin, R. 730; Judd *v.* Porter, 7 Greenleaf R. 337; Hinckley *v.* Morean, 3 Mason R. 88; Titus *v.* Hobart, 5 Mason R. 378; 1 Kent Comm. Lect. 19, p. 420, 422, (2d edit.); 2 Bell Comm. 562, 567, 694; Mason *v.* Haile, 12 Wheaton R. 370; 2 Kent Comm. Lect. 37, p. 394 to 401, (2d edit.) Phillips *v.* Allan, 8 B. & Cresw. 479; Ex Parte Burton, 1 Atk. R. 255; Huberus, Lib. 42, tit. 3, § 5; Heineccii Elem. ad Pand. P. 6, Lib. 42, tit. 3,

§ 340. The general form, in which the doctrine is expressed, that a discharge of a contract by the law of the place, where it is made, is a discharge everywhere, seems to preclude any consideration of the question, between what parties it is made; whether between citizens, or between a citizen and a foreigner, or between foreigners. The continental jurists recognise no distinction in the cases. The English decisions are understood to maintain the universality of the doctrine, whatever is the allegiance or country of the creditor.[1] And a like doctrine would seem generally to be maintained in America.[2] There are, however, some cases, in which a more limited doctrine would seem to be laid down; and which appears to confine it to cases of a discharge from contracts between citizens of the same state. Thus, in one case, it was laid down by the Supreme Court of Massachusetts, that if, when the contract was made, the promisee was not a citizen of the state, where it was made, he would not be bound by laws of such state in any other state; and, therefore, that a discharge there would not bind him or his rights.[3] In another case the same learned Court said, that a discharge of the contract can only operate, where the law is made by an authority, common to the creditor and the debtor in all respects; where both are citizens

---

§ 253; White v. Canfield, 7 John. R. 117; James v. Allen, 1 Dall R. 188; Quin v. O'Keefe, 2 H. Bl. 553; Le Roy v. Crowninshield, 2 Mason R. 160; Wright v. Paton, 10 John. R. 300; Peck v. Hozier, 14 John. R. 346; Walsh v. Nourse, 5 Binn. R. 381.

1 See 12 Wheaton R. 360; 5 East R. 124.

2 See 1 W. Black. R. 258; 13 Mass. R. 1; 2 John. R. 235; 2 Kent Comm. Lect. 37, p. 392, 393, (2d edit.); 16 Martin R. 277, 1 Cowen R. 103, 107.

3 Baker v. Wheaton, 5 Mass. R. 511.

and subjects.[1] But this qualification of the doctrine (which was only incidentally argued in those cases) was afterwards deliberately overruled by the same Court; and the general doctrine established in its universality.[2] It seems, however, again to be asserted in a more recent decision of the same Court, upon grounds not very intelligible.[3] And it has been expressly denied by other learned state courts.[4] In commenting upon some of the cases, in which, upon questions of discharge, considerable importance has been attached to the circumstance, that one or both of the parties were inhabitants of the state or country, where the contract was made, the Supreme Court of New York have said, "that all these cases stand upon a principle, entirely independent of that circumstance. It is that of the *lex loci contractûs;* that the place, where the contract is made, must govern the construction of the contract; and that, whether the parties to the contract are inhabitants of that place, or not. The rule is not founded upon the allegiance due from citizens or subjects to their respective governments; but upon the presumption of law, that the parties to a contract are conusant of the laws of the country, where the contract is made."[5]

§ 341. Under the peculiar structure of the constitution of the United States, prohibiting the states from passing laws impairing the obligation of contracts, it has been decided, that a discharge, under the insolvent laws of the state, where the contract was made, will not operate as a discharge of any contracts, except

1 Watson *v.* Bourne, 10 Mass. R. 337, 340.
2 Blanchard *v.* Russell, 13 Mass. R. 1, 10, 11, 12.
3 Braynard *v.* Marshall, 8 Pick. R. 194.
4 Ory *v.* Winter, 16 Martin R. 277; Sherrill *v.* Hopkins, 1 Cowen R. 103, 107.
5 Sherrill *v.* Hopkins, 1 Cowen R. 102, 108.

such as are made between citizens of the same state. It cannot, therefore, discharge a contract made with a citizen of another state.[1] But this doctrine is wholly inapplicable to contracts and discharges in foreign countries, which must, therefore, be decided upon principles of international law.

§ 342. The converse doctrine is equally well established, viz. that a discharge of a contract by the law of a place, where the contract was not made, or to be performed, will not be a discharge in any other country.[2] Thus, it has been held in England, that a discharge of contract, made there, under an insolvent act of the state of Maryland, is no bar to a suit upon the contract in the courts of England. On that occasion, Lord Kenyon said, "It is impossible to say, that a contract made in one country, is to be governed by the laws of another. It might as well be contended, that, if the state of Maryland had enacted, that no debts due from its own subjects to the subjects of England should be paid, the plaintiff would have been bound by it. This is the case of a contract lawfully made by a subject in this country, which he resorts to a court of justice to enforce; and the only answer given is, that a law has been made in a foreign country to discharge these defendants from their debts, on condition of their having relinquished all their property to their creditors. But how is that an answer to a subject of this country, suing on a lawful contract made here? How can it be

---

1 Ogden *v.* Saunders, 12 Wheaton R. 358 to 369; Boyle *v.* Zacharie, 6 Peters R. 348; 2 Kent Comm. Lect. 37, p. 392, 393, (2d edit.); 3 Story Comm. on Const. § 1384; 1 Kent Comm. Lect. 9, p. 418, 422, (2d edit.)

2 See 2 Bell Comm. 691 to 695; Phillips *v.* Allan, 8 B. & Cres. 479; Lewis *v.* Owen, 4 Barn. & Ald. 654.

pretended, that he is bound by a condition, to which he has given no assent, either express or implied?"[1] In America the same doctrine has obtained the fullest sanction.[2] And it is also clearly established in Scotland.[3]

§ 343. The subject of negotiable paper is generally governed by the same principles. Wherever the contract between the particular parties is made, the law of the place will operate for its discharge; and so, *vice versâ*. A nice question, however, has recently arisen on this subject, in a case already mentioned. A negotiable note was made at New York between persons resident there, and payable generally; and the payee subsequently indorsed the note to a citizen of Massachusetts, by whom a suit was brought in the state court of the latter state against the maker. One point at the argument was, whether a discharge of the maker under the insolvent laws of New York operated as a bar to the suit? The case was decided upon another ground. But the Court expressed a clear opinion, that it did not; and said; "It is a debt payable anywhere by the very nature of the contract; and it is a promise to whoever shall be the holder of the note." "The promisor became immediately upon the indorsement, the debtor to the indorsee, who was not amen-

---

1 Smith *v.* Buchanan, 1 East. R. 6, 11; Lewis *v.* Owen, 4 B. & Ald. 654; Phillips *v.* Allan, 8 B. & Cresw. 477.

2 Van Raugh *v.* Van Arsdaln, 3 Cain. R. 154; Frey *v.* Kirk, 4 Gill & John. R. 509; Green *v.* Sarmiento, Peters Cir. R. 74; Le Roy *v.* Crowninshield, 2 Mason R. 151; Smith *v.* Smith, 2 John. R. 235; Bradford *v.* Farrand, 13 Mass. R. 18; 2 Kent Comm. Lect. 37, p. 392, 393; Id. Lect. 39, p. 458, 459, (2d edit.)

3 2 Bell Comm. 692, 693.

able to the laws of New York, where the discharge was obtained.[1]"

§ 344. It is difficult (as has been already intimated) to perceive the ground, upon which this doctrine can be maintained, as a doctrine of public law.[2] The Court admit, that a debt contracted in New York, and not negotiable, would be extinguished by such a discharge; although such debt is by its very nature payable everywhere, as debts have no locality. As between the original parties, the maker and the payee, the same result would follow. How, then, can the indorsement vary it? It does not create a new contract between the maker and the indorsee in the place of the indorsement. The rights of the indorsee spring from, and under, the original contract, and are a component part of it. The original contract promises to pay the indorsee, as much as the payee, and from the first of its existence. The indorsement is but a substitution of the indorsee for the payee; and it transfers over the old liability, and creates no new liability of the maker.[3] If the indorsement created a new contract in the place, where it was made, between the maker and the indorsee, then the validity, obligation, and interpretation of the contract would be governed by the law of the place of the indorsement, and not by that of the place, where the note was originally made. It would not, then, amount to a transfer of the old contract, but to the creation of a new one, which, from a conflict of laws, not unusual in different states, would, or might, involve obligations and duties wholly

---

1 Braynard v. Marshall, 8 Pick. R. 194. See 12 Wheaton R. 358, 362, 363, 364.

2 Ante § 340.

3 Pothier, De Change. art. 22.

different from, and even incompatible with, the original contract. Nay, the maker might, upon the same instrument, incur the most opposite responsibilities to different holders, according to the law of the different places, where the indorsement might be made.

§ 345. Such a doctrine has never been propounded in any common law authority, or been supported by the opinion of any foreign jurist. The same principle would apply to general negotiable acceptances, as to negotiable notes; for the maker stands in the same predicament as the acceptor. Yet, no one ever supposed, that an indorsement after an acceptance ever varied the rights or obligations of the acceptor. It is, as to all persons, who become holders, in whatever country, treated as a contract made by the acceptor in the country, where such acceptance is made. Yet, the acceptance being general, payment may be required in any place, where the holder shall demand it. The other point, that the indorsement was to a citizen of another state, is equally inadmissible. The question is not, whether he is bound by the laws of New York generally; but, whether he can, in opposition to them, avail himself of a contract, made under the sovereignty of that state, and vary its validity, obligation, interpretation, and negotiability as governed by those laws. If the payee had been a citizen of Massachusetts, and the note had been made by the maker in New York, there could be no doubt, that the contract would still be governed by the laws of New York, in regard to the payee. What difference, then, can it make, that the indorsee is a citizen of another state, if he cannot show, that his contract has its origin there? In short, the doctrine of this case is wholly repugnant to that maintained by the same Court in another case, which was most maturely considered, and in which the argument in its favour was repelled. The Court there declared their opinion to be, that full effect ought to be given to such discharges, as to all contracts made within the state, where they are authorized, although the creditor is a citizen of another state.[1]

§ 346. The Supreme Court of Louisiana, have adopted the same conclusion; and held, that, where a negotiable promissory note was made in one state, and was indorsed in another state to a citizen of the latter, the contract was governed by the law of the place, where the note was made, and not by that of the place, where the indorsement was made. "We see nothing," said the Court, "in the circumstance of the rights of one of the parties being transferred to the citizen of another state, which can take the case out of the general principle." "It is a demand made under an agreement (note) entered into in a foreign state; and consequently the party, claiming rights under it, must take it with all the limitations, to which it was subject in the place, where it was made; and that, although he be one of our citizens."[2] And this is certainly in conformity to what is deemed settled doctrine in England, as well as in some other states in America.[3] It was taken for granted in Slacum *v.* Pomeroy (6 Cranch 221), where, in the case of a negotiable bill of exchange, the drawer's responsibility was supposed to be governed by the law of the place, where the bill was drawn, notwithstanding an indorsement in another

1 Blanchard *v.* Russell, 13 Mass. R. 1, 11, 12. See also Prentiss *v.* Savage, 13 Mass. R. 20, 23, 24.

2 Ory *v.* Winter, 16 Martin R. 277; Sherrill *v.* Hopkins, 1 Cowen R. 103.

3 See 13 Mass. R. 12; 12 Wheaton R. 360; 5 East R. 123, 130.

country; and in De la Chaumette *v.* The Bank of England (9 B. & Cresw. R. 208; S. C., 2 B. & Adolph. 385), where the right to a bank of England note was supposed to be governed by the law of England, notwithstanding a transfer of the same in France.[1]

§ 347. Pardessus has laid down a doctrine equally large. He says, that it is by the law of the place, where a bill of exchange is payable, that we are to ascertain, when it falls due, the days of grace belonging to it, the character of these delays, whether for the benefit of the holder, or of the debtor; in one word, every thing, which relates to the right of requiring payment of a debt, or the performance of any other engagement, when the parties have not made any stipulation to the contrary. And it is of little consequence, whether the person, who demands payment, is the creditor, who made the contract, or an assignee of his right, such as the holder of a bill of exchange by indorsement. This circumstance makes no change in regard to the debtor. The indorsee cannot require payment in any other manner, than the original creditor could. And he applies this doctrine to the case of successive indorsements of bills of exchange, made in different countries, stating, that the rights of each holder are the same, as those of the original payee against the acceptor.[2] He adds, also, that the effects of an acceptance are to be determined by the law of the place, where it has been made;[3] and that every indorsement subjects the indorser to the law of the place,

1 See also 2 Bell Comm. 692, 693. — "Quid si de literis cambii incidat questio," says J. Voet, "quis locus spectandus? Is locus, ad quem sunt destinatæ, et ibidem acceptatæ." J. Voet. De Stat. § 9, ch. 2, § 14.

2 Pardessus, Droit Comm. art. 1495, 1498 to 1500.

3 Id. 1495.

where it has been made; and it governs his responsibility accordingly.[1]

§ 348. Notwithstanding the principle, that a discharge of the *lex loci contractûs* is valid everywhere, and *vice versâ*, is generally admitted, as a part of private international law; yet it cannot be denied, that any nation may by its own peculiar jurisprudence refuse to recognise it, and act within its own tribunals upon an opposite doctrine. But, then, under such circumstances its acts and decisions will be deemed of no validity or force beyond its own territorial limits. Thus, if a state should by its laws provide, that a discharge of an insolvent debtor under its laws should be a discharge of all contracts, and even of those made in a foreign country, its own courts would be bound by such provisions.[2] But they would be held nullities in every other country.[3]

§ 349. And even in relation to a discharge according to the laws of the place, where the contract is made, there are some necessary limitations and exceptions engrafted upon the general doctrine, which every country will enforce, whenever those laws are manifestly unjust, or injurious to the fair rights of its own citizens. It has been said by a learned Judge with great force, that "As the laws of foreign countries are not admitted *ex proprio vigore*, but merely *ex comitate*, the judicial power will exercise a discretion with respect to the

1 Pardessus, Droit Comm. art. 1499.

2 See Penniman *v.* Meigs, 9 John. R. 325; Babcock *v.* Weston, 1 Gallis. R. 168; Murray *v.* De Rottenham, 6 John. Ch. R. 52; Holmes *v.* Remsen, 4 John. Ch. R. 471.

3 See Van Raugh *v.* Van Ardaln, 3 Cain. R. 154; Smith *v.* Buchanan, 1 East. R. 6; Smith *v.* Smith, 2 John. R. 235; Green *v.* Sarmiento, Peters Cir. R. 74; McMenomy *v.* Murray, 3 John. Ch. R. 435; Wolff *v.* Oxholm, 6 Maule & Selw. R. 92.

laws, which they may be called upon to sanction; for if they should be manifestly unjust, or calculated to injure their own citizens, they ought to be rejected. Thus, if any state should enact, that its citizens should be discharged from all debts due to creditors living without the state, such a provision would be so contrary to the common principles of justice, that the most liberal spirit of comity would not require its adoption in any other state. So, if a state, under the pretence of establishing a general bankrupt law, should authorize such proceedings, as would deprive all creditors living out of the state of an opportunity to share in the distribution of the effects of the debtor, such a law would have no effect beyond the territory of the state, in which it was passed."[1]

§ 350. The same reasoning was again asserted by the same learned Judge in another case calling for an exposition of the doctrine. "This rule," said he, "must, however, from its very nature, be qualified and restrained: for it cannot be admitted, as a principle of law or justice, that, when a valid personal contract is made, which follows the person of the creditor, and may be enforced in any foreign jurisdiction, that a mode of discharge, manifestly partial or unjust, and tending to deprive a foreign creditor of his debt, while he is excluded from a participation with the domestic creditors in the effects of the debtor, should have force in any country, to the prejudice of their own citizens. The comity of nations does not require it, and the fair principles of a contract would be violated by it.

§ 351. "Thus if a citizen of this state, being in a foreign country, should, for a valuable consideration,

---

1 Blanchard *v.* Russell, 13 Mass. R. 6

receive a promise to pay money, or to perform any other valuable engagement, from a subject of that country; and the law should provide for a discharge from all debts upon a surrender of effects, without any notice, which could by possibility reach creditors out of the country, where such a law should exist; we apprehend, that the contract ought to be enforced here, notwithstanding a discharge obtained under such law. For although the creditor is to be presumed to know the laws of the place, where he obtains his contract; yet that presumption is founded upon another, which is, that those laws are not palpably partial and unjust, and calculated to protect the creditors at home at the expense of those, who are abroad. Such laws would come within the well known exception to the rules of comity, viz. that the laws, which are to be admitted in the tribunals of a country, where they are not made, are not to be injurious to the state, or the citizens of the state, where they are so received."[1]

§ 352. Before we quit this head of contracts, it may be well to bring together some principles applicable to negotiable instruments, which have not been brought under review in the preceding discussions, and which are important illustrations of the operation of foreign law.

§ 353. Questions have arisen, whether negotiable notes and bills made in one country are transferrable in other countries, so as to found a right of action in the holder against the other parties. Thus, a question occurred in England, in a case, where a negotiable note, made in Scotland and negotiable there, was in-

---

[1] Prentiss *v.* Savage, 13 Mass. R. 23, 24. See also Fergusson on Marr. and Div. 296, 397; Wolff *v.* Oxholm, 6 Maule & Selw. 92.

dorsed, and a suit brought in England by the indorsee against the maker, whether the action was maintainable; and it was held by the Court, that it was.[1] In another case a promissory note made in England, and payable to the bearer, was transferred in France, and the question was made, whether the French holder could maintain an action thereon in England; such notes being by the law of France negotiable; and it was held that he might.[2] But, in each of these cases, the decision was expressly put upon the provisions of the English statute (3 and 4 Ann. ch. 9,) respecting promissory notes, leaving wholly untouched the general doctrine of international law.

§ 354. Several cases may be put upon this subject. In the first place, suppose a note negotiable by the law of the place, where it is made, is there transferred by indorsement; can the indorsee maintain an action in his own name against the maker in a foreign country (where both are found), in which there is no positive law on the subject of negotiable notes applicable to the case? If he can, it must be upon the ground, that the foreign tribunal would recognise the validity of the transfer by the indorsement according to the law of the place, where it is made. According to the doctrine maintained in England, as *choses in action* are by the common law (independent of statute) incapable of being transferred over, it might be argued, that he could not maintain an action, notwithstanding the instrument was well negotiated, and transferred by the law of the place of the contract.[3]

---

1 Milne *v.* Graham, 1 B. and Cresw. R. 192. But see Carr *v.* Shaw, Bayley on Bills, 16, note.

2 De la Chaumette *v.* Bank of England, 2 B. & Adolp. R. 385; S. C. 9 B. & Cresw. 208; and see Chitty on Bills, p. 551, 552, (8th edit.)

3 See 2 Black. Comm. 442; Jeffrey *v.* McTaggart, 3 B. & Cres. 22, 23; Innes *v.* Dunlop, 8 T. R. 595. See also Jeffrey *v.* McTaggart, 6 M. & Selw. R. 126.

So far, as this principle of the non-assignability of *choses in action* would affect transfers in England, it would seem reasonable to follow it. But the difficulty is in applying it to transfers made in a foreign country, by whose laws the instrument is negotiable, and capable of being transferred, so as to vest the property and right in the assignee. In such a case it would seem, that the more correct rule would be, that the *lex loci contractûs* ought to govern; because the holder under the indorsement has an immediate and absolute right in the contract vested in him, as much as he would have in goods transferred to him. Under such circumstances to deny the legal effect of the indorsement is to construe the obligation, force, and effect of a contract, made in one place, by the law of another place. The indorsement in the place, where it is made, creates a direct contract between the maker and the first indorsee; and if so, that contract ought to be enforced between them every where. It is not a question, as to the form of the remedy; but as to the right.

§ 355. This view of the doctrine appears to have been taken in a recent case in England, much stronger in its circumstances, than a case of negotiable notes, which stands in some measure upon the custom of merchants. A suit was brought by the assignee of an Irish judgment against the judgment debtor in England, the judgment being made expresssly assignable by Irish statutes; and the objection was taken, that no action could be maintained by the assignee, because it would contravene the general principle of the English law, that *choses in action* were not assignable. But the Court intimated a strong opinion against this ground of argument; and the cause finally was disposed of upon another point; but in such a manner, as left the opinion in full force.[1] It is matter of surprise, that in some of the more recent discussions in England upon the negotiation of notes in foreign countries, this doctrine has not been distinctly insisted on. For, even in England, negotiable notes are not treated, as mere *choses in action;* but they are deemed to have a closer resemblance to personal chattels on account of their transferability; so that the legal property in them passes upon the transfer, as it does in the case of chattels.[2] If so, no one could doubt, that a title of transfer of personal property in a foreign country, good by the laws of the country, where it is made, ought to be held good everywhere.

§ 356. In the next place, let us suppose the case of a negotiable note, made in one country, and actually indorsed in another, by whose laws a transfer of notes by indorsement is not allowed. Could an action be maintained by the indorsee against the maker, in the courts of either country? If it could be maintained in the country, whose laws do not allow such a transfer, it must be upon the ground, that the original negotiability by the *lex loci contractûs*, is permitted to avail, in contradiction to the *lex fori.* On the other hand, if the suit should be brought in the country, where the note was made, the difficulty would be, that the transfer is bad, by the law of the place, where the indorsement took place. But, at the same time, it may be truly said to be entirely in conformity to the intent of the parties, and to the law of the original contract.[3]

---

1 O'Callagan *v.* Thomond, 3 Taunt. 82.

2 McNeil *v.* Holloway, 1 B. & Ald. R. 218.

3 See Chitty on Bills, ch. 6, p. 218, 219, (8th London edition.) See Kaims on Equity, B. 3, ch. 8, § 4.

§ 357. In the next place, let us suppose the case of a note not negotiable by the law of the place, where it is made, but negotiable by the law of the place, where it is indorsed; could an action be maintained, in either country, by the indorsee against the maker? It would seem, that in the country, where the note was made, it could not; because it would be inconsistent, within its own laws. But the same difficulty would not arise in the country, where the indorsement was made; and, therefore, if the maker used terms of negotiability in his contract, capable of binding him to the indorsee, there would not seem to be any solid objection to giving the contract its full effect there. And so it has been accordingly adjudged in the case of a note made in Connecticut, payable to A *or order*, but by the laws of that state, not negotiable there, and indorsed in New York, where it was negotiable. In a suit, in New York, by the indorsee against the maker, the exception was taken, and overruled. The Court, on that occasion, said, that personal contracts, just in themselves, and lawful in the place, where they are made, are to be fully enforced, according to the law of the place, and the intent of the parties, is a principle, which ought to be universally received and supported. But this admission of the *lex loci* can have reference only to the nature and construction of the contract, and its legal effect, and not *to the mode of enforcing it*. And the Court ultimately put the case expressly upon the ground, that the note was payable to the payee *or order;* and therefore, the remedy might well be pursued according to the law of New York against a party, who had contracted to pay to the indorsee.[1]

[1] Lodge *v.* Phelps, 1 John. Cases, 139; S. C. 2 Caines Cases in Err. 321. See Kaims on Equity, B. 3, ch. 8, § 4.

But, if the words, "or order," had been omitted in the note, so that it had not appeared, that the contract between the parties originally contemplated negotiability, as annexed to it, a different question might have arisen, which would more properly come under discussion in some other place; since it seems to concern the interpretation and obligation of contracts, though it has sometimes been treated as belonging to remedies.[1]

§ 358. Another case may be put, which has actually passed into judgment. A negotiable note was given by a debtor, resident in Maine, to his creditor, resident in Massachusetts. After the death of the creditor, his executrix, appointed in Massachusetts, indorsed the same in that state to an indorsee, who brought a suit, as indorsee, against the maker in the state courts of Maine. The question was, whether the note was, under the circumstances, suable by the indorsee; and the Court held, that it was not; for that the executrix could not herself have sued upon the note, without taking out letters of adminstration in Maine; and therefore she could not, by her indorsement, transfer the right to her indorsee.[2]

§ 359. It does not appear, by the report, whether the note was made in Massachusetts or in Maine. It is not, perhaps, in the particular case material, as the law, as to the negotiability of such a note, is, in both states, the same. If it had been different, it might have given rise to a different inquiry. But, in either state, the creditor could certainly, in his lifetime, by his indorsement have transferred the property in the

---

1 See Chitty on Bills, ch. 6, p. 218, 219, (8th London edit.); 3 Kent Comm. Lect. 44, p. 77, (2d edit.)

2 Stearns *v.* Burnham, 5 Greenl. R. 261; S. P. Thompson *v.* Wilson, 2 New Hampshire, R. 291.

note to the indorsee; and as clearly his executrix could do the same; for it is settled, that an executor or administrator can so transfer any negotiable security.[1] If, then, by the transfer in Massachusetts, the property passed to the indorsee, it is difficult to perceive, why that transfer was not as effectual in Maine, as in Massachusetts; and, by the law of both states, an indorsee may sue on negotiable instruments in his own name. In truth, such instruments are not treated, as mere *choses* in action, but rather as chattels personal. *Choses* in action are not assignable by law; and actions must be brought thereon in the name of the original parties. But negotiable notes are transferable by indorsement; and when transferred, the indorsee may sue in his own name. Upon the reasoning of the above case, the note would cease to be negotiable, after the death of the payee; which is certainly not admissible doctrine.[2] The decision, in a recent case, in the Supreme Court of the United States, is founded upon the doctrine, that an assignment by an executor of a *chose* in action in the state, where he is appointed, and which is good by its laws, will enable the assignee to sue in his own name in any other state, by whose laws the instrument would be assignable, so as to pass the note to the assignee, and enable him to sue thereon.[3]

§ 360. As to bills of exchange, it is generally required, in order to fix the responsibility of other parties, that, upon their dishonour, they should be duly

---

1 See Rawlinson *v.* Stone, 3 Wilson R. 1; S. C. 2 Str. R. 1260.

2 Rawlinson *v.* Stone, 3 Wilson R. 1; S. C. 2 Str. R. 1260; Bayley on Bills, ch. 5, p. 78. — The effect of assignments of debts and other personal property will come more fully under review in the succeeding chapter, when we enter upon the subject of the law, which regulates the transfer of personal property.

3 Harper *v.* Butler, 2 Peters Sup. Ct. R. 239.

protested by the holder, and due notice thereof given to such parties. And the first question, which naturally arises, is, whether the protest and notice should be in the manner, and according to the forms of the place, in which the bill is drawn, or of that, in which it is payable. By the common law, the protest is to be made, at the time, in the manner, and by the persons prescribed, in the place, where the bill is payable.[1] But, as to the necessity of making a demand and protest, and the circumstances, under which notice may be required or dispensed with, these are incidents of the original contract, which are governed by the law of the place, where the bill is drawn.[2] They constitute implied conditions, upon which the liability of the drawer is to attach, according to the *lex loci contractûs*; and, if the bill is negotiated, the like responsibility attaches upon each successive indorser, according to the law of the place of his indorsement; for each indorser is treated, as a new drawer.[3] The same doctrine, according to Pardessus, prevails in France.[4]

---

1 Chitty on Bills, p. 193, 506, 507, 508, (8th London edit.)

2 Id. 506, 507, 508, (8th London edit.)

3 Bayley on Bills, ch. A. (4th edit.) by Phillips & Sewall; Chitty on Bills, ch. 6, p. 266, 267, 370, (8th London edit.); Ballingalls *v.* Gloster, 3 East R. 481.

4 Pardessus, Droit Comm. art. 1496, 1497, 1498, 1499; Henry on Foreign Law, 53, Appx. p. 239 to 248. — Boullenois admits, that the protest ought to be according to the law of the place, where the bill is payable. But, in case of a foreign bill, indorsed by several indorsements in different countries, he contends, that the time, within which notice or recourse is to be had upon the dishonour, is to be governed by a different rule. Thus, he supposes, a bill drawn in England on Paris in favour of a French payee, who indorses it to a Spaniard (in Spain,) and he to a Portuguese (in Portugal,) and he to the holder; and then says, that the holder is entitled to have recourse against the Portuguese within the time prescribed by the law of France, because the holder is there to receive payment; the Portuguese is to give notice to the Spaniard

§ 361. Upon negotiable instruments, it is the custom of most commercial nations, to allow some time for payment beyond the period fixed by the terms of the instrument. The period of indulgence is commonly called the *days of grace;* as to which, the rule is, that the usage of the place, on which a bill is drawn, and where payment of a bill or note is to be made, governs as to the number of the days of grace to be allowed thereon.[1]

§ 362. This head, respecting contracts in general, may be concluded by remarking, that contracts respecting personal property and debts, are now universally treated, as having no *situs* or locality; and they follow the person of the creditor in point of right, (*inhærent ossibus creditoris*);[2] though the remedy on them must be according to the law of the place, where they are sought to be enforced. The common language is, *Mobilia non habent sequelam; actor sequitur forum rei; debita sequuntur personam debitoris.*[3] Indeed the doctrine is so firmly established, that it would be a waste of time to go over the authorities;[4] and especially as the same subject will

---

within the time prescribed by the law of Portugal, because that is the only law, with which he is presumed to be acquainted, &c. &c.; and so in regard to every other indorser, he is to have recourse within the period prescribed by the law of the place, where the indorsement was made, and not of the domicil of the party indorsing. 1 Boullenois, p. 370, 371, 372.

1 Bank of Washington *v.* Triplett, 2 Peters Sup. R. 30, 34; Chitty on Bills, (8th London edit.) p. 407; Id. 193.

2 Thorne *v.* Watkins, 2 Ves. 35; 1 Boullenois, 348; Livermore's Diss. p. 162, 163.

3 Kaims on Equity, B. 3, ch. 8, § 3, 4; Dwarris on Statutes, P. 2, p. 650; Livermore's Diss. p. 162, 163, 167.

4 See Bouhier, Coutum. de Bourg. ch. 21, § 172, p. 408; Id. ch. 22, § 79, p. 429; Id. ch. 25, § 5, 6, p. 490; Pothier, Des Choses, Tom. 8, P. 2, § 3, p. 109, 110; Id. Coutum. d'Orléans, Tom. 10 n. 24, p. 7;

occur, in a more general form, in the succeeding chapter. Debts, in the vocabulary of the civil law, are often known by the title of *nomina debitorum*.[1]

§ 363. But a question of a very different character may arise, as to contracts respecting real estate or immoveables. Are they governed by the law of the place, where the contract is made? Or by the law of the place, where the property is situate? Take, for instance, a case, in England or America, arising under the Statute of Frauds, by which all contracts respecting real estate, or any interest therein, are required to be in writing, and otherwise they are void. If a contract is made in France by parol, or otherwise, in a manner not conformable to the law *rei sitæ*, for the purchase of lands in England or America, and the contract is conformable to the law of France on the same subject; is the contract valid in both countries? Is it valid in the country, where the land lies, so as to be enforced there? If not; is it valid in the country, where the contract was made?

§ 364. If this question were to be decided exclusively by the law of England, it might be stated, that by the law of England, the contract would be utterly void; and it would be so held in a suit brought to enforce it in that realm, upon the ground, that all real contracts must be governed by the *lex rei sitæ*.[2] Lord Mansfield took occason, in a celebrated case, to examine, and state the principle. "There is a distinction," said

---

2 Bell. Comm. 684, 685; Bruce *v.* Bruce, 2 Bos. & Pull. 230; Sill *v.* Worswick, 1 H. B. 690, 691; In Re, Ewing, 1 Tyrush. R. 91; Thome *v.* Watkins, 2 Ves. 35; 4 Cowen R. 517, note; Blanchard *v.* Russell, 13 Mass. R. 6; Livermore's Diss. 163, 164 to 171.

[1] Ersk. Inst. B. 3, tit. 9, § 4; Cujacii Opera, Tom. 7, p. 491; Dig. Lib. 10, tit. 2, l. 2, § 6; Vicat. Vocab. Voce, Nomen.

[2] See 2 Dwarris on Statut. 648.

he, "between local and personal statutes. Local ones regard such things, as are really upon the spot in England; as the Statute of Frauds, which respects lands situate in this kingdom. So stock-jobbing contracts, and the statutes thereupon, have a reference to our local funds. And so the statutes for restraining insurances upon the exportation of wool respect our own ports and shores. Personal statutes respect transitory contracts, as common loans and insurances." [1] And in another report of the same case, after a second argument, he said: "In every disposition or contract, where the subject matter relates locally to England, the law of England must govern; and must have been intended to govern. Thus, a conveyance or will of land, a mortgage, a contract concerning stocks, must all be sued upon in England; and the local nature of the thing requires them to be carried into execution according to the law here." [2]

§ 365. The doctrine has been laid down in equally emphatic terms in the Scottish courts. Lord Robertson in a highly interesting case said: "Although the rule, as to the *lex loci contractûs* is of very general application, particularly as to the constitution and validity of personal contracts and obligations, it is not universal. *In the first place, it does not apply to contracts or obligations relative to real estates.*" [3] Lord Bannatyne, on the same occasion, affirmed the like principle.[4] And it has received an unequivocal sanc-

---

1 Robinson *v.* Bland, 1 W. Black. R. 234, 246.

2 Robinson *v.* Bland, 2 Burr. R. 1079; S. P. 1 W. Black. R. 259. See also Ersk. Inst. B. 3, tit. 9, § 4; Henry on Foreign Law, 12 to 15; Scott *v.* Alnutt, 2 Dow & Clarke, 404. See also 2 Dow R. 230, 250.

3 Fergusson on Marr. and Div. 395; Id. 397. See Ersk. Inst. B. 3, tit. 2, § 40, p. 515.

4 Fergusson Id. 401; 2 Kaims Equity, B. 3, ch. 2, § 2.

tion in America; where it has been broadly declared to be a well settled rule, that any title or interest in land or real estate can only be acquired or lost agreeably to the law of the place, where the same is situate.[1]

§ 366. This doctrine may be farther illustrated by the case of Scotch heritable bonds. By heritable bonds in that law are meant bonds for the payment of money, which are secured by a conveyance or charge upon real estate. Such bonds usually contain not only a charge upon real estate, but a personal obligation to pay the debt. In general, by the Scotch law, mere personal bonds and other debts, on the decease of the creditor, pass to his personal representative; but heritable bonds belong to the heir; because the charge on the real estate, being *jus nobilius*, draws to it the personal right to the debt. According to the Scotch law, no contract or other act disposing of an heritable bond will be good, unless it is according to the law of Scotland; and no contract, intended to create such a heritable bond, will be valid, as such, unless it be made with the solemnities of the Scotch law.[2]

§ 367. The same reasoning seems to have governed in the House of Lords, in a recent case, where certain entailed estates in Scotland were sold for the

---

1 Cutter *v.* Davenport, 1 Pick. R. 81; Hosford *v.* Nichols, 1 Paige R. 220; Wills *v.* Cowper, 2 Hamm. R. 124; S. C. Wilcox R. 278.

2 Ersk. Inst. B. 2, ch. 2, § 9 to 20, p. 198 to 204; Id. B. 3, tit. 2, § 39, 40, 41, p. 514, 515; Jerningham *v.* Herbert, 1 Tamyn R. 103; 2 Bell Comm. 7, 8; Id. 690. — Yet Mr. Erskine in his Institutes seems to admit, that obligations to convey things in Scotland, although not perfected in the Scottish form, yet if perfected according to the *lex domicilii* of the parties, are binding in Scotland, not as conveyances, but as contracts, under some circumstances.

redemption of the land tax, and the surplus money of the proceeds of the sale was vested, according to a statute on the subject, in trustees, who were required to pay the interest of it to the heir of entail in possession, until the money should be reinvested in land. The heir of entail next entitled sold his reversionary and contingent right to the interest of this fund by a deed in the English form, and executed in England, where the parties were domiciled, but without the solemnities required by the law of Scotland. It was admitted, that the fund was to go to the heirs in entail, and that the principal thereof was consequently heritable, and could only be passed according to the solemnities of the law of Scotland. But the House of Lords adjudged the intermediate interest of the surplus, before the investment in lands, to be moveable property, and alienable by the proprietor as such; and therefore they held the assignment of it according to the English law good.[1]

§ 368. From what has been already stated in the preceding discussions, it will be seen, that foreign jurists are by no means agreed in admitting this doctrine. On the contrary some of them maintain, that the validity of a contract is, in all cases, to be governed by the law of the place, where it is made, whether it regards moveables or immoveables. Thus, in respect to the capacity of persons to contract, their doctrine is, that, if they are of age to contract in the place of their domicil, but are not, in the place, where their immoveable proverty is situate, the contract to sell or alienate the latter will be valid everywhere; and

---

1 Scott v. Alnutt, 2 Dow & Clarke, 404, 412.

so, *vice versâ*.[1] Others hold a different opinion, and insist, that, whatever may be the law of the domicil as to capacity, and although it governs the person universally, yet it does not apply to immoveable property in another country.[2]

§ 369. So, in respect to express nuptial contracts, we have seen, that many foreign jurists hold them obligatory upon all property, whether moveable or immoveable, belonging to the parties in other countries, if they are valid by the law of the place of the nuptial contract. And in respect to implied nuptial contracts, all those jurists, who maintain, that the law of the domicil furnishes, in the absence of any express contract, the rule to ascertain the rights and intentions of

---

1 Ante, § 51 to 54, 58 to 60, 62, 63; Rodemburg, tit. 1, ch. 3; Id. tit. 2, ch. 3; Liverm. Diss. p. 48, 49, § 44, 45, 46; Id. p. 56, § 55, 56; Id. p. 58, § 58, 59; 1 Boullenois, 27, 145, 152, 153, 154, 175 to 177; 1 Froland Mém. 156, 160.

2 Ante § 54, 61; Liverm. Diss. p. 49 to 54, § 46 to 53; Id. p. 58, § 59. See 1 Boullenois, 127, 128, 129, 130, 135, 150, 151, 152 to 156; Voet. ad Pand. Lib. 1, tit. 4, § 7, p. 40; 2 Froland, 821. — There are some nice distinctions put by different authors upon this subject, which are stated with great clearness and force by Mr. Livermore, (Dissert. p. 58, § 58 to 62,) and upon which we may have occasion to comment more fully hereafter. At present it is only necessary to say, that Boullenois, Bouhier, and others hold, that, while the law of the domicil, as to general capacity, governs as to contracts and property everywhere, the law of the *situs* of immoveable property governs, as to the quantity, which the party, having full capacity, may sell, convey, or dispose of. See Livermore, Diss. p. 58, § 58 to 63; 1 Boullenois, Prin. Gén. 8, p. 7; Id. 127 to 133; Id. 172, 175 to 178; Id. 183, 184, 188, 189. Bouhier, Cout. de Bourg. ch. 21, § 68 to 70; Id. § 81 to 84. See also, 1 Boullenois, 101, 102, 107, 111, 112; 2 Henrys, Œuvres, Lib. 4, ch. 6, Quest. 105. Rodemburg seems to admit, that a contract respecting real property, which is entered into according to the forms of the *lex loci contractûs* may be good to bind the party personally, although it is not according to the forms prescribed by the *lex rei sitæ*. Rodemburg, tit. 2, ch. 3, p. 19; 1 Boullenois, 414, 415, 416. See also, Voet. De Statut. § 4, ch. 2, 15, p. 127.

the parties, by way of tacit contract, necessarily give to it the same universal operation.[1]

§ 370. Merlin seems to think, that, though in general the French law must govern in all cases of immoveables in France, even when the owners are foreigners; yet that there are exceptions to the rule. As, for instance, if the foreign law, in the country, where a contract is made respecting them, has been adopted by the contracting parties, and converted by them into an express contract; in such a case, he holds, that the contract is binding, because the foreign law, as such, does not act upon the immoveables in France; but solely by way of contract. And he applies the same principle to cases, where there is no express adoption of the foreign law, but it arises by way of tacit contract from the place of the contract.[2]

§ 371. On the other hand, Pothier treats as real, not only lands and houses and inheritable property, but all rights in them, and growing out of them; such as ground rents, or other rents annexed to lands and inheritances, which fall under the denomination of *jus in re;* and also all rights to inheritances, which fall under the denomination of *jus ad rem*, such as contracts or debts (*créances*) respecting the sale and delivery of immoveable property, which are deemed to have the same situation, as the things, which are the object of them. And he asserts the general principle, that all things, which have a *real* or *fictitious* situation, are subject to the law of the place, where they are situate, or are supposed to be situate. *Toutes ces choses, qui ont une situation réelle, ou feinte, sont*

---

[1] Ante, § 143 to 171; 1 Boullenois, 121, 673, 759 to 767.

[2] Merlin, Répertoire, Loi, § 6, n. 2, 3.

sujettes à la loi ou coutume du lieu, où elles sont situées, ou censées d'être.[1] And this is also the doctrine maintained by Rodemburg and Boullenois.[2] And Merlin, in a general view assents to it.[3] Pothier admits, that, when a debt is executed, and an hypothecation is made of immoveable property, as collateral security, the debt is still to be deemed a moveable, although the hypothecation might, *per se*, be an immoveable; because the debt is the principal, and the hypothecation the accessory; and *accessorium sequitur naturam principalis*. But he insists, that contracts, which have for their objects any inheritable property, or other immoveable, are to be deemed immoveables; such as, for instance, upon a contract for the purchase of real estate, the right of the vendee against the vendor for the delivery of the same.[4]

§ 372. Burgundus holds, that in all, which relates to the form, and solemnities, and perfection of contracts, and

---

1 Pothier, Coutum. d'Orléans, ch. 1, § 2 n. 24; Id. ch. 3, n. 51; Id. Traité des Choses, § 3.

2 1 Boullenois, Princ. Gén. 34, 35, 36, p. 8, 9; Id. 121, 129, 223, 224, 225, 374, 381, 488; 2 Boullenois, 472; Rodemburg, De Div. Stat. tit. 2, ch. 2, n. 2, p. 15; Henry on Foreign Law, 14 note; Id. 15. — Cochin lays down the following doctrine: "Les formalités, dont un acte doit être revêtu, se règlent par la loi, qui exerce son empire dans le lieu, où l'acte a été passé; mais, quand il s'agit d'appliquer les clauses, qu'il renferme, aux biens des parties contractantes, c'est le lieu de la situation de ses biens, qui doit seule être consultée." And he illustrates by reference to a donation, in Paris, of property, situate in places, where donations *inter vivos* are prohibited, holding, that such donations, although clothed with all the proper Parisian formalities, are nullities. He then adds, "Ce n'est donc pas la loi du lieu, où l'acte a été passé, qui en détermine l'effet." Cochin, Œuvres, Tom. 5, p. 697. See also 1 Boullenois, Prin. Gén. 31, p. 8.

3 Merlin, Répertoire, Meubles, § 5; Id. Biens, § 2 n. 2; Id. Loi. § 6, n. 3.

4 Pothier, Coutum. d'Orléans, ch. 3, art. 2, n 50, n. 51; Id. Traité des Choses, § 2. See Merlin, Répertoire, Biens § 1, n. 13, § 2, n. 1; Id. Meubles, § 2, 3; Liverm. Diss. p. 162, 163.

their legality, the law of the place, where they are made, is to give the rule. But, in what respects the subject matter of the contract, the law of the place, where it is locally situate, is to govern.[1] But when he comes to illustrate his doctrines by examples, it must be confessed, that both his classification and his decisions are open to much question.[2]

§ 373. But, whatever may be the rule in cases, where the law of the *situs* does not prohibit the contract, as for instance, in a sale of land, it is very clear, that, if prohibited there, it is invalid to all intents and purposes. So the doctrine is laid down by Rodemburg.[3] And Boullenois lays it down among his general maxims; *Une convention, toute légitime qu'elle soit en elle-même, n'a pas son exécution sur les biens, lorsqu'ils sont situés en coutumes prohibitives de la convention.*[4]

---

1 2 Boullenois, 449, 450, 451, 452 to 458.

2 2 Boullenois, 450, 451, 452 to 455.

3 Rodemburg, De Div. Stat. tit. 3, ch. 4. p. 79; 2 Boullenois, 401, 402.

4 1 Boullenois, Pr. Gén. 41, p. 9, 10.

CHAPTER IX.

PERSONAL PROPERTY.

§ 374. We next come to the consideration of the operation of foreign law in relation to personal, real, and mixed property, according to the known divisions of the common law, or to moveable and immoveable property, according to the known divisions of the civil law, and continental jurisprudence. For all the purposes of the present commentaries it will be sufficient to treat the subject under the heads of personal or moveable property, and real or immoveable property, since the class of mixed property appertains to the latter.

375. We have already had occasion to state, that in the civil law the term, "*bona*", includes all sorts of property, moveable and immoveable; as the corresponding word, "*biens*," in French also does.[1] But there are many cases, in which a broad distinction is taken by foreign jurists between moveable and immoveable property, as to the operation of foreign law. We have also had occasion to explain the general distinction between personal, real, and mixed laws in the sense, in which the terms are used in continental jurisprudence; personal, being those, which have principally persons for their object, and only treating of property incidentally; real, being those, which have principally property for their object, and speaking of persons only in relation to property; and mixed, being those, which concern both persons and property.[2]

1 See Livermore's Dissert. 81. § 106; 1 Boullenois, p. 28, 127.; Rodemburg, De Divers. Stat tit. 1 ch. 2. p. 6; Merlin, Répert., Biens, § 1.

2 Ante § 12 to 16; 1 Boull. Pr. Gén. p. 4 to 9; Id. p. 29; Id. 122, 123, 124, 125, 126, 127; P. Voet. De Stat. § 4, ch. 2, n. 2, p. 117.

§ 376. According to this distribution all laws respecting property, whether it be moveable or immoveable, would fall under the denomination of real laws; and, of course, upon the principles of foreign jurists, would seem to be limited in their operation to the territory, where the property is situate. This, however, is a conclusion, which upon a larger examination will be found to be erroneous, the general doctrine held by foreign jurists being, that the right and disposition of moveables is to be governed by the law of the domicil of the owner, and not by the law of their local situation.

§ 377. The grounds, upon which this doctrine, as to moveables, is supported, are differently stated by different jurists; but the differences are more nominal than real. Some of them are of opinion, that all laws, which regard moveables are real; but at the same time they maintain, that by a fiction of law all moveables are supposed to be in the place of the domicil of the owner, *a quo legem situmque accipiunt.* Others are of opinion, that such laws are personal, because moveables have in contemplation of law no *situs*, and are attached to the person of the owner, wherever he is; and, being so adherent to his person, they are governed by the same laws, which govern his person; that is, by the law of his place of domicil.[1] The former opinion is main-

---

1 "Mobilia (says J. Voet) vero ex lege domicilii ipsius defuncti, vel quia semper domino presentia esse finguntur, vel ex comitate passim usu inter gentes receptà." Voet. ad Pand. Lib. 38, tit. 17, § 34, p. 596. And in another place he adds, "Sed considerandum, quàdam fictione juris, seu malis, præsumptione, hanc de mobilibus determinationem conceptam niti; cum enim certo stabilique hæc (mobilia) situ careant, nec certo sint alligata loco, sed ad arbitrium domini undiquaque in domicilii locum revocari facile ac reduci possint, et maximum domino plerumque commodum adferre soleant, cum ei sunt præsentia; visum fuit hanc inde conjecturam surgere, quod dominus velle censeatur, ut illuc omnia sua sint mobilia, aut saltem esse intelligantur, ubi fortunarum suarum

tained by P. Voet, Rodemburg, and Boullenois, and the latter by D'Argentré, Burgundus, Hertius, and Bouhier.[1] Voet says, *Verum mobilia ibi censeantur esse, secundum juris intellectum, ubi is, cujus ea sunt, sedem atque larem suarum fortunarum collocavit.*[2] So Rodemburg; *Mobilia quippe non ideo subjacent statuto (reali), quod personale illud sit; sed quod mobilia, certo ac fixo situ carentia, ibi quemquam situm velle habere, ac existimare intelligimus, ubi larem ac fortunarum fixit summam. In domicilii loco mobilia intelligantur existere.*[3] Boullenois affirms the same doctrine; and gives this reason for it, that, as moveables have no such fixed and perpetual *situs*, as lands, it is necessary, that their *situs* should depend upon the pleasure of the owner, and that they have the very *situs* he wishes, when they have that of his own domicil.[4]

§ 378. On the other hand D'Argentré says, *De mobilibus alia censura est, quoniam per omnia ex conditione personarum legem accipiunt,* et situm habere *negantur, nisi affixa et cohærentia, nec loco contineri dicuntur propter habilitatem motionis et translationis. Quare statutum de bonis mobilibus vere* personale est, *et loco domicilii judicium sumit, et quodcumque judex domicilii de eo statuit, ubique locum obtinet.*[5] Bouhier is quite as explicit. As moveables (says he) have no fixed *situs*,

---

larem summamque constituit; id est, in loco domicilii." Voet. ad Pand. Lib. 1, tit. 4 P. 2, § 11, p. 44. Hertius says, "Nam mobiles ex conditione personæ legem accipiunt, nec loco continentur," 1 Hertii Opera, De Collis. Leg. § 4. n. 6, p. 122, 123.

1 Livermore's Dissert. p. 128, 129; 1 Boullenois, 338, 339, 340; 1 Hertii Opera, De Collis. Leg. § 4, n. 6, p. 122, 123.

2 Voet. De Stat. § 4, ch. 2, n. 2, p. 118; Id. § 9, ch. 1, § 8, p. 255.

3 Rodemburg, De Divers. Stat. Lib. 1, ch. 2, sub finem; 1 Boullenois 25, 28, 140.

4 1 Boullenois, 223, 224, 338; Id. Prin. Gén. 33, p. 8.

5 Livermore's Diss. 129, 130; 1 Boullenois, 339.

and are easily transported from one place to another according to the pleasure of the owner, therefore it is supposed, by a sort of fiction, that they adhere to his person; and from hence comes the maxim in our customary law, that moveables follow the body or person of the owner; *Meubles suivent le corps, ou la personne,— Mobilia sequuntur personam.*[1]

§ 379. But, whether the one opinion, or the other is adopted, it has been truly remarked by Boullenois, that the same conclusion is equally true, that moveables follow the person.[2] The probability is, that the doctrine itself had not its origin in any distinction as to real or personal laws, or in any fictitious annexation of them to the person of the owner, or their incapacity to have a fixed *situs*: but in an enlarged policy growing out of their transitory nature and the general convenience of nations. If the law *rei sitæ* were generally to prevail in regard to moveables, it would be utterly impossible for the owner, in many cases, to know, in what manner to dispose of them during his life, or to distribute them at his death; not only from the uncertainty of their situation in the transit to and from different places, but from the impracticability of knowing with minute accuracy the law of transfers *inter vivos*, or of testamentary dispositions and successions in the different countries, in which they might happen to be. Any change of place at a future time might defeat the best considered will; and a sale or donation might be rendered inoperative from the ignorance of the parties of

---

1 Bouhier. Cout de Bourg. ch. 25, § 2, p. 490; 1 Boullenois, 338.—"Les meubles (says Cochin), quelque part qu'ils soient, suivent le domicile." Cochin, Œuvres, Tom. 5, p. 85; 2 Henrys, Œuvres, Lib. 4, ch. 6, Quest. 105, p. 612. Id. 720.

2 Boullenois, 339. See also Voet. ad Pand. Lib. 38, tit. 17, § 34; 4 John. Ch. R. 487.

the law of the actual *situs* at the time of their acts. These would be serious evils, pervading the whole community, and equally affecting the subjects and the interest of all civilized nations. But in maritime nations, depending upon commerce for their revenues, their power, and their glory, the mischief would be incalculable. A sense of general utility, therefore, must have first suggested the doctrine; and as soon as it was promulgated, it could not fail to recommend itself to all nations by its simplicity, its convenience, and its enlarged policy.[1]

§ 380. But, be the origin of the doctrine what it may, it has so general a sanction among all civilized nations, that it may be treated as a part of the *jus gentium*. Lord Loughborough has stated it with great clearness and force in one of his most elaborate judgments. "It is a clear proposition," said he, "not only of the law of England, but of every country in the world, where law has the semblance of science, that personal property has no locality. The meaning of that is, not that personal property has no visible locality; but that it is subject to that law, which governs the person of the owner; both with respect to the disposition of it, and with respect to the transmission of it, either by succession or by the act of the party; it follows the law of the person. The owner in any country may dispose of his personal property. If he dies, it is not the law of the country, in which the property is, but the law of the country, of which he was a subject, that will regulate the succession."[2] And this doctrine has

---

1 See Harvey *v.* Richards, 1 Mason R. 412.

2 Sill *v.* Worswick, 1 H. Black. 690.

been constantly maintained both in England and America with unbroken confidence.[1]

§ 381. Foreign jurists are not less expressive in its favour. *Constat inter omnes* (says Bretonnier), *que les meubles suivent les personnes, et se règlent suivant la coutume du domicile.*[2] And he speaks the common language of the continental jurists.[3] Pothier, after remarking, that moveables have no locality, adds, that "all things, which have no locality, follow the person of the owner, and are consequently governed by the law or custom, which governs his person, that is to say, by that of the place of his domicil."[4] And Merlin adopts language equally general and exact. "Moveables," says he, "are governed by the law of the domicil of the owner, wherever they may be situate; and this law of course changes with his change of domicil."[5] Bynkershoek asserts the principle to be so well established, that no one has dared to question it; *Adeo recepta hodie sen-*

---

1 The authorities on this point are very numerous. See Henry on Foreign Law, 13, 14, 15; 4 Cowen R. 517, note; 2 Kent, Comment. Lect. 37, p. 428. &c. (2d Edit.); Id. 405; Kaims on Equity, B. 3, ch. 8, § 3 and 4. Erskine's Inst. B. 3, tit. 2, § 40. p. 515; Dwarris on Statutes, 649, 650; *In re* Ewing 1 Tyrwh. R. 91; 1 Rose's Bank. Cas. 478; 5 B. & Cres. 451, 452; 2 Bell, Com. 2 to 10; Piper *v.* Piper, Ambler R. 25; Potter *v.* Brown, 5 East R. 130; Holmes *v.* Remsen, 4 John. Ch. R. 460; Guier *v.* O'Daniel, 2 Binney, R. 349, note; Bruce *v.* Bruce, 2 Bos & Pull. 229, note; Livermore's Dissert. p. 128, to 132; De Sobrey *v.* De Laistre, 2 Harr. & John. R. 191, 224; Hunter *v.* Potts, 4 T. R. 182, 192; Phillips *v.* Hunter, 2 H. Black. 402, 405; Goodwin *v.* Jones, 3 Mass. R. 514, 517; Blake *v.* Williams, 6 Pick. R. 286, 314.

2 2 Henrys, Œuvres, Lib. 4, Quest. 127, p. 720.

3 See 1 Boullenois, 328, 339, 340; Bouhier, ch. 22, p. 429, § 79, ch. 25, p. 490, § 2; 5 Cochin, Œuvres, 85; Livermore's Diss. 129, 130; Huberus, Lib. 1. tit. 3, § 15.

4 Pothier, Coutum. d'Orléans, ch. 1, § 2, Tom. 10, p. 7; Id. Traité de Choses, § 3, Tom. 8. p. 109.

5 Merlin, Répert. Biens, § 1, n. 12; Id. Meubles, § 1; Id. Loi. § 6, n. 3.

tentia est, ut nemo ausit contra dicere.[1] Huberus says, *Verum in mobilibus nihil esse causæ, cur aliud quam jus domicilii sequamur, quia res mobiles non habent affectionem versus territorium, sed ad personam patris-familias duntaxat, qui aliud, quam quod in loco domicilii obtinebat, voluisse obtinere non potest.*[2] So that there seems an entire harmony on this point between foreign and domestic jurists.

§ 382. When, however, we speak of moveables, as following the person of the owner, and as governed by the law of his domicil, we are to limit the doctrine to the cases, in which they may be properly said to retain their original and natural character. For moveables may become annexed to immoveables, either by incorporation, or as incidents, and then they take the character of the latter. Thus, in the language of the common law, moveables, annexed to the freehold, are deemed a part of the latter. Such are the common cases of fixtures of personal property in houses, mills, and other hereditaments, whether for use, or for ornament. In the law of foreign countries a similar distinction is recognised; and wherever moveables become thus fixed by operation of law, or the express determination of the owner, they become a part of the immoveable property.[3] Voet ranks them among immoveables. *Idemque statuendum in mobilibus, per patris-familias destinationem perpetui usûs gratiâ ad certum locum, domum puta, vel*

---

1 2 Kent Comm. Lect. 37, p. 429, (2d edit.)

2 Huberus P. 1, Lib. 3, tit. 13, De Success. (S).

3 Pothier, Traité des Choses, § 1; Id. Coutumes d'Orléans, ch. 3, art. 46, 47, 48; Merlin, Répert. Biens, § 1, n. 13, § 2, n. 1; Id. Meubles, § 2, 3; 1 Bell Comm. 618; 2 Bell Comm. 2, 3, 4; 1 Boullenois, 340, 341; 1 Kaims on Equity, B. 3, ch. 8, § 3; Erskine's Inst. B. 3, Tit 9, § 4.

fundum, delatis, ita ut perpetuo illuc istius usûs causâ mansura sint, etiamsi nunquam immobilibus naturaliter jungenda sint.[1] And among the class of immoveables are also ranked (as we have seen) heritable bonds by the Scottish law, and ground rents, and other rents charged on lands.[2]

§ 383. It follows as a natural consequence of the rule, which we have been considering (that personal property has no locality), that the laws of the owner's domicil should in all cases determine the validity of every tranfer, alienation, or disposition made by the owner, whether it be *inter vivos*, or *post mortem.*[3] And this is regularly true, unless there is some positive or customary law of the country, where they are situate, providing for special cases (as is sometimes done), or, from the nature of the particular property, it has a necessarily implied locality.[4] Lord Mansfield has mentioned, as among the latter class, contracts respecting the public funds or stocks, the local nature of which, requires them to be carried into execution according

1 Voet. ad Pand. Lib. 1, tit. 8, n. 4.

2 1 Bell Comm. 648; 2 Bell Comm. 2, 3, 4; Erskine's Instit. B. 2, ch. 2, § 9 to 20; Pothier Traité des Choses, § 3; Ante § 366, 367, note.

3 Livermore's Dissert. 130 to 137.

4 Mr. Chief Justice Tilghman on one occasion said; "The proposition" (that personal property has no locality, but is transferred according to the law of the country, in which the owner is domiciled,) "is true in general, but not to its utmost extent, nor without several exceptions. In one sense personal property has locality, that is to say, if tangible, it has a place, in which it is situated, and if invisible (consisting of debts), it may be said to be in the place, where the debtor resides; and of these circumstances the most liberal nations have taken advantage, by making such property subject to regulations, which suit their own convenience." "Every country has a right of regulating the transfer of all personal property within its territory; but when no positive regulation exists, the owner transfers it at his pleasure." Moreton v. Milne, 6 Binn. R. 361.

to the local law.[1] The same rule may properly apply to all other local stock or funds, although of a personal nature, or so made by the local law, such as Bank and Insurance stock, Turnpike, Canal, and Bridge shares, and other incorporeal property, owing its existence to, or regulated by, peculiar local laws.[2] No positive transfer can be made of such property, except in the manner prescribed by the local regulations. But, nevertheless, contracts to transfer such property would be valid, if made according to the *lex domicilii* of the owner, or the *lex loci contractûs*, unless such contracts were specially prohibited by the *lex rei sitæ*; and the property would be treated, as personal, or as real, in the course of administration, according to the local law.[3]

§ 384. Subject to exceptions of this nature, (and there may be other cases, such as the statutable transfer of ships, and of goods in the warehouses or

---

1 Robinson *v.* Bland, 2 Burr. R. 1079; S. C. 1 W. Black. R. 247.

2 2 Bell Comm. 4, 5; 1 Bell Comm. 65, 67, 68. — Erskine, in his Institutes (B. 3, tit. 9, § 4) puts the like exceptions. "We must except (says he) from this general rule, as Civilians have done, certain moveables, which by the destination of the deceased are considered as immoveable. Among these may be reckoned the shares of the trading companies, or of the public stocks of any country, for example, the Banks of Scotland, England, and Holland, The South Sea Company, &c., which are, without doubt, descendible, according to the law of the state, where such stocks are fixed. But the bonds or notes of such companies make no exception from the general rule. They are accounted part of the moveable estate of the deceased." Ante § 364, 365.

3 Though stock abroad may be, as to its transfer, affected by the local laws, it is not to be treated, as of course, as partaking of the character of real estate, and descendible as such. On the contrary, if it be by the local law personal estate, it may be disposed of by an administration, as such; and the title passes, if it be made in the forms prescribed by the foreign law. See Attorney General *v.* Dimand, 1 Tyrwhitt R. 243. In the matter of Ewing, 1 Tyrwhitt R. 91. Erskine's Inst. B. 3, tit. 9, § 4; 1 Bell Comm. 65; 2 Bell Comm. 4, 5. Ante § 364, 365.

4 Abbott on Shipp. P. 1, ch. 2, § 10; 1 Chitty on Comm. and Manuf. 556, 558, 566, &c.; 2 Kent Comm. Lect. 45, p. 145, 146, (2d edition.)

docks of a government, which would fall within the same predicament,) the general rule is, that a transfer of personal property, good by the law of the owner's domicil, is valid, wherever it may be situate.[1] But it does not follow, that a transfer made by the owner, according to the law of the place of its actual *situs*, would not as completely devest his title, nor even that a transfer by him in any other foreign country, which would be good, according to the law of that country, would not be equally effectual, although he might not have his domicil there. For purposes of this sort, his personal property may, in many cases, be deemed subject to his disposal, wherever he may happen to be at the time of the alienation. Thus, a merchant, domiciled in America, may, doubtless, transfer his personal property according to the law of his domicil, wherever the property may be. But, if he should direct a sale of it, or make a sale of it in a foreign country, where it is situate at the time, according to the laws thereof, either in person, or by an agent, the validity of such a sale could scarcely be doubted. And if a merchant is temporarily abroad, he is understood to possess a general authority to transfer such property, as accompanies his person, wherever he may be; so always, that he does not violate the law of the country, where the act is done.[2] The general convenience and freedom of commerce require this enlargement of the rule; for, otherwise, the sale of personal property, actually situate in a foreign country, and made accord-

---

1 1 Kaims on Equity, B. 3, ch. 8, § 3. — In the case of a moveable subject (says Erskine), lying in Scotland, the deed of transmission, if perfected according to the *lex domicilii*, is effectual to carry the property, for moveables have no permanent situation. Ersk. Inst. B. 3, tit. 2, § 40, p. 515.

2 See 1 Kaims on Equity, B. 3, ch. 8, § 3.

ing to the forms prescribed by its laws, might be declared null and void in the country of the domicil of the owner. In the ordinary course of trade with foreign countries, no one thinks of transferring personal property according to the forms of his own domicil; but it is transferred according to the forms prescribed by the law of the place, where the sale takes place.

§ 385. A question, involving other considerations, may be presented; and that is, whether a transfer of personal property is good, which is made according to the law of the owner's domicil, but not in conformity to the law of the place, where it is situate? And whether there is any difference in such a case, between the transfer being made by the owner in his place of domicil, or its being made in the place *rei sitæ?* For instance, let us suppose, that, by the law of the domicil of the owner, a sale of goods is complete, and perfect, to pass the title without any delivery; and that, by the law of the place of their *situs*, the sale is not complete, until delivery. In such a case, if the transfer of the goods is made in the domicil of the owner, would it be valid without any delivery, so as to pass the title against third persons? If it would, in such a case; what would be the effect, if the transfer was made in the place, where the goods were situate, without any delivery?

§ 386. The former question has been much discussed in the courts of Louisiana, from a supposed difference between the rule of the common law, and that of the civil law, on this subject. By the common law, a sale of goods was, on these occasions, asserted to be complete without delivery.[1] But by the law of

---

[1] The common law deems a sale, as between the parties, complete without delivery; but not as to third persons. If, therefore, a sale is

Louisiana, delivery is necessary to complete the transfer, according to the well known rule of the civil law, *Traditionibus et usucapionibus dominia rerum, non nudis pactis, transferuntur.*[1] Upon the fullest examination, and repeated arguments, the Supreme Court of Louisiana have held the doctrine, that the transfer of personal property in that state is not complete, so as to pass the title against creditors, unless a delivery is made in conformity to the laws of that state, although the transfer is made by the owner in his foreign domicil, and would be good without delivery by the laws of that domicil.[2]

§ 387. The reasoning, by which this doctrine is maintained, is most fully developed in a case, in which a transfer of a part of a ship was made in Virginia, the ship, at the time of the sale, being locally at New Orleans; and, before any delivery, she was attached by the creditors of the vendor. It was, therefore, a case of conflict between the creditor and the purchaser. The learned Judge, who delivered the opinion of the

---

made, the purchaser, in order to complete his title against creditors and other purchasers, must take possession within a reasonable time. And, where the property is at sea at the time, and is incapable of delivery, there the title is complete without delivery. But it may be lost by an omission to take possession within a reasonable time after its arrival in port. See Meeker *v.* Wilson, 1 Gallison R. 419; 1 Black. Comm. 446, 448; 2 Kent Comm. 492, 493, 498; Id. 515 to 522; Bohlen *v.* Cleveland, 5 Mason R. 174; 3 Chitty on Comm. and Manuf. ch. 5, § 2, p. 272, &c; Lanfear *v.* Sumner, 17 Mass. R. 110; Bigelow's Digest, *Sale*, A. B.

1 Cod. Lib. 2, tit. 3, l. 20; Olivier *v.* Townes, 14 Martin R. 93, 102; Norris *v.* Mumford, 4 Martin R. 20; Dumford *v.* Brooks's Syndics, 3 Martin R. 222, 225.

2 The point appears to have been first decided in Norris *v.* Mumford, 4 Martin R. 20; and it has been repeatedly since adjudged in other cases, and particularly in Ramsay *v.* Stevenson, 5 Martin, 23; Fisk *v.* Chandler, 7 Martin R. 24; and Olivier *v.* Townes, 14 Martin R. 93. Mr. Livermore has contested the doctrine asserted in these decisions with great earnestness. Livermore's Dissert. p. 137 to 140.

Court, on that occasion, said, "The position assumed in the present case is, that by the laws of all civilized countries, the alienation of moveable property, must be determined according to the laws, rules, and regulations in force, where the owner's domicil is situated. Hence, it is insisted, that, as by the law existing in the state, where the vendor lived, no delivery was necessary to complete the sale, it must be considered as complete here; and, that it is a violation of the principle just referred to, to apply to the contract rules, which are peculiar to our jurisprudence, and different from those contemplated by the parties to the contract.

§ 388. "We readily yield an assent to the general doctrine, for which the appellee contends. He has supported it by a variety of authorities drawn from different systems of jurisprudence. But some of those very books furnish also the exception, on which we think this case must be decided, namely, that 'when those laws clash with, and interfere with the rights of the citizens of the countries, where the parties to the contract seek to enforce it, as one or other of them must give way, those prevailing, where the relief is sought, must have the preference." Such is the language of the English books, to which we have been referred; and Huberus, whose authority is more frequently resorted to on this subject than that of any other writer, because he has treated it more extensively, and with greater ability, in his Treatise *De Conflictu Legum*, tells us, *Effecta contractuum, certo loco initorum, pro jure loci illius alibi quoque observantur, si nullum inde civibus alienis creetur prejudicium, in jure sibi quæsito;* The effects of a contract entered into at any place, will be allowed according to the law of that place, in other countries, if no inconvenience will result therefrom, to the citizens of that other country, with respect to the right, which they demand. This distinction appears to us founded on the soundest reasons. The municipal laws of a country have no force beyond its territorial limits; and when another government permits these to be carried into effect within her jurisdiction, she does so upon a principle of comity. In doing so, care must be taken, that no injury is inflicted on her own citizens; otherwise justice would be sacrificed to courtesy. Nor can the foreigner or stranger complain of this. If he sends his property within a jurisdiction, different from that, where he resides, he impliedly submits it to the rules and regulations in force in the country, where he places it. *What the law protects, it has a right to regulate.* A strong evidence of this is furnished by the doctrine in regard to successions. The general principle is, that the personal property must be distributed according to the law of the state, where the testator dies; but, so far as it concerns creditors, it is governed by the law of the country, where the property is situated. If an Englishman or a Frenchman dies abroad, and leaves effects here, we regulate the order, in which his debts are paid, by our jurisprudence, not by that of his domicil."

§ 389. "We proceed to examine, whether, giving effect to the law of Virginia, on the contract now set up, would be working an injury to this state, or its citizens. In doing this, we must look to the general doctrine, and the effect it would have on our ordinary transactions, as well as its operation in this particular case. If we held here, that this sale can defeat the attachment, we should, on the same principle, be obliged to decide, that the claimant would hold the object sold in preference to a second purchaser, to whom it was delivered; the rule being, that, when the debtor can sell, and give to the buyer a good title, the creditor can seize; or, in other words, where the first sale is not complete as to third persons, the creditor may attach and acquire a lien.[1] In relation to moveable property, our law has provided, that delivery is essential to complete the contract of sale, as to third parties. This valuable provision, by which all our citizens are bound in their dealings, protects them from the frauds, to which they would be daily subjects, were they liable to be affected by previous contracts, not followed by the giving of possession. The exemption contended for here, in behalf of the residents of another state, would deprive them of that protection, wherever their rights, as purchasers, came in contact with strangers; a protection, which, it may be remarked, it is of the utmost importance, owing to our peculiar position, that we should carefully maintain. This City is becoming a vast storehouse for merchandise sent from abroad, owned by non-residents, and deposited here for sale; and our most important commercial transactions are in relation to property so situated. If the purchasers of it shonld be affected by all the previous contracts made at the owners' domicil, although unaccompanied by delivery, it is easy to see, to what impositions such a doctrine would lead; to what inconvenience it would expose us; and how severely it would check and embarrass our dealings. However anxious we may be to extend courtesy, and afford protection to the people of other countries, who come themselves, or send their property, within our jurisdiction, we cannot indulge our feelings so far, as to give a decision, that would let in such consequences,

1 McNeil *v.* Glass, 13 Martin R. 261.

as we have just spoken of. It would be giving to the foreign purchaser an advantage, which the resident has not; and that, frequently, at the expense of the latter. This, in the language of the law, we think, would be a *great inconvenience* to the citizens of this state; and, therefore, we cannot sanction it."[1]

§ 390. There is certainly great force in this reasoning upon general principles. And no one can seriously doubt, that it is competent for any state to adopt such a rule in its own legislation, since it has perfect jurisdiction over all property, personal as well as real, within its territorial limits.[2] Nor can such a rule, made

---

[1] Olivier *v.* Townes, 14 Martin R. 97 to 103. But see 1 Kaims on Equity, B. 3, ch. 8, § 3.—The doctrine of this case seems supported by that of Lanfear *v.* Sumner (17 Mass. R. 110), although in the latter case the Court do not found their judgment upon any supposed conflict between foreign and domestic laws. There can be little doubt, that the sale and assignment in Philadelphia, in that case, was a complete transfer by the *lex loci contractûs*; and there was certainly legal diligence in endeavouring to obtain possession after the sale. The Court, however, thought, that delivery was essential to perfect the transfer by the law of Massachusetts; and, as there had been no delivery, until the property was attached by the attaching creditor in Massachusetts, they decided in favour of the title of the latter, against the vendee. The Court also said, that where each of the parties claimed the same goods by a legal title, he, who first obtained possession, would hold against the other; and for this principle, they relied on Lamb *v.* Durant, 12 Mass. R. 54; and Caldwell *v.* Ball, 1 Term Rep. 205. The former is certainly in point. But in the latter the decision was in favour of the party, who first had acquired a legal title by the prior indorsement of the bills of lading to him. "Whoever (said Ashurst J.) was first in possession (not of the goods, but) of either of these bills of lading, had the legal title vested in him." Buller J. said, "Both parties claim under T; but F & Co. have the first legal right, for two bills of lading were first indorsed to them." But see Conard *v.* Atlantic Insurance Company, 1 Peter's Sup. R. 386, 445; Nathan *v.* Giles, 5 Taunt. R. 558; Bohlen *v.* Cleveland, 5 Mason R. 174.

[2] See Livermore's Dissert. 137, 138, 159, 161, 162; Hall *v.* Campbell, Cowper R. 208; Hunter *v.* Potts, 4 T. R. 182, 192; Phillips *v.* Hunter, 2 H. Black. 402, 405; Sill *v.* Worswick, 1 H. Black. R. 673, 690, 691; Davis *v.* Jaquin, 5 Harr. & John. R. 100.

for the benefit of innocent purchasers and creditors, be deemed justly open to the reproach of being founded in a narrow or selfish policy. But, how far a court of justice ought, upon its own general authority, to interpose such a limitation, independently of legislation, has been thought to admit of more serious question; since the doctrine, which it unfolds, aims a direct blow at the soundness of the policy, on which the general rule, that personal property has no locality, is itself founded.[1] It is not, indeed, very easy to reconcile it with the doctrine maintained by Lord Loughborough (which has been already cited),[2] or with other cases to the same effect. Nor is it easy to say, to what extent it may be pressed in subversion of the general rule; since every country has so many minute regulations in regard to the transfers of personal property incorporated into its municipal code, each of which may be properly deemed beneficial to its own government, or to the interests of its citizens.

§ 391. Another case, illustrative of the doctrine, may be stated. A ship belonging to New York, and owned there, was transferred, while at sea, according to the law of the owner's domicil; and it subsequently arrived at New Orleans, and was attached by creditors, before any delivery to the vendee; and the question was, whether the attachment overreached the title by the transfer. The Supreme Court of Louisiana held, that it did not; and that the transfer was valid to all intents and purposes. The Court took the distinction, that

1 See Livermore's Dissert. p. 137 to 140.

2 Ante § 380; 1 H. Bl. 690. See also 1 Kaims on Equity, B. 3, ch. 8, § 3; Erskine's Inst. B. 3, tit. 2, § 40; Bruce *v.* Bruce, 2 Bos. & Pull. 229, note, 231; Hunter *v.* Potts, 4 T. R. 182, 192; Phillips *v.* Hunter, 2 H. Black. 402, 405.

the transfer was complete before the Louisiana laws could locally attach upon it. "In the present case (said the Court), the ship, the subject of the sale, was a New York ship, and the vendor and vendee resident in New York. If, therefore, according to the *lex loci contractûs*, that of the domicil of both parties, the sale transfers the property without a delivery, it did *eo instanti*, or not at all. In transferring it, it did not work any injury to the rights of the people of another country; it did not transfer the property of a thing within the jurisdiction of another government. If two persons in any country choose to bargain, as to the property, which one of them has in a chattel not within the jurisdiction of the place, they cannot expect, that the rights of persons in the country, in which the chattel is, will be permitted to be affected by their contract. But, if the chattel be at sea, or in any other place, if any there be, in which the law of no particular country prevails, the bargain will have its full effect, *eo instanti*, as to the whole world. And the circumstance of the chattel being afterwards brought into a country, according to the laws of which the sale would be invalid, would not affect it."[1] But, if the ship had been, at the time of the sale, in New Orleans, and she had been attached before an actual delivery to the vendee, the title of the attaching creditor would have prevailed.[2]

§ 392. But, suppose persons, claiming as purchasers, under different transfers of the same personal property, one by a transfer from a partner in the place, where the property is locally situate, and another by a

---

1 Thuret *v.* Jenkins, 7 Martin R. 318, 353, 354.

2 Price *v.* Morgan, 7 Martin R. 707.

transfer made by the other partner in the domicil of the firm; and by the law of the latter place delivery is not essential to complete the transfer; but by the law of the former it is; which title is to prevail? According to the doctrine held in Louisiana, the title of the purchaser in the place *rei sitæ* ought to prevail.[1] And that doctrine seems confirmed by the reasoning in decisions of the Supreme Court of Massachusetts, although the precise point as to the conflict of laws was not litigated, and the law of Massachusetts was supposed to require a delivery to complete the title.[2]

§ 393. A case somewhat different has been put by the Supreme Court of Louisiana. "If (say the Court) A and B be partners in New Orleans, and C purchases from A a quantity of cotton in the warehouse of the firm; will his right thereto, if he take instant possession of it, be affected by a sale made a few days before by B in Natchez, or Mobile? Will not C be listened to in his own state, when he shows, that by the *lex fori*, by that *loci contractûs*, by that of the domicil of his vendors, and of his own, the sale and delivery vested the property?"[3] The case is certainly very strongly put. But, after all, it must entirely depend upon the point, whether the prior transfer at Natchez or Mobile conveyed a perfect title by the law of those places, without delivery; and if so, whether the *lex rei sitæ* ought to prevail against it? If no delivery were required by the law of Louisiana to perfect the title, the Natchez or Mobile purchaser would prevail, even in the courts

---

1 Ramsay *v.* Stevenson, 5 Martin R. 23, 77, 78; Thuret *v.* Jenkins, 7 Martin R. 353.

2 See Lamb *v.* Durant, 12 Mass. R. 54; Lanfear *v.* Sumner, 17 Mass. R. 110; Ante § 386, 389, note.

3 Thuret *v.* Jenkins, 7 Martin R. 353.

of Louisiana, against the purchaser in New Orleans, whatever might be the apparent hardship of the case under the circumstances.

§ 394. On the other hand, let us take the case of a shipment of goods from England to New Orleans, on account and risk of a merchant domiciled in England, who owes debts in New Orleans; and a subsequent transfer of the bill of lading in England to a purchaser, after their arrival at New Orleans, but before the unlading thereof. Could a creditor of the shipper at New Orleans in such a case, by an attachment, oust the title of the purchaser, because there had been no delivery to the purchaser under the bill of lading? By the law of England,[1] and, indeed, by that of many other commercial states, the legal title of the goods passes by the mere indorsement and delivery of the bill of lading, without any actual possession of the goods by the purchaser.[2] Would such a title so acquired be devested by the want of a delivery according to the laws of Louisiana? If so, it would most materially impair the confidence, which the commercial world have hitherto reposed in the universal validity of the title acquired under a bill of lading. No opinion is intended to be expressed on the point; but it is presented in order to show, that the doctrine is not without its embarrassments.

§ 395. If, however, the doctrine of the law *rei sitæ* is to prevail over that of the law of the place of the trans-

---

1 Lickbarrow *v.* Mason, 2 T. R. 63; Abbott on Shipp. P. 3, ch. 9, § 16.

2 By the old French law, bills of lading were not negotiable, so as to pass a title in the property to the assignee, but only gave him a right of action subordinate to the rights of third persons; 1 Émérigon Assur. ch. 11, § 3. By the Code of Commerce (art. 281), bills of lading are now negotiable, so as to pass the property to the indorsee. See 3 Pardessus, P. 3, tit. 4, ch. 3, art. 727.

fer, what is to be said in relation to assignments of *choses in action*, due by debtors, resident in a foreign country? Would an attachment before notice defeat such assignments in favour of the attaching creditor, although notice of the assignment should be given within a reasonable time?[1] By the law of some countries an assignment of a debt is good without notice, and takes effect *instanter;* by the law of other countries notice is necessary to perfect the title. Would an assignment of a debt in the creditor's domicil, where it would be good without notice, be ineffectual, if the debtor resided in a country, where notice would be necessary? Suppose an attachment made by a creditor, in the intervening period between the time of the assignment and the notice; would the assignment or the attachment be entitled to a preference?[2] By the Scottish law a creditor may assign his debt to another person; but the transfer is not complete, so as to vest the title absolutely in the assignee, until notice of the assignment, or, (as the Scotch phrase is) until an intimation of the assignment is given to the debtor. If, therefore, an assignment is made, a creditor of the original creditor may, before such intimation, arrest or attach the debt in the hands of the debtor, and will thereby acquire a preference over the assignee. That doctrine, it would seem, has been actually applied in Scotland to debts due by Scottish debtors to foreign creditors, and assigned in the domicil of the latter.[3]

---

1 See Sill *v.* Worswick, 1 H. Black. 691, 692; Bohlen *v.* Cleveland, 5 Mason R. 174. See Holmes *v.* Remsen, 4 John. Ch. R. 460; Lewis *v.* Wallis, Sir Thom. Jones's R. 223; 1 Kaims, Equity, B. 3, ch. 8, § 3, p. 344.

2 See *In re* Wilson, cited 1 H. Black. 691, 692.

3 Selkrig *v.* Davis, 2 Rose Bank. Cas. 315; Stein's Case, 1 Rose Bank. Cas. 481; 2 Bell Comm. 21, 22, 23. But see *In re* Wilson, cited

§ 396. According to our law, a different doctrine would prevail; for an assignment operates, *per se*, as an equitable transfer of the debt. Notice is, indeed,

---

1 H. Black. 691, 692. — I have stated the law of Scotland, as I understand it to be stated in the opinion of Lord Eldon, in Selkrig *v.* Davis (2 Rose Bank. Cas. 315), though it would seem to be exactly like the Massachusetts law stated in the next section (§ 396). And so it was understood by Lord Hardwicke, and Lord Loughborough. The following passage from the judgment of the latter, in Sill *v.* Worswick (1 H. Black. R. 691, 692,) gives a very exact view of their opinions. "A question of this nature came before Lord Hardwicke very largely in the bankruptcy of Captain Wilson. With the little explanation I am enabled to give of that case, in which the Court of Session entirely concurred with Lord Hardwicke, the distinctions will be apparent. There were three different sets of creditors, who claimed, subject to the determination of the Court, on the ground, that Wilson had considerable debts due to him in Scotland. By the law of Scotland, debts are assignable, and an assignment of a debt notified to the debtor, which is technically called an *intimation*, makes a specific lien *quoad* that debt. An assignment of a debt not intimated to the debtor, gives a right to the assignee to demand that debt; but it is a right inferior to that of the creditor, who has obtained his assignment and intimated it. By the law of Scotland also, there is a process for the recovery of debts, which is called an *arrestment*. Some of Wilson's creditors had assignments of specific debts intimated to the debtors and completed by that intimation, prior to the act of bankruptcy. Others had assignments of debts not intimated before the bankruptcy. Others had arrested the debts due to him subsequent to the bankruptcy, and were proceeding under those arrestments to recover payment of those debts. The determination of Lord Hardwicke, and that of the Court of Session, entirely concurred. The first class I have mentioned, namely, the creditors, who had specific assignments of specific debts, intimated to the debtors prior to the bankruptcy, were holden by Lord Hardwicke to stand in the same situation, as creditors claiming by mortgage antecedent to the bankruptcy. All, therefore, he would do with respect to them was, that, if they recovered under that decree, they could not come in under the commission without accounting to the other creditors, for what they had taken under their specific security. With respect to the next class of creditors, Lord Hardwicke was of opinion, and the Court of Session were of the same opinion, that their title, being a title by assignment, was preferable to the title by arrestment; and they likewise held, that the arrestments, being subsequent to the bankruptcy, were of no avail, the property being by assignment vested in the assignees under the commission.

indispensable to charge the debtor with the duty of payment to the assignee; so that, if, without notice, he pays the debt to the assignor, or it is recovered by process against him, he will be discharged from the debt. But an arrest or attachment of the debt in his hands, by any creditor of the assignor, will not entitle such creditor to a priority of right, if the debtor receives notice of the assignment, *pendente lite*, and in time to avail himself of it in discharge of the suit against him.[1]

§ 397. In such a case of conflict of laws, the difficulty of applying any other than the general principle, that moveables are transferable according to the law of the domicil of the owner, is apparent. Let us take the case of a Massachusetts creditor, assigning in that state a debt contracted there, and due to him by a person then domiciled in Scotland. The transfer is in equity complete in the place, where it is made, without notice; but in the place, where the debt is due, it is not complete without notice. To give effect, in such a case, to the law

---

It is in this sense, that an expression has been used by Lord Mansfield, in one or two cases, in which his language, rather than his decision, has been quoted, with respect to the law of Scotland, namely, that the effect of the assignment under a commission of bankruptcy was the same, as a voluntary assignment. For so the law of Scotland treats it, in contradistinction to the assignment perfected by intimation, and to an assignment, which the party might be compelled to make. But it does not follow, that it is an assignment without consideration. On the contrary, it is for a just consideration; not, indeed, for money actually paid, nor for a consideration immediately preceding the assignment. In that respect, therefore, it is a voluntary assignment. But taking it to be so, it excludes, and is preferable to all others attaching; it is preferable to all the arresters; it is preferable to all creditors, who stand under the same class; and to all, who have not taken the steps to acquire a specific lien till after the act of bankruptcy committed."

1 Foster *v.* Sinkler, 4 Mass. R. 450; Blake *v.* Williams, 13 Mass. R. 286, 307, 308, 314; Wood *v.* Partridge, 11 Mass. R. 488; Dix *v.* Cobb, 4 Mass. R. 508; Bohlen *v.* Cleveland, 5 Mason R. 174; Holmes *v.* Remsen, 4 John. Ch. R. 460, 486.

of Scotland, in opposition to that of Massachusetts, would be to give a locality to the debt, and to subject it to the exclusive operation of the law of the debtor's domicil. And it might involve this most serious difficulty, that, if the debtor were afterwards found in Massachusetts, or in any other country than Scotland, he might be compelled to pay the debt to the assignee, although it might have been recovered from him in Scotland by a creditor, in a proceeding by attachment of the debt in his hands, he having had notice of the assignment, *pendente lite*.

§ 398. The reasoning of Lord Kenyon, in a celebrated case,[1] would certainly lead to the conclusion, that an assignment of personal property, whether it were of goods or debts, according to the law of the owner's domicil, would pass the title, in whatever country it might be, unless there were some prohibitory law in that country. His language is, "Every person having property in a foreign country may dispose of it in this; though, indeed, if there be a law in that country, directing a particular mode of conveyance, that ought to be adopted. But in this case no law of that kind is stated; and we cannot conjecture, that it is not competent to the bankrupt himself, prior to his bankruptcy, to have disposed of his property, as he pleased." The same doctrine is maintained by Lord Hardwicke, and Lord Loughborough. And all these learned Judges apply it equally to the cases of assignments of goods and debts, and to voluntary assignments by the party; and also (as we shall more fully see hereafter) to assignments by operation of law, as in bankruptcy. The question of prior notice, or intimation, does not seem to

---

[1] Hunter *v.* Potts, 4 T. R. 182, 192. See Livermore's Dissert. p. 140 to 159; Id. p. 159, § 249.

have been thought by them material, for they treat the transfer, as complete, from the time of the assignment; and, if that has priority, in point of time, over an arrest, or attachment, it is to prevail. The law of England would certainly give effect to such an assignment of any goods or debts in England, which were assigned by the owner in a foreign country.[1]

§ 399. Lord Kaims, in commenting on the subject says, "That, considering a debt as a subject belonging to the creditor, the natural fiction would be (if any were admissible) to place it with the creditor, as in his possession, upon the maxim, *Mobilia non habent sequelam.* Others are more disposed to place it with the debtor."[2] But, in fact, a debt is not a *corpus* capable of local position, but purely a *jus incorporale.* And, therefore, where the debtor and creditor live in different countries, and are subjected to different laws, he thinks the law of the domicil of the creditor ought to prevail.[3]

---

1 See Solomons *v.* Ross and other cases cited, 1 H. Black. 131, 132, note; Sill *v.* Worswick, 1 H. Black. 665, 690, 691; *In re* Wilson, cited Ibid p. 691, 692, 693; Lewis *v.* Wallis, T. Jones R. 223. See also Selkrig *v.* Davis, 2 Rose Bank. Cas. 97; S. C. Id. 291, 315, 316, 317; Kaims on Equity, B. 3, ch. 8, § 4; Scott *v.* Alnutt, 2 Dow & Clarke R. 404, 412; Livermore's Diss. p. 159; Ogden *v.* Saunders, 12 Wheaton R. 364, 365. See also Merlin, Répertoire, Faillité, p. 412, 414, 415.

2 Kaims on Equity, B. 3, ch. 8, § 4. See Morrison's Case, 4 T. R. 185; 1 H. Black. 677.

3 On this point I cannot do better than insert a passage from Mr. Livermore's Dissertations (p. 162, § 251), illustrative of the same principles. "It was formerly doubted by some, whether personal actions should be considered as moveables, and whether they should not be considered to have a location in the domicil of the debtor. But the common opinion seems to be well settled, that, considered *actively*, and with respect to the interest of the creditor and his representatives, they must be considered, as attached to the person of the creditor; and this, although the payment of the debt is secured by an hypothecation upon an immoveable property. Such is the doctrine of Dumoulin. 'Nomina et jura, et quæcumque incorporalia, non circumscribantur loco, et sic non opus est accedere ad certum locum. Tum si hæc jura alicubi esse

He then adds, "When the creditor makes a voluntary conveyance, it is to be expected, that he should speak in the style and form of his own country; and, consequently, that the rule of his own country should be the rule here. In a word, the will of a proprietor, or of a creditor, is a good title *jure gentium*, that ought to be effectual everywhere. Thus, an assignment made by a creditor in Scotland, according to our forms, of a debt due to him by a person in a foreign country, ought to be sustained in that country, as a good title for demanding payment; and a foreign assignment of a debt due here, regular according to the law of the country, ought to be sustained by our judges."[1] In another place he adds, "An equitable title in opposition to one, that is legal, can never found a real action *(actio in rem.)* It cannot have a stronger effect than to found an action against the proprietor to grant a more formal right, or, in his default, that the Court shall grant it. But in the case of a debt, where the question is not about property, but payment, an equitable title coincides, in a good measure, with a legal title. An assignment made

---

censerentur, non reputarentur esse in re pro illis hypothecatâ, nec in debitoris personâ, sed magis in personâ creditoris, in quo activè resident, et ejus ossibus inhærent.' So also Casaregis, after saying, that moveables are attached to the person of the owner, and, at his death, will be distributed according to the laws of his domicil, proceeds to consider, what will be the rule with respect to debts, and determines, that they follow the person of the creditor. 'An ita dicendum de nominibus debitorum, actionibus, ac juribus, quæ bona neque dicuntur mobilia, neque immobilia, sed tertiam speciem bonorum componunt, et dicuntur incorporalia? Et respondeo affirmativè, nam statutum benè comprehendit nomina debitorum, licèt forensium, quia eorum obligationes non circumscribuntur locis, ideoque attenditur statutum, cui subjectus est testator. Et hæc verior est sententia; nam debitorum nomina, tanquam personæ cohærentia, debent regulari secundum statuta loci, cui creditor est subjectus.'"

[1] Kaims on Equity, B. 3, ch. 8, § 4.

by a foreign creditor, according to the formalities of his country, will be sustained here, as a good title for demanding payment from the debtor; and it will be sustained, though informal, provided it be good *jure gentium*; that is, provided, that the creditor really granted the assignment. Such effect hath an equitable title; and a legal title can have no stronger effect."[1] This is in perfect coincidence with the law of England and America.[2]

§ 400. But where there has been an attachment by a creditor according to the local law *rei sitæ*, before any assignment by the party, or by operation of law *in invitum*; in such a case, the attaching creditor is entitled to priority over the assignee. For, in such case, the rule prevails, *Qui prior est in tempore, potior est in jure*; and the creditor is equitably entitled to the benefits of his diligence. A case to this effect is reported by Casaregis, and reasoned out without great force upon general principles. The doctrine does not, indeed, seem in its nature susceptible of any well founded doubt; and it is in entire conformity to the principles on the same subject recognised in England and America.[3]

§ 401. There are some other matters, connected with this subject, which deserve attention. Upon the sale of goods on credit, by the law of some commercial countries, a right is reserved to the vendor to retake them, or

---

1 Kaims on Equity, B. 3, ch. 8, § 4, sub finem. See also Huberus, Lib. 1, tit. 3, § 9.

2 See Holmes *v.* Remsen, 4 John. Ch. R. 460, 486; S. P. 20 John. R. 229, 267; Moreton *v.* Milne, 6 Binn. R. 353, 361, 369; Blake *v.* Williams, 6 Pick. R. 286, 307, 314.

3 Mr. Livermore, in his Dissertations (p. 159 to 162), has given the case and the reasoning of Casaregis at large. See Selkrig *v.* Davis, 2 Rose Bank. Cases, 291, 310.

he has a lien upon them for the price, if unpaid; and, in other countries, he possesses only a right of stoppage *in transitu*, in cases of insolvency of the vendee.[1] The civil law did not generally consider the transfer of property to be complete by sale and delivery alone, without payment or security for the price, unless the vendor agreed to give a general credit to the purchaser; but it allowed the vendor to reclaim the goods out of the possession of the purchaser, as being still his own property. *Quod vendidi* (say the Pandects) *non aliter fit accipientis, quam aut si pretium nobis solutum sit, aut satis eo nomine datum, vel etiam fidem habuerimus emptori sine ullâ satisfactione.*[2] The present Code of France gives a privilege, or right of revendication against the purchaser for the price of goods sold, so long as they remain in the possession of the debtor.[3] And, in respect to ships, a privilege is given by the same Code to certain classes of creditors (such as vendors, builders, repairers, mariners, &c.) upon the ship, which takes effect even against subsequent purchasers, until the ship has made a voyage after the purchase.[4] And, by the general maritime law, acknowledged in many countries, hypothecations and liens are recognised to exist for seamen's wages, and for repairs of foreign ships, and for salvage.

§ 402. The question, then, naturally arises, whether,

---

1 Abbott on Shipp. P. 1, ch. 1, § 6; Id. P. 3, ch. 9, § 2; 1 Domat, Civil Law, B. 1, tit. 2, § 3, n. 1, 2; Id. § 12, n. 13; Id. B. 3, tit. 1, § 5, n. 3, 4, note; Merlin, Répert. Revendication, § 1, n. 6; Code Civil, art. 2102; 4 Pardessus, art. 939, 940, 1204; 2 Kent Comm. Lect. 39, p. 540, (2d edit.)

2 Digest, Lib. 18. tit. 1, l. 19; Id. Lib. 14, tit. 4, l. 5, n. 18.

3 Code Civil, art. 2102, n. 4.

4 Code of Commerce, art. 192, 193; 3 Pardessus, art. 942, 950. See also, 1 Valin, Comm. 340; Abbott on Shipp. P. 1, ch. 1, § 6.

if such privileges, hypothecations, or liens, are recognised in the country, where the contracts, or acts, which give rise to them, are made, they are to be deemed obligatory in every other place, where the property may be found, even against innocent purchasers, or creditors, who would otherwise, by the law of *rei sitæ*, have a preference of right? Would an attachment, for instance, of foreign creditors prevail against them in the tribunals of the domicil of such creditors? Upon the general principles already stated, as to the operation of contracts, and the rule, that moveables have no locality, these privileges, hypothecations, and liens, ought to prevail over the rights of subsequent purchasers and creditors. Having once attached rightfully *in rem*, they ought not to be displaced by the mere change of local situation of the property.[1] And so the doctrine was held in an important case in England, where the right of stoppage *in transitu* was supposed to depend upon doctrines of foreign law, materially different from that of England; and the right conferred by the foreign law was upheld against the claims of English creditors.[2]

§ 403. Hitherto we have been considering cases of voluntary transfers *inter vivos;* and we are now naturally led to the consideration of involuntary tranfers by operation of law, in the domicil of the owner, such as are statutable transfers under Bankrupt and Insolvent Laws. The great question here is, whether an assignment under such laws has a universal operation, so as to transfer the moveable property of the bankrupt or insolvent in all other countries, to the same extent

1 See Livermore's Dissert. p. 159, § 249.

2 Inglis *v.* Underwood, 1 East. R. 515; Abbott on Shipp. P. 3, ch. 9, § 3.

as a voluntary transfer made by him would, and thus to withdraw it from the process of the local foreign laws, by way of arrest, attachment, or otherwise, issued in favour of the local foreign creditors. This question has been very gravely discussed both at home and abroad; and the Courts of England and America have arrived at opposite conclusions respecting it. The Courts of the former uniformly maintain the doctrine of the universal operation of such assignments; and many (but not all) of the Courts of the latter confine their operation to the territory, where the party is declared Bankrupt. The question is worthy of a very full examination, and a summary of the reasoning on each side, will, therefore, be here brought under review.

§ 404. Those, who maintain, that assignments under the Bankrupt laws are, and ought to be, of universal operation to transfer moveable property, in whatever country it may be locally situate, adopt reasoning to this effect. The general principle certainly is, that personal property has no locality; but, that, as to its disposition, it is subject to the law, which governs the person of the owner, that is, to the law of his domicil.[1] There can be no doubt, that he may, by a voluntary assignment or sale, made according to the law of his domicil, transfer the title to any person, wherever the property may be locally situate.[2] Now, an assignment under the bankrupt laws of his domicil is by operation of law a valid transfer of all the Bankrupt's property,

[1] Sill *v.* Worswick, 1 H. Black. 690, 691; Hunter *v.* Potts, 4 T. R. 182.

[2] *In re* Wilson cited 1 H. Black. 691, 692.

as valid, as if made personally by him.[1] The law upon his bankruptcy transfers his whole property to the assignees, who thus become, *lege loci*, the lawful owners of it, and entitled to adminster it for the benefit of all his creditors. The mode of transfer is wholly immaterial; the only proper question is, whether it is good according to the law of his domicil. This rule is admitted in all cases of the succession to intestate estates, where the property passes by operation of law, as well as where it passes by the voluntary act or testament of the owner.[2]

---

1 Sill *v.* Worswick, 1 H. Black. 691, 692; Hunter *v.* Potts, 4 T. R. 182, 192; Phillips *v.* Hunter, 2 H. Black. 402, 405; Goodwin *v.* Jones, 3 Mass. R. 517. — "It is a proposition, (said the Court in Phillips *v.* Hunter, 2 H. Black. 402, 403,) not to be disputed, that previous to the bankruptcy the Bankrupts themselves might have transferred or assigned this property, though abroad, as absolutely, as if it had been in their own tangible possession in this country; and it seems, that the assignees under their commission were entitled, by operation of law, to do with it after the bankruptcy, what the Bankrupts themselves might have done." In Potts *v.* Hunter, (4 T. R. 182, 192) the Court said, "The only question here is, whether or not the property in that Island (Rhode Island) passed by the assignment, in the same manner, as if the owner (the Bankrupt) had assigned it by his voluntary act. And that it does so pass cannot be doubted, unless there were some positive law of that country to prevent it." "On the general reason of the thing, if there be no positive decision to the contrary, no doubt could be entertained, but that by the laws of this country, uncontradicted by the laws of any other country, where personal property may happen to be, the commissioners of a Bankrupt may dispose of the personal property of a Bankrupt here, though such property be in a foreign country." In Goodwin *v.* Jones, (3 Mass. R. 517,) Mr. Chief Justice Parsons said, "The assignment of a Bankrupt's effects may be considered as his own act, as it is in the execution of laws, by which he is bound, he himself being competent to make such assignment, and voluntarily committing the act, which authorized the making of it." See also Livermore's Dissert. p. 159, § 249, 250. The same doctrine was affirmed by Lord Mansfield in Wadham *v.* Marlow, cited 1 H. Black. 437, 438, 439, note; S. C. and P. 8 East. R. 314, 316, note z.

2 Sill *v.* Worswick, 1 H. Black. 690, 691.

§ 405. And the principle applies with equal force and convenience to the disposition of the effects of Bankrupts; for the just and equal distribution of the funds of that class of debtors becomes the common concern of the whole commercial world. In cases of intestacy, it is presumed to be the intent of the Intestate, that his moveables, which by fiction of law have no locality, independent of his person, should be brought home, and distributed according the law of his domicil. It is equally to be presumed, as the understanding of the commercial world, that the Bankrupt's effects should follow his person, and be distributed in the place of his domicil, where the credit was bestowed, or the payment expected.[1] An assignment under the Bankrupt laws ought to be deemed in all respects of equal force with a voluntary assignment of the party; for, by implication of law, he consents to all transfers made of his property according to the law of his domicil. Great inconveniences would follow from a different proceeding. Different commissions might issue in different countries, and have concurrent operation *simul et semel* in different countries. And, thus, it would be in the power of the Bankrupt to throw his property under either commission at pleasure, and to give local preferences to different creditors. Such a state of things, and such conflicting systems, would lead to great inconvenience and confusion; and be the source of much fraud and injustice, and disturb the equality and equity of any bankrupt system.[2]

---

1 Holmes *v.* Remsen, 4 John. Ch. R. 460, 470; Hunter *v.* Potts, 4 T. R. 182, 192.

2 Holmes *v.* Remsen, 4 John. Ch. R. 471: Phillips *v.* Hunter, 2 H. Black. 402. — In Phillips *v.* Hunter, (2 H. Black. 402, 403,) the Court said, "The great principle of the Bankrupt laws is justice found on

§ 406. There is great wisdom, therefore, in adopting the rule, and it has accordingly received a very general sanction. It is true, that a nation may adopt, if it pleases, a different system, and prefer an attaching domestic creditor to a foreign assignee; but such a course of legislation can hardly be deemed consistent with the general comity of nations. But, until such a legislation interposes some obstruction, the true rule is, to follow out the lead of the general principle, that makes the law of the owner's domicil conclusive upon the disposition of personal property.[1] And this especially

---

equality. This being the principle of those laws, it seems to follow, that the whole property of the bankrupt must be under their (the assignees) control without regard to the locality of that property, except in cases, which directly militate against the particular laws of the country, in which it happens to be situated." "If the bankrupt laws were circumscribed by the local situation of the property, a door would be open to all the partiality and undue preferences, which they were framed to prevent; it being easy to foresee, how frequently property would be sent abroad with that unjust view immediately previous to and in contemplation of bankruptcy."

[1] Holmes *v.* Remsen, 4 John. Ch. R. 471, 472; Hunter *v.* Potts, 4 T. R. 182, 192. Sill *v.* Worswick, 1 H. Black. 691, 693. — In Phillips *v.* Hunter (2 H. Black. 402, 405,) the Court said; "It is true, that the laws of the country, where the property is situated, have the immediate control over it, in respect to its locality, and the immediate protection afforded to it; yet the country, where the proprietor resides, in respect to another species of protection afforded to him and his property, has a right to regulate his contract relating to that property." And in Hunter *v.* Potts (4 T. R. 182, 192.) the Court said, "Every person having property in a foreign country may dispose of it in this; though, indeed, if there be a law in that country, directing a particular mode of conveyance, that must be adopted." "If (said Lord Longhborough) the bankrupt happens to have property, which lies out of the jurisdiction of the law of England, if the country, in which it lies, proceeds according to the principles of well regulated justice, there is no doubt, that it will give effect to the title of the assignees." "But if the law of that country preferred him (a creditor) to the assignees, though I must suppose that determination wrong, yet I do not think, that my holding a contrary opinion, would revoke the determination of that country, however I might disapprove of the principle, on which that law so decided." Sill *v.* Worswick, 1 H. Black. 691, 693.

applies to contracts made in the very country, where the party is declared bankrupt.[1]

§ 407. There are many authorities in favour of that doctrine. As early as 1723, Lord Talbot, then at the bar, gave an opinion, that the statutes of Bankruptcy did not extend to the plantations; yet that the personal property of an English Bankrupt in the plantations passed to the assignees.[2] Lord Hardwicke, in Wilson's Case, adopted and acted on the doctrine, that the assignment in Bankruptcy conveyed the personal property of the Bankrupt in foreign countries; and that their title would overreach that of an attaching creditor after the assignment, although at that time not made known to the debtor.[3] In Solomons *v.* Ross in 1704, where the laws of Holland, having in like manner, as under a commission of bankruptcy, taken the administration of the property from the owner, and vested it in persons, who are called curators of Desolate Estates, it was decided in Chancery, that they had immediately upon their appointment a title to recover the debts due to the insolvent in England, in preference to the diligence of the particular creditor seeking to attach those debts. The case of Jollet *v.* Deponthieu in 1769[4] decided the same point. These are cases, in which the rule was asserted in favour of foreign assignees.[5] A like decision in favour of English assignees was made in

---

1 Sill *v.* Worswick, 691, 693, 694; Phillips *v.* Hunter, 2 H. Black. 404, 405.

2 Livermore's Diss. 140; Beames, Lex Mercatoria 5, 6. (6th edit.)

3 Cited in 1 H. Black, 691, 692, and probably decided between 1752, and 1756; 4 T. R. 186, 187.

4 Solomons *v.* Ross. 1 H. Black. 131, note; Id. 691; S. C. Cooke's Bank. Laws (4th edit.), 306.

5 1 H. Black. 132, note; Id. 691.

the Chancery of Ireland in 1763.[1] Lord Thurlow gave it the sanction of his own great name in a case in 1787.[2]

§ 408. The question was most elaborately considered in two cases decided in 1791, in which it was solemnly held, that the operation of the Bankrupt laws is to vest in the assignees all the personal property of the Bankrupt, wherever situate; and that whenever that property shall be brought into England by any person, who has obtained it, the assignees will have a right to recover it of him, for the benefit of all the creditors; and consequently, that an attachment and recovery of such property, made by a creditor in a foreign country after such assignment, will be held inoperative; upon the principle, that the title, which is prior in point of time, ought to obtain preference in point of right and law.[3] Upon a writ of error the general doctrine maintained in these cases was affirmed; but in its actual application it was restricted to attachments made by British creditors against British debtors. In this state the doctrine remained until a very recent period, when in the case of a bankruptcy of an English partner in a Scotch partnership it was discussed anew. A commission of bankruptcy was issued in England; and subsequently an arrest, attachment, or sequestration was made, by a creditor, of debts due to the Bankrupt in Scotland. The question then arose, whether the assignees, or the attaching creditor, was entitled to priority; and this depended on the question, whether an English commission of Bankruptcy passed to the as-

1 Neale *v.* Cottingham, 1 H. Black, R. 132, note; S. C. cited in Hunter *v.* Potts, 4 T. R. 194, and Cooke's Bank. Laws (4th edit. 1799,) p. 303. See also Quelin *v.* Morrisson, 1 Knapp Appeal Rep. 265.

2 Ex parte Blakes, 1 Cox R. 398.

3 Sill *v.* Worswick, 1 H. Black, 665, 690, 691, 694; Hunter *v.* Potts, 4 T. R. 192; S. C. in Err. 2 H. Black, 402.

signees the title to property, or debts locally situate, or due in Scotland. The Court of Session in Scotland held, that it did;[1] and upon appeal, this judgment was affirmed by the House of Lords. "One thing (said Lord Eldon) is quite clear, that there is not in any book any dictum or authority, that would authorize me to deny, at least, in this place, that an English commission passes, as with respect to the bankrupt and his creditors in England, the personal property he has in Scotland, or in any foreign country."[2]

---

1 The Court of Session, in Scotland, gave very elaborate opinions on this subject, in the Royal Bank of Scotland *v.* Cuthbert, commonly cited as Stein's case, 1 Rose's Bank. Case, Appx. 412. 2 Rose, Bank. Cas. 91, 78. See also Smith *v.* Buchanan, 1 East R. 6; 2 Bell. Comm. 684 to 687.

2 Selkrig *v.* Davis, 2 Rose Bank. Cas. 291, 314; S. C. 2 Dow R. 230, 250; 2 Rose Bank. Cas. 97 — See also *Ex parte* Dobrey, 8 Ves. 82; 2 Bell Comm. 684 to 687; Holmes *v.* Remsen, 4 John. Ch. R. 460; S. C. 20 John. R. 229. — The Judgment of Lord Eldon, which was affirmed apparently with entire equanimity, contains many striking remarks upon the difficulties attendant upon any other system of international jurisprudence. The following extracts are particularly valuable for the consideration of the American Courts.

"In whatever way a Scottish sequestration may be enforced, the distribution of a bankrupt's effects under it is perfectly different from what it is under an English commission of bankruptcy. The Scottish law cuts down all securities, that have been made or given within a certain number of days prior to the issuing of the sequestration, whether they have been given *bonâ fide*, or given, as we should say, in contemplation of bankruptcy. On the other hand, in our law, though the approximation of the security to the date of the commission may be evidence, that it was given in contemplation of bankruptcy, yet it is but evidence; and the security may be perfectly good. Again, in England, a man cannot become a bankrupt, without committing an Act of bankruptcy. The commission must be founded on that act of bankruptcy: and there are various other differences, applying to the property of a bankrupt, as administered under an English commission, or, *vice versâ*, as distributed by the rules, and according to the forms, of a Scottish sequestration. If, my Lords, you attempt to obviate these inconveniences by a co-existing sequestration and commission, the difficulty is tenfold greater, unless the one should be used merely as the means of assisting the distribution of the funds on the other. What personal

§ 409. And this is now the settled law of England, in which the following propositions are firmly established; first, that an assignment under the bankrupt law of

---

property shall belong to the one proceeding, and what to the other proceeding, is no ordinary difficulty. The counsel for the appellant say there is no dfficulty. — That a debt owing to the house in Scotland, wherever the debtor lives, ought to go to the Scotch sequestration; and, in like manner, that the debt owing to the house in England, wherever the debtor lives, should go to the commission. But the house may be constituted of persons, of whom it may be difficult to say, whether a man is a Scotchman or an Englishman. It may happen, that a house is composed of persons, some of whom reside in Sccotland and some in England. I should wish to know, not only how the joint debts due to one firm, and the joint debts due to the other, are to be distributed; but, where separate debts are due to each, whether the separate debts are to be a fund of distribution under the English commission, or under the Scottish sequestration, or what is to become of them?

"All these difficulties certainly belong to this case. But, notwithstanding that, one thing is quite clear; there is not in any book, any dictum or authority, that would authorize me to deny, at least in this place, that an English commission passes, as with respect to the bankrupt and his creditors in England, the personal property he has in Scotland or in any foreign country. It is admitted, that the assignment under the English commission, as between the bankrupt and the English and Scotch proprietors, passes the Scotch property, and vests it in the assignees, when the Scotch creditors have not used legal diligence. I think the case was put at the bar thus: That the commission of bankruptcy operated so as to bring into the fund the Scotch personal property, provided that such personal property was not arrested by legal diligence in Scotland, prior to the intimation of the assignment in Scotland. It was therefore argued, that this was to be put on the same footing as the case of the assignation of a particular debt to a particular individual. Now, your Lordships need not be told that, by the law of Scotland, if B assign a debt, which is due from C to B, a creditor of B may arrest that debt in the hands of the debtor, notwithstanding the assignment, unless the assignee has given an intimation formally to the person, by whom the debt is owing. That must be admitted. Upon that it has been insisted here, that no intimation has been given, and that this subsequent arrestment in 1798 ought to have the preference of the title of the assignees, under the commission, that was sued out in the year 1782." * He afterwards proceeded to decide, that no intimation was necessary; and if necessary, it was given.† See Quelin *v.* Morrison, 1 Knapp Rep. 265.

* 2 Rose Bank. Cas. 314 to 316. † Id. 318, 319.

a foreign country passes all the personal property of the bankrupt locally situate, or owing in England; secondly, that an attachment of such property by an English creditor, after such bankruptcy, with or without notice to him, is invalid to overreach the assignment; thirdly, that in England the same doctrine holds under assignments by her own bankrupt laws, as to personal property and debts of the bankrupt in foreign countries; fourthly, that, upon principle, all attachments made by foreign creditors, after such assignment in a foreign country, ought to be held invalid; sixthly, that a British creditor will not be permitted to hold the property acquired by a judgment under any attachment made in a foreign country after such assignment; and seventhly, that a foreign creditor, not subjected to British laws, will be permitted to retain any such property acquired under any such judgment, if the local laws (however incorrectly upon principle) confer on him an absolute title.[1] There is no inconsiderable weight of American authority on the same side; but it must be admitted, that the preponderating authority is certainly now the other way.[2]

---

[1] 2 Bell Comm. 687 to 184: Id. 689, 690; Holmes *v.* Remsen, 4 John Ch. R. 460; S. C. 20 John. R. 229; Dwarris on Statutes, 650, 651.

[2] Mr. Chief Justice Parsons certainly held this opinion in Goodwin *v.* Jones, 3 Mass. R. 517. And Mr. Chancellor Kent has sustained it in one of his most elaborate judgments, which will well reward a diligent perusal, Holmes *v* Remsen, 4 John. Ch. Rep. 460. This is also, as we shall see, the law in France and Holland. See Parish *v.* Seton, Cooper's Bank. Law, 27; Holmes *v.* Remsen, 4 John. Ch. R. 484; S. P. 20 John. R. 258; Blake *v.* Williams, 6 Pick. R. 312, 313; Merlin Répertoire, Faillite et Banqueroute, Art. 10. Mr. Chancellor Kent, in his Commentaries (2 Kent Comm. Lect. 37, p. 404 to 408, 2d edition), has with great candor admitted, that the American doctrine is now established the other way by a preponderance of authority; though he has an undisguised distrust of the validity of its foundation. There are not a few jurists in America, each of whom may be disposed to use on this occasion the language of a great orator

§ 410. The reasoning, which is urged in support of what may be deemed the American Doctrine, is to the following effect. It is admitted, that the rule is, that personal property, including debts, has no locality, but follows, as to its disposition and transfer, the law of the domicil of the owner. But every country may by positive law regulate, as it pleases, the disposition of personal property found within it; and may prefer its own attaching creditors to any foreign assignee; and no other authority has any right to question the determination. When there is no positive law, the general rule is to govern, with the exception of such cases as fall within the known principle of Huberus, that it is not prejudicial to the State, or to the just rights of its citizens. And this is the very ground, upon which the objection to the ubiquity of operation of the bankrupt laws of a country, as respects personal estate, is to be rested.[1]

§ 411. There is a marked distinction between a voluntary conveyance of property by the owner, and a conveyance by operation of law in cases of bankruptcy *in invitum*. Laws cannot force the will, nor compel any man to make a conveyance. In place of a voluntary conveyance, all that the Legislature of a country can do, when justice requires it, is to assume the disposition of it *in invitum*. But their statutable conveyance cannot operate upon any subject, but what is within their territory. This makes a solid distinction between a voluntary conveyance and an involuntary legal convey-

---

of antiquity, "Ego assentior Scævolæ." See Livermore's Diss. 153, 154 to 158.

There are in Mr. Henry's Appendix to his work on Foreign Law, p. 251 to 258, some curious opinions given by Counsel in 1715, as to the effect of attachments after a foreign bankruptcy.

1 Blake *v.* Williams, 6 Pick. 286; Olivier *v.* Townes, 14 Martin R. 93, 97 to 100; Milne *v.* Moreton, 6 Binn. 353.

ance. The former has no relation to place, the latter on the contrary has the strictest relation to place. And this distinction is insisted on with great force by Lord Kaims.[1] It is, therefore, admitted, that a voluntary assignment by a party, according to the law of his domicil, will pass his personal estate, whatever may be its locality. But it by no means follows, that the same rule should govern in cases of assignments by operation of law.

§ 412. The true rule in such cases is, that the assignees are in the same situation, as the bankrupt himself, in regard to foreign debts. They take subject to every equity, and subject to the remedies provided by the laws of the foreign country, where the debt is due; and when permitted to sue in a foreign country, it is not as assignees, having an interest, but as representatives of the bankrupt. They stand upon the footing of administrators only, with a right to sue for the benefit of all the creditors. But our law will not regard the *choses in action* of the debtor, as exclusively appropriated to their use; and the preference can be gained only by pursuing the remedies, which our laws afford. This was formerly the rule in England, as appears from Mawdesley *v.* Park.[2]

§ 413. Nor can it be truly said, that an assignment by the bankrupt laws is with the consent of the bankrupt, because he assents by implication to such laws. This is a very unsafe and dangerous principle, on which to risk the doctrine; for in the same way it may be said, that a man, committing a crime, for which his estate

---

[1] Kaims on Equity, B. 3, ch. 8, § 6; Remsen *v.* Holmes, 20 John. R. 258, 259; Moreton *v.* Milne, 6 Binn. 353, 369.

[2] Cited, 1 H. Black, 680.

is forfeited, voluntarily consents to its transfer. But the principle, whether correct or not, can only apply to cases, where the debtor and creditor belong to the same country. It is wholly inapplicable to foreign creditors.

§ 414. Besides; national comity requires us to give effect to such assignments only so far, as may be done without impairing the remedies, or lessening the securities, which our laws have provided for our own citizens. The rule is, *Quatenus sine prejudicio indulgentium fieri potest.*[1] And after all, this is mere comity, and not international law. All comity of this sort must be built up in a great measure upon the doctrine of reciprocity; and this is extremely difficult, from the known diversities in the jurisprudence of different nations.[2] It would prejudice the rights and remedies of our citizens in our own courts, to suffer the assignments under foreign bankrupt laws to prevail over their own diligence, in seeking remedies against their debtors in our own courts. If there is in such cases a conflict between our own and foreign laws, as to the rights of our citizens, and one of them must give way, our own laws ought to prevail.[3] The most convenient and practical rule is, that statutable assignments, as to creditors, shall operate intra-territorially only. If our citizens conduct themselves according to our laws in regard to the property of their debtors, found within our jurisdiction, it is reasonable, that they should reap the fruits of their diligence, and not be sent to a foreign country to receive such a dividend of their debt-

---

1 Huberus, Lib. 1, tit. 3, De Conflict. § 2.

2 Blake *v.* Williams, 6 Pick. R. 269, 313, 314, 315; Milne *v.* Moreton, 6 Binn. 353, 375; Remsen *v.* Holmes, 20 John. R. 229, 263, 264.

3 Potter *v.* Brown, 5. East. R. 131.

or's effects, as the foreign laws allow. If each government in cases of insolvency should sequester, and distribute the funds within its own jurisdiction, the general result will be favorable to the interest of creditors, and to the harmony of nations. This is the rule adopted in all cases of administration of the property of deceased persons; and there is no real difference between the principle of those cases, and of cases of bankruptcy.[1]

§ 415. Down to the time of the American revolution, this may fairly be deemed to have been the English doctrine. It has since been changed. Even in England the principle has not as yet been applied in favor of any foreign countries, except such as have bankrupt laws in form or substance; and we have none in our country.[2] It can make no difference in the case, whether the debt of the attaching creditor accrued here, or in foreign countries; for in either case the question is not, as to the validity of the contract; but as to a collateral matter, that is to say, the effect to be given to it, in a conflict between rights growing out of our own laws, and those of a foreign country.[3]

§ 416. Neither is it true, that even the voluntary conveyances of parties in all cases are to be held valid, where they are prejudicial to the rights and remedies of our own citizens. In Massachusetts, for instance, it has been held, that a voluntary assignment by a debtor of all his property, made in Pennsylvania for the benefit of creditors generally, shall not prevail over a

---

1 Remsen *v.* Holmes, 20 John. R. 229, 265; Milne *v.* Moreton, 6 Binn. R. 353, 361; Blake *v.* Williams, 6 Pick. 286.

2 Remsen *v.* Holmes, 20 John. R. 229; Blake *v.* Williams, 6 Pick. R. 286; Milne *v.* Moreton, 6 Binn. R. 353; Wallis *v.* Paterson, 1 Harr. & McHen. R. 463; Abraham *v.* Plestero, 3 Wendell R. 538, 549, 550.

3 Milne *v.* Moreton, 6 Binn, 360.

subsequent attachment of the funds of the debtor made after the assignment; because such an assignment would be void by the laws of Massachusetts, if made in that state, as being in fraud of creditors; and it is unjust and unequal in its effects, and prejudicial to the citizens of the state. In such a case, therefore, the party, who shall by process first attach the debt, or seize the property, ought to prevail, whether creditor, or assignee.[1]

§ 417. It is admitted in the reasoning in the American cases, that the old law of France and Holland is in coincidence with the British doctrine.[2] The modern law of those countries is equally decisive in its support; and very recent cases have given it a complete confirmation in their tribunals. The principal grounds of their decisions may be summed up in the following propositions. (1.) That the law of the domicil may rightfully devest the debtor of the administration of his property, and place it under the administration of assignees or syndics. (2.) That laws, whose effects are to regulate the capacity and incapacity of persons, their

1 Ingraham *v.* Geyer, 13 Mass. R. 146; S. C. cited, 6 Pick. R. 307. See also Olivier *v.* Townes, 6 Pick. R. 97 to 101. — This summary of the American reasoning is principally extracted from the three leading cases of Milne *v.* Moreton, 6 Binney R. 353, Remsen *v.* Holmes, 20 John. R. 229, and Blake *v.* Williams, 6 Pick. R. 286, where the subject is very elaborately discussed. — The same doctrine will be found supported in other American cases, cited in 2 Kent Comm. Lect. 37, p. 406 to 408, (2d edit.) See also Olivier *v.* Townes, 14 Martin R. 93, 99; Harrison *v.* Sterry, 5 Cranch R. 289; Ogden *v.* Saunders, 12 Wheaton R. 213; Saunders *v.* Williams, 5 New Hamp. R. 213; Plestero *v.* Abraham, 1 Paige R. 237; S. C. 3 Wendell R. 538; Fox *v.* Adams, 5 Greenl. R. 245; Wallis *v.* Paterson, 1 Har. & McHen. R. 236, 463; Ogden *v.* Saunders, 12 Wheaton, 213, 359, 360, 361, 362.

2 4 John. Ch. R. 484; 20 John. R. 258; 6 Pick. R. 312, 313; Ante, § 409, note. Henry on Foreign Law, p. 127 to 135; Id. 153 to 160; Id. 248 to 250.

personal actions, and their moveables, everywhere belong to the category of personal statutes. (3.) That it is a matter of universal jurisprudence, and especially of that of France and the Netherlands, that the debts, actively considered, of an inhabitant against a foreigner, are deemed a part of his moveable property, and have their locality in the place of domicil of the creditor.[1] At the same time, it is admitted, that a purchaser from the bankrupt, in a foreign country, of property there locally situate, would be entitled to hold it against the assignees, if at the time, he had no knowledge of any bankruptcy, or of any intent to defraud creditors.[2]

§ 418. The American doctrine has been followed out to another result. Suppose (as was the case in Holmes *v.* Remsen) after a commission and assignment in bankruptcy in England, the bankrupt should voluntarily make a confirmatory conveyance in aid of the commission; the question is, whether it will have the effect of a voluntary assignment, so as to defeat a subsequent attachment in America? It has been held by a learned judge in New York, that it will not; because, by the law of England, the commission devests the title of the bankrupt in all his property throughout the world; and he no longer has any capacity to convey it; but in regard to that property, he is to be treated as *civiliter mortuus*.[3] There is great difficulty in maintaining this doctrine. For if the statutable assignment does, *per se*, transfer the personal property of the bankrupt in foreign countries to the assignees, and devest all his title to it, then it

---

1 Merlin, Répertoire, Faillite and Banqueroute § 2, 3, art. 10, p. 412; Henry on Foreign Law, p. 127 to 135; Id. 175.

2 Merlin, Id. p. 415, 416.

3 Mr. Justice Platt, Remsen *v.* Holmes, 20 John. R. 267.

would seem, that a subsequent attachment of it must be wholly inoperative, because he has no longer any attachable interest in it. We are not at liberty to treat the property, as still in him for one purpose, and out of him for another. The doctrine of Mr. Chancellor Kent is certainly here far more satisfactory, giving to such a voluntary assignment a full confirmatory effect.[1]

§ 419. There are some other questions, arising from the operation of foreign bankrupt laws, and other analogous systems of proceeding, for the benefit of creditors generally, *in invitum*, which have come under judicial cognizance, and deserve attention. In the first place, suppose a British subject is declared bankrupt, while he is on a voyage *in transitu* from England to America; and he has a large shipment of property with him; is he entitled to hold it, when it arrives in America? Or, can his assignees maintain a suit against him, or against other persons, holding it for his use, not being creditors? It has been held, by the learned Chancellor of New York (Walworth), that the assignees are entitled to recover, upon the ground, that the assignment operates as a good conveyance to them against the bankrupt, and those holding for his use. On that occasion, the learned Judge stated the distinction between that case, and the preceding cases. "In those cases," said he, "the contest was between foreign assignees and domestic creditors, claiming under the laws of the country, where the property was situate, and where the suits were brought. The question in those cases was, whether the personal property of the debtor was to be considered as having locality, for the purpose of giving a remedy to the creditors residing in the country, where the property was in fact situated, at the time

1 Holmes *v.* Remsen, 4 John. Ch. R. 489.

of the foreign attachment. In this case, the controversy is between the bankrupt and his assignees and creditors, all residing in the country, under whose laws the assignment was made. Even the property itself at the time of assignment was constructively within the jurisdiction of that country, being on the high seas, in the actual possession of a British subject. Under such circumstances the assignment had the effect to change the property, and devest the title of the bankrupt, as if the same had been sold in England under an execution against him, or he had voluntarily conveyed the same to the assignees for the benefit of his creditors."[1] Upon an appeal, however, this doctrine was not in terms confirmed by the appellate Court; and some of the judges dissented from the doctrine of the Chancellor. But the case was ultimately reversed on another point.[2]

§ 420. It is obvious, that the great question involved in this case, was, whether an assignment under a foreign bankrupt law operates as a transfer of personal property in this country. It matters not, in respect to the bankrupt himself, or others claiming under him, not

---

1 Plestero *v.* Abraham, 1 Paige, R. 236.

2 Abraham *v.* Plestero, 3 Wend. 538. — It is difficult to perceive, how the doctrine of the Chancellor, as to the operation of the British bankrupt laws upon British subjects and their property *in transitu*, can be answered. It must be admitted to be operative to devest the bankrupt's title to the extent of an estoppel, as to his own personal claim in opposition to it; for the law of America, be it what it may, had not then operated upon it. It was not locally within our jurisdiction. No one could doubt the right of the assignee to personal property locally in England at the time of the assignment. In what respect does such a case differ from a case, where it has not passed into another jurisdiction? Is there any substantial difference between its being on board of a British and its being on board of an American vessel on the high seas? See ante, § 391.

being creditors or purchasers, whether it operates as a legal or as an equitable transfer. In either way it will devest him of his beneficial interest. Upon this point, it is impossible not to feel, that the general current of American authority is in perfect coincidence with that of England, in favour of the title of the assignees.[1] In most of the cases, in which assignments under foreign bankrupt laws have been denied to give a title against attaching creditors, it has been distinctly admitted, that the assignees might maintain suits in our courts under such assignments for the property of the bankrupt. This is avowed in the most unequivocal manner in the leading cases in Pennsylvania and New York already cited, and it is silently admitted in those in Massachusetts.[2] And unless the admission can be overthrown, it surrenders the principle; for no one will contend, that the assignees can sue either in law or equity in our courts, unless they possess some title under the assignment. The point has hitherto been a struggle for priority and preference between parties, claiming against the bankrupt under opposing titles; the assignees for the general creditors, and the attaching creditors for their separate rights.

§ 421. It is true, that Mr. Chief Justice Marshall, in delivering the opinion of the Court in Harrison *v.* Sterry,[3] used the following language: "As the bankrupt law of a foreign country is incapable of operating a legal

---

1 See 1 H. Black, 691; 6 Maule & Selw. 126; 1 East R. 6; Coke's Bank. Laws, (4th edit.) 304; Doug. R. 161, 170.

2 Holmes *v.* Remsen, 4 John. Ch. R. 485; S. C. 20 John. R. 262, 263; Milne *v.* Moreton, 6 Binn 363, 374; Livermore's Diss. 142, 152; Blake *v.* Williams, 6 Pick. R. 305; Ingraham *v.* Gayer, 13 Mass. R. 146, 147; Goodwin *v.* Jones, 3 Mass. R. 517. But see contra, Orr *v.* Amory, 11 Mass. R. 25.

3 5 Cranch 289, 302. See also Ogden *v.* Saunders, 12 Wheaton R. 61, 362, 363, 364.

transfer of property in the United States, the remaining two thirds of the funds are liable to the attaching creditors, according to the legal preference obtained by their attachments." But the very terms of this statement show, that the Court were examining the point, only as between the conflicting rights of the assignees and attaching creditors, and not in relation to the bankrupt himself. And this is manifestly the light, in which the doctrine was contemplated by the majority of the Court in a subsequent case.[1]

§ 422. In cases of partnership, where there are different firms in different countries, or some of the partners reside in one, and some in another country, there are still more embarrassing difficulties attendant upon questions of foreign bankrupt assignments. If one partner is declared bankrupt under a foreign commission, his share and interest only in the funds there can pass to his assignees, as against the partners in another country. And of course they must take, subject to an account between all the partners, and stand precisely, as the bankrupt does, on a settlement of all claims as between debtor or creditor.[2] Let us suppose the case of a partnership in the British West Indies, and in England; and one of the partners resides in England, and becomes bankrupt; and an assignment is made; and afterwards a British West India creditor of the firm attaches a debt, due to the firm in the West Indies, and procures a judgment and satisfaction there. Can he be compelled to refund the same upon a suit brought by the assignees against him in England? Sir William Grant, in a case of this sort, decided in the negative; and on

---

1 Ogden *v.* Saunders, 12 Wheaton 359 to 365.

2 Harrison *v.* Sterry, 5 Cranch, 289, 302.

that occasion seemed to have great difficulty in reconciling his mind to the decisions upon the more general question of satisfaction obtained abroad by a creditor in case of a sole bankruptcy. He held, that the bankruptcy of the partner resident in England could not affect the partners remaining in the West Indies, in a country not subject to the bankrupt law, so as to devest them of the management of the partnership concerns, or of the disposition of the partnership property. If they applied the partnership assets in the payment of the partnership debts; or, if, in a legal course of proceeding against them, the debts were recovered according to the law of the country, no jurisdiction could exist in England to force the partnership, or the creditor to refund, what he had so received, or so recovered. Under such circumstances the foreign partners and foreign creditors must be left to their general rights and remedies.[1] The same doctrine seems to be acknowledged in other nations, where there are partnerships and partners resident in different countries.[2]

§ 423. But, whatever may be the rule in relation to foreign bankrupt assignments, there is no doubt, that there are some assignments, which take effect by mere operation of law in foreign countries, and are admitted to have universal validity and effect upon personal property, without respect to its locality. Such is the case of a transfer of personal property arising from marriage. Thus, a marriage, contracted by citizens of Massachusetts, is a gift in law to the husband of all the personal, tangible property of the wife, and operates as a transfer of it to him, wherever it may be situate,

---

1 Brickwood *v.* Miller, 3 Marrivale, R. 279.

2 See Merlin, Répertoire, Faillite et Banqueroute, § 2, art. 10, p. 414.

at home or abroad. And the right, thus acquired by the law of the matrimonial domicil, will be held of perfect force and validity in every other country, notwithstanding the like rule would not arise in regard to domestic marriages by its own municipal code. This doctrine was adverted to by Lord Meadowbank, in a very important case already referred to, as perfectly clear and established. "In the ordinary case," says he, "of a transference by contract of marriage, when a lady of fortune, having a great deal of money in Scotland, or stock in the banks, or public companies there, marries in London, the whole property is, *ipso jure*, her husband's. It is assigned to him. The legal assignment of a marriage operates without regard to territory all the world over."[1] Lord Eldon, on several occasions, has given this doctrine the fullest sanction of his own judgment, averring, that notice was not even necessary to give full effect to such a title.[2] The same doctrine was fully admitted in Remsen *v.* Holmes;[3] and it is treated by elementary writers as beyond controversy.[4] We have already seen, that foreign jurists press the doctrine to its fullest extent.[5]

---

1 Ante, § 59, note; Royal Bank of Scotland *v.* Cuthbert, 1 Rose Bann. Cas. Appx. 481.

2 Selkrig *v.* Davis, 2 Rose Bank. Cas. 97, 99; Id. S. C. 291, 317.

3 20 John. 267.

4 2 Ball. Comm. 23; Liverm. Diss. p. 140, § 223.

5 Ante, § 145, 146.

CHAPTER X.

REAL PROPERTY.

§ 424. Having disposed of the more important questions, which have arisen respecting personal property, we are next led to the consideration of the operation of foreign law in regard to real, or immoveable property. And, here, the general principle is, that the laws of the place, where such property is situate, exclusively govern in respect to the rights of the parties, the modes of transfer, and the solemnities, which should accompany them. The title, therefore, to real property can be acquired, passed, and lost only according to the *lex rei sitæ*. This, in a general sense, though not universally, (as we shall presently see) is admitted by all courts and jurists, foreign, as well as domestic. P. Voet states the rule in a brief but clear manner; *Ut immobilia statutis loci regantur, ubi sita.*[1] And the same rule would seem equally to apply to express and implied liens upon immoveable estate.[2]

§ 425. And, here it may be proper to advert a little more particularly to some of the definitions of foreign jurists, in regard to personal and real laws. We have already seen, that laws purely personal are those, which solely affect the person, without any reference to property.[3] And laws purely real directly and indirectly regulate property, and the rights of property, without intermeddling with, or changing the state of

1 Voet. De Stat. § 9, ch. 1, n. 3, p. 253.

2 See 1 Boullenois, p. 683 et seq. 689, 818; Rodemburg De Divers. Statut. tit. 2, ch. 5, § 16, p. 47; 1 Hertii Opera, De Collis. Leg. § 4, n. 64, p. 150.

3 Boullenois, Pr. Gén. 10, p. 4.

the person.[1] There are other laws, again, which are deemed personal and real, containing a mixed operation upon persons and property, and which are therefore called mixed.[2] Thus a particular law, which shall authorize a minor or other person, ordinarily incapacitated, to dispose of property under particular circumstances, would be deemed a mixed law; because, so far as it affects the particular capacity of a person, it is personal, and so far as it enables him to do a particular act respecting property, it is real.[3] In illustration of these distinctions Boullenois considers the Law, known as the *Senatûs-consultum Velleianum*, prohibiting married women from making contracts, as purely personal; a law declaring, that no person of full age shall devise more than a third or fourth of his property, as purely real; and a law allowing a minor (otherwise incapacitated), when married, to make a testament or donation in favour of his wife, as mixed.[4] These distinctions are very important in examining the doctrines of foreign jurists, as they often enter very deeply into the elements of their particular opinions.[5]

§ 426. Now, in regard to laws purely real, Boullenois lays down the rule in the broadest terms, that they

---

1 Boullenois, Pr. Gén. 22, p. 6; Id. Pr. Gén. 21, p. 7.

2 Id. Pr. Gén. 15, p. 5.

3 Id. Pr. Gén. 15, 16, p. 5.

4 1 Boullenois, Pr. Gén. 14, 15, 26, p. 5, 6, 7; Id. 25 to 28; Id. 206, 456, 457, 477, 488. — This definition of mixed laws is given by Boullenois, who has drawn it from Rodemburg. But it is very different (as he informs us, from the sense in which D'Argentré, Burgundus, and Voet use the same phrase. 1 Boullenois, Prin. Gén. 16, p. 5; Id. Obser. 6, 122 to 140; Rodemburg, De Div. Stat. tit. 1. ch. 2; 1 Boul. 25 to 48. See also, 1 Froland, Mém. ch. 6. p. 114.

5 J. Voet has devoted a whole title to the subject of personal, real, and mixed laws, which will reward the diligence of the student in a thorough perusal. 1 Voet. ad Pand. Lib. 1. tit. 4. p. 2. p. 38 et seq. The same subject is elaborately discussed by Froland, 1 Froland, Mém. ch. 4. p. 49. ch. 5, p. 31, ch. 6, p. 114.

govern all real property within the territory, but have no extension beyond it. *Les lois réelles n'ont point d'extension directe ne indirecte hors la jurisdiction et la domination du législateur.*[1] In regard to mixed laws he lays down the rule expressively, that of right they act only upon real property within the territory, to which the persons are subject; but that sometimes they act upon real property situate elsewhere; and then it is only because the laws are conformable to each other, and by a sort of kindred title only, (*à titre de paternité seulement.*)[2] Rodemburg lays down a like rule in regard to real laws (dismissing as unnecessary the class of mixed laws); *Statuta realia inter et personalia hoc interest, quod illa in res scripta territorii sui concludantur metis, hæc extra eas vim et effectum protendant.*[3] P. Voet contends, that no personal laws can regularly extend to immoveable property situate in a foreign country; *Non tamen statutum personale sese regulariter extendet ad bona immobilia alibi sita;* and he treats it as utterly unimportant, whether it assume to do so directly or indirectly, openly or consequentially.[4] J. Voet resolutely maintains the same opinion.[5] D'Argentré holds the following language; *Quæ realia, aut mixta sunt, haud dubie locorum et rerum situm sic spectant, ut aliis legibus quam territorii judicari non possunt.*[6] Huberus says, *Communis et recta sententia est,*

---

1 1 Boullenois, Pr. Gén. 27, p. 7; Id. 230. — Froland lays down the rule in even more brief terms. Le statut réel ne sort point de son territoire. 1 Froland, Mém. 156. And he applies the same rule to mixed statutes. Id. 157.

2 1 Boullenois, Prin. Gén. 20, 21, p. 6; Id. 223, 224.

3 Rodemburg, De Div. Statut. tit. 1, ch. 3; 1 Boullenois, 145 to 152; Id. 230.

4 Voet. De Stat. § 4, ch. 2, 6, 7, p. 123, 124.

5 Voet. ad Pand. Lib. 1 tit. 4, § 7, p. 40.

6 Livermore's Dissert. 77.

in rebus immobilibus servandum est jus loci, in quo bona sunt sita.[1]

§ 427. But it is wholly unnecessary to repeat the opinions of foreign jurists, since in the general proposition they all concur, (though some of them insist upon exceptions, to some of which we may hereafter allude,) that the law of the *situs* exclusively governs as to immoveable property.[2] Pothier has laid it down in the most general form, declaring, that real laws have an exclusive dominion over all things submitted to their authority, whether the persons owning them live within or without the territory.[3] And Vattel has laid it down, as a principle of international law, that immoveables are to be disposed of according to the laws of the country, where they are situate.[4]

§ 428. The consent of the tribunals, acting under the common law, both in England and America, is, if possible, still more uniform on the subject. All the authorities recognise the principle in its fullest import, that real estate is exclusively subject to the laws of the government, within whose territory it is situate.[5] So

1 Huberus, Tom. 1, P. 1, Lib. 3, tit. 13, (5.) De Success.

2 The learned reader may consult Livermore's Dissert. p. 28 to 106. Hertii Opera, Tom. 1, De Collis. § 4, n. 9, p. 125; Ersk. Inst. B. 3, tit. 2, § 40, p. 515; Bouhier, Cout. de Bourg. ch. 23, § 36, 37 to 63, p. 456 to 457; 2 Bell. Comm. 690; Fergusson on Marr. and Div. 395. Le Brun, Communauté. Lib. 1, ch. 2, p. 9, 10; D'Aguesseau, Œuvres, Tom. 4, p. 660; Cochin, Œuvres, Tom. 1, p. 545; Id. Tom. p. 555; Henry on Foreign Law, p. 12, 14, 15; Id. App. p. 196; Voet. ad Pand. Lib. 1, tit. 4. P. 2, § 3, 5, 6, p. 39, 40; 1 Froland, Mém. ch. 4, p. 49, ch. 7, p. 155; 2 Kaims on Equity, B. 3, ch. 8, § 2.

3 Pothier, Coutum. d'Orléans, ch. 1, § 2, n. 22, 23, 24, ch. 3, n. 51.

4 Vattel, B. 2, ch. 8, § 110; Id. § 103.

5 The authorities are very numerous, in which it has been decided or taken for granted, and among them in England are, Sill *v.* Worswick, 1 H. Black. 665; Hunter *v.* Potts, T. R. 41, 182; Phillips *v.* Hunter, 2 H. Black.

that we may here fully adopt the language of Voet, *De realibus quidem, cum plerorumque consensus sit, id pluribus docere supervacuum fuerit.*[1] And so firmly is this principle established, that in cases of bankruptcy the real estate of the bankrupt, situate in foreign countries, is universally admitted not to pass under the assignment, although, as we have seen, there are great diversities of opinion as to moveables.[2] And Lord Eldon has gone so far as to declare, that there exists no legal or equitable obligation (although there is a moral obligation) in the bankrupt to make a conveyance thereof to his assignees; and that the creditors are without redress, unless by way of remedy *in rem*, where the real estate is situate, or by withholding a certificate of discharge until the bankrupt executes such a conveyance.[3]

§ 429. It may, however, be of some utility to examine into the application of the general rule in some of its more important aspects. We shall, therefore, consider it, first in relation to the capacity of persons to

402; Selkrig *v.* Davis, 2 Rose Bank. Cas. Id. 29; 2 Dow R. 230; Coppin *v.* Coppin, 2 P. Will, 290, 293; Broadie *v.* Barry, 2 Ves. and Beames, R. 130; Birthwhistle *v.* Vardill, 5 B. and Cres. 438; 2 Bell. Comm. 690; and in America, U. S. *v.* Crosby, 7 Cranch, 115; Clarke *v.* Graham, 6 Wheaton, R. 597; Kerr *v.* Mason, 9 Wheaton, R. 566; Harper *v.* Hampton, 1 Harr. and John R. 687; Goodwin *v.* Jones, 3 Mass. R. 514, 518; Cutter *v.* Davenport, 1 Pick. R. 81, 86; Holmes *v.* Remsen, 4 John. Ch. R. 460; S. C. 20; John R. 254; Hosford *v.* Nichols, 1 Paige R. 220; Blake *v.* Williams, 6 Pick. 286; Milne *v.* Moreton, 6 Binn. R. 359. See also 4 Cowen Rep. 510, 527, note; Dwarris on Stat. 649, 650: Wiles *v.* Cowper, Wilcox's Ohio Rep. 279; S. C., 2 Hammond R. 124; Henry on Foreign Law, 8, 9; McCormick *v.* Sullivant, 10 Wheaton, R. 192; Darby *v.* Mayer, 10 Wheaton, R. 465.

1 Voet. ad Pand. Lib. 1, tit. 5, P. 2, § 7, p. 40.

2 Selkrig *v.* Davis, 2 Rose Bank. Cas. 97; Id. 291; 2 Dow, R. 230, 250; 2 Bell Comm. 690.

3 Selkrig *v.* Davis, 2 Rose Bank. Cas. 97; Id. 291; S. C. 2 Dow, 230, 250. But see Stein's case, 1 Rose, 462.

take or to transfer real estate; secondly, in relation to the forms and solemnities necessary to transfer it; thirdly, in relation to the extent of interest to be taken or transferred; and fourthly, in relation to the subject matter, or what are properly to be deemed immoveables.

§ 430. First, in relation to the capacity of persons to take or transfer real estate. It may be laid down, as a general principle of the common law, that a party must have a capacity to take according to the law of the *situs*, otherwise he will be excluded from all ownership. Thus, if the laws of a country exclude aliens from holding lands, either by succession, purchase, or devise, such a title becomes wholly inoperative as to them, whatever may be the law of the place of their domicil.[1] On the other hand, if by the local law aliens may take, and hold lands, it is wholly immaterial, what may be the law of their own domicil of origin or of choice.

§ 431. So, if a person is incapable from any other circumstance of transferring his immoveable property by the law of the *situs*, his transfers will be held invalid, although by the law of his domicil no such personal incapacity exists. On the other hand, if he has capacity to transfer by the law of the *situs*, he may make a valid title, notwithstanding an incapacity may attach to him by the law of domicil. This is the silent, but irresistible result of the principle adopted by the common law, which has no admitted exception. We may illustrate the principle by an application to cases of common occurrence under the dominion of the common law. By that law a person is deemed a minor, and is incapable of conveying real estate, until he has

[1] See Buchanan *v.* Deshon, 1 Gill R. 280; Sewall *v.* Lee, 9 Mass. R. 363.

arrived at twenty-one years of age. But by the law of some foreign countries minority continues until twenty-five or even until thirty years of age. Let us then suppose a foreigner, owning lands in England or America (where the common law prevails), who is by the law of his domicil in his minority, but is over twenty-one years of age. It is clear, that he may convey his real estate in England or America, notwithstanding such domestic incapacity; for he is of the age required by the local law.[1] On the other hand, let us suppose a married woman, domiciled in a foreign country, and by the law of that country incapable of alienating her real estate without the consent of her husband, should own real estate in England or America, where she is incapable of alienating it without such consent; she could not alienate it without the consent of her husband; and her separate act would be held *ipso facto* void, by the law of the *situs*.

§ 432. But, however clear this may seem according to the principles of the common law on this subject, a very different doctrine is, as we have already seen, maintained by foreign jurists on this very point.[2] They contend, that the capacity or incapacity of persons to transfer property, or to do any other act, depends altogether upon the law of the place of their domicil. If they have a capacity or incapacity there, it governs all their property elsewhere, whether moveable or immoveable. Thus, Boullenois maintains, that, if a man has immoveable property in a place, where majority is attained at twenty-five, and by the law of his domicil he is of age at twenty, he may at twenty sell or alien-

1 See Saul *v.* His Creditors, 17 Martin R. 569, 597.

2 Ante § 51, 52 to 61, 65.

ate such immoveable property. And on the other hand, if by the law of the *situs* of the immoveable property, he is of age at twenty, but by the law of his domicil not until twenty-five, he cannot sell or alienate such property until the age of twenty-five.[1] Rodemburg adopts the same doctrine, and maintains it with abundance of zeal.[2] And there are many others, who adhere to the same opinion.[3] The ground work of

---

1 Ante § 52, 71. — There is a curious distinction maintained by many jurists on this subject, which deserves notice. — They say, that, if the local law fixes the age of majority at a particular period, and declares, that, until the party has arrived at that period, he shall not alienate immoveable property,— in that case the local law governs; for it does not turn upon the mere fact of being a major or not. But if the local law only says, that no person, who is not a major, shall alienate, then, if the party is a major by the law of his domicil, though not by that of the *rei sitæ*, he may alienate the property, because the only point is majority or not, and that must be ascertained by the *lex domicilii;* for the state or capacity of a person by the law of his domicil extends everywhere. Boullenois dwells much on this distinction, and it has received the support of Merlin. 1 Boullenois 57, 102, 175, 183, 499, 700, 705, 720; Boullenois, Quest. Mixt. p. 19; 2 Merlin, Répertoire, Testament, § 1, 6, art. 3, p. 318, art. 2, p. 317, 318; Id. art. 3; 2 Froland, Mém. 824, 825; Livermore's Diss. p. 48, 50, 58, 59, 60.

2 Rodemburg, De. Div. Stat. tit. 2, ch. 1, p. 10; 1 Boullenois, 77, 78, 154, 155, 194, 295; 1 Hertii Opera, De. Collis. Leg. § 4, n. 23, p. 133; Livermore's Dissert. p. 40, § 31; Id. p. 48, § 44, p. 49, § 45, 46; Bouhier, Cout. de Bourg. ch. 24, § 91 to 108, p. 476, 477, 478.

3 Ante § 51, 52, 53, 54, 60; 1 Froland, Mém. 65, 66; 2 Froland, Mém. 1576 to 1594; Merlin, Répertoire, Testament, § 1, 5, art. 2, p. 517, 518; 1 Boullenois, 705 to 731. — This is manifestly the opinion of Mr. Livermore, (Diss. p. 40 to 42; Id. p. 48 to 50); so of Merlin, (Répertoire, Majorité, § 5; Autorisation Maritale, § 10, art. 2; Id. Puissance Paternelle, § 7, p. 142 to 146); of Froland, (1 Froland, Mém. 156, 171; 2 Froland, Mém. 1595); of Bouhier, (Bouhier, Cout. de Bourg. ch. 23, § 90 to 96, p. 461; Id. ch. 24, § 91, &c.; Id. 1 Boullenois, p. 724); of Pothier, (Pothier Cout. d'Orléans, ch. 1, § 1, n. 7, p. 2); of Huberus, (Huberus, Lib. 1, tit. 3, § 12; Ante § 60); and of Hertius, (Hertii Opera, De Collis. § 4, n. 8, p. 123, 124.) But Merlin in another place admits, that a law, which prohibits a prodigal from making a testament, is personal; but at the same time it will not prevent the prodigal from making a valid will of immove-

their argument is, that capacity and incapacity must be uniformly the same everywhere; that the law of the domicil ought to regulate it; and that it would be utterly incongruous to make a minor in one place a major in another, thus investing him with opposite personal qualities.[1]

§ 433. This notion is combated with great vigor and ability by other foreign jurists. Burgundus admits,

able property in a foreign country, which allows it (as in Bourbourg); for which he gives two reasons, first, that a law is real, which permits one act to be done by a person, who is otherwise incapable; and secondly, because a real law always prevails, when it comes in conflict with a personal law. He applies the same rule to an unemancipated son, who cannot by the law of his domicil make a testament, but yet may alienate any of his property acquired in Hainault, for its laws form an exception to the general incapacity of the son, and therefore they are real. Merlin, Répertoire, Testament, § 1, n. 5, art. 1, p. 310. This opinion seems to coincide with that of Hertius, (1 Hertii Opera, De Collis. Leg. 4, n. 22, p. 133.) It seems also supported by Rodemburg, (Rodemburg, De Div. Stat. p. 1, tit. 1, ch. 2, cited by Merlin, ubi supra.) — But Merlin says, that, if by the laws of the country of his domicil an unemancipated son cannot make a testament, and by the laws of another country he has a general capacity; in such a case such laws are personal and in conflict, and therefore the law of the domicil is to govern. Merlin, Id. p. 311. See also 1 Boullenois, 77, 78. Boullenois lays down some rules upon this subject, which seem also to have received the approbation of Bouhier. (1.) When the personal statute of the domicil is in conflict with the personal statute of another place, the law of the domicil is to prevail. (2.) When the personal statute of the domicil is in conflict with the real statute of the same or another place, it yields to the real statute; when the real statute of the domicil is in conflict with the real statute of the *situs* of the property, each one has its own authority in its own territory. 1 Boullenois, Pr. Gén. 29, 30, 31; Id. 101, 102; Bouhier, Cout. de Bourg. ch. 23, § 90, 96, p. 461; Id. ch. 24, § 91, &c. p. 476; Livermore's Diss. p. 58, 59.

1 Mr. Henry says, that the personal statutes of one place may act indirectly and by comity on immoveable property situate in another, as a decree of lunacy may by its effects deprive a party of a power to alienate his foreign property; and so of the disability created by bankruptcy. Henry on Foreign Law, 15. This seems inadmissible as a doctrine of the common law.

that personal laws, as to capacity, govern all personal acts, such as personal contracts; but, in regard to immoveable property, he says, that it is sufficient, that a person be of the age required by the law of the *situs*, to authorize him to make a valid transfer, although he may be incapable by the law of his domicil.[1] His language is: *Cum enim unicuique provinciæ suæ propriæ sint leges, possessionibus injunctæ atque indictæ, sane incapacitas foris adepta in considerationem venire non potest; sed omnis sive qualitas, sive personæ habilitas, quoad eadem bona pertinet, a loco sitûs proficiscitur.*[2] Boullenois after some fluctuations of opinion comes to the result, that the capacity to make a testament, so far as it regards the person, is personal; but so far as it regards immoveables, is real, and governed by the law of the *situs* of the property.[3] Stockmans, Dumoulin, and P. Voet maintain the same opinion.[4] Dumoulin says, *Si statutum dicat, quod minor 25 annis non possit testari in immobilibus, tunc non respicit personam, nec agit in personam principaliter, sed in certas res, ad finem conservandi patrimonii, et sic est reale; unde statutum loci inspicitur, sive persona subdita sit, sive non.*[5] Paul Voet adds, that personal laws do not regularly extend, so as to affect immoveable property in a foreign country,

---

1 See Rodemburg, De Div. Stat. tit. 2, ch. 1, p. 11, 12; 1 Boullenois, 127, 128, 129, 199, 201, 202; Livermore's Diss. p. 50 to 52; Bouhier, Cout. de Bourg. ch. 24, § 91, 94 to 107, p. 476, 477, 478.

2 1 Boullenois, p. 129, 130, 150.

3 1 Boullenois, 718, 719, 720. See Id. 81, 82, 83, 84, 101, 102. See also Merlin, Répertoire, Testament § 1, n. 8, art. 1, p. 310; Cochin, Œuvres, Tom. 4, p. 555.

4 Livermore's Diss. 52, 53, 54; 1 Froland, Mém. 65, 66; 2 Froland, 819 to 823.

5 Bouhier, Cout. de Bourg. ch. 29, § 102, p. 477, 478; 1 Froland, Mém. 65.

either directly or consequentially.[1] John Voet has gone into an elaborate consideration of the subject, and strongly denies, that personal laws can operate out of the territory. *Nullâ tamen ratione* (he says) *sufficiente, cum hæc nitantur, nec a legibus Romanis huic sententiæ patrocinium accedere possit; verius est, personalia, non magis quam realia, territorium statuentis posse excedere, sive directo, sive per consequentiam.* And he proceeds to put very strong cases, whether any foreign country will permit its own territorial laws to be overthrown by the laws of another country on the subject of prodigals, infamous persons, minors, illegitimacy, or legitimacy, and heirship.[2]

1 P. Voet. de Stat. § 4, ch. 2, n. 7, p. 124.— P. Voet admits, that personal laws accompany the person everywhere, as to property, within the territory of the government of which he is a subject; but not as to any property elsewhere. "Statutum personale ubique locorum personam comitatur, in ordine ad bona infra territorium statuentis, ubi persona affecta domicilium habet. Non tamen statutum personale sese extendit ad bona immobilia alibi sita." Voet. De Statut. § 4, ch. 2 n. 6, p. 123. This qualification of his opinion ought to have been stated, ante, § 51, S. P. Voet. ad Pand. Lib. 1, tit. 4, § 2, 9, p. 43.

2 The passage deserves to be quoted at large. "Ita nec ratio ulla est, cur magis qualitas et habilitas, privato per statutum data vel denegata, vires extenderet per ea loca, in quibus diversum quid aut contrarium circa personarum qualitatem lege cautum est. Quod si hæc cuiquam minus videantur sufficere, is velim mihi rationem modumve expediat, per quem legislator personam, domicilii intuitu sibi suppositam, habilem, inhabilemve ad actus gerendos declarans, alterius loci legislatorem potestate parem cogeret, ut is alienis decretis statutisve pareret, aut rata irritave haberet, quæ judex domicilii talia esse jussit in personâ domicilium illic fovente; maxime si fateatur (ut fateri necesse est) pari in parem nullam competere cogendi potestatem. Exponat, obsecro, prodigo declarato, vel infamiâ notato, vel legitimato, vel in ipso pubertatis tempore habili ad testamentum condendum declarato per magistratum Hollandum, ac Ultrajectum se conferente vel immobilia possidente; exponat, inquam, quâ juris viâ magistratus Ultrajectinus adstringi posset, ut istum ratione bonorum, in Ultrajectino solo sitorum, pro tali agnosceret; adeoque contractus prodigi Hollandici haberet irritos; dignitates Hollando infamato denegaret; successionem in bona Trajectina ad

§ 434. The opinion of these latter jurists is in coincidence with that of the common law, as already stated; and it has been applied to the case of heirship and legitimacy in England in a recent case, of which we have had occasion to take notice in another place.[1] Upon that occasion Lord Chief Justice Abbott said, "The rule as to the law of domicil has never been extended to real property; nor have I found, in the decisions of Westminister Hall, any doctrine giving a countenance to the idea, that it ought to be so extended. There being no authority for saying, that the right of inheritance follows the law of the domicil of the parties, I think it must follow that of the country, where the land lies." And this doctrine was concurred in by the other Judges.[2]

§ 435. Secondly, in relation to the forms and solemnities of passing the title to real estate. We have already had occasion to examine the point, whether contracts respecting real estate must not be in the form prescribed by the local law, in order to have validity; as, for instance, a contract for the sale of land in England to be in writing according to the Statute of Frauds. The result of that examination was, that, in

---

spurium Hollandum legitimatum pertinentia, tanquam in legitime nati patrimonium, pateretur proximis deferri; testamentum masculi, ante conditum annum ætatis octavum et decimum, juberet ratum esse." Voet. ad Pandectas, Lib. 1, tit. 4, pars. 2. De Statutis, § 7, p. 40.

There are some jurists, who adopt an intermediate opinion, holding, that, in order to transfer real property, the party must have capacity according to the *lex domicilii* and the *lex rei sitæ*. Thus, if in the country *rei sitæ* the age to convey is twenty-one years, and in the country of the domicil the age is twenty-five years, a party cannot convey, although he is twenty-one years of age, nor unless he is twenty-five. Ante § 432, note.

1 Ante § 87.

2 Doe dem. Birthwhistle *v.* Vardill, 5 Barn. & Cres. 438.

countries acting under the common law, the affirmative is admitted; though foreign jurists are divided on the point.[1] It would seem clear, also, that no conveyance or transfer of land can be made, either testamentary or *inter vivos*, except according to the formalities prescribed by the local law. Thus, in England, no instrument not under seal can operate a conveyance of land, so as to give a perfect title thereto. An instrument, therefore, not under seal, executed in a foreign country, where no seal is required to pass the title to lands, would be held invalid to pass land in England.[2] The same rule is established in America, where it is held, (as we have seen,) that the title to land can be acquired and lost only in the manner prescribed by the law of the place, where the property is situate.[3]

§ 436. Erskine in his Institutes states this to be the law of Scotland. "In the conveyance (says he) of an immoveable subject, or of any right affecting heritage, the grantor must follow the solemnities established by the law, not of the country, where he signs the deed, but of the state, in which the heritage lies, and from which it is impossible to remove it. For though he be subject with respect to his person to the *lex domicilii*, that law can have no authority over property, which hath its fixed domicil in another territory, and which cannot be tried, but before the Courts, and according to the laws of that state, where it is situated. And this

1 Ante § 363 to 373.

2 See Dundas *v.* Dundas, 2 Dow & Clarke, 349; Coppin *v.* Coppin, 2 P. Will. 291, 293; 2 Fonbl. Equity, B. 5, Ch. 1. § 6, note, p. 444, 445.

3 Ante § 427, 428; U. S. *v.* Crosby, 7 Cranch. 115; Cutter *v.* Davenport, 1 Pick. R. 81, 86; Hosford *v.* Nichols, 1 Paige R. 220; Wills *v.* Cowper, 2 Hamm. R. 124; S. C. Wilcox's Rep. 278; Kerr *v.* More, 9 Wheaton R. 566; McCormick *v.* Sullivant, 10 Wheaton R. 192; Darby *v.* Mayer, 11 Wheaton R. 465.

rule is so strictly adhered to in practice, that a disposition of an heritable jurisdiction in Scotland, executed in England after the English form, was not sustained, even as an obligation to compel the grantor to execute a more formal conveyance."[1] And he is well borne out in this doctrine by other authorities.[2]

§ 437. Boullenois admits, that, when an incapacity to do an act, or make a conveyance of a thing, except by certain formalities, is created by the *lex rei sitæ*, that law must be observed in regard to that thing, although the party be otherwise capable by the law of his domicil.[3] And he adds, in another place, that, if these formalities are attached to things, and not to persons, then the laws, which prescribe them, are real; and, consequently, the law of the place of their situation must govern.[4] And accordingly he lays it down, as a fundamental rule, *Quand la loi exige certaines formalités, lesquelles sont attachées aux choses mêmes, il faut suivre la loi de la situation.*[5] Yet, strangely enough, he departs from this general doctrine in relation to testaments, upon some subtile distinctions, which he takes, between extrinsic and intrinsic forms, between the solemnities required to the perfection and authenticity of an act, and those, which relate to the capacity to do it, or to dispose of the thing, which is the subject of it.[6] Sandius has given us some quite as subtile distinctions, in-

1 Ersk. Inst. B. 3, tit. 3, § 40, p. 515; Id. § 41; 2 Kaims on Equity, B. 3, ch. 8, § 2, p. 328.

2 Ante § 366, 367; Jerningham *v.* Herbert, 1 Tamlyn R. 103; Fergusson on Marriage and Div. 395, 397.

3 2 Boullenois, 476, 477, 488. See Merlin, Répertoire, Testament, § 1, 5, art. 1, 2, 3.

4 1 Boullenois, 467; Id. 499, 500. See Livermore's Diss. p. 58 to 60; Henry on Foreign Law, 50.

5 2 Boullenois, 467, Rule 4. See 1 Boullenois, 151.

6 1 Boullenois, 424, 425, 426.

sisting, that there is a wide distinction between the solemnities of an alienation and the thing, of which the alienation is the subject; *Multum intersit inter solennitates dispositionis et rem, de quâ sit dispositio;* the solemnities are but the form, and the thing the subject of the alienation; and therefore such a statute regards the alienation itself, rather than the thing; *Solennitates sunt forma, res est subjectum dispositionis; quare tale statutum magis efficere videtur dispositionem ipsam, quam rem.*

§ 438. Cujas and Burgundus maintain with great clearness the general doctrine, that the law *rei sitæ* must govern as to the solemnities of alienation, *inter vivos* and testamentary.[1] This is also the opinion of other distinguished jurists.

§ 439. Froland treats, as clearly real, all laws, which respect the alienation of immoveable property, and that it is consequently governed by the *lex rei sitæ. Il faut s'attacher aux coutumes des lieux où les fonds sont situés.*[2] Cochin lays down the rule, that, though the formalities of an act may be, and indeed ought to be according to the law of the place of the act; yet, when such an act is to be applied to property in another country, the law *rei sitæ* must govern. *Les formalités, dont un acte doit être revêtu, se règlent par la loi, qui exerce son empire dans le lieu, où de l'acte a été passé; mais quand il s'agit d'appliquer les clauses, qu'il renferme, aux biens des parties contractantes, c'est la loi de la situation de ces biens, qui doit seule être consultée.*[3]

§ 440. But there are many jurists, who maintain an opposite opinion, holding, that, if the act or instrument have the formalities, which are prescribed by the law

---

1 1 Boullenois, 129, 151, 422, 425; Cujacii Opera, Tom. 3 to Observat. Lib. 14, ch. 12.

2 1 Froland, Mém. 156; Id. 65.

3 Cochin Œuvres. Tom. 5, p. 697.

of the place, where it is made, it ought to have universal operation;[1] and they apply it especially to the case of testamentary dispositions of real property.[2] They found themselves upon the extreme inconvenience, which would otherwise result from requiring a party to make different testaments for property lying in different countries, and the almost utter impossibility, in many cases, of ascertaining at a critical moment, what are the peculiar solemnities prescribed by the laws of each of these countries.[3] They seem wholly to have overlooked, on the other side, the inconvenience of a nation suffering property, locally and permanently situate within its territory, to be subject to be transferred by any other laws, than its own; and thus introducing into the bosom of its own jurisprudence all the innumerable diversities of foreign laws, to regulate its own titles to such property, many of which laws can be but imperfectly ascertained, and many of which may become matters of subtile controversy.[4] And some of these jurists

---

1 Voet. de Statut. § 4, ch. 2, § 6, p. 123, § 7, p. 124; Livermore's Diss. 89; Voet, ad Pand. Lib. 1, tit. 4, P. 2, § 5, 6, p. 39, § 10, p. 43, 44; Livermore's Diss. 127, 130; 1 Boullenois, 426, 427 to 433.

2 See Rodemburg, de Div. Stat. tit. 2, ch. 3, p. 19; 1 Boullenois, 414 to 421; Id. 422 to 433; 1 Hertii Opera. § 4, n. 10, p. 125; Voet, ad Pandect. Lib. 1, tit. 4, p. 2, 13, p. 43; Bouhier, Cout. de Bourg. ch. 23, § 81 to 89, p. 460: Vinnius ad Instit. Lib. 2, tit. 10, § 14, n. 5; 1 Boullenois, 426, 427: Merlin, Répertoire, Loi. § 6, art. 6, 7.

3 Rodemburg, De Div. tit. 2, ch. 3, p. 19; 1 Boullenois, 414, 415, 416, 417. Vinnius ad Inst. Lib. 2 tit. 10, § 14, n. 5; 1 Boullenois, 426, 427; Hertii Opera, De Collis. Leg. § 4, n. 10, p. 126; Id. n. 23, p. 133.

4 Cochin says, it is one of the most uniform principles, that the form of acts depends upon the law of the place, where they are passed; so that, if a man is domiciled at Paris, and there has all his property (*biens*), but he makes his testament in another province under a different law, the law of the latter is alone to be regarded in its form, though the succession to the testator, either of heirship or testamentary, may be regulated by the law of Paris. Cochin, Œuvres, Tom. 2, p. 72. D'Aguesseau treats with some sarcasm those, who venture to suggest a doubt on the point.

press their doctrine so far, as to doubt, whether a transfer according to the solemnities of the place, where the property is locally situate, would be good, if not executed also according to the law of the place, where the act is done.[1]

§ 441. The opinion of these jurists is supported by Dumoulin. His language is; *Et omnium doctorum sententia, ubicunque consuetudo vel statutum locale disponit de solemnitate, vel formâ actûs, ligare etiam exteros, ibi actum illum gerentes, et gestum esse validum, et efficacem ubique, etiam super bonis sitis extra territorium consuetudinis vel statuti.*[2] And in another

---

"We leave such discussions (says he) to the ultramontane Doctors. We say with D'Argentré, that these questions are not worthy to occupy a moment's attention. No one can doubt, that the formalities of a testament ought to be governed by the law of the place, where the act is done." D'Aguesseau, Œuvres, Tom. 4, p. 637.

1 Rodemburg, De Div. Stat. tit. 2, ch. 3, p. 21; 1 Boullenois, 417; Id. 428, 429, 430.

2 Mr. Livermore manifestly entertained the opinion, that it was sufficient for a testament of immoveable property to have the formalities prescribed by the law of the testator's domicil. After adverting to Dumoulin's division of statutes into those, which relate to the solemnities and forms of acts (*nudam ordinationem vel solemnitatem actûs*), and those, which concern the merits and decision of causes, (*quæ meritum causæ vel decisionem concernunt,*) he added: "The statutes of the first class, I do not consider to be either personal, real, or mixed. They do not act directly upon persons, nor upon property; but upon the act for the purpose of determining its authenticity. The laws of some countries require, that a testament shall be made in presence of seven witnesses. In other countries, the law requires only the presence of a notary and two witnesses. These laws dispose of the solemnities of all testaments made within their jurisdiction; but they neither affect the capacity of the testator, nor do they dispose of his property. The law of the testator's domicil determines his capacity to make a testament; the law of the place, where his immoveable property is situated, determines, whether it may be disposed of by testament, or not; the will of the testator disposes of his property; and the sole purpose and effect of the statute, which requires a certain number of witnesses to a testament, is to show, whether that will has been expressed, or not."

place he says, *Aut statutum loquitur de his, quæ concernunt nudam ordinationem vel solemnitatem actûs, et semper inspicitur statutum vel consuetudo loci, ubi actus celebratur, sive in contractibus, sive in judiciis, sive in testamentis, sive in instrumentis aut aliis conficiendis; ita quod testamentum factum coram duobus testibus in locis, ubi non requiritur major solemnitas, valet ubique.*[1]

§ 442. Paul Voet holds the opinion, that the solemnities of contracts and other instruments are to be according to the laws of the place, where the act is done, and not of the *rei sitæ;* for he holds laws respecting solemnities not to be *in rem*, or *in personam*, but of a mixed nature. *Statutum quippe circa solemnia, nec est in rem, nec in personam, sed mixti generis.*[2] And, therefore, he insists, that, if a testament is made according to the solemnities of the place *rei sitæ*, but not of the testator's domicil, it will not be valid, as to property situate elsewhere. *Finge, quempiam testari in loco domicilii adhibitis solemnibus rei sitæ, non sui domicilii; valebitne testamentum ratione bonorum alibi sitorum? Respondeo, quod non. Neque enim aliter testamentum valere potest, quam si ea servetur solemnitas, quam requirit locus gestionis. Quid, si quispiam testatur secundum solemnia sui loci, puta coram notario et duobus testibus, an vires capiet testamentum ratione bonorum extra territorium statuentis jacentium, puta in Friziâ, ubi plures solemnitates requiruntur? Aff. (affirmo). Idque procedit, sive testator prius retinuerit, sive alio transtulerit. Quod, si forensis secundum loci statutum testamentum condat, ubi tantum hos-*

---

[1] 1 Boullenois, 423, 424.

[2] P. Voet. De Statut. § 9, ch. 2, n. 3, p. 263.

pitatur, an valebit alibi, ubi vel immobilia vel domicilium habet? Respondeo, quod ita.[1]

§ 443. Huberus supports the same opinion. "In Holland," says he, "a testament may be made before a notary and two witnesses. In Friezeland it is not valid, unless established by seven witnesses. A Batavian made a testament in Holland, under which property situate in Friezeland was demanded. The question is, whether the judges in Friezeland ought to sustain the demand under that testament. The laws of Holland cannot bind the Friezians; and, therefore, by the first axiom the testament would not be valid in Friezeland; but by the third axiom it would be valid; and, according to that, judgment was pronounced in favour of the testament. But a Friezian goes into Holland, and there makes a testament according to the local law (*more loci*), contrary to the Friezian law, and returns into Friezeland and dies there; is the testament valid? It is valid by the second axiom, because while he was in Holland, although temporarily, he was bound by the local law; and an act, valid in its origin, ought to be valid everywhere by the third axiom; and this without *any discrimination of moveable or immoveable property.* So the law is, and is practised.[2] On the other hand, a Friezian makes his will in his own country before a notary and two witnesses; and it is carried into Holland, and property situate there is demanded. It will not be allowed, because the testament was from the beginning a nullity, being made contrary to the local law. The same law will govern, if a Batavian should make a testament in Friezeland, although it would be

---

1 P. Voet. De Stat. § 9, ch. 2, n. 1, 2, 3, § 262, 263.

2 The axioms here referred to by Huberus are those already stated in § 29.

valid in Holland; for it is true, that such an instrument would from the beginning be a nullity, for the reasons just stated.[1]

§ 444. Rodemburg admits, that the general principle is, that all statutes respecting the solemnities of acts to transfer property are real, and therefore, that they ought to be governed by the *lex rei sitæ; Quicumque enim fuerit, sive incola, sive exterus, qui rem alienare intendit, necesse habet respicere ad solemnitatem territorii, cui bona sunt obnoxia;* but yet, at the same time, he yields to the exception in favour of testaments, upon the ground of public convenience.[2] It is hardly possible to conceive of a stronger illustration of the difficulty of undertaking to build up systems of jurisprudence upon mere theory and private notions of general convenience. The common law has wisely adhered to the doctrine, that the title to real property can pass only in the manner, and by the forms, and to the extent, allowed by the local law. It has thus cut off innumerable disputes, and given simplicity, as well as uniformity, to its operations.

§ 445. Thirdly; in relation to the extent of the interest to be taken or transferred. And, here, there seems a perfect coincidence between the doctrine of the common law, and that maintained by foreign jurists. It is universally agreed, that the law *rei sitæ* is to prevail in relation to all dispositions of immoveable

---

[1] Huberus, Lib. 1. tit. 3, § 4, 15.

[2] Rodemburg, De Div. Stat. tit. 2, ch. 3, p. 19, 21; 1 Boullenois, p. 414 to 418; Id. 422, 423. — Vattel affirms, "that the validity of a testament, as to its form, can only be decided by the domestic judge, whose sentence, delivered in form, ought to be everywhere acknowledged." But at the same time he admits, that the validity of the bequests may be disputed, as not being according to the *lex rei sitæ*. Vattel, B. 2, ch. 7, § 85; Id. § 111.

property, and the nature and extent of the interest to be alienated. If the local law, therefore, prescribes, that no person shall dispose, by deed or by will, of more than a half, or third, or quarter of his immoveable property; or, that he shall dispose only of a life estate in such property; such laws are obligatory, and no other or farther alienation can be made.[1] And it follows, that if the local law prohibits the alienation of certain kinds of immoveable property, or takes from the owner the power of charging them with liens or mortgages, that law exclusively governs in every such case. D'Aguesseau fully assents to this doctrine, and says, that no one can be ignorant, that, when the question is, what portion of immoveable property may be devised, it is necessary invariably to follow the law of the place, where the property is locally situate.[2]

§ 446. Another illustration may be borrowed from the English jurisprudence, prohibiting alienations and devises of real estate in mortmain, or for charitable purposes. If an American citizen, owning lands in England, or a Scotchman owning lands in England, should alienate, or devise such land in violation of the mortmain acts, the instrument, whether *inter vivos* or testamentary, would be held void. And the same principle would apply to a trust created in personal property, to be invested in lands in England for like purposes.[3]

§ 447. Fourthly; in relation to the subject matter, or what are to be deemed immoveables. And here, as

---

1 1 Boullenois, Prin. Gén. 30, p. 8; Id. 205; and 1 Froland, Mém. 156; Rodemburg, De Div. Stat. tit. 2, ch. 2.

2 D'Aguesseau, Œuvres, Tom. 4, p. 637, 638.

3 Attorney General *v.* Mill, 3 Russell R. 328; S. C. 2 Dow & Clarke, 393.

we have already seen, not only lands and houses, but servitudes and easements, and other charges on lands, as mortgages and rents, and trust estates, are deemed to be, in the sense of law, immoveables, and governed by the *lex rei sitæ*.[1] But in addition to these, which may be deemed universally to partake of the nature of immoveables, or (as the common law phrase is) to savour of the realty, all other things, though moveable in their nature, which by the local law are deemed immoveables, are, in like manner, governed by the local law. For every nation, having authority to prescribe rules for the disposition and arrangement of all property within its own territory, may impress upon it any character, which it shall choose; and no other nation can impugn, or vary that character. So, that the question, in all these cases, is not so much, what are or ought to be deemed, *ex suâ naturâ*, moveables, or not; as what are deemed so by the law of the place, where they are situated. If they are there deemed part of the land, or annexed (as the common law would say) to the freehold, they must be so treated in every place, in which any controversy shall arise respecting their nature and character.[2]

---

1 Poth. Cout. d'Orléans, ch. 1, § 2. — P. Voet puts on this point the very sensible distinction, that whether rents are to be deemed personal, or real, depends upon the question, whether they are charged on real property, or not. "Vel enim talium redituum nomine sunt affecta immobilia, id est, super immobilibus sunt constituti et immobilibus erunt adscribendi, adeoque statutum loci spectabitur: vel immobilia affecta non sunt illis reditibus, tumque mobilibus poterunt accenseri; atque adeo statutum loci personæ, cujus illi sunt reditus, inspici debebit." P. Voet. De Stat. § 9, ch. 1, n. 13, p. 259. And he includes among immoveables all moveables, which are intentionally annexed permanently to the freehold. "Nisi tamen perpetui usûs gratiâ ex destinatione patris-familias in uno loco manere debeant; quo casu immobilibus comparabuntur." Id. n. 8, p. 255.

2 See Ersk. Institutes, B. 3, tit. 9, § 4.

§ 448. Hitherto we have spoken of alienations and acquisitions made by the acts of the parties themselves. And the question next arises, whether the same principles apply to estates and rights acquired by operation of law. And it may be affirmed without hesitation, that, independent of any contract, express or implied,[1] no estate can be acquired by operation of law in any other manner, or to any other extent, or by any other means, than those prescribed by the *lex rei sitæ*. Thus, no estate in dowry, tenancy by the courtesy, or inheritable estate, or interest, can be acquired, except by such persons, and under such circumstances, as the local law prescribes. Thus, if the law of a state, where a man was domiciled at his death, should confer a title of dower on his wife, though an alien, that would not prevail in any other state, where an alien is not dowable.

§ 449. Many questions upon this subject have arisen, in the course of the discussions upon the matrimonial rights, conferred by the *lex domicilii*, over immoveable property, situate in foreign countries. In the different Italian States, and formerly in some of the provinces of France, which were governed by the Roman Law, there existed various regulations with regard to dowry or dotal property, *lucrum dotis*. By the laws and customs of some places, the husband gained by survivorship the whole of the dotal effects; by others, a third, by others, a fourth, and by others, nothing.[2] And one of the questions, which has been most elaborately discussed among foreign jurists, is, whether, in such a case, the law of the matrimonial domicil ought to govern the

1 See Livermore's Diss. 72, 73.

2 Livermore's Diss. 71; 1 Domat, B. 1, tit. 9, § 1; Code Civil of France, art. 1540 to art. 1573; 2 Boull. 89, 90.

rights of the parties, as to immoveable property in foreign countries, as it does in the matrimonial domicil. It has been agreed on all sides, that, where there is in the country *rei sitæ* a prohibitory law against any such dotal rights, and against any contract to create them, the law of the matrimonial domicil cannot prevail.[1] But the question has been, whether, in the absence of any such prohibitory law, or any express contract, the law of the matrimonial domicil ought not to prevail, so as to give the same dotal rights everywhere.[2]

§ 450. Baldus held, that in such cases, the law or custom of the matrimonial domicil ought to govern, as to property everywhere. *Consuetudines et statuta,* (said he,) *vigentia in domicilio mariti, non curo, ubi res sint positæ, quæ in dotem datæ sunt.*[3] And Dumoulin held the same doctrine, upon his favourite theory, that in all such cases the law of the matrimonial domicil constituted a tacit contract between the parties.[4]

---

1 Livermore's Diss. 71 to 75; 2 Boullenois, 89, 90, 91, 92; ante § 176 to 180, 184, 188; Voet. De Stat. § 4, ch. 3, § 9, p. 134, 135; 1 Froland, Mém. 62, 63, 64.

2 Even Paul Voet, who is a strong advocate for the realty of statutes, admits, that cases of express contract may govern, as to property locally situate in a foreign country. "Si statuto in uno territorio contractus accesserit, seu partium conventio, etiam si in rem sit conceptum, sese extendit ad bona extra jurisdictionem statuentium sita; non ut afficiat immediate ipsa bona, quam ipsam personam, quoad illa." P. Voet. De Stat. § 4, ch. 2, § 15, p. 127.

3 Livermore's Diss. 71, 72; 1 Froland, Mém. 62.

4 Livermore's Diss. 73, 74: 1 Froland, Mém. 61, 62, 63. — Dumoulin, in treating of the question, what law ought to prevail in fixing the rights of the husband, in regard to the dotal effects of his wife, in case of a change of domicil before the dissolution of the marriage, ultimately decides in favour of the law of the matrimonial domicil. His language is, "Hinc infertur ad questionem quotiodianam de contractu dotis et matrimonii, qui censetur fieri, non in loco, in quo contrahitur, sed in loco domicilii viri, et intelligitur, non de domicilio originis, sed de domicilio habitationis ipsius viri, de quo nemo dubitat, sed omnes consentiunt." 1 Froland, Mém. 61; Id. 62.

There are many jurists, who maintain the same opinion.[1]

§ 451. Boullenois contends, that, even if there be such a tacit contract, it does not render the laws of the place in regard to dowry personal; for, if that were so, (he adds,) then the dowry of persons contracting at Paris would be the same in all other provinces in the realm, as it is in Paris, which no one has ever yet contended.[2] Burgundus manifestly holds the opinion, that the law *rei sitæ* must govern in such cases.[3] And many jurists concur with him.[4]

§ 452. Similar questions have arisen in relation to the rights of community, and of mutual donations between husband and wife, whether they extend to mmoveable property elsewhere, or not; and the general result of the reasoning among foreign jurists turns upon the same considerations, which have been mentioned in relation to dowry. But this subject has been already discussed in another place, and need not be here again examined.[5]

§ 453. Similar questions have also arisen in considering the effect of mutual donations by married

---

1 Ante, § 145, 146, 147, 148 to 156.

2 1 Boullenois, 121; 2 Boullenois, 88 to 92. But see ante, § 155.

3 Ibid.

4 Ante, § 148, 152, 153, 167, 168; 1 Froland, Mém. 66, 67, 156; Id. 316 to 323, 338, 341; 2 Froland, Mém. 816. — Froland expresses himself in the following terms: "Et delà vient que dans le cas où il s'agit de successions, de la manière de les partager, de la quotité des biens, dont il peut disposer entre vifs ou par testament, d'aliénation d'immeubles, de douaire de femme ou d'enfans, de légitime, de retrait lignager, féodal ou conventionnel, de droit de puissance paternelle, de droit de viduité, et autres choses semblables, il faut s'attacher aux coutumes des lieux, où les fonds sont situez." 1 Froland, Mém. 156; Id. 49, 60 to 81.

5 See ante, § 145 to 158; 1 Froland, Mém. 66, 67, 68, 69; Id. 177, P. 2, ch. 1, per tot.; Cochin, Œuvres, Tom. 5, p. 80; Merlin, Répertoire, Testament § 1, n. 5, art. 1, p. 309, 310.

couples, when they are admitted by the law of the matrimonial domicil, but are unknown to, or prohibited by, the law of the place *rei sitæ*. But they proceed upon the same general principles.[1] Cochin says, it is not the law of the place, where an act is done, which determines its effect. If, (says he.) property is situate in a place, whose laws prohibit donations *inter vivos*, or reduces them to a particular portion, no one supposes the donation to be less a nullity, or less subject to reduction, because the act is done in a place, where no such prohibition exists.[2]

§ 454. The doctrine of the common law seems uniformly to be, that in all such cases the law of the place *rei sitæ* is to govern.[3] Hence, if persons, who are married in Louisiana (where the law of community exists), own immoveable property in Massachusetts (where such community is unknown); upon the death of the husband, the wife would take her dower only in the immoveable property of her husband, and the husband, upon the death of the wife, would take, as tenant by the courtesy only, in the immoveable property of his wife.

§ 455. Another class of cases illustrating this subject may be derived from the known rights of fathers over the property of their children according to the provisions of the civil law, and the customary law of countries, deriving their jurisprudence from the civil law. By the ancient Roman law all the sons were in subjection to the authority of the father, until they were

---

1 Liverm. Diss. 114, 115; 1 Voet. ad Pand. Lib. 1, tit. 4, n. 3, p. 39; 2 Froland, Mém. ch. 18, p. 840, &c., ch. 19, p. 904; Rodemburg, De Div. Stat. tit. 2, ch. 5, p. 33, 34; 1 Boullenois, 660, 661, 663, 767; 2 Boullenois, 430, 431, 432.

2 Cochin, Œuvres, Tom. 5, p. 697.

3 Ante, § 157, 158, 159, 174 to 179, 186, 187.

emancipated by the father, or by some other mode known to the law. During such subjection they were incapable of acquiring any property for themselves by succession, donation, purchase, or otherwise; and whatever they thus acquired belonged of right to their father, saving only what was called the son's *peculium*, which consisted of property acquired by his service in the army, or by his skill at the bar, or in the exercise of some public employment.[1] This sort of property was, therefore, known by the name of *peculium castrense*, when it was acquired in war, and of *peculium quasi castrense*, when it was acquired in any other manner.[2] In the time of Justinian the law was altered, and the father was no longer entitled to the property acquired by his unemancipated son; but he was entitled to the usufruct or profits thereof during his life. And the rule thus modified has found its way sometimes without, and sometimes with modifications, into the jurisprudence of many provinces and states of continental Europe.[3]

§ 456. Under this aspect of the law with regard to the paternal power, the question has often been discussed among foreign jurists, whether the laws respecting the paternal power are personal or real; or, in other words, whether the rights of the father, allowed and secured by the law of the place of his domicil, extend to the immoveable property of his sons, sit-

[1] 1 Domat, Civ. Law. Prelim. Book, tit. 2, § 2, p. 24, note; Id. B. 2, tit. 2, § 2, p. 667 to 669, 670, n. 1, 2, 3; Bouhier, Cout. de Bourg. ch. 16, § 8 to 12, p. 295; 1 Brown, Civ. Law, p. 122, 123; 2 Froland, Mém. 806 to 813; 2 Henrys, Œuvres, par Bretonnier. Lib. 4, Quest. 127, p. 712, &c. 717; Merlin, Répertoire, Puissance Paternelle, § 7, p. 142.

[2] 1 Domat, Book, 2, § 2, p. 668.

[3] 1 Domat, Book, 2, § 2, p. 668; Civil Code of France, art. 384 to 387; 1 Froland, Mém. 69; 2 Froland, Mém. ch. 17, p. 789; Bouhier, Cout. de Bourg. ch. 16, p. 294.

uate in other countries, whose jurisprudence confers no such paternal rights.[1]

§ 457. Bretonnier holds the doctrine, that all laws respecting the paternal power are personal, and consequently have effect upon all property, wherever situate, and especially as to the profits and usufruct of it, because the latter partake of the nature of moveables. After stating the question, whether fathers, domiciled in a country using the Roman law (*dans le pays de droit écrit*), whose sons have property in another country, having a different customary law, are entitled to the profits of the latter, that is to say, whether the paternal power extends everywhere, he proceeds to say, *Cette question ne me semble pas susceptible d'une grande difficulté; parceque la puissance paternelle est un droit personnel, et par conséquent il ne peut étre borné par aucun territoire; car c'est une maxime certaine même dans les pays de coutume, qui les statuts personnels sont universels, et produisent leur effet partout. D'ailleurs les fruits sont des choses mobiliares: Or, constat inter omnes, que les meubles suivent les personnes, et se règlent suivant la coutume du domicile.*[2]

§ 458. Hertius seems to hold a like doctrine, as to the personality of such laws; and puts a question, whether a daughter, who is emancipated by marriage, may afterwards make a testament of property situate elsewhere; and whether the father would have a right to the usufruct of her property, situate in a place, where she would be deemed unemancipated. He answers;

1 2 Froland, Mém. 808, 813 to 829.

2 Henrys, Œuvres, par Bretonnier, Tom. 2, p. 720. See 2 Boullenois, 46, 47.

Questio est duplex ; verum ex codem principio decidenda. Jus nempe datum est personæ, quod etiam per consequentiam in bona alterius civitatis, licet immobilia, operatur.[1] Yet Hertius, in another place, holds, that an unemancipated son, who by the law of his domicil may make a testament, cannot make a testament of property situate in a foreign country. *Nam statutum est in rem conceptum, et conditio filii-familiæ non est in dispositione.*[2] The ground of this opinion probably is, that there general incapacity is admitted to exist by the law of the domicil, and the special exception is local and real.[3]

§ 459. Bouhier maintains with earnestness and ability, that the paternal power is altogether personal, and that it extends to the immoveable property of the unemancipated child, situate in a foreign country, where the like law, as to the paternal authority, does not exist.[4] And he is supported by the opinion of Le Brun, D'Argentré, and others.[5]

§ 460. On the other hand, Froland maintains, that the paternal power in regard to the immoveable property of a child is purely real. *Ce statut est constamment réel; il ne s'étend point sur les biens situez dans une coutume, qui n'a pas disposition pareille.*[6] Boullenois, while he admits, that the laws, which give the paternal power, are personal, so far as they respect the state or situation of the parties, contends at the same

---

1 1 Hertii Opera, De Collis. Leg. § 4, n. 17, p. 130.

2 1 Hertii Opera, De Collis. Leg. § 4, n. 22, p. 133.

3 Merlin, Répertoire, Testament, § 1, n. 5, art. 1, p. 310.

4 Bouhier, Cout. de Bourg. ch. 24, § 37 to 87, p. 468 to 475.

5 Id. ch. 24, § 41, p. 468; Le Brun, De la Communauté, Lib. 1 ch. 2, n. 8.

6 1 Froland, Mém. 69; Id. 49, 60, 156; 2 Froland, Mém. ch. 17, p. 789 to 819.

time, that, so far as those laws give rights over immoveable property, they are real, and are to be governed by the law of the place, where the property is situate.[1] And he proceeds to vindicate his opinion in a most elaborate manner.

§ 461. D'Aguesseau insists, that "that, which characterizes a real statute, and distinguishes it essentially from a personal statute, is not, that it relates to certain personal qualities, or certain personal circumstances, or to certain personal events; otherwise we should be compelled to say, that all laws, which concern the paternal power, the right of guardianship, the right of widowhood (*le droit de viduité*), and the prohibition of donations between married persons, are all personal laws. And accordingly it is beyond doubt, that in our jurisprudence all these laws are real, which are to be governed, not according to the law of the domicil, but according to that of the place, where the property is situate."[2]

§ 462. Merlin has examined the same subject in a a formal discussion, and he endeavours to hold a middle course between the opinions of Bouhier and Boullenois, agreeing with the latter, that the usufruct arising under the paternal power is a real right, and governed by the *lex rei sitæ*, and at the same time holding with Bouhier, that the father cannot possess the right, unless by the law of the place of his domicil the paternal power is recognised. He then lays down three principles, which he supposes will remove all the difficulties upon this thorny subject. (1.) The law, which subjects the son to the power of his

---

1 1 Boullenois, p. 68; 2 Boullenois, p. 30 to 33; Id. p. 39 to 47; Boullenois, Quest. Mixtes, Quest. 20, p. 406.

2 D'Aguesseau, Œuvres, Tom. 4. p. 660.

father, has no need of the action (*ministère*) of man for its execution; and it is therefore personal from the very nature of its object. (2.) The law, which declares an unemancipated son (*un fils de famille*) incapable of alienating his immoveable property, without the authority of his father, is personal, though its object is real; because it determines the state of the person in regard to what he can, and cannot do. (3.) The law, which gives to a father the usufruct of the property of his son ought to be real, because its object is real, and it makes no regulation concerning the capacity or incapacity of the unemancipated son to do any thing.[1] In another place (as we have seen) he

[1] Merlin, Répertoire, Puissance Paternelle, § 7, p. 142, 144. — The reasoning of Merlin on this subject is marked with uncommon clearness and force of statement; and I have, therefore, thought that an extract from it might not be unacceptable to the reader.

"Or, que trouvons-nous dans la puissance paternelle? Trois choses.

"Premièrement, elle détermine l'état des enfans; et à cet égard, elle forme un statut personnel qui suit les enfans partout. Ainsi, une mère domiciliée en Hainaut, conserve sous sa puissance les enfans qu'elle a eus dans cette province, lors même que le hasard ou certaines circonstances les ont fait passer dans une autre coutume qui n'accorde pas les mêmes droits aux femmes qu'aux hommes sur la personne de leurs enfans.

"En second lieu, la puissance paternelle imprime dans les enfans qui y sont assujétis, une incapacité de faire certains actes: comme cette incapacité est la suite de leur état, elle les suit également partout et influe sur tous leurs biens, quelle qu'en soit la situation. Ainsi, un fils de famille né dans une coutume où il ne peut pas contracter sans l'autorité de son père, ne peut vendre de lui-même les biens qu'il possède dans une autre coutume qui n'admet pas la puissance paternelle; et réciproquement un fils de famille domicilé dans une coutume qui n'admet pas la puissance paternelle, peut, sans l'autorisation de son père, aliéner les biens qu'il possède dans les pays de droit écrit. Par la même raison, un fils né à Senlis, où la coutume proscrit formellement toute puissance paternelle, quoique nourri et entretenu par son père, peut acquérir pour lui-même en Hainaut et dans les pays de droit écrit. Et réciproquement, un fils de famille né en Hainaut ou dans un pays de droit écrit, ne peut s'approprier les biens qu'il acquiert dans la coutume de Senlis,

holds, that a law, which prohibits an unemancipated son to make a testament, is personal ; but he, at the same time asserts, that this will not prevent him from making

lorsque ses acquisitions ne réunissent pas toutes les circonstances requises pour qu'elles tombent dans le pécule castrense, quasi-castrense ou adventice.

"Troisièmement, la puissance paternelle donne au père, dans les pays de droit écrit et dans quelques coutumes, la jouissance des biens de ses enfans. Cette jouissance est, à la vérité, un accessoire de la puissance paternelle ; mais elle ne forme dans les enfans ni capacité ni incapacité : le statut qui la défère, n'a pas besoin, pour son exécution, du ministère de l'homme ; il agit seul ; l'homme n'a rien à faire. On ne peut donc pas appliquer ici les raisons qui ont déterminé l'espèce de concordat tacite dont nous avons parlé. Quel inconvénient y a-t-il à restreindre cette jouissance au territoire des lois ou coutumes qui l'accordent ? Quoi ! parcequ'un père jouira des biens que ses enfans ont dans une province, et qu'il ne jouira pas de ceux qu'ils ont dans une autre, l'ordre public serait troublé, le commerce serait dérangé ! Non. Il n'y a pas en cela plus de trouble ni plus de confusion, qu'à succéder à un défunt dans une coutume, et de ne pas lui succéder dans une autre.

"Il est donc constant que le système du président Bouhier ne peut pas se soutenir, et que le statut qui donne à un père l'usufruit des biens des enfans qu'il a sous sa puissance, n'est pas personnel. Mais est-il purement réel, comme le prétend Boullenois, ou bien est-il personnel-réel, c'est-à-dire, faut-il, pour qu'il produise son effet, que le père soit domicilié dans une coutume qui admet la puissance paternelle ? C'est la difficulté qui nous reste à résoudre.

"Le principal peut subsister sans les accessoires : mais les accessoires ne peuvent jamais subsister sans le principal. Ce principe est aussi clair qu'indubitable, et il nous conduit droit à la décision de notre question.

"Ainsi, la puissance paternelle peut avoir lieu sans l'usufruit dont nous parlons ici. La coutume de Douai nous en fournit un exemple, puisqu'elle admet l'une chap. 7, art. 2, et qu'elle exclut l'autre par son silence, comme l'a décidé le parlement de Flandre, par un arrêt du 27 janvier 1739 rendu au rapport de M. de Casteele de La Briarde, en faveur du marquis de Sin, contre les sieurs et demoiselles d'Aoust.

"Mais l'usufruit ne peut avoir lieu sans la puissance paternelle, dont il n'est que l'accessoire. Un père ne peut donc en jouir, s'il n'a ses enfans sous sa puissance, et par conséquent s'il n'est domicilié dans une coutume qui admet la puissance paternelle. Un père qui émanciperait son fils au moment même de sa naissance, n'aurait certainement aucun droit à l'usufruit des biens que cet enfant acquerrait ensuite, soit dans la coutume du domicile qu'il avait alors, soit dans toute autre province. Or, ce que ce père est supposé faire, la loi le fait elle-même dans les cou-

a testament of moveable property in other countries, where it is permitted; because this case is a mere exception from his general incapacity, and also falls within the rule, that, in a conflict of real and personal laws, the latter must yield.[1]

§ 463. Without going farther into an examination of the opinions of foreign jurists upon this subject, it is sufficiently obvious, what difficulties they are compelled to encounter at almost every step, in order to carry into effect their favourite system of the division of laws into real and personal. The common law has avoided all these difficulties by a simple and uniform test. It declares, that the law of the *situs* shall exclusively govern in regard to all rights, interests, and titles, in and to immoveable property. Of course it cuts down all attempts to introduce all foreign laws, whether they respect persons or things, or give or withhold the capacity to acquire or to dispose of immoveable property.[2]

tumes qui n'admettent pas la puissance paternelle ; elle émancipe cet enfant dès qu'il voit le jour, et conséquemment elle soustrait les biens qu'il aura dans la suite, à l'usufruit que son père en aurait eu sans cette émancipation." Merlin, Répertoire, Puissance Paternelle, § 7, p. 145, 146.

1 Merlin, Répertoire, Testament, § 1, n. 5, art. 1, p. 310.

2 See Brodie *v.* Barry, 2 Ves. & Beames R. 127.

CHAPTER XI.

WILLS AND TESTAMENTS.

§ 464. HAVING taken these general views of the operation of foreign law in regard to moveable property, and immoveable property, and ascertained, that the general principle adopted in relation to the former is, that it is governed by the law of the domicil of the owner, and in relation to the latter, that it is governed by the law of the place, where it is locally situate; we now come to make a more immediate application of these principles to two of the most important classes of cases arising, constantly and uniformly, in all civilized human societies. One is, the right of a person to dispose of his property after his death; the other is the right of succession to the same property, in case no postmortuary disposition is made of it by the owner. The former involves the right to make last wills and testaments; and the latter the title of descent and the distribution of property *ab intestato*. We shall accordingly in this chapter discuss the subject of foreign law exclusively in relation to testaments, successions, and distributions of moveable and immoveable property.

§ 465. And first in relation to testaments of moveable property. It is now a well settled principle in the English law, that a will of personal property, regularly made according to the law of the testator's domicil, is sufficient to pass such property in every other country, in which it is situate. But this doctrine, though now very firmly established, was for a great length of time much agitated in Westminster Hall.[1] In

[1] See Brodie *v.* Barry, 2 Ves. and Beames, R. 127, 131; Bempde *v.* Johnstone, 3 Ves. R. 192, 200.

Sill vs. Worswick,[1] Lord Loughborough laid down the doctrine, that, with respect to the disposition of moveable property, with respect to the transmission of it, either by succession, *or the act of the party*, it follows the law of the person.[2] The owner in any country may dispose of his personal property. In Bruce *v.* Bruce,[3] Lord Thurlow asserted the same doctrine as to succession to personal property, and by implication as to wills; and Lord Ellenborough put it as clear, in Potter *v.* Brown.[4] He observed, "It is every day's experience to recognise the law of foreign countries, as binding on personal property; as in the sale of ships, condemned as prize by the sentences of foreign courts, the succession to personal property by will or intestacy of the subjects of foreign countries." But antecedently to this period many learned doubts and discussions had existed on the subject.[5] And, in the Duchess of Kingston's case, a will of personal property executed in France, but not in conformity to the laws of that country, was admitted to probate in the Ecclesiastical courts of England in 1791, being duly executed according to the English Forms, although she was domiciled in France at the time of making the will and also at the time of her death.[6]

§ 466. At so late a period as 1823, Sir John Nicholl doubted, whether a will of personal property made

---

1 Ommarey *v.* Bingham, cited 5 Ves. 757; 3 Hagg. Eccles. R. 414, note; Stanley *v.* Barnes, 3 Hagg. Eccles. R. 373; Hogg *v.* Lashley, 3 Hagg. Eccles. R. 415, note.

2 H. Black. 690.

3 2 Bos. & Pull. 229, note.

4 5 East R. 130.

5 See Bemde *v.* Johnstone, 3 Ves. 198, 200; Somerville *v.* Somerville; 5 Ves. 750; Balfour *v.* Scott, 6 Brown Parl. Cas. 550. Tomlin's Edit.; S. C. 2 Addams, Eccles. R. 15, note.

6 See 2 Addams, Eccles. R. 21.

abroad by an English subject domiciled abroad, ought to be held valid, unless it was executed in conformity to the forms prescribed by the English law. The ground of his doubt was, whether an English subject was entitled *exuere patriam* so far as to select a foreign domicil in complete derogation of his native domicil, and thus to render his property in England distributable by succession or testament according to the foreign law. He took a distinction between testacy and intestacy (assuming, for the sake of argument, that in the latter case the foreign law might prevail), thinking, that cases of testacy might be governed by very different considerations from those of intestacy. And, even, if a will, executed according to the law of the place of the testator's domicil, would in such a case be valid, he contended, that it by no means followed universally, and upon principle, that a will, to be valid, must strictly conform to that law, which would have regulated the succession to the testator's property, if he had died intestate. And, therefore, he held, that a will of personal property, made by a British subject in France, according to the forms of the English law, was good as to such property situate in England. He admitted, that as to British subjects domiciled in any part of the United Kingdom, the law of their domicil must govern in regard to successions and wills; and so, the like law must govern in regard to successions and wills of foreigners resident abroad. The restriction, which he sought to establish, was, that a British subject could not, by a foreign domicil, defeat the operation of the law of his own country, as to personal property situate in the latter.[1]

---

[1] Curling *v*. Thornton, 2 Addams Eccles. R. 6, 10 to 25.

§ 467. To this opinion the same learned judge firmly adhered in a still later case. But upon an appeal, the decision was overturned by the High Court of Delegates, and the doctrine fully established, that the law of the actual foreign domicil of a British subject is exclusively to govern in relation to his testament of personal property; as it would in the case of a mere foreigner.[1] This case is the stronger, because it was the case of a will, and several codicils, made according to the law of Portugal, and also of several codicils made, not according to the law of Portugal, where the testator was domiciled. The will and codicils executed according to the Portuguese law were held valid; the others were held invalid.

§ 468. The same doctrine is as firmly established in America. The earliest case, in which it was directly in judgment, is Desesbats *v.* Berquiers[2] in the Supreme Court of Pennsylvania in 1808; and this case may be truly said to have led the way to the positive adjudication of this important and difficult doctrine. There, a foreign testator, domiciled abroad, had made a will of his personal estate, invalid according to the law of his domicil, but valid according to the law of Pennsylvania; and the question was, whether it was competent and valid to pass personal property situate in Pennsylvania. The Court decided, that it was not; and asserted the general doctrine, that a will of personal estate must, in order to pass the property, be executed according to the law of the place of the testator's domicil at the time of his death. If void by that law, it is a nullity everywhere, although it is executed with the

---

1 Stanley *v.* Barnes, 3 Hagg. Eccles. Rep. 373 to 465.

2 1 Binney, R. 336.

formalities required by the law of the place, where the personal property is locally situate. The Court asserted, that in this respect there was no difference between cases of succession by testament, and by intestacy.[1] The same doctrine has been repeatedly recognised by other American courts, and may now be deemed, as of universal authority here.[2]

§ 469. In Scotland the doctrine was formerly involved in many doubts. By the law of Scotland, illegitimate persons are not deemed capable of making a will; and hence a will of moveables in Scotland, made by such a person, domiciled in England, was formerly held in Scotland to be invalid.[3] And in like manner a nuncupative will, being in Scotland invalid, was formerly held invalid to pass moveables in Scotland, although the will was made in England (where such a will is valid) by a person domiciled there.[4] But the general doctrine is now the same in Scotland, as in England. The law of the domicil universally prevails, as to successions and wills of moveables in other countries.[5]

§ 470. Foreign jurists are as generally agreed, as to the doctrine in regard to moveables, upon the ground, maintained by all of them, that *mobilia sequuntur personam*.[6] J. Voet lays down the rule in the following

---

1 1 Binn. R. 336.

2 See Holmes *v*. Remsen, 4 John. Ch. R. 460, 469; Harvey *v*. Richards, 1 Mason, R. 381, and cases cited, p. 408, note; Dixon's Ex'ors *v*. Ramsay's Exo'rs, 3 Cranch, R. 319; De Sobry *v*. De Laistre, 2 Harr. and John. R. 193, 224.

3 Ersk. Inst. B. 3, tit. 2, § 41, p. 515; 2 Kaims, Equity, B. 3, ch. 8, § 3.

4 2 Kaims, Equity, B. 3, ch. 8, § 3, p. 345.

5 See Bempde *v*. Johnstone, 3 Ves. 198, 201; Somerville *v*. Somerville, 5 Ves. R. 757; Brodie *v*. Barry, 2 Ves. & Beames, 127, 131, and the cases cited § 465; Ersk. Inst. B. 3, tit. 2, § 40, 41; 2 Kaims, Equity, ch. 8, § 3.

6 See 6 Boullenois, Observ. 28, p. 696 to 721; Cochin, Œuvres, Tom 5. p. 85.

terms. *In successionibus, testandi facultate, contractibus, aliisque, mobilia, ubicunque sita, regi debere domicilii jure, non vero legibus loci illius, in quo naturaliter sunt constituta.*[1]

§ 471. Vattel has spoken in terms, admitting of more question, as to the extent of their meaning. After observing, that a foreigner in a foreign country has by natural right the liberty of making a will, he remarks, "As to the form or solemnities appointed to settle the validity of a will, it appears, that the testator ought to observe those, which are established in the country, where he makes it, unless it be otherwise ordained by the laws of the state, of which he is a member; in which case he will be obliged to observe the forms, which they prescribe, if he would validly dispose of the property, which he possesses in his own country. The foreign testator cannot dispose of his property, moveable or immoveable, which he possesses in his own country, otherwise than in a manner conformable to the laws of that country. But as to moveable property, specie, and other effects, which he possesses elsewhere, which he has with him, we ought to distinguish between the local laws, whose effect cannot extend beyond the territory, and those laws, which peculiarly affect the character of citizens. The foreigner, remaining a citizen of his own country, is still bound by these last mentioned laws, wherever he happens to be, and is obliged to conform to them in the disposal of his personal property, and all his moveables whatsoever. The laws of this kind, made in the country, where he resides at the time, but of which he is not a citizen, are not obligatory with respect to him. Thus, a man, who makes his

---

1 J. Voet. ad Pand. Lib. 1, tit. 4, P. 2, § 11, p. 44.

will, and dies in a foreign country, cannot deprive his widow of the part of his moveable effects, assigned to that widow by the laws of his own country. A Genevan, obliged by the laws of his country to leave a portion of his personal property to his brothers or cousins, if they are his next heirs, cannot deprive them of it by making his will in a foreign country, while he continues a citizen of Geneva. But a foreigner, dying at Geneva, is not obliged in this respect to conform to the laws of the Republic. The case is quite otherwise in respect to local laws. They regulate, what may be done in the territory, and do not extend beyond it. The testator is no longer subject to them, when he is out of the territory; and they do not affect that part of his property which is also out of it. The foreigner is obliged to observe those laws in the country, where he makes his will, with respect to the goods he possesses there." [1]

§ 472. Vattel is in this passage principally considering the effect of the law of a foreign country upon a foreigner, who is resident there. And there can be no doubt, that every country may by its laws prescribe whatever rules it may please, as to the disposition of the moveable property of its citizens, either *inter vivos* or testamentary. But it is equally clear, that such rules are of no obligation, as to moveable property in any other country; and can be in force there only by the comity of nations. So that a will of such moveable property, made in the foreign country, where he is domiciled, and according to its laws, will be held valid, whatever may be the validity of such will in the country, to which the testator owes his allegiance by birth. But the discussion, in which we are engaged, does not respect the effect of any

---

[1] Vattel, B. 2, ch. 8, § 111.

local prohibitory laws over moveable property within the territory; but the general principles, which regulate the disposition of it, when no such prohibitory laws exist. And, here, by the general consent of foreign jurists, the law of the domicil of the testator governs as to transfers *inter vivos* and testamentary. [1]

§ 473. But it may be asked, What will be the effect of a change of domicil after a will is made of personal property, if it is valid by the law of the place, where the party was domiciled, when it was made, and not valid by the law of his domicil at the time of his death? The terms, in which the general rule is laid down, sufficiently establish the principle, that in such case the will is void, for it is the law of the actual domicil, which must govern.[2]

§ 474. We next pass to the consideration of wills made of immoveable property. And here the doctrine of the common law is clearly established, that the law of the place, where the property is locally situate, is to govern as to the capacity of the testator, the extent of his power to dispose of the property, and the forms and solemnities to give the will its due attestation and effect.[3]

§ 475. The doctrine of foreign jurists does not, as we have seen, entirely accord with that of the com-

---

1 See Ante § 465; Hertii Opera, De Collis. Leg. § 4, n. 6, p. 112; Pothier, Cout. d'Orléans, ch. 1, § 2, n. 24; Voet. ad Pand. Tom. 2, Lib. 38, tit. 17, § 34.

2 See Desesbats *v.* Berquier, 1 Binn. R. 336; Potinger *v.* Wightman, 3 Meriv. R. 59, 68; Henry on Foreign Law, Appx. 196; 2 Boullenois, ch. 1, p. 2, &c.; Id. 7, &c.; Id. 54; Id 57; Ante § 55 to 74

3 Coppin *v.* Coppin, 2 P. Will. 291, 293; 2 Fonb. Eq. p. 444, 445, note; U. States *v.* Crosby, 7 Cranch, 115; Holmes *v.* Remsen, 4 John. Ch. R. 460; S. C. 20 John. R. 229; McCormick *v.* Sullivant, 10 Wheaton R. 192, 202; Wills *v.* Cowper, 2 Hamm. R. 124; Henry on Foreign Law, p. 13, 15; Ante, § 428.

mon law; but even among them there is great weight of authority in favour of the general principle. Putting out of view the questions, as to the form and solemnities of acts, and the capacity of the testator, (upon which we have already commented,) here seems a general coincidence of opinion, that the *lex rei sitæ* must govern as to wills of immoveable property. Thus John Voet says, *Bona defuncti immobilia et quæ juris interpretatione pro talibus habentur, deferri secundum leges loci, in quo sita sunt.*[1] Dumoulin's opinion is to the same effect;[2] so is that of Hertius.[3] D'Aguesseau deems it a mere waste of time to do more than state the general rule.[4] Paul Voet has stated the doctrine in an expressive manner, *Non tamen statutum personale sese extendit regulariter ad bona immobilia alibi sita.*[5] In another place he says, *Immobilia statutis loci ubi sita, mobilia loci statutis, ubi testator habuit domicilium.*[6] In another place he says, *Quid, si itaque contentio de aliquo jure in re, seu ex ipsâ re descendente; vel ex contractu, vel actione personali, sed ad rem scriptâ, an spectabitur loci statutum, ubi dominus habet domicilium, an statutum rei sitæ? Respondeo, statutum rei sitæ.*[7] And in another place he adds, *Sive in rem sive in personam loquatur statutum, ad bona extra territorium non extenditur. Consideratur namque bonorum dominus, ut duplex homo; quoad bona nempe sita in uno territorio est unus homo; et quoad alterius*

1 Voet. ad Pand. Lib. 38, tit. 17, § 34, p. 596.

2 1 Froland, Mém. 65; Id. 779.

3 1 Hertii Opera, De Collis. Leg. § 4, n. 9, p. 125.

4 D'Aguesseau, Œuvres, Tom. 4, p. 636, 637. See Cochin, Œuvres, Tom. 4. p. 555.

5 P. Voet. De Stat. § 4, ch. 2, n. 6, p. 123.

6 P. Voet. De Stat. § 4, ch. 3, n. 10, p. 135.

7 Id. § 9, ch. 1, n. 2, p. 252.

territorii bona est alius homo.[1] And this is certainly the doctrine of the common law; for a man may have a capacity to take real estate in one country, when he is totally disabled to take it in another. Boullenois, (as we have seen), lays it down among his general principles, that, when the personal laws of the domicil are in conflict with the real laws of the same or of a foreign country, the personal are to yield; and that, when the real laws of the domicil are in conflict with the real laws of another country, both have effect within their own territory according to the laws thereof.[2]

§ 476. Huberus expounds the subject at large, and says, that his observations as to the validity of acts done according to the *lex loci*, "do not apply to immoveable property, since it is considered, not as depending upon the free disposition of the head of the family *(pater-familias)*; but as having certain marks impressed upon it by the laws of every commonwealth, in which it is situate, which remain indelible therein, whatever the laws of other governments, or the dispositions of private persons may establish to the contrary. For it would cause great confusion and prejudice to the commonwealth, where immoveable property is situate, that the laws promulgated concerning it should be changed by any other acts." "Hence, (he adds,) a Frizian, having lands and houses in the province of Groningen, cannot make a will thereof, because the laws there prohibit any will to be made of such real estate; and the Frizian laws cannot affect real estate, which constitutes an integral part of a foreign territory."[3] And yet, with this clear principle in view, he proceeds to declare, "that this does not

1 1 Boullenois, 154.
2 1 Boullenois, Pr. Gén. 30, 31, p. 8.
3 Huberus, Lib. 1 tit. 3, § 15.

contradict the rule, which he had already laid down, that if a will is valid by the law of the place, where it is made, it ought to have effect even in regard to real property, situate in foreign countries, by whose laws such property may be passed by a will; because the diversity of laws in that respect does not affect the soil, neither speaks of it, but simply directs the manner of making the will, which being rightly done, the law of the commonwealth does not prohibit the instrument to have validity in regard to immoveables, inasmuch as no characteristic or incident impressed by the laws of the country are injured or diminished."[1]

§ 477. Burgundus lays down the doctrine in general terms, that in every thing, which regards land and other real inheritances, it is the law of the situation, which is to decide.—And he applies it specially to wills. *Solemnitates testamenti ad jura personalia non pertinent, quia est quædam qualitas bonis ipsis impressa, ad quam tenetur respicere, quisquis in bonis aliquid alterat. Nam si ex solemni testamento nascitur jus in ipsâ re, quomodo id potest præstare alterius regionis consuetudo, quæ alienis fundis alterationis necessitatem imponere non potest. Hoc enim esset jus dicere extra territorium, cui impune non paretur.*[2] There is a great deal of solid sense in these remarks; and they form a satisfactory answer to the distinction propounded by Huberus.

§ 478. The Scottish law is in perfect coincidence with the common law on this subject. Erskine, in a passage already cited, has stated, that in the conveyance of an immoveable subject, or of any right affecting heritage, the owner must follow the solemni-

---

1 Huberus, Lib. 1, tit. 3, § 15; Id. § 4, 5.

2 1 Boullenois, p. 151; See also Henry on Foreign Law, p. 97, 98.

ties established by the law, not of the country, where he signs the instrument, but of the state, in which the heritage lies. And even if all due solemnities are observed, still no estate will pass, unless in conformity with the local law. Hence, (he adds), a foreign testament bequeathing heritable subjects, situate in Scotland, is not sustained in Scotland, though by the law of the country where the testament was made, a heritage might have been actually settled; because by the Scottish law no heritable subject can be disposed of in that form.[1]

§ 479. Vattel (as we have seen) adopts the same rule, as a general one of the *jus gentium*. As to bequests, he asserts in the most positive terms, that, when they respect immoveables, they must be conformable to the law of the country, where they are situated.[2] If it were necessary, many opinions of other foreign jurists might be cited to the same effect; but it would encumber these pages to give them a more extended review.

---

1 Erskine's Inst. B. 3, tit. 2, § 41, p. 515, 516; 2 Kaims, Equity, B. 3, ch. 8, § 3.

2 Vattel B. 2, ch. 7, § 85, ch. 8, § 103, 110, 111.

CHAPTER XII.

SUCCESSION AND DISTRIBUTION.

§ 480. Having considered the operation of foreign law, in regard to testaments of moveable and of immoveable property, we next proceed to the right of succession in cases of intestacy, or, as the phrase is, of succession *ab intestato.* And, here, the preceding discussions have left little more to be done, than to state the general principle applicable to each species of property.

§ 481. First, in relation to moveable property. The universal principle, now recognised by the common law, though it was formerly much contested, is, that the succession to personal property is governed exclusively by the law of the actual domicil of the intestate at the time of his death. It is of no consequence, what was the country of birth, or of any former domicil, or what is the actual *situs* of the personal property at the time of his death; it devolves upon those, who are entitled to take it, as heirs or distributees, according to the law of his actual domicil.[1] Hence, if a Frenchman dies intestate in America, all his personal property, whether it be in America or in France, is distributable according to the statute of distributions of the state, where he then resided, notwithstanding it may differ essentially from the distribution prescribed by the law of France. And this doctrine is maintained with equal broadness by the generality of foreign jurists.[2]

---

1 Rodemburg, De Div. Stat. P. 2, tit. 2, ch. 2, p. 59; 2 Boullenois, p. 54: Erskine, Inst. B. 3, tit. 9, § 4.

2 The authorities to sustain this point, have been already cited,

§ 482. Paul Voet has put the principle in a compendious manner. *Verum an, quod de immobilibus dictum, idem de mobilibus statuendum erit? Respondeo, quod non. Quia illorum bonorum nomine nemo censetur semet loci legibus subjecisse. Ut quæ res certum locum non habent, quia facile de loco in locum transferuntur; adeoque secundum loci statuta regulantur, ubi domicilium habuit defunctus.*[1]

§ 483. Secondly, in relation to immoveable property. And here a very different principle prevails. The descent and heirship of real estate is exclusively governed by the law of the country, within which it is actually situate. No person can take except those, who are recognised as legitimate heirs by the laws of that country; and they take in the proportions, and order, which those laws prescribe. This is the indisputable doctrine of the common law. And, however much foreign jurists may differ on other points, they are here generally agreed; and admit, that the descent and distribution of real estate must be governed

ante § 465 to 497. But a few may be here referred to. Pipon v. Pipon, Ambler R. 25; Thorne v. Watkins, 2 Ves. R. 35; 1 Chitty on Comm. and Manuf. 661; Sill v. Worswick, 1 H. Black. 690, 691; Bruce v. Bruce, 2 Bos. & Pull. 229, note; Hunter v. Potts, 4 T. R. 182; Potter v. Brown, 5 East R. 130; Livermore's Dissert. 162, 163; Olivier v. Townes, 14 Martin R. 99; Shultz v. Pulver, 3 Paige R. 182; De Sobry v. De Laistre, 2 Harr. & John. R. 193, 224, 228; Holmes v. Remsen, 4 John. Ch. R. 460; S. C. 20 John. R. 229; De Couche v. Savatier, 3 John. Ch. R. 190; Erskine's Inst. B. 3, tit. 2, § 40, 41; Id. B. 3, tit. 9, § 4; 2 Kaims, Equity, B. 3, ch. 8, § 3, 4, p. 333, 345; 1 Boullenois, 358; 2 Boullenois, 54; Id. 57; Fergusson on Marr. and Div. 346, 361; Vattel, B. 2, § 85, 103, 110, 111; 1 Hertii Opera, De Collis. Leg. § 4, n. 26, p. 135; Huberus, Lib. 1, tit. 3, § 15; Henry on Foreign Law, p. 13, 14, 15; Id. 46, 196; Voet. ad Pand. Lib. 38, tit. 17, § 34, p. 596; Harvey v. Richards, 1 Mason R. 418; 2 Froland, Mém. 1294; 2 Dwarris on Statut. 649.

1 Voet. De Stat. § 9, ch. 1, n. 8, p. 255.

by the *lex rei sitæ.*[1] On this head it might be sufficient to adopt the language of John Voet in his classification of real and personal statutes. He reduces to the class of real statutes whatever regards inheritances. *Quo pertinent jura successionum ab intestato; quonam ordine ad bona quæque ab intestato, quisque in capita, vel stirpes, vel lineas, vel jure primogenituræ admittendus sit; quâ ratione legitimi aut illegitimi, agnati, cognati vocentur; quæque his sunt similia plura.*[2] Rodemburg is equally decisive. *Jus rebus succedendi immobilibus semper a loco rei sitæ metiendum.*[3] And Dumoulin gives the rule in the most consise but energetic terms. *Mobilia sequuntur personam; immobilia situm.*[4]

§ 484. It may be proper to add, that in the interpretation of wills of immoveable property, and moveable property, if the description of persons, who

---

1 The authorities to this point also have been already cited, ante § 424 to 448. See Doe dem. Birthwhistle *v.* Vardell, 5 B. & Cres. 438; U. S. *v.* Crosby, 7 Cranch R. 115; Kerr *v.* Moon, 9 Wheaton R. 566, 570; McCormick *v.* Sullivant, 10 Wheaton R. 192; Darby *v.* Mayer, 10 Wheaton R. 469; Hosford *v.* Nichols, 1 Paige R. 220; Cutler *v.* Davenport, 1 Pick. R. 81; Wills *v.* Cowper, 2 Hamm. R. 124; 1 Hertii Opera, De Collis. Leg. § 4, n. 26, p. 135; 1 Boullenois, 25, 223, &c.; 1 Froland, Mém. 60, 61, 65; Voet. De Stat. § 4, ch. 2, n. 6, p. 123; Voet. ad Pand. Lib. 1, tit. 4, P. 2, § 3, p. 39; Ersk. Inst. B. 3, tit. 2, § 40, 41, p. 515; D'Aguesseau, Œuvres, Tom. 4, p. 637; Huberus, Lib. 1, tit. 3, § 15; 2 Dwarris on Statut. p. 649; Rodemburg, P. 2, tit. 2, ch. 2, p. 59, 63; 2 Boullenois, 54, 57, 383; 2 Froland, Mém. ch. 27, p. 1288.

2 Voet. ad Pand. Lib. 1, tit. 4, P. 2, § 3, p. 39.

3 Rodemburg, De Div. Stat. P. 2, tit. 2, ch. 2, p. 59; 2 Boullenois, 54, 57.

4 2 Froland, Mém. 1289.—Paul Voet is equally as expressive. "Quid si, circa successionem ab intestato, statutorum sit difformitas? Spectabitur loci statutum, ubi immobilia sita, non ubi testator moritur." (P. Voet. De Statut. § 9, ch. 1, n. 3, p. 252.) "Quid si testamento bona immobilia relicta diversis subjaceant statutis? Idem dicendum; nil enim interest, testatus quis, an intestatus decedat, ut locus sit regulæ." (Id. n. 4, p. 253.)

are to take, be by some general designation, such as "heirs," or "next of kin," "issue," or "children," they are to be ascertained by the *lex loci* in regard to immoveable property, and by the *lex domicilii* in the case of moveable property, unless the context furnishes some guide for a different interpretation. The like rule applies to descents and distributions of immoveable and moveable property.[1]

§ 485. But these general principles still leave behind them, even in the common law, some very embarrassing difficulties; and in the complex systems of foreign law the latter are greatly multiplied. Sir William Grant adverted to this subject in an important case, and said; "Where land and personal property are situated in different countries, and governed by different laws, and a question arises upon the combined effect of those laws, it is often very difficult to determine, what portion of each law is to enter into the decision of the question. It is not easy to say, how much is to be considered as depending on the law of real property, which must be taken from the country, where the land lies, and how much upon the law of personal property, which must be taken from the law of the domicil, and to blend both together, so as to form a rule applicable to the mixed question, which neither law separately furnishes sufficient materials to decide."[2]

§ 486. Two cases of a curious nature were on the same occasion mentioned by Sir William Grant, as illustrative of his remarks, which cannot be better stated than in his own language. "I have argued,

---

1 See Thorne *v.* Watkins, 2 Ves. 35; Brown *v.* Brown, 3 Hagg. Ecc. R. 455, note; Voet. De Stat. § 3, ch. 3, n. 2, p. 100.

2 Brodie *v.* Barry, 2 Ves. & Beames R. 130, 131.

in the House of Lords, cases, in which difficulties of that kind occurred. Two of the most remarkable were those of Balfour *v.* Scott, and Drummond *v.* Drummond. In the former, a person domiciled in England died intestate, leaving real estate in Scotland. The heir was one of the next of kin; and claimed a share of the personal estate. To this claim, it was objected, that, by the law of Scotland, the heir cannot share in the personal property with the other next of kin, except on condition of collating the real estate; that is, bringing it into a mass with the personal estate, to form one common subject of division. It was determined, however, that he was entitled to take his share without complying with that obligation. There, the English law decided the question."

§ 487. "In Drummond *v.* Drummond, a person, domiciled in England, had real estate in Scotland; upon which he granted a heritable bond, to secure a debt contracted in England. He died intestate; and the question was, by which of the estates this debt was to be borne. It was clear, that by the English law the personal estate was the primary fund for the payment of debts. It was equally clear, that by the law of Scotland the real estate was the primary fund for the payment of the heritable bond. Here was a direct *conflictus legum.* It was said for the heir, that the personal estate must be distributed according to the law of England, and must bear all the burthens, to which it is by that law subject. On the other hand, it was said, that the real estate must go according to the law of Scotland; and bear all the burthens, to which it is by that law subject. It was determined, that the law of Scotland should prevail; and that the real estate must bear the burthen."

§ 488. "In the first case, the disability of the heir did not follow him to England; and the personal estate was distributed, as if both the domicil and the real estate had been in England. In the second, the disability to claim exoneration out of the personalty did follow him into England; and the personal estate was distributed, as if both the domicil and the real estate had been in Scotland." [1]

§ 489. Another illustration is furnished by the very case then in judgment before him, which turned upon the question, whether an heir at law of heritable property in Scotland, being a legatee of personal property, which was in England, under a will of the testator, which intended to dispose of all his real property in England and Scotland, but which will, not being conformable to the law of Scotland, was not capable of passing real estate there, should be put to his election to take the legacy under the will, or to surrender to the purposes of the will the Scotch heritable property. Sir William Grant decided in the affirmative; and said, "Now, what law is to determine, whether an instrument of any given nature or form is to be read against an heir at law for the purpose of putting him to an election, by which the real estate may be affected? According to Lord Hardwicke and the Judges, who have followed him, that is a question belonging to the law of real property; for they have decided it by a statute, which regulates devises of land. Upon that principle, if the domicil were in Scotland, and the real estate in England, an English will, imperfectly executed, ought not to be read in Scotland for the purpose of putting the heir to an election; and, upon the same principle, if, by the law of Scotland, no will could be read against

---

1 2 Ves. & Beam. p. 132.

the heir, it would follow, that a will of land, situated in Scotland, ought not to be read in England, to put the Scotch heir to an election. Doubting much the soundness of that principle, I am glad, that the case of Cunningham *v.* Gayner relieves me from the necessity of deciding the question; as, whichever law is applied to the decision of the present case, the result will be the same, &c. If the law of Scotland is resorted to, the case alluded to determines, that the English will may be read against the Scotch heir, for the purpose of putting him to an election."[1]

§ 490. Another illustration of the difficulties, attendant upon the administration of this branch of testamentary law, is to be found in the application of local rules to the interpretation of wills, whether arising from the *lex domicilii*, or the *lex rei sitæ*, as the case may regard moveable or immoveable property. A question of this sort was recently discussed in the House of Lords upon a will made in Virginia, by which the testator bequeathed to his sister, Mary Brown, "the remaining one fourth share of the balance of his estate, at her death to be equally divided among her children, if she should have any." The question was, what estate Mary Brown took under the will, whether a life estate, or an absolute property. And, it appearing, that the courts of Virginia had construed the bequest to give her an absolute estate, upon the footing of that decree, the House of Lords, deeming it a question of American law, established the same construction.[2]

§ 491. In another case, the same principle was

---

1 Brodie *v.* Barry, 2 Ves. & Beames R. 127, 133.

2 Gordon *v.* Brown, 3 Hagg. Ecc. R. 455, note.

adopted; and the Court laid down the rule, that in the construction of a will the *lex domicilii* must govern, unless there is sufficient on its face to show a different intention in the testator. The facts were these. A lady, a native of Scotland, was domiciled in England. On a visit to Edinburgh she made a will entirely in the Scotch form, and it was deposited with the writer at Edinburgh. She had personalty in England only, and died in England. Scotland, then, was the *domicilium originis et forum contractûs*; but, on the other hand, England was the *forum domicilii* and the *locus rei sitæ*. The question was, whether by the legatee's death in the lifetime of the testatrix the legacy lapsed according to the law of England, or survived to the legatee's representatives according to the law of Scotland. The Court decided, that being domiciled in England, it was to be presumed, that she intended the law of England to be applied; and, that there was not enough in the will to repel that presumption.[1]

---

1 Anstruther *v.* Chalmers, 2 Simons R. 1; 3 Hagg. Ecc. R. 444.

CHAPTER XIII.

FOREIGN GUARDIANSHIPS AND ADMINISTRATIONS.

§ 492. The order of our subject next leads us to the consideration of the operation of foreign laws in relation to persons acting *in autre droit*, such as guardians, tutors, and curators *inter vivos*, and executors and administrators *post mortem*.

§ 493. And first, in relation to guardians. By the Roman law guardianship was of two sorts, (1) *tutela*, and (2) *cura*. The first lasted in males, until they arrived at fourteen years of age, and in females, until they arrived at twelve years of age, which was called the age of *puberty* of them respectively. From the time of puberty, until they were twenty-five years of age, which was their full majority, they were deemed minors, and subject to curatorship. During the first period of tutelage, their guardian was called *tutor*, and they were called *pupils*; during the second period, their guardian was called *curator*, and they were called *minors*.[1] In England the guardian performs the offices of both tutor and curator under the Roman law.[2] In France, the tutorship lasts until the full age of majority.[3]

§ 494. In treating of guardianship, two questions naturally arise; (1) Whether the authority of a guardian

---

[1] 1 Domat, Civil Law, B. 2, tit. 1, p. 260; Halifax, Analysis of Civil Law, ch. 9, p. 15, 17, 18; 1 Brown, Civil Law, B. 1, ch. 5, p. 129, 130. See also Ersk. Inst. B. 1, tit. 6, § 1, p. 128.

[2] Halifax, Analysis of Civil Law, ch. 9, p. 15, 17, 18; 1 Brown, Civil Law, B. 1, ch. 5, p. 129, 130.

[3] 1 Domat, Civil Law, B. 2, tit. 1, p. 261.

over the person of his ward is local, and confined to the place of his domicil, or extends everywhere? (2) Whether the authority of the guardian over the property of his ward is local, or extends everywhere?

§ 495. In regard to the first point, (the authority of the guardian over the person of his ward,) Boullenois maintains, that the laws, which regulate it, are strictly personal; and, therefore, that the authority extends to the ward in foreign countries, as well as at home; and is of equal validity and right, according to the law of the domicil, in every other place. "*Je mets* (says he) *au nombre des statuts personnels, ceux, qui mettent les enfants sous la puissance de leur père, ou de leur tuteur.*"[1] From this, it would seem to follow, that the tutor is to be recognised, as fully entitled to assert any claims over the moveable property of his ward, and to sue for the debts due to his ward in foreign countries, without having any confirmation of the guardianship by the local authorities.

§ 496. And so Merlin expressly holds, asserting, that the foreign guardian, in such a case, is competent to maintain any suit for the debts due to his ward in France and the Netherlands, without any interposition of the local authorities, to confirm the guardianship.[2] "*Il est* (says he) *de principe, que les procurations revêtues de la forme requise par la loi du lieu, où elles se passent, ont leur effet partout. Aussi ne s'est on jamais avisé de prétendre, que le tuteur nommé à un mineur, ou à un interdit, par le juge de son domicil, ne pût agir dans un pays étranger contre les*

1 1 Boullenois, B. 51, 68; Ante § 57.

2 Merlin, Répertoire, Absens. ch. 3, art. 3, p. 37; Id. Faillite, § 2, n. 2, art. 9, 10, § 2, p. 412. See also, Id. Autorisation Maritale, § 10, art. 2; Ante, § 53, 54.

débiteurs d'un ou de l'autre, qu'après avoir fait déclarer le jugement de sa nomination exécutoire dans ce pays.[1]"

§ 497. Vattel lays down a similar doctrine in more comprehensive terms. "It belongs," says he, "to the domestic Judge to nominate tutors and guardians for minors and idiots. The law of nations, which has an eye to the common advantage and the good harmony of nations, requires, therefore, that such nomination of tutor or guardian be valid and acknowledged in all countries, where the pupil may have any concerns."[2] This is also the opinion of Huberus, as we have already seen;[3] and it is stoutly maintained by Hertius. *Hinc tutor,* (says he,) *datus in loco domicilii, etiam bona alibi sita administrat;* adding, however, this qualification, *quoniam ipsi fatemur, si externa civitas circa bona immobilia aliquid directe disposuit, eam legem servari oportere.*[4] And, indeed, this same doctrine is commonly asserted by all foreign jurists, who give to personal laws an ubiquity of operation.

§ 498. On the other hand, P. Voet, who denies, that laws, respecting either persons or property, have in the sense of the civil jurisprudence (*si de ratione juris civilis sermo instituatur*) any extra-territorial authority, lays down the following rules; (1) that a personal statute does not affect the person beyond the territory of his domicil, so that he is not to be reputed such without the territory, as he was within; (2) that a personal statute accompanies the person everywhere, in regard to property within the territory of the govern-

---

1 Merlin, Repertoire, Faillite, § 2, n. 2, art. 10, p. 414.

2 Vattel, B. 2, ch. 9, § 85.

3 Ante, § 58, 59.

4 1 Hertii Opera, De Collis. Leg. § 4, n. 8, p. 123, 124.

ment, where he has his domicil, and to which he is subjected.[1]

§ 499. It would seem from Morrison's case,[2] that the House of Lords deemed the authority of an English guardian sufficient to institute a suit for the personal property of his ward in Scotland, upon the ground, that the administration of his personal estate granted by the usual authority, where he resided, must be taken to be everywhere of equal force with a voluntary assignment by himself. The courts of Scotland had unequivocally decided the other way. Whether this decision has been since acted upon in England does not distinctly appear. It has certainly not received sanction in America in the states acting under the jurisprudence of the common law. The rights and powers of guardians are considered as strictly local; and not as entitling them to exercise any authority over the person or personal property of their wards in other states, upon the same general reasoning and policy, which has circumscribed the rights and authorities of executors and administrators.[3]

§ 500. In regard to the other point, whether guardians appointed in foreign countries have any authority over the property of their wards, situate in other countries, the general consent of foreign jurists is, that as to immoveable property (whatever may be the rule, as to moveable property) the rights and authority of guardians are circumscribed by the laws of the territory of their appointment, and do not extend to other countries. In other words, the laws *rei sitæ* are to govern; and a guardian in one country can claim nothing in an-

---

1 P. Voet. De Stat. § 4, ch. 2, n. 6, p. 123.

2 Cited in 4 T. R. 140, and 1 H. Black, 677, 682.

3 Morrill *v.* Dickey, 1 John. Ch. R. 153; Kraft *v.* Vickery, 4 Gill & John. R. 332.

other, except in the form and manner, and under the regulations prescribed by the local law. Burgundus states the doctrine with great clearness. *Proinde confitendum est, si aliquid circa rem alterare minor velit, ut puta alienandi vel hypotecandi facultatem exigere, ibi sane veniam impetrari debere, ubi bona sunt sita.* But he adds a qualification, that, if the question simply respects the administration of the property, *hoc casu postulare debebit a judice domicilii, cui in personas plenum jus est attributum.*[1] This is a qualification by no means admissible.

§ 501. Boullenois after stating, that in France the principal object of guardianship is not so much the custody of the person, as of property, adds, that it has in view the administration and direction of property (*biens*), and that the rights, which it grants, are all real rights. *La garde consiste, ou en droits de propriété, ou en fruits d'usufruit; et il n'y a rien de plus réel, que ces sortes de droits. Par conséquent elle ne peut être régie, que par la loi de la situation, &c. De là il semble qu'il faudroit nécessairement en conclure, que chaque coutume, qui admet la garde, et où il y a des biens, a seule le droit de déférer la garde à qui bon lui semble; et qu'il n'y a que ceux, à qui elle la défère, qui puissent être gardiens, quelque domicile d'ailleurs, qu'aient ceux, qui tombent en garde, et ceux, qui sont appelés à la garde.*[2] He admits, that there are jurists, who assert the contrary.[3]

§ 502. Hertius, as we have seen, asserts the same doctrine as to immoveable property;[4] and it is almost

---

1 1 Boullenois, 150; Id. 129.
2 2 Boullenois, 320, 321, 339, 340.
3 Ibid.
4 Ante, § 497. 1 Hertii Opera, De Collis. Leg. § 4, n. 8, p. 123, 124.

unnecessary to add, that the Voets are of the same opinion.[1] Froland arranges himself on the side of those, who assert the reality of the laws, which respect guardianship, distinguishing, however, as to the quality of persons entitled, the right of possessing the property, and the formalities accompanying.[2]

§ 503. Lord Kaims lays down the Scottish doctrine to be, that it is of no importance in what place curators of minors are chosen; and accordingly, a choice made in England of curators, whether English or Scotch, will be held effectual in Scotland. He admits, that the powers of a guardian to a lunatic in England are limited, extending only to his person, and not to his estate; or rather, that different guardians are, or may be appointed by the Court of Chancery for each. But the authority of any guardian or curator, however appointed, in a foreign country, is not understood by him to extend to any real estate in Scotland.[3]

§ 504. There is no question, that, according to the rules of the common law, the rights of foreign guardians are not admitted over immoveable property, situate in other countries. Those rights are strictly territorial; and are not recognised, as having any influence upon such property in other countries, whose systems of jurisprudence embrace different regulations, and require different duties and arrangements. No one has ever supposed, that a guardian, appointed in any one state of this Union, had any right to receive the profits or to assume the possession of the real estate of his ward, in any other state, without having

---

1 Voet. De Stat. § 4, ch. 2, n. 6, p. 123; Voet. ad Pand. Lib. 1, tit. 4, P. 2, § 3, 7, p. 39, 40.

2 1 Froland, Mém. ch. 16, p. 717, 749, 750, 752.

3 2 Kaims, Equity, B. 3, ch. 8, § 1, p, 325; Id. § 4, p. 348.

received a due appointment from the proper tribunals of the state, where it is situate. The case falls within the well known principle, that rights to real property can be acquired, changed, and lost only according to the law *rei sitæ.*[1]

§ 505. Whether a guardian has authority to change the domicil of his ward from one country to another, seeing, that it may have a most important operation, as to the succession to his moveable property, in case of his death, has been much discussed. In favour of the affirmative there are many foreign jurists, among whom (we have seen) are Bynkershoeck, Boullenois, and Bretonnier; and in favour of the negative, Pothier and Mornac.[2] Rodemburg and J. Voet maintain the affirmative, as well in respect to a change of domicil by a parent, as by a guardian; excepting however cases, where the change of domicil is for a fraudulent purpose.[3]

§ 506. The same question has occurred in England; and it has been held, that a guardian may change the domicil of his ward, so as to affect the right of succession, if it is done *bonâ fide* and without fraud.[4] And this seems recognised as the true doctrine in America.[5]

§ 507. Secondly; in relation to executors and administrators. According to the Roman law, which made no distinction in this respect between moveable

---

1 Ante, § 424.

2 Ante, § 46, note 5; 2 Boullenois, p. 49, 50, 51, 52, 53.

3 Rodemburg, De Div. Stat. P. 2, tit. 2, ch. 1, § 6, p. 57; Id. ch. 2, § 2, p. 59; 2 Boull. 2, 5; Id. 54, 55, 56; Voet. ad Pand. Lib. 5, tit. 1, § 100. See other citations in 3 Merivale R. 72, 73, note.

4 Potinger *v.* Wightman, 3 Merivale, R. 67.

5 Guier *v.* O'Daniel, 1 Binn. R. 349, note; Cutts *v.* Haskins, 9 Mass. R. 543; Holyoke *v.* Haskins, 5 Pick. R. 20.

and immoveable property, the title, *heirs*, was indiscriminately applied to all persons, who were called to the succession, whether they were so called by the act of the party, or by operation of law. Thus, the person, who was created universal successor by a will, was called the testamentary heir (*hæres factus*), and the next of kin by blood in cases of intestacy was called the heir at law (*hæres natus*) or heir by intestacy. The heirs, whether consisting of one or more persons, and whether testamentary or by intestacy, were entitled by succession to all the estate of the deceased, whether it was real or personal, and were chargeable with all the burthens and debts due from him. [1] But inasmuch as the succession in either case might be onerous, as well as profitable, the law allowed the heir, whether he were so by testament, or by law, to renounce it, if he pleased; or he might accept it with the benefit of an inventory, the effect of which was to exonerate the heir from any farther liability, than the amount of the assets, or property inventoried. [2] These explanations are important in or-

[1] 1 Domat, B. 1, tit. 1, p. 557; Id. § 1, n. 1, 2, p. 558.— Domat says, that in France in the Provinces, which are governed by the testamentary law, and not by the Roman law (*droit écrit*) the title of heirs is given only to the heirs by blood, or heirs at law, and that the testamentary heirs are called universal legataries. But this distinction is merely nominal, and the same rules are applied to the universal legataries, as to the heirs by blood. 1 Domat, B. 1, tit 1, p. 557, 558. Erskine in his Institutes, B. 2, tit. 2, § 3, p. 192, says, that in Scotland, "heritable subjects are those (immoveables), which on the death of the proprietor descend to the heir; and moveables those, which go to executors, who are on that account sometimes styled *hæredes in mobilibus*. It may be also observed, that those, who undertake to gather in, and distribute among such as are interested in the succession, the moveable estate of a person deceased in virtue of a nomination, either by the testator, or by the Judge, frequently get the name of executors, because it is their office to execute the last will of the deceased." See Id. B. 3, tit. 9, § 1, 2, 26.

[2] 1 Domat, B. 1, tit. 1, § 5. n. 3, 4, p. 593.

der fully to understand the reasonings of the foreign jurists, and to apply them to the present subject; for the civil law distinctions everywhere pervade the jurisprudence of continental Europe.

§ 508. It will be at once seen, that the executor under the common law in many respects corresponds with the testamentary heir of the civil law; and that the administrator in many respects corresponds with the heir by intestacy. The principal distinction between them, which is important here to be considered, is, that executors and administrators have no right, except to the personal estate of the deceased; whereas the Roman heir was entitled to administer both the real and personal estate; and all the assets were treated as of the same nature, without any distinction of equitable and legal assets.[1]

§ 509. From what has already been said, the heir, testamentary or by intestacy, of immoveable property, can take only according to the *lex loci rei;* or, in other words, he is not admissible as heir, so as to administer the estate in any foreign country, unless he is duly qualified according to the principles and forms of the local law.[2] In this respect, he does not differ, either in regard to rights or responsibilities, from an heir or devisee, chargeable at the common law or by statute with the bond debts of the ancestor or testator. It is for the same reason, that a power to sell immoveable property, given to an executor, cannot be executed, unless upon due probate of the will in the place, where

1 1 Brown, Civil Law, 344, note.

2 See 2 Kaims, Eq. B. 3, ch. 8, § 3, p. 332; Vattel, B. 2, ch. 8, § 109, 110, 111; 1 Boullenois 242; Id. Pr. Gén, 37, p. 9; Doe dem. Lewis *v.* McFarland, 9 Cranch, 151.

the property is situate, and showing, that it may be lawfully done by the *lex loci.*[1] And if the party claims not under a power, but as a devisee, in trust to sell for the payment of debts, it is also necessary to have a like probate of the will. But it is not necessary in the latter case to take out letters of administration, although the devise in trust be to the party by the description of executor; for in such case he takes, as devisee, and not as executor; and his title is under the will, and not under the letters testamentary.[2]

§ 510. But in regard to moveable estate a like rule may not necessarily prevail in foreign countries, governed by a jurisprudence, which is drawn from or modelled upon the civil law; for moveables being treated as having no *situs*, and to be governed by the law of the domicil of the testator or intestate, the title of the heir, taking its effect directly from that law, is, or at least may be, consistently held to carry the right to such property, wherever it may be locally situate, in the same manner as it would by an assignment by the owner *inter vivos.*[3]

§ 511. Lord Kaims seems to take a distinction between the case of a testamentary heir, and an heir by intestacy, asserting that the nomination of an executor (*hæres de mobilibus*, or *hæres fiduciarius*[4]) by the proprietor in his testament, as to moveables, is effectual all the world over *jure gentium*, and will be sustained in Scotland; whereas letters of administration in a foreign country are strictly territorial, and, when granted in a foreign country, are not recognised in

1 Wells *v.* Cowper, 2 Hamm. R. 124.
2 Doe dem. Lewis *v.* McFarland, 9 Cranch, 151.
3 2 Kaims, Equity, B. 3, ch. 8, § 4.
4 Ersk. Inst. B. 3, tit. 9, § 2, 26.

Scotland, unless they are confirmed there by a proper judicial proceeding.[1] It may be so; but Erskine lays it down as clear law, that in Scotland neither executors nor administrators, foreign or domestic, are entitled to administer the estate of the deceased, until they have been duly confirmed by the competent Judge.[2] What perhaps Lord Kaims meant to say, was, that the title of executor was a good title *jure gentium*, and when established in the manner, and by the process prescribed by the law of the place, where it was sought to be exercised, ought to be held of universal obligation. And so it probably is in all civilized nations, except such (if there now are any) as adopt the *droit d'aubaine*, and confiscate the moveable property of all foreigners dying, and leaving such property within their territories.

§ 512. In regard to the title of executors and administrators, derived from a grant of administration in the country of the domicil of the deceased, it is to be considered, that that title cannot *de jure* extend, as a matter of right, beyond the territory of the government, which grants it, and the moveable property therein. As to such property, situate in foreign countries, the title, if acknowledged at all, is acknowledged *ex comitate;* and of course it is subject to be controlled or modified, as every nation may think proper, with reference to its own institutions and policy, and the rights of its own subjects. And, here, the rule, to which reference has been so often made, applies with great force, that no nation is under any obligation to enforce foreign laws, prejudicial to its own rights, or those of its subjects. Persons, domiciled and dying in

---

1 2 Kaims, Equity, B. 3, ch. 8, § 3; Id. § 4, p. 347, 348.

2 Ersk. Inst. B. tit. 9, § 27, 29.

foreign countries are often deeply indebted to creditors, living in other countries, in which they leave personal assets. In such cases it would be a great hardship upon such creditors to allow a foreign executor or administrator to withdraw those funds, without the payment of such debts, and thus to leave the creditors to seek their remedy in the domicil of the foreign executor or administrator, and perhaps there meet with obstructions and inequalities in the enforcement of their own rights from the peculiarities of the local laws.

§ 513. It has hence become a general doctrine of the common law, recognised both in England and America, that no suit can be brought by or against any foreign executor or administrator in the courts of the country, in virtue of his foreign letters testamentary, or of administration. But new letters of administration must be taken out, and new security given, according to the general rules of law prescribed in the country, where the suit is brought.[1] The right of the foreign execu-

---

1 The authorities to this point are now exceedingly numerous and entirely conclusive. See Lee *v.* Moore, Palmer R. 163; Tourton *v.* Flower, 3 P. Will, 369, 370; Thorne *v.* Watkins, 2 Ves. 35; Atty. Gen. *v.* Cockerell, 1 Price R. 179; Lowe *v.* Fairlie, 2 Madd. R. 101; 1 Hagg. Eccl. R. 93, 239; Mitford's Plead. 177 (4th edit.); Fenwick *v.* Sears, 1 Cranch 259; Dixon's Executors *v.* Ramsay's Executors, 3 Cranch, 319, 323; Kerr *v.* Moon, 9 Wheaton R. 565; Armstrong *v* Lear, 12 Wheaton R. 169; Thompson *v.* Wilson, 2 N. Hamp. R. 291; Dickinson's Administrators *v.* McCraw, 4 Randolph R. 158; Glenn *v.* Smith, 2 Gill. & John. R. 493; Stearns *v.* Burnham, 5 Greenleaf R. 261; Goodwin *v.* Jones, 3 Mass. R. 514; Borden *v.* Borden, 5 Mass. R. 67; Stevens *v.* Gaylord, 11 Mass. R. 256; Langdon *v.* Potter, 11 Mass. R. 313; Dangerfield *v.* Thurston, 20 Martin R. 232; Riley *v.* Riley, 3 Day's Conn. Cas. 74; Champlin *v.* Tilley, Id. 303; Trecothick *v.* Austin, 4 Mason R. 16, 32; *Ex parte* Picquet, 5 Pick. 65; Holmes *v.* Remsen, 20 John. R. 229, 265; Smith, Administrator *v.* The Union Bank of Georgetown, 5 Peters R. 518; Campbell *v.* Tousey, 7 Cowen R. 64; Logan *v.* Fairlie, 2 Sim. & Stu. 284.

tor or administrator to take out such new administration is usually admitted, as a matter of course, unless some special reasons intervene; and the new administration is treated as merely ancillary or auxiliary to the original foreign administration, so far as regards the collection of the effects and the proper distribution of them.[1] Still, however, the new administration is made subservient to the rights of creditors, legatees, and distributees resident within the country; and the residuum is transmissible to the foreign country only, when the final account has been settled in the proper domestic tribunal, upon the equitable principles adopted in its laws.[2]

---

1 Harvey *v.* Richards, 1 Mason R. 381; Stevens *v.* Gaylord, 11 Mass. R. 256; Case of Miller's Estate, 3 Rawle R. 312.

2 See Harvey *v.* Richards, 1 Mason R. 381; Dawes *v.* Boylston, 9 Mass. R. 337; Selectmen of Boston *v.* Boylston, 4 Mass. R. 318, 384; Richards *v.* Dutch, 8 Mass. R. 506; Dawes *v.* Head, 3 Pick. R. 128; Hooker *v.* Olmstead, 6 Pick. R. 481; Davis *v.* Estey, 8 Pick. 475; Jennison *v.* Hapgood, 10 Pick. R. 77; Stevens *v.* Gaylord, 11 Mass. R. 256; Case of Miller's Estate, 3 Rawle 312. — Many complicated questions may grow out of original and ancillary administrations, some of which have been stated in the cases of Harvey *v.* Richards, 1 Mason R. 381, and Dawes *v.* Head, 3 Pick. 128. The following extract, from the opinion of Chief Justice Parker, in the latter case, deserves an attentive perusal. The question there arose, how assets under an ancillary administration were to be disposed of in cases of insolvency, and of debts due to creditors belonging to the same country, as the deceased debtor. The Chief Justice after disposing of these particulars, said "Thus this action is determined without touching the questions, upon which it was supposed it would turn, which are of a novel and delicate nature, and though often glanced at, do not appear to have been decided, either in this or any other state of the union. We wish to avoid any thing, which may be construed into a conclusive adjudication, and yet are of opinion, that it will be useful to throw out for consideration the results of our reasonings upon this subject.

"If the technical difficulties, upon which this cause has been decided, had not occurred, but the estate had been rendered insolvent here, and a decree of distribution for a proportion had been issued, or if the debt

§ 514. But although a foreign executor or administrator is not suable in another state for assets received abroad; yet, if he comes into such state and col-

---

of Lenox and Sheafe had been ascertained by a judgment, and the pleadings to a suit on the bond had been the same in that case as now, the question would be, whether the funds, collected here by an ancillary administration, should be appropriated to the payment of such debts, as might be regularly proved here, notwithstanding it was made to appear, that the whole estate was insufficient to pay all the debts, and that the effects here were wanted by the executor abroad, to enable him duly to administer the estate. It has been contended, that this should be done, because the administrator has given bond here in the same manner, as if this were the original administration, and because the statute, which authorizes this administration, requires, that the Judge of Probate shall settle the estate in the same way and manner, as he would, if the original will had been proved here. With respect to the bond, it will be saved by a faithful administration of the estate according to law; and with respect to the settlement by the Judge of Probate, this must be understood to authorize him to require the administrator to account, and that the due course of proceedings in the probate office shall be observed. It certainly cannot be construed to mean, that in all cases a final settlement of the estate shall take place here; if it did, then, if there were no debts here, and none to claim as legatees or next of kin, it would be necessary for all such to prove their right and receive their distributive shares here, notwithstanding the settlement must in such case be made according to the laws of the country, where the deceased had his domicil. But we think in such case it would be very clear, that the assets collected here should be remitted to the foreign executor or administrator; for it seems to be a well settled principle, that the distribution is to be made according to the laws of the country, where the deceased was domiciled; and if any part is to be retained for distribution here, it will be only by virtue of some exception to this general rule, or because the parties interested seek their remedy here; in which case it might be within the legal discretion of the court here to cause distribution, or to remit, according to the circumstances and condition of the estate.

"An exception to the general rule grows out of the duty of every government and its courts to protect its own citizens in the enjoyment of their property and the recovery of their debts, so far as this may be done without violating the equal rights of creditors living in a foreign country. In relation to the effects found within our jurisdiction and collected by the aid of our laws, a regard to the rights and interests of our citizens requires, that those effects should be made answerable for

lects property and debts, which are assets there, he is liable to be treated as an executor *de son tort*, to the extent of such assets. And in such case, if he

---

debts due to them, in a just proportion to the whole estate of the deceased and all the claims upon it, whatever they may be. In the several cases which have come before this Court, where the legal character and effects of an ancillary administration have been considered, the intimations have been strong, that the administrator here shall be held to pay the debts due to our citizens. The cases *Richards* v. *Dutch*, *Dawes, Judge, &c.* v. *Boylston*, *Selectmen of Boston* v. *Boylston*, and *Stevens* v. *Gaylord*, are of this character. In all these cases, however, we must suppose the Court had reference to a solvent estate, and in such case there seems to be no question of the correctness of the principle; for it would be but an idle show of courtesy to order the proceeds of an estate to be sent to a foreign country, the province of Bengal for instance, and oblige our citizens to go or send there for their debts, when no possible prejudice could arise to the estate, or those interested in it, by causing them to be paid here; and possibly the same remark may be applicable to legacies payable to legatees living here, unless the circumstances of the estate should require the funds to be sent abroad. Whether citizens of other states claiming payment of their debts of the administrator here, are to be put upon the same footing with citizens of Massachusetts, by virtue of the privileges and immunities secured to them by the constitution of the United States, is a point which we do not now decide. But without doubt the courts of the United States, having full equity powers, would enforce payment upon the principles above stated, where there is no suggestion of insolvency of the estate. There would be no doubt, we think, that payment of debts by the administrator here, after sufficient proof, that they were due, and an allowance of his account therefor by the Probate Court with proper notice, would be faithful administration according to the condition of his bond, and would be a proper way of accounting to the principal administrator abroad.

"In regard to effects thus collected within our jurisdiction, belonging to an insolvent estate of a deceased person having his domicil abroad, the question may be more difficult. We cannot think, however, that in any civilized country advantage ought to be taken of the accidental circumstance of property being found within its territory, which may be reduced to possession by the aid of its courts and laws, to sequester the whole for the use of its own subjects or citizens, where it shall be known, that all the estate and effects of the deceased are insufficient to pay his just debts. Such a doctrine would be derogatory to the character of any government. Under the English bankrupt system, foreigners as well as subjects may prove their debts and share in the distribu-

has brought the assets collected abroad with him into such state, it has been decided in New-York, that he is chargeable with all the assets received abroad, which

tion. Without doubt, in other foreign countries, where there is a *cessio bonorum*, or other process relating to bankrupts' estates, the same just principle is adopted. It was so under our bankrupt law, while that was in force, and no reason can be suggested, why so honest and just a principle should not be applied in the case of insolvent estates of deceased persons. It is always practised upon in regard to persons dying within our jurisdiction, having had their domicil here; that is, creditors of all countries have the same rights as our own citizens, to file their claims and share in the distribution. There cannot be then a right in any one or more of our citizens, who may happen to be creditors, to seize the whole of the effects, which may be found here, or claim an appropriation of them to the payment of their debts, in exclusion of foreign creditors.

"It is said this is no more than what may be done by virtue of our attachment law, in regard to the property of a living debtor, who is insolvent. But the justness of that law is very questionable, and its application ought not to be extended to cases, by analogy, which do not come within its express provisions.

"What then is to be done with the effects collected here belonging to an insolvent estate in a foreign country? Shall they be sent home in order to be appropriated according to the laws of that country? This would often work great injustice, and always great inconvenience, to our own citizens, whose debts might not be large enough to bear the expense of proving and collecting them abroad; and in countries, where there is no provision for an equal distribution, the pursuit of them might be wholly fruitless. As in Great Britain, our citizens, whose debts would generally be upon simple contract, such as bills of exchange, promissory notes, accounts, &c., would be postponed to creditors by judgment, bond, &c., and even to other debts upon simple contract, which might be preferred by the executor or administrator. It would seem too great a stretch of courtesy to require the effects to be sent home and our citizens to pursue them under such disadvantages. What then shall be done to avoid, on the one hand, the injustice of taking the whole funds for the use of our citizens to the prejudice of foreigners, when the estate is insolvent, and on the other, the equal injustice and greater inconvenience of compelling our own citizens to seek satisfaction of their debts in distant countries?

"The proper course would undoubtedly be, to retain the funds here for a *pro ratâ* distribution according to the laws of our state among the citizens thereof, having regard to all the assets, either in the hands of the principal administrator or of the administrator here, and having regard also to the whole of the debts, which by the laws of either coun-

he still retains in his hands, or which he has expended, or disposed of in such state, unless expended or disposed of in the due course of administration, whether

---

try are payable out of those assets, disregarding any fanciful preference which may be given to one species of debt over another, considering the funds here as applicable to the payment of the just proportion due to our own citizens; and, if there be any residue, it should be remitted to the principal administrator, to be dealt with according to the laws of his own country, the subjects of that country, if there be any injustice or inequality in the payment or distribution, being bound to submit to its laws. The only objection, which can be made to this mode of adjusting an ancillary administration upon an insolvent estate, is the difficulty and delay of executing it. The difficulty would not be greater than in settling many other complicated affairs, where many persons have interests of different kinds in the same funds. The powers of a court of chancery are competent to embrace and settle all cases of that nature, even if the powers of our Court of Probate are not sufficiently extensive; which however is not certain. The administrator here should be held to show the condition of the estate abroad, the amount of property subject to debts, and the amount of debts, and a distribution could be made upon perfectly fair and equitable principles. The delay would undoubtedly be considerable, but this would not be so great an evil as either sending our citizens abroad upon a forlorn hope to seek for the fragments of an insolvent estate, or paying the whole of their debts out of the property without regard to the claims of foreign creditors. And if the Probate Court has not sufficient power to make such an equitable adjustment, a bill in equity, in which the administrator here should be the principal respondent, would probably produce the desired result, as then time and opportunity could be given to make known the whole condition of the estate, and all persons interested might be heard before any final decree; in the mean time the administrator could be restrained from remitting the funds until such decree should be passed." 3 Pick. R. 143 to 148. The following extracts are made from the opinion of the Court in Harvey *v.* Richards. "One objection urged against the exercise of the authority of the Court is, that, as national comity requires the distribution of the property according to the law of the domicil, the same comity requires, that the distribution should be made in the same place. This consequence, however, is not admitted; and it has no necessary connexion with the preceding proposition. The rule, that distribution shall be according to the law of the domicil of the deceased, is not founded merely upon the notion, that moveables have no *situs*, and therefore follow the person of the proprietor, even interpreting that maxim in its true sense, that personal property is subject to that law, which governs the person of the owner. Nor is it, perhaps, founded upon the presum-

they were received in such state, or in the foreign country. There is great difficulty in supporting this decision to the extent of making the foreign executor

ed intention of the deceased, that all his property should be distributed according to the law of the place of his domicil, with which he is supposed to be best acquainted and satisfied; for the rule will prevail even against the express intention of the deceased, unless the mode, in which that intention is expressed, would give it legal validity as a will. It seems, indeed, to have had its origin in a more enlarged policy, founded upon the general convenience and necessities of mankind; and in this view the maxim above stated flows from, rather than guides, the application of that policy. The only reason, why any nation gives effect to foreign laws within its own territory, is the endless embarrassment, which would otherwise be introduced in its own intercourse with foreign nations. The rights of its own citizens would be materially impaired, and, in many instances, totally extinguished, by a refusal to recognise and sustain the doctrines of foreign law. The case now under consideration is an illustration of the perfect justice and wisdom of this general practice of nations. A person may have moveable property and debts in various countries, each of which may have a different system of succession. If the law *rei sitæ* were generally to prevail, it would be utterly impossible for any such person to know in what manner his property would be distributed at his death, not only from the uncertainty of its situation from its own transitory nature, but from the impracticability of knowing, with minute accuracy, the law of succession of every country, in which it might then happen to be. He would be under the same embarrassment, if he attempted to dispose of his property by a testament; for he could never foresee, where it would be at his death. Nay more, it would be in the power of his debtor, by a mere change of his own domicil, to destroy the best digested will; and the accident of a moment might destroy all the anxious provisions of an excellent parent for his whole family. Nor is this all. The nation itself, to which the deceased belonged, might be seriously affected by the loss of his wealth, from a momentary absence, although his true home was in the centre of its own territory. These are great and serious evils, pervading every class of the community, and equally affecting every civilized nation. But in a maritime nation, depending upon its commerce for its glory and its revenue, the mischief would be incalculable. The common and spontaneous consent of nations, therefore, established this rule from the noblest policy, the promotion of general convenience and happiness, and the avoiding of distressing difficulties, equally subversive of the public safety and private enterprise of all. It flowed from the same spirit, that dictated judicial obedience to the foreign commissions of the admiralty. *Sub mutuæ vicissitudinis obtentu, damus petimusque vicissim,* is the language of the civilized world

or administrator liable in such state for assets received abroad, and brought into the state by him. If he cannot sue in his representative character in another state,

---

on this subject. There can be no pretence, that the same general inconvenience or embarrassment attends the distribution of foreign effects according to the foreign law by the tribunals of the country, where they are situate. Cases have been already stated, in which great inconvenience would attend the establishment of any rule, excluding such distribution. It may be admitted also, that there are cases, in which it would be highly convenient to decline the jurisdiction and remit the parties to the *forum domicilii.* Where there are no creditors here, and no heirs or legatees here, but all are resident abroad, there can be no doubt, that a court of equity would direct the remittance of the property upon the application of any competent party.

"The correct result of these considerations upon principle would seem to be, that whether the Court here ought to decree distribution or remit the property abroad, is a matter not of jurisdiction, but of judicial discretion, depending upon the particular circumstances of each case; that there ought to be no universal rule on this subject; but that every nation is bound to lend the aid of its own tribunals for the purpose of enforcing the rights of all persons having title to the fund, when such interference will not be productive of injustice or inconvenience, or conflicting equities.

"It is farther objected, that a rule, which is to depend for its application upon the particular circumstances of each case, is too uncertain to be considered a safe guide for general practice. But this objection affords no solid ground for declining the jurisdiction, since there are an infinite variety of cases, in which no general rule has been or can be laid down, as to legal or equitable relief, in the ordinary controversies before judicial tribunals. In many of these, the difficulty is intrinsic in the subject matter; and where a general rule cannot easily be extracted, each case must, and indeed ought to, rest on its own particular circumstances. The uncertainty, therefore, is neither more nor less than belongs to many other complicated transactions of human life, where the law administers relief *ex æquo et bono.*

"Another objection, addressed more pointedly to a class of cases like the present, is the difficulty of settling the accounts of the estate, ascertaining the assets, what debts are sperate, what desperate, and, finally ascertaining what is the residue to be distributed, and who are the next of kin entitled to share. And to add to our embarrassment, we are told, that we cannot compel the foreign executor to render any account in our courts. I agree at once, that this cannot be done, if he is not here; but I utterly deny, that the administrator here cannot be compelled to account to any competent Court for all the assets, which he has received under the authority of our laws. And if the foreign executor

without new letters of administration, because he derives his authority from a foreign government, to which he is solely responsible in his administration, it is not easy to perceive, how he can be sued in such state for assets in his hands, received abroad under the sanction

chooses to lie by, and refuses to render any account of the foreign funds in his hands, so far as to enable the Court here to ascertain, whether the funds are wanted abroad for the payment of debts or legacies, or not, he has no right to complain, if the Court refuses to remit the assets, and distributes them among those who may legally claim them. And as to settling the estate, or ascertaining who are the distributees, there is no more difficulty than often falls to our lot in many cases, arising under the ordinary probate proceedings.

"All these objections are, in fact, reasons for declining to exercise the jurisdiction in particular cases, rather than reasons against the existence of the jurisdiction itself. It seems, indeed, admitted by the learned counsel for the defendant, that, if there be no foreign administration, it would be the duty of the Court to grant relief upon an administration taken here. Yet every objection, already urged, would apply with as much force in that as in the present case. The property would be to be distributed according to the foreign law of the deceased's domicil. The same difficulty would exist, as to ascertaining the debts and legacies, and the assets and distributees entitled to share. But it is said in the case now put, the administration here would be the principal administration, whereas in the case at bar, it is only an auxiliary or ancillary administration. I have no objection to the use of the terms principal and auxiliary, as indicating a distinction in fact as to the objects of the different administrations; but we should guard ourselves against the conclusion, that therefore there is a distinction in law as to the rights of parties. There is no magic in words. Each of these administrations may be properly considered as a principal one, with reference to the limits of its exclusive authority; and each might, under circumstances, justly be deemed an auxiliary administration. If the bulk of the property, and all the heirs and legatees and creditors were here, and the foreign administration were only to recover a few inconsiderable claims, that would most correctly be denominated a mere auxiliary administration for the beneficial use of the parties here, although the domicil of the testator were abroad. The converse case would of course produce an opposite result. But I am yet to learn, what possible difference it can make in the rights of parties before the Court, whether the administration be a principal or an auxiliary administration. They must stand upon the authority of the law to administer or deny relief, under all the circumstances of their case, and not upon a mere technical distinction of very recent origin."

of the foreign administration, and by the authority of the foreign government, to which he is accountable for all such assets. The learned Court, however, who decided the point, seem to have taken it for granted, that a foreign executor or administrator was of course suable here for all assets found in his hands. "If a foreign executor" they say "is liable to be sued here, *of which we apprehend there can be no question*, he must from the very nature of the case, *primâ facie*, be responsible for the assets, which are shown to have been in his possession within this state." With great deference, that was the very point to be established by reasoning, since no authority could be shown, which supported it. On the other hand, there are authorities, which indicate a very different doctrine.[1]

§ 515. But, although a foreign executor or administrator is not entitled to maintain a suit in our courts, in virtue of his original letters of administration; yet, if a debtor here chooses voluntarily to pay him a debt, which he may lawfully receive under that administration; the debtor will be discharged.[2] And on the other

---

1 See Selectmen of Boston *v.* Boylston, 2 Mass. R. 384; Goodwin *v.* Jones, 3 Mass. R. 514; Davis *v.* Estey, 8 Pick. R, 475; Dawes *v.* Head, 3 Pick, 128; Doolittle *v.* Lewis, 7 John. Ch. R. 45, 47.

2 The proposition is thus guardedly laid down, in Stevens *v.* Gaylord, 11 Mass. R. 256. But a more important question may arise, whether a voluntary payment of a debt to a foreign administrator, when there is no domestic administrator appointed, would not be a good discharge of the debtor. Debts are not only due in the domicil of the debtor, but in the domicil of the creditor; and indeed, unless a particular place of payment is appointed, they are due and may be demanded any where. If a debtor were found in the foreign country, where the creditor died, and where an administrator was appointed, he would certainly be suable there, and could not protect himself by a plea, that he was liable to pay only to the administrator appointed in the place of his (the debtor's) domicil. Lord Hardwicke, in Thorne *v.* Watkins, (2 Ves. 35) said, that all debts follow the person, not

hand, if a foreign executor or administrator brings or transmits property here, which he has received under the administration abroad, or if he is here personally present, he is not personally, or in his representative capacity, liable to a suit here; nor is such property liable here to creditors; but they must resort for satisfaction to the forum of the original administration.[1] And where property is remitted by a foreign executor to this country to pay legacies, no suit can be maintained for it, if there is no specific appropriation of it, without an administration taken out here.[2]

§ 516. And here it is necessary to attend to a distinction, important in its nature and consequences. If a foreign administrator has, in virtue of his administration, reduced the personal property of the deceased, there situated, into possession, so that he has the legal title thereto, according to the laws of that country; if that property should afterwards be found in another country, or carried and converted there against his will, he may maintain a suit for it in his own name, without taking out letters of administration; for he is to all intents and purposes the legal owner, although he is so in the

---

of the debtor in respect of the right or property, but of the creditor to whom due. In Doolittle *v.* Lewis, (7 John. Ch. R. 49) Mr. Chancellor Kent held, that a voluntary payment to a foreign executor or administrator was a good discharge of the debt. See Shultz *v.* Pulver, 3 Paige R. 182; Hooker *v.* Olmstead, 6 Pick. R. 481; Atkyns *v.* Smith, 2 Atk. R. 63; Trecothick *v.* Austin, 4 Mason R. 16, 33.

1 Currie administrator *v.* Bircham, 1 Dowl. & Ryl. R. 35; Davis *v.* Estey, 8 Pick. R. 475. But see Dowdale's case, 6 Co. R. 47; Campbell *v.* Todfey, 7 Cowen R. 64. — In Scrimshire *v.* Scrimshire (2 Hagg. Consist. R. 420), Sir Edward Simpson said, "If an Englishman makes a will abroad, and makes a foreigner executor, and has no effects in England, and the executor proves the will lawfully abroad, that probate or sentence of the proper court, establishing the will as to effects there of a man domiciled there, would be a bar to a discovery in chancery of effects abroad."

2 Logan *v.* Fairlie, 2 Sim. & Stu. R. 284.

character of trustee. And in like manner, if a specific legacy is bequeathed of property in a foreign country, and the legatee has, under an administration there, been admitted to the ownership, he may afterwards sue in his own name for any injury or conversion of such property in another country, where the property or party may be found, without any probate of the will there.[1]

§ 517. The like principle will apply, where an executor or administrator, in virtue of an administration abroad, becomes possessed of negotiable notes belonging to the deceased, which are payable to bearer; for then he becomes the legal owner and bearer by virtue of his administration, and may sue thereon in his own name; and need not take out letters of administration in the state, where the debtor resides, in order to maintain a suit against him.[2] And for a like reason, it would seem, that negotiable paper of the deceased, payable to order, actually endorsed by a foreign executor or administrator in the foreign country, and capable there of passing by such endorsement, would confer a complete legal title on the indorsee, so that he ought to be everywhere treated, as the legal indorsee, and allowed to sue thereon accordingly; as he would be, if it were a transfer of personal goods or chattels of the deceased situate in such foreign country.[3]

§ 518. Where there are different administrations, granted in different countries, those, which are in their

---

[1] See Commonwealth *v.* Griffith, 2 Pick. R. 11; Bollard *v.* Spencer, 7 T. R. 354; Shipman *v.* Thompson, Willes R. 103; Slack *v.* Walcott, 3 Mason R. 508, 518.

[2] Robinson *v.* Crandall, 9 Wendell R. 425. But see Stearns *v.* Burnham, 5 Greenleaf R. 261; Thompson *v.* Wilson, 2 New Hamp. R. 291; McNeilage *v.* Holloway, 1 B. and Ald. 218; ante § 354, 358, 359.

[3] Ib. and ante § 358, 359.

nature ancillary, are, as we have seen, generally held subordinate to the original administration. But each administration is deemed so far independent of the others, that property received under one cannot be sued for under another, though it may at the moment be locally situate within the jurisdiction of the latter. Thus, if property is received by a foreign executor or administrator abroad, and afterwards remitted here, an executor or administrator appointed here could not assert a claim to it here, either against the person, in whose hands it might happen to be, or against the foreign executor or administrator.[1] The only mode of reaching it, if necessary for the purposes of due administration, would be to require its transmission or distribution, after all claims against the foreign administration had been ascertained and settled.

§ 519. But suppose a case, where the personal estate of the deceased has not, at the time of his decease, any positive locality in the place of his domicil, or in any foreign territory; but is strictly *in transitu* to a foreign country, and afterwards arrives in the country of its destination. It may be asked, in such case, to whom would the administration of such property rightfully belong? Would it belong to the administrator in the place of the domicil of the deceased, or to the administrator appointed in the place, where it had arrived? And if (as may well happen in case of a ship and cargo sent abroad) the property or its proceeds should return to the domicil of the original owner, would the administrator, there appointed, be entitled to take it, and bound to account for it, in the due course

1 Currie administrator *v.* Bircham, 1 Dowl. & Ryl. R. 35. See Jauncey *v.* Seeley, 1 Vern. R. 397.

of administration? Practically speaking, no doubt is entertained on this subject; and the property, whenever it returns to the country of the domicil of the owner, whether by remittance or otherwise, is understood to be under the administration of the administrator appointed there. Nor has there been a doubt hitherto judicially expressed, that property so sent abroad, and returned, might and should be so administered, and that all parties would be protected by their doings in regard to it.

§ 520. Indeed, according to the common course of commercial business, ships and cargoes, and the proceeds thereof, locally situate in a foreign country at the time of the death of the owner, always proceed on their voyages, and return to the home port, without any suspicion, that all the parties concerned are not legally entitled so to act; and they are taken possession of, and administered by the administrator of the *forum domicilii*, with the constant persuasion, that he may not only rightfully do so, but that he is bound to administer them, as part of the funds appropriately in his hands. A different course of adjudication would be attended with almost inextricable difficulties, and would involve this extraordinary result, that all the personal property of the deceased must be deemed to have a fixed *situs*, where it was at the moment of his death; and, if removed from it, must be returned thither for the purpose of a due administration. Nay, debts due in a foreign country would be absolutely required to be retained there, until a local administration was obtained; and could not without peril be voluntarily remitted to the creditor's domicil. And, if the debtor should in the mean time remove to another country, it might become matter of extreme doubt, whether a payment to a local administrator there would discharge him from the debt.[1]

§ 521. A case illustrative of these remarks has recently occurred. The personal estate of an intestate consisted in a considerable degree of stage coaches and stage horses, belonging to a daily line, running from one state to another; and letters of administration were taken out by the same person in both states, one being that of the intestate's domicil. A question arose, under which administration the property was to be accounted for, part of it being in one state, and part in the other, and part *in transitu* from one to the other, at the moment of the intestate's death. The learned Chancellor of New York said, that, if administration had been granted to different individuals in the two states, the property must have been considered as belonging to that administrator, who first reduced it to possession within the limits of his own state. But that in the case before him, as both administrations were granted to the same person, if an account of administration were to be taken, it would be necessary to settle that by ascertaining what had been inventoried and accounted for by him under the administration in the other state.[2]

§ 522. Where administrations are granted to different persons in different states, they are so far deemed independent of each other, that a judgment obtained against one will furnish no right of action against the other, to affect assets received by the latter in virtue of his own administration; for, in contemplation of law, there is no privity between him and the other administrator.[3]

---

1 See Stevens *v.* Gaylord, 11 Mass. R. 256.

2 Orcutt *v.* Orms, 3 Paige R. 459.

3 Lightfoot *v.* Bickley, 2 Rawle R. 431.

It might be different, if the same person were administrator in both states.[1] On the other hand, a judgment, recovered by a foreign administrator against the debtor of his intestate, will not form the foundation of an action against the debtor by an ancillary administrator appointed in another state.[2] But the foreign administrator might himself in such a case maintain a personal suit against the debtor in any other state; because the judgment would, as to him, merge the original debt, and make it personally due to him in his own right, he being responsible therefor to the estate.[3]

§ 523. So strict is the principle, that a foreign administrator cannot do any act, as administrator, in another state, that, where the local laws convert real securities in the hands of an administrator into personal assets, which he may sell or assign, he cannot dispose of such real securities, until he has taken out letters of administration in the place *rei sitæ*.[4] Thus, mortgages are declared by the laws of Massachusetts to be personal assets in the hands of administrators; and disposable by them accordingly. But the authority cannot be exercised by any, except administrators, who have been duly appointed within the state.[5] On the other hand, if an administrator sell real estate for the payment of debts, pursuant to the authority given him under the local laws *rei sitæ*, he is not responsible for the proceeds as assets in any other state; but they are to be

---

1 Lightfoot *v.* Bickley, 2 Rawle R. 431.

2 Talmage *v.* Chapel, 16 Mass. R. 71.

3 Ibid.

4 Goodwin *v.* Jones, 3 Mass. R. 514, 519. See Bissell *v.* Briggs, 9 Mass. R. 467, 468. But see Doolittle *v.* Lewis, 7 John. Ch. R. 45, 47.

5 Cutter *v.* Davenport, 1 Pick. R. 80.

disposed of, and accounted for, solely in the place and manner pointed out in the local laws.[1]

§ 524. In relation to the mode of administering assets by executors and administrators, there are in different countries very different regulations. The priority of debts, the order of payments, the marshalling of assets for this purpose, and, in cases of insolvency, the mode of proof, as well as of distribution, differ in different countries.[2] In some countries, all debts stand in equal order; and, in cases of insolvency, the creditors are to be paid *pari passu.* In others, there are certain classes of debts entitled to a priority of payment, and are therefore deemed privileged debts. Thus, in England bond debts and judgment debts possess this privilege; and the like law exists in some of the states of this Union. Similar provisions may be found in the law of France in favour of particular classes of creditors.[3] On the other hand, in Massachusetts, and in many other states of the Union, all debts, except those due to the government, possess an equal rank, and are payable *pari passu.* Let us suppose, then, that a debtor dies domiciled in a country, where such priority of right and privilege exists; and he has assets situate in a state, where all debts stand in an equal rank, and administration is duly taken out, in the place of his domicil, and also in the place of the *situs* of the assets. What rule is to govern in the marshalling of the assets? The law of the domicil? Or the law of the *situs?* The established rule now is, that in regard to creditors the administra-

1 Peck *v.* Mead, 2 Wendell R. 471; Hooker *v.* Olmstead, 6 Pick. R. 481, 483; Goodwin *v.* Jones, 3 Mass. R. 514, 519, 520.

2 Harvey *v.* Richards, 1 Mason R. 421.

3 Merlin, Répertoire, Privilége; Civil Code of France, art. 2092 to 2106.

tion of the assets of deceased persons is to be governed altogether by the law of the country, where the executor or administrator acts, and from which he derives his authority to collect them; and not by that of the domicil of the deceased. The rule has been laid down with great clearness and force on many occasions.[1]

§ 525. The ground, upon which this doctrine has been established, seems entirely satisfactory. Every nation, having a right to dispose of all the property actually situate within it, has (as has often been said) a right to protect itself and its citizens against the inequalities of foreign laws, which are injurious to their interests. The rule of a preference, or of an equality in the payment of debts, whether the one or the other course is adopted, is purely local in its nature, and can have no just claim to be admitted by any other nation, which in its domestic arrangements pursues an opposite policy. And in a conflict between our own and foreign laws, the doctrine avowed by Huberus is highly reasonable, that we should prefer our own. *In tali conflictu magis est ut jus nostrum, quam jus alienum, servemus.*[2]

§ 526. It seems, that many foreign jurists maintain a different opinion, holding, that in every case the privileges of debts and the order of payment are to be gov-

---

[1] See Harrison *v.* Sterry, 5 Cranch 299; Milne *v.* Moreton, 4 Binn. R. 353,361; Olivier *v.* Townes, 14 Martin, 93, 99; De Sobry *v.* De Laistre, 2 Harr. & John. R. 193, 224; Smith administrator *v.* Union Bank of Georgetown, 5 Peters R. 518, 523; Dawes *v.* Head, 3 Pick. R. 128; Holmes *v.* Remsen, 20 John. R. 265; Case of Miller's Estate, 3 Rawle R. 312. — Where there are administrations and assets in different States, and the estate is insolvent, the general principle adopted by the Courts of Massachusetts is, to place creditors there, as to the assets in the state, upon a footing of equality with other creditors in the state, where the party had his domicil at his death. Davis *v.* Estey, 8 Pick. R. 475.

[2] Huberus, Lib. 1, tit. 3, § 11; See also Smith adm'r *v.* Union Bank of Georgetown, 5 Peters R. 517.

erned by the laws of the domicil of the debtor, at the time of his contract, or of his death. They found themselves upon the general rule, that the creditor must pursue his remedy in the domicil of the debtor, and that debts follow his person, and not that of the creditor.[1] This rule was acknowledged in matters of jurisdiction in the Roman law, in which it is said; *Juris ordinem converti postulas, ut non actor rei forum, sed reus actoris sequitur. Nam ubi domicilium reus habet, vel tempore contractûs habuit, licet hoc postea transtulerit, ibi tantum eum conveniri oportet.*[2] But it by no means follows, that, because this was the rule in the municipal jurisprudence of Rome, therefore it ought to be adopted, as a portion of modern international law. Nor does it necessarily follow, even if the rule were admitted to govern, as to the forum, where the suit should be brought against the debtor, in his

1 Livermore's Diss. p. 164 to 171. — Mr. Livermore has, in his Dissertations (p. 164 to 171), controverted the correctness of the American doctrine; and he holds, that the law of the debtor's domicil, at the time when the debt was contracted, furnishes the true rule. Mr. Henry lays down the rule, that when the law of the domicil of the creditor and debtor differ, as to classing debts and rights of action among personal or real property, the law of the domicil of the debtor must prevail in suits on them. Henry on Foreign Law, 34, 35. Mr. Dwarris states the same rule, and quotes the maxims, "Actor sequitur forum rei," and "Debita sequuntur personam debitoris." He admits, indeed, that debts and rights of action attend upon the person of the creditor, "inhærent ossibus creditoris"; but, to recover them, one must follow the *forum rei*, and person of the debtor. If the question regard the distribution of the creditor's estate, the law of his domicil is to be observed. If the question is, in what degree or proportion the representatives of the debtor should be charged with payment from his effects, then it is of a passive nature, and the law of the domicil of the debtor should be followed. Dwarris on Statut. 650. It would be difficult to point out, in the English law, any authority in support of this doctrine. See also Dumoulin's and Casaregis's opinions in Livermore's Diss. 162, 163.

2 Cod. Lib. 3, tit. 13, l. 2.

lifetime, that upon his death, in a conflict of the rights and privileges of creditors (*concursus creditorum*) of different countries, the municipal law of the country of the debtor, should overrule the jurisprudence of the *situs* of the effects.

§ 527. This, however, is affirmed to be the doctrine of Coquille, Mevius, Carpzovius, Burgundus, Rodemburg, and Gail.[1] But it is manifest, from the language used by them, that it is a matter of no small difficulty; and a diversity of laws and opinions may well be presumed to exist in regard to it. Boullenois holds the same doctrine;[2] and Hertius affirms it, saying, *Ad jura igitur domicilii debitoris, ubi fit concursus creditorum et quo omnes cujusquoque generis lites adversus illum debitorem propter connexitatem causæ trahuntur, regulariter respiciendum erit.*[3] Yet he seems to admit, that cases may exist, where undue preferences, given by the local laws of one state in favour of its own subjects, may be met with a just retaliation by others.[4] He cites a passage from Huberus, which would seem to show, that the latter was of a different opinion. A creditor (says he) upon a bill of exchange, exercising his right in a reasonable time, has a preference in Holland to all other creditors upon the moveable property of his debtor. He has property of the like kind in Friezeland, where no such law exists. Will such a creditor be there preferred to other

1 Livermore's Diss. p. 166 to 171; Rodemburg, De Div. Stat. tit. 2, ch. 5, § 16, p. 47; 1 Boullenois, 684, &c.; Id. 818, &c. 832, 833, 834; Bouhier, Cout. de Bourg. ch. 21, § 204, ch. 22, § 151.—Not having access to the particular works, in which these authors maintain this doctrine (except that of Rodemburg), I must rely on Mr. Livermore for the correctness of this statement of their opinions.

2 1 Boullenois, 818, 834.

3 1 Hertii Opera, De Collis. Leg. § 4, n. 64, p. 150.

4 Id.

creditors? By no means, since those creditors, by the laws there received, have already acquired a right. *Creditor ex causâ cambii, jus suum in tempore exercens, præfertur apud Batavos omnibus aliis debitoribus [creditoribus?] in bona mobilia debitoris. Hic habet ejusmodi res in Friziâ, ubi hoc jus non obtinet. An ibi creditor etiam præferetur aliis creditoribus? Nullo modo; quoniam heic creditoribus vi legum hic receptarum jus quidem quæsitum est.*[1]

§ 528. In the course of administrations, also, in different countries, questions often arise, as to particular debts, whether they are properly and ultimately payable out of the personal estate, or are chargeable upon the real estate of the deceased; and in all such cases, the law of the domicil of the deceased will govern in cases of intestacy; and, in cases of testacy, the intention of the testator. A case, illustrating this doctrine, occurred in England many years ago. A testator, who lived in Holland, and was seised of real estate there, and of considerable personal estate in England, devised all his real estate to one person, and all his personal estate to another, whom he made his executor. At the time of his death, he owed some debts by specialty, and some by simple contract in Holland, and had no assets there to satisfy those debts; but his real estate was by the laws of Holland made liable for the payment of simple contract, as well as specialty debts, if there were not personal assets to answer the same. The creditors in Holland sued the devisee, and obtained a decree for the sale of the lands devised for the payment of their debts. And then the devisee brought a suit in England against the

---

[1] I quote the passage as I find it in Hertius, not having found the original reference. Should not *debitoribus* be *creditoribus*?

executor (the legatee of the personalty) for reimbursement out of the personal estate. The Court decided in his favour, upon the ground, that in Holland, as in England, the personal estate was the primary fund for the payment of debts, and should come in aid of the real estate, and be charged in the first place.[1]

§ 529. In the Scottish law a very different principle prevails; for there, heritable bonds are primarily payable out of the real estate; and, as we have seen, the personal estate of a person domiciled, and dying in England, is held exonerated from the charge of a heritable bond, made by him upon real estate in Scotland, to secure a debt contracted in England; and the Scottish estate must bear the burthen.[2]

---

1 Anonymous, 9 Mod. R. 66; S. P. Bowaman *v.* Reeve, Preced. Ch. 511.

2 Ante, § 486, 487, 488; Drummond *v.* Drummond, 6 Brown, Parl. Cases, 550, (edit. 1803); S. C. cited 2 Ves. & Beames, 131.

CHAPTER XIV.

JURISDICTION AND REMEDIES.

§ 530. We are next led to the consideration of the subject of remedies. And, in the nature of things, these may well be classed into three sorts; first, those, which purely regard property, moveable and immoveable; secondly, those, which purely regard persons; and, thirdly, those, which regard both persons and property. The Roman jurisprudence took notice of this distinction, and accordingly divided all remedies, as to their subject, into three kinds; (1) Real actions, otherwise called vindications, which were those, in which a man demanded something, that was his own, and were founded on dominion, or *jus in re;* (2) Personal actions, denominated also conditions, which were those, in which a man demanded, what was barely due to him, and were founded on obligation, or *jus ad rem;* (3) Mixed actions, which were those, in which some specific thing was demanded, and where also some personal obligations were claimed to be performed.[1] The real actions of the Roman law, were not like the real actions of the common law, confined to real estate; but included personal, as well as real property. But the distinction, as to classes of remedies and actions, equally pervades the common law, as it does the civil law. Thus, we have real actions, personal actions, and mixed actions, the first embracing

---

1 Halifax on Roman Law, B. 3, ch. 1, § 4, 5, p. 85, 86; 1 Brown, Civil Law, 439, 440. — In Pothier's work on the Customs of Orléans, there will be found a correspondent division of actions into the same classes. Pothier, Coutumes d'Orléans, Introd. Gén. ch. 4, art. 109 to 122.

those, which concern real estate, where the proceeding is purely *in rem;* the next, embracing all suits *in personam* for contracts and torts; and the last, those mixed suits, where the person is liable by reason of, and in connexion with, property.[1]

§ 531. In considering the nature of actions, we are necessarily led to the consideration of the proper tribunal, in which they should be brought; or, in other words, what tribunal is competent to entertain them in point of jurisdiction. And, here, the subject naturally divides itself into the consideration of the matter of jurisdiction, in regard to the mere municipal and domestic administration of justice; and into the matter of jurisdiction *inter gentes*, upon principles of public law.

§ 532. In the Roman jurisprudence, and among nations, who have derived their jurisprudence from the civil law, many embarrassing questions, as to jurisdiction, seem to have arisen.[2] The general rule of the Roman Code is, that the plaintiff must bring his suit or action in the place, where the defendant has his domicil, or had it at the time of the contract. *Juris ordinem* (said the Emperor Diocletian) *converti postulas; ut non actor rei forum, sed reus actoris sequitur. Nam, ubi domicilium reus habet, vel tempore contractûs habuit, licet hoc postea transtulerit, ibi tantum eum conveniri oportet.*[3] But it is not to be understood, that the rule extended to all cases, where the party defendant is found, without any regard to the situation of the thing sought, as if the ob-

---

[1] 3 Black. Comm. 294; Comyn's Dig. Action, N.

[2] See 1 Voet. ad Pand. Lib. 5, tit. 1, § 303; Id. § 64, 66, 74, 91, 92; Huberus, Lib. 5, tit. 1, De Foro Compet.; Strykius, Tom. 6, 11, 1, 8, Tom. 7, 1, p. 5; 1 Boullenois, 601, 618, 619, 635.

[3] Cod. Lib. 3, tit. 13, l. 2.

ject was to show more favour to the party defendant, than to the plaintiff; but solely, that the adjudication may be, where it can be enforced. Thus, we find the doctrine laid down in the Code, that, although the general rule is, that the plaintiff must bring his suit in the domicil of the defendant; yet this was dispensed with in certain suits *in rem*, which were to be brought in the place *rei sitæ*. *Actor rei forum, sive in rem, sive in personam sit actio, sequitur. Sed et in locis, in quibus res, propter quas contenditur, constitutæ sunt, jubemus in rem actionem adversus possidentem moveri.*[1]

§ 533. Huberus thus explains the doctrine; *Cujus ratio non tam est, quod reus sit actore favorabilior, etsi verissima; sed quod necessitatis vocandi et cogendi alium ad jus æquum, non nisi a superiore proficisci queat; superior autem cujusque non est alienus, sed proprius rector. Vocandi, inquam, et cogendi; quandoquidem sine coactione judicia forent elusoria; nec alibi forum lege stabilitur, quam ubi illa cogendi facultas adhiberi potest; non tamen ut ubicunque illa valet sit forum, sed ubi res et æquitas patitur.*[2] And, hence he thinks, that the rule of the civil law *rei sitæ* applies, not only to immoveables, but to moveables, although many jurists confine it to the former.[3] *Sed heic aliam potius rationem sequimur, quod in foro stabiliendo maxime consideretur, an in promptu*

---

1 Cod. Lib. 3, tit. 19, l. 3.

2 Huberus, Lib. 5, tit. 1; De Foro Compet. § 38, p. 722. See also 1 Boullenois, 618, 619.

3 The subject is a good deal controverted among the civilians; but the present work does not require me to engage in the task of discussing the various opinions, which are held by them. The learned reader will find many of them referred to in J. Voet. ad Pandect. Lib. 5, tit. 1, § 77, &c. p. 337.

sit effectum dare citationi in cogendis partibus ad obsequium jurisdictionis; quæ facultas æque locum habet in mobilibus, ubi detinentur, quam in immobilibus, ubi sitæ sunt.[1]

§ 534. But he admits, that, as the *forum domicilii* was of universal operation, actions *in rem* might be brought in the *forum domicilii*, as well as in the *forum rei sitæ*. . *Videlicet hoc semper tenendum, domicilii forum esse generale, quod in cunctis actionibus, adeoque etiam in actionibus in rem, obtinere, sciendum est ut de dd. legibus constat.*[2] Again he says; *Summa igitur hæc esto. Domicilium in omnibus rebus et actionibus præbet forum. Res sita preterea in actionibus in rem singularibus, non excluso domicilio.*[3] And he supposes the same rule to apply in modern times in the civil law countries. *Hæc ego de foro domicilii, reique sitæ alterne conjuncto, moribus hodiernis eodem modo putem obtinere, quemadmodum jure Cæsaris præscriptum est; ut maxime in rem agatur, ubi res sita est; possit tamen omnino etiam, ubi reus habitat.*[4]

§ 535. In regard to mixed actions, although there is no text of the Roman law directly in point, he thinks, that they may be brought, either in the place of domicil of the defendant, or of the *rei sitæ*. *De mixtis actionibus, exceptâ hæreditatis petitione, quæ partim in rem, partim in personam esse dicuntur, non sunt textus speciales ubi sunt instituendæ. Ideoque id ex earum proprietate colligunt interpretes, cum partim imitantur naturam personalium, partim, in rem actiones, illas et apud domicilium et apud rem sitam esse moven-*

---

1 Huberus, Lib. 5, tit. 1, § 48. 2 Id. § 49. 3 Id. § 50.
4 Id. § 50.

das, &c. Proinde sic est statuendum. Posse quidem illas actiones utroque loco, domicilii, sitûsque moveri; verum, si faciendæ sunt adjudicationes manuque divisio regenda sit, partes ad judicem loci remittendas esse, res ipsa loquitur.[1]

§ 536. The civil law contemplated another place of jurisdiction, the place, where a contract was made, or to be fulfilled, or where any other act was done, if the defendant or his property could be found there, although it was not the place of his domicil. *Illud sciendum est, eum, qui ita fuit obligatus, ut in Italiâ solveret, si in provinciâ habuit domicilium utrobique posse conveniri, et hic, et ibi.*[2] Huberus explains this thus. *Sequitur causa fori tertia, quam rem gestam esse diximus, eamque vel e contractu vel ex delicto admisso, &c. Sed contractus ita forum tribuit, si contrahens in eodem loco reperiatur; quod convenit requisito communi inde ab initio collocato nullam esse fori causam, nisi cum facultate cogendi conjunctam; qualis non est ex historiâ contractûs, si vel reus ibi non inveniatur, vel bona duntaxat sita non habeat, in quæ missio fieri possit, quando reus se in loco contractûs non sistit.*[3] These distinctions of the Roman law have found their way into the jurisprudence of all the continental nations of modern Europe.

§ 537. Accordingly we find it laid down by foreign jurists generally, that there are, properly speaking, three places of jurisdiction; first, the place of domicil of the party defendant, commonly called the *forum domicilii;* secondly, the place, where the thing in con-

---

1 Huberus, Lib. 5. tit. 1, § 51.

2 Dig. Lib. 5, tit. 1, l. 19, § 1, 4. See also as to all these distinctions, Pothier, Pand. Lib. 5, tit. 1, art. 29 to 44; Cod. Lib. 3, tit. 18, l. 1.

3 Huberus, Lib. 5, tit. 1, § 53, 54.

troversy is situate, commonly called the *forum rei sitæ;* and thirdly, the place, where the contract is made, or other act done, commonly called *forum rei gestæ,* or *forum contractûs. Vis illa compellandi partes ad æquum jus* (says Huberus) *imprimis est in loco domicilii; est etiam in loco rei sitæ; et rei gestæ, si reus illic haberi posse; alias secus.* The same distinctions are fully laid down by Huberus, Voet, and Boullenois, to whom we may generally refer for more copious information.[1] They are also recognised in the Scottish law.[2] They have been brought into view, because they constitute the basis of the reasoning of many foreign jurists, in discussing the great doctrines respecting the competent tribunals to hold jurisdiction of causes; and the proper operation of judgments and decrees *(rei judicatæ.)* And they are known, as fundamental elements, in the actual jurisprudence of many of the nations of continental Europe.[3]

---

1 Huberus, Lib. 5, tit. 1, De Foro Compet; Voet. ad Pand. Lib. 5, tit. 1, De Judiciis, p. 303, § 64 to 149; 1 Boullenois, Observ. 25, p. 601; Id. 618, 619; Id. 635; Henry on Foreign Law, ch. 8, p. 54, ch. 9, p. 63.

2 Erskine, Inst. B. 1, tit. 2, § 16 to 22, p. 29 to 39.

3 See Code de Procédure Civile of France, B. 1, tit. 1, art. 1 to 4; Henry on Foreign Law, ch. 8, p. 54, ch. 9, p. 63, ch. 10, p. 71; Pardessus, Droit Comm. Tom. 5, art. 1353; 1 Boullenois, 601, 618, 619; Id. 635.—In France, jurisdiction would seem generally to belong either to the place of domicil, or to the place *rei sitæ.* Jurisdiction in the place of the contract, or other act done, does not seem to have been recognised under the old jurisprudence, and it does not exist in the modern Code.* "Le lieu (says Boullenois), où se passent les actes, celui où les parties s'obligent de payer, et leur soumission, ne déterminent pas la justice où elles doivent plaider." † Dumoulin says, "Cæterum ex eo solo, quod quis promisit solvere certo loco, licet ibi conveniri possit de jure sicut ibi contraxisset; tamen hoc non observatur in hoc regno; non sortitur quis forum ratione contractûs, etiam vere et realiter facti in loco." ‡

* Code de Procédure Civile, art. 1, 2.

† 1 Boullenois, 829, 830, 831, 832; 2 Boullenois, 455, 456, 457.

‡ Id. See also Pothier, Traité de la Procédure Civile, ch. 1.

§ 538. In the corresponding distribution of actions by the common law into personal actions, real actions, and mixed actions,[1] the two latter are, in point of jurisdiction, confined to the place *rei sitæ;* and the former are generally capable of being brought, wherever the party can be found. Or, as the judicial phrase is, in the common law, real and mixed actions are *local;* and personal actions are *transitory.*[2]

§ 539. Considered in an international point of view, jurisdiction, to be rightfully exercised, must be founded either upon the person being within the territory, or the thing being within the territory; for, otherwise, there can be no sovereignty exerted, upon the known maxim, *Extra territorium jus dicenti impune non paretur.*[3] Boullenois puts this among his general principles. The laws of a sovereign rightfully extend over persons, who are domiciled within his territory, and over property, which is there situate.[4] Vattel lays down the true doctrine, in clear terms. "The sovereignty, (says he,) united to the domain, establishes the jurisdiction of the nation in its territories, or the country, which belongs to it. It is its province, or that of its sovereign, to exercise justice in all places under its jurisdiction, to take cognizance of the crimes committed, and the differences that arise, in the country."[5] On the other hand, no sovereignty can extend its process beyond its own territorial limits, to subject either persons or property to its judicial decisions. Every exertion of authority of this sort, beyond this limit, is a

---

1 3 Black. Comm. 117, 118.

2 3 Black. Comm. 294; Com. Dig. Action, N; 1 Chitty, Comm. & Manuf. 647, 648, 649.

3 Dig. Lib. 2, tit. 1, l. 20.

4 1 Boullenois, Pr. Gén. 1, 2, p. 2, 3.

5 Vattel, B. 2, ch. 8, § 84.

mere nullity, and incapable of binding such persons or property in any other tribunals.[1] This subject, however, deserves a more exact consideration.

§ 540. In the first place, let us consider the subject of jurisdiction, a little more particularly, in regard to persons. These may be, either citizens (native or naturalized), or foreigners. In regard to the former, while within the territory of their birth, or adopted allegiance, the jurisdiction of the sovereignty over them is complete and irresistible. It cannot be controlled; and it ought to be respected everywhere. But as to citizens of a country, domiciled abroad, the extent of jurisdiction, which may be lawfully exercised over them *in personam*, is not so clear upon acknowledged principles. It is true, that nations generally assert a claim to regulate the rights, duties, obligations, and acts of their own citizens, wherever they may be domiciled. And, so far as these rights, duties, obligations, and acts afterwards come under the cognizance of the tribunals of the sovereign power of their own country, either for enforcement, or for protection, or for remedy, there may be no just ground to exclude this claim. But when such rights, duties, obligations, and acts, come under the consideration of other countries, and especially of the country, where such citizens are domiciled, the duty of recognising and enforcing such claim of sovereignty, is neither clear, nor generally admitted. The most, that can be said, is, that it may be admitted *ex comitate gentium*; but it may also be denied *ex justitiá gentium*, wherever it is deemed injurious to the interests of foreign nations, or subversive of their policy or institutions.

---

1 Picquet *v.* Swan, 5 Mason R. 35, 42.

No one, for instance, could imagine, that a judgment of the parent country, confiscating the property, or extinguishing the personal rights or capacities of a native, on account of such foreign residence, would be recognised in any other country. And, it could be as little expected, as a matter of right, that any other country would enforce a judgment against such persons in the parent country, obtained *in invitum*, on account of a supposed contumacy in remaining abroad, to which he had never appeared, and of which he had received no notice; however it might be in conformity to the local laws. This is the result deducible from the axioms of Huberus already quoted; and, especially, from the first and second of those axioms.[1] Whatever authority should be given to such judgments, must be purely *ex comitate*.

§ 541. In regard to foreigners, resident in a country, although some jurists deny the right of a nation generally to legislate over them, it would seem clear, upon general principles of international law, that such a right does exist; and the extent, to which it should be exercised, is a matter purely of municipal arrangement and policy. Huberus lays down the doctrine in his second axiom. All persons, who are found within the limits of a government, whether their residence is permanent or temporary, are to be deemed subjects thereof.[2] Boullenois says, that the sovereign has a right to make laws to bind foreigners, in relation to their property within his domains; in relation to contracts, and acts done therein; and, in relation to judicial proceedings, if they implead before his tribu-

---

1 Ante § 29.

2 Id.; Huberus, Lib. 1, tit. 3, § 2; Henry on Foreign Law, ch. 8, p. 54, ch. 9, p. 63, ch. 10, p. 71.

nals.[1] And, further, that he may, of strict right, make them for all foreigners, who merely pass through his domains, though commonly this authority is exercised only as to matters of police.[2] Vattel asserts the same general doctrine, and says, that foreigners are subject to the laws of a state, while they reside in it.[3] And, in relation to disputes, which may arise between foreigners, or between a citizen and a foreigner, he holds, that they are to be determined by the judge of the place, and, according to the laws of the place of the defendant's domicil.[4]

§ 542. There are nations, indeed, which wholly refuse to take cognizance of controversies between foreigners, and remit them for relief to their own domestic tribunals, or to that of the party defendant; and, especially, as to matters originating in foreign countries. Thus, in France, with few exceptions, the tribunals do not entertain jurisdiction of controversies between foreigners respecting personal rights and interests.[5] But this is a matter of mere municipal policy and convenience, and does not result from any principles of international law. In England, and America, on the other hand, suits are maintainable, and are constantly maintained between foreigners, where either of them is within the territory of the state, in which the suit is brought.

§ 543. But, though every nation may thus rightfully exercise jurisdiction over all persons within its domains; yet, we are to understand, that, in regard to

---

1 Boullenois, Pr. Gén. 4, 5, p. 3.

2 Id. 5, p. 3.

3 Vattel, B. 1. ch. 19, § 213; Id. B. 2, ch. 8, § 99, 101, 103.

4 Id. B. 2, ch. 8, § 103.

5 See Pardessus, Droit Comm. Tom. 5, art. 1476 to 1478, p. 238; Henry on Foreign Law, Appendix, 214 to 216.

suits, the doctrine applies to suits purely personal, or connected with property within the same sovereignty. For, although the person may be within the jurisdiction; yet, it is by no means true, that, in virtue thereof, every sort of suit may be maintainable against him. A suit cannot, for instance, be maintainable against him, so as absolutely to bind property situate elsewhere; and *a fortiori* not absolutely to bind the rights and titles to immoveable property. It is true, that some nations do, in maintaining suits *in personam*, attempt, indirectly, to bind property situate in other countries; but it is always with the reserve, that it binds the person in their own courts in regard to such property. And, certainly, there can be no pretence, that it binds the property itself, or the rights over it, established by the local laws, where it is situate. If a Court of Chancery, in England, should compel a bankrupt by decree, to convey his personal and real estate, situate in foreign countries, to the assignees under the commission, (as it was at one time thought they might, though now the doctrine is repudiated,)[1] such a decree would not operate to transfer the property, so as to affect the rights of creditors, or the regular operation of the laws of the state *rei sitæ*.

§ 544. The doctrine of the English Courts of Chancery, on this head of jurisdiction, seems carried to an extent, which may, in some cases, perhaps, not find a perfect warrant in the general principles of public law; and, therefore, as to its recognition in foreign countries, it must have a very uncertain basis, even as founded in the comity of nations.

---

[1] *Ex parte* Blades, 1 Cox R. 398; Selkrig *v.* Davies, 2 Rose, Bank. Cases, 97; Id. 291; S. C. 2 Dow R. 231.

That doctrine is, that the Court of Chancery, having authority *agere in personam*, may act indirectly upon real estate, situate in a foreign country, through the instrumentality of this authority over the person; and, it may compel him to give effect to its decrees respecting such property, whether they go to the entire disposition of it, or only to affect it with burthens.[1] Lord Hardwicke asserted the jurisdiction in several cases,[2] and, especially in Penn *v.* Lord Baltimore, (1 Ves. 444.) In Cranstown *v.* Johnston, (3 Ves. 170; 5 Ves. 276; S. C.) the Court asserted the jurisdiction over a British creditor, who had fraudulently obtained a judgment, in the British West Indies, against his debtor, and had, on an execution, sold his debtor's real estate there, and become the purchaser thereof, and set aside the purchase for the fraud. It is observable, that, here, all the parties were British subjects, and the original judgment was in a British Island. Lord Kenyon, the Master of the Rolls, on that occasion said; "Upon the whole, it comes to this; that by a proceeding in the island, an absentee's estate might be brought to sale, and for whatever interest he has, without any particular, upon which they are to bid; the question is, whether any court will permit the transaction to avail to that extent. It is said, this Court has no jurisdiction, because it is a proceeding in the West Indies. It has been argued, very sensibly, that it is strange for this Court to say, it is void by the laws of the island, or for want of notice. I admit, I am bound to say, that, according to those laws, a creditor may do this. To that law he has had recourse,

---

1 See 1 Eq. Abrid., C. p. 133; Arglasse *v.* Muschamp, 1 Vern. R. 75, 135; Kildare *v.* Eustace, 1 Vern. 419.

2 See Foster *v.* Vassall, 3 Atk. 589.

and wishes to avail himself of it; the question is, whether an English Court will permit such an use to be made of the law of that island, or any other country. It is sold, not to satisfy the debt, but in order to get the estate, which the law of that country never could intend, for a price much inadequate to the real value; and to pay himself more than the debt, for which the suit was commenced, and for which only the sale could be holden. It was not much litigated, that the Courts of equity here have an equal right to interfere with regard to judgments or mortgages upon the lands in a foreign country, as upon lands here. Bills are often filed upon mortgages in the West Indies. The only distinction is, that this Court cannot act upon the land directly, but acts upon the conscience of the person living here. Archer *v.* Preston, Lord Arglasse *v.* Muschamp, Lord Kildare *v.* Eustace, 1 Eq. Abr. 133; 1 Vern. 75, 135, 419. Those cases clearly show, that with regard to any contract made, or equity between persons in this country, respecting lands in a foreign country, particularly in the British dominions, this Court will hold the same jurisdiction, as if they were situated in England. Lord Hardwicke lays down the same doctrine, 3 Atk. 589. Therefore, without affecting the jurisdiction of the Courts there, or questioning the regularity of the proceedings, as in a court of law, or saying, that this sale would have been set aside either in law or equity there, I have no difficulty in saying, which is all I have to say, that this creditor has availed himself of the advantage he got by the nature of those laws, to proceed behind the back of the debtor upon a constructive notice, which could not operate to the only point, to which a constructive notice ought, that there might be actual notice without wilful default; that he has gained an advantage, which neither the law of this, nor of any other country would permit. I will lay down the rule as broad as this; this Court will not permit him to avail himself of the law of any other country to do what would be gross injustice."

§ 545. To the extent of this decision, there does not seem any well-founded objection;[1] and the same doctrine has been repeatedly acted upon by the equity courts of America.[2] But even in England, the Court of Chancery will not act directly upon lands in the plantations, so as to affect the title, or possession, or rents and profits.[3] Nor will it entertain jurisdiction over contracts with regard to lands in foreign colonies, so as to touch the title there; or, to prevent a sale thereof by an injunction;[4] though it has been repeatedly held, in very general terms, that there is no doubt of the jurisdiction of the Court of Chancery, as to land in the West Indies or other foreign places, if the persons are in England.[5]

§ 546. But it is not an uncommon course for a nation, by its municipal code, to provide for the institution of actions against non-resident citizens, and foreigners, by citations *viis et modis* (as it is called), or by attachment of their property, nominal or real, within the limits of their territorial sovereignty; and to proceed to judgment against the party defendant, whether he ever appears to the suit, or not. In respect

---

1 S. P. Jackson *v.* Petrie, 10 Ves. 164.

2 See Massie *v.* Watts, 6 Cranch 148, 158; Ward *v.* Amedon, Hopkins R. 213.

3 Roberdeau *v.* Rous, 1 Atk. 543. See 1 Vern. R. 75, 135, 419.

4 White *v.* Hall, 12 Ves. Jr. 321.

5 Jackson *v.* Petrie, 10 Ves. 165.

to such suits *in personam*, by mere personal citations, *viis et modis*, such as by posting them up on the Royal Exchange, in London, as is done in the Admiralty in England, or by an edictal citation (as it is called), posted up at the Key in Leith, at the market cross of Edinburgh, and the pier and shore of Leith, according to the practice of Scotland,[1] there is no pretence to say, that such modes of proceeding can confer any legitimate jurisdiction over foreigners, who are non-residents, and do not appear, whether they have notice of the suit or not. The effects of all such proceedings are purely local; and, elsewhere, they will be held as nullities.

§ 547. Lord Ellenborough has put this doctrine with great clearness and force, in a recent case, where a judgment was obtained in the Island of Tobago, against a party, stated in the proceedings, to be "formerly of the City of Dunkirk, and now of the City of London, merchant," and who was cited to appear at the ensuing court, to answer the plaintiff's action, by a summons, which was returned served "by nailing up a copy of the declaration at the Court House door," and on which service, judgment was afterwards given by default of the defendant to appear and defend it. It was attempted to maintain the judgment, as authorized by the local law, in cases of persons absent from

---

1 Ersk. Instit. B. 1, tit. 2, § 17, 18; Id. B. 4, tit. 1, § 8. — After a decree is obtained *in personam*, in Scotland, it seems, that letters of *horning*, as they are called, issue, requiring the defendant to comply with the decree, which may be served by personal service, or, if the party cannot be found, by application at his place of domicil, or dwelling-house; and, if he is out of the kingdom, then he is charged by a copy put up at the market cross in Edinburgh, and at the pier and shore of Leith. Ersk. Inst. B. 2, tit. 5, § 55; Id. B. 4, tit. 3, § 9. See Douglas *v.* Forrest, 4 Bing. R. 686, 690.

the island. Lord Ellenborough, in delivering the judgment of the Court, said, "By persons absent from the island, must necessarily be understood persons, who have been present, and within the jurisdiction, so as to have been subject to the process of the Court; but it can never be applied to a person, who, for aught appears, never was present within, or subject to the jurisdiction. Supposing, however, that the act had said in terms, that though a person sued in the island, had never been present within the jurisdiction, yet, that it should bind him upon proof of nailing up the summons at the court door; how could that be obligatory upon the subjects of other countries? Can the Island of Tobago pass a law to bind the rights of the whole world? Would the world submit to such an assumed jurisdiction? The law itself, however fairly construed, does not warrant such an inference; for 'absent from the island' must be taken only to apply to persons, who had been present there, and were subject to the jurisdiction of the Court, out of which the process issued; and, as nothing of that sort was in proof here to show, that the defendant was subject to the jurisdiction at the time of commencing the suit, there is no foundation for raising an assumpsit in law upon the judgment so obtained."[1] This doctrine has been fully recognised in the American courts.[2]

§ 548. In a recent case, the validity of judgments rendered against persons, who were non-residents, and

---

1 Buchanan v. Rucker, 9 East. 192, 194. See Cranston v. Johnston, 3 Ves. 170; S. C. 5 Ves. 276; Cavan v. Stewart, 1 Starkie R. 525; Becquet v. MacCarthy, 2 Barn. & Adolph. 951.

2 Tenton v. Garlick, 8 John. R. 194; Borden v. Fitch, 15 John. R. 121; Bissell v. Briggs, 9 Mass. R. 462; Mills v. Durgee, 7 Cranch 481, 486; Picquet v. Swan, 5 Mason R. 35, 43, 44; Buttrick v. Allen, 8 Mass. R. 473.

had no actual notice of the suit, and did not appear and answer the same, came before the Court of Common Pleas in England, upon a Scottish judgment rendered against a Scottish absentee, upon due attachment of his heritable property in Scotland, and due proclamation by what is technically called *horning*, in Scotland, and a judgment by default for non-appearance. The question was, whether a judgment so rendered was void, or not. It was held, that the judgment was valid. This was, partly, the result of the articles of union between Scotland and England, and partly of the recognition of such practice, as valid, by a British Act of Parliament; and partly of the fact, that the judgment was against a Scottish subject. On that occasion, Lord Chief Justice Best, in delivering the opinion of the Court said, "A natural born subject of any country, quitting that country, but leaving property under the protection of its laws, even during his absence, owes obedience to those laws, particularly when those laws enforce a moral obligation. The deceased, before he left his native country, acknowledged, under his hand, that he owed the debts; he was under a moral obligation to discharge those debts, as soon as he could." And after adverting to the case of Buchanan *v.* Rucker, and some others, he added, "To be sure, if attachments issued against any persons, who were never within the jurisdiction of the court issuing them, would be supported and confirmed in the country, in which the person attached resided, the legislature of any country might authorize their courts to decide on the rights of parties, who owed no allegiance to the government of such country, and were under no obligation to attend its courts, or obey its laws. We confine our judgment to a case, where the party owed allegiance to the country, in which the judgment was so given against him, from being born in it; and, by the laws of which country, his property was, at the time those judgments were given, protected. The debts were contracted in the country, in which the judgments were given, whilst the debtor resided in it." [1]

§ 549. A still more common course, in many states and nations, is, to proceed against non-residents, whether they are citizens or foreigners, by an arrest, or attachment of their property within the territory. Sometimes the arrest or attachment is purely nominal, as of a chip or cane, or both. In other cases the arrest or attachment is *bonâ fide* of real or personal property within the territory, or of debts in the hands of debtors of the non-resident, who live within the country.[2] In such cases, for all the purposes of the suit, the existence of such property, within the territory, constitutes a just ground of proceeding, to enforce the rights of the plaintiff, to the extent of subjecting such property to execution upon the decree or judgment. But it is to be treated to all intents and purposes, if the defendant has never appeared and contested the suit, as a mere proceeding *in rem*, and not personally binding on the party as a decree or judgment *in personam*. In other countries, it is uniformly so treated, and considered, as having no extra-territorial force or obligation.[3]

---

1 Douglas *v.* Forrest, 4 Bing. R 686, 702, 703. See also Becquet *v.* MacCarthy, 2 Barn. & Adolph. R. 951.

2 See Henry on Foreign Law, ch. 8, ch. 9, ch. 10, p. 54, 63, 71; Douglas *v.* Forrest, 4 Bing. R. 686, 700, 701.

3 See Phelps *v.* Holker, 1 Dall. 261; Kilburn *v.* Woodworth, 5 John. R. 37; Pawling *v.* Bird's Ex'ors, 13 John. R. 192; Bissell *v.* Briggs, 9 Mass. R. 462; Robinson *v.* Ex'ors of Ward, 8 John. R. 86. But see

§ 550. In the next place, let us consider the subject of jurisdiction, in regard to property. It will be unnecessary to discuss the matter at large, as to personal property, since the general doctrine is not controverted, that, though moveables are, for many purposes, to be deemed to have no *situs*, except that of the domicil of the owner; yet, this being but a legal fiction, it yields, whenever it is necessary for the purposes of justice, that the actual *situs* of the thing should be examined. A nation, within whose territory

Douglas *v.* Forrest, 4 Bing. R. 686, 702, 703; Shumway *v.* Stillman, 6 Wendell R. 447; 1 Boullenois, 609, 610, 619, 620, 622, 623, 624, 628; 6 Harri. & John. R. 191; Taylor *v.* Phelps, 1 Gill & John. R. 492.— Mr. Chief Justice Parsons, in his very able opinion, in Bissell *v.* Briggs (9 Mass. R. 468), has made some pointed remarks on this subject, from which the following extract is made. "To illustrate this position, it may be remarked, that a debtor, living in Massachusetts, may have goods, effects, or credits, in New Hampshire, where the creditor lives. The creditor there may lawfully attach these, pursuant to the laws of that state, in the hands of the bailiff, factor, trustee, or garnishee of his debtor; and, on recovering judgment, those goods, effects, and credits, may lawfully be applied to satisfy the judgment; and the bailiff, factor, trustee, or garnishee, if sued in this state for those goods, effects, or credits, shall, in our courts, be protected by that judgment, the Court in New Hampshire having jurisdiction of the cause for the purpose of rendering that judgment, and the bailiff, factor, trustee, or garnishee producing it, not to obtain execution of it here, but for his own justification. If, however, those goods, effects, and credits are insufficient to satisfy the judgment, and the creditor should sue an action on that judgment in this state to obtain satisfaction, he must fail; because the defendant was not personally amenable to the jurisdiction of the Court rendering the judgment. And, if the defendant, after the service of the process of foreign attachment, should either in person have gone into the state of New Hampshire, or constituted an attorney, to defend the suit, so as to protect his goods, effects, or credits from the effect of the attachment, he would not thereby have given the Court jurisdiction of his person; since this jurisdiction must result from the service of the foreign attachment. It would be unreasonable to oblige any man living in one state, and having effects in another state, to make himself amenable to the courts of the last state, that he might defend his property there attached."

personal property is actually situate, has as entire dominion over it, while there, in point of sovereignty and jurisdiction, as it has over immoveable property. It may regulate its transfer, subject it to process and execution, and provide for, and control the uses and disposition of it, to the same extent, that it may exert its authority over immoveable property. One of the grounds, upon which, as we have seen, jurisdiction is assumed over non-residents, is, through the instrumentality of their personal property, as well as of their real property, within the local sovereignty. And hence it is, that, whenever personal property is taken by arrest, attachment, or execution within a state, the title so acquired under the laws of the state is held valid in every other state;[1] and the same rule is applied to debts due to non-residents, which are subjected to the like process under the local laws of a state.[2]

§ 551. In respect to immoveable property, every attempt of a foreign tribunal to found a jurisdiction over it, must, from the very nature of the case, be utterly nugatory, and its decree must be for ever incapable of execution *in rem.* We have seen, indeed, that by the Roman law a suit might in many cases be brought, either where the property was situate, or where the party had his domicil. This might well be done within any of the vast domains over which the Roman

---

1 Lord Kenyon expressed his opinion to the following effect, in Ogden *v.* Folliott, (3 T. R. 733). "I have always understood it to be clear (said he), that all judicial acts, done in one country, over the property of the subjects within their jurisdiction, are conclusive on the property of those parties in any other country."

2 See Bissell *v.* Briggs, 9 Mass. R. 462, 468, 469. But see Folliott *v.* Ogden, 1 H. Black. R. 123, 135; S. C. 3 T. R. 726, 733.

empire extended; for the judgments of its tribunals would be everywhere respected and obeyed. But among the independent nations of modern times, there would be insuperable difficulties in such a course. And hence, even in countries acknowledging the civil law, it has become a very general principle, that suits *in rem* should be brought, where the property is situate; and this principle is applied with almost universal approbation in regard to immoveable property. The same rule is applied to mixed actions, and to all suits, which touch the realty. [1]

§ 552. Boullenois has treated this whole subject with becoming fullness and accuracy. He has divided actions into those, which are purely personal, those purely real, and those, which are mixed and partake of the character of both, following, in these respects, as he avows, the division of Burgundus. The first pronounce sentence solely in regard to persons *ad dandum vel faciendum aut non faciendum;* the next in regard to things, their ownership, possessions, liens, or titles; the last in regard to persons and things, adjudging upon the title to property or the profits thereof, and also as to damages *in personam.*[2] Personal actions may rightfully be brought between natives in any competent tribunal of the realm; between foreigners also, who have submitted to the jurisdiction, wherever the laws allow its exercise; and between natives and foreigners in like manner.[3] But in all these cases the

1 Henry on Foreign Laws, ch. 8, § 3, p. 59, ch. 9, § 1, p. 63; 1 Boullenois, Observ. 25, p. 601, &c.; Id. 618, 619; Id. 635, &c.; Id. 819.

2 Boullenois, 601, 602.

3 Boullenois makes a distinction in suits between natives and foreigners to this effect. If a foreigner sues a native, then the jurisdiction is well founded against the latter in the place of his domicil; and the for-

domicil of the party defendant is commonly supposed to be within the jurisdiction.[1] Real actions ought to be brought in the place *rei sitæ;* and this is to be, not only, when the property in controversy is situate in the same kingdom; but also when the parties, being domiciled in one country, engage in a litigation, as to property locally situate in another country.[2] If, therefore, a judgment should be rendered in one country respecting property in another, it will be of no force in the latter. It is true, that property within a country does not make the owner generally a subject of the sovereign, where it is locally situate; but it subjects him to his jurisdiction *secundum quid, et aliquo modo.*[3] Mixed actions, so far as they regard the realty, are to be brought in the place *rei sitæ;* but if the personal damages or claims be separable in their nature and character they may be sued for as personal actions.[4] There are many other jurists, who adopt similar distinctions.[5]

§ 553. Vattel explicitly avows the same doctrine. "The defendant's judge," (that is, the competent court), says he, "is the judge of the place, where the defendant has his settled abode, or the judge of the place where the defendant is, when any sudden diffi-

---

eigner is bound by the judgment. If the foreigner is defendant, and has submitted to the jurisdiction, then the same result follows. If he has not submitted, or has not appeared to the suit, then the judgment is not obligatory. 1 Boullenois, 609, 610. He founds himself in this opinion upon the general rule, *Actor sequitur forum rei;* and he quotes with approbation the remark of J. Galli; *Quis manens extra regnum non tenetur in parlemento respondere super actione personali.* Id. 612.

[1] 1 Boullenois, 601, 602, 603, 606, 609. See also, Id. Prin. Gén. 34, p. 8, 9.

[2] 1 Boullenois, 618, 619, 620, 622, 623. Id. Princ. Gén. 35, 37, p. 9.

[3] Id. p. 623, 624, 625.

[4] Id. p. 635, 636.

[5] Id. Observ. 25, p. 601, to 651; 1 Hertii Opera, De Collis. Leg. § 70, p. 132; Voet. ad Pand. Lib. 4, tit. 1, § 28, p. 241.

culty arises, provided it does not relate to an estate in land, or to a right annexed to such an estate. In this case, as property of that kind is to be held according to the laws of the country, where it is situated, and as the right of granting it is vested in the ruler of the country, controversies relating to such property can only be decided in the state, in which it depends."[1]

§ 554. It will be perceived, that in many respects the doctrine, here laid down, coincides with that of the common law. It has been already stated, that by the common law personal actions, being transitory, may be brought in any place, where the party defendant can be found;[2] that real actions must be brought in the *forum rei sitæ;* and mixed actions are properly referrible to the same jurisdiction.[3] Among the latter are actions for trespasses and injuries to real property, which are deemed local; so that they will not lie elsewhere than

1 Vattel, B. 2, ch. 8, § 103.

2 See Mostyn *v.* Fabrigas, Cowper R. 161, 176, 177; Robinson *v.* Bland, 2 Burr. R. 1074; S. C. 1 W. Black. 259; Ante § 364.

3 Ante § 364; 4 Cowen R. 527, note. — Lord Mansfield, in Mostyn *v.* Fabrigas (Cowper R. 161, 176) said, "There is a formal and a substantial distinction as to the locality of trials. I state them as different things. The substantial distinction is where the proceeding is *in rem;* and where the effect of judgment cannot be had, if it is laid in a wrong place. That is the case of all ejectments, &c. With regard to matters, that arise out of the realm, there is a substantial distinction of locality too; for there are some cases, that arise out of the realm, which ought not to be tried any where, but in the country, where they arise. As if two persons fight in France, and both happening casually to be here, one should bring an action of assault against the other, it might be a doubt, whether such an action could be maintained here; because, though it is not a criminal prosecution, it must be laid to be against the peace of the king; but the breach of the peace is merely local, though the trespass against the person is transitory." His Lordship here doubtless alluded to a case of a personal trespass between foreigners; for in a subsequent part of the same opinion he expressly held, that, as between subjects, not only upon contracts, but for personal torts, an action might be maintained in England; and indeed that was the very point decided in the case then in judgment.

in the place *rei sitæ*. This distinction was recognised as long ago as 1665, in the case of Skinner *v.* the East India Company (cited in Cowper R. 167, 168), where the twelve Judges certified, that for torts to the person and to personal property done abroad, a remedy lay in a suit *in personam* in England; but that for torts to real property or fixtures abroad no suit lay. Lord Mansfield and Lord Chief Justice Eyre held at one time a different doctrine; and allowed suits to be maintained in England for injuries done by pulling down houses in foreign unsettled regions, viz. the desert coasts of Nova Scotia and Labrador.[1] But this doctrine has been since overruled as untenable by the actual jurisprudence of England;[2] however maintainable it might be upon general principles, when the suit is for personal damages only.[3]

§ 555. The grounds, upon which the exclusive jurisdiction is maintained over immoveable property are the same, upon which the sole right to establish, regulate, and control the transfer, descent, and testamentary disposition of it have been admitted by all nations. The inconveniences of an opposite course would be innumerable, and would subject the property to the most distressing conflicts arising from opposing titles, and compel every nation to administer almost all other laws, except its own, in the ordinary administration of justice.[4]

---

1 Cited by Lord Mansfield in Mostyn *v.* Fabrigas, Cowper R. 180, 181.

2 Doulson *v.* Matthews, 4 T. R. 503.

3 The doctrine of this last case was very fully examined and affirmed by Mr. Chief Justice Marshall, in the case of Livingston *v.* Jefferson, before the Circuit Court of Virginia, in 1811, (4 Hall's American Law Journal, 78.) It was an action *quare clausum fregit*, brought against Mr. Jefferson on account of an alleged trespass to lands (the Batture) in New Orleans. The suit was dismissed for want of jurisdiction.

4 Ante § 364, § 365.

§ 556. Having stated these general principles in relation to jurisdiction, (the result of which is, that no nation can rightfully claim to exercise it, except as to persons and property within its own domains,) we are next led to the consideration of the question, in what manner suits arising from foreign causes are to be instituted, and proceedings to be had, until the final judgment? Are they to be according to the law of the place, where the parties, or either of them, live? Or are they to be according to the modes of proceeding and forms of suit prescribed by the laws of the place, where the suits are brought? Fortunately, here, there is scarcely any ground left open for controversy, either in the opinions of jurists, or in the actual practice of nations. It is universally admitted and established, that the forms of remedies, and the modes of proceeding, and the execution of judgments, are to be regulated solely and exclusively by the laws of the place, where the action is instituted; or, as the civilians uniformly express it, according to the *lex fori*.

§ 557. The reasons for this doctrine are so obvious, that they scarcely require any illustration. The business of the administration of justice by any nation is, in a peculiar and emphatic sense, a part of its public right and duty. Each nation is at liberty to adopt such a course of proceeding, as best comports with its convenience and interests, and the interests of its own subjects, for whom its laws are particularly designed. The different kinds of remedies, and the modes of proceeding best adapted to enforce rights and guard against wrongs, must materially depend upon the structure of its own jurisprudence. What would be well adapted to the jurisprudence, customary or positive, of one nation, for rights, which it recognised, or for duties, which it enforced, might be wholly unfit for that of another nation, either as having gross defects, or steering wide of the appropriate remedial justice. A nation, acknowledging the existence of peculiar rights and privileges, either personal or real, such as seignorial rights, or trusts in the realty, would naturally introduce correspondent remedies. While others, in which these did not exist, might well dispense with the formalities, which they might require. The jurisprudence of one nation may be very refined and artificial, with a multitude of intricate and perplexed proceedings; that of another may be rude, uninformed, and harsh, consisting of an undigested mass of usages. It would be absolutely impracticable to apply the process and modes of proceeding of the one to the other. Besides, there would be an utter confusion in all judicial proceedings by attempting to engraft, upon the remedies of one country, those of all other countries, whose subjects should be parties or interested therein. No tribunal on earth, however learned, could hope, by any degree of diligence, to master the laws and processes and remedies and the qualifications and limitations belonging to them. A whole life might be passed in obtaining little more than a few unconnected elements; and litigation would thus become immeasurably complicated, as well as almost without end. All, that a nation can, therefore, be justly required to do, is to open its own tribunals to foreigners, in the same manner and to the same extent, as they are open to its own subjects; and to give them the redress, as to rights and wrongs, which it deems fit to acknowledge in its own municipal code for natives and residents.

558. The doctrine of the common law is so fully established on this point, that it would be useless to

do more than state the universal principle, which it has promulgated; that, in regard to the merits and rights involved in actions, the law of the place, where they originated, is to govern; *in iis quæ spectant decisoria causæ, et litis decisionem, inspiciuntur statuta loci, ubi contractus fuit celebratus;* [1] but that all forms of remedies and judicial proceedings are to be according to the law of the place, where the action is instituted, without any regard to the domicil of the parties, the origin of the right, or the country of the act.[2]

§ 559. Nor are foreign jurists less pointed in their recognition of it. Thus Bartolus, in speaking upon contracts, says: *Quæro quid de contractibus? Pone contractum celebratum per aliquem forensem in hac civitate; litigium ortum est, et agitur lis in loco originis contrahentis. Cujus loci statuta debent servari vel spectari? Distingue; aut loquimur de statuto, aut de consuetudine, quæ respiciunt ipsius contractûs solennitates, aut litis ordinationem, aut de his, quæ pertinent ad jurisdictionem ex ipso contractu evenientis executionis. Primo casu, inspicitur locus contractûs. Secundo casu, aut quæris de his, quæ pertinent ad litis contestationem, et inspicitur locus judicii; aut de his, quæ pertinent ad ipsius litis decisionem, et tunc, aut de his,*

---

1 2 Boullenois, 462.

2 The authorities are exceedingly numerous. Among them we may cite the following. See 4 Cowen R. 528, note (10), and authorities there cited; 2 Kent Comm. Lect. 27, p. 118, &c. (2d edition); Robinson *v.* Bland, 2 Burr. 1084; De la Vega *v.* Vianna, 1 Barn. & Adolp. R. 284; Fenwick *v.* Sears, 1 Cranch 259; Nash *v.* Tupper, 1 Cain R. 402; Pearsall *v.* Dwight, 2 Mass. R. 84; Smith *v.* Spinola, 2 John. R. 189; Van Reimsdyk *v.* Kane, 1 Gallis. R. 371; Lodge *v.* Phelps, 1 John. Cas. 412; Thrasher *v.* Everhart, 3 Gill. & John. 234; Peck *v.* Hozier, 14 John. R. 346.

quæ oriuntur secundum ipsius contractûs naturam tempore contractûs, aut de his, quæ oriuntur ex post facto, propter negligentiam vel moram; primo casu inspicitur locus contractûs, &c.[1]

§ 560. Rodemburg asserts the same distinction: *Primum utamur vulgatâ doctorum distinctione, quâ separantur ea, quæ litis formam concernunt ac ordinationem, ab iis, quæ decisionem aut materiam; lis ordinanda secundum morem loci, in quo ventilatur.*[2] Boullenois affirms the same doctrine; *A l'égard* (says he) *du principe de décision, quantum ad litis decisoria, il se tire, ou de la loi du contrat, ou de la loi de la situation, ou de la volonté présumée des parties, lorsqu'elles ont contracté ensemble. Diversitas fori non debet meritum causæ variare. A l'égard des formalités judiciares, quantum ad litis ordinationem, la règle est de suivre la procédure et les usages observés dans le lieu, où l'on plaide.*[3] Hertius states the same point in his compendious way: *Jura judicii tantum in illis observanda esse, quæ ad ordinem processûs judicialis pertinent.*[4]

§ 561. Strykius states it in the following language: *Quotiescunque circa judicii ordinationem controvertitur, statuta loci judicii, omnibus cæteris posthabitis, introspiciantur. In modo procedendi consuetudo judicii attendenda, ubi lis agitatur. In modo vero decidendi, seu in ipsâ causæ decisione, consuetudo litigantium, seu ubi actus est gestus, attendendus.*[5] Hu-

1 2 Boullenois, 455, 456.

2 Rodemburg, De Div. Stat. tit. 2, P. 5, n. 16, p. 47; 1 Boullenois, 660, 685, 818.

3 1 Boullenois, 535 to 546; Id. Prin. Gén. 49, p. 11.

4 1 Hertii Opera, De Collis. Leg. § 4, n. 70, p. 153.

5 Strykii Tract. et Disp. Tom. 2, p. 27; De Jure Princ. ext. Territ. ch. 3, n. 34.

berus says: *Adeoque receptum est optimâ ratione, ut in ordinandis judiciis loci consuetudo, ubi agitur, etsi de negotio alibi celebrato, spectatur.*[1] Dumoulin says: *An instrumentum habeat executionem, et quo modo debeat exequi, attenditur locus ubi agitur, vel fit executio. Ratio, quia virtus executoria et modus exequendi concernit processum. In his quæ pertinent ad processum judicii, vel executionem faciendam, vel ad ordinationem judicii, semper sit observanda consuetudo loci, in quo judicium agitatur.*[2] Émérigon says: *Pour tout ce concerne l'ordre judiciare, on doit suivre l'usage du lieu, où l'on plaide. Pour tout qui est de la décision du fond, on doit suivre en règle générale les lois du lieu où le contrat a été passé. Cette distinction est consignée dans tous nos livres.*[3]

§ 562. We may conclude this reference to the opinions of foreign jurists by a citation from J. Voet, who states at once the rule and the reason of it. *Quia vero regionum, civitatum, vicorum varia, imo contraria sæpe jura sunt, observandum est, quantum quidem ad ordinem judicii formamque attinet, judicem nullius alterius sed sui tantum fori leges sequi: sed in litis ipsius definitione, si de solennibus contractûs, testamenti, vel negotii alterius quæstio sit, validum pronunciare debet ac solenne negotium, quoties adhibita invenit solennia loci, in quo illud gestum est, licet aliæ, aut majores, in loco judicii ad talem actum solennitates requisitæ essent.*[4]

---

1 Huberus, Lib. 1, tit. 3; De Confl. Leg. § 7.

2 1 Boullenois, 523, 524.

3 1 Émérigon, Traité des Assur. ch. 4, § 8, n. 2, p. 122; Le Roy *v.* Crowninshield, 2 Mason R. 163. See also to the same effect, P. Voet. De Stat. § 10, ch. 1, § 1, 6, p. 281, 285, 286.

4 Voet. ad Pand. Lib. 5, tit. 1, § 51, p. 328.

§ 563. There are many questions, however, which may arise, as to what are, and what are not matters belonging to the remedy, *ad litis ordinationem*, and what are, and what are not matters properly belonging to the merits, *ad litis decisionem*. Many cases of this sort may be found collected, and discussed by foreign jurists upon the peculiarities of their own jurisprudence. But they could not be made intelligible to a lawyer under the common law, without occupying a space in explanations, wholly disproportionate to their importance in a treatise, like the present.[1]

§ 564. It may be of more utility to introduce a few illustrations, arising peculiarly under the common law modes of proceeding; first, in regard to persons, who may sue; secondly, in regard to process; and thirdly, in regard to certain defences against actions, founded on local laws or customary practice, and arising from matters *ex post facto*.

§ 565. In the first place, in regard to persons, who may sue. We have already had occasion to take notice of a peculiarity of the common law, that *choses in action* are not, with the exception of promissory notes and bills of exchange, assignable. Hence, if any such *chose in action*, as a bond, covenant, or debt is assigned, no action can be maintained in a common law court by the assignee. And this rule is applied to assignments of *choses in action*, made in foreign countries, although the assignee might be entitled to found an action thereon in such foreign country in his own name, in virtue of such assignment. For such have been thought to belong not so much to the

---

[1] See 1 Boullenois, 535 to 569.

right and merit of the claim, as to the form of the remedy. Thus it has been held, that a Scotch assignee of a bankrupt could not maintain a suit in his own name in England for a *chose in action* of the bankrupt, which was admitted to pass under the assignment.[1] In America, contradictory decisions have been made upon the same point, some decisions affirming, and others denying, the right of the assignee to sue in his own name; though the weight of authority must now be admitted to be against the right.[2]

§ 566. And the reasoning of these decisions seems equally to apply to the case of a foreign assignee by the voluntary act of the party. But in a case, where the assignee of an Irish judgment brought a suit in his own name in England, such judgment being assignable in Ireland, so as to vest a title at law in the assignee, the Court of Common Pleas held, that he was entitled to recover, because (it should seem) a legal title by the *lex loci* vested in him, and the case was not to be governed by the law of England, as the assignment was in Ireland.[3] The distinction, though nice, is at the same time clear; for the remedy is sought upon a legal right vested *ex directo* by the local law in the assignee, against the judgment debtor. The case, however, seems to

---

1 Jeffrey *v.* McTaggart, 6 M. & Selw. 126, and Wolff *v.* Oxholm, 6 M. & Selw. 99. But see Smith *v.* Buchanan, (1 East 11,) the *dictum* of Lord Kenyon.

2 See ante, § 358, 359, 419, 420; Milne *v.* Moreton, 6 Binn. R. 374; Goodwin *v.* Jones, 3 Mass. R. 559; James *v.* Boynton, 9 Mass. R. 357; Orr *v.* Amory, 11 Mass. R. 25; Ingraham *v.* Gayer, 13 Mass. R. 146, 147; Byme *v.* Walker, 7 Serg. & Rawle, 483; Bird *v.* Caritat, 2 John. R. 342; Bird *v.* Pierpont, 1 John. R. 118; Murray *v.* Murray, 5 John. Ch. R. 60; Brush *v.* Curtis, 4 Connect. R. 312; Raymond *v.* Johnson, 11 John. R. 488; Holmes *v.* Remsen, 4 John. Ch. R. 460, 485.

3 O'Callaghan *v.* Thomond, 3 Taunt. 82, 84.

stand alone; and therefore can scarcely be thought unexceptionable in point of authority. The *dictum* of Lord Loughborough, in Folliott *v.* Ogden, (1 H. Black. 135,) and that of Lord Ellenborough in Wolff *v.* Oxholm, (4 M. & Selw. 99,) are against it.[1]

§ 567. Another illustration may be taken from the forms of action upon instruments under seal. Thus in Virginia a contract to pay money with a scrawl instead of a seal, is treated as a sealed instrument, so that debt lies upon it in that state. But in New York, where such a scrawl is not treated as a seal, the remedy must be, as upon an unsealed simple contract.[2] On the other hand, a single bill is deemed in Virginia not to be a specialty; in Maryland it is otherwise. A remedy brought in Maryland upon such a single bill, executed in Virginia, cannot be by an action of assumpsit, as upon a simple contract, but must be by action of debt as upon a specialty.[3]

§ 568. In the next place, as to process. There is no controversy, that in a general sense the mode of process constitutes a part of the remedy. But the question has arisen, whether upon contracts made in a foreign country, and which by the laws of that

---

1 See ante, § 358, 359. See Trasher *v.* Everhart, 3 Gill. & John. 234; McRay *v.* Mattoon, 10 Pick. R. 52; Pearsall *v.* Dwight, 2 Mass. R. 96.—This subject is ably discussed on different sides in two articles in the American Jurist, viz. in the number for January 1833, (9 Vol. 42,) and in the number for January 1834, (11 Vol. 101,) to which I gladly refer, as giving a more satisfactory view of this subject, than with reference to the plan of the present work, I have been able to give.—It may be thought, that the case of foreign executors and administrators, as assignees by operation of law of the deceased's estate, stands upon a similar ground. But it appears to me to proceed on principles materially different, applicable to rights, and not merely to remedies. See ante, § 512, 513.

2 Warren *v.* Lynch, 5 John. R. 239. See also Andrews *v.* Herriot, 4 Cowen, 508. But see Meredith *v.* Hindsdale, 2 Caines R. 362.

3 Trasher *v.* Everhart, 3 Gill. & John. R. 234.

country are precluded from being enforced by a personal arrest or imprisonment, the like exemption applies in suits to enforce them in another country, where such process constitutes a part of remedial justice. Such a contract existed, or was supposed to exist, in the case of Melan *v.* Fitz James, (1 Bos. & Pull. 138,) where a bond given in France, and sued in England, was understood to bind the property, and not the person of the party. On that occasion Lord Chief Justice Eyre said: "If it appears, that this contract creates no personal obligation, and that it could not be sued as such, by the laws of France, (on the principle of preventing arrests so vexatious, as to be an abuse of the process of the court,) there seems to be a fair ground, on which the Court may interpose to prevent a proceeding so oppressive, as a personal arrest in a foreign country, at the commencement of a suit, in a case, which, as far as one can judge at present, authorizes no proceeding against the person in the country, in which the transaction passed. If there could be none in France, in my opinion there can be none here. I cannot conceive, that what is no personal obligation in the country, in which it arises, can ever be raised into a personal obligation by the laws of another. If it be a personal obligation there, it must be enforced here in the mode pointed out by the law of this country. But what the nature of the obligation is, must be determined by the law of the country, where it was entered into; and then this country will apply its own law to enforce it." And accordingly the Court discharged the party from the arrest.

§ 569. There does not seem the least reason to doubt the entire correctness of the doctrine thus laid down. If the contract creates no personal obligation but an obligation *in rem* only, it cannot be, that its nature can be changed, or its obligation varied by a mere change of domicil. That would be to contradict all the principles maintained in all the authorities, that the validity, nature, obligation, and interpretation of a contract are to be decided by the *lex loci contractûs.*[1] A suit *in personam* in England could not be maintained, except upon some contract, which bound the person. If it bound the property only, the proceeding should be *in rem;* and, if in express terms the party bound his property only, and exempted himself from a personal liability, no one would doubt, that a suit *in personam* would not be maintainable. And the same principle would apply, if the laws of a country should declare, that certain classes of contracts should not bind the person at all, but only property, or a particular species of property. Such laws do probably exist in some countries. But it does not follow, because a personal remedy is not given by the laws of a country, that therefore there is no personal obligation in a contract.[2]

§ 570. The real difficulty lies, not in the principle itself, but in its application. There is a great distinction between a contract, which *ex directo* excludes personal liability, and a contract made in a country, which binds the party personally; but where the laws do not enforce the contract *in personam* but only *in rem.* In the latter case the remedy constitutes no part of the contract. The liability is general, so far as the acts of the parties go; and the mode of enforcing is a mere matter of municipal regulation. It

---

1 Ante §. 263.

2 Talleyrand, *v.* Boulanger, 3 Ves, Jr. R. 446; Flack *v.* Holm, 1 Jac. & Walk. 405.

is strictly a part of the *lex fori*, and may be changed from time to time, as the legislature may choose.[1] And this was the view of the matter taken by Mr. Justice Heath in the case alluded to; for he, in dissenting from the opinion of the Court, did not deny the principles of the decision, but held, that the contract was *personal.* "We all agree (said he) that in construing contracts we must be governed by the laws of the country, in which they are made; for all the contracts have reference to such laws. But, when we come to remedies, it is another thing. They must be pursued by the means, which the law points out, where the party resides. The laws of the country, where the contract was made, can only have reference to the nature of the contract, not to the mode of enforcing it. Whoever comes voluntarily into a country, subjects himself to all the laws of that country; and therein to all the remedies directed by those laws, on his particular engagements."[2]

§ 571. The doctrine of this case has been sometimes followed in America.[3] But the better opinion now established, both in England and America, is, that it is of no consequence, whether the contract authorized an arrest or imprisonment of the party in the country, where it was made, if there is no exemption from personal liability. He is still liable to arrest or imprisonment, in a suit upon it in a foreign country, whose laws authorize such a mode of proceeding, as a part of the remedy.[4] In a very recent case in England, where the

---

1 See Ogden *v.* Saunders, 12 Wheaton R. 213.

2 Bos. & Pull. 142; Hinkley *v.* Morean, 3 Mason R. 88; Titus *v.* Hobart, 5 Mason R. 378.

3 Symonds *v.* Union Insur. Co. 4, Dall 417.

4 See Imley *v.* Ellesson, 2 East R. 453; Peck *v.* Hozier, 14 John. R. 346; Robinson *v.* Bland, 2 Burr. 1089; Hinkley *v.* Morean, 3 Mason R. 88; Titus *v.* Hobart, 5 Mason R. 378.

plaintiff and defendant were both foreigners, and the debt was contracted in a country, by whose laws the defendant would not have been liable to arrest, and application was made to discharge the defendant from arrest on that account, the Court refused the application. Lord Tenterden on that occasion in delivering the opinion of the Court said; "A person, suing in this country, must take the law, as he finds it. He cannot by virtue of any regulation in his own country enjoy greater advantages than other suitors here. And he ought not, therefore, to be deprived of any superior advantage, which the law of this country may confer. He is to have the same rights, which all the subjects of this kingdom are entitled to." [1]

§ 572. And the like principles apply to the form of judgments to be rendered, and of executions to be granted in suits. They must conform to the *lex fori*, although the party defendant may, in his domestic forum, have been entitled to a judgment, exempting his person from imprisonment, in virtue of a discharge under an insolvent law existing there, and of which he had there judicially obtained the benefit.[2] And it will make no difference in such case, whether the contract sued on was made in the state granting such discharge, or not; or whether the parties were citizens of that state, or not. The effect of such a discharge is purely local. It is addressed solely to the courts of the state, under whose authority the exemption is allowed. But it has nothing

---

1 De la Vega *v.* Vianna, 1 Barn. and Adolph. R. 284. See also Whittemore *v.* Adams, 2 Cowen R. 626; Willing *v.* Consequa, 1 Peters Cir. R. 317; Courtois *v.* Carpentier, 1 Wash. Cir. R. 376; Bird *v.* Caritat, 2 John. R. 345; Wyman *v.* Southward, 10 Wheaton R. 1. See Henry on Foreign Law, p. 81 to 86.

2 Hinkley *v.* Morean, 3 Mason R. 88; Titus *v.* Hobart, 5 Mason R. 378.

to do with the process, proceedings, or judgments of the courts of other states, which are governed altogeer by their own municipal jurisprudence. Wherever a remedy is sought, it is to be administered according to the *lex fori;* and such judgment is given, as the laws of the state, where the suit is brought, authorize, and not such, as the laws of other states authorize or require.[1]

§ 573. The general doctrine is stated in ample terms by P. Voet. *Sed revertar unde fueram digressus, ad concursum statutorum variantium circa judicia. Ubi occurrunt nonnulla circa solemnia in judiciis servanda, circa tempora, cautiones, probationes, causarum decisiones, executiones, et appellationes. Finge enim alia servari solemnia, in loco domicilii litigatoris, alia in loco contractûs, alia in loco rei sitæ, alia in judicii loco; quænam spectanda solemnia? Respondeo; spectanda sunt solemnia, id est stylus judicis fori illius, ubi litigatur. Idque in genere verum est, sive loquamar de civibus, sive forensibus: statuta quippe circa solemnia meo sensu mixti erant generis; adeoque vires exserunt tam intra quam extra territorium, tam in ordine ad incolas, quam ad exteros.*[2]

§ 574. The same doctrine is fully confirmed by J. Voet, as a received doctrine of foreign law. *Multis præterea in locis id obtinet, ne duo ejusdem provinciæ seu territorii incolæ se invicem, aut bona, sistant in alio territorio, &c. Quod si quis, neglectâ statuti dispositione, concivem aut bona ejus alibi stiterit* [arrest] *litis movendæ gratiâ, non peccabunt quidem istius loci judices, si arrestum confirment; cum non ligentur alieni*

1 Hinkley *v.* Morean, 3 Mason R. 88; Titus *v.* Hobart, 5 Mason R. 378.

2 Voet. de Statut. § 10, ch. 1 § 6, p, 285.

territorii legibus, talem arrestationem concivium vetantibus; sed qui ita detentus litigare coactus est, recte petet a suo judice, condemnari concivem, ut arresti vinculum, contra statuti domicilii prohibitionem alibi impositum, remittat, litique alibi cœptæ cum impensis renunciet, ac solvat mulctam statuto dictatam.[1] And he proceeds to add, that in some places the practice is in such cases to remit the parties to the domestic *forum;* which, however, is not as a matter of right or duty, but of comity; *quod tamen vel ex comitate magis, quam necessitate fit.*[2] And this indeed seems the general doctrine maintained by foreign jurists; and Boullenois has collected their opinions at large.[3] He treats the question of imprisonment purely as one *modus exequendi;* and applies the same principle to mesne process and process in execution.[4]

§ 575. In the next place, as to defences arising from matters *ex post facto.* These may be of the nature of counter claims or set-offs to actions; or they may be laws regulating the time of instituting suits, called, in the foreign law, statutes of prescriptions, and, in the common law, statutes of limitations. The latter will deserve a very exact consideration. The former may be disposed of in a few words. It is held in our courts, that a set-off to any action, allowed by the local law, is to be treated as a part of the remedy; and that therefore it is admissible in claims between persons belonging to different states or countries, although it may not be admissible by the law of the country, where

---

1 See Henry on Foreign Law, 84, 85.

2 Voet. ad Pand. Lib. 2, tit. 4, § 45, p. 129; cited also 1 Barn. & Adolp. R. 288, n.

3 1 Boullenois, 523, 524, 525, 528, 529.

4 Id.; Henry on Foreign Law, p. 24, 85.

the debt, which is sued, was contracted.[1] The liens, implied hypothecations, and priorities of satisfaction, given to creditors by the law of particular countries and the order of payment of their debts, are generally treated, as belonging to the subject of proceedings *ad litis ordinationem*, and not to the merits of the claim.[2]

§ 576. In regard to statutes of limitation or prescription, there is no doubt, that they are strictly questions, affecting the remedy, and not questions upon the merits. They go, *ad litis ordinationem*, and not *ad litis decisionem*, in a just juridical sense.[3] The object of them is to fix certain periods, within which all suits shall be brought in the courts of a state, whether they be brought by subjects or by foreigners. And there can be no reason, and no sound policy, in allowing higher or more extensive privileges to foreigners, than to subjects. Laws, thus limiting suits, are founded in the noblest policy; they are statutes of repose, to quiet titles, to suppress frauds, and to supply the deficiency of proofs from the ambiguity and obscurity of transactions. They presume, that claims are extinguished, because they are not litigated within the prescribed period. They take away all solid grounds of complaint, because they rest on the negligence or *laches* of the party himself. They quicken diligence, by making it in some measure equivalent to right. They discourage litigation, by burying in one common receptacle all the accumulations of past times, which are unexplained, and have now

---

1 Gibbs *v.* Howard, 2 New Hamp. R. 296; Ruggles *v.* Keeler, 3 John. R. 263. See Pothier on Oblig. art. 641, 642.

2 Rodemburg, De Diversit. Statut. tit. 2, ch. 5, n. 15, 16, p. 47, 49; 1 Boullenois, 634, 639, 685, 818. See also P. Voet. De Statut. § 10, ch. 1, n. 35, p. 282 to 289.

3 1 Boullenois, 530.

become inexplicable. It has been said by Voet with singular felicity, that controversies are limited, lest they should be immortal, while men are mortal; *ne autem lites immortales essent, dum litigantes mortales sint.*[1]

§ 577. It has accordingly become a formulary in international jurisprudence, that all suits must be brought within the period prescribed by the local law (*lex fori*), otherwise the suit will be barred; and this rule is equally as well recognised in foreign jurisprudence, as it is in the common law.[2] Not, indeed, that there are no diversities of opinion upon this subject; but the doctrine is established by a decisive current of well considered authorities. Thus, Huberus lays down the doctrine in clear terms. *Ratio loci est, quod præscriptio et executio non pertinent ad valorem contractûs, sed ad tempus et modum actionis instituendæ, quæ per se, quasi contractum, separatum negotium constituit.*[3] Boullenois holds a s milar doctrine, asserting, that the bar of presumption is a part of the *modus procedendi.*[4] Many other jurists might be cited in support of it, if it

---

1 Voet. ad Pand. Lib. 5, tit. 1, § 53, p. 328.

2 The authorities in the common law are very numerous. A considerable number of them are cited in 4 Cowen R. 528, note 10; Id. 530; Van Reimsdyk *v.* Kane, 1 Gallis. R. 371; Le Roy *v.* Crowninshield, 2 Mason R. 351; British Linen Company *v.* Drummond, 10 Barn. & Cresw. 903; De la Vega *v.* Vianna, 1 Barn. & Adolp. R. 284; De Couche *v.* Savatier, 3 John. Ch. R. 190; Lincoln *v.* Battelle, 6 Wend. R. 475.

3 Huberus, Lib. 1, tit. 3, De Conflict. Leg. § 7; 1 Hertii Opera, De Collis. § 4, n. 65, p. 150, 151. Hertius seems of a different opinion; saying, that, if the prescription only of the place, where the suit was brought, could prevail, the times of prescription would be very uncertain; for a man might frequently be sued in different places. 1 Hertii Opera, De Collis. Leg. § 4, n. 65, p. 150. See also the opinions of other jurists to the same point in 1 Boullenois 528, 529, 530; 2 Boullenois, 487, 488; Erskine's Inst. B. 3, tit. 7, § 48, p. 633, 634; Voet. ad Pandect. Lib. 44, tit. 3, § 10, 12.

4 1 Boullenois, 530.

were necessary to go at large into the subject.[1] The doctrine of the Scottish courts is in precise conformity to that of the common law.[2]

§ 578. But if the question were entirely new, it would be difficult upon principles of international justice or policy to establish a different rule. Every nation must have a right to settle for itself the times and circumstances, within and under which suits shall be litigated in its own courts. And there can be no pretence to say, that foreigners are entitled to crowd the tribunals of any nation with suits of their own, which are stale and antiquated, to the exclusion of the common administration of justice between its own subjects. As little right can they have to insist, that the times, provided by the laws of their country, shall supersede those of the nation, in which they have chosen to litigate their controversies.

§ 579. The reasoning often insisted upon by foreign jurists, in opposition to this plain and intelligible doctrine is, in the first place, that the statute of limitations really operates, as a peremptory bar, and therefore does not in fact touch the mode of proceeding, but the merits of the case; *non tangit modum procedendi, sed tangit meritum causæ.*[3] And in the next place, that it subjects the party to different prescriptions in different places, and therefore leaves his rights in uncertainty.[4] The latter objection may be answered by the consideration, that, if he chooses to reside within

---

1 See 1 Boullenois, 350, 550; 2 Boullenois, 455, 456; Casaregis Disc. 179, § 59, 60; Voet. De Statut. § 10, ch. 1, § 1, p. 281.

2 Erskine's Inst. B. 3, tit. 7, § 48, p. 633; 2 Mason R. 174; Kaims on Equity, B. 3, ch. 8, § 4, 6; Voet. De Statut. § 10, ch. 1, n. 1, p. 280, 281.

3 1 Boullenois, 529.

4 1 Hertii Opera, De Collis. Leg. § 4, n. 65, p. 150, 151.

any particular territory, he subjects himself to the laws of that territory, as to all suits brought against him. And that, as the law of prescription of a place, even in case of a contract, made in such place, makes no part of the contract itself, but merely acts upon it *ex post facto*, in case of a suit, it cannot properly be deemed a right stipulated for in the contract. Even foreign jurists do not pretend, that a prescription constitutes a part of the contract; but only, that it acts upon, and appertains to, the decision of the cause. *Hoc pertinet ad decisionem causæ*, says Baldus. *Præscriptio utique ad contractum et meritum causæ pertinet, non ad progressum*, says Gerhard Titius.[1]

§ 580. The other objection is well founded in its form, but it does not shake the ground of the general doctrine. It is true, as Baldus contends, that the statute of limitations does go to the decision of the cause; *Exceptio peremptoria pertinet ad decisionem causæ*. But that is not the question. The question is, whether it is a matter of the original merits, for instance, of the original validity, interpretation, or discharge of a contract, or a matter touching the mode of remedial justice, which is provided to redress grievances. Suppose a nation were to declare (as France has done in regard to foreigners in some cases), that no suits should be maintained in its courts between foreigners; this would be a peremptory exception. But could it be denied, that France had a right so to regulate the jurisdiction of its own tribunals; or that it was an enactment touching remedies? Considered in their true light, statutes of limitation or prescription are ordinarily simple regulations of suits, and not of rights. They regulate the times

---

[1] 1 Boullenois, 529, 530; Erskine's Inst. B. 3, tit. 7, § 48, p. 633, 634.

in which rights may be asserted in courts of justice, and do not purport to act upon those rights. Boullenois has truly said, *L'exception ne tombe, que sur l'action et la procédure intentée.*[1] Pothier treats prescription (*fin de non recevoir*) not so much, as an extinguishment of the claim, as an extinguishment of the right of action.[2] And this is precisely the manner in which the subject is contemplated at the common law,[3] as well as by many foreign jurists.[4]

§ 581. And here, again, upon the same mistaken foundation already discussed, some foreign jurists maintain the doctrine in relation to contracts, that, if they are made in one place, and to be performed or paid in another place, the law of prescription of the latter place is to govern. Such is the opinion of Everhard. *Aut quærimus,* (says he,) *quis locus inspiciatur, quoad præscriptionem statutoriam vigentem in uno loco, et non in alio, ubi statuta locorum sunt diversa. Et certum est, quod inspicitur locus distinctæ solutionis.* Bartolus, Burgundus, and Christinæus hold the same opinion.[5] Of course, the doctrine of these authors must be

1 1 Boullenois, 530; Erskine's Inst. B. 3, tit. 7, § 48, p. 633, 634.

2 Pothier on Oblig. art. 641, 642.

3 Sturgis *v.* Crowninshield, 4 Wheaton R. 122, 200, 207.

4 Voet. ad Pand. Lib. 44, tit. 3, § 10; D'Aguesseau, Œuvres, Tom. 5, p. 374; 2 Mason R. 170, 171.

5 2 Boullenois, 488. — It is surprising, that Mr. Henry should have cited this doctrine of foreign authors, as sound law (apparently copying it from Boullenois) without considering, that the whole course of English opinion on this subject disclaimed it. (Henry on Foreign Law, ch. 8, § 2, p. 55). Pardessus says, that, when a debtor pleads a statute of prescription, the right to use this plea, and the time, within which it should be pleaded, will be regulated by the law of the place, where he has promised to pay; or, if this place has not been determined, then at the domicil of the debtor, at the time when he contracted the obligation; because, prescription being a plea given to the debtor against the demand of his creditor, it is naturally in the domicil of the debtor, or of his gov-

understood to be limited to prescription in personal actions; for as to prescription in cases of immoveable property, it is beyond doubt, that it is governed purely by the *lex loci.*[1] The common law has firmly fixed its own doctrine, that the prescription of the *lex fori* must prevail in all cases of personal as well as of real actions.[2]

§ 582. But although statutes of limitation, or prescription of the place, where a suit is brought, may properly be held to govern the rights of parties in such suits, or as the proposition is commonly stated, the recovery must be sought, and the remedy pursued within the times prescribed by the *lex fori,* without regard to the *lex loci contractûs,* or the origin of the cause; yet there is a distinction, which deserves consideration, and which has been often propounded. It is this. Suppose the statutes of limitation of a particular country do not only extinguish the right of action, but the claim or title itself, *ipso facto,* and declare it a nullity after the lapse of the prescribed period; and the parties are resident within the jurisdiction during all that period, so that it

---

ernment, that he should find this protection. Pardessus, Tom. 5, P. 6, tit. 9, ch. 2, § 2, art. 1445, p. 275; Henry on Foreign Law, Appendix, p. 237. Pardessus goes on to state, that these rules apply to the case, where several securities for the same debt reside in jurisdictions, where the laws respecting prescription are different. Each, in becoming security, must be supposed to have intended to enjoy all the real pleas or exceptions existing in favour of the principal debtor, without renouncing the particular prescription in his own favour, to extinguish his obligation as security, which is regulated by the law of his domicil at the moment, when he signed the contract. Pardessus, Id. art. 1495, p. 275, 276; Henry on Foreign Law, 238. This is certainly pressing the doctrine to a very great extent.

1 1 Boullenois, 350; Dumoulin's opinion, Voet. ad Pandect. Lib. 44, tit. 3, § 12.

2 See British Linen Company *v.* Drummond, 10 Barn. & Cres. 603; De Couche *v.* Savatier, 3 John. Ch. R. 190, 218, 219; De la Vega *v.* Vianna, 1 Barn. & Adolp. 284; Lincoln *v.* Battelle, 6 Wend. R. 475.

has actually operated upon the case; in such a case may not such statute be set up in any other country, to which the parties remove, by way of extinguishment, or transfer of the claim or title? This is a point which does not seem to have received as much consideration in the decisions of the common law, as it would seem to require. That there are countries, in which such regulations do exist, is unquestionable. There are states, which have declared, that all right to debts, due more than a prescribed term of years, shall be deemed extinguished; and that all titles to real and personal property, not pursued within the prescribed time, shall be deemed for ever fixed in the adverse possession.[1] Suppose, for instance, (as has occurred) personal property is adversely held in a state for a period, beyond that prescribed by the laws of that state, and after that period has elapsed, the possessor should remove into another state, which has a longer period of prescription, or is without any prescription; could the original owner assert a title there against the possessor, whose title by the local law, and the lapse of time, had become final and conclusive before the removal? It has certainly been thought, that, in such a case, the title of the possessor cannot be impugned.[2] If it cannot, the next inquiry is, whether the bar of a statute extinguishment of a debt *lege loci* ought not equally to be held a peremptory exception? This subject may be

1 See Voet. ad Pand. Lib. 44, tit. 3, § 5, 6, 9; Erskine's Inst. B. 3, tit. 7, § 1, 2, 7, 8; Beckford *v.* Wade, 17 Ves. 86; Lincoln *v.* Battelle, 6 Wend. R. 475.

2 See Beckford *v.* Wade, 17 Ves. 88; Newby *v.* Blakeley, 3 Hen. & Mum. R. 57; Brent *v.* Chapman, 5 Cranch, 358; Shelby *v.* Grey, 11 Wheaton R. 311, 371. But see Lord Dudley *v.* Warde, Ambler R. 113.

thought by some to be open for future discussion. But it should be stated, that, as far as the decisions in the American courts go, they do not sustain the distinction. In all the cases, however, in which the point has been discussed, the statutes under consideration did not extinguish the right, but merely the remedy.[1]

§ 583. What has been thus far stated on this head may be concluded by quoting a passage from J. Voet, the correctness and force of which, in point of principle, are submitted to the reader. *Quod si restitutio concedenda sit non ex causâ, quæ ipsum negotium ab initio comitabatur, (uti comitatur metus, dolus, error) sed ex eâ, quæ post supervenit, (qualis est usucapio rerum, aut præscriptio jurium et actionum, propter absentiam non interrupta) ita generaliter definiendum existimo, illius loci leges in restitutione faciendâ attendendas esse, secundum cujus loci leges impleta summo jure fuit per absentiam usucapio vel præscriptio. Quid enim, obsecro, aut justius aut æquius, quam ut ex eorundem legislatorum præscripto remedium adversus læsionem indulgeatur, ex quorum præscripto et summo jure primitus læsio nata fuit? Quibus consequens est, ut, si immobilium rerum usucapio impleta sit, serventur in restitutione faciendâ jura regionis, in quâ immobiles res sitæ sunt: adeoque, ut in amittendo, sic et in recuperando dominio regantur immobilia ex*

1 On this subject, see Decouche *v.* Savatier, 3 John. Ch. R. 190, 218, 219; Van Reimsdyk *v.* Kame, 1 Gallis. R. 371; Le Roy *v.* Crowninshield, 2 Mason R. 151, and the cases there cited; Lincoln *v.* Battelle, 6 Wend. R. 475; 1 Domat, B. 3, § 4, art. 1, p. 464; Id. art. 10, p. 466. J. Voet says in one place, "Si præscriptioni implendi alia prefinita sint tempora in loco domicilii actoris, alia in loco, ubi reus domicilium fovet, spectandum videtur tempus, quod obtinet ex statuto loci, in quo reus commoratur." Voet. ad Pand. Lib. 44, tit. 3, § 12.

sitûs sui lege, juxta vulgatam regulam in materiâ statutariâ. Sin mobilia usucapta fuerint, in restitutione magis erit, ut serventur leges domicilii ejus, qui per usucapionem dominium amiserat; ut ita mobilia, quæ censentur illic esse, ubi domicilium fovet dominus, ex lege domicilii redeant uti fuerant amissa. Sed si actiones in personam temporis lapsu, per absentiam contingente, extinctæ sint; probabilius fuerit, in illis restituendis ob justam absentiæ causam spectandum esse jus loci, in quo debitor commoratur, contra quem restitutio petitur: cum etiam ex istius loci lege præscriptio implenda fuerit.[1]

[1] Voet. ad Pandect. Lib. 4, tit. 1. § 29, p. 241; Henry on Foreign Law, 56, 59.

CHAPTER XV.

FOREIGN JUDGMENTS.

§ 584. We come in the next place to the consideration of foreign judgments, or the effect *rei judicatæ.* As to the effect to be given to foreign judgments, there has been much diversity of practice, as well as of opinion among nations. We do not speak here of cases, where the point was, whether the court, pronouncing judgment, had jurisdiction or not; but, assuming the jurisdiction to be unquestionable, what effect ought to be given to such judgment. Ought it to be held conclusive upon the parties? Or ought it to be open to impeachment by new evidence, or to be re-examined upon the original merits? The subject may be considered in two general aspects; first, in regard to judgments *in rem;* and secondly, in regard to judgments *in personam.* The latter is again divisible into three heads; first, where the judgment is set up by way of defence to a suit in a foreign tribunal; and, secondly, where the judgment is sought to be enforced in a foreign tribunal against the original defendant, or his property; and, thirdly, where the judgment is between subjects, or between foreigners, or between foreigners and subjects. These divisions will require, in some degree, a separate examination.

§ 585. Vattel has said with great force, that it is the province of every sovereignty to administer justice in all places within its territory and under its jurisdiction, to take cognizance of crimes committed there, and of the controversies, that arise within it. Other nations ought to respect this right; and, as the administration of justice necessarily requires, that every definitive sentence, regularly pronounced, be esteemed just, and executed as such, when once a cause, in which foreigners are interested, has been decided in form, the sovereign of the defendants ought not to hear their complaints. To undertake to examine the justice of a definitive sentence is an attack upon the jurisdiction of the sovereign, who has passed it.[1] Hence Vattel deduces the general rule, that, in consequence of this right of jurisdiction, the decision made by the judge of the place within the extent of his authority, ought to be respected, and to take effect even in foreign countries.[2]

§ 586. Reasonable as this doctrine seems to be, it is difficult to affirm, that it has obtained the universal assent of modern nations in their intercourse with each other. But the support, which it has received from the common law, is far more extensive and uniform, than it has received in the jurisprudence of continental Europe. In order, however, to found a proper ground of recognition in any other country, it is indispensable to establish, that the court pronouncing judgment had a lawful jurisdiction over the cause, and the parties. If the jurisdiction fails as to either, it is (as we have already seen) treated as a mere nullity, having no obligation, and entitled to no respect beyond the domestic tribunals. And this is equally true, whether the proceedings be *in rem*, or *in personam*.[3]

---

1 Vattel, B. 2, ch. 7, § 84.

2 Id. § 85.

3 Ante, § 539, 546, 547; Buchanan *v.* Rucker, 9 East. 192; Bissell *v.* Briggs, 9 Mass. R. 462; Shumway *v.* Stillman, 6 Wend. R. 447;

§ 587. This subject was a good deal considered in a celebrated case, *in rem*, before the Supreme Court of the United States; and upon that occasion Mr. Chief Justice Marshall, in delivering the opinion of the Court, used the following language, "The power of the Court then is, of necessity, examinable to a certain extent by that tribunal, which is compelled to decide, whether its sentence has changed the right of property. The power, under which it acts, must be looked into; and its authority to decide questions, which it professes to decide, must be considered.

§ 588. "But although the general power by which a court takes jurisdiction of causes must be inspected, in order to determine, whether it may rightfully do, what it professes to do, it is still a question of serious difficulty, whether the situation of the particular thing, on which the sentence has passed, may be inquired into, for the purpose of deciding whether that thing was in a state which subjected it to the jurisdiction of the court passing the sentence. For example; in every case of a foreign sentence condemning a vessel as prize of war, the authority of the tribunal to act as a prize court must be examinable. Is the question, whether the vessel condemned was in a situation to subject her to the jurisdiction of that court, also examinable? This question, in the opinion of the court, must be answered in the affirmative.

§ 589. "Upon principle, it would seem that the operation of every judgment must depend on the

---

4 Cowen R. 524, n.; 1 Starkie on Evid. P. 2, § 68, p. 214.; Henry on Foreign Law, 18, n.; Id. 73; Id. 23; Cavan *v.* Stuart, 1 Stark. 525; Hall *v.* Williams, 6 Pick. 232; Wood *v.* Tremere, 6 Pick. R. 354.

power of the court to render that judgment; or, in other words, on its jurisdiction over the subject matter which it has determined. In some cases, that jurisdiction unquestionably depends, as well on the state of the thing, as on the constitution of the court. If by any means whatever a prize court should be induced to condemn, as prize of war, a vessel which was never captured, it could not be contended that this condemnation operated a change of property. Upon principle, then, it would seem that, to a certain extent, the capacity of the court to act upon the thing condemned, arising from its being within, or without their jurisdiotion, as well as the constitution of the court, may be considered by that tribunal which is to decide on the effect of the sentence.

§ 590. "Passing from principle to authority, we find, that in the courts of England, whose decisions are particularly mentioned, because we are best acquainted with them, and because, as is believed, they give to foreign sentences as full effect as are given to them in any part of the civilized world, the position that the sentence of a foreign court is conclusive with respect to what it professes to decide, is uniformly qualified with the limitation that it has, in the given case, jurisdiction of the subject matter."[1]

§ 591. Let us now consider the operation of judgments in the different classes of cases, which have been already adverted to. And first, in relation to judgments *in rem.* If the matter in controversy is land, or other immoveable property, the judgment pronounced in the *forum rei sitæ* is held of universal

---

[1] Rose *v.* Himely, 4 Cranch, 269, 270.

obligation, as to all the matters of right and title, which it professes to decide in relation thereto. And this results from the very nature of the case; for no other court can have a competent jurisdiction to inquire into, or settle such right or title. By the general consent of nations, therefore, the judgment of the *forum rei sitæ* is held absolutely conclusive.[1] *Immobilia ejus jurisdictionis esse reputantur, ubi sita sunt.*[2]

§ 592. And the same principle is applied to all other cases of proceedings *in rem*, as to moveable property, within the jurisdiction of the court, pronouncing the judgment.[3] Whatever it settles as to the right or title, or whatever disposition it makes of the property by sale, revendication, transfer, or other act, will be held valid in every other country, where the same question comes directly or indirectly in judgment before any other foreign tribunal. This is very familiarly known in the cases of proceedings *in rem*, in foreign courts of Admiralty, whether they be causes of prize, or bottomry or salvage, or forfeiture, of which such courts have a rightful jurisdiction, founded in the actual or constructive possession of the subject matter.[4] And the same rule is applied to other courts proceeding *in rem*, as to the Court of Exchequer in England; and other courts exercising

---

[1] 1 Boullenois, 618, 619, 623.

[2] Id. p. 619; 1 Hertii Opera, De Collis. § 4, n. 73, p. 153, 154.

[3] See Kaims on Equity, B. 3 ch. 8, § 4.

[4] Croudson *v.* Leonard, 4 Cranch, 434; Williams *v.* Armroyd, 7 Cranch. R. 423; Rose *v.* Himely, 4 Cranch, 241; Hudson *v.* Guestier, 4 Cranch 293; 1 Starkie on Evid. P. 2, § 81, p. 238, &c.; Marshall on Insur. B. 1, ch. 9, § 6, p. 412, 435. Cases cited in 4 Cowen R. 520, n. 3; Grant *v.* McLachlin, 4 John. R. 34.

a like jurisdiction upon seizures.[1] And in cases of this sort it is wholly immaterial, whether the judgment be of acquittal or of condemnation. In both cases it is conclusive.[2] And proceedings by way of foreign attachment against personal property, or against debts in favor of creditors, are entitled to the same consideration.[3]

§ 593. In all these cases, the same principle prevails, that the judgment acting *in rem* shall be held conclusive upon the title and transfer and disposition of the property itself, in whatever place the same property may afterwards be found, and by whomsoever the latter may be questioned; and whether it be directly or incidentally questioned. But it is not so universally settled, that the judgment is conclusive upon all the points, which are incidentally disposed of by the judgment; nor of the facts or allegations, upon which it professes to be founded. In this respect different rules are adopted by different states, both in Europe and America. In England such judgments are held conclusive, as to all points and facts, which they professedly or incidentally decide. And in some of the American states the same doctrine prevails. While in other American States the judgments are held conclusive only *in rem*, and may be controverted as to all the incidental grounds and facts, on which they profess to be founded.[4]

---

1 Ibid. and Starkie on Evid. P. 2, § 67, 80, 81, p. 336; Hoyt *v.* Gelston, 3 Wheaton R. 246; Williams *v.* Armroyd, 7 Cranch 423.

2 Ibid.

3 See cases cited in 4 Cowen R. 520, 521. n.; Holmes *v.* Remsen, 20 John R. 229; Hull *v.* Blake, 13 Mass. R. 153; McDaniel *v.* Hughes 3 East. R. 366; Phillips *v.* Hunter, 2 H. Black. 402, 410.

4 See 4 Cowen R. 522, n. and cases cited; Vandenheuvel *v.* U. Insur. Co. 2 Cain. Cases in Err. 217; 2 John. Cases, 451; Id. 481; Robinson

§ 594. A similar doctrine has been contended for, and in many cases successfully, in favour of sentences of a peculiar character, such as those, which touch the general capacity of persons; and those, which concern marriage and divorce. Thus, foreign jurists strongly contend, that a decree of a foreign court declaring the state of a person, and placing him, as an idiot, minor, or prodigal, under guardianship, ought to be deemed of universal authority and obligation.[1] And so it ought, and doubtless would be deemed, in regard to all acts done, and authority exercised, within the jurisdiction of the sovereign, whose tribunals have pronounced the sentence. But the necessity of giving it universal effect, so as to make the guardianship operative and effectual in all other countries, in regard to the person, and his property in those countries, is not so obvious. But we have already had occasion to consider this subject in another place.[2]

§ 595. As to sentences confirming marriages or granting divorces, they may well stand upon a distinct ground. If pronounced by competent tribunals in regard to persons within the jurisdiction, there is great reason to say, that they ought to have universal conclusiveness. Lord Hardwicke is reported to have said, in a case before him, in which the validity of a

---

v. Jones, 8 Mass. R. 536; Moley v. Shattuck, 3 Cranch, 488; 2 Kent Com. Lect. 37, p. 120, 121, and cases there cited; Tarleton v. Tarleton, 4 M. and Selw. 20.

1 1 Boullenois, 603, Burgundus's opinion. — Indeed, Burgundus seems to have been of opinion, that the only judgments, which ought to have any force or operation extra-territorially, are those, which respect the state and condition of persons. "Mihi sola," says he, "illa sententia, quæ de statu personæ fertur, explicare vires extra territorii limites videtur." 1 Boullenois, 603.

2 Ante, § 495, 500.

marriage in France was asserted to have been established by the sentence of a court in France, having proper jurisdiction, "It is true, that if so, it is conclusive, whether in a foreign court, or not, from the law of nations in such cases; otherwise the rights of mankind would be very precarious."[1]

§ 596. On the other hand Lord Stowell, in a case before him, in which the validity of a foreign sentence of divorce was set up, as a bar to proceedings in the English Ecclesiastical Courts between the same parties, said: "Something has been said on the doctrine of law, regarding the respect due to foreign judgments; and undoubtedly a sentence of separation, in a proper court, for adultery, would be entitled to credit and attention in this court; but I think the conclusion is carried too far, when it is said, that a sentence of nullity of marriage is necessarily and universally binding on other countries. Adultery and its proofs are nearly the same in all countries. The validity of marriage, however, must depend, in a great degree, on the local regulations of the country, where it is celebrated. A sentence of nullity of marriage, therefore, in the country, where it was solemnized, would carry with it great authority in this country; but I am not prepared to say, that a judgment of a third country, on the validity of a marriage, not within its territories, nor had between subjects of that country, would be universally binding. For instance, the marriage, alleged by the husband, is a French marriage; a French judgment on that marriage would have been of con-

1 Roast *v.* Garvin, 1 Ves. 157. See also a case in the time of Charles 2d, cited by Lord Hardwicke in Boucher *v.* Lawson, Cas. T. Hard. 89; 2 Swanst. R. 349.

siderable weight; but it does not follow, that the judgment of a court at Brussells, on a marriage in France, would have the same authority, much less on a marriage celebrated here in England. Had there been a sentence against the wife for adultery in Brabant, it might have prevented her from proceeding with any effect against her husband here; but no such sentence any where appears."[1]

§ 597. This subject, however, has already been considered at large in the preceding discussions, relative to divorces. The result of the doctrine therein stated is, that the English courts are not disposed to admit, that any valid sentence of divorce can be pronounced in regard to a marriage celebrated in England between English subjects. But in Scotland, and in America, a different doctrine is maintained; and it is held, that a sentence of divorce pronounced between parties actually domiciled in the country, by a competent tribunal, having jurisdiction over the case, is valid, and ought to be held everywhere a complete dissolution of the marriage, in whatever country it was originally celebrated.[2] Of course we are to understand, that the sentence is obtained *bonâ fide* and without fraud; for fraud in this, as in other cases, will vitiate any judgment, however well founded in point of jurisdiction.[3]

§ 598. In the next place, as to judgments *in personam*. And here a distinction is commonly taken between suits brought by a party to enforce a foreign

---

[1] Sinclair *v.* Sinclair, 1 Hagg. Consist. Rep. 297. See also Scrimshire *v.* Scrimshire, 2 Hagg. Consist. Rep. 397, 410.

[2] See ante, § 212, 215 to 230.

[3] See Starkie on Evid. P. 2, § 77, 79, 83; Duchess of Kingston's case, 11 State Trials, 261, 262.

judgment; and suits brought against a party, who sets up a foreign judgment in bar of the suit by way of defence. In the former case it is often urged, that no sovereign is bound *jure gentium* to execute any foreign judgment within his dominions; and therefore, if execution of it is sought in his dominions, he is at liberty to examine into the merits of the judgment, and to refuse to give effect to it, if, upon such examination, it should appear unjust and unfounded. He acts in executing it upon the principles of comity; and has, therefore, a right to prescribe the terms and limits of that comity.[1] But it is otherwise, (it is said,) where the defendant sets up a foreign judgment, as a bar to proceedings; for, if it has been pronounced by a competent tribunal, and carried into effect, the losing party has no right to institute a new suit elsewhere, and thus bring the matter again into controversy; and the other party is not to lose the protection, which the foreign judgment gave him. It is then *res judicata*, which ought to be received, as conclusive evidence of right; and the *exceptio rei judicatæ* under such circumstances is entitled to universal conclusiveness and respect.[2] This distinction has been very generally recognised as having a foundation in international justice.[3]

§ 599. Lord Chief Justice Eyre has stated it with his usual force in an elaborate judgment. "If we had

1 2 Kent Comm. Lect. 37, p. 119, 120; (2 edit.) and cases there cited.

2 Id., and cases there cited.

3 Id., and cases there cited; Burrows *v.* Jemino, 2 Str. R. 733; S. C. cited Cas. T. Hard. 87; Boucher *v.* Lawson, Cas T. Hard. 89; 2 Swanst. R. 326, note; Tarleton *v.* Tarleton, 4 M. & Selw. 20; Taylor *v.* Phelps, 1 Gill. and John. R. 492; Griswold *v.* Pitcairn, 4 Connect. R. 85.

the means," said he, "we could not examine a judgment of a court in a foreign state brought before us in this manner (that is, by the defendant as a bar.) It is in one way only, that the sentence or judgment of the court of a foreign state is examinable in our courts, and that is, when the party, who claims the benefit of it, applies to our courts to enforce it. When it is thus voluntarily submitted to our jurisdiction, we treat it, not as obligatory to the extent, to which it would be obligatory perhaps in the country, in which it was pronounced; nor as obligatory to the extent, to which by our law sentences and judgments are obligatory; not as conclusive, but as matter *in pais;* as a consideration *primâ facie* sufficient to raise a promise. We examine it as we do all other considerations of promises; and for that purpose we receive evidence of what the law of the foreign state is, and *whether the judgment is warranted by that law.* In all other cases, we give entire faith and credit to the sentences of foreign courts and consider them as conclusive upon us."[1] The same distinction is found applied in the same manner in the jurisprudence of Scotland.[2]

§ 600. Lord Kaims has marked out, and supported another distinction between suits sustaining, and suits dissmissing a claim. "In the last place," says he, "come foreign decrees; which are of two kinds, one sustaining the claim, and one dissmissing it. A foreign decree sustaining the claim, is not one of those universal titles, which ought to be made effectual everywhere. It is a title, that depends on the authority of the court, whence it issued, and therefore has no

[1] Phillips *v.* Hunter, 2 H. Black. R. 410.
[2] Erskine's Inst. B. 4, tit. 3, § 4.

coercive authority *extra territorium*. And yet as it would be hard to oblige the person, who claims on a decree, to bring a new action against his party in every country, to which he may retire; therefore, common utility, as well as regard to a sister court, have established a rule among all civilized nations, that a foreign decree shall be put in execution, unless some good exception be opposed to it in law or in equity; which is making no wider step in favour of the decree, than to presume it just, till the contrary be proved. But this includes not a decree decerning for a penalty; because no court reckons itself bound to punish, or to concur in punishing, any delict committed *extra territorium*.

§ 601. "A foreign decree, which, by dismissing the claim affords an *exceptio rei judicatæ* against it, enjoys a more extensive privilege. We not only presume it to be just, but will not admit any evidence of its being unjust. The reasons follow. A decreet-arbitral is final by mutual consent. A judgment-condemnator ought not to be final against the defendant, because he gave no consent. But a decreet-absolvitor ought to be final against the plaintiff, because the judge was chosen by himself; with respect to him at least, it is equivocal to a decreet-arbitral. Public utility affords another argument extremely cogent. There is nothing more hurtful to society, than that law-suits be perpetual. In every lawsuit there ought to be a *ne plus ultra*; some step, ought to be ultimate; and a decree dissmissing a claim is in its nature ultimate. Add a consideration, that regards the nature and constitution of a court of justice. A decree dismissing a claim, may, it is true, be unjust, as well as a decree sustaining it. But they differ widely in one capital point; in declining to give redress against a decree dismissing a claim, the court is not guilty of authorizing injustice, even supposing the decree to be unjust; the utmost that can be said is, that the court forbears to interpose in behalf of justice; but such forbearance, instead of being faulty, is highly meritorious in every case, where private justice clashes with public utility. The case is very different with respect to a decree of the other kind; for to award execution upon a foreign decree without admitting any objection against it, would be, for aught the court can know, to support and promote injustice. A court, as well as an individual, may in certain circumstances have reason to forbear acting, or executing their office; but the doing injustice, or the supporting it cannot be justified in any circumstances."[1]

§ 602. It does not appear, that this distinction of Lord Kaims, between judgments sustaining suits, and judgments dismissing them, has been recognised in the common law.[2] And there seems quite as much reason, that a defendant should be protected against a new litigation, after there has been a final sentence in his favour, as there is, that a plaintiff should be protected in the enjoyment of any right, which is established by a sentence in his favour. The sentence for the defendant may, in its legal operation, as completely establish a right in him, or as completely establish the non-existence of any right in the

1 2 Kaims on Equity, 365.

2 See the cases cited in Starkie on Evid. P. 2, § 80; Gelston v. Hoyt, 13 John. R. 561; S. C. 3 Wheaton R. 246; The Bennett, 1 Dodson R. 175, 180.

plaintiff, as the contrary sentence would establish an adverse right in the plaintiff, and the non-existence of any repugnant right in the defendant.

§ 603. In the next place, as to judgments *in personam*, which are sought to be enforced by a suit in a foreign tribunal. There has certainly been some fluctuation of opinion in the English Courts upon this subject. It is admitted on all sides, that in such cases, the foreign judgments are *primâ facie* evidence to sustain the action, and are to be deemed right, until the contrary is established.[1] But the question is, whether they are to be deemed conclusive; or whether the defendant is at liberty to go at large into the original merits, and show, that the judgment ought to have been different. If the latter course be the correct one, then a still more embarrassing consideration is, to what extent, and in what manner, the original merits can be properly inquired into.

§ 604. Lord Nottingham, in a case, where an attempt was made to examine a foreign sentence of divorce in Savoy, in the reign of Charles the 2d, held, that it was conclusive, and its merits not examinable. "We know not," said he, "the laws of Savoy. So, if we did, we have no power to judge by them. And, therefore, it is against the law of nations not to give credit to the sentences of foreign countries, till they are reversed by the law, and according to the form, of those countries, wherein they were given. For what right hath one kingdom to reverse the judgment of another? And how can

---

1 See Walker *v.* Witter, Doug. R. 1, and cases there cited; Arnold *v.* Redfern, 3 Bing. R. 353; Sinclair *v.* Fraser, cited Doug. R. 4, 5, note; Ripple *v.* Ripple, 1 Rawle R. 386.

we refuse to let a sentence take place, until it be reversed? And what confusion would follow in Christendom, if they should serve us so abroad, and give no credit to our sentences."[1] Lord Hardwicke manifestly held the same opinion, saying, "that where any court, foreign or domestic, that has the proper jurisdiction of the cases, makes the determination, it is conclusive to all other courts.[2]

§ 605. On the other hand Lord Mansfield thought, that foreign judgments gave a ground of action, but that they were examinable.[3] The same doctrine was held by Lord Chief Baron Eyre,[4] and Mr. Justice Buller,[5] the latter relying upon the decision of the House of Lords in Sinclair *v.* Fraser, as giving the true line of distinction between foreign and domestic judgments. In that case the House of Lords revived a decision of the court of Sessions of Scotland, in which the latter Court held the plaintiff bound in a suit upon a foreign judgment to prove before the court the general nature and extent of the demand, on which the judgment had been obtained. The reversal expressly declared, that the judgment ought to be received as evidence, *primâ facie*, of the debt; but that it lies upon the defendant to impeach the justice thereof,[6] or to show the same to have been irregularly or wrongly obtained. But it may be remarked of this last decision, that it does

---

1 2 Swanston R. note 326, 327.

2 Boucher *v.* Lawson, Cas. T. Hard. 89. See also Roach *v.* Garvan, 1 Ves. 157.

3 Walker *v.* Witter, Doug. 1; Id. 6, note 3. Herber *v.* Cooke, Willis, R. 36, note.

4 Phillips *v.* Hunter, 2 H. Black. 410; ante § 2.

5 Gallbraith *v.* Neville, cited Doug. R. 6, note (3.)

6 Doug. R. 4, 5, note (1.)

not go to the extent of establishing the doctrine, that the merits of the judgments *ab origine* are re-examinable *de novo;* but only that its justice may be impeached, or its irregularity or fraud shown.

§ 606. Lord Kenyon seems clearly to have been of a different opinion, and expressed serious doubts whether foreign judgments were not binding on the parties here.[1] And Lord Ellenborough on an occasion, in which the argument was pressed before him, that a foreign judgment was re-examinable, and that the defendant might impeach the justice of it, pithily remarked, that he thought he did not sit at *nisi prius*, to try a writ of error upon the proceedings of the court abroad.[2] In a very late case the Vice-Chancellor, upon a full examination of the authorities, held the opinion, that the true doctrine was, that foreign judgments were conclusive evidence, and not re-examinable; and that this was the true result of the old authorities. And he decided accordingly.[3] There is much reason to contend, that the present inclination of the English courts of common law is to sustain the conclusiveness of such judgments.[4]

§ 607. And it is very difficult to perceive what could be done, if a different doctrine were maintainable to the full extent of opening all the evidence and merits of the cause anew, on a suit upon the foreign judgment. Some of the witnesses may be since dead; some of the vouchers may be lost or

---

1 Galbraith *v.* Neville, Doug. R. 5, note (3.) See also Guinness *v.* Carwell, 1 Barn. & Adolph. 459.

2 Tarleton *v.* Tarleton, 4 M. & Selw. 21.

3 Martin *v.* Nicolls, 3 Simon R. 458.

4 See Guinness *v.* Carroll, 1 Barn. & Adolph. 459; Becquet *v.* McCarthy, 2 Barn. & Adolph. R. 951.

destroyed; the merits, as formerly before the court upon the whole evidence, may have been decidedly in favor of the judgment; upon a partial possession of the evidence they may now appear otherwise. Suppose a case purely sounding in damages, as an action for an assault, for slander, for conversion of property, for a malicious prosecution, for criminal conversation; is the defendant to be at liberty to re-try the whole merits, and to make out, if he can, a new case upon new evidence? Or is the court to review the former decision like a court of appeal upon the old evidence? In case of covenant, or debt, or breach of contract, are all the circumstances to be re-examined anew? And if they are, by which laws and rules of evidence and principles of justice is the validity of the original judgment to be tried? Is the court to open the judgment and to proceed *ex æquo et bono?* Or is it to administer strict law, and stand to the doctrines of the local administration of justice? These and many more questions might be put to show the intrinsic difficulties of the subject. Indeed showing the judgment to be *primâ facie* evidence for the plaintiff would be a mere delusion, if the defendant might still question it by opening any of the original merits on his side; for under such circumstances it would be equivalent to granting a new trial. It can well be understood, that a defendant may be at liberty to impeach the original justice of the judgment, by showing, that the court had no jurisdiction, or that he never had notice of the suit, or that it was procured by fraud, or that upon its face it is founded in mistake: or that it was irregular, and bad by the local law *rei judicatæ.* To such an extent the doctrine is intelligible and practicable. Beyond this the right to impugn the judgment is in legal effect the right to re-try it at large, and to put the defendant upon proving the original merits.[1]

§ 608. The general doctrine maintained in the American courts in relation to foreign judgments certainly is, that they are *primâ facie* evidence, but that they are impeachable.[2] But how far and to what extent this doctrine is to be carried, does not seem to be definitely settled. It has been declared, that the jurisdiction of the court may be inquired into, and its power over the parties and things; and that the judgment may be impeached for fraud.[3]

§ 609. By the constitution of the United States it is declared; that full faith and credit shall be given in each state to the public acts, records, and judicial proceedings of every other state. And Con-

---

1 See Arnot *v.* Redfern, 2 Carr and Payne, 88.; S. C. 3 Bing. R. 353; Novelli *v.* Rossi, 2 Barn. & Adolph. 757; Douglas *v.* Forrest, 4 Bing. R. 686; Obicini *v.* Bligh, 8 Bing. R. 335; See also Starkie on Evidence P. 2, § 67; Philips on Evidence (6th edit.) p. 333; Buttrick *v.* Allen, 8 Mass. R. 273; Huberus, Lib. 1. tit. 3. De Conflictu, § 6.

2 Many of the cases are collected; 2 Kent Comm. Lect. 37, p. 118, &c. (2d edition); in 4 Cow. R. 520, note 3; and in Mr. Metcalf's notes to his valuable edition of Starkie on Evidence, P. 2, § 67, 68. (edit. 1830. p. 214 to 216). See also Bissell *v.* Briggs, 9 Mass. R. 462; Borden *v.* Fitch, 15 John. R. 121; Green *v.* Sarmiento, 1 Peters Circt. R. 74; Field *v.* Gibbs, 1 Peters Civ. R. 155; Aldrich *v.* Kinney, 4 Connect. R. 380; Shumway *v.* Stillman, 6 Wend. R. 447; Hall *v.* Williams, 6 Pick. 247; Starbuck *v.* Murray, 5 Wend. R. 148; Davis *v.* Peckars, 6 Wend. R. 327; Buttrick *v.* Allen, 8 Mass. R. 273; Pawling *v.* Bird's Ex'rs., 13 John. R. 192; Hitchcock *v.* Aicken, 1 Cain. R. 460; Watson's Dig. *Judgment I;* Bigelow's Dig. *Judgment H.;* Johnson's Digest, *Debt H;* Coxe's Digest, *Judgment;* Hoxie *v.* Wright, 2 Vermont Rep. 263; Bellows *v.* Ingraham, 2 Vermont Rep. 575; Barney *v.* Patterson, 6 Harris and John. 182.

3 Ibid.

gress, in pursuance of the power given them by the constitution in a succeeding clause, have declared, that judgments of state Courts shall have the same faith and credit in other states, as they have in the state, where they are rendered.[1] They are therefore put upon the same footing as domestic judgments. But this does not prevent an inquiry into the jurisdiction of the Court, in which the original judgment was rendered, to pronounce the judgment, or into the right of the state to exercise authority over the parties on the subject matter. The constitution did not mean to confer any new power upon the states; but simply to regulate the effect of their acknowledged jurisdiction over persons and things within their territory.[2]

§ 610. In the next place, as to judgments *in personam* between citizens and between foreigners, and between foreigners and citizens. The common law recognises no distinction whatever, as to the effect of foreign judgments; whether they are between citizens or foreigners, they are all deemed of equal obligation, whoever are the parties. The cases, which have been already cited, refer to no such distinction, and apply the same rules indiscrminately to all persons.

§ 611. We have hitherto been principally considering the doctrines of the common law. But it cannot be affirmed, that the same doctrines are gene-

---

1 Constitution, Art. 3, § 4; Act of Congress of 26th May, 1790, ch. 11; 3 Story's Comm. on Constit. ch. 29. §1297 to 3107.

2 See Story's Comment. on the Constit. ch. 29, § 1297 to 1307, and cases there cited;—Hall *v.* Williams, 6 Pick. R. 237; Bissell *v.* Briggs, 9 Mass. R. 462; Shumway *v.* Stillman, 6 Wend. R. 447; Evans *v.* Tarleton, 9 Sergt. and R. 260; Benton *v.* Burgot, 10 Sergt. and R. 240; Hancock *v.* Barrett, 1 Hall Sup. Ct. R. 155; S. C. 2 Hall Sup. Ct. R. 302; Wilson *v.* Niles, 2 Hall Sup. Ct. R. 358; Hoxie *v.* Wright, 2 Vermont R. 263; Bellows *v.* Ingraham, 2 Vermont R. 573; Aldrich *v.* Kinney, 4 Connect. R. 380.

rally maintained either by foreign Courts or foreign Jurists. Many foreign Jurists contend for the doctrine of Vattel, that the judgments of a competent tribunal are to be held of equal validity in every other country.[1] Thus Huberus lays down the rule; *Cuncta negotia et acta, tam in judicio quam extra judicium, &c., secundum jus certi loci rite celebrata, valent, etiam ubi diversa juris observatio viget.*[2] And again. *Similem usum habet hæc observatio in rebus judicatis. Sententia in aliquo loco pronunciata, vel delicti venia ab eo, qui jurisdictionem illam habet, ubique habet effectum, &c. Idem obtinet in sententiis rerum civilium.*[3] The doctrine seems well founded in the more expressive language of the civil law. *Res judicata pro veritate accipitur.*[4]

§ 612. D'Argentré holds a like opinion. *De omni personali negotio constat judicis ejus cognitionem esse cui persona subsit, ut, quocunque persona abeat, id jus sit quod ille statuet.*[5] Gaill holds, that any other rule would involve absurdity; *absurdum fore, si post sententiam definitivam, alia esset ferenda sententia, et processum in infinitum extrahi litemque ex lite oriri debere.*[6]

§ 613. We have already had occasion to take notice of the doctrines of Boullenois upon the right of jurisdiction;[7] and he applies them in an especial manner to the authority of foreign judgments. In regard to judgments *in rem* or partly *in rem* and partly *in*

---

1 Henry on Foreign Law, 75, 76.
2 Huberus, Lib. 1, tit. 3, De Conflict. Leg. § 3.
3 Idem § 6.
4 Dig. Lib. 1, tit. 5, c. 25.
5 Henry on Foreign Law, 74; 1 Boullenois, 605.
6 Henry on Foreign Law, 74, 75; 1 Boullenois 605, 606.
7 Ante, § 552.

personam, he deems the jurisdiction to belong exclusively to the tribunals of the place *rei sitæ*, and consequently that the judgment rendered there, ought to be of universal obligation.[1] But, in regard to judgments in personal actions, he makes the following distinctions. If the foreign judgment is in a suit between natives of the same country, in which it is pronounced, and it is rendered by a competent tribunal, in such case it ought to be executed in every other country without any new inquiry into the merits.[2] The reason assigned is, that the judgment has emanated from a lawful authority, and has been rendered between persons, who are subject to that authority; and consequently, the judgment ought not to be submitted to examination or discussion in any other tribunal, which for such purposes must be wholly incompetent. If the foreign judgment is rendered in a suit between mere strangers, who are found within the territorial authority of the court rendering it, whenever the jurisdiction is rightfully exercised over the parties, in such case the judgment is equally conclusive, and not examinable by any other tribunal.[3] But he thinks that such jurisdiction cannot be rightfully exercised merely because the strangers are found there, unless they are domiciled, and have made themselves subject to the laws, or have made some contract there, or some contract to be executed there, which is the subject matter of the suit.[4] Lastly, if the judgment is rendered in a suit between a native of the country, where the judgment is pronounced, and a stranger;

---

1 1 Boullenois, 618, 619, 620, to 624; Idem 635, 636.

2 1 Boullenois, 603, 605.

3 1 Boullenois, 606, 607.

4 1 Boullenois, 606, 607, 608, 609, 610.

sequitur forum rei, belongs to the law of nations.[1] Vattel affirms this maxim in explicit terms.[2]

§ 617. The doctrine thus promulgated by Émérigon has continued down to a very recent period.[3] But by the present code of France the ordinance of 1629 seems to be abolished; and foreign judgments are now deemed capable of execution in that country.[4] But the merits of the judgment are examinable, and no distinction seems to be made, whether the judgment is in a suit between foreigners, or between Frenchmen, or between a foreigner and a Frenchman; or whether it is in favor of one party or the other; or whether it is rendered upon default or upon confession, or upon full trial and contestation of the merits.[5] Toullier considers it as now the established jurisprudence of France, that no foreign judgment can be rendered executory in France, but upon a full cognizance of the cause before the French tribunals, in which all the original grounds of the action are to be debated and considered anew.[6] And the same principle is applied to cases, where foreign judgments are set up by the defendant by way of bar

---

1 Émérigon, Traité des Ass. ch. 4, § 8, n. 2, p. 122, 123; 2 Kent Comm. Lect. 37, p. 121, 122, note. — The same doctrine is explicitly avowed to be the law of France in many other authorities. See Henry on Foreign Law, Appx. 209.

2 Vattel, B. 2, ch. 8, § 103.

3 Merlin, Répertoire, Jugement, § 6; Id. Stat. § 5, n. 6, p. 380; Id. Questions de Droit, Jugement, § 14; 2 Kent Comm. Lect. 37, p. 121, 122, note; Toullier, Droit Civ. Franç. ch. 6, § 3, p. 76, 81, 82, 86.

4 Code de Procédure Civile, art. 546; Code Civil, art. 2123, 2128; 10 Toullier, Droit Civ. Franç. ch. 6. § 3, n. 76, 77, 78, 84, 85, 86.

5 Toullier, Droit Civ. Franç. ch. 6, § 3, n. 76, 77, 78, 80, 81, 84, 85, 86; Pardessus, Droit Comm. Tom. 5, art. 1488.

6 Id. n. 85. 86. 2 Kent Comm. Lect. 37, p. 121, 122, note (2d edit.); Pardessus, Droit Comm. Tom. 5, art. 1488.

to a new action. The judgments are equally re-examinable upon the merits.[1]

§ 618. It is difficult to ascertain, what the prevailing rule is in regard to foreign judgments in other of the continental nations of Europe; whether they are deemed conclusive, or only *primâ facie* evidence. Holland seems at all times, upon the principle of reciprocity, to have given great weight to them, and in many cases, if not in all cases, a weight equal to that given to domestic judgments, where the rule of reciprocity with regard to Dutch judgments has been adopted by the foreign country, whose judgment is under review. This is certainly a very reasonable rule; and may, perhaps, hereafter work itself firmly into the structure of international jurisprudence.[2]

---

[1] Toullier, Droit Civ. Franç. ch. 6, § 3, n. 76 to 86; Merlin, Répertoire, Jugement, § 6; Id. Questions de Droit, Jugement, § 14; Pardessus, Droit Comm. Tom. 5, art. 1488; 2 Kent Comm. Lect. 37.

[2] Henry on Foreign Law, ch. 10, § 2, p. 75, 76.

CHAPTER XVI.

PENAL LAWS AND OFFENCES.

§ 619. We are next led to the consideration of the operation of foreign Laws in regard to penalties and offences. And this will not require an expanded examination, as the topics are few, and the doctrines maintained by foreign jurists and by tribunals acting under the common law involve no intricate inquiries into the peculiar jurisprudence of different nations.

§ 620. The common law considers crimes as altogether local, and cognizable and punishable exclusively in the country, where they are committed. No other nation, therefore, has any right to punish them; or is under any obligation to take notice of, or to enforce any judgment, rendered in such cases by the tribunals having authority to hold jurisdiction within the territory, where they are committed.[1] Hence it is, that a criminal sentence of attainder in the courts of one sovereign, though it creates a personal disability to sue, does not carry the same disability with the person into other countries. Foreign jurists maintain on this particular point a different opinion, holding, that the state or condition of a person in the place of his domicil accompanies him everywhere.[2] Lord Loughbo-

---

1 Rutherf. Inst. B. 2, ch. 9, § 12; Martens' Law of Nations, B. 3, ch. 3, § 22, 23, 24, 25; Merlin, Répertoire, Souveraineté, § 5, n. 5, 6, p. 379 to 382; Commonwealth *v.* Green, 17 Mass. R. 515, 545, 546, 547, 548.

2 Ante, § 91, 92; 1 Hertii Opera, De Collis. Leg. § 4, n. 8, p. 124; 1 Boullenois, 64, 65. — Boullenois states this doctrine in strong terms. "A l'égard des statuts, qui prononcent une morte civile pour crimes ou une note d'infamie, l'état de ces misérables se porte par tout, indépendamment de tout domicile; et cela par un concert and un concours général des nations, ces sortes de peines étant une tache, une plaie

rough in declaring the opinion of the Court in Folliott *v.* Ogden,[1] said, "Penal laws of foreign countries are strictly local, and affect nothing more than they can reach, and can be seized by virtue of their authority. A fugitive, who passes hither, comes with all his transitory rights. He may recover money held for his use, and stock, obligations, and the like; and cannot be affected in this country by proceedings against him in that, which he has left, beyond the limits of which such proceedings do not extend." And Mr. Justice Buller in the case on a writ of error said, "It is a general principle, that the penal laws of one country cannot be taken notice of in another."[2] And the same doctrine was affirmed by Lord Ellenborough in a more recent case.[3]

§ 621. The same doctrine has been frequently recognised in America. "We are required (said Mr. Chief Justice Spencer in an important case) to give effect to a law (of Connecticut), which inflicts a penalty for acquiring a right to a *chose in action.* The defendant cannot take advantage of, nor expect the Court to enforce, the criminal laws of another state. The penal acts of one state can have no operation in another state. They are strictly local, and affect nothing more than they can reach.[4]" Upon this ground also the Supreme Court of Massachusetts have held, that a person, convicted of an infamous offence in one state,

---

incurable, dont le condamné est affligé, et qui l'accompagne en tous lieux. C'est ce que dit D'Argentré." (1 Boullenois, 64, 65.)

1 1 H. Black. p. 135.

2 Ogden *v.* Folliott, 3 T. R. 733, 734.

3 Wolff *v.* Oxholm, 6 M. & Selw. R. 99.

4 Scoville *v.* Canfield, 14 John R. 338, 340. See also The State *v.* Knight, Taylor's N. C. Rep. 65.

is not thereby rendered incompetent as a witness in other states.[1]

§ 622. The same doctrine is stated by Lord Kaims as the doctrine in Scotland. "There is not (says he) the same necessity for an extraordinary jurisdiction to punish foreign delinquencies. The proper place for punishment is where the crime is committed. And no society takes concern in any crime but what is hurtful to itself."[2]

§ 623. The same doctrine is laid down by Martens as a clear principle of the law of nations. After remarking, that the criminal power of a country is confined to the territory, he adds, "By the same principles a sentence, which attacks the honor, rights, or property of a criminal, cannot extend beyond the Courts of the territory of the sovereign, who has pronounced it. So that he, who has been declared infamous, is infamous in fact, but not in law. And the confiscation of his property cannot affect his property situate in a foreign country. To deprive him of his honour and property judicially there also, would be to punish him a second time for the same offence."[3]

§ 624. Pardessus has affirmed a similar principle. "In all the States of Christendom, by a sort of general consent and uniformity of practice, the prosecution and punishment of penal offences are left to the tribunals of the country, where they are committed. The principle of the French Legislation, that the laws of police and bail are obligatory upon all, who are within the terri-

---

1 Commonwealth *v.* Green, 17 Mass. R. 515, 540, 541, 546, 547.

2 Kaims on Equity, B. 3, ch. 8, § 1. See also Ersk. Inst. B. 1, tit. 2, § 23.

3 Martens' Summary of the Law of Nations, B. 3. ch. 3, § 24, 25.

tory, is a principle of common right in all nations."[1] Bouhier also admits the locality, or, as he terms it, the reality of penal laws; and of course he limits their operation to the territory of the sovereignty, within which they are committed.[2]

§ 625. On the other hand Hertius, and P. Voet, seem to maintain a different doctrine, holding, that crimes committed in one state, may, if the criminal is found in another state, be upon demand punished there.[3] Voet says, *Statutum personale ubique locorum personam comitatur, etiam in ordine ad pœnam a cive petendam, si pœna civibus sit imposita.*[4] Some of the foreign jurists enter into elaborate discussions of the question, whether, if a fugitive criminal is arrested in another country, he is to be punished according to the law of his domicil, or according to the law of the place, where the offence was committed.[5] If any nation should suffer its own courts to entertain jurisdiction of foreign offences in such cases, the rule of Bartolus would seem to furnish the true answer. *Delicta puniuntur juxta mores loci comissi delicti, et non loci, ubi de crimine cognoscitur.*[6]

---

1 Pardessus, Droit Comm. Tom. 5, art. 1467. See also Merlin, Répertoire, Souveraineté, § 5, n. 5, 6, p. 379 to 382.

2 Bouhier, Cout. de Bourg. ch. 34, p. 583. See also Matthæi, Comm. ad Pand. Lib. 48, tit. 20, § 17, 18, 20.

3 Hertii Opera, De Collis. Leg. § 4, n. 18, 21, p. 130, 131, 132.

4 P. Voet. de Statut. § 4, ch. 2, n. 6, p. 123. See Id. § 11, ch. 1, n. 4, 5, p. 294, 295, 296.

5 See 1 Hertii Opera, De Collis. Leg. § 4, n. 19, 20, 21, p. 131, 132; Voet. de Stat. § 11, ch. 1, § 1, 4, 5, p. 291 to 297.

6 Henry on Foreign Law, 47. — Martens deems it clear, that a Sovereign, in whose dominions a criminal has sought refuge, may, if he chooses, punish him for the offence, though committed in a foreign country; though he admits, that the more common usage in modern times is to remand the criminal to the country, where the crime was committed. Martens' Law of Nations, B. 3; ch. 3, § 22, 23. See also Vattel, B. 2. ch. 2, § 76; Grotius de Jure Belli et Pac. B. 2, ch. 21, § 2, 3, 4, 5; Burlemaqui, P. 4, ch. 3, § 24, 25, 26.

§ 626. There is another point, which has been a good deal discussed of late; and that is, whether a nation is bound to surrender up fugitives from justice, who escape into its territories, and seek there an asylum from punishment. The practice has, beyond question, prevailed as a matter of comity, and sometimes of treaty, between some neighbouring states, and sometimes also between distant states, having much intercourse with each other.[1] Voet remarks, that under the Roman Empire this right of having a criminal remitted for trial to the proper *forum criminis* was unquestionable. It resulted from the very nature of the universal dominion of the Roman Laws. *Jure tamen civili notandum, remissionibus locum fuisse de necessitate, ut reus ad locum, ubi deliquit, sic petente judice, fuerit mittendus, quod omnes judices uni subessent imperatori. Et omnes provinciæ Romanæ unitæ essent accessorie, non principaliter.*[2] But he remarks, that according to the customs of almost all Christendom (except Saxony) the remitter of criminals, except in cases of humanity, is not admitted; and, when done, it is to be upon letters rogatory, so that there may be no prejudice to the local jurisdiction. *Moribus nihilominus (non tamen Saxonicis) totius fere Christianismi nisi ex humanitate non sunt admissæ remissiones. Quo casu, remittenti magistratui cavendum per litteras reversoriales, ne actus jurisdictioni remittentis ullum pariat præjudicium. Id quod etiam in nostris Provinciis Unitis est receptum*[3] And he adds, *Neque enim Provinciæ Fœderatæ uni supremo parent;*[4] a remark

1 See Vattel, B. 2, ch. 6, § 76.
2 Voet. De Stat. § 11, ch. 1, n. 6, p. 297.
3 Voet. De Stat. § 11, ch. 1, n. 6, p. 297.
4 Id. See also Matthæi, Comm. de Criminibus, Dig. Lib. 48, tit. 14, § 3.

strictly applicable to the American States. It is manifest that he treats it purely as a matter of comity and not national duty.

§ 627. It has been treated, however, by other distinguished jurists, as a strict right, and as constituting a part of the law and usage of nations, that offenders charged with a high crime who have fled from the country, in which the crime had been committed, could be delivered up and sent back for trial by the sovereign of the country where they are found. Vattel manifestly contemplates the subject in this latter view, contending that it is the duty of the government, where the criminal is, to deliver him up, or to punish him; and if it refuses so to do, then it becomes responsible as in some measure an accomplice in the crime.[1] And this opinion is maintained with great vigor by Grotius, by Heineccius, by Burlemaqui, and by Rutherforth.[2] There is no inconsiderable weight of common law authority on the same side; and Mr. Chancellor Kent has adopted the doctrine in a case which called directly for its decision.[3]

§ 628. On the other hand Puffendorf explicitly denies it as a matter of right.[4] Martens is manifest-

---

1 Vattel, B. 2, ch. 6, § 76.

2 Grotius de Jure Belli et Pacis, ch. 21, § 2, 3, 4, 5; Heineccii Prælect. in Grot. h. t.; Burlemaqui, Pt. 4, ch. 3, § 19 to 24; Rutherf. Inst. B. 2. ch. 9, § 12.

3 In the matter of Washburn, 4 John. Ch. R. 106; 1 Kent Comm. Lect. 2, p. 36, (2nd. ed.); Rex *v.* Hutchinson, 3 Keble, 785; Rex *v.* Kimburley, 2 Strange R. 848; East India Company *v.* Campbell, 1 Ves. Sen. 246; Mure *v.* Kaye, 4 Taunton R. 34; Per Heath J.; Wynne's Eunomus, Dialog. 3, § 67; Lundy's Case, 2 Vent. R. 314; Rex *v.* Ball, 1 Amer. Jurist, 287.

4 For this reference to Puffendorf's opinion, I must rely on Burlemaqui (Pt. 4, ch. 3, § 23, 24.), not having been able to find it in his Treatise on the Law of Nations. The only reference to the point, which I have met with in that work is in B. 8, ch. 3, § 23, 24.

ly of the same opinion, contending that, with respect to crimes committed out of his territories, no sovereign is obliged to punish the criminal, who seeks shelter in his dominions, nor to execute a sentence pronounced against his person or property.[1] Lord Coke expressly maintains that the sovereign is not bound to surrender up fugitive criminals from other countries, who have sought a shelter in his dominions.[2] Mr. Chief Justice Tilghman has adhered to the same doctrine in a very elaborate judgment.[3] And the reasoning of Mr. Chief Justice Parker in Commonwealth *v.* Green,[4] leads to a similar conclusion.[5]

---

1 Martens' Law of Nations, B. 3, ch. 3, § 23.

2 3 Coke Inst. 180.

3 Comwth. *v.* Deacon, 10 Serg. & R. 125; 3 Story, Comm. on Constit. § 1802. See also Merlin, Répertoire, Souveraineté, § 5, n. 5, 6, p. 379 to p. 382,

4 17 Mass. R. 515, 540, 541, 546, 547, 548.

5 All the reasoning on each side will be found very fully collected in the cases of the matter of Washburn, 4 John. Ch. R. 106.; Commonwealth *v.* Deacon, 10 Serg. & Rawle, 123; and Rex *v.* Ball, 1 Amer. Jurist, 297. The latter case is the decision of Mr. Chief Justice Reid of Canada. See also 1 Amer. State Papers, 175; Commonwealth *v.* De Longchamps, 1 Dall. 111, 115.

CHAPTER XVII.

EVIDENCE AND PROOFS.

§ 629. We come in the last place to the consideration of the operation of foreign laws in relation to evidence and proofs. And, here, the question materially arises, in what manner contracts, instruments, or other acts made or done in other countries are to be proved. Is it sufficient to prove them in the manner and by the solemnities and proofs, which are deemed sufficient by the law of the place, where the contracts, instruments, or other acts, were executed? Or is it necessary to prove them according to the law of the place where the action or other judicial proceeding is instituted?

§ 630. Various cases may be put to illustrate these questions. A contract or other instrument is executed and recorded before a Notary Public in a foreign country, in which by law a copy of the contract or other instrument certified by him is sufficient to establish its existence and genuineness; would that certificate be admissible in the courts of common law of England or America to establish the same facts?[1] Again; persons who are interested, and even parties in the suit are in some foreign countries admissible witnesses to prove contracts, instruments, and other acts, material to the merits of the suit; would they be admissible as witnesses in suits brought in the course of common law in England and America to prove the like facts in relation to contracts, instruments, or other acts made or done in such foreign

[1] See Mascardus, De Probat. Vol. 2, Conclus. 927, p. 336.

countries material to the suit? These are questions more easily put than answered.

§ 631. There are certain formalities of proof, which are required by the laws of foreign countries in regard to contracts, instruments, and other acts, which are indispensable to their validity there; and they are therefore held of universal obligation; and must be duly proved in every foreign tribunal, in which they are in litigation, before any right can be founded on them.[1] An illustration of this doctrine may be drawn from the known rule of the common law, that a bill of exchange upon its dishonour must be protested before a notary; and if not proved to be so protested, no remedy can be had against the drawer or indorsers.[2] Another illustration may be drawn from the registration of deeds and other instruments, which cannot be given in evidence unless proved to be duly registered. Another illustration may be drawn from cases of contract under the statute of frauds, which must be in writing, and must state a consideration in order to be valid in point of legal obligation or evidence. And another illustration may be drawn from the known doctrine as to stamps, by which it is held that no instrument can be given in evidence unless it is properly stamped. In all these cases the proper proofs must doubtless be given in conformity with the local law.[3] And if given in the mode which the local law requires, there is some difficulty in asserting that such proofs ought not to be deemed everywhere a full authentication of the instrument.[4]

---

1 See Trasher *v.* Everhart, 3 Gill. & John. R. 234, 242.

2 See Boyden *v.* Taylor, 2 Harr. & John. 396.

3 Ante, § 260.

4 See Erskine's Inst. B. 3, tit. 2, § 39, 40.

§ 632. Boullenois appears to hold this doctrine, and recognises the maxim, *Solemnitates testimoniales non sunt in potestate cotrahentium, sed in potestate juris.*[1] Voet appears to entertain a different opinion, and puts the case, whether an instrument executed before a notary, who by the *lex loci* is competent for this purpose, but by the law of another place is incompetent, would have public authenticity in the latter place? After giving the opinions of several jurists in the affirmative, he proceeds to give his own to this effect; that it is not so much a question of solemnities, as of the efficacy of proof, which although it may be sufficient in one place, may not be so everywhere; and that the tribunals of one country cannot give such validity and force to any instrument, that it shall have operation elsewhere.[2]

§ 633. Voet also in another place, speaking upon the subject of the operation of the *lex fori*, as to modes of proceeding in suits, uses the following language. *Si de probationibus et quidem testibus, sic eas adhibebit, sic examinabit hosce, prout exigit forum judicis, ubi producuntur. Si de instrumentis, sic exhibenda, sic edenda, ut fert loci statutum, ubi exhibenter, vel eduntur.*[3] The generality of these expressions leads to the conclusion, that he deemed the modes of proof and the law of evidence of the *lex fori* must regulate all suits whether these arose from foreign contracts, instruments, or other acts or not. But perhaps he may have intended to give them a more limited application.[4]

1 1 Boullenois, 492; Ante, § 260.

2 Voet. de Stat. § 10, ch. 1, n. 11, p. 287, 288.

3 Ibid. § 10, ch. 1, n. 11, p. 287.

4 Erskine in his Institutes says, that in suits in Scotland with foreigners upon obligations made in a foreign country, they may prove payment or extinguishment *lege loci*. If, for instance, the law of the foreign country allows the payment of a debt constituted by writing to be proved by

§ 634. Bouhier states a case, where a suit was brought in France by an Englishman against another person for money supposed to be lent by him to the latter; and he offered proof thereof by witnesses. It was objected, that by the ordinance of Moulins (art. 54), such parol proof was inadmissible. But the Court admitted it upon the ground that the law of England, where the contract was made, admitted such parol proof, and therefore it was admissible in a controversy on the contract in France. Bouhier holds the decision to be correct, if the contract was made, as he supposes it to have been, in England.[1]

§ 635. There are very few traces to be found in the reports of the common law, of any established doctrines on this subject. We have already seen in regard to witnesses generally, that their competency is governed in common cases by the *lex fori.* But, suppose the only witness to a contract, written or verbal, was incompetent on account of interest by the common law, but competent by the law of the place of the contract; in a suit in a tribunal of the common law on the contract, ought his testimony to be rejected? Again; suppose that books of account, which (as is well known [2]) are by the laws of some states admissible and of other states inadmissible as evidence, are offered in the forum of the latter

---

witnesses, that manner of proof will also be allowed by the Scottish courts as sufficient for extinguishing such debt, although by the Scottish law obligations formed by writing are not extinguishable by parol evidence. Erskine's Inst. B. 3, tit. 5, § 7. This seems a mixed case of the law of the place governing as to the discharge of contracts, and also of the mode of proof of the discharge.

1 1 Bouhier, Cout. de Bourg, ch. 21, § 205, p. 415. See also Strykius, Tom. 2, Diss. 1, ch. 3, § 18 to 25, p. 21, 27.

2 See Pothier on Oblig. P. 4, ch. 1, art. 2, § 4, n. 719; Cogswell *v.* Dolliver, 2 Mass. R. 217; 1 Starkie on Ev. P. 2, § 130, 131; Strykius, Tom. 7, Diss. 1, c. 4, § 5.

to establish debts contracted in the former; ought they to be rejected?[1] Cases, *vice versâ*, may easily be put, which will present questions quite as embarrassing.

§ 636. In regard to wills of personal property made in a foreign country, it would seem to be almost matter of necessity to admit the same evidence to establish their validity and authenticity abroad, as would establish them in the domicil of the testator; for otherwise the general rule that personal property shall pass everywhere by a will made according to the law of the place of the testator's domicil, might be sapped to its very foundation, if the law of evidence in any country, where such property was situate, was not precisely the same as in the place of his domicil. And, therefore, parol evidence has been admitted in courts of common law to prove the manner in which the will is made and proved in the place of the testator's domicil, in order to lay a suitable foundation to establish the will elsewhere.[2]

§ 637. Passing from this most embarrassing, and as yet (in a great measure) unsettled class of questions, let us consider in what manner courts of justice arrive at the knowledge of foreign laws. Are they to be judicially taken notice of? Or are they to be proved as matters of fact? The established doctrine now is, that no court takes judicial notice of the laws of a foreign country, but they must be proved as facts.[3]

---

1 Upon this very point foreign jurists have delivered opposite opinions, as appears from Hertius, who however abstains from giving any opinion on the subject. 1 Hertii Opera, De Collis. Leg. § 4, n. 68, p. 152. Voet thinks they are to be deemed *primâ facie* evidence but, not conclusive. Voet. De Stat. § 5, ch. 2, n. 9, p. 160.

2 De Sobry *v.* De Laistre, 2 Harr. & John. 191, 195.

4 See Mostyn *v.* Fabrigas, Cowp. 174; Male *v.* Roberts, 3 Esp. R.

§ 638. But it may be asked whether they are to be proved as facts to the jury, if the case is a trial at the common law, or as facts to the court? It would seem to the latter; for all matters of law are properly referrible to the court, and the object of the proof of foreign laws is to enable the court to instruct the jury what is, in point of law, the result from foreign law to be applied to the matters in controversy before them. The court are therefore to decide what is the proper evidence of the laws of a foreign country; and when evidence is given of those laws, the court are to judge of their applicability, when proved, to the case in hand.[1]

163; Douglas *v.* Brown, 2 Dow & Clark R. 171; De Sobry *v.* De Laistre, 2 Harr. & John. R. 193; Trasher *v.* Everhart, 3 Gill. & John. R. 234; Brackett *v.* Norton, 4 Connect. R. 517; Talbot *v.* Leeman, 1 Cranch, 38; Church *v.* Hubbart, 2 Cranch, 187, 236, 237; 4 Cowen R. 515, 516, note; Starkie on Evid. P. 2, § 33; Id. § 92; Id. P. 4, p. 569; Conseequa *v.* Willings, Peters Cir. R. 229; Legg *v.* Legg, 8 Mass. R. 99; Hosford *v.* Nichols, 1 Paige R. 220.

1 De Sobry *v.* De Laistre, 2 Harr. & John. 193, 219. But see Brackett *v.* Norton, 4 Connect. R. 517. — In Trasher *v.* Everhart (3 Gill. & John. 234, 242), the Court said, "It is in general true that foreign laws are facts, which are to be found by the jury. But this general rule is not applicable to a case, in which foreign laws are introduced for the purpose of enabling the Court to determine whether a written instrument is evidence. In such the evidence always goes in the first instance to the Court, which, if the evidence be clear and uncontradicted, may, and ought to decide what the foreign law is, and, according to its determination on that subject, admit or reject the instrument of writing as evidence to the jury. It is offered to the Court to determine a question of law, — the admissibility or inadmissibility of certain evidence to the jury. It is true, that if, what the foreign law is, be a matter of doubt, the Court may decline deciding it, and may inform the Jury, that if they believe the foreign law, attempted to be proved, exists as alleged, then they ought to receive the instrument in evidence. On the contrary, if they should believe that such is not the foreign law, they should reject the instrument as evidence." Is not foreign law offered in all cases to instruct the Court in matters of law material to the point

§ 639. As to the manner of proof this must vary according to circumstances. The general principle is, that the best testimony or proof shall be required which the nature of the thing admits of; or, in other words, that no testimony shall be received, which presupposes better testimony attainable by the party who offers it. And this applies to the proof of foreign laws as well as of other facts. But to require proof of such laws by such species of testimony, as their institutions and usages do not admit of, would be unjust and unreasonable. In this as in all other cases no testimony is required which can be shown to be unattainable.[1]

§ 640. Generally speaking authenticated copies of written laws or other public instruments of a foreign government are expected to be produced. For it is not to be presumed that any civilized nation will refuse to give such copies duly authenticated, which are usual and necessary for the purposes of administering justice. It cannot be presumed that an application to authenticate an edict or law will be refused; but the fact of refusal must be proved. But if such refusal is proved, then inferior proofs may be admissible.[2] Where our own government has promulgated a foreign law or ordinance of a public nature as authentic, that may be sufficient evidence of its existence.[3]

---

in issue? Can the Court properly leave it to the jury to find out what the law is, and apply it to the case? Lord Mansfield in Mostyn v. Fabigas (Cowper R. 174) said, "The way of knowing foreign laws is by admitting them to be proved as facts; and the Court must assist the jury in ascertaining what the law is."

1 Church v. Hubbart, 2 Cranch R. 237.

2 Church v. Hubbart, 2 Cranch 237, 238.

3 Talbot v. Leeman, 1 Cranch 38.

§ 641. In general foreign laws are required to be verified by the sanction of an oath, unless they can be verified by some other such high authority as the law respects, not less than the oath of an individual.[1] The usual modes of authenticating foreign laws (as of foreign judgments) are by an exemplification of a copy under the great seal of a state; or by a copy proved to be a true copy; or by the certificate of an officer authorized by law, which certificate must itself be duly authenticated.[2]

§ 642. But foreign unwritten laws, customs, and usages, may be proved, and indeed must ordinarily be proved by parol evidence. The usual course is to make such proof by the testimony of competent witnesses, instructed in the law under oath.[3] Sometimes, however, certificates of persons in high authority have been allowed as evidence.[4]

§ 643. It seems, that the public seal of a foreign sovereign affixed to a writing purporting to be a written edict, or law, or judgment, is, of itself, the highest evidence of its authority; and courts of other countries will judicially take notice of such public seal, which is therefore considered as proving itself.[5] But the seal of a foreign court does not prove itself, and therefore must be established as such by

---

1 Church *v.* Hubbart, 2 Cranch, 237.

2 Church *v.* Hubbart, 2 Cranch, 238; Packard *v.* Hill, 2 Wend. R. 411; Lincoln *v.* Battelle, 6 Wend. R. 475.

3 Church *v.* Hubbart, 237; Dalrymple *v.* Dalrymple, 2 Hagg. Rep. App'x. p. 15 to 144; Brush *v.* Wilkins, 4 John. Ch. R. 520; Mostyn *v.* Fabrigas, Cowper R. 174.

4 *In re* Dormay, 3 Hagg. Eccl. R. 767, 769.

5 Lincoln *v.* Battelle, 6 Wend. R. 475; Griswold *v.* Pittcairn, 2 Conn. 85; Church *v.* Hubbart, 2 Cranch, 238, 239; Anon. 7 Mod. R. 66; United States *v.* Johnson, 4 Dall. 416.

competent testimony.[1] There is an exception to this rule, in favour of courts of admiralty, which being courts of the law of nations, the courts of other countries will judicially take notice of their seal without positive proof of its authenticity.[2]

§ 644. The mode, by which the laws, records, and judgments of the different states composing the American Union, are to be verified, has been prescribed by Congress, pursuant to an authority given in the Constitution of the United States. It is, therefore, wholly unnecessary, to dwell upon this subject, as these regulations are properly a part of our municipal law; and do not strictly belong to a treatise on international law.[3]

§ 645. And here these commentaries on this interesting branch of public law, are brought to a close. It will occur to the learned reader, upon a general survey of the subject, that many questions are still left in a distressing state of uncertainty, as to the true principles, which ought to regulate and decide them. Different nations entertain different doctrines and different usages in regard to them. The jurists of different countries hold opinions opposite to each other, as to some of the fundamental principles, which ought to have a universal operation; and the jurists of the same nation are sometimes as ill agreed among themselves. Still, however, with all these

---

1 Starkie on Evid. P. 2, § 92; Delafield v. Hurd, 3 John. R. 310; De Sobry v. De Laistre, 2 Harr. & John. R. 193; Henry v. Adey, 3 East R. 221; 4 Cowen R. 526, note.

2 See Yeaton v. Fry, 5 Cranch, 335; Thompson v. Stewart, 3 Conn. R. 171.

3 See on this subject the Act of Congress of 26th of May 1790, ch. 11, and the Act of Congress of the 27th of March 1804, ch. 56; 3 Story's Comm. on Const. § 1297 to 1307; 4 Cowen R. 526, 527, note.

deductions, it is manifest, that many approximations have been already made towards the establishment of a general system of international jurisprudence, which shall elevate the policy, subserve the interests, and promote the common convenience of all nations. We may thus indulge the hope, that, at no distant period, the comity of nations will be but another name for the justice of nations; and that the noble boast of the great Roman Orator may be in some measure realized: — *Non erit alia lex Romæ, alia Athenis, alia nunc, alia posthac; sed et omnes gentes et omni tempore una lex et sempiterna et immortalis continebit.*[1]

---

[1] Cicero, Fragm. de Repub.

INDEX.

A.

D.

J.

O.

P.

R.

S.

T.

U.

V.

W.

www.ingramcontent.com/pod-product-compliance
Lightning Source LLC
Chambersburg PA
CBHW021626200126
38285CB00009B/5